ARCHAEOLOGY

· OF THE ·

LAND OF THE BIBLE

VOLUME II

732–332 BCE

THE ANCHOR BIBLE REFERENCE LIBRARY is designed to be a third major component of the Anchor Bible group, which includes the Anchor Bible commentaries on the books of the Old Testament, the New Testament, and the Apocrypha, and the Anchor Bible Dictionary. While the Anchor Bible commentaries and the Anchor Bible Dictionary are structurally defined by their subject matter, the Anchor Bible Reference Library will serve as a supplement on the cutting edge of the most recent scholarship. The series is open-ended; its scope and reach are nothing less than the biblical world in its totality, and its methods and techniques the most up-to-date available or devisable. Separate volumes will deal with one or more of the following topics relating to the Bible: anthropology, archaeology, ecology, economy, geography, history, languages and literatures, philosophy, religion(s), theology.

As with the Anchor Bible commentaries and the Anchor Bible Dictionary, the philosophy underlying the Anchor Bible Reference Library finds expression in the following: the approach is scholarly, the perspective is balanced and fair-minded, the methods are scientific, and the goal is to inform and enlighten. Contributors are chosen on the basis of their scholarly skills and achievements, and they come from a variety of religious backgrounds and communities. The books in the Anchor Bible Reference Library are intended for the broadest possible readership, ranging from world-class scholars, whose qualifications match those of the authors, to general readers, who may not have special training or skill in studying the Bible but are as enthusiastic as any dedicated professional in expanding their knowledge of the Bible and its world.

David Noel Freedman
General Editor

THE ANCHOR BIBLE REFERENCE LIBRARY

ARCHAEOLOGY
· OF THE ·
LAND OF THE BIBLE

VOLUME II

*The Assyrian, Babylonian,
and Persian Periods*
732–332 BCE

EPHRAIM STERN

Doubleday

NEW YORK   LONDON   TORONTO   SYDNEY   AUCKLAND

THE ANCHOR BIBLE REFERENCE LIBRARY

PUBLISHED BY DOUBLEDAY
a division of Random House, Inc.
1540 Broadway, New York, New York 10036

THE ANCHOR BIBLE REFERENCE LIBRARY, DOUBLEDAY,
and the portrayal of an anchor with the letters ABRL are registered
trademarks of Doubleday, a division of Random House, Inc.

Library of Congress Cataloging-in-Publication Data applied for

ISBN 0-385-42450-7
Copyright © 2001 by Ephraim Stern
All Rights Reserved
Printed in the United States of America
March 2001
First Edition

1   3   5   7   9   10   8   6   4   2

To my wife, Tamar

Contents

PREFACE

T his book is the fruit of many years of teaching at the Institute of Archaeology of the Hebrew University of Jerusalem. It represents a summary of the personal views I have developed during those years regarding the evolution of the material culture of the Land of the Bible in the Assyrian, Babylonian, and Persian periods.

This volume differs from the preceding volume by Amihai Mazar in that it deals with a relatively short period. It thus treats the finds more intensively, and I hope that nothing of significance among the tens of thousands of finds and discoveries has been left out. Despite this, I have omitted some of the introductory material and definitions found in Mazar's book, such as the geographical background, the structure of the tell and the ruin, basic terms in stratigraphy, etc. Nor have I dealt with the structure and history of Jerusalem in the 8th to 6th centuries BCE (particularly the surrounding tombs), to avoid repeating what has already been published.

The present volume deals with the archaeology of the Land of the Bible during only four hundred years: from 732 BCE, i.e., the start of the Assyrian conquest, to 332 BCE, the year of the conquest by Alexander the Great, an event that brought the Persian period to an end. In terms of material culture, these years constitute a single period during which the region was under the control of three powers of Mesopotamian origin: Assyria, Babylonia, and Persia. In fact, to complete the period, we should have extended it up to the days of Ptolemy II Philadelphus (285–245 BCE). He, as is well known, was the ruler who brought genuine Hellenism to the region and diverted the orientation of the lands under his control from the eastern to the Greek culture. However, while the period is homogeneous from the point of view of material culture, in other aspects there are considerable differences within it. The fate of the region varied greatly from period to period because of the different policies of the occupying powers toward it, a fact that is clearly reflected in the complexity of the archaeological finds.

In the first stage, from the Assyrian to the Babylonian conquests (732–604 BCE), the region was divided between eight peoples (or seven after the conquest): Aramaeans, Phoenicians, Israelites, Judahites, Philistines, Ammonites, Moabites, and Edomites. It was subject to various foreign influences: Assyrian, Egyptian, and Greek. Since each people created its own particular material culture from these various components, the first book of this volume, which deals with the Assyrian period, is divided into chapters according to these cultural entities.

In the second period, that of the Babylonian kingdom (604–539 BCE), the picture changes radically. The Babylonians, who conquered the region in waves between 604 and 582 BCE, caused widespread destruction, looting, and carrying to Babylon everything that was portable. The land was left in ruins, plundered of its wealth and its inhabitants, throughout the rule of the Babylonians, who displayed meager interest in it. Indeed, apart from two limited areas, one in Benjamin and one in Ammon, little remained in the region, and this period, the subject of the second book, is a virtual vacuum.

The third power, the Achaemenian Persians (538–332 BCE), did not conquer the region by force but found it desolate. The Persians conducted a different policy from their two predecessors: they permitted each people or organized ethnic group to return to the territory that was theirs before the Babylonian conquest, or to settle in deserted regions. Thus the Jews returned to Judah, while the coastal port cities in the former Philistia were settled mainly by Phoenicians. The material culture of the Land of the Bible was now divided not into seven but into two regional cultures: that of the coastal area, which was in effect part of the *koine* that included the entire coast of the eastern Mediterranean, and that of the hills, which reflected to a great extent the cultures of the two peoples of the interior, the Jews and the Samaritans.

Much effort has been devoted to the bibliography to enable the interested reader to continue to study each of the periods and the subjects treated here. The bibliography is as up-to-date as possible and is organized according to the various periods and chapters of the book.

This book would not have been possible without the dedicated work of my fellow archaeologists. Very many of them, too numerous to name here, assisted me in tracking down finds and enabled me to include the results of their research, in many cases unpublished. I am most grateful to all of them.

I am also grateful to Prof. D. N. Freedman for his editorial comments on the entire text; to the Annenberg Research Institute in Philadelphia; to the Dorot Foundation and to its director, Dr. E. S. Frerichs, for their support; to Alan Paris, who helped me prepare the manuscript for publication; to Ruhama Bonfil, who prepared all the maps; to Sara Halbreich, who drew most of the line drawings; to Z. Radovan, who took all of the photographs at my own excavations at Tel Dor and Tel Mevorakh and photographed at many other sites; and finally to the editorial staff of Doubleday, particularly Dr. Mark J. H. Fretz, senior editor of religious publishing, and Andrew R. Corbin, editor. My sincere thanks to all of them.

Ephraim Stern
Jerusalem, December 1998

ACKNOWLEDGMENTS AND CREDITS

The photographs and line drawings in this book are published with the kind permission of the following scholars and institutions (illustrations identified by their numbers):

The Institute of Archaeology of the Hebrew University of Jerusalem: I.50; I.63; I.75; I.77; I.78; I.80; I.81, I.87; I.89; I.90; I.117; I.121; III.2; III.4; III.15; III.52

Israel Antiquities Authority: I.22; I.42; I.43; I.46; I.47; I.52; I.105; III.30; III.41; III.48; III.50

Israel Exploration Society; illustrations reproduced from the book *The Architecture of Ancient Israel* (edited by H. Katzenstein), from *Qadmoniot*, and from *Israel Exploration Journal*: I.15; I.19; I.79; III.54

Israel Museum: I.21; I.103

Reuben and Edith Hecht Museum, Haifa University: I.82; I.83; I.87

R. Arav: I.27; I.28

N. Avigad, Institute of Archaeology, the Hebrew University of Jerusalem: I.48; I.76; I.79; I.102; III.22; III.51

D. Barag, Institute of Archaeology, the Hebrew University of Jerusalem: I.50

G. Barkai, Bar-Ilan University, Ramat Gan: I.86

I. Beit-Arieh, Institute of Archaeology, Tel Aviv University: I.67; I.68; I.69; I.72; I.107; I.108; I.109; I.111; I.112; I.113; II.3

A. Ben-Tor, Institute of Archaeology, the Hebrew University of Jerusalem: I.24; I.29; III.7; III.38

A. Biran, Hebrew Union College–Jewish Institute of Religion, Jerusalem: I.26; I.29; I.35; I.39; I.96

M. Broshi, Israel Museum, Jerusalem: III.9; III.43

M. Cogan, Department of Israelite History, the Hebrew University of Jerusalem: I.8

R. Cohen, Israel Antiquities Authority: I.70; I.71; I.99; I.110; I.114; I.115; I.118

M. Dothan, Haifa University: I.6; III.45; III.63

A. Eitan, Israel Antiquities Authority: I.62

J. Elgavish, the Municipality of Haifa: III.3; III.8

H. Eshel, Institute of Archaeology, the Hebrew University of Jerusalem: III.2

R. Frankel, Institute of Archaeology, Tel Aviv University: III.23; III.31

S. Gitin, W. F. Albright Institute of Archaeology, Jerusalem, and T. Dothan, Hebrew University (Tel Miqne Expedition): I.17; I.55; I.57; I.59; I.60; I.61; I.97

Z. Herzog, Institute of Archaeology, Tel Aviv University: I.19; I.73; I.74; III.20

M. Kochavi, Institute of Archaeology, Tel Aviv University: I.93

E. Linder, Haifa University: I.40

I. Magen, Archaeological Officer for Judea and Samaria: I.25; III.36

A. Mazar, Institute of Archaeology, the Hebrew University of Jerusalem: I.64; I.66

E. Mazar, Institute of Archaeology, the Hebrew University of Jerusalem: I.44; III.18; III.19

Y. Meshorer, Israel Museum, Jerusalem: III.55–62

J. Naveh (with A. Yardeni), Institute of Archaeology, the Hebrew University of Jerusalem: I.55; I.56; I.65; III.4

E. D. Oren, Department of Archaeology, Ben-Gurion University, Beer-Sheba: I.5; I.11; I.12; I.58; I.92; I.94; I.95; I.98; III.37; III.47

J. B. Pritchard, Director, The University Museum, the University of Pennsylvania Expedition to Gibeon: II.7

R. Reich, Haifa University: I.14

E. Stern, Institute of Archaeology, the Hebrew University of Jerusalem: I.9; I.20; I.32; I.33; I.34; I.36; I.37; I.38; I.41; I.45; III.5; III.10; III.11; III.13; III.14; III.24; III.25; III.27; III.28; III.29; III.32; III.34; III.35; III.39; III.49

M. and H. Tadmor, Jerusalem: I.10

D. Ussishkin, Institute of Archaeology, Tel Aviv University: I.2; I.3; I.4; I.85; I.88; III.16; III.21

G. E. Wright, Director of the Drew-McCormick Expedition to Shechem: III.47

All maps prepared for this book by Ruhama Bonfil

List of Tables, Maps, and Illustrations

Tables

Maps

Illustrations

LIST OF ABBREVIATIONS

I. PERIODICALS, BOOKS, AND FESTSCHRIFTS

AAA	Annals of Archaeology and Anthropology of the University of Liverpool
AASOR	Annual of the American Schools of Oriental Research
ADAJ	*Annual of the Department of Antiquities of Jordan*
AFO	*Archiv für Orientforschung*
Aharoni [1978]	Y. Aharoni, *The Archaeology of the Land of Israel* (rev. ed.), Philadelphia 1978
Aharoni [1987]	Y. Aharoni, *The Land of the Bible: A Historical Geography* (rev. ed.), London 1987
Ahituv [1992]	Sh. Ahituv, *Handbook of Ancient Hebrew Inscriptions,* Jerusalem 1992 (Hebrew)
AJA	*American Journal of Archaeology*
AJBA	*Australian Journal of Biblical Archaeology*
Albright Festschrift	H. Goedicke (ed.), *Near Eastern Studies in Honor of W. F. Albright,* Baltimore 1971
ALUOS	*Annual of Leeds University Oriental Society*
Amiran [1969]	R. Amiran, *Ancient Pottery of the Holy Land,* Jerusalem 1969
ANET	J. B. Pritchard (ed.), *Ancient Texts Relating to the Old Testament* (3rd ed.), Princeton 1969
APEF	*Annual of the Palestine Exploration Fund*
Architecture	H. Katzenstein et al. (eds.), *The Architecture of Ancient Israel,* Jerusalem 1992
AS	*Anatolian Studies*

'Atiqot	Journal of the Israel Department of Antiquities and Museums and the Israel Antiquities Authority
AUSS	*Andrews University Seminary Studies*
Avigad, *Corpus*	N. Avigad and B. Sass, *Corpus of West Semitic Stamp Seals,* Jerusalem 1997
BA	*Biblical Archaeologist*
BARev	*Biblical Archaeology Review*
BASOR	*Bulletin of the American Schools of Oriental Research*
BAT I–II	*Biblical Archaeology Today: Proceedings of the International Congress on Biblical Archaeology,* I: Jerusalem 1985; II: Jerusalem 1993
BBSA	*Bulletin of the British School of Archaeology in Jerusalem*
Belliddo Festschrift	A. Blanco et al., *Homenaje a García Belliddo,* vol. I: *Revista de la Universidad,* vol. 25, Madrid 1976
Ben-Tor [1991]	A. Ben-Tor (ed.), *The Archaeology of Ancient Israel,* New Haven 1991
Berytus	*Berytus,* Bulletin of the American University of Beirut
BMB	*Bulletin du Musée de Beyrouth*
CAH	*Cambridge Ancient History* (3rd ed.)
Cathedra	*Cathedra for the History of Eretz Israel and Its Yishuv,* Bulletin of the I. Ben-Zvi Institute (Hebrew)
CHJ	W. D. Davies and L. Finkelstein (eds.), *The Cambridge History of Judaism,* vol. I: *Introduction, The Persian Period,* Cambridge 1984
Cross Festschrift	P. D. Miller, P. D. Hansen, and S. D. McBride (eds.), *Ancient Israelite Religion: Essays in Honor of F. M. Cross,* Philadelphia 1987
Dothan [1982]	T. Dothan, *The Philistines and Their Material Culture,* New Haven 1982
Dothan Festschrift	M. Helzer et al. (eds.), *Studies in the Archaeology and History of Ancient Israel, Presented to M. Dothan,* Jerusalem 1993
EI	*Eretz-Israel,* Archaeological, Historical and Geographical Studies
ESI	*Excavations and Surveys in Israel*
Gibson [1971]	J. C. L. Gibson, *Textbook of Syrian Semitic Inscrip-*

	tions, vol. I: *Hebrew and Moabite Inscriptions,* Oxford 1971
Gitin [1995]	S. Gitin (ed.), *Recent Excavations in Israel, Paper No. 1 of American Institute of Archaeology,* Boston 1995
Glueck Festschrift	J. A. Sanders (ed.), *Near Eastern Archaeology in the Twentieth Century: Essays in Honor of Nelson Glueck,* New York 1970
HEI	J. Shavit (ed.), *The History of Eretz Israel,* Jerusalem 1984 (Hebrew)
Hestrin-Dayagi [1973]	R. Hestrin and M. Dayagi, *Inscriptions Reveal,* Jerusalem 1973
Horn Festschrift	L. T. Geraty and L. G. Herr (eds.), *The Archaeology of Jordan and Other Studies: Presented to Siegfried H. Horn,* Berrien Springs, Mich. 1986
HTR	*Harvard Theological Review*
HUCA	*Hebrew Union College Annual*
IEJ	*Israel Exploration Journal*
IMJ	*Israel Museum Journal*
IMN	*Israel Museum News*
INJ	*Israel Numismatic Journal*
Iraq	*Iraq,* Bulletin of the British School of Archaeology in Iraq
Isserlin Festschrift	R. Y. Ebied and M. J. L. Young (eds.), *Oriental Studies Presented to Benedikt S. J. Isserlin,* Leiden 1980
JANES	*Journal of the Ancient Near Eastern Society of Columbia University*
JAOS	*Journal of the American Oriental Society*
JARCE	*Journal of the American Research Center in Egypt*
JBL	*Journal of Biblical Literature*
JCS	*Journal of Cuneiform Studies*
JEA	*Journal of Egyptian Archaeology*
JHS	*Journal of Hellenic Studies*
JJS	*Journal of Jewish Studies*
JNES	*Journal of Near Eastern Studies*
JPOS	*Journal of Palestine Oriental Society*
JQR	*Jewish Quarterly Review*
JSRS	*Judea and Samaria Research Studies* (Hebrew)
Kenyon [1979]	K. M. Kenyon, *Archaeology in the Holy Land* (rev. ed.), London 1979

Kenyon Festschrift	P. R. S. Moorey and P. Parr (eds.), *Archaeology in the Levant: Essays for Kathleen M. Kenyon,* Warminster (England) *1978*
King Festschrift	M. Coogan et al. (eds.), *Scripture and Other Artifacts: Essays in the Bible and Archaeology in Honor of Philip J. King,* Louisville, Ky. 1994
LA	*Liber Annus Studi Biblici Franciscani*
Levant	*Levant,* Journal of the British School of Archaeology in Jerusalem, London
Levine Festschrift	B. *Levine Festschrift,* New York University (forth-coming)
Marx Jubilee Volume	S. Liebermann (ed.), *A. Marx Jubilee Volume on the Occasion of His 70th Birthday,* New York 1950
Mazar [1990]	A. Mazar, *Archaeology of the Land of the Bible 1000–586 B.C.E.,* New York 1990
MDOG	*Mitteicungen des Deutschen Orient Gesellschaft*
Michmanim	*Michmanim,* Journal of the Hecht Museum, Haifa
Moscati Phoenicians	S. Moscati, *The World of the Phoenicians,* London and New York, 1968
Muse	*Muse,* Journal of the Museum of Art and Archaeology, University of Missouri
NC	*Numismatic Circular*
NEAEHL	E. Stern (ed.), *The New Encyclopedia of Archaeological Excavations in the Holy Land,* Jerusalem 1993
OA	*Oriens Antiquus*
OP	*Opuscula Atheniensia*
Orientalia	*Orientalia,* Pontifical Biblical Institute, Rome
PEFA	*Palestine Exploration Fund Annual*
PEFQS	*Palestine Exploration Fund Quarterly Statement*
PEQ	*Palestine Exploration Quarterly*
QDAP	*Quarterly of the Department of Antiquities in Palestine*
Qedem	Monographs of the Institute of Archaeology, the Hebrew University of Jerusalem
Qedem Reports	*Reports of the Institute of Archaeology,* the Hebrew University of Jerusalem
RA	*Revue d'assyriologie et d'archéologie orientale,* Paris
RB	*Revue Biblique,* Paris
RDAC	*Report of the Department of Antiquities, Cyprus,* Nicosia

Richardson Festschrift	L. M. Hopfe (ed.), *Uncovering Ancient Stones: Essays in Memory of H. N. Richardson,* Winona Lake, Ind. 1994
Rose Festschrift	L. G. Perdue et al. (eds.), *Archaeology and Biblical Interpretation: Essays in Memory of D. Glen Rose,* Atlanta 1987
RSF	*Rivista di studi fenici*
SCE	E. Gjerstad, *The Swedish Cyprus Expedition,* vols. III, IV, Stockholm 1937–1938
ScrHier	*Scripta Hierosolomitana*
Sefunim	*Bulletin of the National Maritime Museum,* Haifa
Semitica	*Journal de l'Université de Paris, Institut d'Etudes Semitique*
SHAJ I; II; III; IV; V	*Studies in the History and Archaeology of Jordan,* Amman, I: 1982; II: 1985; III: 1987; IV: 1992; V: 1995
Stern [1982]	E. Stern, *The Material Culture of the Land of the Bible in the Persian Period, 538–332 BCE,* Warminster (England) 1982
Symposia	F. M. Cross (ed.), *Symposia Celebrating the 75th Anniversary of the American Schools of Oriental Research*
TA	*Tel Aviv,* Journal of the Tel Aviv University Institute of Archaeology
Tadmor Festschrift	M. Cogan and I. Epha'l (eds.), *Studies in Assyrian History and Ancient Near Eastern Historiography Presented to H. Tadmor,* Jerusalem 1991 (*ScrHier* 33)
Trans	*Transeuphratène, Institut Catholic de Paris*
Tufnell Festschrift	J. Tubb (ed.), *Palestine in the Bronze and Iron Ages: Papers in Honor of Olga Tufnell,* London 1985
UF	*Ugarit-Forschungen*
Van Beek Festschrift	J. D. Seger (ed.), *Retrieving the Past: Essays on Archaeological Research and Methodology in Honor of Gus W. Van Beek,* Winona Lake, Ind. 1996
VT	*Vetus Testamentum,* Leiden
WHJP	B. Mazar (ed.), *The World History of the Jewish People,* Jerusalem, n.d.
Wright Festschrift	F. M. Cross et al. (eds.), *Magnelia Dei: The Mighty Acts of God: Essays on the Bible and Archaeology in Memory of G. E. Wright,* New York 1976

Yadin [1963]	Y. Yadin, *The Art of Warfare in Biblical Lands,* Ramat Gan 1963
ZA	*Zeitschrift für Assyriologie und vorderasiatische Archäologie*
ZAW	*Zeitschrift für die alttestamentliche Wissenschaft,* Berlin
ZDPV	*Zeitschrift des deutschen Palästina-Vereins*

II. Excavations in Palestine

Abu Ghosh	F. M. Abel, Découverte d'un Tombeau Antique à Abou-Ghosh, *RB* 30 (1921), 97–102.
Abu Hawam, Tell I	R. W. Hamilton, Tell Abu-Hawam Interim Report, *QDAP* 3 (1933), 78–79.
Abu Hawam, Tell II	R. W. Hamilton, Excavations at Tell Abu-Hawam, *QDAP* 4 (1934), 1–69.
Abu Hawam, Tell III	G. Finkielsztein, Tell Abu-Hawam, Réexamen des Périodes Helléniques et Perse, *RB* 96 (1989), 224–234.
Abu Hawam, Tell IV	J. Balensi et al., Le Niveau Perse à Tell Abu-Hawam. Résultats Récents et Signification dans le Contexte Régional côtier, *Trans* 2 (1990), 125–136.
Acco	M. Dothan, *NEAEHL,* vol. I, 17–23.
Achzib I	M. W. Prausnitz, *NEAEHL,* vol. I, 32–35; E. Mazar, ibid., 35–36.
Achzib II	M. W. Prausnitz, Die Nekropolen von Akhzib und die Entwicklung der Keramik von 10 bis 7 Jh. V. Chr., in: H. G. Niemeyer (ed.), *Phönizier im Westen,* Mainz 1982, 31–44.
'Amal, Tel	G. Edelstein and N. Feig, *NEAEHL,* vol. IV, 1447–1450.
Amman I	F. Zayadin, Recent Excavations on the Citadel of Amman, *ADAJ* 18 (1973), 17–75.
Amman II	F. Zayadin et al., The 1988 Excavations on the Citadel of Amman Lower Terrace Area, *ADAJ* 33 (1989), 357–363.
'Anathoth I	A. Bergman, Soundings at the Supposed Site of OT Anathoth, *BASOR* 62 (1936), 22–25.
'Anathoth II	Y. Nadelman, The Identification of Anathot and the Soundings at Khirbet el-Sidd, *IEJ* 44 (1994), 62–74.

Anthedon	W. F. M. Petrie, *Anthedon, Sinai,* London 1937.
Apollonia I	I. Roll and E. Ayalon, *Apollonia and Southern Sharon,* Tel Aviv 1989 (Hebrew).
Apollonia II	I. Roll and E. Ayalon, *NEAEHL,* vol. I, 72–75.
Arad I	Y. Aharoni, *Arad Inscriptions,* Jerusalem 1981.
Arad II	Z. Herzog et al., The Israelite Fortress at Arad, *BASOR* 254 (1984), 1–34; 267 (1987), 77–80.
Arad III	Z. Herzog, *The Arad Fortresses,* Tel Aviv 1977, 113–296 (Hebrew).
Aroer I (in Judah)	A. Biran, *NEAEHL,* vol. I, 89–92; A. Biran and R. Cohen, 'Aroer in the Negev, *EI* 15 (1981), 250–273 (Hebrew).
Aroer II (in Moab)	E. Olavarri-Goicoechea, *NEAEHL,* vol. I, 92–93.
Ashdod I	M. Dothan and D. N. Freedman, Ashdod I: The First Season of Excavations 1962, *'Atiqot* VII, English series, Jerusalem 1967.
Ashdod II–III	M. Dothan, Ashdod II–III: The Second and Third Seasons of Excavations 1963, 1965, *'Atiqot* IX–X, English series, Jerusalem 1971.
Ashdod IV	M. Dothan and Y. Porath, Ashdod IV: Excavations of Area M, *'Atiqot* XV, English series, Jerusalem 1982.
Ashdod V	J. Porath, A Fortress of the Persian Period, *'Atiqot* 7, Hebrew series, Jerusalem 1974, 43–55.
Ashkelon I	W. J. Phythian-Adams, Report on the Stratification of Askalon, *PEFQS* (1923), 60–84.
Ashkelon II	J. H. Iliffe, A Hoard of Bronzes from Askalon c. Fourth Century B.C., *QDAP* 5 (1935), 61–68.
Ashkelon III	L. E. Stager, *NEAEHL,* vol. I, 103–112.
Ashkelon IV	L. E. Stager, Ashkelon and the Archaeology of Destruction: Kislev 604 BCE, *EI* 25 (1996), 61*–74*.
'Atlit	C. N. Johns, Excavations at 'Atlit (1930–31); the South-Eastern Cemetery, *QDAP* 2 (1933), 41–104.
Ayelet ha-Shaḥar	R. Reich, The Persian Building at Ayyelet ha-Shahar: The Assyrian Palace of Hazor, *IEJ* 25 (1975), 233–237.
Azor	M. Dothan, An Inscribed Jar from Hazor, *'Atiqot* III, English series, Jerusalem 1961, 181–184.
Baluʿa	U. F. Worschech et al., Preliminary Report on the Second and Third Campaigns at the Ancient Site of

	el-Baluʿa, *ADAJ* 33 (1987), 111–121; 36 (1992), 167–174; 38 (1994), 195–203.
Batash, Tel	G. L. Kelm and A. Mazar, *Timnah: A Biblical City in the Sorek Valley,* Winona Lake, Ind. 1995.
Bat Yam	Y. Shapira, An Ancient Cave at Bat Yam, *IEJ* 16 (1966), 8–10.
Beersheba I	Y. Aharoni (ed.), *Beer-Sheba I: Excavations at Tel Beer-Sheba, 1969–1971 Seasons,* Tel Aviv 1973.
Beit Lei	J. Naveh, Old Hebrew Inscriptions in a Burial Cave, *IEJ* 13 (1963), 74–92.
Beit Mirsim, Tell	W. F. Albright, *The Excavations of Tell Beit Mirsim, III: The Iron Age,* AASOR 21–22 (1943).
Bethel	J. L. Kelso, *The Excavations of Bethel 1934–1960,* AASOR 39 (1968).
Bethsaida	R. Arav and R. A. Freud, *Bethsaida, a City by the North Shore of the Sea of Galilee,* Kirksville, Mo. 1995.
Beth-Shean I	F. W. James, *The Iron Age at Beth Shan,* Philadelphia 1966.
Beth-Shean III	G. M. Fitzgerald, *Beth-Shan Excavations III: The Arab and Byzantine Levels,* Philadelphia 1931.
Beth-Shemesh	S. Bunimovitz and Z. Lederman, Beth Shemesh: Culture Conflict on Judah's Frontier, *BARev* 23 (1997), 42–49; 75–79. Also idem, Six Seasons of Excavations at Beth-Shemesh—a Border Town in Judah, *Qadmoniot* 30 (1997), 22–37 (Hebrew).
Beth-Zur I	O. R. Sellers, *The Citadel of Beth-Zur,* Philadelphia 1933.
Beth-Zur II	O. R. Sellers et al., *The 1957 Excavations at Beth Zur,* AASOR 38 (1968).
Beth-Zur III	R. Reich, The Beth Zur Citadel II: A Persian Residency? *TA* 19/1 (1992), 113–123.
Bliss-Macalister [1902]	F. J. Bliss and R. A. S. Macalister, *Excavations in Palestine (1898–1900),* London 1902.
Buseirah I	C. M. Bennett, in: J. F. A. Sawyer et al. (eds.), *Midian, Moab and Edom,* Sheffield 1983, 9–17.
Buseirah II	C. M. Bennett, Excavations at Buseirah, Southern Jordan, *Levant* 5 (1973), 1–11; 6 (1974), 1–24; 7 (1975), 1–15; 9 (1977), 9–10.

Daliyeh I	P. W. Lapp and N. Lapp, *Discoveries in the Wadi Ed Daliyeh,* AASOR 41 (1974).
Daliyeh II	M. J. W. Leith, *Wadi Daliyeh I: The Wadi Daliyeh Seal Impressions. Discoveries in the Judaean Desert,* XXIV, Oxford 1997.
Dan, Tel	A. Biran, *Biblical Dan,* Jerusalem 1994.
Deir ʿAlla, Tell	H. J. Franken, *Excavations at Tell Deir ʿAlla I*, Leiden 1969.
Dibon I	W. L. Reed, *The Excavations at Dibon (Dhiban) in Moab: The Second Campaign,* AASOR 37 (1964).
Dibon II	A. D. Tushingham, *The Excavations at Dibon (Dhiban) in Moab,* AASOR 40 (1972).
Dor I	E. Stern, *Dor the Ruler of the Seas,* Jerusalem 1994.
Dor II	E. Stern et al., Excavations at Tel Dor Final Report, vols. IA and IB: Areas A and C, *Qedem Reports* 1–2 (1995).
Dothan, Tel	P. J. Free, The Sixth Season at Dothan, *BASOR* 156 (1959), 22–29.
Eid, Khirbet	Y. Barouch, Kh. El Eid—an Iron Age Fortress in the North of Mount Hebron, *JSRS* 6 (1996), 49–56 (Hebrew).
Ekron I	S. Gitin, Tel Miqne-Ekron in the 7th Century B.C.E.: The Impact of Economic Innovation and Foreign Cultural Influence on a Neo-Assyrian Vassal City-State, in: S. Gitin (ed.), *Recent Excavations in Israel: A View to the West,* Archaeological Institute of America, Colloquia and Conference Papers No. 1, Boston 1995, 61–79.
Ekron II	S. Gitin, T. Dothan, and I. Naveh, A Royal Dedication Inscription from Ekron, *IEJ* 47 (1997), 1–96.
El-Sahab, Tell	F. Zayadin, Archaeological Excavations at Sahab, *ADAJ* 17 (1972), 23–26; 19 (1973), 55–61; 20 (1975), 69–82.
En-Gedi I	B. Mazar et al., En Gedi: The First and Second Seasons of Excavations 1961–1962, *ʿAtiqot* V, English series, 1966.
En-Gedi II	B. Mazar and I. Dunayevsky, En Gedi: the Fourth and Fifth Seasons of Excavations, Preliminary Report, *IEJ* 17 (1967), 133–143.

'En Gev I	B. Mazar et al., En Gev Excavations in 1961, *IEJ* 14 (1964), 1–49.
'En Gev II	M. Kochavi, *NEAEHL,* vol. II, 411–412.
'En Ḥofez	Y. Alexandre, En Hofez, *ESI* 16 (1997), 53–54.
'Erani, Tel I	S. Yeivin, *First Preliminary Report on the Excavations at Tel "Gat" (Tell Sheykh 'Ahmed el-'Areyny),* Jerusalem 1961.
'Erani, Tel II	A. Ciasca, Un Deposito di Statuette da Tell Gat, *Oriens Antiquus* 2 (1963), 45–63.
'Eton, Tel I	E. Ayalon, Trial Excavation of Two Iron Age Strata at Tel 'Eton, *TA* 12 (1985), 54–62.
'Eton, Tel II	O. Zimhoni, The Iron Age Pottery of Tel 'Eton and Its Relation to the Lachish, Tell Beit Mirsim and Arad Assemblages, *TA* 12 (1985), 63–90.
Far'ah, Tell el- (S) I	W. F. M. Petrie, *Beth Pelet,* vol. I, London 1930.
Far'ah, Tell el- (S) II	J. L. Starkey and G. Lankester-Harding, *Beth Pelet* II, London 1932.
Far'ah, Tell el- (N)	A. Chambon, *Tell el-Far'ah 1: L'Age du Fer,* Paris 1984.
Ful, Tell el- I	W. F. Albright, *Excavations and Results at Tell el-Ful (Gibea of Saul),* AASOR 4 (1924).
Ful, Tell el- II	L. A. Sinclair, *An Archaeological Study of Gibeah (Tell el-Full),* AASOR 34–35 (1960), 1–52.
Ful, Tell el- III	P. W. Lapp, *The Third Campaign at Tel el-Ful: The Excavations of 1964,* AASOR 45 (1981).
Ful, Tell el- IV	R. A. S. Macalister, Some Interesting Pottery Remains, *PEFQS* (1915), 35–37.
Ful, Tell el- V	P. M. Arnold, *Gibeah—the Search for a Biblical City,* Sheffield 1990.
Gezer I-III	R. A. S. Macalister, *The Excavations of Gezer,* vols. I–III, London 1912.
Gezer (HUCA) 1–2	W. G. Dever et al., *Gezer 1–2,* Jerusalem, 1970, 1974.
Gezer (HUCA) 3	S. Gitin, *Gezer 3: The Ceramic Typology of the Late Iron Age Persian and Hellenistic Periods,* Jerusalem, 1990.
Ghrareh	S. Hart, Excavations at Ghrareh, 1986, Preliminary Report, *Levant* 20 (1988), 89–99.
Gibeon I	J. B. Pritchard, *Hebrew Inscriptions and Stamps from Gibeon,* Philadelphia 1959.

Gibeon II	J. B. Pritchard, *The Water System of Gibeon,* Philadelphia 1961.
Gibeon III	J. B. Pritchard, *Winery Defences and Soundings at Gibeon,* Philadelphia 1964.
Gibeon IV	J. B. Pritchard, *Gibeon Where the Sun Stood Still,* Princeton 1962.
Gilʿam	E. Stern, Excavations at Gilʿam, *ʿAtiqot* 6, Hebrew series, 1970, 31–54.
Hadid, Tel	N. Naʾaman, The Assyrian Deportations to Palestine: Cultural and Historical Aspects, in: *Proceedings of the 22nd Archaeological Conference in Israel,* Tel Aviv 1996, 12 (Hebrew).
Halif, Tel	J. D. Seger, *NEAEHL,* vol. II, 553–559.
Harasim, Tel	S. Givon (ed.), *Tel Harasim (Nahal Barkai), Preliminary Reports, Seasons 1–8,* Tel Aviv 1990–1998.
Haror, Tel	E. D. Oren, *NEAEHL,* vol. II, 580–584.
Hashavyahu, Mezad I	J. Naveh, The Excavations at Mesad Hashavyahu, Preliminary Report, *IEJ* 12 (1962), 89–113.
Hashavyahu, Mezad II	R. Reich, A Third Season of Excavations at Mezad Hashavyahu, *EI* 20 (1989), 228–232 (Hebrew).
Hazeva I	R. Cohen and Y. Yisrael, On the Road to Edom: Discoveries from ʿEn Hazeva, *Israel Museum Catalogue,* no. 370, Jerusalem 1995.
Hazeva II	R. Cohen and Y. Yisrael, Smashing the Idols: Piecing Together an Edomite Shrine in Judah, *BARev* 22 (1996), 40–52. Also *idem,* The Iron Age Fortress at ʿEn Haseva, *BA* 58 (1995), 223–235.
Hazor I–IV	Y. Yadin et al., *Hazor I–IV,* Jerusalem 1958–1962.
Hazor V	A. Ben-Tor et al., *Hazor V: An Account of the Fifth Season of Excavation, 1968,* Jerusalem 1997.
Hebron	A. Ofer, Excavations at Biblical Hebron, *Qadmoniot* 87–88 (1990), 88–93 (Hebrew).
Heshbon	L. A. Geraty, *NEAEHL,* vol. II, 626–630.
Hesi, Tell el- I	W. F. M. Petrie, *Tell el-Hesy (Lachish),* London 1891.
Hesi, Tell el- II	F. J. Bliss, *A Mound of Many Cities,* London 1894.
Hesi, Tell el- III	W. J. Bennett, Jr., and J. A. Blakely, *Tell el-Hesi,* vol. 3: *The Persian Period (Stratum V),* Winona Lake, Ind. 1989.

Huga, Horvat	R. Gophna, Some Iron Age II Sites in the Southern Philistia, *'Atiqot* 6, Hebrew series, 1970, 25–30.
Ibsan, Khirbet	R. Amiran, Achaemenian Bronze Objects from a Tomb at Kh. Ibsan in Lower Galilee, *Levant* 4 (1972), 135–138.
'Ira, Tel	I. Beit-Arieh, *NEAEHL,* vol. II, 626–646.
Jaffa I	J. Kaplan and H. Ritter-Kaplan, *NEAEHL,* vol. II, 555–659.
Jaffa II	H. Ritter-Kaplan, The Ties Between the Sidonian Jaffa and Greece in the Light of Excavation, *Qadmoniot* 58–59 (1982), 64–68 (Hebrew).
Jawa, Tell	P. M. M. Daviau, Excavations at Tell Jawa, Jordan (1993, 1994), *ADAJ* 38 (1994), 173–193; 40 (1996), 83–99.
Jelul, Tell	L. G. Herr et al., Madaba Plains Project 1994: Excavations at Al-'Umayri, Tall Jalul and Vicinity, *ADAJ* 40 (1996), 71–75.
Jemmeh, Tell I	W. F. M. Petrie, *Gerar,* London 1928.
Jemmeh, Tell II	G. Van Beek, *NEAEHL,* vol. II, 667–674.
Jemmeh, Tell III	R. Reich, A Note on the Relative Chronology of Buildings A and B at Tell Jemmeh, *EI* 25 (1966), 264–267 (Hebrew).
Jericho I	E. Sellin and C. Watzinger, *Jericho,* Leipzig 1913.
Jericho III–IV	K. M. Kenyon and T. A. Holand (eds.), *Excavations in Jericho,* vol. III: *The Architecture and Stratigraphy of the Tell,* London 1981; vol. IV: *The Pottery Type Series and Other Finds,* London 1982.
Jerusalem I	N. Avigad, *Discovering Jerusalem,* Jerusalem 1980.
Jerusalem II	Y. Shiloh, Excavations at the City of David I: 1978–1982, Interim Report of the First Five Seasons, *Qedem* 19 (1984).
Jerusalem III	E. and B. Mazar, Excavations in the South of the Temple Mount, *Qedem* 29 (1989).
Jerusalem IV	D. T. Ariel and A. De Groot, Excavations at the City of David IV: 1978–1985, *Qedem* 35 (1996).
Jerusalem V	H. J. Franken and M. L. Steiner (eds.), *Excavations in Jerusalem 1961–1967,* vol. II: *The Iron Age Extramural Quarter on the South West Hill,* Oxford 1990.
Jerusalem VI	I. Eshel and K. Prag (eds.), *Excavations by K. M. Kenyon in Jerusalem 1961–1967,* Oxford 1995.

Jezreel, Tel	D. Ussishkin and J. Woodhead, Excavations at Tel Jezreel, 1994–1996, Third Report, *TA* 24 (1997), 3–180.
Jibʿit, Khirbet	Z. Ilan and E. Dinnur, Jibʿit, an Ancient Settlement in the Border of the Samaritan Desert, in: Z. A. Ehrlich (ed.), *Samaria and Benjamin,* vol. I (1987), 114–130 (Hebrew).
Jokneam, Tel	A. Ben-Tor, *NEAEHL,* vol. III, 805–811.
Judeideh, Tell	S. Gibson, The Tell el-Judeideh (T. Goded) Excavations, *TA* 21 (1994), 194–234.
Kabri	A. Kempinski and W. D. Niemeir (eds.), *Excavations at Kabri Preliminary Reports, Nos. 1–8, Seasons 1988–1993,* Tel Aviv, 1989–1994.
Kadesh-Barnea I	M. Dothan, The Fortress of Kadesh Barnea, *IEJ* 15 (1965), 134–151.
Kadesh-Barnea II	R. Cohen, Kadesh-Barnea: A Fortress from the Time of the Judaean Kingdom, *Israel Museum Catalogue,* no. 233, 1983.
Kedesh, Tel	E. Stern and I. Beit-Arieh, Excavations at Tel Kedesh (Tell Abu-Qudeis), *TA* 6 (1979), 1–25.
Keisan, Tell	J. Briend and J. B. Humbert (eds.), *Tell Keisan (1971–1976): Une cité phénicienne en Galilee,* Paris 1980.
Ketef Jericho	S. H. Eshel and H. Misgav, A Fourth Century B.C.E. Document from Ketef Jericho, *IEJ* 38 (1988), 158–176.
Kheleifeh, Tell el-	G. D. Pratico, *Nelson Glueck's 1938–1940 Excavations Tell el-Kheleifeh: A Reappraisal,* AASOR Archaeological Reports 3, Atlanta 1993.
Kinneret I	V. Fritz, *Kinneret, Ergebnisse der Ausgrabungen auf dem Tel el-ʿOreme am See Gennesaret 1982–1985,* Wiesbaden 1990.
Kinneret II	V. Fritz, Excavations at Tell el ʿOreimeh (Tel Kinrot), 1982–1985 *TA* 20 (1993), 187–215.
Kochavi [1972]	M. Kochavi (ed.), *Judaea, Samaria and Golan, Archaeological Survey 1967–68,* Jerusalem 1972 (Hebrew).
Kudadi, Tell	N. Avigad, *NEAEHL,* vol. III, 882.
Lachish III	O. Tufnell, *Lachish III: The Iron Age,* Oxford 1953.
Lachish V	Y. Aharoni, *Investigations at Lachish: The Sanctuary and the Residency,* Tel Aviv 1975.

Lachish VI	D. Ussishkin, Excavations at Tel Lachish 1973–1977, Preliminary Report, *TA* 5 (1978), 1–98.
Lachish VII	D. Ussishkin, Excavations at Tel Lachish 1978–1983, Second Preliminary Report, *TA* 10 (1983), 97–175.
Luzifar	Y. Barouch, Khirbet Luzifar—a Fortified Site from the Persian Period in the Hills of Hebron, *JSRS* 1 (1995), 97–108 (Hebrew).
Maʿagan Mikhaʾel	E. Linder, *NEAEHL*, vol. III, 918–919; *idem, BAT II*, 640.
Madaba Plains I–III	L. A. Geraty, et al. (eds.), *Madaba Plains Project,* vols. I–III, Berrien Springs, Mich. 1989, 1991, 1997.
Makmish	N. Avigad, Excavations at Makmish, Preliminary Report, *IEJ* 10 (1960), 90–96.
Malḥata, Tel I	M. Kochavi, *NEAEHL*, vol. III, 934–936.
Malḥata, Tel II	I. Beit-Arieh, Tel Malhata, *ESI* 14 (1994), 128–129.
Mareshah	A. Kloner, Maresha, *Qadmoniot* 95–96 (1992), 70–85 (Hebrew).
Masos, Tel	V. Fritz and A. Kempinski (eds.), *Ergebnisse uber die Ausgrabungen auf der Hirbet el-Msas (Tel Masos),* Wiesbaden 1983.
Mazar, Tell el- I	K. Yassine, *Tell El-Mazar I, Cemetery A,* Jordan 1984.
Mazar, Tell el- II	Tell El-Mazar Field I. Preliminary Report of Area G, H, L and M: The Summit, in: *Archaeology of Jordan: Essays and Reports,* Amman 1988, 75–113.
Megadim, Tel I	M. Broshi, *NEAEHL*, vol. III, 1001–1003.
Megadim, Tel II	S. R. Wolff, Tel Megadim, *AJA* 100 (1996), 748.
Megiddo I	R. S. Lamon and G. M. Shipton, *Megiddo I,* Chicago 1939.
Megiddo, Cult	H. G. May, *Material Remains of the Megiddo Cult,* Chicago 1935.
Meqabelein	G. Lankester-Harding, The Iron Age Tomb at Meqabelein, *QDAP* 14 (1950), 44–48.
Mevorakh, Tel	E. Stern, The Excavations of Tel Mevorakh, vol. I, The Hellenistic, Persian and Israelite Strata, *Qedem* 9 (1978).
Michal, Tel	Z. Herzog et al., *Excavations at Tel Michal, Israel,* Minneapolis 1988.
Michmash, Meẓad	S. Riklin, A Fortress at Michmas on the North-

	Eastern Boundary of the Judaean Desert, *JSRS* 4 (1994), 69–74 (Hebrew).
Migdol	E. Oren, A New Fortress on the Edge of the Eastern Nile Delta, *BASOR* 256 (1984), 7–44.
Mikhmoret I	B. S. J. Isserlin, Excavating in an Ancient Port in Israel: The Leeds University Trial Excavation at Mikhmoret, ALUOS 2 (1961), 3–5.
Mikhmoret II	Y. Porath, S. M. Paley, and R. Stieglitz, *NEAEHL,* vol. III, 1043–1046.
Mizpe Yammim I	R. Frankel, *NEAEHL,* vol. III, 1061–1063.
Mizpe Yammim II	R. Frankel and R. Ventura, The Mispe Yamim Bronzes, *BASOR* 311 (1998), 39–56.
Naḥal Tut	Y. Alexandre, Nahal Tut, *ESI* 15 (1996), 49–50.
Nahariya, Tel	O. Yogev, *NEAEHL,* vol. III, 1088–1090.
Naṣbeh, Tell en- I	C. C. McCown, *Tell en-Nasbeh I,* Berkeley 1947.
Naṣbeh, Tell en- II	J. C. Wampler, *Tell en-Nasbeh II,* Berkeley 1947.
Naṣbeh, Tell en- III	J. R. Zorn, Tell en-Nasbeh: A Re-evaluation of the Architecture and Stratigraphy of the Early Bronze Age, Iron Age and Later Periods. Ph.D. diss., University of California, Berkeley, 1993.
Nebi Samuel	I. Magen and M. Dadon, Nebi Samuel in the Iron and Persian Period, *Proceedings of the 22nd Archaeological Conference in Israel,* Tel Aviv 1996, 19–20 (Hebrew).
Nebi Yunis	F. M. Cross, The Ostracon from Nebi Yunis, *IEJ* 14 (1964), 185.
Nimra, Khirbet	H. Hizmi and Z. Shabtai, A Public Building from the Persian Period at Jabel Nimra, *JSRS* 3 (1993), 65–86 (Hebrew).
Nimrin, Tell	J. W. Flanagan and D. W. McCreery, First Preliminary Report of the 1989 Tell Nimrin Project, *ADAJ* 34 (1990), 131–152; R. H. Dornemann, ibid., 153–181.
Philadelphia	A. Raban, The Phoenician Jars from the Wrecked Ship off Philadelphia Village, *Sefunim* 5 (1976), 48–58 (Hebrew).
Qadum	E. Stern and I. Magen, A Persian Period Pottery Assemblage from Qadum in the Samaria Region, *BASOR* 253 (1984), 9–27.
Qasile, Tell	A. Mazar, Excavations at Tell Qasile, Part Two, The Philistine Sanctuary, *Qedem* 20 (1985).

Qiri, Tel	A. Ben-Tor et al., Tell Qiri, a Village in the Jezreel Valley, *Qedem* 24 (1987).
Qitmit	I. Beit-Arieh, *Horvat Qitmit, an Edomite Shrine in the Biblical Negev,* Tel Aviv 1995.
Qom, Khirbet el-	W. G. Dever, *NEAEHL,* vol. IV, 1233–1235.
Rabud, Tell	M. Kochavi, Khirbet Rabud-Debir, *TA* 1 (1974), 1–33.
Radum, Horvat	I. Beit-Arieh, *NEAEHL,* vol. IV, 1254–1255.
Ramat Raḥel I	Y. Aharoni et al., *Excavations at Ramat Raḥel (1959–1960),* Rome 1962.
Ramat Raḥel II	Y. Aharoni et al., *Excavations at Ramat Raḥel (1961–1962),* Rome 1964.
Rishon le-Zion	Y. Levi, Rishon Lezion in: S. R. Wolf (ed.), Archaeology in Israel, *AJA* 100 (1996), 744.
Ruqeish, Tell er- I	W. Culican, The Graves at Tell er-Reqeish, *AJBA* 1 (1973), 66–105.
Ruqeish, Tell er- II	E. Oren, *NEAEHL,* vol. IV, 1293–1294.
Ṣafi, Tell-es	E. Stern, *NEAEHL,* vol. IV, 1522–1529.
Ṣafut, Tell	D. Wimmer, Tell Safut Excavations 1982–1985, Preliminary Survey *ADAJ* 31 (1987), 159–174.
Saʿidiyeh, Tell es-	J. B. Prichard, *Tell Es-Saʿidiyeh: Excavations on the Tell, 1964–1966,* Philadelphia 1985.
Samaria HA I–II	G. A. Reisner, C. S. Fisher, and D. G. Lyon, *Harvard Excavations at Samaria 1908–1910* (I—Text; II—Plates), Cambridge, Mass. 1924.
Samaria I	J. W. Crowfoot, K. M. Kenyon, and E. L. Sukenik, *Samaria-Sebaste I: The Buildings,* London 1942.
Samaria III	J. W. Crowfoot, G. M. Crowfoot, and K. M. Kenyon, *Samaria-Sebaste III: The Objects,* London 1957.
Saʾsaʾ	H. Smithline, Saʾsa, *ESI* 16 (1997), 20–22.
Seraʿ, Tel	E. Oren, *NEAEHL,* vol. IV, 1329–1335.
Shavei Zion I	E. Linder, A Cargo of Phoenicio-Punic Figurines, *Archaeology* 26 (1973), 182–187.
Shavei Zion II	E. Linder, The Figurines from Shavei Zion—a Reexamination, in: M. Yedaʿaya, *The Western Galilee Antiquities,* Haifa (1986), 409–415 (Hebrew).
Shechem I	G. E. Wright, *Shechem: The Biography of a Biblical City,* New York and Toronto 1965.
Shechem II	E. Stern, Achaemenian Tombs from Shechem, *Levant* 12 (1980), 90–111.

Shechem III	N. Lapp, The Strata V Pottery from Balatah (Shechem), *BASOR* 257 (1985), 19–43.
Shilḥa, Ḥorvat	A. Mazar, D. Amit, and Z. Ilan, Hurvat Shilha: An Iron Age Site in the Judaean Desert, in: J. D. Seger (ed.), *Retrieving the Past: Essays on Archaeological Research and Methodology in Honor of Gus W. Van Beek,* Winona Lake, Ind. 1996, 193–211.
Shiqmona I	J. Elgavish, *Archaeological Excavations at Shiqmona, Field Report No. 1: The Levels of the Persian Period, Seasons 1963–1965,* Haifa 1968 (Hebrew).
Shiqmona II	J. Elgavish, *Shiqmona, on the Seacoast of Mount Carmel,* Tel Aviv 1994 (Hebrew).
Sinai	E. Oren, *NEAEHL,* vol. IV, 1393–1394.
Taanach, Tel I	W. E. Rast, *Taʿanach I: Studies in the Iron Age Pottery,* Cambridge, Mass. 1978.
Taanek I–III	E. Sellin, Tell Taʿanek I–III, Vienna 1904–1905.
Tawilan, Tell	C. M. Bennett and P. Bienkowski, *Excavations at Tawilan in Southern Jordan,* Oxford 1995.
Tirat Yehuda	Z. Yeivin and G. Edelstein, Excavations at Tirat Yehuda, *ʿAtiqot* 6, Hebrew series, 1970, 56–69.
Tov, Ḥorvat	R. Cohen, Horvat Tov, *ESI* 7–8 (1988–1989), 179–180.
Tuwein, Khirbet et-	A. Mazar, Khirbet Tuwein, *PEQ* 114 (1982), 87–109.
ʿUmeiri, Tel I–III	L. G. Herr et al. (eds.), *Madaba Plains Project I–III,* Berrien Springs, Mich. 1989–1991.
Umm el-Biyara I	C. M. Bennett, Fouilles d'Umm el-Biyara, *RB* 73 (1966), 372–403.
Umm Uthainah	H. Hadad, Umm Uthainah Tomb, *ADAJ* 28 (1984), 7–16 (Arabic).
ʿUsa, Ḥorvat	A. Ben-Tor, Excavations at Ḥorvat ʿUsa, *ʿAtiqot* 3, Hebrew series, 1966, 1–24.
ʿUza, Ḥorvat	I. Beit-Arieh and B. C. Cresson, Ḥorvat ʿUza, a Fortified Outpost on the Eastern Negev Border, *BA* 54 (1991), 126–135.
Vered Jericho	A. Eitan (interview), *BARev* 12 (1984), 30–34; *idem,* Rare Sword of the Israelite Period Found at Vered Jericho, *IMJ* 12 (1994), 61–62.
Yavneh-Yam	M. Fischer, Yavneh Yam, in: S. R. Wolf, Archaeology in Israel, *AJA* 102 (1988), 786–787.

Zippor, Tel	O. Negbi, A Deposit of Terracottas and Statuettes from Tel Sippor, *'Atiqot* VI, English series, 1966.
Zori [1977]	N. Zori, *The Land of Issachar, Archaeological Survey,* Jerusalem 1977 (Hebrew).

III. Excavations in Neighboring Lands

Al-Mina I	C. L. Woolley, Excavations at Al-Mina, Sueida, *JHS* 58 (1938), 1–30, 133–170.
Al-Mina II	C. L. Woolley, *A Forgotten Kingdom,* Harmondsworth 1953.
Defenneh	W. F. M. Petrie, *Nebesheh and Defenneh,* London 1886.
Naukratis I	W. F. M. Petrie, *Naukratis I (1884–5),* London 1886.
Sarepta	J. B. Pritchard, *Sarepta: A Preliminary Report on the Iron Age Excavations of the University Museum of the University of Pennsylvania, 1970–72,* Philadelphia 1975.
Sarepta I–IV	P. A. Anderson, *Sarepta I: The Late Bronze and Iron Age Strata of Area II, Y;* I. A. Khalifeh, *Sarepta II: The Late Bronze and Iron Age Periods of Area II, X;* R. B. Koehl, *Sarepta III: The Imported Bronze and Iron Age Wares from Area II, X;* J. B. Pritchard, *Sarepta IV: The Objects from Area II, X;* Beyrouth 1988, 1988, 1985, 1989.
Sukas I	P. J. Riis, *Sukas I: The North-East Sanctuary and the First Settling of Greeks in Syria and Palestine,* Copenhagen 1970.
Sukas II	G. Ploug, *Sukas II: The Aegean, Corinthian and Eastern Greek Pottery and Terracottas,* Copenhagen 1973.
Sukas VI	P. J. Riis, *Sukas VI: The Greco-Phoenician Cemetery at the Southern Harbor,* Copenhagen 1979.
Tanis II	W. F. M. Petrie, *Tanis II,* London 1888.
Umm el-'Amed	M. Dunand and R. Duru, *Oumm el-'Amed: Une ville de l'époque Hellénistique aux Echelles de Tyr,* Paris 1962.

GLOSSARY

GENERAL

alabastron (-a): elongated bottle, rounded at the bottom, with a flattened lip and a narrow orifice, used in antiquity to hold oils and perfumes, named after Egyptian alabaster bottles of that shape

amphoriskos (-oi): small glass or ceramic amphora

ankh: Egyptian logogram for "life" shaped like a cross with a loop instead of an upper vertical arm

aryballos (-oi): small, usually round Greek flask with flattened lip

bamah (-ot): (Heb.) cultic high place: cultic platform within a sanctuary

bichrome: of two colors, usually red and black

bothros: see *favissa*

caryatid: A figure of a woman in stone, metal, or pottery, supporting a heavy burden

cartouche: oval or oblong ornament with the hieroglyphic names and titles of an Egyptian king

casemate wall: double fortification wall with partitioned compartments, sometimes used for storage or dwellings

cist grave: boxlike burial chamber lined with stone or brick

chiton: basic tuniclike garment worn in ancient Greece

favissa (-ae): repository for discarded cultic objects

fibula (-ae): clasp in the shape of a safety pin or brooch

glacis: diagonal coating of an earthen rampart or fortification wall for defensive and constructional purposes, constructed of stone, compact earth, brick, etc.

haemation: long, loose outer garment worn in the ancient world by both men and women

Hippodamian plan: town planning in which the streets intersect at right angles, sometimes ascribed to Hippodamos of Miletus (5th century BCE), but actually not invented by him

insula (-ae): city block, usually quadrangular, with multiple dwellings

kernos (-oi): pottery vessel consisting of several small vessels and/or figurines joined on a ring or attached to the rim of a vase

King's Highway: one of the two most important highways that connected Egypt with Mesopotamia, crossing Transjordan from north to south, closer to the desert's fringe

koine: large international or intercultural area featuring common cultural traits

laginos (-oi): Greek drinking cup or bowl

Lamashtu: a female demon who attacked pregnant women and newborn children in particular. Lamashtu is usually depicted with lion's head and wings. Lamashtu amulettes and plaques were inscribed with incantations to block the ill effects of Lamashtu.

lekythos (-oi): Greek cylindrical, round, or squat vase with one handle, used for oils and ointments

mas oved: (Heb.) annual labor obligation for the king

mazzeba (-ot): (Heb.) ritual standing stones

mortarium (-ia): thick, heavy pottery bowls, mainly from the Late Iron Age and Persian period

omphalos: central boss projecting in the base of various vases, mainly bowls

pithos (-oi): large storage jar

protoma (-i): bust or front parts of an animal

pyxis (pixides): small, usually cylindrical box or container, usually lidded

quadriga (-e): Greek and Roman chariot, led by four horses

rhyton (-a): vessel for liquids; drinking vessel, usually shaped like a funnel, cone, animal or the head of an animal, or deity

shaft tomb: subsurface tomb reached through a vertical shaft

situla (-e): Egyptian cultic bottle, made of various materials, mainly faience or bronze

skyphos (oi): Greek drinking cup with handles

stela (-ae): upright slab or pillar, often with inscription or artistic depiction

thymiaterion (-ia): large stand used for incense burning

tophet: (Heb.) a site where children were burned and buried

Tridacna squamosa: large seashell, common in the Red Sea, and used in antiquity as a cosmetic palette

uraeus (-i): Egyptian symbol of kingship; a rearing cobra on a king's forehead or crown; also used as architectural decoration

Way of the Sea: one of the two most important highways that connected Egypt and Mesopotamia, crossing Palestine along the Mediterranean coastline and then branching north and northwest. The "Via Maris" of later periods.

White Painted ware: Cypriot pottery group of the Cypro-Geometric and Cypro-Archaic periods, decorated with geometric or figurative designs in black or brown on a white background

Wild Goat style: East Greek pottery group mainly from the 7th century BCE, decorated with the figures of various animals, especially wild goats

GEOGRAPHIC TERMS

Hebrew	Arabic	English
Tel	Tell	Mound
Horvah	Khirbeh	Ruin
Nahal	Nahr, Wadi	River, Brook
Har	Jebel	Mountain
'En	'Ain	Spring

TABLE 1

Kings of Judah, Assyria, the Neo-Babylonian Kingdom, and Persia

Judah		Assyria		Neo-Babylonian Kingdom		Persia (Achaemenids)	
Hezekiah	727–698	Tiglath-pileser III	744–727				
		Shalmaneser V	726–722				
		Sargon II	721–705				
Manasseh	698–642	Sennacherib	704–681				
		Esarhaddon	680–669				
Amon	641–640	Ashurbanipal	668–627				
Josiah	639–609			Nabopolassar	625–605		
Jehoahaz	609						
Jehoiakim	608–598			Nebuchadnezzar II	604–562		
Jehoiachin	597						
Zedekiah	596–586			Amel Marduk	561–560		
				Nergal Shar Usur	560–556	Cyrus II	559–529
				Nabonidus	556–539		
						Cambyses II	528–523
						Darius I	522–486
						Xerxes	485–465
						Artaxerxes I	464–424
						Darius II	423–405
						Artaxerxes II	404–359
						Artaxerxes III	358–338
						Arses (Xerxes II)	338–335
						Darius III	335–331

ARCHAEOLOGY

· OF THE ·

LAND OF THE BIBLE

VOLUME II

732–332 BCE

BOOK ONE

THE
ASSYRIAN
PERIOD

(732–604 BCE)

· Chapter 1 ·

THE ASSYRIAN CONQUEST
AND DOMINATION OF PALESTINE

The conquest of Palestine by the Assyrians was a gradual process that occurred in three major stages:

1. Penetration, destruction, and deportations began in the days of Tiglath-pileser III and Shalmaneser V (734–722 BCE). Areas conquered include the Golan and the Gilead in the northern part of Transjordan, where the Aramaic kingdom of Geshur was destroyed, and the territory of the Israelite kingdom, which was utterly destroyed; a third area affected by this first Assyrian movement was the coastal region consisting of southern Phoenicia and Philistia.

2. In the days of Sargon II (721–705 BCE) and the beginning of Sennacherib's reign (704–700 BCE), the conquest of Philistia was consolidated, Judah (except for Jerusalem) had been conquered and destroyed, and the way to Palestine was henceforth closed to the Egyptians. It is possible that during this stage the first Assyrian provinces—the Gilead, Megiddo, Dor, and Samaria—were established and most of their ruined settlements were rebuilt.

3. This was the most important stage in the conquest, and occurred in the latter part of Sennacherib's rule (700–681 BCE) and during the reigns of Esarhaddon (680–669 BCE) and Ashurbanipal (668–627 BCE), climaxing during these kings' campaigns to Egypt (674–663 BCE). At this time, Assyrian settlements and fortresses along the Via Maris (Way of the Sea) across Philistia were erected (fortresses have been discovered at Rishon le-Zion, Tell Jemmeh, Sheikh Zuweid, Ruqeish, Tel Seraʿ, Tel Haror, and elsewhere).

We may assume that up to Sennacherib's campaign to Judah, during which he also battled against the Egyptians, the Assyrians were often forced to reconquer various parts of the country that rebelled against them. From this campaign on, they faced almost no internal opposition and were able to dedicate all of their efforts against the Egyptians or other outsiders, such as the desert dwellers on their eastern frontier.

In contrast to its gradual beginning, the end of the Assyrian period in Palestine came suddenly: with the death of Ashurbanipal in 627 BCE. This year also witnessed the start of long, internal conflicts within the royal family that weakened the empire and caused the Assyrians to abandon the entire territory west of the Euphrates, including the whole of Palestine. It is probable that the hegemony over Palestine was lost even earlier, as we do not possess any documents attesting to Assyrian presence here after 645 BCE.

Assyrian hegemony in Palestine did not, therefore, exceed eighty to ninety years, not a long chapter in the country's history.

THE ASSYRIAN ARMY

THE CONQUEST OF Palestine, the destruction of its settlements, and the deportation of its inhabitants were implemented by the Assyrian army. This was a newly built organization that set out regularly to conquer new territories or defend ones already under its control. Its main advantage was superb organization, which enabled it to cover large distances in a relatively short time with its sophisticated equipment and to position large units against a few rivals simultaneously, even under difficult conditions. The Assyrian army had probably already incorporated within its units many of the military improvements usually associated with much later periods: Persian-Achaemenian, Greek, Hellenistic, or even Roman.

Detailed descriptions have survived in Assyrian military documents and in numerous reliefs depicting their battle method, both in the open field and while besieging fortified towns. These sources provide us with enough evidence to study the formation of Assyrian military units in detail. This army for the first time employed large units of cavalry alongside the age-old chariots, both equipped with light and heavy armor. Their heterogeneous infantry units included heavily armed spearmen, lance throwers, archers, and slingmen. The place of each weapon was fixed according to its range. In addition, a sophisticated intelligence network and an efficient signal system were employed. The army was also equipped with the best means to cross land and water obstacles and to hastily build fortified camps while en route to the enemy's territory. In time of siege, it possessed all elements needed to overcome

I.1   The siege of the city of Ekron by Sargon II

a strongly fortified town, such as battering rams, siege towers, and the know-how to build huge ramparts so as to bring all these siege machines close to the enemy's fortifications.

In many cases (such as the siege of Lachish), units of mercenaries who specialized in the use of weapons not utilized by the regular Assyrian army were employed, such as slingmen as well as large numbers of slaves and servants taken from lands previously subjugated.

From the many Assyrian sources describing their military campaigns, several depict scenes of siege of Palestinian and Transjordanian towns, such as the siege against Ashtaroth-Karnaim in the Bashan and the siege against Gezer, both in 734 BCE. These scenes survived in reliefs found in the palace of Tiglath-pileser III at Nimrud, as well as reliefs depicting the sieges laid against Ashdod, Gibbethon, Ekron, Raphia, and perhaps Samaria, uncovered on the walls of the palace of Sargon II in his capital at Khorsabad (Dur Sharukin). But the most impressive description is the one found in the palace of Sennacherib at Kuyunjik (Nineveh), composed of a series of orthostats that describe in detail the fierce fighting at and siege of the Judaean city of Lachish in 701 BCE. The main scene shows the attack on the gate and walls of Lachish. The protruding city gate is presented in minute detail, with its crenellations and its special reinforcement by a superstructure of warriors' shields. The battering rams were moved over specially constructed ramps covered with wooden logs. They were "prefabricated," four-wheeled, turreted machines. The scene vividly shows the frenzied fighting of both attacker and defender in the final stage of the battle. In a desperate effort to stop the operation of the battering rams, the defenders fling down lighted torches. The battering squads counter this by pouring water over the exterior of the machines with the aid of implements that look like long ladles. The grim outcome of the attack is illustrated by the captured women and children passing by the impaled bodies of prisoners. As to the Assyrian army itself, the scenes show its units arrayed opposite Lachish. The battle is depicted in three registers. The top one shows slingmen and auxiliary archers, the middle one auxiliary archers, heavy archers, and assault troops with spears. The bottom register shows, again, slingmen, heavily armored archers, auxiliary archers, and assault troops equipped with spears. Another scene describes the main assault, with the city gate and its vicinity as the focal area of the battle, from which we may extrapolate the "battle system" of the Assyrian army in such situations: behind the battering rams come the archers and the slingmen; in front are spearmen and shield bearers. Some of the psychological means used by the Assyrian troops against their enemies are also described, such as the cruel torture of some of the captives in front of their comrades standing on the city walls, or reading proclamations to the besieged people describing what will happen to them if they do not surrender.

The long and intensive activity of the Assyrian army in Palestine left many traces in the country's archaeological record. We should point first to the destruction levels at many sites attributed to the Assyrians. At others, some actual weapons used by this army have been uncovered: A most impressive find, unique in the entire Near East, is the huge Assyrian siege ramp built in 701 BCE at Lachish. The width of this ramp at its base is 55 to 60 m., narrowing at its top. It towered to a height of 16 m. and was composed of many tons of fieldstone gathered from the surrounding area. Its upper stratum—about 1 m. thick—was made of small stones, packed together with hard clay and wooden logs, on which the Assyrian soldiers could walk and push forward their siege engines.

Around the rampart, and especially in the area from which the Assyrians broke into the town, many hundreds of round slingstones of lime or flint the size of tennis balls were recovered. With these were found hundreds of arrowheads, bronze armor scales, and even remains of typical Assyrian bronze helmets. These are indeed unique remains of the Assyrian assault on a Judaean city.

More remains of Assyrian military equipment have been uncovered at other major Assyrian sites in Palestine, such as Gezer, where some lanceheads and arrowheads peculiar to this army were found, or in the storerooms of the Assyrian fort at Tel Seraʿ, in which some bronze weapons and a sock-

I.2 The Assyrian siege rampart at Lachish, looking north from the Assyrian camp toward the city

eted crescent-shaped bronze standard belonging to an Assyrian chariot were excavated.

The results of the activity of the Assyrian army in Palestine are well attested, as mentioned above, in the reports of the excavations conducted in all parts of Palestine:

In the Galilee and the northern coastal region, the first regions to fall into Assyrian hands, the conquest brought generalized destruction to all settlements. The result is visible at all sites excavated. According to the excavators' reports, all Israelite and the neighboring Aramaic settlements, which flourished in the Late Iron Age, were completely razed. Among these are Dan, Hazor, Chinnereth, Bethsaida, Tel Hadar, 'En Gev, Beth-Shean, Kedesh, Megiddo, Jokneam, Qiri, Acco, Keisan, Shiqmona, and Dor. Some of these settlements never recovered from this description and were abandoned for many years (Beth-Shean, Kedesh, 'En Gev, Tel Hadar, and Bethsaida).

In 721 BCE, when the Assyrians conquered the **southern part of the**

I.3 Assyrian slingstones throwers from the siege of Lachish

I.4 Arrowheads from Lachish
dated to the Assyrian siege

I.5 Tel Seraʿ, bronze crescent-shaped standard, bronze bell, iron chain, and forklike device from the Assyrian-period fort

Israelite kingdom and its capital, Samaria, this region, too, suffered total destruction. This is reflected in all excavations and surveys conducted there: at Taanach, Dothan, the city of Samaria, at Tell el-Farʿah (N), Shechem, Bethel, and Gezer (probably destroyed as early as 733 BCE during the first campaign of Tiglath-pileser III). This event is also reflected in the Bible (2 Kings 17:3–6; 18:9–12) and complemented by the inscriptions of Sargon II. These sources are, however, mutually contradictory, and it is difficult to draw a precise picture from them: either concerning the siege against Samaria, which lasted about three years, or regarding the conquest of Samaria. It is even possible—as H. Tadmor has pointed out—that there was a double conquest of the city: one in 722 BCE by Shalmaneser V and a second in 720 by Sargon II.

As to **Philistia,** here the Assyrian conquest is reflected in remains found at the excavations of Rishon le-Zion, Tel Mor, Ashdod, Ashdod-Yam, Tell el-Ḥesi, Ḥorvat Ḥuga, the fortress close to the mouth of the Shiqmah River, Tell esh-Sheikh Zuweid, Tel Haror, and Tel Sera'. From the Assyrian reliefs, we learn of the subjugation of four additional towns: Ekron, Gibbethon, and the towns located at Raphia and el-'Arish.

Judah. This kingdom felt the fierce blow of the Assyrian army somewhat later, during Sennacherib's campaign in 701 BCE, when Lachish and forty-six other towns were destroyed. The result of this invasion is evident at all Judaean settlements, except perhaps for Jerusalem. Destruction layers attributed to the Assyrian presence have been uncovered at Lachish, Tel Batash, Tell Beit Mirsim, Tel Halif, Tel 'Erani, as far as Tel Sheva, Arad, and the entire Beersheba Valley and Mount Hebron.

In the kingdoms of **Transjordan,** the settlements of the northern provinces that had already been taken by Tiglath-pileser III in 733/2 BCE have not yet been excavated, and it remains impossible to measure the might of the Assyrian blow there. The only evidence for the Assyrian invasion in this region is a relief depicting the conquest of the city of Ashtaroth-Karnaim and excavations at Tell Rumeith in the Golan and at Israelite settlements in the Valley of Sukkoth, which were also destroyed by Tiglath-pileser III. As already mentioned, four border towns belonging to Aram Geshur—Chinnereth, Bethsaida, Tel Hadar, and 'En Gev—were also destroyed by the Assyrians, but these are located on the Israelite border, along the northeastern coast of the Sea of Galilee.

At the same time, the kingdoms of **Ammon, Moab,** and **Edom** chose to surrender without a battle, willingly accepting Assyrian domination for the benefits it promised. The period of Assyrian domination in these kingdoms appears to have been one of continuing economic and cultural prosperity.

THE ASSYRIAN ADMINISTRATIVE SYSTEM

DURING THE EIGHTY years or so of Assyrian domination in Palestine, the country was divided administratively into four types of units: (1) the Assyrian provinces that were under direct Assyrian rule, (2) the autonomous vassal kingdoms, (3) the Phoenician and Philistine harbor towns along the coast, and (4) the nomadic tribes that linked the country with the surrounding deserts.

Usually, the Assyrians annexed the small kingdoms they captured and turned them into provinces directly ruled by Assyrian officials sent by the court. These provinces, which encompassed territories inhabited by various nations, were of varying size and importance. At the head of each of them stood a governor supported by a small army unit. The title of the governor was *peḥa (bel piḥati), šaknu,* or *sgn.* Other administrative titles of lower-level officials that appear in Assyrian documents from the province of Samaria are the *rab alani,* the official in charge of a district, and the *ḥazannu,* i.e., governor of a city.

The creation of a province—according to the Assyrian system, which was already fully developed in the days of Tiglath-pileser III—was followed by large-scale deportations of the local inhabitants. It seems that the reason for these deportations was—as N. Na'aman recently put it—to populate cities and settlements in Assyria itself while at the same time weakening the enemy's country by destroying its national framework, which was naturally hostile to the conqueror. The Assyrians also transferred some of the enemy's military units and incorporated them into their own army.

According to Assyrian sources, dated to the reigns of Tiglath-pileser III and Sargon II, about 50,000 people were deported from Palestine and sent to Mesopotamian towns.

Later, Sennacherib, when destroying Lachish and another forty-six Judaean settlements, claimed that he had captured no fewer than 200,000 people and deported them. In order to replace the deportees, these kings sent new inhabitants from the eastern parts of the Assyrian empire (Babylon, Cutha, Ava, Hamath, and Sepharvaim—cf. 2 Kings 17:24) to populate the new towns that Sargon had founded in the territories of Megiddo, Samaria, and Dor. It seems that in Palestine, the movement of deportees into the new towns continued through the entire Assyrian period, including the reigns of both Esarhaddon and Asnapar (Ashurbanipal: Ezra 4:2, 9–10). These newcomers were indeed the main political, military, and cultural support for the Assyrian governors during their period of domination, and continued to function as such later, under the subsequent empires, in particular under Persian rule (see below).

1. According to E. Forer, the Assyrians established no fewer than six provinces in Palestine: three in the northern part of Transjordan, in territories previously under Aramaic and Israelite control (Hauran, Gilead, and Karnaim), and three in western Palestine (Megiddo, Samaria, and Dor), all established by Tiglath-pileser III, who also conquered them, except for the province of Samaria, established in the days of Sargon II. Recently, I. Eph'al, in a comprehensive discussion of Assyrian domination of Palestine, claimed that according to Assyrian records, some of which have only recently been

published, Tiglath-pileser III did not establish any provinces in Transjordan; nor do we possess direct evidence for the establishment of the province of Samaria by Sargon II.

Eph'al also pointed out that the only certain Assyrian sources that deal with the administration of the Assyrian provinces in Palestine and mention the names of governors with their titles are of a later date. In these documents, reference to "the governor of Karnaim" and perhaps also the name Gilead may point to administrative provinces existing there. At the same time, no mention of the Hauran appears anywhere.

Considering the titles of the governors (which were listed in the Assyrian "eponym" or annual lists of the years 690, 679, and 646 BCE), and according to the other published Assyrian administrative lists, Eph'al concluded that "we have clear information about the existence of only two Assyrian provinces in western Palestine (Megiddo and Samirina), and two in Transjordan (Karnaim and Gilead)," but he adds that "because the Assyrian documents that we possess are few and accidental, it is impossible to be sure either of the existence or the extent of other Assyrian provinces in Palestine."

It was only in 1995 that a new list of Assyrian provinces in Syria-Palestine was published by F. M. Fales and J. N. Postgate. This list repeats again the names of Samaria and Megiddo, but it adds, for the first time, a third province in western Palestine, the province of **Dor.** Before the publication of this document, the problem of Dor as capital of a separate province was the topic of a long and intensive dispute. This matter was finally resolved by the results of the recent archaeological excavations in the ancient city, where important Assyrian finds have been recovered, lending support to the idea that Dor was a provincial capital in those days, now confirmed by the recent publication.

2. The Phoenician cities incorporated in the Dor province, or those located south of it, along the coast of western Galilee, became almost autonomous trading centers that used their fleets to trade with both Egypt and the North African coast, as well as with Greece and the west. This greatly benefited the Assyrian sovereigns, who appointed special inspectors at each harbor and maintained strict supervision of this trade activity.

3. As for the desert nomads, they, too, were subjugated by the Assyrians, who kept close tabs on the incense and spice trade. The two parties benefited from this trade. The Assyrian domination of desert territories was not firmly established: it was strengthened or weakened according to changing needs and circumstances.

It is noteworthy that although the Assyrians made some efforts to develop the Phoenician overseas trade with Egypt and the west, as well as that of the nomads in South Arabia, they themselves never participated in it directly, benefiting from it indirectly by the appointment of officials who were located in all important harbors and in desert forts along the trade routes. They inspected the stream of merchandise coming and going and made sure that the Assyrian government received its proper share.

· Chapter 2 ·

The Assyrian Impact
on the Material Culture
of Palestine

Assyrian Inscribed Remains and Seals

As compared with the Babylonian and the Persian periods, Assyrian domination of Palestine and its administrative system left rich and important traces in the archaeological record of the country, despite a relatively short duration. The most distinguished remains are several documents written in Assyrian cuneiform script.

The overall number of such artifacts is quite surprising, for a variety of scripts was common in the country during the Assyrian period: each of the many nations of the country spoke its national language and wrote in its own alphabetic script, while Aramaic served as the *lingua franca,* or common language, for all, including the Assyrian authorities. These cuneiform documents serve, therefore, as important evidence for the intensity of Assyrian rule in the country: scores of scribes were required to read or write this peculiar script, which was probably imposed on the locals.

The Assyrian cuneiform inscriptions found in Palestine are of three different types: (1) monumental stone stelae, inscribed to commemorate historical events, (2) clay tablets which served local officials' supervision of daily life in the provinces, and (3) short cuneiform inscriptions on seals belonging to high-ranking officials, which were intended to designate their position in the imperial or the local hierarchy.

Of the monumental Assyrian inscriptions found here, four are known; three of them are attributed to Sargon II (who, as explained above, probably established the Assyrian provinces of Megiddo, Samaria, and Dor). The best known among these is one uncovered at Ashdod, connected with the story of

I.6 Sargon II's stelae from Ashdod and Samaria

the city's conquest by the Assyrian army commander, "the Tartan," in 712 BCE (Isaiah 20:1: "In the year that Tartan came unto Ashdod, when Sargon the king of Assyria sent him, and fought against Ashdod and took it"). A second monumental inscription was found in the town of Samaria the capital of the Assyrian province. It belongs, perhaps, to the period of the rebuilding of the city in the days of Sargon II. The other two inscribed cuneiform Assyrian stelae were found by chance on the western slopes of the Samaria Hills. One in Ben-Shemen (close to the Assyrian center recently uncovered at Hadid) is also attributed to Sargon, and the fourth, found in the ruins of the village of Kakun on the eastern side of the Sharon Plain, is the only one attributed to Esarhaddon.

Although Aramaic was the common language and script in those days, as is evident from the many finds of ostraca written in this language, it is also clear that most of the Aramaic (and Hebrew) documents were written on papyri, which did not survive (not a single Aramaic papyrus from the Assyrian period is known; the only evidence for their common use here is the clay bullae utilized to seal them). Some of the bullae found in the capital city of Samaria definitely belonged to the Assyrian royal administration: they bear impressions containing royal emblems. It is tempting to assume that the papyrus documents sealed with these bullae were sent by the Assyrian court to the governor of the Assyrian province of Samaria.

In addition, there are some clay cuneiform tablets that probably constitute but a small percentage of Assyrian written texts. Made of hard material, these tend to be better preserved than the papyri. In the city of Samaria, a

I.7 Drawing of a royal Assyrian
bulla from Samaria

clay tablet was found mentioning the title of an Assyrian official, a *rab alani* who was probably the governor of a district. Two legal tablets of the years 651 and 649 BCE were found at Gezer in the Samaria province. These contain twenty-one personal names, twelve of which are Akkadian (mostly Babylonians); five are West Semitic (two of which were Aramaean and one Israelite); and one, that of the city governor *(ḥazannu),* is Egyptian. These documents may indicate a group of inhabitants brought from Mesopotamia to Gezer. The same tablets also contain some evidence concerning the legal rights of the local people during this period. The tablets from Gezer probably originated in the remains of a large structure that was once an Assyrian administrative center. Recently, a third Assyrian cuneiform tablet from Gezer was observed in the archives of the museum of Istanbul but was not yet properly published.

Close to Gezer in a place called **Hadid,** another complete Assyrian legal tablet was recently uncovered. It is a document of sale, which contains only Babylonian and Aramaic names and no Hebrew ones. It may refer to an early period, close to the arrival of the new deportees to Palestine. The document is dated to the period between 701 and 689 BCE, and it, too, came from a large building considered by the excavator to have been an administrative center, still only partially excavated and in which the Assyrian stela mentioned above also probably originated.

Additional Assyrian administrative tablets were found at Tell Keisan in the Acco Valley, which served also as an Assyrian center. One consists of a list of Assyrian weights *(minda)* used for distribution of rations to various people. Another cuneiform tablet, only a few small pieces of which survived, was discovered during the 1930s at Sepphoris in the Lower Galilee.

Recently, a new clay cuneiform tablet was found near the city of Lachish. This is a different type of document: on one of its sides, it is inscribed, while on the other side is a relief. The publisher of the tablet believes that it was an apotropaic amulet, or a charm of the Lamashtu type, against bad omens etc. He also suggests that it might have been lost by one of the Assyrian soldiers who carried it all the way from home during the campaign against Lachish in 701 BCE.

There are some Assyrian-style seals found here, both cylinder seals and stamp seals, which give us the titles of their owners in the Assyrian hierarchy. Noteworthy is a cylinder seal published by H. and M. Tadmor, found in the province of Dor, in which they read the name and title of *belu asharedu rab ekalli,* i.e., "the overseer of the palace." Other seals belonging to Assyrian officials have been found in many of the major centers of the Assyrian provinces in Palestine: Tell Keisan, Beth-Shean, Megiddo, Dor, Samaria, Shechem, Gezer, etc. Some were recovered along the main roads often used by the Assyrian military forces, such as the Assyrian cylinder seal recently found at Caesarea, or the *belu asharedu* seal, mentioned above, which was found along the Via Maris (Way of the Sea), near the modern site of the

I.8 Assyrian Lamashtu tablet
from the region of Lachish

I.9 Assyrian cylinder seal from Tel Dor

I.10 Assyrian cylinder seal belonging to "the overseer of the palace"

Wingate Institute. A few others were recovered in the territory of Judah, at sites such as Tel Sheva and Arad. These usually depict Assyrian cult scenes. In some cases, only the seal impressions survived. Others depict the image of the Assyrian goddess Ishtar of Arbel, who is recognized by a circle of stars surrounding her and who was probably identified here with the local 'Astarte. Most of the seals found here were imported from Assyria, for they are made of stones such as agate or carnelian, which are not native to Palestine. There are many local imitations as well.

ASSYRIAN ARCHITECTURE AND CITY PLANNING

THE HUGE DESTRUCTION that the Assyrians wrought in many parts of Palestine, followed by mass deportations out of and into the country, settling new peoples in these regions, and most important, the tremendous building activities that followed their decision to rebuild the destroyed towns left clear traces in the material culture and the archaeological record of the Assyrian period in Palestine.

Although they ruled for a relatively short period, the Assyrians' impact on every aspect of Palestine's culture may be regarded as revolutionary: it appears to have brought an end to the age-old Israelite-Phoenician tradition and the introduction of the Mesopotamian-Assyrian one instead.

The Assyrians left their mark, as we have seen, upon the military practice of war and siege and upon the civil administration, but their main impact has survived more clearly in the remains of the new cities that they built in a surprisingly short time. Here, new city plans were introduced, as well as new types of dwelling, palace, and monumental architecture, imitating Assyrian prototypes. Their impact can also be detected in burial customs, temples and cult, glyptic art on stone, clay, glass, faience, and metal objects; in short—almost all the elements of culture.

Even more important was the influence of the new Assyrian style on local artisans, who began to imitate it from then on and through later periods, even years after Assyrian domination had ceased.

The conquest of Galilee, Samaria, and the entire coastal region by the Assyrians, as well as the immigration of many new peoples into these areas, caused a tremendous momentum in building, aimed at providing needed dwellings for these masses. This massive building activity is uncommon over the long history of Palestine. These new constructions followed new plans and rules, partly adopted from Mesopotamian tradition, which was previously completely unknown in this region. At the same time, in the areas occupied by the independent states, such as Judah, the previous Israelite-Phoenician style continued.

As a rule, the towns of the Assyrian provinces were not fortified. This may reflect Assyrian strategy in the region. It is only in the case of the three capitals of the provinces—Megiddo, Samaria, and Dor—that remains of city walls and gates have been found. At Megiddo and Dor, the fortification systems must have been rebuilt but a short time after the destruction of the previous ones. We cannot yet say if this occurred in 733/2 BCE or, more likely, twelve years later, after the final destruction of the kingdom of Israel in 720 BCE. We prefer the later date, and attribute the massive building activity to the Assyrian king Sargon II, whose monumental stelae were found at three sites in the land of Samaria.

It is noteworthy that the fortifications of Megiddo and Dor built by the Assyrians follow an identical plan: both city walls are of the offset-inset type, inner gates follow the two-chamber plan, and both had an outer gate. This correlation between plan and date between the two neighboring towns perhaps points to both having been built by the same hand.

In Samaria, no construction belonging to the Assyrian-period city wall has yet been uncovered or identified, but it seems certain that the city's fortifications were rebuilt or maintained, because the walls of the Israelite period survived into the Hellenistic period and even to the Roman period.

The best example of the plan of a complete city built by the Assyrians is undoubtedly that of Megiddo Stratum III. This town consisted of dwellings that occupied the entire area of the previous Israelite town. At the north end, close to the city gate, a complex of public buildings was erected. The general plan of the stratum left by the American excavators depicts a very well planned town, divided into regular blocks *(insulae)* arranged between intersecting streets, and composed of dwellings built according to an identical plan. The public buildings (palaces, storehouses, etc.) are concentrated at the north end of the town, near the gate area. Together, they create a kind of administrative center. There is also a water system and a large public silo, both located inside the town. Each of these different types of construction was built as a separate *insula.* Together, they reflect a virtually Hippodamian

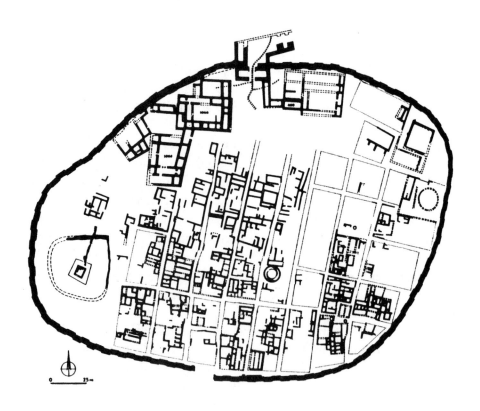

I.11 Plan of Megiddo Stratum III: the Assyrian town

plan. We do not yet know if the other towns reconstructed at the same time by the Assyrians enjoyed a similar superb level of planning, but this seems plausible.

In most cases, we are dealing with the rebuilding of old centers according to the requirements of the new administration. This means that a network of large centers, including the provincial capitals such as Megiddo, Samaria, and Dor, was reconstructed, as were many smaller, secondary centers, remains of which have been found at Ayelet ha-Shaḥar in the province of Megiddo, at Tell Keisan in the Phoenician Acco Valley, at Tel Dothan in the Samaria Hills, and at Gezer and Tell Hadid on their western slopes.

To this new rebuilding belong many military fortresses located along the main roads and especially along the Via Maris in Philistia. These forts (some of which were erected before the conquest of Egypt by the Assyrians, others at the time of the conquest) include a recently excavated one near modern Rishon le-Zion, the forts at Tell el-Ḥesi, Ḥorvat Ḥuga, at a fort at the mouth of the Shiqmah River, Tell Jemmeh, Tel Seraʿ, Tel Haror, and Sheikh Zuweid.

In addition to the renewal of the earlier network of settlements, new centers were constructed at sites not existing previously, in order to achieve better control over international trade routes, which now came into being. These new centers were connected to the Phoenician maritime trade and to the Arab and Edomite fortresses that controlled the desert trade routes. The Assyrians contributed to trade by erecting a new harbor town near Sidon called Kur Essarhadon, where an Assyrian governor was appointed to take revenues due from the city as well as from the nearby towns of Tyre and Sidon. Even before that, the Assyrians built another harbor town at the southern end of the Palestinian coast, called the Closed Karum of Egypt, i.e., a town built by Sargon II on the border of Egypt in order to achieve better access to trade routes between Palestine and Egypt, in particular those involving trade in incense and spices brought there by the Edomites and the Arabs (see below). The identification of this Assyrian harbor is today a matter of controversy. Some authorities believe that it was located at Sheikh Zuweid, excavated long ago by W. M. F. Petrie, where an Assyrian center was uncovered; others identify it as a site excavated recently by E. Oren at Ruqeish. Here, a large town encircled by huge defensive walls has been uncovered. It was built at the beginning of the Assyrian period and remained in use until the Persian period. The town was populated mainly by Phoenician residents who were probably brought here by the Assyrians. Remains of another Assyrian-built port have recently been excavated on the coast of Gaza, but these have not yet been published.

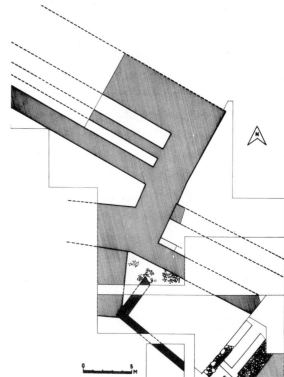

I.12 Tel Sera᷍, section of
the Assyrian fort

We have already noted that the Assyrian building methods in Palestine imitated those practiced in Assyria itself and were entirely unknown here previously. These methods can be divided into two types of construction:

1. The less common of the two utilized purely Assyrian methods, i.e., Assyrian house plans, Assyrian building materials, and even Assyrian architectural decorations that were probably brought from Assur itself or were made here under the supervision of experienced Assyrian architects and artisans. This royal Assyrian architecture is distinguished by a series of architectural elements. These features were studied by G. Loud and G. Turner and recently by R. Reich, in a survey they made of Assyrian architecture in the Assyrian imperial centers, and in their provinces in Syria and Palestine.

According to Reich, in Palestine the degree to which a building is Assyrian in character should be judged on the basis of the architectural criteria established by Loud and Turner. A survey reveals the existence of buildings that were constructed according to a strict Assyrian formula, which is: typical layout, architectural features such as an elevated podium, the use of burnt square bricks, horn-shaped stone thresholds, shallow niches in the walls, vaulted openings and roofs, etc. It may be assumed that these structures were designed by an Assyrian architect brought especially for this purpose.

I.13 Ruqeish, section of the city wall

2. On the other hand, there are also buildings that exhibit Assyrian characteristics but are not, in fact, exact replicas of Assyrian buildings. This may perhaps indicate only Assyrian influence, or the experience acquired by local architects working with the Assyrians. In the provinces of Megiddo and Samaria, Assyrian building features have been identified with certainty at only a few sites and in only a few buildings.

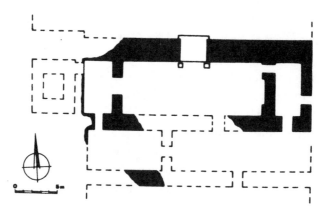

I.14 Plan of the Assyrian palace at Ayelet ha-Shaḥar

Of the buildings of the first type, i.e., structures of purely Assyrian concept and materials, the building uncovered at Hazor (or rather, at nearby Ayelet ha-Shaḥar) may serve as a good example. According to Reich, it was a part of an administrative center that also contained a large residence of a local governor. This building was constructed according to Assyrian rules, a fact that made it easily identifiable, despite its reuse during the Persian period (see below). The series of rooms uncovered here once belonged to the reception wing of the residence and contained the main audience hall in the center (this was, according to Reich, the largest room in the building, a kind of throne room for the local governor). The building is identical in plan, design, and construction method to ones known from the heart of the Assyrian empire, or from sites within the area of Assyrian territories in northern Syria, such as Arslan Tash, Til Barsip, and Zinjirli. The long walls of the Ayelet ha-Shaḥar residence were considerably thicker than the other walls and probably carried vaults of mud bricks that did not survive.

Other features, such as the anteroom of the audience hall (and especially the typical pair of door sockets for the heavy double doors), the use of shallow niches, the thick plaster floor, the drainage system consisting of sections of terra-cotta pipes, and the thick walls of *terre-pisée* (beaten earth), are all unmistakable characteristics of royal Assyrian architecture. This residence would appear to have been erected in the days of Sargon II.

Other buildings of the pure Assyrian type are known from Tell Jemmeh, Sheikh Zuweid, and Tel Seraʿ, all located in Philistia.

At **Tell Jemmeh,** in the excavations carried out by G. Van Beek, part of a building containing a number of adjoining rooms was uncovered. Although a clear plan pointing to Assyrian origin cannot yet be gleaned from these remains, the building technique and the small finds—which included Assyrian Palace ware—do attest to the source of influence. The building was con-

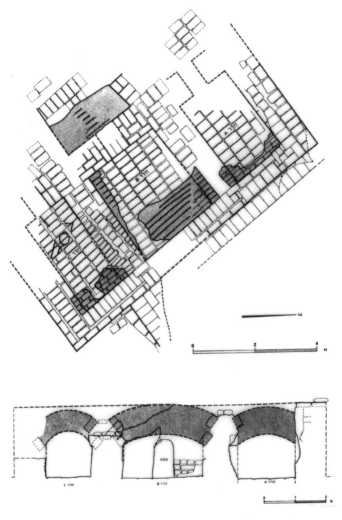

I.15 Plan of the Assyrian structure at Tell Jemmeh

structed in its entirety—walls, floors, and roof—of rectangular mud bricks, which were laid as headers and stretchers in the walls. The brick vaults were laid in the pitched-brick technique, in which the vault was composed of arches built of square bricks. The first arch is slightly inclined and rests on the back wall, as do the other arches. The bricks were bonded with mud mortar and the joint strengthened by means of grooves made in the lower surface of the bricks. Since the brick vaults are an extremely rare find due to poor preservation, parallels for this roof are difficult to find, but it can be assumed that many Assyrian buildings employed brick vaults for roofing the halls and some of the rooms. At Tell Jemmeh, a very low space was left beneath the vaults. Therefore, the rooms in this level were probably not used for dwelling, but for storage.

At **Tel Seraʿ**, too, massive building remains were uncovered at the southern and northern sides of the mound in Stratum VI, which is attributed by the excavator, E. Oren, to the 7th to 6th centuries BCE. These remains belong to a mud-brick structure consisting of brick walls with long, narrow spaces between them. Its location, at the edge of the mound, indicates that it had a defensive function. Finds of Assyrian origin were uncovered in the spaces between the walls. It is therefore possible that the structure served as an Assyrian military fort.

Another example of Assyrian architecture was found many years ago at **Tell el-Sheikh Zuweid** (Tell Abu Salima) by W. M. F. Petrie. Here, another fort was uncovered, apparently built by the Assyrians close to the Egyptian border. It consisted of a series of rooms laid around a central court and was protected by an offset-inset wall, with a stepped base in the outer face. The wall was also supported by an earthen fill, which raised the fortress above the terrain, as was common in Assyrian buildings. The construction material was sun-dried mud brick. Identification of the site as Assyrian is based upon the existence of a small temple erected for the use of the local Assyrian administration and army. The most distinctive Assyrian element here was the floor of the cella, which was paved with square, fired bricks. The steps leading to the cella were similarly paved. Two pedestals stood at either side of the steps, another widespread feature in Assyrian temples. Floors paved with fired bricks were a common element in Assyrian architecture, but so far, this is the only example that has been uncovered in Palestine.

Lately, another Assyrian-type fort raised on a high brick platform has been uncovered west of the modern town of **Rishon le-Zion**, located along the Via Maris. The fort is situated atop a narrow *kurkar* hill, ca. 30 m. above the surrounding area, thus providing a good strategic location. The site was excavated by Y. Levi and contained two strata of occupation: an Assyrian one sealed by a Persian-period fort. In the Assyrian period, the upper part of the site was leveled, and a roughly square fortress (18 x 17 m.) was erected. The building was made of sun-dried mud bricks, and its walls were preserved to a height of up to 3.5 m. A belt of small chambers was built around a central courtyard. These cells, too small to have served as rooms, were probably constructional elements. A glacis was erected against the outer walls of the fort. The excavator concluded that this kind of mud-brick architecture and the pottery finds show strong Assyrian influence. The fort must have housed an Assyrian garrison that according to the excavator was "most likely associated with the activities of Sargon II."

Of the Assyrian-influenced buildings of the second type, i.e., those that exhibit Assyrian characteristics but are not exact replicas of Assyrian prototypes, many more examples have been uncovered in Palestine. This type was already dealt with by R. Amiran and I. Dunayevsky following the discovery of Building 3002 in Area B at Hazor. They published a study dealing with all similar structures found here, in which the plan consists of a large open court occupying the central part of the building, which they designated as "the open-court building," claiming it to be of Mesopotamian origin with local additions.

The best examples of this hybrid Mesopotamian-local type are the Hazor 3002 structure and the Megiddo Stratum III public buildings. Others have been unearthed at Buṣeirah, the Edomite capital, and at other sites in Transjordan.

At **Megiddo,** remains of the buildings uncovered in Stratum III display a strong Assyrian influence, mainly the public buildings situated in the northern part of the city in the vicinity of the city gate. It seems, however, that Stratum III was planned—as pointed out above—and laid out according to the Hippodamian plan; i.e., the town was divided into blocks (*insulae*) by a system of streets, running north-south and east-west. This geometric layout was apparently intended to enlarge the area available for private dwellings for the new population of the city, which was brought by the Assyrian authorities, and which should have been even larger than that of the previous period. Formerly, about 50 percent of the city area, at most, was allocated for private housing. This was now increased to ca. 75 percent. Almost no Assyrian influence could be perceived in the plans of the private dwellings, and it seems that the local population built them within an urban plan that was dictated to them by the authorities.

The public buildings uncovered near the city gate include Buildings 1052,

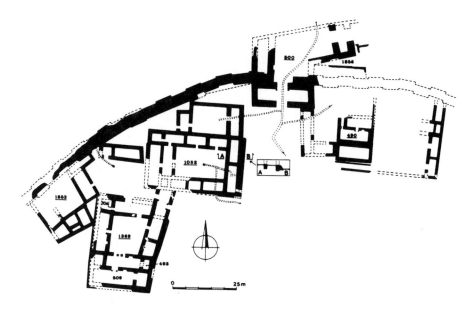

I.16 The Assyrian buildings at Megiddo Stratum III

1369, and 1853 south of the gate, and Building 490 and the Nordburg (excavated by G. Schumacher), northeast of it.

Building 1369 consisted of series of rooms around a large court. South of the court was the reception wing. The building was erected on a raised platform or podium, about 2 m. above its surroundings, supported by a retaining wall. Podiums like this were widespread in Assyria, where they were known as *tamlu* (= *millo* in Hebrew). Although the remains of the walls that were uncovered were of stones, there was probably a mud-brick superstructure, as suggested by the excavators. The reception wing in the south also followed Assyrian design, with the exception of two stone slabs placed in the entrance, on which stood columns to support the lintel. Columns in entrances are extremely rare in Assyrian architecture. Here, they probably represented a local solution to the problem of the roofing of the wide entranceway. In Assyria, a large brick arch was employed instead. Additional Assyrian elements in the building include narrow niches in the reception rooms, a bathroom with a drainage system with the drain hole set in a niche, thresholds with the doorpost sockets in a deep cavity covered by horseshoe-shaped stones with molded profile, a stairwell, the base of which was apparently uncovered in one of the rooms, and the trapezoidal appearance of the building, created by angles not all of which are of 90 degrees.

Building 1052 resembles Building 1369 in that it, too, contains a court surrounded on all sides by a row of rooms, with a double row on the western side, in which the audience halls were situated. Building 1052 seems to have been later than Building 1369.

Several rooms were cleared in Building 490. This structure stood adjacent to the city wall, near the gate. It, too, was constructed on an elevated platform. No remains of the building have survived in the area of the wall or outside it, but it has the same location in the city as the previous Assyrian building, though it is smaller in scale. It seems also that several walls of Building 490 were unearthed by G. Schumacher in the building he called the Nordburg.

In **Buṣeirah,** the capital town of the Edomites, a number of public buildings was uncovered, which exhibited Assyrian architectural elements. On the acropolis (Area A), two buildings were excavated by C. Bennett, one above the ruins of the other. The lower one was a large-scale structure consisting of two suites of rooms arranged around two large courtyards. One of the rooms, located in a row of rooms between the courtyards, served as a temple, as attested by the following details: a wide staircase across the full width of the room ascending to the floor that was raised above the court; two stone bases at the sides of the staircase, which had originally held statues or cult objects. The plan of the entrance was identical to that of Assyrian temples in the imperial centers, in the provinces under direct Assyrian rule, and in the temple at Sheikh Zuweid. The building in the upper stratum is smaller. It consists of a row of rooms around a single courtyard and thus resembles the plan of Building 3002 at Hazor. Only a few datable finds were discovered in the buildings at Buṣeirah, but the fact that the upper building was erected above a building containing Assyrian elements attests that the former should be assigned to the late 7th century BCE.

Another building of public character was discovered in another area (Area C) at Buṣeirah, but only a small part of it has been exposed. The remains uncovered belong to a large hall. An interesting feature linking this building to the Assyrian world is a broad, shallow niche. It lacked the layer of thick plaster covering the floor of the hall, which indicates that it had originally held a stone slab (later removed) very common in Assyrian audience halls. According to R. Reich, these two buildings—the lower one in Area A and the partially excavated one in Area C—represent the two large public buildings erected at Buṣeirah after its conquest by the Assyrians. One served as a residence, and the other probably functioned as a temple.

In recent years, another important Assyrian-influenced building complex has been uncovered at Philistine **Ekron,** designated by its excavator, S. Gitin, as Temple Complex 650 and attributed to Stratum IB, dated to the 7th century BCE. The temple complex, which was found in the "elite zone" in the center of the lower city (Field IV), is a monumental structure (57 x 30 m.) and one of the largest buildings of this kind ever to have been excavated in Palestine. The focus of its architectural plan—also based on the design concept of Neo-Assyrian royal palaces, residences, and temples—is a long and narrow reception hall (M) with a mud-brick platform constituting the throne room (K). This great hall, which had a threshold with a pair of doorpost sockets for heavy double doors, served as a buffer separating two larger courtyard areas: an open courtyard (J) with adjoining rooms (C-I), and a cultic area with a sanctuary (U; and see below). Building 650, erected in the first quarter of the 7th century BCE, was in use (with its sanctuary) until the end of Stratum IB, when it was destroyed with the rest of the city by the Babylonians in 603 BCE.

Other buildings of the hybrid Assyrian-local type, which have been par-

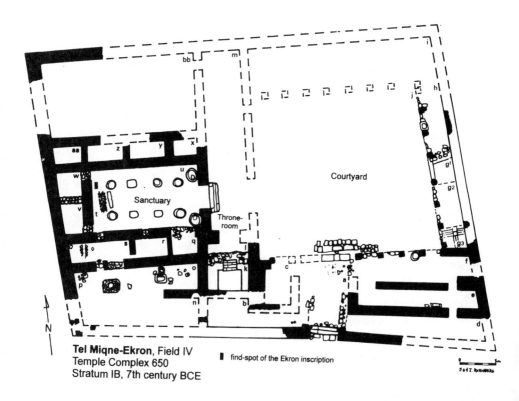

Tel Miqne-Ekron, Field IV
Temple Complex 650
Stratum IB, 7th century BCE

■ find-spot of the Ekron inscription

I.17 Plan of the Assyrian temple-palace at Ekron

tially uncovered, are located at Tel Chinnereth, Tell Keisan, and Tel Dothan in the northern part of Palestine, and at Gezer and Hadid in the central area. There must, however, have been many more such structures during this period.

ASSYRIAN TEMPLES AND CULT

OF THE TEMPLES exhibiting Assyrian influence found in Palestine, there are only three examples. One was excavated at Ekron in Philistia as part of Temple Complex 650; the second, at Sheikh Zuweid, also in Philistia, was found long ago by W. M. F. Petrie; the third was excavated by C. Bennett at Buṣeirah, capital city of Edom. The last two structures were recently reevaluated by R. Reich. The sanctuary at **Ekron,** part of Complex 650 there, had two parallel rows of column bases and a main monumental entrance to the building, but lacked door sockets. Inside, flanking the entrance, were two large stone vats, possibly used for ritual ablutions. At the western end of the sanctuary, opposite the entrance, was a raised stone threshold and a partially stone-paved cella. A royal dedicatory inscription incised on a rectangular-shaped limestone block (60 x 39 x 26 cm.) found in the cella may have been part of the western wall of the sanctuary—and perhaps its focal point. The five-line inscription, written in the local script, mentions five rulers of Ekron, including Achish the son of Padi, who built the temple to his goddess. Padi is mentioned as the king of Ekron in the Assyrian annals of Sennacherib's campaign in 701 BCE. Achish is the Ikausu, the king of Ekron, known from the annals of the Assyrian kings Esarhaddon and Ashurbanipal of the first half of the 7th century BCE.

The sanctuary side rooms (o–t, v–z) contained an olive-oil installation and hundreds of whole and restorable clay vessels, gold, silver, and bronze objects, and a large number of ivory fragments, including an ivory knob with the cartouche of Pharaoh Ramses VIII of the 20th Dynasty (1134 BCE) and a carved ivory statuette head, the largest of its kind in Israel. Other unique finds include a gold cobra (a uraeus) and a faience amulet of Ptah-Pataikos. This, and a carved ivory from the great hall of the adjoining palace (m) depicting a large male figure with a relief of a princess or goddess at his side, and a cartouche of Pharaoh Mernephtah of the 19th Dynasty (1224–1214 BCE) on its back, and other carved Egyptian objects belong to the final phase of the city, reflect the period of time between 640 and 603 BCE during which Egypt controlled Philistia.

According to R. Reich, the identification of the **Sheikh Zuweid** building as Assyrian is based on the existence of a small temple (with a cella, 2.89 x 4.42 m.), which was erected for the use of the local Assyrian administration and army. The most distinctive Assyrian element here was the floor of the cella, which was paved with square, fired bricks. The steps leading to the cella were similarly paved. Two pedestals stood at both sides of the steps, another widespread feature in Assyrian temples.

Of the other Assyrian-influenced temples, the one from **Buṣeirah** was discovered in Area C (ca. 67 x 105 m.), but only a small part of it has been excavated. The remains uncovered belonged to a large hall, about 6.5 m. wide and about 14 m. long. An interesting feature linking this building to the Assyrian world is a broad, shallow niche (0.5 x 2.5 m.). It lacked the layer of thick plaster covering the floor of the hall, which indicates that it originally held a stone slab, as was common in Assyrian audience halls. Assyrian influence on the local cult is also clearly exhibited in the finds and in some written texts. Tiglath-pileser III, for example, states in one of his inscriptions that when he conquered Gaza he introduced the Assyrian cult into one of the existing temples there. This again relates to the Lamashtu plaque found near Lachish, which probably arrived with one of the Assyrian soldiers participating in the campaign against that city.

In addition, many emblems of Assyrian deities are found on seals and bullae recovered at various sites. Among these is the emblem of Ishtar of Arbel, who is depicted as a goddess surrounded by a circle. On a silver amulet from Ekron, she is depicted standing on a lion, with a figure in prayer standing in front of her.

The most common motif in these seals, however, is the moon crescent atop a pole, the emblem of the moon god Sin from Haran. This has been found at many sites of the period all over the country, and in particular, in the territories of the three Assyrian provinces: Megiddo, Samaria, and Dor. Here we shall point to the large group of stamp impressions found in the Phoenician-Assyrian center at Tell Keisan in the Acco Valley, at Tel 'Ira and Tel Arad in Judah, and at Tawilan and 'En Ḥazeva in Edom. At Gezer, for example, this emblem is repeated three times on one of the Assyrian clay tablets found there, and at Tel 'Ira, on a bulla that probably sealed a Judaean papyrus.

It is important to note that a new type of incense burner was introduced all over Palestine in this period: this was a small limestone (or clay) box, standing on four small feet, which originated in Mesopotamia. This new Assyrian type began to replace the old four-horned, larger incense altar, common in the previous period. From the Assyrian period onward, this was the major type in use here.

ASSYRIAN BURIAL CUSTOMS

IT IS NOW clear that the Assyrian conquerors brought some of their Mesopotamian burial customs with them: i.e., the use of clay ossuaries, both ossuaries for regular burials and the smaller types for secondary burials. This Mesopotamian custom continued thereafter in Palestine—as we shall see— through the domination of the subsequent Babylonian and Persian empires.

The ossuaries are made of clay and usually have the shape of a modern bathtub. In Assyria, they are subdivided into several groups that are similar to each other: (1) oval tub ossuaries rounded at both ends, (2) long tub ossuaries rounded at both ends, and (3) bathtub ossuaries, straight at one end and round at the other. Recently, a fourth type, consisting of rope-decorated burial jars, has been proposed.

These ossuaries were covered in a variety of ways, usually with clay slabs, but sometimes with a second ossuary, which was laid upon it, inverted; or with date-palm boards. Some of the ossuaries were decorated with a relief rope ornamentation, surrounding the rim, and also with many handles, used for lowering the ossuary into the depression of the burial site.

The Palestinian ossuaries attributed to the Assyrian period come mainly from two regions. Most have been found in the three provinces under direct Assyrian domination (Megiddo, Samaria, and Dor), where they have been found at the following sites: Hazor, Tell Qitaf, which is near Beth-Shean, Tel Jezreel, Megiddo, Tel Dothan, Tell el-Far'ah (N), and Dor. A second region is in Transjordan, in the territory of the kingdom of Ammon (where they were found in the tomb of Adoni-Nur).

Near some of these coffins, or even inside them, Assyrian pottery vessels have been uncovered, sometimes with other Assyrian and Phoenician artifacts (Dothan and Tell Qitaf), but most of them contained mixed Assyrian and locally made artifacts. We may perhaps assume that some of them were burials of local dignitaries in the service of the Assyrian administration, who also adopted some of their overlord's customs.

The clay coffins continued to be utilized in Palestine during the Babylonian period (at Tell en-Naṣbeh and Jerusalem), as well as in the land of Ammon (at Tell el-Mazar), and during the Persian period, from which a large clay coffin at Shechem has survived (see below).

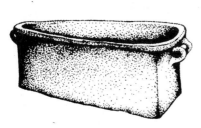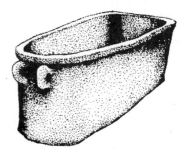

I.18 Drawing of an Assyrian clay coffin from Rabbath-Ammon

ASSYRIAN SCULPTURE AND GLYPTIC

NO MONUMENTAL ASSYRIAN sculpture has yet been recovered in Palestine, though it is possible, according to some Assyrian sources, that such monuments were erected there. The Assyrian glyptic finds (excluding seals and seal impressions; see below) are very few in number. Three that belong to different categories are noteworthy. One is a broken piece of a limestone relief box, from Tell eṣ-Ṣafi in Philistia, which depicts an Assyrian male head; the second includes two Assyrian clay figurine heads of Assyrian deities or kings, from Dan and Tell Keisan in the Acco Valley; and the third is a small bichrome painting on a pottery shard from Ramat Raḥel in Judah, which follows the conventions typical of Assyrian wall painting, and which was interpreted as a model for such a painting thought to have once adorned the Judaean royal palace located there. All these finds reflect Assyrian prototypes mixed with local features, and all may be regarded as local imitations of Assyrian originals. This probably means that the local artisans were, at this time, well acquainted with Assyrian glyptic and painting.

At the same time, Assyrian seals and seal impressions are much more common in Palestine and were probably used by the local administrators. Finds consist of both stamp and cylinder seals, and impressions from both. Here again, most seals were recovered from the territory of the three Assyrian provinces: Megiddo, Samaria, and Dor.

One is a cylinder seal inscribed "belonging to Belu Asharedu the overseer of the palace," a title that, according to M. and H. Tadmor, was utilized in the royal court only. In addition, some figures are depicted on it, such as two people standing in prayer before a god standing upon a crouching animal;

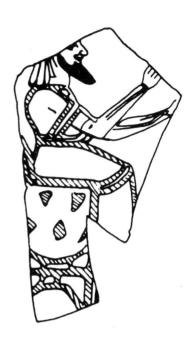

I.19 Drawing of an Assyrian-style seated governor from the Judaean royal palace at Ramat Raḥel

above them are the emblems of the sun disk and the moon crescent and seven stars. Though the seal's original date is earlier than the conquest of Dor by Tiglath-pileser III, the Tadmors believe that this is a typical case of seal "migration"; i.e., it was brought here by a later owner, with the coming of the Assyrian army. At Tel Dor, two more seals have been found: one is a stamp seal and the other is a cylinder seal. Both were imported and are made of agate. One depicts the common Assyrian motif of the king struggling with two monsters; the other shows the Assyrian king standing before the god Assur.

More Assyrian seals and seal impressions have been found at other sites, such as Tell Keisan, Beth-Shean, Shechem, Samaria, and Gezer, all centers of Assyrian administration. They present some additional Assyrian motifs, such as the Assyrian king standing before a fire altar or on an animal. The bulla found in the city of Samaria depicts the Assyrian king struggling with a lion. This is a design exclusively used by the royal Assyrian court.

Only a small number of Assyrian seals has been recovered outside the borders of these provinces. These were probably used as votive offerings in temples or tombs. We shall mention here the imported inscribed chalcedony cylinder seal from a *favissa* at Tel Sheva, which belonged to "Rimuti Ilani son of Hadad Idri," who was a worshiper of the god Apladad. The center of this god's worship was in the middle Euphrates region. According to Tadmor, this seal "migrated" here with the Babylonian army of Nebuchadnezzar II (586 BCE). Another "migratory" Assyrian cylinder seal was found in Judaean Arad. It depicts an Assyrian cultic scene: an enthroned god facing a huge bird, the moon crescent above and seven stars.

Indeed, in the absence of coins in this period, seals may be regarded as the most common expression of Assyrian domination of the country and are a useful criterion for its identification. Even more important is the influence of this new glyptic on the school of local engravers. It is not an exaggeration to claim that Assyrian glyptic revolutionized local seal production.

ASSYRIAN POTTERY VESSELS

ANOTHER COMMON FEATURE of the strata dated to the 7th century BCE at all Palestinian sites is the presence of Assyrian-style pottery. This pottery is called Palace ware, and is well known from excavations in Assyria in the palaces of the Assyrian kings, at cities such as Calah (Nimrud), Nineveh (Kuyunjik), Dur Sharukin (Khorsabad), and elsewhere. Its date there is well established.

The Assyrian Palace ware vessels are distinguished by their white, well-levigated clay and by their typical shapes, mainly thin, carinated bowls that are presumably copies or imitations of metal vessel forms. Especially common and typical, however, are the closed bottles with elongated bodies and pointed or onion-shaped bases. These vessels are usually unpainted, but they were sometimes decorated by the potter pushing a thumb into the sides (the result is called "dimpled"). Most of the Assyrian vessels lack handles. Many of these vessels were adopted in the local Palestinian repertoire throughout the country. These henceforth became a regular part of the Palestinian ceramic corpus. Study of the results of several excavations shows that more Assyrian-style vessels have been uncovered in the northern part of the country, which was under direct Assyrian rule, than in other regions. There hardly seems to be a site in the territories of the provinces of Megiddo, Samaria, and

I.20 An "Assyrian" juglet from Tel Dor

Dor at which these vessels have not been found. Examples are known from Dan, Hazor, Tel Chinnereth, 'En Gev, Beth-Shean, Tell Qitaf, Tel 'Amal, Dothan, Megiddo, Tel Qiri, Jokneam, Tell Keisan, Acco, Shiqmona, Dor, Samaria, Shechem, Tell el-Far'ah (N), Gezer, and elsewhere.

In the Phoenician coastal region, these vessels are characterized by their ornamentation; i.e., many of them are painted in red, brown, or black stripes, typical of the local Israelite-Phoenician decorative tradition. Moreover, some other typically local features were added to some of the vessels, such as handles (missing in the original Assyrian prototypes), rims, and bases. Some of the vessels found at Tell Keisan and Dor are the best examples of such hybridization.

Toward the end of the 7th century BCE, some Assyrian clay vessels began to appear at Judaean sites. Several examples have been uncovered in the Judaean royal palace at Ramat Rahel, and in Jerusalem, Tell en-Nasbeh, Gibeon, Lachish, Tel Batash, Tel Halif, Tel Sheva, Aroer, Tel 'Ira, Tel Masos, Arad, En-Gedi, and elsewhere.

I.21 Assyrian-style bronze and clay bowls found in Samaria region

Large assemblages of Assyrian-style vessels, almost identical in fabric and shape to the original Palace ware, have also been found at some Philistine towns, located on the main highway to Egypt. The first and the most important among these was already discovered by W. M. F. Petrie at Tell Jemmeh. Petrie was also the first scholar to identify them correctly. Later they appeared in great quantities at the same site (Tell Jemmeh) in the second excavation directed by G. Van Beek inside a building erected in true Assyrian style (see above). At the other sides of Philistia, Assyrian-style vessels have been uncovered in the strata dated to the 7th century BCE. These sites are Ashdod, Tel Sera', Sheikh Zuweid, Tel Haror, Tel Qatif (Ruqeish), and Ekron.

The interesting feature of the Assyrian-style vessels from Judah, and particularly those found in the royal palace at Ramat Raḥel, the most elaborate examples, is that they became "Judaized." In the same way that the Assyrian-style vessels in Phoenicia and Israel received local painted decoration, so the

Assyrian-style vessels in **Judah** were modified by the addition of red burnishing, typical of the local tradition. In some cases, their typical pointed bases were turned into low ring bases.

In **Transjordan,** too, Assyrian-style vessels replaced the local ones, which had been made according to Phoenician and Israelite traditions. Assyrian-style vessels are common to the 7th century BCE and early 6th century BCE assemblages in all the Transjordanian kingdoms—Ammon, Moab, and Edom—where they are found in settlements and tombs.

Important groups of Assyrian-style pottery are known at Edomite Tell el-Kheleifeh (Period IV), Tawilan and Buṣeirah, the Moabite tombs of Mount Nebo and Dibon, and the many tombs excavated around Rabbath-Ammon, at Heshbon and Tell el-ʿUmeiri, and at Tell el-Mazar in the Jordan Valley. Here, the Assyrian-style vessels are decorated in the local white-and-black-painted tradition.

We say Assyrian *style,* as it is almost certain that most of the vessels were not imported from Assyria. In most cases, even those that closely resemble the original Palace ware of Assyria are local imitations of the latter. Concerning the bowls, we are even more certain, as, in the assemblages discovered in Assyria proper, they are quite rare, mostly imitating metalware. In Palestine, bowls are very common, and constitute the largest vessel type in the local assemblages.

We should point out that the various Assyrian-style vessels (except, perhaps, the unique assemblage from Tell Jemmeh) constitute a minority among the local vessel repertoire, which continues the tradition of the local pottery of the 8th century BCE with slight changes. In the final report of his excavation at Shechem, G. E. Wright attributed the two different groups of pottery to the two different peoples who inhabited the Samaria province at the time: the Assyrian-style vessels were used by the newcomers, while the local vessels were used by the remaining Israelites.

ASSYRIAN STONE, GLASS, AND METAL ARTIFACTS

IN ADDITION TO the Assyrian-style ceramic vessels, there are, among the Palestinian finds, some stone, glass, and metal artifacts that were also made in the Assyrian style and were intended for use by the Assyrian local administration.

Of each of these kinds, only a small number of examples is known, and we shall enumerate a few typical ones. There are two unique stone vessels found

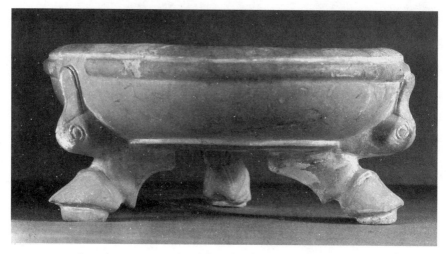

I.22 Assyrian stone bowl found in a tomb near Beth-Shean

in an Assyrian clay ossuary tomb at Tell el-Qitaf near Beth-Shean. One is a basalt bowl with bar handles and three legs of a type quite common among the clay Palace-ware vessels. The other is a beautiful stone bowl, its legs made in the shape of bull hooves surmounted by duck heads.

Assyrian glass vessels include a cup found at **Aroer** in the Beersheba Valley in a 7th century BCE stratum. This vessel has some close analogies at Nimrud. A similar example was recently found at Megiddo in an Assyrian tomb. Some glass pendants recovered at Gezer, of very peculiar shape, are claimed to be Assyrian imports.

The two best examples of metal vessels are a beautifully decorated bronze bowl from Samaria and a bronze beaker from Tell en-Naṣbeh, with close analogies among the bronze vessels of Nimrud.

ASSYRIAN WEIGHTS AND MEASURES

WE DO NOT yet know the extent or nature of Assyrian influence on the various aspects of the daily life of local inhabitants in Palestine. Excavation results have not provided satisfying solutions to this problem. Nothing in the way of weights and measures has yet been recovered in the area of the three Assyrian-dominated provinces of Megiddo, Samaria, and Dor, or even at sites such as Ayelet ha-Shaḥar, Tell Keisan, Dothan, Gezer, Tell Jemmeh, and Tel Seraʿ, where Assyrian-style buildings have been excavated. The few Assyrian documents found here do not shed much light upon this matter, except perhaps the Tell Keisan tablet that contains a list of Assyrian weights (*minda*) used for distributing rations. There are only possible examples of such weights. The most important are the bronze weights made in the shape of ducks found off the Carmel coast, which may be Assyrian or Babylonian. There are also some nonepigraphic stamp seals of the same shape from private collections. At Arad and some other sites in Philistia, more nonepigraphic bronze weights have been uncovered in 7th century BCE contexts, some in the shape of a crouching lion, undoubtedly imitating an Assyrian prototype.

Chapter 3

The Assyrian Provinces
of Megiddo and Samaria

Introduction

The kingdom of Israel was conquered by the Assyrians in two waves. In the first (733/2 BCE), the entire Galilee and the large valleys were captured by Tiglath-pileser III. In the second wave, the Samaria Hills and the kingdom's capital city of Samaria were occupied by Shalmaneser V and Sargon II in 723/2–720 BCE. It was probably the latter king who divided the area of the previous Israelite kingdom between the two newly established Assyrian provinces, Megiddo in the north and Samaria or Samirina in the south, and appointed Assyrian governors to both. In any case, the names of two of these governors are mentioned later in the Assyrian records of the years 695 and 646 BCE.

After the conquest and the initial destructions came—following Assyrian objectives—the large-scale deportations, which were aimed at achieving the following:

1. Breaking up of the existing national units by sending large numbers of their population to distant areas and replacing them in their native lands with deportees from elsewhere who had no prior connection with the original inhabitants and who were completely dependent upon the Assyrian authorities for their security and welfare.
2. Rebuilding and repopulating of settlements and towns in regions that were severely damaged at the time of their initial conquest in the Assyrian campaigns—in particular, the major cities that later became the

capitals of the newly established provinces, and even enlarging them by comparison with the previous Israelite towns.

It seems that as a result of this bi-directional movement of the deportees, great changes occurred in the ethnic composition of the local population during the Assyrian domination of Megiddo and Samaria. But even so, there is—so far as we can judge today—a major difference between the fate of the province of Megiddo and that of Samaria. In the former, all evidence points to the fact that the entire region was destroyed and never repopulated by the Assyrians (except, perhaps, for the provincial capital of Megiddo). This situation becomes evident upon comparison of the number of settlements during the 7th century BCE with the number of settlements in the preceding period. In Samaria, in contrast, where the movement of the deportees was bi-directional, not only was overall damage smaller, but the arrival of the new population brought a new era of growth and prosperity, as well as better conditions than those existing during the final Israelite phase. It does seem, however, that the settlement of the new population was anticipated with careful planning, as well as with the efficient support of the local Assyrian administration.

According to the Assyrian and biblical sources, Tiglath-pileser III deported all residents of the area he occupied in the north of Palestine in order to weaken any future internal resistance. In 2 Kings 15:29, some of the settlements of the Upper Galilee that he destroyed are mentioned: Ijon, Abel-beth-Maachah, Janoah, Kedesh, Hazor and Gilead, "all the land of Naphtali." It also states that he carried their inhabitants as captives to Assyria.

In Tiglath-pileser's own inscriptions, more settlements of the Lower Galilee, as well as of the Beth Nethopha Valley, which suffered a similar fate, are mentioned. It is stated that 13,200 people were forced into exile.

Sargon II (on the period of Shalmaneser V we have no sources at all), on the contrary, initiated a new policy, the main purpose of which was to incorporate the land of Palestine within the empire. He was probably the one who established the Assyrian provinces of Megiddo and Samaria (and Dor; see below) and brought waves of new settlers into the country. In 720 BCE, when he conquered the capital city of Samaria, he first exiled 27,280 individuals from it and the surrounding area, "placed them in Halah and in Habor by the river of Gozan, and in the cities of the Medes" (2 Kings 17:6), and must have emptied Samaria of its original inhabitants. But he claims that later he

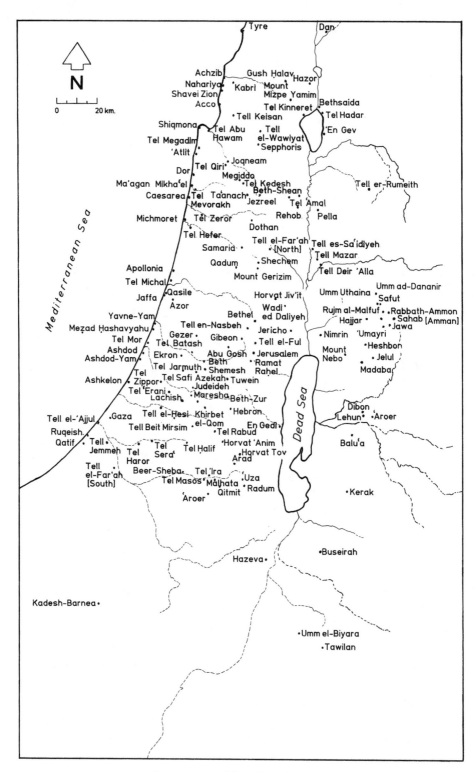

I.23 Excavated Late Iron Age sites

rebuilt the city and made it "even more than before." This was probably done in 715 BCE, i.e., only five years or so after its complete destruction, initially with people from Arab tribes such as Thamud and Epha.

According to 2 Kings 17:24, he brought new inhabitants to Samaria from "Babylon, and from Cutha, and from Ava, and from Hamath, and from Sepharvaim, and placed them in the cities of Samaria instead of the children of Israel: and they possessed Samaria, and dwelt in the cities thereof." This event is usually attributed to Sargon II, who left his stela in Samaria in 710–709 BCE, but others prefer to date it to the days of Sennacherib in the period after 701 BCE.

Though our sources are quite meager from this point on, deportations to Palestine appear to have continued in the days of the subsequent Assyrian kings, Esarhaddon and Ashurbanipal during the first half of the 7th century BCE, as indicated in Ezra 4:1–2 and 4:9–10, which attribute deportations of people from Babylon, Shushan, and Elam to the days of Asnapper (Ashurbanipal), i.e., as late as 647–645 BCE, the period close to the collapse and total withdrawal from the entire area by Assyria.

We have already mentioned the great impact of the Assyrian conquest on the cultures of Palestine in general, and more specifically dealt with the huge construction projects undertaken following the change in Assyrian policy. It seems, however, that this major change in the region's population left but a modest mark in the archaeological record. Almost nothing has been uncovered that can be attributed to the countries of the different groups of deportees, who are said to come from the Iranian plateau or Elam. Even in the capital cities of the two Assyrian provinces, only a handful of finds can be attributed to them. This is difficult to understand. In any case, in the present stage of the research, the evidence provided by the written sources is superior to that of the archaeological record concerning the identification of the new ethnic elements that settled in Samaria. The two Neo-Assyrian cuneiform clay tablets found at Gezer and dated to 651–649 BCE should again be recalled: of twenty-one names mentioned, about twelve were Babylonian, one Israelite, one Egyptian, and five general West Semitic names. It is possible that the Babylonian names belong to the new deportees who were brought there by the Assyrians but a short time before. Many more Babylonian names are mentioned in the earlier Neo-Assyrian clay tablet discovered recently at the nearby site of Hadid. The tablet is dated to the period of Sargon II. More Babylonian names have survived on some Aramaic ostraca found in the Samaria region in a later context (see below).

The New Settlement Picture
in the Megiddo Province

THE ASSYRIAN CONQUEST of the Galilee, the large valleys, and the land of Samaria brought with it the general destruction of all Israelite settlements and the deportation of most of their inhabitants. The result of this conquest and the mass deportations that followed is clearly apparent in all the excavations carried out in these regions, as well as in the many intensive surveys conducted there in recent years.

Some of the large towns and settlements in those areas were destroyed and not rebuilt (Beth-Shean, Rehob, Chinnereth, Bethsaida, Tel Hadar, 'En Gev, Tel Kedesh, Tel Qashish). Elsewhere (with the exception of the capital city of Megiddo), towns were poorly rebuilt and remained unfortified.

At **Tel Dan,** the last Israelite city (Stratum II) was destroyed by the Assyrians. A new, probably unfortified town was reconstructed (Stratum I). In this stratum, a unique pottery assemblage revealing Assyrian, Phoenician, and Greek influences was recovered. This assemblage may perhaps serve as a "case study" for the character of Galilee pottery of the 7th century BCE; for, till now, the pottery finds at other Galilean sites of the period are poor and not indicative.

At **Hazor,** Stratum V was the last Israelite city destroyed by the Assyrians. It is true that Y. Yadin's expedition believed that after the Assyrian conquest a poor and short-lived settlement was established there by squatters or by some of the previous inhabitants who survived the destruction (Stratum IV). This stratum did not produce any significant finds.

On the destruction level of this temporary settlement, a new Assyrian fortress was erected in the form of the open-court house of Mesopotamian origin, which was, to the excavator's mind, the only structure built on the mound. From this stratum (III), not a single artifact was recorded from this building at the site where some Assyrian burial jars were found, which probably indicate use as an Assyrian cemetery that was established on the mound.

Outside the mound, however, and close to its northeast side (in the vicinity of Ayelet ha-Shahar), a purely Assyrian brick structure was erected, perhaps the palace of the local Assyrian governor (see above). It is interesting to note, however, that this palace was erected in a low and open area without a protecting wall.

At **Tel Chinnereth** on the north coast of the Sea of Galilee, a similar pic-

I.24 View of the "Assyrian" fortress on the summit of Tel Hazor

ture emerged: above the destruction level of the last Israelite (or Aramaean?) settlement at the site, the foundation of a large structure was uncovered in one of the excavated areas. This building was interpreted by its excavator as an Assyrian administrative center. It continued to exist into later periods.

At **Taanach,** City IV was destroyed by Tiglath-pileser III. A short-lived settlement (V) replaced it, lasting for approximately fifty years (700–650 BCE).

At **Tel Jezreel,** remains of a 7th century BCE settlement are attested by a few graves of the period. Among these, two "Assyrian" clay coffins were recorded (see above). The tombs contained local as well as Phoenician art objects.

At **Jokneam,** the last Israelite stratum (VIII) was destroyed by the Assyrians. During the period of the Assyrian conquest, the previous strong city wall went out of use. Atop it, remains of small walls and ovens were found. In the area inside the wall, the excavators found evidence for a small settlement dated from the late 8th to the late 7th centuries BCE.

Our survey clearly shows that the Assyrian remains found in the province of Megiddo are few and scattered and originate in but a few of the previous Israelite centers. Except for the city of Megiddo, the provincial capital (see below), Assyrian remains have been identified at Dan, Hazor, Chinnereth, and Jezreel, while other sites were either abandoned (Beth-Shean, Rehob) or replaced by small villages (Jokneam).

The survey of the Lower Galilee during the Iron Age conducted by Z. Gal provided similar results: Gal concludes that "the entire northern part of the kingdom of Israel was destroyed. It appears as if the lower Galilee was significantly deserted and its inhabitants exiled. The events of 733/2 BCE provide a tragic landmark in the history of the Israelite settlement in Galilee, whatever had not been destroyed by the wars was removed and laid waste by the exiles, and the region was not occupied during the 7th–6th centuries BCE!"

This picture corresponds to the evidence from the excavated sites, and both point to the same conclusion: that the entire Galilee and the major valleys were half deserted during the Assyrian period.

The one exception was the rebuilding of the provincial capital city of **Megiddo,** which the Assyrians probably repopulated with new inhabitants from other lands.

The problem of the exact date of the establishment of the Megiddo and Samaria provinces (as well as the province of Dor; see below) has been discussed above. It was concluded that none of these was established by Tiglath-pileser III. It seems now that both became Assyrian centers only in the days of Sargon II, after the collapse of the Israelite monarchy, and at the time of the arrival of the first deportees from abroad to the country during the reign of Sargon II, ca. 715 BCE.

The study of the Assyrian town at Megiddo, i.e., Megiddo Stratum III, has an important bearing on the understanding of the entire Assyrian period. This town is unique in being the only completely excavated site that provides evidence for the formidable Assyrian effort to reconstruct the towns they had destroyed and razed but a short time before.

At Megiddo, after the complete destruction of the last Israelite city (Stratum IVA) at the hands of Tiglath-pileser III, the new Assyrian town that emerged presents a radical change both in local city planning and in the individual plans of residential and public structures.

The city plan was composed of rectangular and square *insulae* in "pseudo-Hippodamian" fashion. This lasted, almost unchanged, up to the end of City II. Some elements even remained in City I (see below). In the center of the Stratum III city, a round public granary was built. The rest of the residential buildings were built according to the new Assyrian open-court house plan.

As to the fortifications, the inset-offset city wall of the previous periods was maintained and even rebuilt. The transition to Stratum III was also followed by the change in the plan of the gate: it was reduced to a one-chamber structure, a feature typical of the late 8th and early 7th centuries BCE in Syria-Palestine. The second major change was the construction of the large Assyrian public open-court buildings on both sides of this gate. The main complex, the western one, originally belonged to an earlier stage of the stratum.

As already noted, these large public buildings were constructed in accordance with Assyrian tradition on a podium about 2 m. higher than central court 1374; the entrance to the main reception suite was through a doorway flanked by two pillars, with a typical niche at a right angle to the entrance. Reception suite 509 had a typical side chamber, 512. Other typical Assyrian features were the bathrooms and the horseshoe door sockets.

With the Assyrian occupation of Megiddo, the city regained its public and central character and became the capital for Assyrian activity in the entire Galilee.

In Stratum III, the period of Assyrian rule at Megiddo, we should have expected an abundance of Assyrian material, but this is not the case: very few finds have been recovered. The excavation's methods and the system for publishing the finds may be partly to blame. In any case, the material found in this stratum, though it includes some Assyrian finds such as pottery vessels and clay ossuaries, was very much mixed with that of the strata above and below it.

Even so, the small amount of Assyrian-period finds permits us to conclude that in the entire Galilean area, in addition to Assyrian influence there are two other new cultural factors, which begin to be felt immediately after the Assyrian conquest. One is the **Phoenician** influence, which can be traced in the pottery and small finds, such as inscriptions and ostraca, as well as art objects. The other influence is **Greek,** and mainly **East Greek,** reflected in the many imported vessels found here. These influences become even stronger in the subsequent periods.

THE PROVINCE OF SAMARIA

IN 722 BCE, Shalmaneser V besieged the city of Samaria, and in 720 BCE, the Assyrians under Sargon II conquered the town of Samaria, destroyed it, and brought an end to the Israelite monarchy and deported its inhabitants to Assyria. But only five years later—as we have already seen—they reestablished it as an Assyrian province headed by an Assyrian governor.

At all excavated sites in Samaria, remains of the total destruction of the country at the hands of the Assyrians were found. Towns such as Dothan, Shechem, the town of Samaria, Bethel, Tell el-Far'ah (N), and Gezer (which had previously suffered destruction at the hands of Tiglath-pileser III) are all reported by their excavators as having been destroyed in this conquest.

In contrast to the Megiddo province and the Galilee region, here the Assyrian authorities changed their policy shortly afterward and made major efforts to rebuild the entire area and replace its exiled inhabitants with new immigrants, whom they brought in from various parts of the Assyrian empire and settled in the towns and villages of Samaria over the course of the 7th century BCE. These settlers undoubtedly received considerable support from the local authorities, as we are told in 2 Kings 17:24: "And the king of Assyria brought men from Babylon, and from Cutha . . . and placed them in the cities of Samaria instead of the children of Israel: and they possessed Samaria, and dwelt in the cities thereof."

As already pointed out, the results of the excavations in all the large towns in the land of Samaria clearly show that they were destroyed by the Assyrians and were all reconstructed subsequently. The overall picture emerging from the excavations in Samaria shows, however, that these reconstructed towns were unfortified settlements, occupying but a part of the areas of the previous Israelite towns, except perhaps for the capital city of Samaria, where the old city wall was retained. This may reflect the general policy of the local Assyrian administration to retain fortifications only in the provincial capitals. The many surveys carried out recently in this region by I. Finkelstein, S. Dar, A. Zertal, and others point to similar findings: all show that the main new settlements were built in the eastern part of the Manasseh Hills and in the area covering the triangle between Shechem, the town of Samaria, and Tell el-Far'ah (N). Most of the settlements reestablished here were villages that covered an area of 1 to 5 acres. The majority were established during the 7th century BCE; some continued to exist until the Persian period. The rest were established later in the Persian period.

Following the results of the survey conducted in the western Samaria Hills by I. Finkelstein, it has become clear that at the end of the 8th century BCE, many agricultural estates and small villages were established there. In Finkelstein's opinion, these results reflect a more secure situation after the Assyrian conquest of the region and the establishment of the Samarian province. This enabled the inhabitants of towns to leave their relative safety and settle in smaller villages or even agricultural estates, in search of more land for cultivation. The typical Samarian agricultural estate was usually a solitary structure surrounded by a low wall. It includes a large open courtyard with a few rooms on one of its sides in which some of the necessary installations, water cisterns and wine- and oil presses, were located. The results of the various surveys may also attest to a period of "population explosion."

The strata excavated in the Samaria region that produced Assyrian-style pottery vessels and other Assyrian-influenced finds, such as inscriptions, seals, clay burial coffins, stone and metal vessels, were encountered at Dothan (Stratum I), the town of Samaria (7), Tell el-Far'ah (N) (Stratum VIIE), Shechem (Stratum VI), and Gezer (Stratum IV). In some cases (the town of Samaria, Shechem, Tell el-Far'ah [N], and Gezer), two phases were identified in these strata, while in others (Dothan and Bethel) settlement occurred only during one part of this period.

Apart from the usual Assyrian clay vessels uncovered in the 7th century BCE strata, the pottery assemblage displays remarkable continuity with local traditions. Perhaps only one type of pottery was introduced, i.e., the "wedge-decorated" bowls which may have started in this period and were influenced by Mesopotamian prototypes. This ware was, perhaps, brought by the new inhabitants of the region.

At the same time, here, as we noted in the Galilee, a growing Phoenician influence is apparent in the many Phoenician pottery vessels and other Phoenician artifacts. This tendency will become even stronger in subsequent periods. As usual, this is followed by the appearance of Greek imports from various sources, of which the East Greek component is the most popular.

In conclusion, the settlement picture in the new Assyrian province of Samaria, according to both historical records and recent archaeological research, clearly shows that shortly after the first wave of conquest, destruction, and exile, the Assyrians made a tremendous effort to rebuild the region. This activity seems to have been heavily dependent upon the local administration. Besides the construction, the administration took care of the groups of deportees sent here from the other parts of the empire. In the first stage of this enormous project, only the capital city of Samaria was restored and fortified. With it, a network of unfortified secondary centers, such as Dothan, Shechem, Tell el-Far'ah (N), Gezer, and Hadid, was established. In the second stage, many small towns and villages and agricultural estates were reestablished. Some of these were newly established in previously unpopulated areas, attesting to a period of population growth and prosperity.

Temples and Cult Objects

NO WRITTEN DOCUMENTS outside the Bible tell us about the local cults introduced in the Samarian province during the Assyrian period. Perhaps 2 Kings 17:24–41 refers to the reconstruction of the major temple at Bethel by the Assyrian authorities. It was probably later destroyed by the Judaeans, at the end of the 7th century BCE when Bethel was itself annexed to Judah (cf. 2 Kings 23:15–20). Possible remains of another cult place in Assyrian Samaria are dated to the 7th century BCE, by Y. Magen, who excavated recently on Mount Gerizim, as well as three proto-Aeolic capitals found not far away, which depict, in addition to the usual triangle and volutes, the edge of a Phoenician palmette and, in one capital, the facade of a temple guarded by seven uraei (cobras). These capitals, although found in a Persian context, may have originally belonged to the older Assyrian-period cult place.

I.25 Proto-Aeolic capital found on Mount Gerizim

The only other cultic remains are the clay figurines and two Aramaic plaster texts found at Tell Deir ʿAlla in the Sukoth Valley near the Jordan Valley. The contents of the plaster texts present a local version of the story of Balʿam the son of Beʾor the seer (Numbers 22–24). Most scholars believe that the stratigraphy and the find spot point to the pre-Assyrian Israelite period. Others, however, attribute these texts to the Assyrian period.

The texts were written with black and red ink on the plaster covering two stelae (and cf. Deuteronomy 27:2–3), which fell down when the house was destroyed. The texts here resemble the earlier Israelite plaster texts found in northern Sinai at Kuntillet-ʿAjrud. It seems, therefore, that writing holy texts with ink on the walls of Israelite and latter sanctuaries must have been a common practice among the peoples of Palestine (as in a much later period, if we recall the plaster texts recently found on the walls of the nearby 4th century CE synagogue at Rehob).

The problem of the Deir-ʿAlla texts is whether they are Israelite, Ammonite, or pertain to another group. About one thing, there is no conflict: the contents of the texts reflect a rich, pagan worldview similar to that described in the inscriptions found at Kuntillet ʿAjrud and Khirbet el-Qom in the Judaean Hills (see below).

The texts, written in a local West Semitic dialect, tell about the main goddess whose name is *Shgr-ʿAshtar*, probably one of the many names of ʿAstarte (cf. Deuteronomy 7:13). El also appears as the main god, with other *shadai* gods and goddesses, as well as mountain gods who gathered in an assembly.

I.26 Tel Dan, 7th century BCE cult chapel with stone stelae found near the city's gate

Whether these texts belong to the pre-Assyrian-conquest period and were written by the Israelite inhabitants of the Gilead, or are from the Assyrian period and are Ammonite, they probably reflect the local version of a pagan cult that gives us a rare look into a hitherto unknown and almost utterly lost world of literature.

Except for this remarkable find and, perhaps, the remains of a structure uncovered at Tell el-Far'ah (N) which was interpreted by its excavator as a sanctuary because it consisted of some *mazzebot* and the remains of a large house recently uncovered at the foot of Tel Shiloh, the only other cultic remains found in the two Assyrian provinces are the usual clay figurines. The major figurine find comes, in fact, from the northern part of the Megiddo province, mainly from Megiddo (Strata III–II). Others were uncovered at Tel Dan (Stratum I). From other sites, such as Hazor, Beth-Shean, Jezreel, Tel Qiri, and Jokneam, no important remains have survived, and it is difficult to distinguish between what was there before the Assyrian conquest and the period right after. As to Samaria, nothing really important has been recovered at the towns of Samaria or Shechem or elsewhere. At Tell el-Far'ah (N), a clay figurine depicting a double-flute player is reported, and at Shiloh, an Egyptian female figurine inscribed with a hieroglyphic dedication inscription to Isis was found.

I.27 Bethsaida, view of the gate of the last Aramaic town destroyed by the Assyrians. Note the stelae flanking the gate.

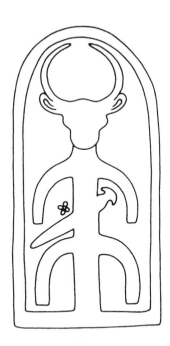

I.28 A stone stela from the gate of Bethsaida depicting the image of the Aramaic god Hadad

The northern figurines from Dan and Megiddo are usually made of clay, but some examples are made of stone, faience, and even glass. The clay statuettes consist mostly of female figurines, i.e., the naked ʿAstarte fertility figurines of the usual type, sometimes supporting their breasts, pregnant, or nursing a small child. Another group is composed of various music instrumentalists, most playing the tambourine.

The technique by which these were executed is a transitional one between styles: some of them have handmade bodies, while the heads are pressed in molds, but most have hollow bodies; some are made in the Phoenician "bell" shape, but most are hollow-molded in front and their backs are plain, in the Greek style. In all cases, the head, which was made in a mold, has a tang which was inserted into the solid handmade or hollow-molded body.

There is a surprisingly large quantity of flat, solid plaques, molded in front, more frequent here than in any other region of Palestine. Perhaps the reason for this is that they were made under Assyrian influence. There are also clay heads of male gods, though small in number, and many horse figurines that may have once been part of figurines depicting horses and riders. Some might have depicted the male warrior god, but at least one of the male statuettes is of a flute player.

Not a few figurines depict animals, produced in the solid handmade and the hollow-molded varieties. This group has survived mainly in a great number of body parts and heads. In addition to the horse heads, there are also bull and ram heads.

I.29 Clay and faience heads of deities found at Tel Dan and Jokneam

The peculiarity of the figurines found in the northern Assyrian provinces of Palestine is mainly in the differences in their facial features, which are unlike those of figurines found in other parts of the country and continue earlier Israelite examples.

The female figurines are characterized by their headdresses, which, though also imitating Egyptian veils, as the Phoenician and the Judaean figurines, nevertheless have differently rendered features: the hair is usually short and is marked by dense groups of straight lines, sometimes also used to indicate body features. This statuette is of a type unique to the northern region of the country.

Male figurines' heads are covered with round turbans, and the ears and eyes protrude. They, too, constitute a separate type, different from those in the other parts of the country.

Also peculiar to this region is the common use of faience statuettes in different colors. The best examples, made in both Egypto-Phoenician style and Syro-Phoenician style, have been found at Tel Dan and at Jokneam. These depict bearded males and female heads wearing the Egyptian veil.

· Chapter 4 ·

THE PHOENICIANS

THE HISTORICAL BACKGROUND OF PHOENICIA
IN THE ASSYRIAN PERIOD

In 743–738 BCE, Tiglath-pileser III succeeded in crushing the independent states in Syria and turned them into directly ruled Assyrian provinces. He also received heavy tribute from the rest of the kings of Syria and Palestine, including Ethba'al and, later, Hiram of Tyre, who probably ruled over Sidon as well, and from Shephatba'al the king of Byblos. The reorganization of the ports of the northern coast of Phoenicia with its central city of Sumuru into an Assyrian province was the first sign of Tiglath-pileser's intentions to subdue all the large harbor towns of the country. This was also the beginning of a period of constant struggle between the Assyrian empire and the Phoenician city-states. The Assyrians tried to capture and hold the entire area, while the Phoenicians, who did not succeed in uniting their forces into one strong military body, adopted a double strategy against them: while they accepted Assyrian suzerainty, whenever possible they rebelled.

In 734 BCE, Tiglath-pileser III attacked the Phoenician coast in a brief campaign. He defeated those Phoenician towns that stood in his way and penetrated straight to Gaza at the southern end of Palestine. The Phoenician kings along the way surrendered, but before the end of the same year the Assyrians returned to recapture some of Hiram's cities, because he had made an alliance with their rival, Rezin of Damascus. The Tyrian king again surrendered and paid heavy tribute, as did his son and successor, Matan.

The result of this unsuccessful rebellion against the Assyrians was harsh and painful for the Phoenicians. Tiglath-pileser enlarged the territory of the Assyrian-ruled province of Summur and reduced the autonomy of the rest of

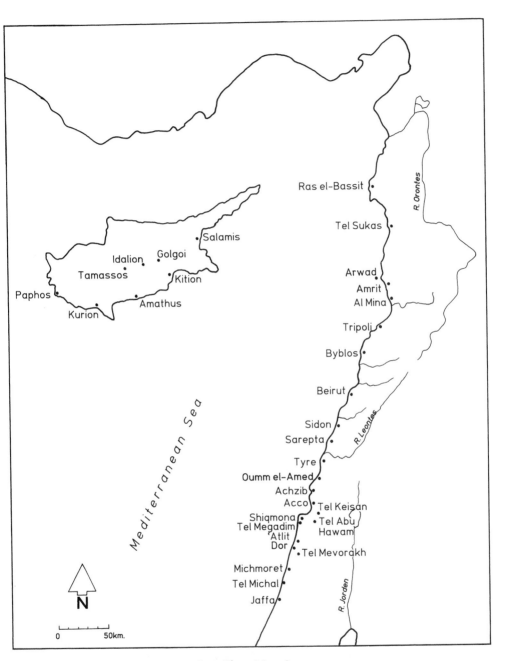

Ras el-Bassit

Tel Sukas

Arwad
Amrit
Al Mina

Tripoli

Byblos

Beirut

Sidon
Sarepta

Tyre
Oumm el-Amed
Achzib
Acco
Tel Keisan
Shiqmona
Tel Megadim
Tel Abu
Hawam
Atlit
Dor
Tel Mevorakh
Michmoret
Tel Michal
Jaffa

Salamis

Idalion
Golgoi
Tamassos
Kition
Paphos
Amathus
Kurion

Mediterranean Sea

R. Orontes
R. Leontes
R. Jordan

N

0   50km.

I.30 Phoenician sites

the coastal towns. At Tyre, he placed an Assyrian official, supported by a military unit, whose task was to supervise the local ruler. One of these official's letters has been found. It is an Assyrian report on cedar wood trade.

Josephus Flavius presents another tradition quoted from Menandros, according to which Shalmeneser V (726–722 BCE) started a war against rebellious Phoenicia headed by the king of Tyre. Some of the country's other cities, including Sidon, however, rebelled against the Phoenician leader and joined the Assyrians against him. Menandros says that the Assyrians laid siege to Tyre, which lasted five years. There is no information about the end of this war. We may assume that when Sargon II came to power, he reached an agreement with the Tyrians, because there is no record of a war against them during his reign.

There is no information regarding the wars conducted by Sargon II in Phoenicia, but from his own inscriptions we can deduce that he subjugated the island of Cyprus, where he left a victory stela at Kition, and fought the Greeks at sea. He thereby developed Assyrian military and economic activity overseas, but hurt the Syro-Palestinian harbor cities' interests, especially those of the Sidonians. It is not surprising that in the third year of Sennacherib, Sidon became the center of a large-scale uprising that encompassed many regions in the west.

In the year 701 BCE, Sennacherib set out to crush the uprising. In his annals, he claims that Luli king of Sidon fled to *yadnana* (Cyprus) and disappeared there (cf. Isaiah 23:1–12; Ezekiel 28:8). Sennacherib replaced him with Ethba'al to rule over Sidon. The other small towns of this region, such as Beth-Zayit, Sarepta, Usu (the coastal town of Tyre), Achzib, and Acco, surrendered to him.

Assyrian domination was consolidated in this territory during the days of Esarhaddon. Control over the maritime trade was consolidated, too. That is why the kings of Tyre and Sidon constantly attempted to regain independence. In 677 BCE, Esarhaddon had to crush a new rebellion led by Ebed-milkat king of Sidon. The Assyrian king reconquered Sidon, killed its monarch, and deported its inhabitants to Assyria. He then organized its territory into a province and resettled it with deportees brought from various parts of the empire. The southern part of the previously Sidonian territory was annexed to that of the Tyrian king. Near destroyed Sidon, Esarhaddon established a new town, naming it Kur Esarhaddon, and forced the kings of Arwad, Byblos, and Tyre to participate in its construction.

The erection of a new Assyrian trade colony near Sidon similar to the Assyrian Karum that existed in this period close to the city of Arwad in the

I.31 Aerial view of the Phoenician city of Byblos

north, and the treaty of Esarhaddon with Ba'al king of Tyre, attest to the deep interests of the Assyrians in Mediterranean trade. While the treaty with Ba'al is fragmentary and parts of it difficult to understand, it seems that many Phoenician towns along the Syrian and Palestinian coast such as Acco and Dor were considered Assyrian territory. We assume that Ba'al the Tyrian king may have received some trade rights in these towns. At the same time, the treaty says that an Assyrian official is to be posted in the city of Tyre itself. He attended the town elders' assemblies and oversaw all activities of the vassal king.

In 674 BCE, it was the turn of Ba'al of Tyre and Yakinlin king of Arwad to rebel against the Assyrians, and in 671 BCE, Esarhaddon again battled in Phoenicia, recapturing the entire coast and leaving Ba'al to rule over the Tyrian island only.

Ashurbanipal, like Esarhaddon, counted the kings of Tyre, Byblos, and

Arwad among the "twenty-two kings of the coast" who assisted him in his first campaign against Egypt (667/6 BCE). But after the second campaign of Ashurbanipal against Egypt, Tyre rose against him. This time the Assyrian king laid siege to the city. When Tyre surrendered, he expelled the royal family to Assyria.

With the death of Ashurbanipal and, later, after the collapse of Assyrian domination over the entire west, the rich cities of Phoenicia became the prey of new empires: Egypt and Babylon fought each other for hegemony over the coast. The archaeological evidence of the presence of the Egyptians here includes the memorial stela left in Sidon by Pharaoh Necho. Elsewhere, many scarabs and other finds belonging to the 26th Dynasty of Sais have been uncovered. An example is an Egyptian scarab found in one of the Achzib tombs.

This situation continued until 604 BCE, the time of the arrival of the Babylonian armies to the region (see Book Two).

EXCAVATIONS AND SITES

IN PHOENICIAN TERRITORY within Palestine, i.e., the coast of western Galilee and the Acco plain, the following sites have been excavated to date: Achzib, Kabri, Acco, and Tell Keisan. Farther to the south, along the Carmel coast, the sites of Shiqmona and Dor contain strata of this period, but farther to the south of those sites, along the coast of the Sharon Plain, which previously belonged to the Israelite monarchy, none of the excavated sites (Tel Mevorakh, Mikhmoret, Apollonia, and Tel Michal) contain Persian-period strata. It seems that this region did not recover from the Assyrian conquest, and Jaffa and its surroundings already belonged to the Philistine-Ashkelon enclave in this period. At the end of the 7th century BCE, during the reign of Josiah king of Judah, Judah also penetrated the region, leaving traces at Tell Qasile.

A heterogeneous picture emerges from the results of these excavations: from **Achzib,** there are mainly cemeteries and tombs, some with rich finds. In the recent excavation conducted in the north side of the mound (Area E) at **Kabri,** a solid fortification system was uncovered. It consisted of a strong city wall and of a tower built according to typical Phoenician style. This system was probably destroyed by the Assyrians in the late 8th century BCE. On top of this settlement, another one was established in the 7th to 6th centuries BCE, probably under Tyrian suzerainty. This settlement consisted of two phases: only some walls and floors were unearthed from the first; the second consisted of the remains of a large casemate building. According to the excavators' estimate, the area of this settlement was about five acres and it should be identified with the Phoenician town of Rehob, which was, together with Achzib, one of the most important cities along the north coast of Palestine. This stratum was destroyed at the end of the 7th century BCE.

There are many finds from this period, including local Phoenician and imported Greek pottery, some of the Wild Goat style. Some typical Phoenician figurines and amulets and one imported Neo-Babylonian seal were found.

In the city of **Acco,** it was discovered that during the Late Iron Age (8th to 7th centuries BCE) a new and intensive rebuilding took place within the town. The excavator claims that the entire city was leveled. In Area A, masonry walls, perhaps of public buildings, appeared for the first time in addition to the usual fieldstone and brick. In one of these buildings, also occupied in the Assyrian period and perhaps destroyed in the campaign of Sennacherib in 701 BCE, a silver hoard was found. Another destruction level was observed there, which was attributed to the days of Ashurbanipal. Here, too, remains of metalworking activities were found. From the end of the period, a Phoenician medallion inscribed with its owner's name was found.

In another area, foundations of stone constructions were uncovered, perhaps belonging to a casemate wall, which may be the one described in one of Ashurbanipal's inscriptions.

More important was the discovery of a residential quarter in Area K, consisting of solid stone walls. Here was found a large pottery kiln in which many local Phoenician vessels survived. Some of them were decorated with motifs, never before observed on Phoenician vessels in Palestine and previously known only from Cyprus. Also in this stratum were many clay figurines and three Aramaic ostraca.

In the Acco plain east of the city, intensive excavations were carried out at **Tell Keisan,** revealing the remains of a large Phoenician town of the 7th century BCE. The period of Assyrian domination is well attested at this site, perhaps indicating the presence of an Assyrian administrative center there. A clay tablet inscribed in Assyrian cuneiform was recovered; it contains a list of names and numbers. Numerous Assyrian pottery vessels and local imitations were also present. The latter have peculiar local decoration. These vessels were found together with the ordinary Phoenician red-burnished pottery, which consisted of both thin and heavy Samarian bowls and Achzibian jugs and juglets. There were also some Assyrian-style seals and even an "Assyrian" clay figurine head. The date of this stratum (V) should be fixed to not later than about 640 BCE, when the Assyrians withdrew from the entire region, since the Assyrian occupation of the site was in the days of Tiglath-pileser III (733/2 BCE). The next stratum (IV) dates from the second half of the 7th century BCE, i.e., from the period of the Assyrian withdrawal until the coming of the Babylonians in 604 BCE. This stratum already contains much East Greek material: basket-handled amphorae, mortaria bowls, various Greek amphorae, and many vessels decorated with the characteristic Wild Goat style, which provides an exact date for the stratum. Also found here were some Cypriot vessels of the White Painted and the Bichrome families. Of the local vessels, the majority were Phoenician red vessels of the Samarian-Achzibian type, which continue here—in Phoenicia—until the end of the 7th century BCE and even into the 6th century (see below).

At **Shiqmona,** too, the excavations uncovered the remains of City 3, the last Israelite town, destroyed by Tiglath-pileser III in 733/2 BCE. Above it a new town was erected (City 4), dated to the 7th century BCE. This town was included in the province of Dor; it was destroyed by the Babylonians early in the 6th century BCE. Unfortunately, most of the finds from these two cities have not yet been published.

The major excavations along the Carmel coast were conducted at **Tel Dor,** the capital of the region and the province, the remains of which were also better preserved than at other excavated sites in this area.

The destroyed stratum of the last Israelite period included a strong forti-

I.32 Aerial view of Tel Dor

fication system and a solid four-chambered gate burned in a conflagration. It became apparent after the study of the pottery (including vessels imported from Greece!) that the destruction had been brought about by the Assyrian armies at the end of the 8th century BCE, during the campaign of Tiglath-pileser III.

From this time on, there are no written documents to tell us how long the city remained destroyed and when—if at all—it was rebuilt. The results of the excavations show, however, that this destruction, which was probably connected with large-scale deportations in accordance with the Assyrian system, did not last a long time. It seems that the Assyrians, who did not possess a fleet, were completely dependent in this matter on the Phoenicians for development of their trade with the west; moreover, for a short time, during the days of Sargon II, the Assyrians ruled over Cyprus, according to their own texts and the archaeological record on the island. There can be no doubt that they reached the island thanks entirely to the active support of the Phoenicians and that their very presence there was dependent upon the Phoenician fleets. It was apparently in their own interest to renew the harbor towns under their rule, for the development of the maritime meant the collection of more taxes and greater wealth. They also needed harbors for the transfer of rations and equipment to their soldiers stationed in the southern part of Palestine, and later to their soldiers and officials in Egypt, the domination of which became one of their major goals. This is why the coastal region of Palestine became such an important transit area.

The results of the recent excavations at Dor clearly show that the city was rebuilt by the Assyrians after a very short time. The excavations on the east side of the mound revealed a new and very strong fortification system that encircled the town. These fortifications were composed of a city wall of the offset-inset type. The use of such a wall apparently began in the earlier stratum, i.e., from the time of the divided monarchy (the period of King Ahab), and was reconstructed by the Assyrians. Of this wall, mainly the solid foundations are preserved, part of which is composed of stone foundations, and corners strengthened with fine masonry (partly built with stones in secondary use incised with mason's marks). Above this solid foundation, the width of which was about 2 m., a brick wall was erected that was probably rather high and coated with clay and lime. The city wall was also strengthened along its entire length with clay glacis, a steep slope also coated with lime to protect it from rain. Remains of the lime coating, sometimes of considerable thickness, were found in all the excavation's areas.

Attached to the wall was a city gate, this time a two-chambered gate. It

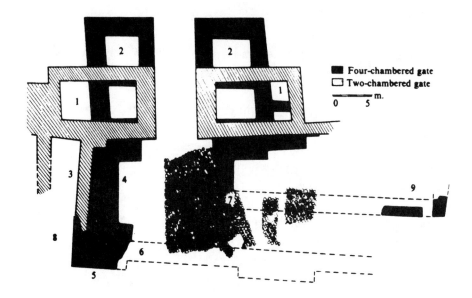

Four-chambered gate
Two-chambered gate

I.33 Tel Dor, plan of the Israelite and Assyrian city gates

was placed immediately above the previous Israelite four-chambered one. The two rooms of the later gate are much wider and project considerably (almost twice the width of the earlier rooms) to the south and north. At the same time, the depth of the new gate is smaller, almost by half, than the previous one. Its stones are also much smaller than the Israelite ones.

The two-chambered gate was preserved with its square flagstone entrance, an area paved with ashlar stones in the main entrance between the two chambers, and a flagstone lane leading from the gate to the interior of the city. Outside the gate, a similar paved way led from this interior gate to an outer one. This paved way is well built and preserved, but of the outer gate only a few stones were found intact.

The vessels found on the floor of the gate are rather late: they date until the beginning of the 4th century BCE, i.e., to the later part of the Persian period; probably their last use dates to the time of the great Phoenician rebellions against Persia, ca. 350 BCE.

When was the two-chambered gate erected? This can be established in two ways. One is the date of destruction of the previous four-chambered gate, and we have already seen that it was destroyed by fire at the time of the conquest of the city by Tiglath-pileser III (733/2 BCE). The two-chambered gate must therefore be later than this. Indeed, while excavating its entrance, on its southern side, the base of a doorjamb and a threshold were uncovered. In the corner of the latter was a stone socket in two parts, the lower part consisting, as was usual, of a round basalt stone with a high gloss from use, and a horseshoe-shaped cover stone of limestone, of a type discussed above and regarded as of Assyrian origin. In Palestine, this type was always restricted to Assyrian buildings. Thus, both the two-chambered gate and the attached offset-inset wall were erected in the Assyrian period.

This discovery is most important because it fits very well with the history of Dor as recorded in the written sources.

The comparison of the fortifications of Dor with those uncovered in the neighboring city of Megiddo, which was also built by the Assyrians as the capital of a province, strengthens these conclusions; for at Megiddo, too, as has been pointed out, above the four-chambered gate dated to the age of Ahab, a two-chambered gate closely resembling that of Dor, with only minor differences in dimensions, was found. The Megiddo two-chambered gate is also only an interior gate, with an outer gate down the slope. The two-chambered gate at Megiddo is—as we have seen—attributed by all authorities to Stratum III, the Assyrian period. Near the Megiddo gate some Assyrian-influenced open-court public buildings were uncovered, as well as a well-planned residential quarter of the same age.

To sum up, we may conclude that the fortification system at Dor includes a two-chambered gate and an offset-inset city wall built by the Assyrians not long after they had destroyed its predecessor, probably at the time when they rebuilt Megiddo as the capital of the province of Duru. The close resemblance between the fortifications of Dor and Megiddo in this period stems from a similar position in the hierarchy of Assyrian administrative organization: each was a provincial capital and the residence of an Assyrian governor.

Assyrian domination over Dor lasted about eighty years. Although this is a relatively short period and the excavated area of the Assyrian city is small, some important Assyrian finds were recovered, among them seals and pottery vessels. Of the two Assyrian seals discovered at Dor, one is a cylinder seal and the other a stamp seal. Both were brought from Assyria, for they are of imported stone. (A third, un-

I.34 Dor, an Assyrian stamp seal

stratified Assyrian seal, also a cylinder seal, has been found recently at nearby Caesarea. It may also have originated at Dor.)

Another Assyrian cylinder seal was found farther south along the coast (but still within the territory of the Dor province). This seal, recently published by M. and H. Tadmor, included an Assyrian cuneiform inscription that provides the name and title of its owner, clearly an important official in the Assyrian royal hierarchy who brought it with him to the place of his service. These seals can also serve as indicators of the importance of both the city of Dor itself and the sea road passing by it toward Jaffa.

Many Assyrian clay vessels have also been recovered at Dor, as well as many local imitations. Most of the vessels found at Dor, as at all the other sites of the period, are thin carinated bowls (or bowl fragments), with high sides and light-colored fabric. They are probably imitations of the well-known Assyrian metal bowls.

The Assyrian domination at Dor was of a short duration. It ended here around 630 BCE. In the next thirty years, until the arrival of the Babylonian armies, the status of the city is unclear. The excavations did not clarify the picture.

The city may have been controlled by one of the Phoenician kings, probably the king of Sidon, and have become an autonomous harbor town. But it is also possible that for a very short time, in the years 610–609 BCE, it was ruled by a Judaean king: King Josiah of Judah, en route to Megiddo to try to stop the army of Pharaoh Necho, king of Egypt on his way to Carchemish to assist the Assyrian army (2 Kings 23:29–30). This may explain the find of a Judaean *sheqel* weight at the site.

As to the excavated Phoenician settlements along the coast south of Dor, a rather surprising picture has emerged: of all these settlements—Tel Mevorakh, Mikhmoret, Apollonia, and Tel Michal—two, Tel Mevorakh and Tel Michal, were destroyed at the end of the 10th century BCE and did not recover before the Persian period. Mikhmoret and Apollonia were erected for the first time in the Persian period as a part of the huge building program that took place in the coastal area, which had been deserted for a lengthy period of time.

It seems, therefore, that this region was not inhabited during the Assyrian period at all. The same is true of the area extending farther to the south: the sites of Tell Qasile and perhaps also Tell Jerishe, both on the banks of the Yarkon River.

Another region in which the Phoenicians were settling during the period of the Assyrian domination is the region of the kingdom of **Gaza,** where the Assyrians built another maritime trading post, or *karum,* at the site of

Ruqeish. Recent excavations at the site have clarified that its entire material culture is typically Phoenician. According to the archaeological finds, the Phoenicians also populated the eastern part of Philistia, at sites such as **Tel Haror** and **Tel Seraʿ,** as well as the northern coast of Sinai. At least one trading post was also erected on the coast of the Red Sea, as is reflected by the Phoenician ostraca found at **Tell el-Kheleifeh** (of somewhat later date). From this point on, the Phoenicians became an important factor in Philistia and south Judah/Idumaea. They thus became the immediate heirs to all the regions previously populated by the Israelites in the north and Philistines in the south.

PHOENICIAN ARCHITECTURE

IN THE FIRST volume of this series (pp. 471–76), A. Mazar discussed in detail the main features of this architectural style and its ornamentation. Phoenician architecture was adopted and imitated by all the peoples of Palestine: Israelites, Judaeans, Philistines, and all the peoples of the eastern Jordan. Each of them modified aspects of it, adding some characteristic features of their own. All faithfully followed this style in all their public buildings and palaces in all the country's capitals and main towns until the arrival of the Assyrians.

The Assyrian conquest, particularly the conquest of the Israelite monarchy, brought an abrupt end to the Phoenician building style throughout the kingdom's territory. All buildings, whether public or private, constructed as a part of the large-scale Assyrian building activity in Samaria were executed in a new Assyrian style.

During the 7th century BCE, after the consolidation of the Assyrian regime, the Phoenician architectural style survived only in Judah, as long as Judah maintained its independence, and in Phoenicia. Its best example is the palace of the Judaean kings at Ramat Raḥel near Jerusalem, a palace that was erected—according to the recent evidence from the excavations conducted there by G. Barkai—a short time before Sennacherib's campaign against Judah and rebuilt immediately after it. This style survived here until the Babylonian conquest in 586 BCE. Only in Phoenicia, i.e., in the narrow coastal strip running from Lebanon to western Galilee, the Carmel, and the Sharon down to Jaffa, did this architectural style continue uninterruptedly through the entire Assyrian and Persian periods and perhaps even into the early Hellenistic age.

The major elements of this Phoenico-Israelite architecture style are:

1. Alternating courses of headers and stretchers built of long, well-dressed blocks
2. Walls constructed of ashlar piers with fieldstones in the spaces between them
3. Proto-Aeolic capitals, Hathor capitals, and Papyrus capitals
4. Recessed openings (both doors and windows)
5. Ornamented window balustrades (free sculpted or in relief on both sides)
6. Ornamented orthostats, depicting the same motifs known from the ivories, some examples of which have been found along the coast at sites such as Tyre, Sarepta, Achzib, Kabri, Acco, Tell Abu Hawam, Dor, Mikhmoret, Tell esh-Shuni (Kudadi), and Jaffa.

During the Assyrian period and later, some specific changes and variations, however, were introduced, such as the transfer in use from the limestone of the Early Iron Age to the coastal sandstone *(kurkar).* More variations of stone laying and wall building were introduced, such as the appearance (at Dor) of the "Punic" style of using monoliths in the walls instead of the standard-built Phoenician piers, as well as the use of the relief orthostats with motifs adopted from the Phoenician "pattern book," such as sphinxes, griffins, "the tree of life," sitting ʿAstarte, and others. A variety of

I.35 Tel Dan, a
Papyrus capital

I.36 Dor, a small stone orthostat depicting a Phoenician nobleman

new capitals appears, with Hathor heads, "Phoenician palmettes," a line of uraei (cobras), as well as papyri capitals, such as those discovered at Tel Dan, Megiddo, and Mount Gerizim (Shechem?) in Palestine, at Byblos in Phoenicia, and at Amathus in Cyprus.

At Amathus, the few Hathor capitals discovered were painted in strong colors (red, blue, and black). It may be assumed that these paints were also used on architectural ornamentation in Palestine and Phoenicia. To this list of architectural features may be added the many stelae depicting gods and priests as well as kings and dignitaries, which were discovered in large numbers at Tyre, Sidon, and Umm el-'Amed in southern Phoenicia, as well as at Achzib in Palestine.

PHOENICIAN TEMPLES AND CULT

THE NUMBER OF excavated sanctuaries attributed to the Phoenicians is surprisingly small. Even smaller is the number of those attributed to the Iron Age. The Phoenician sanctuaries discovered along the Phoenician and Palestinian coasts are dated mostly to the Persian period. Of the sanctuaries dated to the Iron Age, those discovered at Kition are the best known, but they will not be discussed here.

The only sanctuary of the Assyrian period that has been found is Temple

I.37 Dor, typical Phoenician wall

I.38 Dor, typical "Punic" wall in a public building found on the mound's acropolis

1, uncovered in the potters' quarter at Sarepta (biblical Zarephath), above which another one of the Persian period was erected (no. 2). According to the excavators' description, it is a rectangular structure (2.5 x 6.5 m.) oriented east-west, its floor made of hard-packed lime cement. Along the walls were benches coated with plaster. The most interesting element was a built table attached to the western wall, probably intended for votive offerings. The three open sides of the table were coated with lime; in front of it was a large ashlar stone. Another stone was missing. A square (40 x 40 cm.) depression in the floor attests to another missing element, perhaps a stela or an incense altar. Near the table a few cult objects such as clay figurines, masks, ivory carvings, medallions, and lamps were uncovered.

The plan of the two sanctuaries is noteworthy as, even in this late period, it conserves old Canaanite tradition and is almost identical to that of the Late Bronze Age Canaanite temples, such as the Fosse Temple at Lachish, the temple at Tel Mevorakh, a few of the Beth-Shean temples, and others. It even bears similarity to some earlier Canaanite temples, such as the one at Nahariya.

In recent years, a few small prayer chapels have been found, consisting of one relatively small room. These, too, follow an old Canaanite pattern, an example of which is the Area C temple at Hazor. In this room, there was usually the statue of the god or goddess or—sometimes—a line of stone stelae. Chapels of this type were found in various Palestinian excavations, for example, east of the foot of Tel Michal and (of the 7th century BCE) near the Tel Dan city gate. Many more chapels have been found in the Phoenician settlements along the coast, as well as overseas. The rest of the Phoenician sanctuaries are dated to the Persian period and will be discussed below.

On the cult practiced in the Phoenician sanctuaries, there are some biblical and Greek references. Of the Phoenician sources, all found in excavations, there are some inscriptions (the majority of which date to the Persian period). The longest one, an ostracon, was found at Acco, probably at the site of a sanctuary. It is an order issued by the city authorities to the guild of metalworkers to present a precious metal basin, as well as some additional metal implements, some made of gold or silver, to the person appointed as the head of the sanctuary. A few of the names of implements are Greek, written here in Phoenician letters. Another ostracon found in the same place included only numbers.

A similar, somewhat earlier inscription was found incised on a red-burnished Samaria bowl, recovered in one of the Phoenician temples at Kition (Temple 1 = 850–800 BCE), in which we are told about a citizen of the city of Thamasos in Cyprus who came to the Kition temple to present his hair, which was cut and placed in a bowl dedicated to ʿAstarte. Another example of this tradition was discovered in a Phoenician inscription recently found at Kition, which listed accounts of the ʿAstarte temple at the site. Among the sanctuary's employees are "the sacred barbers," perhaps those who directed the ceremony. In the same inscription, many more functionaries of the temple are mentioned, such as scribes, metalworkers, police, and children.

Long lists of cult items are included, especially in the Phoenician inscriptions from Kition, which mention dozens of metal objects, mostly of copper. The lists of tariffs found at Marseilles in France, which probably originated in one of the nearby Punic colonies and were intended for the temple of Baʿal-Zaphon, include the prices of the various animals brought there and re-

I.39 Tel Dan, stone stelae in a 7th century BCE chapel near the city gate

semble similar biblical lists. Additional details can be found in the many Punic inscriptions incised on stone stelae, which deal with similar matters.

We had to go as far as the western Mediterranean to collect our evidence, but there can be no doubt that the cult practiced by the Phoenicians along their own coast as well as that of Palestine is one and the same.

We now come to the question of the nature of the Phoenician cult, its symbols, and its remains, because this cult—like the other components of the peculiar Phoenician culture—became the prototype of all the pagan cults practiced by other Palestinian peoples during this period, including the Judaeans.

The Phoenician cult did not start in the 7th century BCE. Its foundations were laid in the Late Bronze Age and were consolidated during the first centuries of the first millennium BCE, but virtually no written sources from the late 8th and 7th centuries BCE have survived.

The archaeological finds are generally composed of two major types of figurines that appear simultaneously in all assemblages: the first is an adult male, represented as a king sitting on a throne or standing, or as a warrior on a horse; the second is a fertility goddess, sometimes pregnant, supporting her breasts, and other times either holding or nursing a child. Sometimes the child is depicted separately.

This is consistent with S. Moscati's observation that the Phoenician cult was composed of "a triad of deities: a protective god of the city, a goddess, often his wife or companion who symbolizes the fertile earth; and a young god somehow connected with the goddess (usually her son), whose resurrection expresses the annual cycle of vegetation. Within these limits, the names and functions of the gods vary, and the fluidity of this pantheon, where the common name often prevails over the proper name, and the function over the personality, is characteristic. Another characteristic of the Phoenician triad is the flexibility from town to town." (*Moscati Phoenicians,* p. 62.)

The major archaeological sources are the hundreds of dedicatory inscriptions found both on the coasts of the eastern Mediterranean and on its western shores, in which, as a rule, the names of a pair of gods are mentioned: a male god and a goddess. If more names are mentioned, they are either duplicate names or compound names for the same god, such as Baʿal-Melqart, Baʿal-Eshmun, Baʿal-Gebal (Byblos), or Baʿalat-Gebal, Ashtoreth-Tanit, Tanit-Pane-Baʿal. Very seldom do we find inscriptions that mention the name of an additional deity. These additional names are usually names of ancient gods that survived from the remote past. These reappear very rarely and include the Babylonian gods Shadrap and Shamash.

The male god is Baʿal, and this name became a regular component in hundreds of Phoenician personal names, including names of kings and high-ranking officials of the Phoenician city-states. Names such as Ethbaʿal, Elibaʿal, Adonibaʿal, Itenbaʿal, or Baʿalnatan, Baʿalsaleah, etc., also occur— and not surprisingly—in personal names common among the Israelites, Judaeans, Philistines, Moabites, Edomites, and Ammonites (see below), for Baʿal was a title that could be applied to any god.

Secondary titles are often added to the name Baʿal. These were intended to emphasize his important position in the divine hierarchy, or to distinguish one of his many attributes, such as the title Baʿal-Shamem ("lord of heaven") on a papyrus sent in 604 BCE from either Ashkelon or Ekron to the king of Egypt, and on ostraca found at Tel Michal and Tell Jemmeh.

The majority of the Baʿal titles, however, is connected with geographical regions or features, denoting his lordship over certain territories, such as sacred mountains (Baʿal-Zaphon or Baʿal-Lebanon, Baʿal-Zebul, and perhaps also Baʿal-Carmel), but mainly his role as the chief deity of the various Phoenician cities and colonies. Here, a separate name is added for each site: at Sidon he is Baʿal-Sidon or Baʿal-Eshmun; at Tyre, Baʿal-Tyre or Baʿal-Melqart; at Gebal (Byblos), Baʿal-Gebal; and at Carthage, Baʿal-Hamman.

Concerning the territorial significance of these Baʿals, we learn from archaeological finds in Palestine. According to our written sources, both Phoenician and Greek, the coastal region of Palestine was divided between Tyre and Sidon, and there are some ostraca from the Sharon Plain that are connected with Sidon, such as those from Dor and Apollonia, in which the name of Eshmun, the Baʿal of Sidon, is mentioned. There is also a Phoenician building inscription from Jaffa describing the foundation of a temple to Baʿal-Eshmun there. Other evidence, this time from Nebi Yunis (near Ashdod), tells of the establishment of a sanctuary there to the Baʿal of Tyre.

Territorial lordship resembling that of Baʿal was also attributed to the deities of all the other Palestinian peoples: each nation with its specific god, including the god worshiped in the pagan cult of Israel and Judah. For the latter, we may mention here the inscription found at Kuntillet ʿAjrud from an earlier period in which the names *yahweh shomron* and *yahweh teman* are mentioned.

In addition to the geographical and city names, Baʿal has many titles that glorify him: *adon* ("Lord"), *ha-melekh,* or *molekh* ("the King"). Many examples are found among the Carthaginian inscriptions, such as "to the lord, to Baʿal-Hamman" ("lord of incense altar"). These titles are also frequently represented among the personal names—Ebedmelekh ("servant of the king") or

Baʿal-Adir ("Mighty Baʿal")—and were utilized by all other Palestinian nations: Israel, Judah, Philistia, Ammon, Moab, and Edom (see below).

Names of another type helped the Phoenicians to identify their local deities with those of the other cities, for example, the identification of Eshmun with Melqart. That is why we find personal names such as Eshmunmelqart; or an inscription that states that "this stela was erected to the lord Eshmun by the son of Ebed-Melqart the son of Reshefyten," i.e., three generations, each having a different Baʿal. Or an inscription that mentions: "Ebed-Elim the son of Ebed-Melqart the son of Ebed-Reshef." The personal names that included the names of these deities have a similar form, such as Baʿal-Saleh, Melqart-Saleh, Eshmun-Saleh; or Baʿal-Shalem, Eshmun-Shalem, Melqart-Shalem, etc.

The same is true concerning the names of Baʿal's consort Ashtoret (ʿAstarte). Her name is also connected with many Phoenician proper names, both male, like Ebed-ʿAstarte, and female, like Em- ("mother of") ʿAstarte, Bat- ("daughter of") ʿAstarte, Amath- ("servant of") ʿAstarte, Han- ("the beauty of") ʿAstarte. This goddess also ruled over some territory, or over a certain region, a fact supported by evidence from excavations, where names such as ʿAstarte of Lebanon, Baʿalat-Gebal, Baʿalat-Tyre, and ʿAstarte of Sidon have been recovered. Moreover, on one of the Phoenician seal impressions we read: "the son of Abinadab who made an oath to ʿAstarte of Sidon." In a recently found Phoenician inscription incised on a side of a clay bowl, the goddess is called ʿAshtar-Isi, which probably means "the goddess ʿAshtar (is the goddess) Isis," pointing to Egypto-Phoenician religious syncretism. Among other recently discovered inscriptions incised on metal bowls, probably from a temple at Eliachin in the Sharon Plain, one says: "to the ʿAshtorim who are in the Sharon." Here the territory is the Sharon.

Often the name ʿAstarte comes together with the name of her male consort, as, for example, ʿAstarte the name of Baʿal, ʿAstarte the wife of Baʿal, ʿAstarte the face *(areshet)* of Baʿal, or Tanit the face (Pane) Baʿal. She is also honored with the titles commonly attributed to the gods, such as: to *rabat* ("lady") to ʿAstarte.

For many years, it had been accepted that Tanit was a separate deity from ʿAstarte, peculiar to the western Punic colonies, even though many personal names with the component Tanit have been discovered in the east, too (such as Ebed-Tanit). These are also attributed to the Carthaginians, who lived in the east. The first doubt crept in when a Cypro-Phoenician inscription was found reading: "to the lady ʿAstarte and to Tanit in Lebanon." In recent years after more excavations had been conducted along the Phoenician and

I.40 Shavei Zion, Phoenician clay figurine of 'Astarte. Note the "Tanit" emblem on the deity's body.

Palestinian coasts, it became clear that her name is quite common here, too. At first, her emblem was discovered on a monumental stone slab on a tomb facade near Byblos and, later, on stelae from the *tophet* at Tyre. Her emblem also survived on dozens of clay figurines, of various sizes, recovered from the sea near the harbors of Tyre and Shavei Zion along the Phoenician coast. This emblem has also been found on seals, seal impressions, and weights at sites along the entire Palestinian coast. Recently, some bronze and stone medallions depicting her emblem have been found at Ashkelon. It is not known how long she was worshiped in Palestine, but on an Ashkelonite coin dated to the 2nd century CE, her emblem is still depicted and her name, Panebalos, is inscribed, i.e., Tanit-Pane-Ba'al. The final proof of the unity of 'Astarte and Tanit came, however, from a Phoenician inscription found at Temple 1 at Sarepta dated to the 7th century BCE, which was dedicated to "Tanit-'Ashtoret," as well as her unity with Isis, which is derived from the name mentioned above: 'Ashtar-Isi.

It should be added that in this period, especially its later part, when the relations with Egypt had been consolidated, we find a strong influence of the Egyptian cult on the Phoenician one, such as the penetration of Egyptian motifs into Phoenician cultic art, which continue older Egyptian motifs from the Canaanite age. One example of the introduction of figures of Egyptian deities into the local cult is the appearance of the goddess Ba'alat-Gebal as Isis on the stela of Yahumelekh king of Byblos. The figure of Osiris is also common among the Phoenicians, and this phenomenon is reflected, as was already pointed out, in the list of Phoenician names that often included Egyptian deities, such as Ebed-Ibsat (servant of the Egyptian goddess Bestet), Ebed-Osira (Osiris), and Ebed-Ptah. Sometimes, however, Isis is mentioned in the Phoenician inscriptions by her real name, as the local goddess to whom prayers should be addressed.

In addition to the male and female deities, another figure appears in this period, a cult probably started relatively late—in any case, not long before the Assyrian period. It is a boy or a young child, usually depicted as the Egyptian child-god Horus-Harpokrates, either beside his mother, Isis, or alone. Some of his figurines, found at several Palestinian sites, show him with a large head in relation to his body, and he has one lock of hair running from the center of his head to one side. Sometimes he points his finger toward his mouth. Before the Assyrian period, he was usually found among the Phoenician ivories (including the Samaria ivories), but gradually he became more common on Palestinian seals all over the country. It is not clear if his cult began at this time, but from the 7th century BCE onward he appears more frequently in local glyptic art on seals, engraved on metal bowls, in clay and faience figurines, medallions, etc.

Among the Phoenician cult objects, the most common find is the clay figurines. We shall discuss them here in detail, for here, too, all the other Palestinian nations adopted the Phoenician model. During the Late Iron Age, such finds reflect the major cult common in the country as presented above,

I.41 Dor, clay mold of 'Astarte and a figurine cast from it

but many new and previously unknown details were added, most of them from the sphere of the popular apotropaic practices.

The figurines that characterized the Phoenicians are mainly females. In this age, we meet the bell-shaped type, i.e., pottery figurines with hollow, round, wheel-made bodies. Their heads are molded and are attached to their bodies by a tang. The goddess is usually depicted as a nude woman who supports her breasts with both hands. In addition to her bell form, she is characterized by a long "Phoenician wig," which falls to her shoulders. This wig is different from the short Judaean wig. At the end of the period, the appearance of the figurines is changed, and they are usually made by the new technique brought from Greece: a hollow figurine molded in front with back smoothed. Even the features of the figurines change: the majority of the late figurines depicts fertile women either supporting their breasts or in a stage of advanced pregnancy (hand upon belly). A smaller number shows them nursing or playing with a young child on their knees or carrying him on their shoulder. There are usually no inscriptions to help us identify the deities represented, but in a few figurines retrieved from the sea near Shavei Zion, which closely resemble the other figurines discussed above, there appears the symbol of the goddess Tanit-Pane-Ba'al or a dolphin, another of her emblems. We have already seen that according to the Sarepta dedicatory inscription, Tanit and 'Astarte are one and the same goddess.

A separate group among the Phoenician clay figurines of this period consists of those playing various musical instruments. Most of these are made in the usual Phoenician technique—bell-shaped figurines, the heads of which are covered with long Egyptian wigs—but instead of the usual position, i.e., supporting the breasts, hands upon womb, or nursing a child, these are playing one of four musical instruments: a frame drum, a tambourine, a lyre, or a double flute. These four instruments are very common at Phoenician sites including Sarepta, Achzib (mainly in tombs), Acco, Tell Keisan, Shiqmona, Tel Megadim, and Dor, as well as at sites along the Phoenician coast, in Cyprus and the Punic colonies. This "orchestra" was also a favored motif in the period before the Assyrian conquest, as seen in the Phoenician ivories, where the players appear as a group or as individuals, as well as on the decorated Phoenician metal bowls and Phoenician and Israelite seals.

There were also antique Canaanite prototypes for this Phoenician orchestra of the 7th century BCE. They appear as ordinary clay figurines or as decorations on metal or clay cult stands. Most important is the "musicians stand" found at Ashdod, which depicts a whole band; and we have already mentioned the ivories and metal bowls on which, again, a whole band is playing.

I.42 Typical Phoenician clay female figurines playing various musical instruments from Achzib

There is no doubt that this band—like the rest of the Phoenician cult components—was introduced into all the Palestinian sanctuaries and among all its nations (cf. 1 Samuel 10:5: "thou shalt meet a company of prophets coming down from the high place with a psaltery, and a tabret, and a pipe, and a harp, before them").

Figurines of musicians with the same four instruments have also been found in Israel (at Dan, Hazor, Beth-Shean, Taanach, and Tell el-Far'ah [N]), in Judah, Philistia, and in all the kingdoms of Transjordan. Among the Phoenicians, as well as the other Palestinian nations, the musicians were of both genders: in Judah, a male tambourine player was found at Tel 'Ira; at Ashdod in Philistia, a male lyre player; and at Edomite Tel Malḥata, a male double-flute player. These motifs are sometimes found depicted on local clay cultic vessels or engraved on seals, such as the seal of "Ma'adana the king's daughter," which depicts a lyre.

The third group of female figurines, typical of the Phoenicians in this pe-

I.43 Achzib, clay figurine
of a washing woman

riod (from Achzib and various sites in Cyprus to the west), depicts women engaged in everyday activities. There are women washing themselves in a bath; others are kneading loaves of bread on a table. It is not clear if these figurines represent cultic activities, like the musicians, or regular daily chores practiced in the sanctuaries.

Female models are not made only of clay. There are a few figurines of the 7th century BCE in ivory and bone (Sarepta, Achzib, Dor), some identical to the clay figurines. There are also metal figurines attached to metal stands. The same figures also frequently appear on the period's seals and seal impressions.

A mutual identity existed between the Phoenician mother-goddess ʿAstarte and the Egyptian Isis. The Phoenician ʿAstarte commonly appears in the Phoenician glyptic in the form of the Egyptian deity, and without the accompanying inscriptions, we could not differentiate between the two. We have already mentioned the Phoenician Baʿalat-Gebal on the Yahumelekh stela who is depicted as Isis, and the many figurines and amulets of the Egyptian goddess uncovered in Phoenician temples and *favissae* of the 7th century BCE, and later in Palestinian sites such as ʿAtlit, Dor, Tel Michal, and Ashkelon. One of the most popular depictions (in both the Phoenico-Israelite and the other people's cults in Palestine) is in the form of the cow Isis suckling her baby calf. Another schematic way to depict her is in the form of "the tree of life," which probably represented her body, sometimes adding her face on its top. This is often found engraved on ivories, seals, or clay vessels.

Male figurines are relatively rare, and among the many Phoenician clay types, only one, the "horseman," is found. This figurine must represent the figure of the warrior god. Riders of the Phoenician type on large, decorated horses of a specific kind have been recovered from the tombs at Achzib, Kabri, Tell Keisan, Acco, Megiddo, Dothan, Tel Megadim, Shiqmona, and Dor. These horsemen possess long faces and noses; they wear pointed helmets reminiscent of those of the Egyptian god Osiris, and they should be regarded as depictions of gods. Similar figurines, in large quantities, are also well known at Syro-Phoenician coastal sites, as well as from Cyprus. All should be interpreted as the "fighting Baʿal."

The only other Phoenician male figurine was uncovered at the temple at Sarepta: this is a bust wearing a round "turban" of the type common among the male figurines of other Palestinian nations, the Judahites and the Ammonites.

It should be noted that the Phoenician figurines—like all other figurines

I.44 Phoenician horsemen from Achzib

of the period—were painted in strong colors, mainly red and black, emphasizing the details of the faces of both humans and horses.

In the Phoenician settlements were found, in addition to the regular clay figurines, also **clay models** of sanctuaries that usually depict a one-room chapel. Such artifacts, like the others, originated in the Canaanite and early Phoenician cult, whence they spread among the other peoples of the country. During the 7th century BCE, however, it became common again, and many models of the kind have been recovered in almost all Phoenician settlements in Palestine at Achzib, Tell Keisan, Acco, Dor, and in the entire area of the Galilee: at Tel Rechesh located at Jezreel Valley and elsewhere. They are also common in Cyprus and the Punic colonies in the west.

Somewhat different in style is the model discovered at Sarepta in Sanctuary 1, dated to the 7th century BCE. It was broken, but the remaining part depicted a throne flanked on each side by the figure of a sphinx wearing a tall crown. On the seat of the chair was a figure, only the lower part of the torso of which was preserved. There can be no doubt that this small clay model of a chair depicts a real chair of stone of life-sized dimensions, which served as a throne for full-sized sculptures of deities of both genders, a common feature in the Phoenician homeland, some of which were found by chance. These are also supported or flanked by winged sphinxes.

The typical clay models of one-room sanctuaries also had some stone analogies. One miniature stone model of the type, in the center of which is a schematic image of a god, guarded by uraei (Egyptian cobras), was found at Achzib. Another miniature model depicting a stela, the height of which is only 8 cm., and decorated with a proto-Aeolic capital, was found at Acco. Among the stone stelae found in the Phoenician *tophet* cemeteries, a decoration in the shape of a chapel-temple was extremely common: first, a chapel in the Phoenician style and, later, one in a Greek style.

It is now clear that all these miniature models represent real small prayer chapels that were erected in the 7th century BCE and later along the main roads crossing the country and in settlements.

THE PHOENICIAN POPULAR CULT

SIDE BY SIDE with the regular Phoenician cult, practiced in the sanctuaries, there are many finds that point to a common popular cult, an apotropaic cult that was mainly intended to prevent bad luck, evil spirits, disease, etc. This cult had its own objects and artifacts and its own symbols, in which Egyptian emblems and motifs played a particularly important role. Some of these were simply adopted from the Egyptians, and others were somewhat changed. Of the common finds of this cult are the figurines of the three Egyptian deities Bes, Pataikos, and Ptah, who are all depicted as naked dwarfs wearing a feather headdress. The Phoenician version of these three deities was somewhat different, including some additions and alterations. Bes is also depicted on some pottery vessels, but mainly on glass and faience amulets, which were suspended from the neck. These gods also appear on carved ivories and on seals and seal impressions. Other symbols of this cult are grotesque human heads that were intended to ward off evil spirits and the like. Also adopted from Egyptian mythology are the eye of Horus, the ankh, and other symbols. Large assemblages of these glass and faience amulets have been found throughout the Phoenician world, and in Palestine at sites including Sarepta, Kabri, Tell Keisan, Acco, Tell Abu Hawam, 'Atlit, Dor, and Tel Michal.

Similar to these amulets in meaning and function are clay masks, some of which depict heads of actual deities of both genders (both Baʿal and ʿAs-

I.45 Typical Phoenician faience amulets from Dor

tarte), but most of them are also grotesque and were intended to frighten and ward off all danger. To some of them were added curious emblems in the center of the forehead, which had similar apotropaic meaning. During the 7th century BCE, the use of these masks becomes more and more popular, and many masks have been uncovered at all major Phoenician settlements along the eastern coast of the Mediterranean, including Palestinian ones such as Tyre, Sarepta, Achzib, Tell Keisan, Acco, and Dor, but also in inland Galilee at Hazor.

All these heterogeneous assemblages of apotropaic cult objects share common chronological and historical values: they were adopted from the Egyptian cultic sphere during the Canaanite age, and they continued into the Early Iron Age and reached their major distribution in the 7th century BCE along the Phoenician coast whence they passed westward to Cyprus and the Punic colonies.

PHOENICIAN BURIAL CUSTOMS

THE TYPICAL PHOENICIAN burial custom of the Late Iron Age involved burning of the dead and inserting the ashes into clay urns, above which were placed stone stelae. On each stela was inscribed the name of the deceased, as well as the name of the deity to whom it was dedicated. In addition, sometimes an emblem was incised, such as the Egyptian ankh, which was the symbol of life, but more often the figures of the various deities or their emblems were sculpted on them, as well as on the facades of chapels. In modern research, these cemeteries are usually called by the biblical name *tophet*.

At first, *tophet*s were mainly uncovered in the western Punic colonies such as Carthage, Motya (Sicily), and Tharros (Sardinia), and recently also in Cyprus, in the coastal region near Amathus. But during recent years, remains of many similar cemeteries have been discovered along the coasts of the eastern Mediterranean at sites such as Khaldeh and Rashidieh near Tyre, more recently at Tyre itself, and along the Palestinian coast. A few cemeteries that contained both urns and stone stelae were discovered around the Phoenician city of **Achzib;** they are the most important of their kind in Palestine of the Assyrian period. Here, no fewer than four Phoenician cemeteries have been excavated, which contained urns and ashes side by side with ordinary shaft tombs.

Farther south at ʻ**Atlit,** a huge cemetery was found dated to the late 8th

I.46 Phoenician clay cult masks from Achzib

and 7th centuries BCE. It was composed mostly of remains of burnt human bones left with the charred wood of the fire, spread over the surface of a very large area. Some graves here also included clay urns of typical Phoenician form. According to the 'Atlit evidence, the Phoenicians stopped burning their dead in the late 7th century BCE or beginning of the 6th, and started to bury them in rock-cut tombs of various types and even half-cut and half-built graves, above which, in some cases, stone stelae were erected with the names of the dead incised. In one case a human head was also sculpted.

Additional remains of Phoenician *tophet*s that included clay urns were also discovered along the southern Palestinian coast, within the territory of the kingdom of Gaza, near some of the new Phoenician settlements that were established there with Assyrian encouragement and support. These *tophet*s were found at Tell el-'Ajjul and Tell el-Far'ah (S); but the largest of them was recently discovered at Ruqeish, near the *karum*, i.e., the harbor that the Assyrians built on the coast to serve as the main harbor center for the intensive trade with Egypt. Here, dozens of clay urns of various sizes have been

I.47 Phoenician gravestones from Achzib

uncovered, as well as human ashes that were collected in regular store-jars. In contrast to the other *tophet*s on the northern Phoenician coast (those from Byblos, Khaldeh, Rashidieh, Tyre, and Achzib), no stelae have been found yet.

The shaft tombs of 'Atlit, which replaced the urns there, have already been mentioned. At Achzib, too, many Phoenician shaft tombs have been uncovered. In the eastern cemetery of the site, some 8th century BCE shaft tombs were found with later (Persian period) ones. Around the shafts, flights of steps were cut into the rock, to enable lowering of the bodies into the burial chambers. The entrance between the shaft and the rooms was closed with a stone that was carefully fitted. In the chambers were found the remains of many dead, as well as many clay vessels and other personal belongings of the deceased buried with them.

In the southern cemetery of Achzib, too, three additional shaft tombs were recently excavated. All three had a common plan consisting of a small entrance shaft from which one could enter the underground burial chamber. Along the walls of the burial chambers, benches were cut. Despite the initial impression that a homogeneous plan was prepared for all of these shaft tombs, it seems that this did not apply to their size, internal division, and orientation.

The rock-cut shaft tombs intended for multiple burials are but one of the many burial forms peculiar to the Phoenicians, both in their homeland and in the western colonies. For example, there were cemeteries of simple cist tombs as well as beautifully built chamber tombs, with many analogies along both the Phoenician and the Palestinian coasts and in Cyprus and the western colonies.

PHOENICIAN SEALS AND SEAL IMPRESSIONS

WE SHALL FIRST consider Phoenician **stamp seals**, which serve as good examples of the high standard of glyptic art achieved by the Phoenicians. These, like many other elements of Phoenician art, later became the prototype and source of inspiration for the rest of the Palestinian peoples. Beside the ivory carvings, which were earlier in time, and production of which ceased at the time of the Assyrian conquest, these seals are the most complete and beautiful examples of this art.

Of the Phoenician seal inscriptions, some pertain to royalty, or to the officials of the various states. Among them is the unique seal inscribed "belonging to the king of Sarepta" (no name) or that of "*ʿebed* ('servant') of ʿAzarbaʿal," which must have been the name of an unknown Phoenician king. Seals of scribes or priests appear, too, such as "the man of god." Peculiar to the Phoenicians, however, are the many inscribed seals containing a blessing or votive formula, such as "the seal of Manan, blessed by Baʿal."

As to the motifs engraved on the Phoenician seals, it may be assumed that the Phoenicians had, in this case, as in the ivory carvings or the production of metal bowls, a limited assortment of basic motifs, of which there were not more than thirty or forty. These were rendered again and again in endless variations and compositions on all these seals. These motifs were well known in all the production centers, and the differences among these centers are largely ones of style, i.e., seals carved in the southern Phoenician style, which was inspired by the Egyptian, or in the northern Phoenician style, which was more influenced by Hittite or Aramaic prototypes. In most cases, the seals depict a single motif but sometimes two or more. The seal motifs are mainly rendered from the Egyptian sphere, such as various deities—Ra, Horus, Isis, Sekhmet, Nephtis, Bes, Ptah, Pataikos, etc.—as well as Egyptian emblems, such as a winged uraeus, the head of Bes, the four-winged beetle, the eye of Horus, the ankh, the winged sun disk, and others. Sometimes Egyptian pseudo-hieroglyphs and cartouches are added, but they are unreadable and have no meaning at all. In addition, the figures of the kings of Egypt and its priests are depicted in various attitudes: fighting, standing, or leading prisoners of war. Other motifs include an African leading a monkey and winged demons.

In addition to the Egyptianizing motifs, there are also autonomous Phoenician ones, such as the human-headed sphinx that wears the double crown of Egypt, as well as a typical griffin. Sphinxes and griffins near "the tree of life," a hero stabbing a sphinx or a griffin with a spear, people praying to "the tree of life," and the figure of the naked ʿAstarte supporting her breasts are also well known.

Other Phoenician seals depict various animals that were probably adopted as family emblems: roaring lions, walking lions, a lion attacking a bull, a lion fighting a human figure, bulls grazing in a field, a cow suckling a calf, a crocodile, and some hunting and war scenes.

With the arrival of the Assyrians, a real revolution took place in Phoenician glyptic art. It is true that many of the previous motifs continued, but many new ones were added, the majority of which were taken from the Assyrian or even the general Mesopotamian repertoire. Later, Babylonian and Persian motifs were added and even (quite early on) Greek ones. Of the As-

I.48 Typical Phoenician
seal: the seal of Jezebel

syrian motifs, figures wearing Assyrian dress, Assyrian cultic emblems such
as the moon crescent and the stars, the hero struggling with one or more
monsters, and the hero stabbing a lion are common examples. The early
Greek motif most frequently used by the Phoenicians is Hercules, because of
his identification with Melqart, as well as admiration for his physical
strength. Many war scenes include horses and chariots and the like.

PHOENICIAN ART OBJECTS

ONE OF THE characteristics of the Phoenician material culture of the late
8th century BCE until the early 6th is a flowering of the production of decorated objects, especially those associated with cosmetics. These were of limestone, alabaster, shell, glass, faience, metals, and other materials. Many of
them are unique to this period. It is not only their heterogeneous character
that is surprising but their broad distribution as well. As the number of excavations in Phoenicia itself is small, most of these finds were recovered outside the Phoenician homeland, i.e., in Palestine (including Transjordan) and
Syria. Many other finds have been collected from Assyrian palaces, such as
those excavated at Nimrud and Khorsabad, where the objects were brought

as spoils of war. Others have been found in large numbers in the west, especially in Cyprus, where a large Phoenician population was settled, but also in Phoenician settlements in the Greek islands where they were carried by the intensive international trade of this period. Particularly noteworthy is the large Phoenician assemblage of fine objects found in the hereum (the sanctuary for the Greek goddess Hera) at Samos. Others had been found at Rhodes, Crete, and even in mainland Greece. Not a few traveled as far as southern Italy, i.e., to Magna Graecia, which was established at that time, and even up north to central Italy and to the Etruscan territories.

As to Palestinian finds, though they often originated in Phoenicia, the local artisans adopted and imitated these objects and produced them at the local centers of all the nations of the country. We shall examine the major groups of alabaster and shell vessels, the seals, and the metal and faience objects.

Examples of the art of the Phoenician ivory carving, which in the previous period was the finest expression of the Phoenician school, were found at many Palestinian sites. These began to disappear at the end of the 8th century BCE but mainly in the 7th century, under the Assyrian domination of Palestine. This happened not only in Palestine but in the entire eastern Mediterranean coastal region. Perhaps the reason was a lack of raw material. In any case, at that time artisans began using large quantities of cheaper materials, such as bone, stone, and alabaster. The change in materials appears to have been followed by a change in production quality and increased use of simple shallow incised and drilled geometric designs. The same degeneration can be observed in the art of seal glyptic. Most of the period's finds, however, are of the simple cosmetic objects mass-produced for daily use rather than the sophisticated art decoration. A few examples follow.

The most common of the decorated objects of the period are the cosmetic palettes made of hard limestone imitating marble. Some were plain, but the majority was decorated with shallow geometric incisions of two types: concentric circles with dots in their center, and net designs in various shapes. Such decorations may have also been painted or even filled with inlays of colored glass. The palettes appear to have been made on a potter's wheel and were later incised by hand. Recently, similar cosmetic bowls made of blue or green glass have been found. In the mid-8th century BCE, these vessels started to appear at all Palestinian sites. They occur in greater numbers only during the 7th and early 6th centuries BCE. At that time, they are found along the Phoenician coast and in the Assyrian palaces in Nimrud and Nineveh as well as in Palestine. Their production ceased at the end of the Iron Age.

In recent years, the assemblage of these decorated cosmetic bowls or palettes has become more and more varied, especially as regards the variety of motifs, now known to include open and closed lotus flowers.

An additional type of stone bowl popular in Palestine, Syria, and Phoenicia as well as in the Assyrian palaces of the same period is the hemispherical bowl averaging 7 cm. in diameter. These have a hole in their side, usually fitted with a tubelike extension. In most cases, the bottom of the bowl is decorated in low relief, with one of a set repertoire of motifs: a human hand, a volute palmette, a cross, or a pair of lions. The common occurrence of these motifs on the bottom of the bowls makes it possible to group them accordingly. The majority is of various kinds of stone, but some are of ivory. The use and function of these bowls have been addressed by many scholars. An early suggestion that they are censers has been rejected, since no traces of burning have been found on their inner faces. Moreover, some were made of ivory, bone, or other soft materials such as Egyptian blue (a soft blue stone). Other interpretations view them as cosmetic palettes or libation bowls. However, the motifs decorating them appear to have cultic and apotropaic significance. Their style was mostly Phoenician, but V. Fritz correctly designates the lion motif as of Syrian origin.

More types of stone vessels of the same origin and date have recently been uncovered. These are elongated cosmetic palettes with a round depression at

I.49 Decorated Phoenician
stone cup from 'En Gev

I.50 Decorated Phoenician
stone cosmetic palette

one end. This type was previously common among the ivory carvings, where it is known as the "bird nest" type. Good ivory examples were found at Israelite Hazor and Judaean Beth-Zur. These stone vessels appear to have replaced the ivory ones. D. Barag recently published some of them; the most beautiful one, probably from Rabbath-Ammon, depicts the Phoenician "tree of life," which consisted of a few alternating proto-Aeolic capitals and Phoenician palmettes with a winged sun disk on top. Two praying figures flank the tree. The scene is typically Phoenician in all its details, and many analogies are common on the earlier ivories and metal bowls, as well as on Phoenician carved shells and seals. The other two cosmetic palettes of this type are engraved with floral motifs: lotus flowers, palm branches, rosettes, and concentric circles that were drilled in the same technique used in the limestone cosmetic bowls mentioned above.

Similar to them in date, function, and distribution are flat alabaster cosmetic palettes. These were probably used to mix paints or powders. They occur at the same sites on both sides of the Jordan as well as in Phoenicia. The palettes are usually rectangular in shape, flat, and highly polished. One end is engraved in the shape of a goddess's head in northern Phoenician style. Sometimes, as in the case of the alabaster palette found in a Tel Jezreel grave, instead of a curved head there is a perforated projection for hanging, decorated with simple incised lines. Others also have a geometric design consisting either of concentric circles alone or of such circles surrounded by squares. C. Bennett, who first published them, noticed the great similarity between the shape of their heads and the heads decorating the *Tridacna* shells and some of the decorated bone objects.

I.51 Decorated Phoenician
alabaster cosmetic palette

The last decorated type of Phoenician objects to be discussed here is the *Tridacna squamosa* shell, originating in the Red Sea. At the edge of each shell, a female human head is engraved. The reverse depicts her garment and jewelry. The inside is left plain except for the edges, where another motif or a series of motifs is engraved. The decorations, though very detailed, exhibit a schematic quality. At the same time, they preserve and repeat many of the motifs found on the carved ivories of the past. These include cultic scenes, war and hunting scenes, etc. According to R. A. Stucky, all date to the 7th century BCE, and their style is probably north Phoenician. Many engraved *Tridacna* shells have been found all over Palestine, including the Transjordanian states, in Judah, Philistia, the Assyrian provinces of the north, and Phoenicia, as well as the Assyrian palaces where they were brought as spoils of war. Although most scholars agree with Stucky about their Phoenician origin, it should be pointed out that their distribution, as that of most of the Phoenician decorated objects, goes far beyond the Phoenician borders. Many have been uncovered in the East Greek islands, especially in Rhodes and Samos, and several were found in Egypt at Daphne and Naukratis. There are still some scholars who believe that they originated in the Nile Delta region.

Very similar to the *Tridacna* shells are bone implements and medallions decorated with rows of concentric circles and dots, which appear to be of the same age and fabric.

At the end of the 7th century BCE, two additional cosmetic vessels came to be commonly used. The first of these are simple glass juglets: alabastra, *amphoriskoi,* and *aryballoi,* which were used as containers for perfumes, perfumed oils, etc. The glass was usually dark blue, but often painted in white, yellow, and red wavy lines. In addition, some faience vessels in the shape of Phoenician or Egyptian kneeling women were used for the same purpose. They were apparently filled with "sacred Nile water" or other sacred liquids and used in the local cult.

The second type is composed of alabastra with small ledge handles in Egyptian fashion, which were also used for perfumed oils. Examples have been found in Palestine, Phoenicia, and many other regions. These alabastra were in use until the Persian period.

On the basis of style and distribution, most scholars now believe that the origin of all the decorated cosmetic objects of various shapes and materials discussed above is in Phoenicia. However, "Phoenician" does not exclude the possibility that they were manufactured in the Palestinian coastal towns that formed an organic part of the Phoenician school of art in the Assyrian

I.52 Phoenician glass juglet
from 'Atlit

period. D. Barag recently pointed out that many of these objects clearly continue old Canaanite prototypes. He notes, for example, another type of a cosmetic object: a stemmed *pyxis* with vertically perforated lug handles, which was produced in stone, faience, and glass, and which has clear roots in the Canaanite *pyxis* of the late 2nd millennium BCE. This type was still manufactured in the Levant in the 7th century BCE and was found in the Assyrian-period Stratum III at Megiddo.

We shall now discuss the decorated Phoenician **metal** vessels of the Assyrian period, which may be divided into three types: (1) bronze mirrors, (2) bowls and jugs, (3) caryatid censers, and (4) *thymiateria*.

Bronze mirrors occur in houses and tombs of the period. The best examples come from Hazor, Jezreel, and Samaria. Dozens of metal vessels from the second group, mainly bowls but also a few closed vessels (jugs), have been found at all the large centers where Phoenician vessels of the other types discussed above—ivories, *Tridacna* shells, and stone and glass vessels—also occur. These bowls are sometimes made of gold or silver, but usually of bronze. The majority is undecorated, but others are ornamented with floral designs, rosettes, bar handles, etc. The similarity between these and the other Phoenician vessels described above can be established by the more composite motifs depicted on them, which are almost identical to those on the ivories, the *Tridacna* shells, and the various stone vessels. Generally, there is also a close similarity between the distribution of the *Tridacna* shells and that of the decorated metal bowls. The only clear example from Palestine of decorated metal bowls of this style was uncovered at Megiddo (Stratum IV). The others come from sites along the Phoenician coast, as well as the Assyrian palaces where they were brought as war spoils, and naturally from Cyprus, the East Greek islands (especially Samos and Rhodes), Crete, mainland Greece, and even Magna Graecia (i.e., the southern part of Italy) and the Etruscan regions of central Italy.

The Phoenician name for this bowl and its original function are known to us from an inscribed bronze bowl found at an unknown site on the Lebanese coast. The base of the bowl, like many others of the type, is decorated with a rosette design. In this case, it is surrounded by a Phoenician inscription,

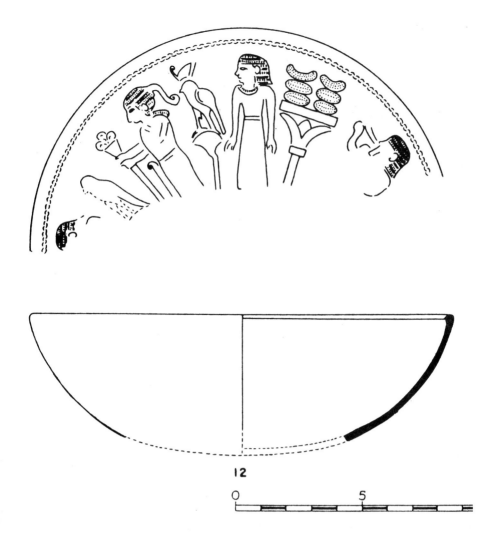

I.53 Decorated Phoenician bronze bowl from Megiddo

which designates it as *quba'im* ("cups," and cf. Isaiah 51:17, 22). This vessel is connected, according to the inscription, with the term *marzeaḥ*, i.e., a sacred feast that is prepared in honor of the Phoenician deity Melqart and the Babylonian Shamash.

In addition to this bowl with a Phoenician inscription, some additional inscribed bowls of this type have been uncovered in Cyprus and elsewhere, but the inscriptions include only the names of the owners, who are always Phoenician. Many Phoenician motifs are depicted on them and are often the same ones portrayed on the carved ivories and the *Tridacna* shells, such as the figures of Ba'al and 'Astarte, sphinxes and griffins, scenes of hunting and war, etc. Their style is peculiar in the way it combines the Egyptian, Assyrian, Greek, and Phoenician motifs. The date of these bowls is mainly from the late 8th century BCE and later.

The third type of Phoenician metal vessels of the period is the caryatid censers, i.e., bowls resting on a long pedestal in the shape of a human figure, usually of 'Astarte or Ba'al, which were also intended to be used in the local cults. Like the bowls and all other decorated Phoenician vessels discussed above, these censers had Late Bronze Age prototypes (the best examples come from Tel Nami on the Carmel coast and from Megiddo). Similar to all other works of art discussed above, these vessels also enjoyed a new heyday in Phoenicia and Palestine in the 7th century BCE, and certainly continued into following periods, during which they reached the East Greek islands as well as Cyprus and the western Punic colonies. A unique group of bronze caryatid censers of the 7th century BCE from the Phoenician coast has been published by P. R. S. Moorey. That this type of cult object was also adopted by other nations in Palestine is proved by a complete caryatid bronze censer of the same date found in an Ammonite tomb near the capital city of Rabbath-Ammon.

The fourth group of Phoenician metal vessels is the *thymiateria* used either as censers or as lamps. Examples of these vessels were found along the Phoenician and Palestinian coasts, in Assyrian palaces, and to the west in Cyprus and the East Greek islands. Some belong to the 7th century BCE, but others are later.

PHOENICIAN POTTERY

OF THE PHOENICIAN pottery groups common in the Early and Middle Iron Ages, the earliest to appear is the Bichrome family. This type of ware had completely disappeared by the 9th century BCE. Even the succeeding Black-on-Red family, which constituted a large part of the Phoenician pottery of the 10th to 8th centuries BCE, had deteriorated by the 7th century BCE and consisted then of a few debased, poorly painted forms. It ceased to appear entirely at the end of the 7th century BCE, when more and more Phoenician decorated vessels belonged to the Red-Slip family. By the time of the Babylonian conquest, they were the only decorated Phoenician pottery types. The Red-Slip family continued through the entire Assyrian period to the end of the 7th century BCE. In the coastal region, it probably continued even later. This pottery family is known by various names—Samaria ware, Achzib ware, in Cyprus simply as Red-Slip—but all are members of a single family, the most common Phoenician pottery type in the Punic world, too. This family is composed, on the one hand, of delicate, well-burnished Samaria bowls, the colors of which alternate from red to white, and on the other, of coarse, heavy, red-burnished bowls as well as red-burnished jugs and juglets. The shapes of these jugs and juglets are divided between those with a mushroom-shaped upper part and those with a pinched mouth. A few of these red-burnished jugs are decorated with several coarse, black lines. In addition to these decorated Phoenician families, there are many simple and undecorated vessels for daily use, such as large jars with flat shoulders and pointed bases, which were also used in the maritime trade; juglets with high loop handles; bowls with very wide rims; and flat, open lamps with one or two pinched spouts. Many such vessels have been rescued from the sea. They serve as important indicators of the first appearance of a ceramic *koine,* which will reach its peak during the Persian period (see below).

Recently, a new type of Phoenician vessel, also dated to the late 8th to 7th centuries BCE, has been uncovered at Acco. These vessels are decorated with designs incised in a layer of paint. The motifs are mainly floral, of the same style observed above on the stone and metal vessels. But a few symbolic elements, such as the eye of Horus, are added here. It should be pointed out that these vessels have many close similarities to decorated Phoenician ware in Cyprus, where they are usually ornamented with the same designs, but mainly painted rather than incised. Some of the Cypriot analogies are similar to the Acco vessels, but others are much more elaborate. These typical Cypriot-Phoenician vessels have not yet been found at any of the Palestinian coastal sites.

Chapter 5

The Philistines

The Historical Background of Philistia in the 7th Century BCE

During the Assyrian domination of Philistia, the country was divided among four semiautonomous political units headed by kings. These were, from north to south: Ashdod, Ashkelon, Gaza, and Ekron. The fifth city of the Philistine Pentapolis was Gath (the final identification of which is not yet agreed upon; it was probably Tell eṣ-Ṣafi). This last city, if it existed at all at this time, would have been a small and unimportant Philistine border village, and, perhaps more likely, under Judaean occupation. In either case, Gath did not participate in any of the recorded events of the period.

The seniority and relative importance of these towns changed from time to time. This hierarchy was not always decided by the local powers. At the beginning of the period, Ashkelon probably enjoyed priority among these kingdoms. Later it was replaced for some unknown reason by Ashdod. Each of these centers had quite a large territory: the kingdom of **Ashdod** included, in addition to the city itself, Ashdod-Yam, reaching almost to Jaffa in the north, to Gath in the east, and to the Lachish River in the south. The kingdom of **Ashkelon** possessed a small northern enclave, which included the towns of Beth-Dagon, Jaffa, Bene-Berak, and Azor. But its regular border stretched from the Lachish River in the north to the Shiqmah River in the south. The kingdom of **Ekron** perhaps included the cities of Elthake and Gibbethon and—for a short period—the Judaean city of Timnah. The kingdom of **Gaza** was the largest of all and was therefore, despite having a king,

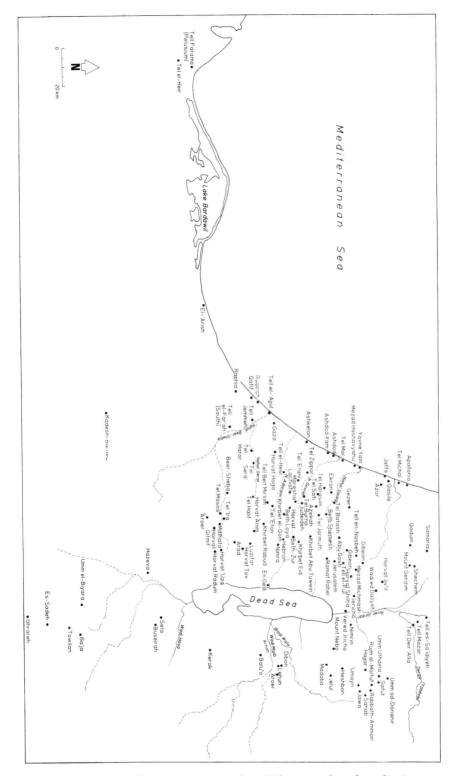

I.54 Excavated Iron Age sites in southern Palestine and northern Sinai

probably under direct Assyrian domination. This kingdom included, in addition to the city itself, some large towns uncovered in the excavations of Tell el-Ḥesi, Tell el-ʿAjjul, Ruqeish (Qatif), Tell Jemmeh, Tel Haror, Tel Seraʿ, Tell el-Farʿa (S), Raphia, and Tell Abu Salima (Sheikh Zuweid), as well as many more smaller settlements, such as those discovered at Ḥorvat Hugah and Mephalsim. Its eastern border was the Judaean foothills, and the southern border was the el-ʿArish River. It seems that Assyria found it important, right from the beginning of its penetration into the areas west of the Euphrates, to occupy the coastal region of the eastern Mediterranean on the way to Egypt, including—as we have seen—the province of Dor and the entire Philistine territory.

The history of the Assyrian conquest of Philistia in many ways resembles the story of the occupation of the northern part of the country and the former Israelite kingdom, but also differs from it in some details. This story, too, is completely dependent (aside from the archaeological sources) on a few biblical narratives, as well as on the Assyrian documents. From all of these, it is clear that from the beginning, the Assyrians had adopted a system of administration here different from that in the north. For various reasons, they organized all the coastal settlements in Philistia in the form of semiautonomous states, headed by local kings who were under the control of an appointed Assyrian officer (sometimes even of an administrator, as we learn from an Aramaic papyrus found at Saqqara in Egypt that was written in Ashkelon or Ekron as late as 604 BCE, where the title "the governor of the land" is mentioned). These rich Philistine towns managed to retain their semi-independent status and their commercial and internal freedom by paying high annual tributes to the Assyrian court. Caught between Assyria and Egypt, they developed a particular flexibility, continually adapting themselves to the fluctuating political situation, at times swearing allegiance to both sides. They thus had the capacity to endure, while greater, stronger kingdoms elsewhere were totally annihilated.

The first Assyrian campaign to Philistia took place during the reign of Tiglath-pileser III in 734 BCE. He descended along the coast to Gaza and "to the city of the Egyptian river," probably el-ʿArish. Gaza was evidently the target of the campaign from the outset. Ḥanun king of Gaza fled to Egypt, was returned, and paid high tribute. It is possible that all other Philistine towns surrendered to the Assyrians, too. But just one year later (733 BCE) Ashkelon rebelled and another campaign against it passed through Gezer (from which there is the relief depicting "the siege of Gezer"). Soon Ashkelon's rebellious king, Mitinti I, was replaced by his son Rukubti. During the rest of Tiglath-pileser III's reign, as well as that of his son Shalmaneser V, Philistia remained quiet.

In 720 BCE, when Sargon II came to power, Gaza again joined a general rebellion. Sargon arrived quickly to quell it. This quick move is decisive evidence for the importance of the area in Assyrian policy. That same year, Sargon recaptured Gaza and deported its king to Assyria. An Egyptian army, on which all the rebellions in Philistia depended, arrived, for the first time since the Assyrian penetration, only to be defeated near Raphia. The city of Raphia itself was completely destroyed by the Assyrians, who also deported all its inhabitants. From now on, Gaza changed its orientation and remained loyal to the Assyrians for the duration of their domination. Gaza also assisted the Assyrians in many of their projects through the reigns of Sennacherib, Esarhaddon, and Ashurbanipal.

In 716 BCE, Sargon returned to Philistia and brought more territories as far as "the city of the river of Egypt" under his rule. He also pacified the nomadic tribes in the neighborhood and established a new Assyrian trade colony within the territory of the kingdom of Gaza. The inhabitants of this colony were composed of Assyrians, as well as various peoples who were transferred from other regions of the empire, including many Phoenicians and perhaps also some Egyptians. This colony is probably the city excavated at the site of Ruqeish (see below).

Within a short time (713 BCE), it became the turn of Ashdod to rebel. Its king, Azuri, was replaced by the Assyrians, and his brother Aḥimetu was appointed in his stead. The city's citizens did not accept him and appointed Yamani (712 BCE), who led the rebellion anew. In the same year, Sargon once more sent his army to Ashdod under the *tartanu,* or military commander (cf. Isaiah 20:1 "In the year that Tartan came unto Ashdod, when Sargon the king of Assyria sent him," and also the discussion above of the Assyrian stela found at Ashdod). The Assyrian officer reconquered the city as well as the town of Ashdod-Yam and the eastern Philistine towns of Gibbethon, Ekron, and Gath (the depiction of the conquest of the first two was found in the reliefs at Sargon's palace at Khorsabad; see above). Some scholars believe that for a short time Ashdod became an Assyrian province; but later sources continue to list the names of its kings. O. Bustenai thinks that the frequent campaigns of Sargon to Philistia attest to the importance of the region in his policy. It was evidently Sargon who placed Philistia under almost direct Assyrian rule by posting his army units to the major Philistine cities, erecting military forts along the coastal highway, and establishing a trade colony on the Egyptian border. It should also be pointed out that besides the port towns along the eastern coast of the Mediterranean, Sargon succeeded in conquering the island of Cyprus, as indicated by the find of his stela in the Cypriot town of Kition. To his reign, more than that of any other Assyrian monarch, we must assign the opening of international trade with Egypt and Greece.

Upon the death of Sargon in 705 BCE, Philistia rebelled again, this time as part of a general rebellion supported by the Egyptian army. The rebellion encompassed Judah under Hezekiah (see below). This time, Ashdod (under Mitinti) and Gaza (under Silbel) did not join. The leading city at this time was Ashkelon, whose king, Rukubti, was exiled by his own citizens and replaced by his brother Ṣidka. The inhabitants of Ekron also joined the rebellion, but without their king, Padi, who was taken by Hezekiah to a prison in Jerusalem.

In 701 BCE, Sennacherib campaigned against Judah and Philistia. In Judah, he conquered and destroyed Lachish and forty-six other towns and also recaptured Ashkelon and the Ashkelonite enclave around Jaffa, which consisted of Jaffa itself, Azor, Beth-Dagon, and Bene-Berak. The king of Ashkelon was deported to Assyria and was replaced by a king with an Assyrian name, Sharruludari (Rukubti's son). Ekron surrendered to the Assyrians without a fight and King Padi returned. An Egyptian army, which came to help the rebels, was defeated near the city of Elthake. Parts of the region of western Judah had been given by the Assyrians to the three Philistine cities that remained loyal to the Assyrians: Ashdod, Gaza, and Ekron.

Philistia remained quiet during the rest of the Assyrian period, i.e., until ca. 640 BCE. Throughout this entire period, i.e., the days of Esarhaddon and his son Ashurbanipal, all the Assyrian wars aimed at the conquest of Egypt. In 679 BCE, Esarhaddon set out on a campaign against Ursa, a site on the border of Egypt, occupied it, and deported its king to Assyria. Two years later he, with the cooperation of Mitinti II son of Ṣidka king of Ashkelon, Aḥim-ilki king of Ashdod, and Ikausu (Achish) king of Ekron, was engaged in construction projects at Sidon and Nineveh.

In 674, 671, and 669 BCE, three campaigns were conducted by the Assyrians against Egypt. In this connection, the Assyrian eponym list of 669 BCE mentions an Assyrian governor who was appointed to oversee the kings of Ashdod, Ashkelon, and Gaza. This explains why, in 668–667 BCE (at the time of Ashurbanipal's military campaigns against Egypt), the names of the four Philistine kings listed above are mentioned as collaborators of the Assyrian monarch. This record is also the last time any of these Philistine kings is mentioned at all.

When Psamtik the son of Necho became the king of Egypt (664–610 BCE), the Assyrians retreated from Egypt, first to Philistia (where they were still active until 649 BCE according to the evidence of the Gezer tablets), and shortly afterward, when the Assyrian administration in Palestine collapsed totally around 640 BCE, the Egyptians penetrated Philistia and replaced the Assyrians, except perhaps in the northern part of the kingdom of Ashdod, which fell for a short time into the hands of Josiah king of Judah (according to the finds at Meẓad Ḥashavyahu and perhaps also those of Tell Qasile; see below). Herodotus (1.105) tells that Psamtik ruled fifty-four years, twenty-nine of which he spent on the siege of Ashdod. Herodotus also mentions that in the third decade of his rule, the Scythians arrived in the area. Even if this event really occurred, it left no distinguishable mark in the archaeological record.

It has already been pointed out that the Philistine kings generally bore West Semitic names, such as Ḥanun, Ṣidka, Mitinti, Aḥimilki, and Padi. Only Ikausu, the king of Ekron, had a definitely non-Semitic name. It is difficult to determine to what extent the inhabitants of Philistia in the 7th century BCE were still the direct descendants of the original Philistines of Aegean origin, who settled Palestine in the Early Iron Age. They were apparently deeply influenced by the local cultures because just as they bore West Semitic names, they probably spoke a language and wrote in a script similar to those current in the area, as indicated by the ostraca found in Philistia. In addition, the monumental inscription recently found at Ekron mentions five of its last kings (of whom three were previously unknown): Achish/Ikausu son of Padi son of *ysd* son of Ada son of Ya'ir, ruler of Ekron. We learn from A. Demsky that the title of the goddess mentioned in the inscription is *potnia,* which should be interpreted as the common Archaic Greek word for "divine." This means that even at this late stage in the history of the Philistines, they still used Greek words inherited from their ancestors.

During the forty years between the withdrawal of the Assyrians from Philistia and its conquest by the Babylonians (640–604/3 BCE), Egypt ruled the region, even though it experienced some initial difficulties in capturing some Philistine centers (as indicated, for example, by the unusually long siege of Ashdod). During the Egyptian domination, too, the various political units there continued to function as semiautonomous states headed by their kings. The names of some of these kings are known to us from the written sources. They all gradually changed their orientation from Assyria toward Egypt. This new orientation became disastrous when the Babylonian armies arrived, after their final victory over the Assyrians and Egyptians at Car-

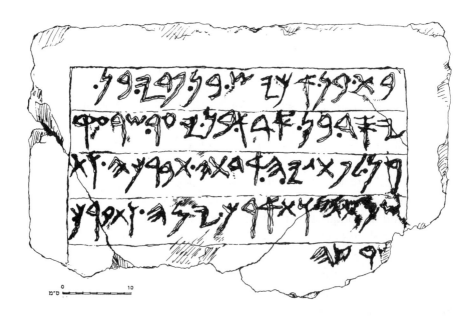

I.55 Ekron, a dedicatory inscription and facsimile from the sanctuary of Temple Complex 650

chemish in 605 BCE. Just a year later the Babylonian king Nebuchadnezzar II arrived in Philistia, first to either Ashkelon or Ekron. A papyrus dated to this year survived at Saqqara in Egypt. It is a copy of a letter sent to the Egyptian monarch announcing the arrival of the Babylonian army and pleading for military aid. When this help did not arrive, the Babylonian king captured the town and entirely destroyed it (cf. Jeremiah 47:4–5). This fits well with both the *Babylonian Chronicle* and the archaeological evidence. The fate of the other Philistine cities was not better: in about a year or so, all were destroyed and their inhabitants deported to Babylon.

PHILISTINE SETTLEMENTS AND STRATIGRAPHY

PHILISTIA IS ONE of the regions of Palestine where remains dated to the late 8th to the end of the 7th centuries BCE have been better explored than elsewhere, both by extensive excavation of all its major sites and by comprehensive surveys. At three out of the four central Philistine cities (Ashdod, Ashkelon, and Ekron), large-scale excavations have uncovered important remains from the period of Assyrian domination. Also extremely important are the excavations of smaller towns such as Jaffa, of an Assyrian fortress in the sands of Rishon le-Zion, Tel Mor, Ashdod-Yam, Meẓad Ḥashavyahu, and elsewhere. This is especially true in regard to the sites of the kingdom of Gaza: Tell el-Ḥesi, Tell el-ʿAjjul, Tell Jemmeh, Tell el-Farʿah (S), Tel Haror, Tel Seraʿ, and Tell er-Ruqeish. Together, they provide a reliable picture of the various elements composing the peculiar regional material culture, as well as the development of settlements during this period. Many surveys conducted in the area include that of the Rubin River and the survey of the Philistine settlements. These uncovered the remains of many more sites, like the ones at Ḥorvat Hugah and Mephalsim. A picture of a flourishing society from the time of the Assyrian conquest to its end emerges, despite the frequent Assyrian military campaigns that were often directed against the rebellious Philistine cities from 734 to 701 BCE. Above, we mentioned the Assyrian campaigns of the years 734, 733, 720, 716, 712, and 701.

After the campaign of 701, Philistia was pacified and did not participate in any rebellion against Assyria. The first signs of economic growth and prosperity, however, are already visible in the days of Sargon II, who erected a trade center, or *karum,* close to the Egyptian border in 716. As in the case of the entire coastal region of Palestine and Transjordan (see below), this picture of settlement growth and cultural development can be attributed to a constellation of new conditions: the peace and security that followed the Assyrian conquest and reorganization; the large-scale building in the Philistine cities; and the erection of new Assyrian military and administrative centers serving both soldiers posted along the important Via Maris, the main road to Egypt, and the Assyrians who dwelled in Egypt. The Assyrians appear to have brought many thousands of people from various parts of their empire, mainly from Phoenicia, to settle in the region for the execution of these projects. They also encouraged the reopening of the trade routes along the coasts from Syria to Egypt, and to destinations in the west, i.e., Cyprus and Greece. Traces of this international commerce may be detected in the archaeological record—in particular, in the heterogeneous character of the pottery vessels, which, in addition to the local or so-called Ashdodite ware, include Assyrian, Phoenician, Egyptian, Edomite, Cypriot, Corinthian, and various East Greek potteries.

The formidable Assyrian construction project that took place in the kingdom of Gaza from the beginning of the Assyrian occupation there was discussed above. Palaces and fortresses were constructed, and perhaps even an Assyrian temple. Such remains have been uncovered in excavations at Tell el-Ḥesi, Ḥorvat Hugah, a fort at the mouth of the Shiqmah River, Tell Jemmeh, Tel Seraʿ, Tel Haror, and Tell Abu Salima (Sheikh Zuweid), and the large, new city at Ruqeish was encircled with strong fortifications. Recently, another possible fortified city was found on the Gaza coast. We have also mentioned the peculiarly Assyrian finds in this region: the Assyrian pottery vessels, remains of military equipment, seals, etc. The typical Assyrian-style construction was but a small part of the overall building effort that took place in the region at this time, as recent excavations clearly show.

Generally, we may assume that prior to the Assyrian conquest of Philistia, the building style in Philistia, as in other parts of Palestine, originated in Phoenicia, with one difference: the rare limestone utilized in Philistia, usually brought from a great distance, was replaced by local sandstone *(kurkar)*. For the same reason, mud brick was frequently utilized for construction in Philistia. It is difficult to deduce this type of construction from W. M. F. Petrie's excavations at Philistine sites, as both his chronological conclusions and his descriptions of the strata are problematic and require revision. We may study Petrie's reports; however, the new excavations and the recent studies of E. Oren show that the use of stone was quite common in local architecture during the period preceding the Assyrian conquest, especially for the exterior surfaces of walls and fortifications and for strengthening corners. Masonry incorporated methods familiar with Phoenico-Israelite tradition, i.e., ashlars with marginal drafts, and the arrangement of building stones in header-stretcher fashion. There are also a few remains of architectural ornamentation in the same style as found elsewhere in this region. Only later were Assyrian-style buildings erected here. Such cases were encountered in excavations at Tel Sera‘, where a Phoenician-style structure was built before the Assyrian one. The same is true at Ekron, where a stone-lined fortification system was uncovered in the upper city.

Except for the huge Assyrian-style constructions in this region, the major parts of which were probably built after the days of Sargon II and Sennacherib, i.e., late 8th century BCE and early 7th, in connection with the seizure of Egypt, there was also a large and surprising increase in the size of Philistine settlements, even those located on the eastern border of the region. The best example of this development may be seen at the city of **Ekron,** where the late Philistine stratum was recently excavated by S. Gitin. According to the new evidence from this excavation, the town suddenly increased in size (having been a small and poor settlement since the end of the 10th century BCE), immediately after the Assyrian conquest (but mainly after the 701 BCE campaign of Sennacherib), and became a very large city. The area of the new city encompassed about 85 acres! It was divided into four quarters, each one having a different role, which together constituted a well-planned city.

A. The **fortifications zone,** which included the upper city's thick, strong wall, as well as the thinner lower town wall, which encircled only one side of the city, also included a long line (ca. 150 m.) of stables. The impressive fortifications included a gate in the lower city wall, as well as a formidable bastion in the southeastern corner of the town and a four-chambered gate in the upper city wall.

B. The economically most important area was the **industrial zone,** located along a narrow strip around the interior of the wall of the upper city, occupying about 20 percent of the city's territory. This zone was divided into smaller subdivisions on the north and south sides of the town. The excavator emphasized that although only about one-third of the site's area was excavated, no fewer than 114 oil presses have been found in the industrial zone so far (mostly identified in a surface survey), and there is no doubt that their total number was much larger. He believes that the capacity of production of these 114 oil presses alone amounted to approximately five hundred tons per year (fifty thousand full oil jars), an impressive statistic. The typical oil press included a rectangular three-room house. In one of its walls, a niche was constructed in which a four-horned stone incense altar was erected (see below).

The industrial zone also produced much evidence for cloth production, in the form of numerous clay loom weights.

This large-scale oil industry at Ekron is somewhat surprising, for the other Philistine coastal towns were mainly engaged in trade and do not show many traces of agricultural produce (except, perhaps, Ashkelon, where new evidence points to the existence of a wine industry). S. Gitin believes that the oil industry at Ekron was a result of Assyrian encouragement and support, for olive oil was not produced in either Assyria or Egypt, where no olive trees were grown. It seems that Philistine production was in competition with that of Judah, which also produced large quantities in surrounding settlements, such as Tel Batash (Timnah) and Gezer, where similar oil presses were uncovered, though, admittedly, not in such large numbers. At Ashdod's industrial zone, the main product was clay vessels, which were found in great quantities. In the city, in Area D Stratum VII (also from the first half of the 7th century BCE), the potters' quarter was preserved, with its streets, houses, and courtyards used as workshops. Its main feature was pottery kilns, mostly of the elongated type, some preserved with their air vents. In one of them, holemouth jars were found. There appear to have been industrial zones in the rest of the Philistine towns, with each dedicated to a different product.

C. Coming back to Ekron, the third area excavated to the north of the industrial zone was a well-planned, dense **residential quarter,** with houses, courtyards, and streets.

D. The fourth quarter was the residential area of the **hierarchy** of Ekron, both civilian and religious. It included the monumental Palace-Temple Complex 650, discussed above, which is located in the center of the lower city. In this building was found also the five-line royal dedicatory inscription that mentions five rulers of the city, including Achish the son of Padi, identified with Ikausu the king of Ekron, known from the Assyrian annals of the days of Esarhaddon and Ashurbanipal during the first half of the 7th century BCE. Finds in this quarter, according to Gitin, were different from those of the residential area for the commoners, for large amounts of high-quality ornamented pottery vessels were found here, more than in any other part of the city. Among these vessels were local red-burnished types, Assyrian fine ware, East Greek painted pottery, a few jewelry hoards, and other works of art.

The heyday of Ekron did not last long: at the end of the Assyrian domination, beginning immediately with the total Assyrian retreat from the region ca. 640 BCE, the entire system collapsed, for the Egyptian successors had a different ideology.

Another example of a rich town that was not an Assyrian fort, but a trad-

ing center built under Assyrian control and with Assyrian encouragement, is
the coastal settlement of **Ruqeish,** south of Gaza. This city, erected—
according to the latest excavation results—at the end of the 8th century BCE,
was identified by its excavator, E. Oren, as Karum of Egypt, which was built
by Sargon II in 716 BCE. (The other candidate for this *karum* was, as we have
seen, at Tell esh-Sheikh Zuweid, excavated by W. M. F. Petrie.) After the
erection of the town, many new settlers were brought there. According to the
Assyrian sources, they came from the Zagros Mountains, from Assyria
proper, and even from Egypt. But the archaeological record clearly indicates
that the most important maritime traders of the age who settled here were
the Phoenicians and Greeks. Perhaps some Edomites and Arabs also settled
there. The area of the city and its port comprised ca. 20 acres. It was fortified
with an enormous brick wall, the impressive remains of which still tower to a
considerable height. From this town, the Assyrians controlled trade with the
west, assisted by the Phoenicians and Greeks, and trade with Egypt and Arabia, with the help of Arabs and Edomites. Material remains reflecting all
these peoples were recovered in the excavation. In 1997, an additional part
of approximately the same age and dimensions was found and partly excavated on the coast at **Gaza.**

Recent excavations at **Ashkelon,** another major Philistine port town, have
proved highly productive and relevant to our interest. Remains of the 7th
century BCE city were uncovered under the heavy destruction layer of 604
BCE, the year when the city was totally razed by the Babylonians. A section of
the inner part of the town was uncovered, including some shops (a butcher
shop, a wine shop, etc.), as well as the remains of some administrative structures and storehouses, probably intended for wheat storage. The quarter was
well planned and built according to an almost Hippodamian plan: the houses
were constructed in blocks *(insulae),* separated by streets intersecting at right
angles; even some of the town's squares have survived. This plan is quite reminiscent of Assyrian Megiddo (Stratum III). In the storerooms, bronze scales
and square or rectangular weights were found, as well as an ostracon written
in Hebrew characters in a local (Ashkelonite) script, dealing with lists of
wheat, wine, and other beverages. Pottery finds from this stratum are similar
to those we have seen at Ekron and elsewhere in the settlements of the kingdom of Gaza of the same period. This is a mixed assemblage, which includes
red Ashdodite vessels, Phoenician vessels including the delicate Samaria
bowls, and a large number of imported East Greek vessels of various origins,
such as vessels decorated in Wild Goat style and vessels from the islands of
Chios, Knidos, and Samos, as well as from Corinthos in mainland Greece

and from Cyprus. As to the fine small artifacts, there are objects of metal, stone, and faience, many of them inspired by Egyptian styles. In the destruction level caused by the Babylonian army, seven decorated bronze *situlae* in Egyptian style have been found. These depict Egyptian cultic scenes in which, for some reason, the god Min is prominent. Faience amulets depicting various Egyptian deities as well as a bronze figurine of the god Osiris and an alabaster perfume vessel were also found.

On the other hand, the clay figurines are made here in a local style peculiar to Philistia. A stone incense altar was found, which resembles the Ekron ones minus the horns. It was probably located on the roof of one of the public buildings. In light of this find, the excavator, L. Stager, has suggested that the Ashkelonites used the sand dunes around the city as vineyards and made the city into a center for wine production and trade, which became one of the sources of its wealth. Like Ekron, Ashkelon was not rebuilt during the Babylonian period.

Farther south on the coast lies the region of **north Sinai.** Assyrian, Egyptian, and biblical sources provide detailed accounts of the military and commercial activities along its roads in the Late Iron Age. More than thirty settlement sites of this period between Wadi el-ʿArish and Wadi Ghazzeh provide evidence for the Assyrian domination of southwestern Philistia at the end of the 8th century and the 7th century BCE. These sites were a springboard for the Assyrian military incursions into Egypt and a buffer zone between Egypt and Assyria. They were also administrative and commercial centers for international trade, including the Arabian spice trade. One such cluster of Late Iron Age settlements was investigated at Ruqeish, yielding new data about Assyria's deployment on the border of Egypt (see above). Assyria coordinated international trade with Egypt and controlled the spice trade from Arabia. An Assyrian fort was excavated by W. M. F. Petrie at Tell Abu Salima (Sheikh Zuweid). This evidence strengthens the assumption of an Assyrian-administered territory in the late 8th and 7th centuries BCE as far as the Brook of Egypt (Wadi el-ʿArish).

In northwestern Sinai, an expedition headed by E. Oren recorded a dense cluster of sites from the Saite period of the late 7th and the 6th centuries BCE. All sources, both written and archaeological (including burial customs), indicate that in this period there were colonies and border garrisons along the eastern Nile Delta, which were inhabited by foreign merchants and mercenaries—Greeks, Phoenicians, Arabs, and Jews—merchants who were encouraged to settle here by the pharaohs of the Saite Dynasty.

Among these settlements, Tell el-Ḥer and site T-21 (Migdol) are the most important. The latter is located on the edge of the Delta plain and is ca. 20 acres in size. At the center of the site is a massive, square mud-brick enclosure (200 x 200 m.) with walls 15 to 20 m. wide. On three sides, small hollow compartments 3 x 2 m. each were constructed at fixed intervals inside the walls, and massive buttresses, also with cellular compartments, were attached outside the walls. The widest wall on the east had rectangular compartments, as well as very long and narrow inner corridors. This architectural technique is known from other sites from the Saite period in the Delta, such as Daphne and Naukratis. A similar fort was recently found by a French-Egyptian expedition not far from Migdol at Qedua West.

PHILISTINE INSCRIPTIONS OF THE 7TH CENTURY BCE

THE NUMBER OF 7th century BCE inscriptions found in the mounds and settlements of Philistia is not large, but it is increasing steadily. There is hardly a settlement without one or more inscribed artifacts from this period. Ostraca inscribed in ink and incised clay shards were recovered at Tell Jemmeh and Tell el-Far'ah (S), some by W. M. F. Petrie and others in more recent excavations. Others were found at Ashdod, Ashkelon, Ekron, Tel Sera', Tel Haror, Azor, and Tell Qasile (which belonged to the kingdom of Ashkelon during this period).

The most important Philistine inscription of the Assyrian period yet found is undoubtedly the monumental dedicatory inscription from Ekron that mentions five of its kings with the title "ruler of Ekron" (discussed above).

According to J. Naveh, who recently studied and published most of the other Philistine records, they are inscribed in two scripts: Aramaic and Philistine. The few 7th century BCE Aramaic ostraca found at Tell Jemmeh, Tell el-Far'ah (S), and Tel Sera' seem, in his mind, to indicate that the Assyrian garrisons stationed in the Philistine towns wrote in Aramaic, the current language and script in the western provinces of the Assyrian empire. On the other hand, the local inhabitants wrote in a script that they learned from their neighbors, adding some features otherwise unknown in the Hebrew script.

Inscriptions that should be classified as "Philistine" (or Philisto-Hebrew, according to F. Cross) are not sufficient to provide a clear picture of the script used; however, they may point to the assumption that, like the eastern neighbors of Israel and Judah (Ammon, Moab, and Edom), who adopted the Aramaic or Hebrew script, the Gazaites, Ashkelonites, and Ashdodites also introduced some local peculiarities to the script that they learned from the Hebrews. But as the script of the Ashdod inscriptions and those of the Tell Jemmeh ostraca do not share the same peculiarities, we may take into consideration that there were perhaps at least two local "Philistine" scripts: that of Gaza and that of Ashdod. It is even probable that the other two Philistine centers, Ashkelon and Ekron, also had their own scripts. J. Naveh is of the opinion that the numbers used by the Philistines, usually in horizontal lines, were adopted from the Phoenicians or the Aramaeans rather than from Judah or Israel. But in at least one case, at Tel Haror, Egyptian hieratic numbers were copied on pottery vessels (in the same manner as in Judah; see below). Recently, a similar ostracon was found in Ashkelon, written in a local Philistine script in Hebrew letters, which deals with an agreement to buy or sell a quantity of wheat, as well as lists of units (bottles) of red wine.

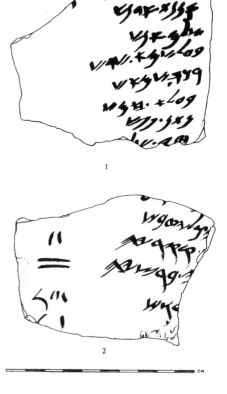

I.56 A 7th century BCE ostracon from Tell Jemmeh indicating "Philistine" names

Of great importance are two ostraca recovered at Tell Jemmeh, dated to the 7th century BCE. Published by J. Naveh, these contain lists of personal names in typical fashion: on one side, common West Semitic names such as Shalem, Natan, Ba'ala, and Ba'al-shama, and on the other, Indo-European names such as *herb, bnksh, wnnt, adnsh,* and *shgsh.* Explanation of these names is rather difficult. Though they are non-Semitic, one cannot decide if they are of Philistine origin or are, perhaps, Greek names of local inhabitants or foreign mercenaries (Ionians, Carians, Lydians, etc.) who may have been employed by the Assyrians or by the king of Gaza. Others believe that they are names of people deported to Philistia from distant regions by the Assyrians. These foreign names also occur in other inscriptions and seals found at Philistine sites, such as an ostracon from Ashdod where the name *dggrt* is mentioned, or one of the Tell Jemmeh seals which is inscribed *drymsh-eli-aqim.* In this connection, we should also recall the name Achish (or Ikausu), the king of Ekron, which was inscribed on a stone dedicatory inscription found recently at the site, as well as in the Assyrian annals.

The most important among the smaller epigraphic finds from Philistia is a seal that has been known for about a hundred years, inscribed "(belonging) to 'bd'li'ab son of Shib'a servant of Mitinti son of Ṣidqa." This seal was long ago identified as the seal of "the servant of the king" of Mitinti II, the king of Ashkelon mentioned in the annals of Esarhaddon and Ashurbanipal as bringing tribute to them in 677 and 667 BCE. Ṣidka is the king of Ashkelon and the son of Mitinti I mentioned in 701 BCE by Sennacherib. In addition to providing the names of the Ashkelonite kings in the Assyrian period, this seal is also important because it shows that in the different Philistine kingdoms—Gaza, Ashkelon, Ashdod, and Ekron—the same administrative system with an identical official hierarchy existed as in the other Palestinian states.

From Ashdod comes a bulla inscribed *lmlk* ("to the king") with the motif of a soldier leading a captive. The other two Philistine seals that are known to us are engraved with regular Phoenico-Egyptian scenes: the winged griffin and pharaoh presenting a *maat* statuette to an enthroned deity.

The same is true in the matter of weights and measures that were in use in Philistia in this period. Up to now, no inscribed weights have been found here except those engraved with the symbol representing the Judaean *sheqel* or the Judaean *pym, nsf,* or *bq'* (see below), of which about sixteen of all known types were uncovered throughout Philistia: at Ashdod, Ekron, Tell Jemmeh, Tell el-Far'ah (S), Tel Haror, Tell Abu Salima, and Mephalsim, as well as at Meẓad Ḥashavyahu and Nebi Rubin (which were probably Judaean fortresses in Philistia). At Ekron, an inscription was found that mentions a Judaean measure: the *bat*. We assume that this weight standard was in use here, otherwise we would have found remains of some local weight standard. The numbering system here was mixed, as in Judah: Phoenician numbers beside hieratic Egyptian numbers. But we also possess some evidence here for the use of foreign weights, such as the crouching-lion bronze weight from Tell Jemmeh, which imitates an Assyrian prototype, or the bronze cubic weights from Ashkelon, which were, according to their incised numbers, undoubtedly Egyptian.

THE PHILISTINE CULT

WE DO NOT know much about the Philistine cult in general or during the Assyrian period in particular, except, perhaps, the Semitic name of their chief god in the 11th to 10th centuries BCE, Dagon. The Philistine cult in the 7th century BCE is not even mentioned in the biblical sources of this period, nor in external sources. All that we know concerns the frequent appearance of the name Ba'al in late Philistine personal names, as written on ostraca, such as Ba'alshama or Ba'ala. The name of one of the kings of the city of Gaza is Silba'al. In the Saqqara papyrus written in 604 BCE at Ashkelon or Ekron, the name Ba'alshmen is mentioned. There is new evidence from Ekron, where the name of 'Astarte, Ba'al's consort, is mentioned (evidently in a peculiar pronunciation: Asherat) in dedicatory inscriptions on jars of the 7th century BCE. The full inscription says *qodesh le'asherat,* "sacred to Asherat." Another inscription from Ekron mentions the word *mqm,* perhaps a holy place, i.e., the local sanctuary. In this connection, Herodotus (1.105) tells about the burning of the famous temple of Aphrodite (the Greek name for 'Astarte) at the time of Pharaoh Psamtik.

Only two examples of the Philistine sanctuaries of the period have been uncovered to date, one at Ashdod and the other at Ekron, and they have nothing in common. At Ashdod in Stratum VIII, which was probably destroyed by the Assyrians in 712 BCE, a small temple consisting of several rooms was discovered. Attached to one of the long sides of the main room was a rectangular brick structure that may have served as an altar. Near it and in adjacent rooms, a large quantity of cult objects, such as clay figurines of domestic animals, was found. Most were fragments of vessels used for libations in the temple *kernoi.* The many male and female figurines that were found here probably belonged to miniature clay offering tables. Figurines of

I.57 Ekron, two parts of an inscription, "dedicated to [the goddess] Asherat," from the city's elite zone

the plaque type, especially female ones, were also found. Some of the finds of Stratum VIII were discovered in pits (*favissae*) in Stratum VII.

At Ekron, too, a temple was uncovered, but this was of a completely different type: Temple Complex 650 was discussed above. According to its excavator, S. Gitin, it was a monumental structure. The focus of its architectural plan—based on the design concept of Neo-Assyrian royal palaces and temples—is a long narrow reception hall with a mud-brick platform or throne room. This great hall served as a buffer separating two larger courtyard areas: an open courtyard with adjoining rooms and a cultic area with a sanctuary. The sanctuary had two parallel rows of four column bases each and a main entrance with a stepped stone threshold. Inside, flanking the entrance, were two large stone vats, possibly used for ritual ablutions. At the western side of the sanctuary, opposite the entrance, was a raised stone threshold and a partially stone-paved cella. A royal dedicatory inscription found in the cella may have been part of the western wall of the sanctuary—and perhaps a focal point. The five-line inscription mentions—as we have seen—five kings of Ekron, including Achish/Ikausu the son of Padi, who is known from Assyrian sources from 676 to 667 BCE, and who built the temple to his goddess. The sanctuary's antechambers contained an olive press and many clay vessels and old ivory carvings and gold objects stored here. Temple Complex 650 at Ekron was erected in the first quarter of the 7th century and was in use to the end of Stratum IB, when it was destroyed with the rest of the city during the Babylonian king Nebuchadnezzar's 603 BCE campaign to Philistia.

Regardless of whether the name of the chief Philistine deity was Dagon or a particular Ba'al (for example, Ba'al-Zebub; cf. 2 Kings 1:2: "go inquire of Ba'al-Zebub the god of Ekron"), or the two names were used simultaneously for the same god in different cities, there is no doubt that his cult and that of his consort Asherat, whose name is written on clay jars found at Ekron, was practiced similarly to that of the other nations of the country. It should be mentioned, however, that in the recently published monumental inscription from Ekron, discussed above, dedicated to this Philistine goddess on the occasion of the building of her temple, J. Naveh read the goddess's name as *pt-gyh*, an unknown deity, perhaps of Greek origin. A. Demsky recently demonstrated that the word is really *pt(n)yh (potnia)*, the common Archaic Greek word for "divine mistress"; i.e., it is not a proper name but a title of honor. This interpretation not only strengthens the connection of the late Philistines with the Greek world but is probably the earliest Greek documentation in Palestine.

Indeed, cult objects found in Philistia show quite clearly that the usual cult of this divine pair was practiced here, too. We shall start our survey as usual with the figurines. At Ashdod, many clay figurines were found in Strata VIII and VII. More figurines were recovered at other Philistine towns, such as Tel Seraʿ and Tel Haror. Even more important were the clay figurine molds found at Tel Batash (which was indeed a Judaean border town, but its figurines had nothing to do with the Judaean style). We may assume that the figurines of the Philistine towns, just like those of all other nations in Palestine, exhibited a particular style that becomes more and more apparent as more are uncovered. This is particularly true concerning the Ashdodite figurines, both male and female, which are often red-slipped, sometimes burnished and painted with black strips (similar to the Ashdodite pottery). The male heads have a unique pointed shape, sometimes covered with a round "turban." Both males and females have large protruding eyes made of separate balls of clay, and long sharp noses. Among the males is a type depicting a lyre player that occurs among the figurines of other nations as well. The female figurines at Ashdod are mostly of the plaque type, depicted in the usual attitude: either supporting their breasts or pregnant. Even so, the Ashdodite figurines of the late 8th and the 7th centuries BCE reflect some kind of continuity of the earlier Philistine tradition: the Philistine-Aegean traditions that are recognized by the peculiar molding of the faces described above and the frequent use of *kernoi,* vessels of an Aegean origin that had long since disappeared from the rest of the country. Of the *kernoi,* mainly heads of horned animals have survived. To this Aegean tradition we may perhaps attribute also a *rhyton* in the shape of a lioness head of the same period from

I.58 Heads of late Philistine clay ʿAstarte figurines from Tel Seraʿ

Ashdod, which was very popular at the beginning of Philistine settlement in the country, five hundred years earlier. In addition, we have here parts of clay cultic stands decorated with figures of male and female deities, such as a hollow figurine of a goddess made of red-slipped and burnished clay, reminiscent of similar figurines of an old Philistine origin found on clay stands at Ashdod and Tell Qasile.

At the same time, it is interesting to note, as we did before with the late Philistine scripts, that the figurines found outside Ashdod, at Ashkelon, Tell Jemmeh, Haror, Seraʿ, Ekron, or Tel Batash, are definitely different from the Ashdodite examples, and probably belong to local subtypes. The group that represents southern Philistia (the kingdom of Gaza) can be seen among the figurines found at Tell Jemmeh, Tel Seraʿ, and Tel Haror, as well as in those found during the survey at Mephalsim and Horvat Hugah. Here, too, the forms resemble those of "pillar figurines"; i.e., their bodies are made by hand and their faces in a mold. The difference is in the depiction of the women's faces, which, though covered with the usual Egyptian veil, are rendered with long curls and with an amulet on the neck. These small changes make the expressions of their faces entirely different from those of the Judaean figurines or those of other peoples.

A third type, which was probably peculiar to the kingdom of Ekron, was found at Tel Batash. These figurines were made in the shape of flat plaques. One of the complete figures depicts a nude female supporting her breasts with her hands. The face is somewhat distorted, perhaps because it was not pressed correctly to the original mold. In profile, however, the delicate facial features of the figure are highlighted. A second complete figure from Batash shows a nude female in frontal view, with arms at her sides. The proportions of this figure are unusual: the head is too large for the slender body, and the hands are too long. The large eyes and the "archaic smile" suggest inspiration from Cypriot or Phoenician sculpture of the Late Iron Age. These details come to characterize a local art form that flourished in this part of Philistia during the 7th century BCE.

Apart from the peculiar style of the figurines, there is a close resemblance between the other Philistine cult finds and those of the other peoples of Palestine. At Ashdod, a large group of miniature votive clay furniture represents the same types uncovered in Judaean Lachish and Tel Sheva, or in the tombs of Rabbath-Ammon. The numerous clay incense stands found there have close parallels at all Iron Age sites in the country. A rather surprising find, not so much for its type as for its quantity, was approximately fifteen stone incense altars equipped with four horns in various sizes at Assyrian-

I.59 Ekron, assemblage of four-horned incense altars, 7th century BCE

period Ekron. This assemblage is the largest group of such altars ever found in Palestine. These altars had a long history in Israel and Judah from the 10th to the 7th centuries BCE. The altars of Ekron are the latest examples found. They are also unique because of their large quantity here: they have been found in almost every house of the 7th century BCE stratum, both in dwellings and in the industrial quarters. Most of them were found inside the buildings near the entrances or in special niches. These rooms contained rich finds, well dated up to the destruction of the town by Nebuchadnezzar II king of Babylon in 603 BCE. The altars from Ekron are divided into a few subtypes with two main ones: freestanding and engaged (the latter are unworked on one side). The interesting feature of this find, besides its quantity and its distribution in the city's quarters, is that not one was found in the temple: all were uncovered in ordinary domestic dwellings. S. Gitin, the excavator, suggested that the cult here was less centralized than at other sites. It should be remembered, however, that in Ashkelon, too, a similar stone altar was recently uncovered (without horns), from the same period. Here, it was originally located on the roof of a public building. These two finds are complementary. The reason for their sudden wide distribution may be connected—as S. Gitin suggested—with the renewal of the incense trade from Arabia on a large scale. Even so, the preservation of these altars in such large quantity at Ekron (and perhaps at Ashkelon, too) is surprising because as such altars increase in other parts of the country, it becomes more and more obvious that in Phoenicia, the provinces of Megiddo and Samaria and Judah, as well as the Transjordanian kingdoms, this type of horned altar was replaced by a new, Assyrian-influenced type that continued to the Persian and even to the Hellenistic periods. This type is also usually made of limestone (but sometimes of clay, closer to the Assyrian original). It is smaller and cube-shaped, standing on four feet, and shall be dealt with in detail below. It seems, however, that the occurrence of these two types together in the 7th century BCE, in all the parts of the country, is ultimately connected with the renewal of trade with the lands exporting incense.

Of the metal cult objects discovered in Philistia, a medallion was found at Ekron in the destruction layer of the Babylonian conquest along with a hoard of silver ingots and the jars inscribed with the words "sacred to Asherat." On the medallion is a depiction of the goddess standing on a lion; beside her is a praying figure; above her head are the winged sun disk, the moon crescent, and seven stars. This is evidently an Assyrian motif adopted by the locals, in the same way that other Assyrian motifs influenced local engravers, especially in seal production. The bronze medallion itself is of a type common in Palestine, with prototypes going back to the Late Bronze Age.

An interesting cult find was uncovered at Ashkelon in the destruction level caused by the Babylonian army. This find is in a purely Egyptian style and perhaps belonged to Egyptian inhabitants of the city. However, because similar finds were also recovered at sites outside Philistia, they may have been locally produced, or produced for the use of the locals. One of these Egyptian finds is a bronze figurine of the Egyptian god Osiris, found in the new excavations but also (with many other Egyptian deities) in a Persian-period context during an excavation conducted at Ashkelon many years ago. Similar figurines are known from Judah and Israel, found at Tel Dan, Gibeon, and Tel Sheva. Here, too, the contexts point to both the Assyrian and the Persian periods. Seven bronze *situlae* (small bottles) were found in the same destruction level at Ashkelon. They are also decorated in a purely Egyptian style (in which the figure of the god Min predominates). With them was found a small bronze medallion depicting a table with two baboons and two wine jars. In the same context, many plain Egyptian faience apotropaic amulets occurred; they usually represent Bes, Pataikos, or other gods. These finds at Ashkelon may be interpreted in two ways: either as an extension of the regular Egyptian cult or, more plausibly, as a local cult using Egyptian artifacts.

I.60 Ekron, 7th century BCE silver medallion with scene depicting the goddess Ishtar ('Astarte) standing on a lion in front of a worshiper with upraised arms. Above are the moon, a winged solar disk, and seven circles.

PHILISTINE BURIAL CUSTOMS

DESPITE THE MANY Assyrian remains in the Gaza kingdom, or in Philistia in general, no Assyrian-style burials have been uncovered there to date, although it is logical to assume that in the future they may be found in the local Assyrian strongholds such as Tell Jemmeh or Tel Seraʿ. Of the regular local graves of the period, only a few have been found. At Ashdod, a few burials connected with Stratum VII were uncovered. They consisted of groups of skeletons and bones in secondary burials with some funerary offerings. The remains belong to some three thousand individuals who probably died, according to the excavator, during the conquest of the city by Sargon II in 712 BCE.

The rest of the 7th century BCE tombs discovered in Philistia are connected, by chance, with the Phoenician population that settled there by Assyrian initiative or moved there of its own will.

At Azor, which, as we have already seen, was included within the Ashkelonite enclave (together with Jaffa), there were many burials of the 7th to 6th centuries BCE. Among them was a group of burial jars, one of which is incised with a Phoenician name: *Islmy*. Among the finds that could not be ascribed to any specific tomb were thick bowls with pinched rims, used for copper smelting. Another such find was a scaraboid in the shape of a negroid head, bearing a prancing horse on its obverse, dated to the Egyptian 26th Dynasty (664–520 BCE).

The major cemetery of the period in Philistia was uncovered at Ruqeish south of Gaza, a site excavated on several occasions. Its unusual pottery will be dealt with separately. This cemetery produced many cremation burials composed of Phoenician clay urns filled with burnt bones and ash. Some of the urns were of the Ruqeish type, but others were of regular coastal jar types, which were usually in the service of the maritime trade. These are definitely the remains of a Phoenician cemetery. Concerning the distribution of the Phoenician population in this region in the 7th century BCE, it is not surprising that cremation burials of the same types were also uncovered at Tell el-Farʿah (S) and Tell el-ʿAjjul.

PHILISTINE POTTERY

AS IN ALL the other regions of Palestine, Philistia, too, had its unique ceramics during this period, both plain and decorated. The pottery of the northern part of Philistia is called Ashdodite, after the site where it was first found. In fact, these vessels were already produced before the 7th century BCE, but no doubt they were also made during the 7th century. The problem is that the distribution area of these vessels is large and they are also found in other Philistine regions. Special Ashdodite decoration is in black paint on the red-burnished face of the vessel, perhaps a continuation of ancient Philistine tradition, but reflecting Phoenician influence as well.

The differences between the pottery of the several Philistine kingdoms has not yet been properly studied, but some of these differences can already be noted. The pottery of the 8th to 7th centuries BCE in the Gaza kingdom is characterized mainly by the "Ruqeish" vessels, named after the site and cemetery where they were first found. Although they were originally assumed to be earlier than the Assyrian period, after E. Oren's excavations at the site it became clear that all date to the 7th century and later. The majority of these vessels is red-burnished. Their unique attribute is the form of their handles, which are often horizontal, probably imitating popular East Greek types. The Ekron pottery of this period also had its unique attributes, different from those of the other two kingdoms, but these have not yet been fully studied. In summarizing the pottery of Tel Batash Stratum II (a Judaean city in close proximity to Ekron), A. Mazar reached similar conclusions. He suggests that the pottery assemblage of Stratum II at Tel Batash, while unusual in its variety and character, is composed of roughly two equal components, a Judaean one and a characteristically Philistine one, as well as a few northern types and local imitations of Assyrian vessels. In his view, this is a phenomenon typical of border regions lying between two adjacent political units, each with its own land and inhabitants. A comparison of the Philistine vessels found here with those from Ashdod clearly shows many pottery types and decorative techniques at Ashdod that are not found at Tel Batash. These are indicative of differences in regional pottery traditions within Philistia. Mazar concludes that the Philistine pottery at Batash perhaps reflects the types used in the neighboring kingdom of Ekron, which differ in many details from those at Ashdod.

Among the Philistine vessels listed were numerous jars used in maritime

I.61 Ekron, assemblage of 7th century BCE pottery, iron agricultural tools, and four-horned incense altar from an olive oil factory building

trade; some are local types that developed gradually in this region during the course of the Iron Age, influenced mainly by Phoenician ceramic tradition. The typical characteristics of these jars are the flat shoulder and the body with pointed base or sack shape, as well as the amphorae with basket handles of Greek origin. Generally, the growing influence of Greek ceramics, mainly East Greek wares, on the local potters is felt. It may even be assumed that these "Greek traits" are the ones that influenced and characterized the entire Philistine repertoire, but it is only fair to point out that the uniqueness of 7th century BCE vessel assemblages found in Philistia is their heterogeneity. Any group of vessels found here will probably include some Ashdodite vessels, a few Ruqeish vessels from the Gaza region, some types peculiar to Ekron or Ashkelon, as well as many "general" coastal-plain pottery types in various sizes, late Phoenician vessels including jars, delicate Samaria bowls, and red-burnished Achzib jugs, as well as some late types of the Cypro-Phoenician family, Assyrian vessels with some of their local imitations, East Greek painted or plain vessels (including large amphorae and basket-handled jars), Cypriot jars and jugs, and Corinthian juglets and alabastra. In the kingdom of Gaza, we may expect, in addition, Edomite vessels. This coastal Philistine pottery did not stop at its political borders, and much of it spread to the east, into the western Judaean sites, where it is found in large quantities. Sometimes (as in the case of an assemblage of 7th century BCE pottery vessels from Tel Batash Stratum II mentioned above) it is hard to know from the pottery alone if the site was inhabited by Judaeans or Philistines. In smaller numbers, these coastal vessels are found even in eastern Judah, at sites such as Lachish (Stratum II), or even in Jerusalem. The Judaean finds in Philistia, however, are much more scarce: while in the north Philistine kingdoms of Ashdod, Ashkelon, and especially Ekron, we can detect some Judaean finds or influences in the local cultures, when we come to the kingdom of Gaza, these are almost entirely absent.

Chapter 6

THE KINGDOM OF JUDAH

OUTLINE OF HISTORY

The history of the Judaean monarchy during the 7th century BCE may be divided, both historically and archaeologically, into three different sub-periods that correlate with its wars against three of the major empires of the ancient Near East: Assyria, Egypt, and Babylon.

The first period is that of the Assyrian domination of the kingdom between 701 and ca. 640 BCE. This period begins with Hezekiah's rebellion against Assyria, which brought the Assyrian campaign headed by Sennacherib in 701 BCE into Judah and resulted in conquest and destruction of Lachish (Stratum III) and forty-six additional Judaean settlements.

The extent of the destruction caused by the Assyrian army in this campaign is comparable to the results of the Assyrian campaign against the kingdom of Israel, with one major difference: Jerusalem, the capital of Judah, survived the war, and the region of Benjamin probably survived as well. Furthermore, in the case of Judah, the royal Judaean family also remained intact. On the other hand, all the area south of Jerusalem was probably destroyed. As more sites are excavated, it becomes more apparent that the Assyrian army destroyed all the Judaean settlements in the Negev, all those of the Shephelah, and even some of the settlements on the crest of the Judaean Hills, such as Beth-Zur and probably even Ramat Raḥel, situated on the immediate outskirts of Jerusalem. There are scholars who believe that some of the destroyed towns such as Tell Beit Mirsim, Tel 'Eton, Beth-Shemesh, and others never recovered from this blow for the rest of the monarchic period. During the period that followed Sennacherib's destruction, Judah lacked the intensive support that the Assyrian empire had previously provided for reconstruction of the destroyed Israelite towns. Assyrian support had included imperial resources, administration, and transfers of new immigrants. Judah had to depend on its own limited resources. The results, as reflected by archaeological evidence, were nonetheless immediately successful and the rebuilding process appears to have been rapid, starting perhaps as early as the last days of Hezekiah and certainly during the reign of Manasseh. This enormous effort was definitely initiated and carried out under direct royal supervision. In a relatively short time, most of the southern region was rebuilt, probably with the assistance of the refugees who survived the Assyrian campaign, or even by others who had come from the north, from territories held previously by the kingdom of Israel. Either way, the result of this effort was a new, dense network of settlements, many more than during the period before the Assyrian conquest, while Jerusalem became a relatively large city, probably also much larger than before, and served as its capital.

In the second period, 640–609 BCE, the days of Josiah, the construction activity continued and became even more intensive, ultimately resulting in the expansion of the kingdom's borders in all directions, including to the east, where settlements were established in areas not previously settled, and to the west, where for a short time a small coastal territory was captured by a Judaean king. It seems that this expansion was made possible at the expense of the ex-Assyrian provinces. The problem is that between the latest Assyrian annals (Ashurbanipal's of ca. 640 BCE) and the beginning of the *Babylonian Chronicle,* from 627 BCE (see below), there is a gap. When the *Babylonian Chronicle* reappears in 627 BCE, the situation is already very different from that of 640, for Assyria is no longer a strong imperial force, but a monarchy fighting for its own survival against the Babylonians in remote territories of Mesopotamia.

This chapter in the history of Judah ended with the death of Josiah in the battle of Megiddo in 609 BCE, during his unsuccessful attempt to stop the Egyptians from coming to the aid of their Assyrian allies. The immediate result of this battle was that, for a short time during the last decade of the 7th century BCE, Judah became an Egyptian vassal.

The third and the last chapter in the kingdom's existence, the period between 604 and 586 BCE, is the story of Judah's continuous struggle against Babylonia until its final collapse, the destruction of Jerusalem, and the deportation of some of its inhabitants to Babylon. During this period of time, when the destiny of all the small, autonomous Palestinian states depended on their loyalty to the relevant imperial forces, but especially on their ability to choose the winner among them, Judah completely failed. This short period was very dynamic and is referred to many times in the books of Kings, Chronicles, Jeremiah, and Ezekiel, as well as in the *Babylonian Chronicle*. According to these sources, King Jehoahaz succeeded Josiah, but Pharaoh Necho placed Jehoiakim on the throne instead. Judah became a vassal of Babylon during the days of Jehoiakim (609–598 BCE), probably by 604. Three years later Jehoiakim rebelled as a result of the Babylonian fiasco against Egypt near the Egyptian border in 601. The Babylonian retaliation came three years later, in 598. Meanwhile, Jehoiakim died and his son Jehoiachin replaced him. Jehoiachin surrendered to the Babylonians but was deported to Babylon. Judah itself also suffered some deportations, and the Babylonians placed Zedekiah on the throne as the last Judaean king. King Zedekiah (597–586 BCE) rebelled again against Babylon, and the results were the destruction of all the kingdom's cities (excluding those of Benjamin), including Jerusalem and the Temple, the deportation of a large number of its inhabitants, and mass flight of survivors to Egypt. Very little is known about the results of the last Babylonian campaign against the various cities of Judah outside Jerusalem itself, and the details of the battle with the Egyptian forces who came to Judah's aid. This information comes primarily from archaeological sources.

A detailed description of the material culture of Judah during the age of the divided monarchy may be found in the first volume of the present series. In that volume, A. Mazar discussed the development of the earlier Judaean material culture, which was a separate branch, different from all the other local cultures in Palestine. In the present discussion, we shall concentrate on the far-reaching changes that occurred in this culture over the last hundred years of its existence, as well as the characteristics that made it so different from its predecessor and those of other peoples. We shall therefore concentrate here on only those elements belonging to the late 8th century or to the 7th and early 6th centuries BCE.

The excavations conducted at sites in Judah with remains from this period are very numerous, and we are unable to include them all here. We shall look at the excavations carried out in the land of Benjamin, north of Jerusalem, at sites such as Bethel, Tell en-Naṣbeh, Tell el-Ful, Gibeon, Gezer, and Meẓad Ḥashavyahu, which bordered the northern front against the Assyrian provinces of Samaria and Dor. Next will come the major excavations on the crest of the Judaean Hills: at Jerusalem, Ramat Raḥel, Beth-Zur, and Tell Rabud. Then the excavations on the eastern border will be examined, including those at Jericho, Vered Jericho, and En-Gedi in the Judaean desert on the shore of the Dead Sea. Finally, the excavations of Beth-Shemesh, Tel Batash, Tel Azekah, Tell Judeideh, Maresha, Lachish, and Tel 'Erani, as well as those at Tell Beit Mirsim and Lahav located in the western Shephelah adjacent to Philistia; and the excavations in the Negev of Judah, in the valleys of Beersheba and Arad, at the sites of Tel Sheva, Tel 'Ira, Tel Masos, Tel Aroer, and Tel Arad; and the major Judaean fortresses in this region, such as Horvat 'Uza, Horvat Radum, Horvat Tov, and Kadesh-Barnea, which were erected to defend the state against the Edomites.

From all these numerous excavations emerges a detailed and comprehensive picture, quite rare in the history of the archaeology of Palestine, of the dense network of Judaean settlements of the period, with their fortifications and defensive systems, their royal, extremely centralized administrative organization, the Judaean army, and the various components of the unusually rich and developed material culture of this state. A picture emerges of a small state that succeeded well in the art of governing its citizens throughout its territory, even in the remotest parts of the kingdom. This government took responsibility for building settlements and supplying all the needs of its people. There are few periods in the history and archaeology of Palestine for which we have such a plentiful and detailed body of information concerning such a short period of time.

The wealth of archaeological finds touches upon almost every aspect of everyday life and the various elements of the material culture of the period: political and administrative organization, town planning, fortifications and fortresses, public and domestic buildings, burial customs, sanctuaries, cult and cult objects, and art and crafts. It is even possible today to divide between the early and the late phases of this relatively short period of time. Moreover, the wealth of inscribed material discovered in the Judaean towns of the 7th to early 6th centuries BCE enables us to complete the picture that emerges from the other aspects of material culture, beyond the reconstructions possible for many other periods, and create a unique composite picture based upon the biblical and other written sources, the inscribed material, and other finds from the excavations. Four main topics will be examined here: (1) the borders of the Judaean state as revealed in the recent excavations, (2) the political, administrative, and military organization of the kingdom as exhibited in inscriptions and other artifacts, (3) the character of the national pagan cult, which is dealt with here in detail in view of its important bearing on the future development of the Jewish religion and the particularly rich finds associated with it, and (4) architecture of the kingdom. Other topics, such as finds in the city of Jerusalem, town planning, domestic architecture, architectural ornamentation, and burial customs will not be dealt with here, for they have been summarized comprehensively by A. Mazar in the first volume of this series and do not basically differ from those of the earlier Iron Age phases.

THE BOUNDARIES OF JUDAH
The Eastern Border

WE SHALL BEGIN our survey of the boundaries of Judah in the east, for the date of their construction and establishment is much clearer than those elsewhere. From north to south, the northernmost site, located almost at the state's northeast corner, was **Jericho.** Here, the results of three major excavations permit us to conclude with certainty that the town was settled and flourishing during the Late Iron Age and that the finds from this period are typically Judaean. This means that during the 7th century BCE Jericho passed from Assyrian rule (for it previously belonged to the Israelite monarchy) to Judaean. A survey conducted in the region by Y. Magen revealed another large, ca. 7.5-acre, single-period settlement of this period about half a kilometer south of Jericho, on the southern side of Wadi Qelt. It should probably be regarded as a "daughter" settlement of Jericho.

Another site was discovered and excavated by A. Eitan about 6 km. south of Jericho at a location called **Vered Jericho.** It stands beside the main road leading from Jericho to the south toward Jerusalem or En-Gedi. Here, a well-preserved structure in the form of a 20 x 20 m. square was uncovered. Its outer wall was about 1 m. wide. Even today this structure is preserved to a height of about 2 m. and more. The walls are built of stone and coated with mud. The upper parts were of mud brick. The structure is composed of two identical four-room house units, and its area is symmetrically organized. The structure may have also had a cultic installation. The finds in the building clearly show that it was used only in one period and that it dates from the end of the 7th to the early 6th centuries BCE. All the material found in it was purely Judaean, including a seal impression, pottery vessels, clay figurines, etc., and it seems that it was a small regional military or administrative fortified center.

South of here, in the areas of the large valley of the **Beq'a** in the Judaean desert, F. M. Cross and R. Milik examined in the 1950s three additional sites: **Khirbet Abu-Tabak, Khirbet Abu-Samrah,** and **Khirbet el-Maqari.** They found here large fortified structures surrounded by agricultural installations,

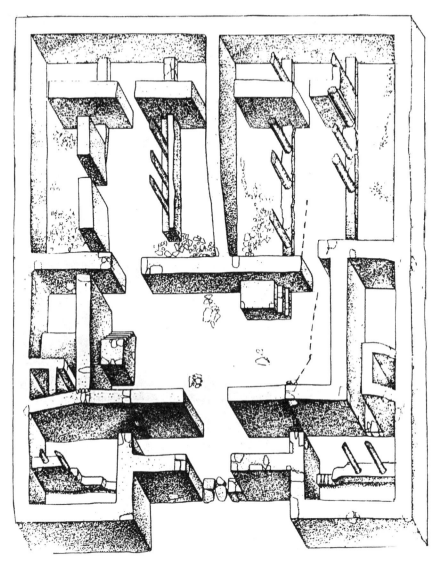

I.62 Isometric plan of the Vered Jericho structure

which may have served as agricultural estates of the Judaean kingdom. All three were single-period Judaean settlements, similar to that at Vered Jericho, and they, too, point to the erection of Judaean settlements in the desert of Judah during the late 7th century BCE. The finds from this survey, as well as those uncovered in the excavations that followed, were later reexamined by L. A. Stager, who supported their dating and even came to the conclusion that during the 7th century BCE, Judah had incorporated the district of the "Wilderness" (Joshua 15:61–62), with all six of its settlements within its borders. Stager also thought that this annexation provided the Judaean monarchy with access to the mineral treasures of the Dead Sea, such as salt, bitumen, and asphalt, as well as to the date plantations first established during this period in the area between Qumran and En-Gedi. The three communities were established here as military strongholds with small settlements to defend the road from Judah that passed through the Beqʿa. These settlements did not exist for more than a few decades and were totally destroyed by the Babylonians in 586 BCE and never rebuilt. Other similar fortresses and settlements of the same date were also discovered along the western coast of the Dead Sea, among them **Rujm el-Bahr, Qumran, ʿAin Awar,** and **ʿAin Turbah.**

The next Judaean settlement is **En-Gedi,** after Jericho, the major town of the eastern Judaean border. En-Gedi was intensively excavated and it is the best example of a Judaean settlement on the eastern border during the last phase of the monarchy.

In the ancient mound of En-Gedi (Tel Goren), five occupational strata were uncovered; the earliest, Stratum V, was also dated to the last days of the Judaean kingdom (630–582 BCE). This first settlement was erected both on the mound's acropolis and on its slopes. The earliest occupational remains were uncovered on the southern slope, consisting of buildings with attached courtyards where huge pottery barrels were found stuck into their floors. In one of the courtyards, a cluster of seven such barrels was uncovered, standing close to each other. Around them, more usual vessels such as jars, bowls, cooking pots, jugs, juglets, and lamps were uncovered, along with clay loom weights. All these vessels are dated to the end of the 7th or early 6th century BCE. To the same period belong the houses uncovered later on the north slope of the mound. The houses here were probably of uniform plan: each structure included a wide courtyard on one side with two small rooms attached to it. The houses were close to each other along the terraces that encircled the mound. Access was via the narrow street on a lower level by a wooden ladder from the street to the entrance of each house. Here, too, in all excavated courtyards, the same clusters of pottery barrels were found, which, when completed, had openings in their lower part and were connected to each other by a network of small tunnels. The excavators explained them as installations for producing the balsam incense that was grown in the oasis (cf. Song of Songs 1:14) and that was a monopoly of the royal house. In the houses, many stamped jar handles with the royal rosette emblem as well

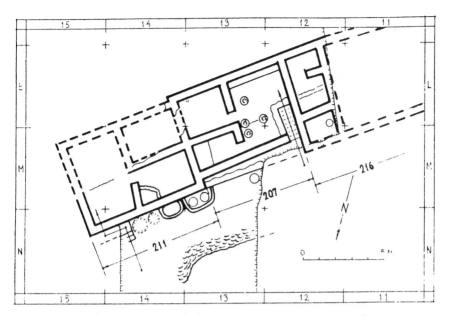

I.63 En-Gedi, plan of the Judaean houses on the northern slope

as the state's *sheqel* weights along with seals and seal impressions of the king-dom's administrators were recovered.

As was explained above, all these finds can be safely attributed to the end of the 7th and early 6th centuries BCE. There was also no doubt that the settlement was of one stratum with no changes or additions. The Babylonian destruction was clearly visible here in the piles of ash and charred wood that fell upon the floors, smashing everything. The typical bronze three-winged Babylonian arrowheads were also found stuck in the walls. According to Josephus (*Antiquities* 10.1.7), this happened in the twenty-third year of Nebuchadnezzar II (582 BCE, and cf. Jeremiah 39:9).

The general picture that emerges from the study of the settlements of Judah's eastern boundary from Jericho to En-Gedi clearly shows that all were established at the end of the 7th century BCE in the time of King Josiah, in a region that was unsettled previously (excluding Jericho-Tell es-Sultan). It also seems that the establishment of these settlements was part of a greater plan intended to defend the entire kingdom. Because the danger of enemy penetration from this direction was relatively small, and the steep mountains made it easy to block any threatening army here, the fortification systems in this area remained rather unsophisticated. The settlements were established not only for defensive purposes but in order to dominate this essential area for economic reasons: this was the only region in Palestine where both the production and trade of local and imported incense and spices took place. It should be pointed out here that the Judaean line of fortresses established by the previous Judaean kings along the Aravah, extending south to the shores of the Red Sea, had been lost to the Edomites. Two of the fortresses of this line that have been excavated, one by R. Cohen at ʿEn Ḥazeva, the other, many years ago, by N. Glueck at Tell el-Kheleifeh, proved to be Edomite and not Judaean in the 7th century BCE (see below).

The Northern Border

From the northeastern limit of the boundary of the Judaean monarchy, fixed at **Jericho,** the line turns to the northwest. At this bend, one of the few sites of the Desert of Benjamin which belonged to Judah was excavated. The site is **Ḥorvat Shilḥa,** which is located along the road from Jericho leading to Michmash on the north side of Wadi Qelt, which should be identified—according to the excavators—with "the Way of the Border" (1 Samuel 13:18). The site, a one-period fortress, is composed of one square structure of the "four-room" type, typical of Judah until its destruction. All pottery vessels found in it were Judaean, dated to the late 7th century BCE. One *lmlk* seal impression of the two-winged type, which still existed in this period, was found. The fortress lasted only a short time and was destroyed by the Babylonians.

Meẓad Michmash. A few kilometers west of Ḥorvat Shilḥa on the road to Michmash, another small Judaean fort was recently excavated by S. Riklin. Located on a hilltop, it is a small square structure (8.5 x 9 m.) of the "four-room" type. It contained typical late Judaean pottery vessels identical to those of Ḥorvat Shilḥa, and was probably erected at the same time along the northern border of the kingdom. It was also destroyed by the Babylonians.

It recently became clear that the large settlement located at the site of **Khirbet Marjameh,** about 15 km. to the northwest, was an Israelite and not a Judaean site and that it was destroyed by the Assyrians and never resettled. At the same time, at another nearby site to the south called **Khirbet Jibʿit,** recent excavations conducted by Z. Ilan showed that it had a Judaean ceramic assemblage identical to that of Ḥorvat Shilḥa and Meẓad Michmash. These three sites can be useful as an indication of the location of the northern boundary of the Judaean monarchy in this region at the end of the 7th century BCE, and the front line of defense for its territory to the north. Another identical single-period settlement-and-fortress was uncovered at **Khirbet e-Sid,** which may be the site of biblical Anathoth, the town of Jeremiah.

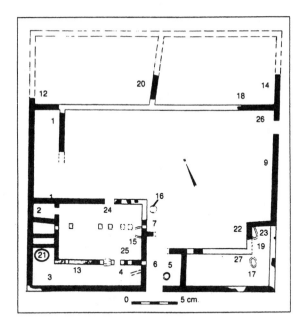

I.64 Line sketch of Ḥorvat Shilḥa complex

From Shilḥa, Michmash, and Jibʿit, the boundary probably extended to **Bethel.** Its sanctuary is mentioned in 2 Kings 23, which states that it was destroyed by King Josiah in about 622 BCE. This information alone is enough to include the city in Judah, but in the excavations of the site, some Judaean finds were reported, including a *sheqel* weight and Judaean figurines. From here, the boundary moved to **Tell en-Naṣbeh** (Mizpah). Here, the excavations uncovered the 7th century BCE settlement stratum, which was relatively rich in finds, including, for example, the well-known seal impression of "Jaazaniahu the *ebed* ('servant') of the king," who might be identified with the Jaazaniah mentioned in 2 Kings 25:23; many Judaean weights, rosette impressions, clay figurines; and a large assemblage of 7th century BCE Judaean ceramics. There can be no doubt, therefore, that this town in Benjamin was, in the late 7th century BCE, within the borders of Judah. For a short time, Mizpah replaced Jerusalem as the capital of Judah, at least from the time of the destruction of Jerusalem by the Babylonians to the murder of Gedaliah the son of Ahikam, who was appointed governor of Judah on behalf of the Babylonians.

From Tell en-Naṣbeh, the northern boundary of Judah continued westward through **Gibeon,** where the excavations uncovered a rich 7th century

BCE assemblage that included Judaean rosette seal impressions, groups of Judaean clay figurines, weights, and pottery vessels. Other Judaean finds were uncovered in cemeteries excavated at the site and in surveys conducted around the city. From here, the border continued to **Nebi Samuel.** On this prominent hill overlooking Jerusalem from the northwest, recent excavations revealed that the first settlement here was also established at the end of the 8th century BCE and lasted until the 7th century BCE. The finds consisted of Judaean pottery of the period, as well as various *lmlk* seal impressions and Hebrew personal name seal impressions. This settlement came to an end in 586 BCE.

The next known site on the northern Judaean frontier is **Gezer.** Here, Macalister's excavations in the beginning of the century encountered a few Judaean finds from the 7th century BCE, including some earlier *lmlk* seal impressions that may indicate that the city was captured by King Hezekiah during his reign when he prepared to rebel against Assyria. It again became Judaean after the collapse of Assyrian control and the destruction, perhaps by Josiah, of the large Assyrian center there. The latest excavation at the site, conducted by W. Dever, strengthens this possibility, for the 7th century BCE stratum uncovered here certainly had a Judaean character.

From here, the northern boundary of Judah moved straight to **Meẓad Ḥashavyahu** located on the coast, near Yavneh-Yam. It appears possible that the Judaean monarchy in its last stage, i.e., the period of Josiah, gained access to the sea. This was probably the northwestern corner of the kingdom. One may assume that the coastal region captured by Judah in those days was even larger and that it encompassed the entire area between Meẓad Ḥashavyahu and **Tell Qasile,** which means that the northern boundary of Judah was on the bank of the Yarkon River in the north, and nearly reached Ashdod in the south. Ashdod may have been an ally of Josiah in his wars against the Egyptians. More confidently, we may speak only about two Judaean settlements. One was at Tell Qasile, which was rebuilt in the late 7th century BCE after a lengthy abandonment. It has but one late Judaean stage (mixed, as usual, with other coastal potteries of the period). More important is the evidence found at the other site, Meẓad Ḥashavyahu, located close to Yavneh. It is interpreted as a Judaean fortress under a Judaean officer, in which soldiers originating in various East Greek islands were garrisoned (and see below, the chapter on the Greek penetration). According to the accepted view, this fortress was established and existed for only one generation or less: between 630 and 609 BCE, from the time of the Assyrian retreat from the Palestinian coast to the battle between Josiah and the Egyptians at Megiddo, where he

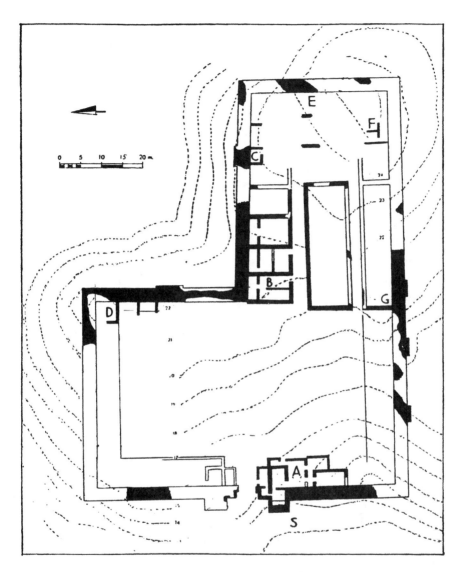

I.65 Plan of Meẓad Ḥashavyahu

was killed while trying to stop the Egyptians from aiding the Assyrians. As mentioned above, the commander of the fortress was a Judaean, judging by a Hebrew ostracon found there in which the Judaean commander is mentioned by his title, as well as other Hebrew ostraca, including one that probably names the commander himself, Ḥashavyahu, and some Judaean *sheqel* weights, including one that belonged to a certain Barchi, according to the

Hebrew inscription incised upon it. It seems that in addition to the regular Judaean soldiers serving here, there were others who were summoned for *mas oved,* an annual tax in the form of labor in the royal fields and at other royal properties. Around 609 BCE, the fort was destroyed, probably by the invading Egyptians, and for a short time the entire coastal region fell into their hands. A recent proposal that the fort was Egyptian with East Greek and Judaean soldiers serving under the Egyptian regime appears to be unacceptable. This totally contradicts both the evidence of the Hebrew ostraca and the absolute lack of Egyptian remains of any kind. It is impossible that an Egyptian fort of any period would be totally devoid of Egyptian remains.

In comparison with the western and southern boundaries of the Judaean monarchy (to be discussed below), which were fortified against Philistia and Edom, it seems that the northern border of Judah was built rather loosely. Though it creates a clear line that enabled the kingdom to defend itself from this direction, the actual defenses were not particularly thick or strong, and did not include a mainline and sublines as did the borders in the west and south. Even so, we may assume that it was somewhat more sophisticated than was initially suspected, and that between the large towns such as Bethel and Tell en-Naṣbeh, there were many smaller forts protecting the intervening areas, serving as watchtowers and warning stations. One such single-period small fort dated to the 7th century BCE has been excavated by O. Negbi at French Hill overlooking Jerusalem from the north, as well as Ḥorvat Shilḥa, Michmash, and Jibʻit mentioned above, and many others identified in the various surveys but never excavated.

The Judaean Western Boundary

According to the results of the comprehensive survey recently conducted in this area by Y. Dagan, this part of Judah suffered a deadly blow during Sennacherib's campaign of 701 BCE. Out of 354 Judaean settlements flourishing before the campaign, only 39 were reestablished during the 7th century BCE, including the 2 major cities in the region: Lachish and Maresha. However, these conclusions are hard to accept for two reasons. One is that as more sites are excavated, the more evidence there is for the existence of 7th century BCE settlements. In 1998, two sites on the extreme western border of Judah facing Philistia, Tell eṣ-Ṣafi and Tel Ḥarasim, which are also located one beside the other, produced rosette seal impressions and a few Judaean clay figurines, which are the best chronological evidence for the existence of a 7th century BCE site. The second reason is that it is already clear that the plan of the western boundary of Judah in the 7th century BCE was much more elaborate than the rest of the borders of Judah, for it still faced Philistia in the first part of the 7th century BCE and Egyptian Philistia in the second part of that century.

The western border of Judah in this period was composed of two different lines: an external line that bordered the Philistine territories in the Shephelah, and an internal line that constituted the real line of defense, and not a mere boundary. This line passed close to the first, but was located on the crest of the first line of the Judaean Hills, climbing toward central Judah and overlooking the Philistine plains from above. It is hard to believe, therefore, that behind such an elaborate system of defensive lines, the interior of the country remained deserted and unsettled!

The outer line was sparsely built. It probably included (from north to south) the site of **Gezer,** to which attention was given in connection with the northern boundary, **Tel Batash, Tell eṣ-Ṣafi, Tel Ḥarasim,** and **Tel ʿErani.** From here, it moved in a southeastern direction toward **Tell e-Shalaf, Tell el-Muleiha, Tel Ḥalif,** and **Beersheba.** Most of these sites served as outposts or guardposts and warning stations, rather than sites intended to defend the area.

The inner line, which was erected only a few kilometers to the east, was the real defensive line oriented toward the west. It was located on the crest of the hills that were facing one another, and its positions were rather densely built. The line may have contained the towns of **Beth-Shemesh, Jarmuth, Azekah, Socoh, Tell Judeideh, Tell Burnat, Maresha,** and **Lachish** and continued to the southeast toward **Tell Beit Mirsim** and **Tel ʿEton.** There can be no doubt that the main military, logistic, and administrative center of this system was located at Lachish, which, in this period, too, was the second most important town in all Judah and served as the headquarters of the commander of the entire western frontier. It was he who commanded all the western forts on behalf of the king in Jerusalem. This defensive system, only parts of which have been uncovered, was rather centralized and included sophisticated watch and warning units commanded—as we know now from the Lachish ostraca—according to strict orders from Jerusalem.

We shall now turn to the detailed discussion of the finds from the sites of the western boundary of Judah, starting with the settlements of the outer defensive line.

Tel Batash (Timnah). This site was included in the discussion of the results of the excavations of its Philistine neighbor, Ekron. Stratum III was a prosperous Judaean city that was destroyed in 701 BCE by Sennacherib. Stratum II, which was reconstructed during the 7th century BCE, was again fortified with the same wall system, which was rebuilt and repaired. Its internal planning was well conceived: a wide street was found inside the wall, toward which some of the structures located on its other side opened. The easternmost building here was a new administrative center that replaced the old one of Stratum III. A few houses of the "four-room" type, found regularly at all Judaean sites of the period, are divided inside by lines of monolithic pilasters. In some of them, stone basins for crushing olives and monolithic vats were uncovered. This kind of planning certainly indicates state planning and construction of the entire city, even though, according to its excavator, A. Mazar, it differs from other Judaean cities of this period, such as Tell Beit Mirsim, Beth-Shemesh, or Tel Sheva, i.e., the Judaean cities that existed before the Assyrian destruction, in which the outer parts of the dwelling houses were incorporated into the casemate fortifications. The houses of Stratum II were also destroyed in a conflagration. On their floors, a rich assemblage from the late 7th century BCE was preserved, partly Judaean and partly typical of the coastal region of Philistia. Pseudo-Assyrian vessels as well as Phoenician and East Greek wares were recovered. This assemblage is closely paralleled by ones of the same age found at Ekron and Ashdod. Among the vessels and the other finds, many are typically Judaean, such as *lmlk* jars (which survived from the previous stratum, or were brought from Jerusalem, among them the two-winged *lmlk* seal impressions of the type found at En-Gedi and Ḥorvat Shilḥa; see above), and some rosette seal impressions that are typical only of the last stage of Judah. Also found were Judaean *sheqel* and *pym* weights. This mixed assemblage is typical for a town located so close to the Philistine boundary. Timnah of Stratum II was also a flourishing town. The similarity between the finds there and those from Ekron led the excavator to suggest that it belonged to its Philistine neighbor at that time. This suggestion appears to be unnecessary in view of the many official Judaean remains here. In any case, the fate of these two towns was identical: both were destroyed by the Babylonians in about 603 BCE and never recovered.

Tell eṣ-Ṣafi. We assume that the boundary passed from Tel Batash to **Tel Ḥarasim** and **Tell eṣ-Ṣafi.** This last town, which should probably be identified with the ex-Philistine city of **Gath,** is not mentioned in this period in the Assyrian records (unless "the royal city of the Philistines" mentioned in one of Sennacherib's tablets dated to his 701 BCE campaign as a town captured previously by Hezekiah king of Judah is the city of Gath, as some scholars believe, even though the name of the city itself had not survived). It is possi-

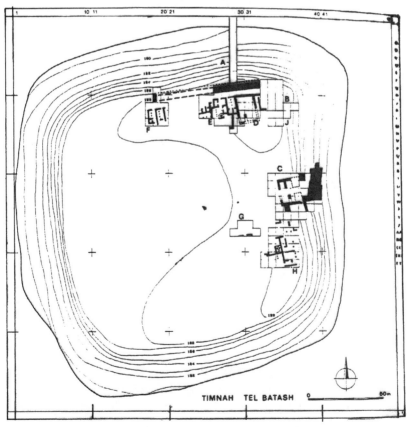

I.66 View and plan of Stratum II at Tel Batash

ble, however, based upon the finds from this period uncovered in the excavations of 1898–1890, which are similar to those from the other Judaean cities in the nearby Shephelah, such as Tell Judeideh, Azekah, and Maresha, that after being destroyed by Sennacherib in 701 BCE, Gath again became a part of the Judaean kingdom. In any case, in the new excavations at Tell eṣ-Ṣafi, which started in 1997, at least three late Judaean rosette seal impressions have already been found. Other finds include a small limestone relief in the Assyrian style, which may depict a part of a war scene. This find provides further evidence for the existence of Gath during this period, now proved beyond doubt by the find of a *lmlk* seal impression on a jar handle with one of the latest emblems of the kingdom—concentric circles beside the two-winged beetle—in the excavations of **Tel Ḥarasim** located 2 to 3 km. north of Tell eṣ-Ṣafi on the same western line of defense.

Farther to the south, on the same line, lies **Tel ʿErani.** This frontier fort of the Judaean monarchy was probably a watch post for Lachish, as it dominates the entire northern Philistine plain. Here, the excavator, S. Yeivin, observed no fewer than five stages dated from the late 8th century BCE to the early 6th. Towns VIII and VII are those destroyed by Sennacherib in 701 BCE. They contained jars (some complete) with handles bearing *lmlk* seal impressions, one Hebrew ostracon, a few Judaean clay figurines of various types, and one Edomite figurine.

In the VI–IVth stages, the settlement was fortified with a wall, and even remains of a gate were observed. Like Tel Batash, its inner area was built with "four-room" houses, in which large numbers of Judaean finds were recovered, including seals and jars as well as Judaean figurines. It is presently difficult to establish an absolute chronology for the five stages, but it is quite clear that the last two stages belong to a Judaean town of the 7th to early 6th centuries BCE.

Another town that may have been a fort in this western frontier of the Judaean monarchy is **Tel Shalaf,** usually identified with Gibbethon, a town captured by Sargon II king of Assyria, according to the reliefs found in his palace at Khorsabad (see above). The city may have been resettled and rebuilt in this period, as well as **Tell el-Muleiha** south of it, but we lack conclusive evidence.

Farther south, another Judaean city was excavated on the western frontier of the kingdom at **Tel Ḥalif.** Here, large-scale excavations showed that the city, which existed through the entire period of the divided monarchy (Stratum VIB), was destroyed in Sennacherib's campaign of 701 BCE. Above it, a new town was established (Stratum VIA), which existed, according to the excavators, only during the period of Assyrian domination (700–650 BCE). The excavators believe that the last stage of the Judaean monarchy is absent here and that settlement was renewed only during the Persian period. The Judaean town that was destroyed by Sennacherib was a flourishing town here, too, surrounded by a casemate wall, the inner space of which was covered with houses of the "four-room" type, just like those of its neighbors. In the Assyrian destruction level, remains of many weapons were uncovered, especially ballista stones and arrowheads. Many loom weights were found, which attest to weaving activity, as well as Judaean pottery. To this stratum also belongs a nearby cemetery. The 7th century BCE stratum (VIA) was a small-scale settlement that lasted a short period of time in which "four-room" structures were built. The excavators believe that it was not destroyed but abandoned. It produced many Judaean finds, including typical figurines.

As pointed out above, all the sites listed here were part of the external western frontier of the Judaean kingdom. All of them must have been surrounded by smaller forts, but only a few of these have been excavated. As we have already indicated, the major western defense line of the kingdom was erected inside Judah's territory, on top of the hills on which the roads pass from the coastal plain into the hill country. This line included Beth-Shemesh (?), Azekah, and perhaps Jarmuth, Socoh, Tel Goded (Judeideh), Maresha and its frontier fortress at Tell Burnat, Lachish, Tel 'Eton, and Tell Beit Mirsim. From here, the border moved southward to the sites overlooking the Beersheba Valley (see below).

The first excavators of **Beth-Shemesh,** Mackenzie and Wright, believed that this town became unimportant in the Late Iron Age, that it was unfortified and was not included in the defense line of the Judaean kingdom at all. But the new excavations showed that at least until 701 BCE when it was destroyed by the Assyrians, it was an important and well-fortified town in which a large and sophisticated water system was constructed, for water storage for use in the event of siege. The water was brought from an external source and stored in underground cisterns (a method recently found at other Judaean towns such as Tel Sheva, Arad, and Kadesh-Barnea; see below). A large number of graves, large Judaean pottery assemblages, clay figurines, *lmlk* seal impressions, personal seal impressions of the kingdom's officials, and royal weights of all types attest to the existence of this town in the period before the arrival of the Assyrians. A question that remains open is whether the town recovered from its destruction during the 7th century BCE after the Assyrians departed, as did the neighboring cities, or was abandoned. The new excavations have provided no definitive answer yet. But recently, pottery of the 7th century BCE was indeed found in the new excavations, mainly in the water system.

Just south of Beth-Shemesh lies the site of **Azekah** (Tel Zakariah). This site is one of four Shephelah sites excavated, together with Tell eṣ-Ṣafi, Tell Judeideh, and Tel Maresha by Bliss and Macalister in 1890. It is difficult to reconstruct from their report the exact state of the mound during the 7th century BCE, i.e., during the period after its destruction by the Assyrian king Sennacherib. The many *lmlk* seal impressions and Judaean figurines and weights found here indicate that in the period preceding Sennacherib's campaign there was a flourishing town here.

Only a very small portion of the published material from Tell Zakariah relates to the 7th century BCE, but its existence as an important Judaean fort in this period is attested at nearby Lachish. One of the Lachish ostraca mentions Azekah as an important fort in the defense line against the Babylonian army in 586 BCE. Additional evidence includes a seal impression on a jar handle found at Azekah that depicts a galloping horse; it is identical to a seal impression found at En-Gedi, which is definitely dated to the 7th century BCE. Typical Judaean clay figurines were also found here.

On either side of Azekah is another site: **Tel Jarmuth** is on the north side; **Tel Socoh** on the south. Neither has been excavated, but while we do not know much about the former during the Judaean period, a few finds have been collected from Tel Socoh pointing to its existence until at least 701 BCE, including the usual Judaean royal seal impressions, clay figurines, and Judaean pottery. In both cases, only future excavation can provide definitive evidence. Farther south, atop a prominent hill, another Judaean fort was excavated at **Tel Goded** (Judeideh) at the end of the 19th century, and many finds collected from the site are dated to the period prior to 701 BCE, among them at least forty *lmlk* seal impressions and many personal seal impressions. Clear evidence of its existence in the 7th century BCE includes several rosette seal impressions and Judaean clay figurines, which are limited to this period, but not many building remains were uncovered. In the gap between Tel Goded and Maresha is another large Judaean fortress at **Tell Burnat**, which may have been a frontline fort of the city of Maresha connected with the outer western frontier behind the town of Tel 'Erani. The site has not yet been excavated but some rosette seal impressions were found there.

The next large town is **Tel Maresha**, also excavated by Bliss and Macalister in 1890. Here, they distinguished a "Jewish" stratum at the lower part of the mound, which otherwise dates mainly to the Hellenistic age. In their final report, the two published about twenty *lmlk* and personal seal impressions, as well as royal weights. Most of the published material dates to the period close to 701 BCE, but there were also 7th century BCE finds. In the recent excavations at the site directed by A. Kloner, a 7th century BCE stratum was uncovered. Among the finds is an ostracon of the period containing a list of names and numbers.

Lachish. We have already discussed in detail the importance of Stratum III at Lachish, the city besieged and destroyed by the Assyrian monarch Sennacherib. As to the last Judaean stratum established atop the mound (Stratum II), after a short period during which Lachish was abandoned, the settlement was renewed and fortified in the days of Manasseh, or, more plausibly, by King Josiah (639–609 BCE). The Stratum II city was poorer, less densely inhabited, and smaller. A weaker fortification system than that of the preceding town was erected. The outer gate was separated from the inner one by a large rectangular courtyard surrounded by rooms with entrances facing it. In one of these rooms, the famous Lachish Letters were found, perhaps in the city's headquarters (see below). The outer revetment wall seems to have been repaired, and a new main wall was constructed at the edge of the mound, above the previous walls. The palace-fort was not rebuilt. It remained a pile of ruins in the center of the city. Several small structures, mostly residential buildings, were uncovered on the eastern side of the mound, near the city gate, and in its southwest corner. There were many open, uninhabited areas throughout this settlement. Stratum II was destroyed in a fire during the conquest of Judah by the Babylonians in 587/6 BCE. Many late 7th century BCE Judaean finds were uncovered in the burnt debris of the stratum, including weights, clay figurines, and more than twenty rosette seal impressions typical of this period, as well as the above-mentioned ostraca.

South and east of Lachish are two more Judaean cities that continue the second, inner defensive line of the kingdom: one is **Tell Beit Mirsim** and the other is **Tel ʿEton.** The settlement at Tell Beit Mirsim, excavated by W. F. Albright, served for many years as a model for a small Judaean town. Albright himself concluded that the last Judaean town here was Stratum A2, which was destroyed by the Babylonians. But a reassessment of the excavation results by Y. Aharoni brought him to the conclusion that the major destruction of this town—as of many others in this region—occurred in 701 BCE under Sennacherib. There is no doubt that the town was later rebuilt, perhaps on a smaller scale, during the 7th century BCE. Its end came at the hands of the Babylonians in 586 BCE. It is quite difficult to separate the parts of the city destroyed by Sennacherib from those rebuilt by the Judaeans and later destroyed by the Babylonians. We do not have a clear picture of the late city's fortifications and plan, though its existence is attested by late Judaean pottery, seals, weights, clay figurines, and the other typical finds.

South of here were a few Judaean towns that have not yet been fully excavated. The most important of these is **Tel ʿEton,** from which some pottery shards found in a small trial trench were recently published. The publisher of the pottery concluded that this town was destroyed by Sennacherib and never recovered. But it seems here, too, that the later uppermost Judaean town was smaller than its predecessors, as in most of the other sites investigated, and the location of the excavated trench may have been beyond that town's boundaries. We assume that here, too, an important fortified Judaean town must have been renewed after Sennacherib's destruction and existed until the end of the Iron Age, as all the other towns in the region.

The dense network of settlements in the inner Shephelah of Judah included some large cities during this period, while others were no more than small forts rather than settlements. This cluster of settlements was organized by the Judaean kingdom during the 7th century BCE in a double defensive line, oriented westward. This system was probably implemented by a headquarters using a sophisticated system of signals and intelligence. It is now becoming more and more clear that even the relatively desolated areas between the Shephelah settlements and those atop the Judaean Hills and along their steep western slopes were partly covered by the kingdom's military authorities with a line composed of clusters of fortresses. These functioned as signal and warning posts, as well as forts that blocked the way into the highlands. One of the best examples of this kind of fort is the one excavated by A. Mazar at **Khirbet et-Tuwein.** Located on the western slopes of the Hebron Hills, this fort may be considered a typical Judaean fortress with a nearby small village. It is an isolated square building (31 x 30 m.). The plan comprises a central courtyard flanked by two rows of rooms, with a gatehouse on the eastern side. It was initially built during the 8th to 6th centuries BCE, destroyed, and resettled in the Persian period. The military considerations in selecting the site for the fortress are obvious. Most significant was the location on the hilltop, giving a fine long-distance view, especially of the inner Shephelah, including Lachish, Maresha, Tell Judeideh, Socoh, Azekah, and Adullam. Similar fortresses are known at three other sites in the vicinity: **Deir Baʿal, Khirbet Tibneh,** and **Khirbet el-ʿId** near Wadi Fukin. **Khirbet el-ʿId** is a rectangular fort excavated by Y. Baruch, located on a hilltop overlooking one of the inner roads leading into the Hebron Hills. Its plan consisted of a large central courtyard surrounded by rooms. Finds consisted of typical Judaean pottery of the 7th century BCE. The site was destroyed in 586 BCE and was never resettled. All four fortresses are visible from one another. The distances between Khirbet el-'Id and the other three forts are 1.5 km. to Deir Ba'al, 2.5 km. to Khirbet et-Tuwein, and 4 km. to Khirbet Tibneh. Khirbet el-'Id was the largest of these (110 x 55 m.) and perhaps the central one in the group. All these fortresses were but a part of the sophisticated defensive system of fortresses (sometimes with attached small villages) built throughout Judah, especially in areas not otherwise settled. These fortresses may have been located so as to facilitate the sending of fire signals.

The Southern Border

Similar to the western border of Judah, the southern one was also built in two defensive lines: an outer one and an inner one. The frontier line was located to the south of Nahal Beersheba, and it consisted of (from east to west) the following fortresses (to which some small settlements were also attached): **Horvat 'Uza** and the nearby **Horvat Radum, Tel Malhata** (with its sanctuary at **Qitmit**), and **Tel Aroer.**

In the inner line, situated on the southern hills climbing toward the southern side of the Judaean Hills, are the following settlements: the pair of forts at **Arad** and **Khirbet Tov,** and (north of Nahal Beersheba) **Tel 'Ira, Tel Masos, Khirbet Yiten, Tel Sheva,** and **Beersheba** itself (probably now lying under the modern city of Beersheba). Outside these lines lies the 7th century BCE Judaean fort discovered at **Kadesh-Barnea,** which was probably not a part of the southern defensive system of the kingdom at all, but was located on a source of fresh water on the main road leading from Judah to Egypt.

We shall now discuss the southern boundary settlements in detail, as we have done with the western ones. First we'll look at those located on the outer frontier line mentioned above: Radum, 'Uza, Tel Malhata, and Aroer. Then we'll examine those along the inner line, on the northern bank of Nahal Beersheba. We shall not, however, discuss here the Qitmit sanctuary, for it was purely Edomite from beginning to end.

Horvat Radum is a small, single-period fort, dated to the last stage of the Judaean kingdom. It is strategically located on the southeastern border of the Judaean Negev. It is a single-stratum site measuring 21 x 25 m., surrounded by a fortification wall with rooms abutting this wall. The fort's gate was protected by an antechamber. Near the gate, a platform and a staircase were exposed. The massive foundations uncovered in the center of the fort's courtyard were interpreted by the excavator as belonging to a square tower,

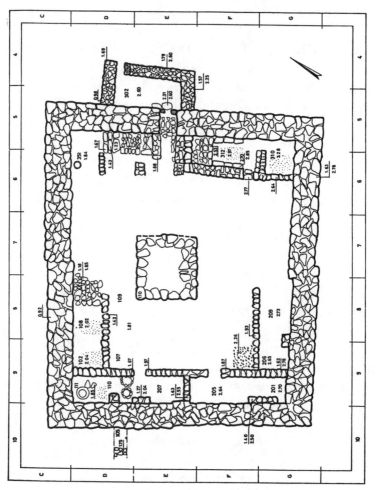

I.67 Ḥorvat Radum, plan and reconstruction of the fortress

i.e., a combination of a tower and a fort structure. Among the finds were four Hebrew ostraca. From a strategic viewpoint, Radum probably served as a fortified outpost for the larger fort (and settlement) at ʿUza located some 2 km. to the north. A similar relationship seems to have existed between the large fort of Arad and the small fort at Tov, located nearby (see below). Studying the map of the region, a fortification line consisting of the four above-mentioned fortresses can be traced, which runs in the direction of Judaea's southeastern border.

During the 7th century BCE, a larger (52 x 42 m.) fortress was erected along the same defensive line in the eastern end of the Arad Valley, some 10 km. southwest of Arad, at the site of **Ḥorvat ʿUza.** This fort was surrounded by a wall that had ten square outer towers: four at the corners of the fort, two

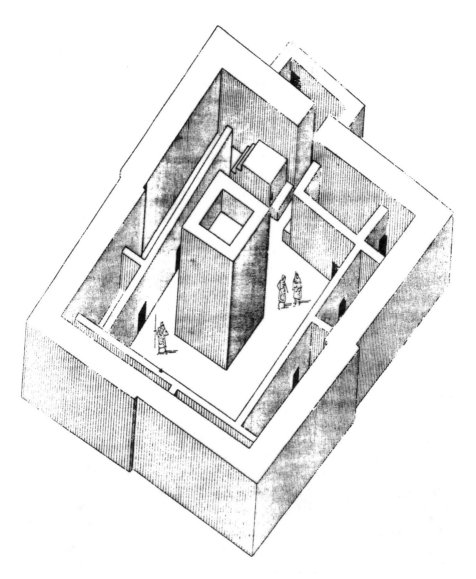

in the center of the southern wall, one in the middle of the eastern wall, two flanking the gate, and one in the west. The fort was surrounded by a revetment. The left wing of the gate consists of two chambers. Two building stages have been identified in the fort, but no distinction could be made between the pottery of the two phases. Both phases date to the 7th century BCE. A small settlement was also built on the bank of the *wadi* outside the fort, on artificial stone terraces. Both the fort and the settlement produced Judaean pottery and twenty-nine ostraca (twenty-seven from the fort and two from the settlement), including a jar with two inscriptions and four Hebrew and one Edomite ostraca in the gate room. The inscriptions are documents of various sorts: a military directive, name lists, distribution of supplies or inventories, and a literary-legal document. All these inscriptions confirm that 'Uza occupied an important position on the southeastern border of the Judaean Negev. The content of the Edomite letter, which includes an order by a commander of the fort, furnishes authentic historical evidence that the fort fell into the hands of the Edomites (see below).

The short distance between Radum and 'Uza suggests a close connection between the two. From 'Uza, it is possible to see the southern end of the Qinah River, in the bed of which passed the road from the Aravah to "the Negev of Judah." This was the reason for the establishment here of the small Radum fortress that served as a frontline post for larger 'Uza.

Next, to the west, along the outer defensive line comes the fort and settlement of **Aroer.** Here, too, the excavations failed to uncover any remains of occupation prior to the 7th century BCE, and three strata from this period were identified. The lowest of these (IV) was defended by a strong offset-inset wall with buildings along it. Stratum IV and its wall do not seem to have had a long duration, and no gap in occupation could be distinguished between Stratum IV and Stratum III. Both continue to use the same buildings.

I.68 Aerial view of the Judaean fort at Ḥorvat 'Uza and Naḥal Kina

I.69 Tel Malḥata, general view and fortifications

Stratum III included Judaean pottery as well as Judaean ʿAstarte figurines and other finds which indicate that it was a prosperous town. It may have been an administrative center along the road. Assyrian influence here is apparent in such finds as a glass bowl of a type often found in the Assyrian royal palaces at Nimrud. It seems that this stage was influenced by the Edomites, too, for a seal inscribed with a name incorporating the name of Qosa, the Edomite deity, was recovered here. The Judaean material included many pottery vessels, an ʿAstarte figurine, and a bone plaque decorated with a proto-Aeolic capital, which may have served as either a calendar or perhaps a game board, a few *lmlk* seal impressions, and a *sheqel* weight. Stratum II was dated to the end of the 7th and early 6th centuries BCE. At this time, a fortress or a tower was built on the mound's summit. It had typical pottery of this period, including some mortaria bowls and a large number of Edomite vessels, but decorated and undecorated. Stratum II was probably destroyed by the Babylonians.

North of **Aroer,** but still south of Naḥal Beersheba, lies the site of **Tel Malḥata.** This site, too, was inhabited in the 7th century BCE. During excavations in 1967 and 1971 conducted by M. Kochavi, a fortified settlement was uncovered, surrounded by a wall and towers, which were first erected before the 7th century BCE but were reconstructed during the late 7th to early 6th centuries BCE. Within it, a storehouse of "four-room" plan was uncovered. This building existed for a lengthy period and was finally destroyed by the Babylonians. In its final stage, it included a row of monolithic pillars and a stone-paved floor. Only the last level of the house was destroyed by fire and produced numerous finds from the early 6th century BCE. Most of the finds from the site date to the town's final destruction level, including a few Judaean *sheqel* and *nsf* weights and Judaean clay figurines as well as a jar or two, with handles bearing a royal Judaean rosette seal impression (a rare example of a complete jar of the type). In the same locus were also found a complete decorated East Greek jug, dated—according to J. N. Coldstream—to ca. 600 BCE. In the same locus, about a quarter of the pottery vessels were Edomite, as were the personal names on an ostracon discovered in this stratum, attesting to contacts with Edom.

During the 1990s, five additional seasons of excavations were conducted at the site under the direction of I. Beit-Arieh. In these excavations, two phases of Stratum III dating from the 7th to the early 6th centuries BCE were uncovered. They had been built above the earlier 8th century BCE Stratum IV. Here were found a few Edomite ostraca. In one of them are incised the Edomite names Ozanel and Danel. Two seals were also found: one depicted an ostrich and in the other was incised the name *haha'*, probably another Edomite name. A rich assemblage of decorated and plain Edomite pottery had been uncovered, as well as many "Assyrian" bowls. Of the small finds, mention should be made of eight Judaean *sheqel, nsf,* and *gerah* stone weights. The excavator also reports the find of many cult objects including a few dozen clay figurines. Some were of the "pillar figurine" type, but others were clearly Edomite, resembling figurines found at Qitmit and Ḥazeva. One is portraying a man playing a double flute. Other cult objects are the small cubic limestone incense altars and fenestrated clay stands. There can be no doubt that this large fortified town served during the 7th to 6th centuries BCE as a central Edomite stronghold in the region.

Projecting deeply southward from this outer defensive line of the Judaean kingdom was the Judaean fort of **Kadesh-Barnea,** located in northern Sinai. This fort was not a part of the regular southern defensive line of the monarchy, and the reason for its establishment by the Judaean kingdom (and later by the Edomites; see below) was the necessity to defend the main road crossing through the desert from Judah to Egypt, during the period when people from both countries often traveled in both directions (as reflected in the Bible). At the beginning of this period, Egypt was the major ally of Judah in all its struggles against the Assyrians, and a large number of Jewish exiles found refuge in Egyptian cities. During the second part of the 7th century BCE, Egypt was the empire that actually ruled the coastal region of Palestine,

I.70 Aerial view of the Judaean fort at Kadesh-Barnea, looking south

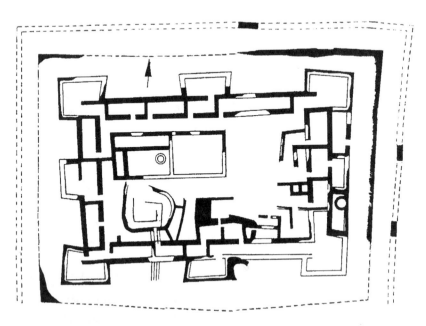

I.71 Plan of the 7th century fort at Kadesh-Barnea

and such a road was essential for maintaining contacts between the two countries.

The fort at Kadesh-Barnea was excavated by two expeditions. The first, in 1956, headed by M. Dothan, has three stages: (1) a pre-fort settlement, (2) a fort from the 8th to 6th centuries BCE, which consists of several phases, (3) a Persian-period fort. The second excavation, conducted by R. Cohen during the 1970s, also detected three stages: (1) a pre-fort settlement, (2) a two-stage fort (the lower fort, which had a massive wall, was built in the 8th century and destroyed in the mid-7th century BCE; the upper fort, surrounded by a casemate wall, was built by King Josiah in the mid-7th century BCE and destroyed by the Babylonians), (3) a Persian-period settlement. In a reassessment of these results, D. Ussishkin has suggested that instead of separating the two forts, we should consider them as a single unit, in existence from the mid-8th to the early 6th centuries BCE. He relies on N. Na'aman, who claims that during the reign of Josiah the territory of Judah was small and did not encompass Kadesh-Barnea. He therefore suggests that the fort at this time was not Judaean but was first built by the Assyrians and later transferred to the Egyptians. He also believes that the soldiers serving in the fort came from vassal states, perhaps including Judah. He also based his assumptions on the discovery of a few Egyptian hieratic documents at the site, but similar documents appear to have been found at other Judaean forts, such as Arad. O. Goldwasser's interpretation, i.e., that the Egyptian script and especially its numbers were deeply rooted and widely used in Judaean administrative tradition—from its beginnings—seems preferable (see below).

Coming now to the inner defensive line of Judah, we shall begin our survey with the fortress of **Arad.** This massive fort, excavated by Y. Aharoni, is divided into two stages. In the earlier one, which started perhaps in the 10th or 9th century BCE, the fort was rectangular, surrounded by a casemate wall (Stratum XI). Later, from Stratum X until the last phase of Stratum VI, it was surrounded by a solid offset-inset wall with one gate located in the east. According to the chronology offered by the excavator, supported by Z. Herzog, Stratum VIII was the stratum destroyed by Sennacherib; Stratum VII, dated to the 7th century BCE, was destroyed in 609 at the time of the Egyptian conquest of the Palestinian coastal region; Fort VI was the one destroyed by the Babylonians. The pottery vessels of Strata VII–VI are all dated to the 7th and early 6th centuries BCE. It is almost impossible to distinguish between them. It also became clear that the casemate wall attributed to Stratum VI replacing the solid one is not Judaean at all, but is a foundation wall of the Hellenistic tower. Therefore, the entire Judaean fort at Arad, from its erection in the 10th to 9th centuries until its final destruction during the 6th century BCE, existed in its original form, i.e., square, surrounded by a solid wall. The two major visible destructions should be assigned to Sennacherib in 701 BCE and to the Babylonians in 586 BCE. These are in accordance with the history of the other Judaean settlements. The rich Judaean finds at this site included all the typical components: ostraca, seals, seal impressions, weights, pottery vessels, and clay figurines, including a small archive belonging to one of the Judaean commanders of the fort, Elyashib son of Ashyahu, including three of his personal seals.

A few kilometers northeast of Arad, another small Judaean fort was excavated by R. Cohen at **Ḥorvat Tov.** It was a square structure (ca. 36 x 36 m.), also dated to the Late Iron Age, with two or three phases. It was surrounded by a solid offset-inset wall and had one gate on the east side flanked by two towers, as well as an inner tower in the center of the fort (as at Radum). The distance between Tov and Arad is about 5.5 km., roughly comparable to that between Radum and 'Uza. Both these forts were part of the inner Judaean defensive line.

Farther to the west lies the strong fortress of **Tel 'Ira.** This fortified city, dated to the late 8th or early 7th century BCE (Stratum VII), was erected over the entire site. In the eastern part, the city gate and some public buildings

I.72 Aerial view of the Judaean fort at Tel 'Ira

were uncovered. Private houses were found in the other areas. The city's strategic position, its considerable area, and its powerful fortifications attest to its great importance among the cities of the eastern and central Beersheba Valley. It is assumed to have been an administrative center of the kingdom of Judah and a major fortified city on its southern border. The Stratum VII structures were built directly on bedrock. The remains of the later stratum, dated to the late 7th century BCE, were found mainly in the casemate rooms encircling the fort. Stratum VII was destroyed in a conflagration. The pottery from Strata VII–VI includes types common in Judah and also a few shards and bowls imitating Assyrian prototypes, as well as Judaean *sheqel* and *pym* weights and a relatively large number of Judaean clay figurines. Some Hebrew ostraca were also found which pertained to a Judaean garrison unit stationed there. The city was identified as Eltolad (Joshua 15:30) by B. Mazar or as Ramot Negev, the site mentioned in the Arad ostracon, by others.

A few kilometers to the west, another Judaean fort of the 7th century BCE is located at **Tel Masos.** It was uncovered on a relatively small part of the mound. Its size and nature were not fully clarified. Four phases of occupation were found in the fortress, all dated to the 7th century BCE. It seems to exhibit a carefully laid-out residential quarter of chambers along a paved street. The finds included Judaean vessels, three ostraca bearing Hebrew personal names, Judaean clay figurines, and also a few Edomite shards. It appears that the fortress lasted no more than fifty to seventy years and was destroyed by violent conflagration, perhaps—as the excavator suggested—by the Edomites, but more likely by the Babylonians.

The excavations conducted by Y. Aharoni at **Tel Sheva** were quite comprehensive, and uncovered the remains of a flourishing Judaean city there from the 10th century BCE until its final destruction at the end of Stratum II during Sennacherib's campaign of 701 BCE (or perhaps even earlier at the hands of Tiglath-pileser III—as some tend to believe). Later, during Stratum I, if anything was built there, it was too poorly constructed or preserved to identify. However, many of the finds published from the excavation can be dated within the 7th century BCE. These include pottery vessels, weights, and a large number of Judaean clay figurines. It is agreed today that biblical Beersheba, also referred to in the Arad Ostraca, is probably buried under the modern town of Beersheba. A small trial excavation at this site uncovered remains of a Judaean city, but these are earlier than the 7th century BCE.

The results of the study of the Judaean towns in the Negev are therefore similar to those that we have seen elsewhere within its boundaries. Here, everything seems to be clearer because of the desert nature of the region.

This is an area that cannot support such a dense network of settlements by agriculture alone, unless they enjoyed strong state support and defense. In this region, as we have seen, many excavations and surveys were conducted, which supply us with abundant and reliable data.

One thing is clear: the total number of settlements in the Negev of Judah dated to the 7th century BCE, whether erected anew in this period after being destroyed by the Assyrians or built for the first time, is much larger than that during the earlier period, i.e., the 9th to 8th centuries BCE. During this earlier period, the only towns were Tel Sheva, Tel Malhata, Arad, and Kadesh-Barnea. During that time, the two fortresses in the Aravah, Tell el-Kheleifeh and 'En Hazeva, were also under Judaean rule. The arrival of the Assyrians to this region in 701 BCE put an end to all Judaean settlements, some of which, such as the one at Tel Sheva, never recovered, while the Aravah fortresses were not returned—according to our view—to Judaean control and their new inhabitants were already Edomites.

The renewal of the large-scale construction initiated by the Judaean state started, so it seems, but a short time after, probably at the beginning of the 7th century BCE during the reign of King Manasseh, as many scholars now agree, but was continued and even intensified by all other Judaean kings of the period, until the final Babylonian destruction. The many settlements erected here were planned as clusters of forts along a line of defense oriented toward the south, which also aimed at the inclusion of the areas of the Arad and Beersheba valleys. This was done mainly in order to gain control over the roads on which the caravans of incense and spice traders passed from the deserts of the east toward the Mediterranean coast. This trade started to develop during this period under the "Assyrian peace," and was a source of friction between Judah and Edom.

This defensive array was built of an outer line erected south of Nahal Beersheba and included the fortress of 'Uza, which served as a major fort, and that of **Khirbet Radum** as a secondary one; **Tel Malhata, Aroer,** and Kadesh-Barnea were built along one of the inner routes to Egypt. This line was apparently captured in its entirety by the Edomites during the later part of the 7th or the early 6th century BCE (see below).

The inner line, however, opposed the Edomite pressure. This line, erected on the northern side of Nahal Beersheba, consisted of the following forts: **Arad** and **Khirbet Tov** (as major and secondary fortresses), **Tel 'Ira, Tel Masos, Horvat Yiten,** and the town of Beersheba itself (buried below modern Beersheba and mentioned in the Bible and the Arad Ostraca). All these Judaean fortresses existed until the Babylonian conquest. Only then, after the entire Jewish population was deported from here, did this line, too, fall into the hands of the Edomites, who resettled it during the Persian period.

There can be no doubt that these two defensive lines were connected with each other in many ways and that all were efficiently connected with the headquarters in Jerusalem, as we have already noted in the case of the other boundaries on the north, east, and west. This system made Judah's defenses look like one huge fortress. Along each of these borders were one or two principal towns, while the permanent major fort of the king of Judah from which he controlled the entire network must have been in Jerusalem or perhaps even in Ramat Raḥel. From his capital, the king could, in times of necessity, support any portion of the border or even a single site by sending soldiers, whether mercenaries or his own troops, when called upon.

Even after this detailed and careful study of the results of all the many excavations and surveys mentioned above, we do not yet have a complete picture of Judah's defensive array, for there are more names of settlements in Judah mentioned in the various ostraca dated to this period than there are excavated and identified archaeological sites. Names such as Qinah, Ramot Negev, Hazar-Susa, Eltolad, Upper and Lower Anim, etc., are mentioned in the ostraca. Even if we assume that some of them should be identified with some of the excavated sites, it is certain that others are not. It should therefore be recognized that the overall number of Judaean fortresses in Judah's southern defensive line was certainly much larger.

The question at this point is, from where were all the people who inhabited this large number of desert settlements recruited? Even assuming that some of these sites were small and that their total population was small, in order to build so many new settlements, people must have been brought here from other parts of the kingdom. It is possible that some of them were Judaean refugees who found temporary refuge in Jerusalem at the time of Sennacherib's campaign against Judah in 701 BCE and were sent to these sites, whether immediately or somewhat later. A second and earlier source may have been, as many authorities have speculated, a wave or several waves of refugees arriving in Judah after leaving their towns in the Israelite monarchy following its destruction by the invading Assyrians during their first initiative there. Another possible source may have been internal immigration movements within the kingdom, which were supported by the Judaean kings during the 7th century BCE—as was noted above, a period of peace, natural growth, and economic prosperity. Finally, some of the people who populated the fortresses in this region (especially the smaller ones) may have been inhabitants of central Judah who were sent there for short periods of service as garrison soldiers, a practice that may have continued until the arrival of the Babylonians. The archaeological evidence clearly shows that the Judaean fortresses in the Negev were not damaged at the time of the final retreat of the Assyrians from Palestine. Their final destruction cannot, therefore, be attributed to Egyptian penetration during the last decades of the 7th century BCE. This Egyptian intervention passed almost unnoticed, leaving very few traces in the finds from this region. It is true that some scholars believe that the use of the Egyptian numerical system in Judaean weights and measures, as well as a few Egyptian ostraca in Judaean Arad and Kadesh-Barnea, attests to their physical presence in the area; but we have already shown that there was only an indirect influence of the Egyptian administration on the Judaean, which may have started in the 10th century BCE. In any case, it was much earlier than the withdrawal of the Assyrians or the actual arrival of the Egyptians. There is no archaeological documentation indicating direct Egyptian domination of the Judaean fortresses. On the contrary, the only Hebrew ostracon from Arad that mentions the king of Egypt (by title, not by name) speaks about him indirectly: "I have come to reign in all . . . Take strength and . . . King of Egypt to . . ." Y. Aharoni interpreted this ostracon as an order from King Jehoahaz the son of Josiah to the commander of Arad to fight against the Egyptians; Y. Yadin read it as a copy of an order from the king of Assyria, Ashurubalit, to the Judaean king to help the Egyptian king. Today it seems to us that both these scholars exaggerated the Judaean king's power—for it was difficult enough for him, it seems, to fend off the invading Edomites with his tiny army, let alone the Egyptians.

The final blow and the total destruction of this region was, as in the other parts of Judah, a result of the Babylonian invasion. The Babylonians removed everything they could. What they were not able to take they totally destroyed when they left, taking some of the surviving Judaean inhabitants with them. The entire region was abandoned for a while and was resettled only in the Persian period, mainly by the Edomites, who seem to have suffered less than others at the hands of the Babylonians (see below).

Jerusalem and the Settlements in the Judaean Hills

The borders of the city of Jerusalem in the period of the Judaean kingdom, its inner plan and fortifications, according to the results of the new excavations in the City of David and the Upper City, as well as in the cemeteries around it, were discussed in detail by A. Mazar in the first volume of this series, and need not be repeated here. As is well attested in the works just mentioned, Jerusalem in this period expanded considerably, both in area and in the size of its population. It is even claimed that the city's built-up area equaled that of all the rest of the Judaean settlements combined and that the entire kingdom was but a large *polis* (perhaps excluding the Negev). This growth had a direct bearing on the rural settlements around the capital both in number and in plan. In recent years, several 7th century BCE Judaean farmhouses have been uncovered in the vicinity of the city, at Naḥal Zimri, the French Hill, Pisgat Zeev, and Khirbet er-Ras, i.e., on the north and south sides of the city. The characteristics of this rural settlement have been studied by G. Edelstein, S. Gibson, and A. Faust, and it is now clear that the typical Judaean farmhouse included an unfortified residential house (of the "four-room" type). The farmhouse at **Khirbet er-Ras,** for example, consisted of a paved room to the west, an open courtyard at its center, and, presumably, another room to the east. The fourth broad room to the south was a storeroom containing three hundred holemouth jars. It also contained some agricultural installations for domestic production, as well as a wine/olive press, basins, and agricultural terraces.

We shall now examine the results of recent excavations at some of the sites of the hill area. This survey is mainly intended to address the problem of the boundaries of the destruction caused by Sennacherib in his campaign of 701 BCE, and to establish whether his army reached this region or if the towns on the crest of the hill south of Jerusalem were spared. We shall examine the sites from south to north.

Tell Rabud. This town was excavated by M. Kochavi and identified by him with Debir (Qiriath Sefer). It was a fortified Judaean town (Stratum IIB), destroyed by Sennacherib in 701 BCE. In its destruction layers, many pottery vessels, *lmlk* seal impressions, and two identical Hebrew seal impressions containing the name of the local official were recovered. The city's wall was rebuilt in the 7th century BCE and even widened in several locations up to 7 m. In the strata of this period (Strata IIA–IB), the town was enlarged, and an additional unfortified section was added to it on a lower terrace on the north side. It was finally destroyed by the Babylonians.

In the biblical city of **Hebron** located at Tell Rumeidah, two strata of the Iron Age were uncovered, though their exact dates have not been clarified. One seal impression with the *lmlk ḥbrn* inscription was found. At the nearby site of **Beth-Zur,** two large-scale excavations made it clear that it was only from the late 8th and 7th centuries BCE until the early 6th that an extensive and prosperous community came into existence here. The city met an abrupt end in 586 BCE. About ten *lmlk* seal impressions were found here, all of them of the later "two-winged" type, as well as five rosette seal impressions. The excavators also attribute two carved ivories of the "bird nest" type to this period. One depicts a man dressed in a local style, while the other depicts a sphinx. At **Khirbet el-Qom,** identified with biblical Makkedah and located west of Hebron, the remains of a fortified town with a few gates were uncovered. The pottery evidence places the last phase of the fortifications in the 7th century BCE, though these were initially constructed much earlier. Among the finds were a pit sealed by a layer of severe destruction, which contained a *lmlk* seal impression, a decanter with an incised Hebrew name, and *sheqel* weights. Also known from this site are tombs of the 8th to 7th centuries with many Hebrew inscriptions, one of which mentions Yahweh and 'Astarte (see below).

At **Ramat Raḥel,** adjacent to the southern side of Jerusalem, the last palace of the Judaean kings was uncovered. This was a monumental structure built of fine limestone masonry and decorated with proto-Aeolic capitals and carved window balustrades. The plan of the palace was rectangular, surrounded with casemate walls within which was a central building with a spacious courtyard. According to the excavator, Y. Aharoni, it consisted of two Iron Age strata: Stratum VB dated to the 8th to 7th centuries BCE, of which very few remains are left. The major stratum, VA, dated to 608–586 BCE, contained the remains of the palace. Recent excavations, however, conducted at the site by G. Barkay, show that the armies of Sennacherib reached even this spot so close to Jerusalem, and the destruction of Stratum VB should be attributed to his campaign in 701 BCE. Stratum VA and the palace are from the 7th century BCE, perhaps as early as the reign of Manasseh or his immediate successors. Finds from this stratum included a large number of seal impressions of various kinds, Judaean weights, pottery vessels, and clay figurines.

The overall picture emerging from the excavations at the sites along the Judaean Hill ridge appears to corroborate that in other parts of the Judaean monarchy: a severe destruction followed Sennacherib's 701 BCE campaign at almost all sites, excluding Jerusalem. Between that date and the arrival of the Babylonians, the country enjoyed a period of rebuilding and relative prosperity.

THE ARCHITECTURE OF THE KINGDOM OF JUDAH

ALMOST ALL RESIDENTIAL houses of the 7th and early 6th centuries BCE found at Judah were built according to the "four-room" plan, which was

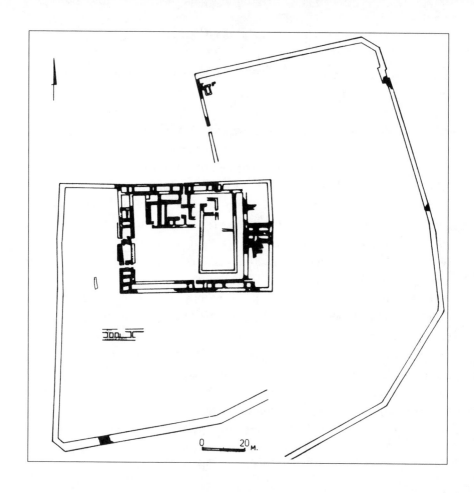

I.73 Plan of the Judaean royal palace at Ramat Raḥel

common during the entire period of the monarchy and even much earlier. The central element common to all these houses is the line of monoliths erected in the lower floor, which divides the space into two parts. In the 7th century BCE, there was considerable flexibility in the plan and in the arrangement of the rooms in each house, according to the needs of the individual owner.

Judah, and probably also Phoenicia, were the only states at the time that conserved the previous Phoenician-Israelite building tradition to the end of the period. Up to now, not even a single example of the new "Assyrian" construction of brick with gabled roofs, common in the other regions (see below), has been encountered within their borders. Even the other more common type of the Assyrian open-court plan, which consisted of many local elements, has not been found. The major example of the latter type, which is also the closest to Judah geographically, is the palace recently uncovered at Philistine Ekron. This continuation of the old Phoenician-Israelite building tradition stands in remarkable contrast with that of the northern Assyrian provinces of Megiddo and Samaria, Philistia, and even developments in the Transjordanian states, which voluntarily changed their old Phoenician building system to the Assyrian one.

As to monumental architecture, since the excavation of the palace of the last Judaean kings at Ramat Raḥel, which is confidently dated to the 7th century BCE, it became clear that in monumental architecture, too, Judah remained faithful to the old principles current during the entire period of the monarchy from the 10th century BCE on. The palace of Ramat Raḥel was built according to strict Phoenician-Israelite conventions, i.e., utilizing all-limestone building materials, stone masonry and margins executed with a broad-headed chisel, the same-size stones, and the same method of laying them in header-and-stretcher fashion observed at other sites. Floor pavements consist of a heavy layer of a limestone waste, which remained from chiseling the edges of the masonry on the spot to fit properly without requiring cement. This continuity is distinguished mainly, however, in the architectural decorations, which are identical with those of the public buildings and palaces of the previous Israelite kingdom, such as the palace of the Israelite kings at Samaria and the public buildings of Dan, Hazor, and Megiddo (and probably Shechem, too). This resemblance is so close that it led both Y. Yadin and Y. Shiloh to the hypothesis that the Judaean palace at Ramat Raḥel had been erected during the 9th century BCE, which, however, we know today was not the case! Recent excavations at the site by G. Barkay proved beyond any doubt that the earliest stratum at the site, Stratum VB, which consisted of a small settlement, was probably destroyed by Sennacherib in 701 BCE while his army laid siege to Jerusalem. The construction of the palace was carried out afterward, during the 7th century BCE and perhaps mainly toward the end of that century.

Nearly all the types of architectural ornamentation known to us from this period are present in the Judaean palace of Ramat Raḥel. These include about a dozen proto-Aeolic capitals (following the southern Judaean order, which differs from the earlier Israelite one, and has been found elsewhere only at Jerusalem and in Moab). Two typical window balustrades were also uncovered there: one is a freestanding sculpted balustrade, the other a thin balustrade in low relief on both sides. Both depict the "fallen leaves" motif, which occurred frequently on balustrades found elsewhere. Similar proto-Aeolic capitals were found in K. Kenyon's excavations in the City of David in

I.74 Ramat Raḥel, a window ballustrade from the Judaean palace

Jerusalem. Limestone balustrade fragments identical to those from Ramat Raḥel were uncovered by Y. Shiloh in the City of David. These finds mean that the same kind of architecture was in use in Jerusalem during this period.

Two other related finds are an ivory game board found at **Aroer** in the Negev of Judah, the upper part of which is decorated with a proto-Aeolic capital of the same type as those discovered at Jerusalem and Ramat Raḥel, and fragments of small decorations from wooden furniture discovered at the City of David in Jerusalem within the destruction level of 586 BCE, which are identical to the Phoenician-Israelite ivory carvings of the previous Israelite monarchic period. This type of carving thus continued in Judah until its end, though in this case, wood replaced ivory, which was apparently no longer available.

The only find from Ramat Raḥel, which may indicate Assyrian influence on the architecture of this Judaean palace, is a fragment of a colored wall painting depicting an Assyrian figure sitting on a throne. This is a local imitation of an Assyrian prototype. The publisher of this unique fragment thought that it served as a small-scale model for a larger painting that was drawn on one of the palace's walls in the method well known in Neo-Assyrian palaces elsewhere. This is possible, but no local parallels exist.

THE WRITTEN EVIDENCE

O N E O F T H E surprising results of the excavations of Judah in the 7th century BCE is the unusual amount of epigraphic material from a period that lasted not much more than one hundred years. This material is abundant in comparison with both the preceding and the following periods. The Judaean state appears to have experienced an "explosion" of writing in comparison with the rest of the Palestinian states of the period, which also enjoyed the prosperity of the age, and in comparison with the written finds in the Assyrian provinces in general. Taking into consideration the size of the Judaean kingdom during this period, this large body of written artifacts is truly astonishing.

We shall now describe the various Judaean inscriptions according to type, but the rarity of this phenomenon should be examined first. It seems that the major reason stems from the fact that the Judaean kingdom of this period was an extremely centralized administrative unit in which each activity needed the approval of the king in Jerusalem or of one of the senior officials. In order to make this possible, a sophisticated bureaucratic network of administrators was established to deal with all aspects of the kingdom's activity. The remains of this bureaucracy and its echo can be traced in the archaeological record in the form of the many official seals and seal impressions issued by the royalty, the seals of the various officials and administrators of the kingdom, the system of taxation, and the surprisingly accurate system of weights and measures. Remains of a well-organized system for reporting among the various components of this administration were also unearthed. It seems to have been almost impossible, even in the remotest small fort, to send any amount of rations without recording them in a detailed manner. If we add to this the ordinary daily reports and reporting on special events, we obtain a picture of a sophisticated bureaucracy involving every aspect of state life. The question arises, however, why this administration did not appear earlier. There are hints that a comparable system existed in earlier times within the state of Israel, as reflected in the Samaria Ostraca and the seals of the many officials of the kingdom of Israel. But it seems that the consolidation of this bureaucratic system occurred only later in the south, in the late Judaean monarchic period. In any case, we must remember that we have but a tiny fraction of the written documents of the time, and probably the less important ones: for the major writing material of this period (as attested by hundreds of bullae) was papyrus. Only two or three examples from this period have survived: one from Judah, the others from Philistia and Moab (see below).

Of the epigraphic finds from Judah of the 7th century BCE, the major ostraca archives were unearthed at Lachish, Arad, and Tel 'Ira. But it seems that there is hardly an excavated Judaean site at which ostraca or other written documents were not found. Epigraphic finds come from the Judaean sites of Gibeon, Jerusalem, Ramat Raḥel, En-Gedi, Jericho, Gezer, Beth-Shemesh, Tel Batash, Meẓad Ḥashavyahu, and almost all the settlements excavated in the south, including Arad, 'Uza, 'Ira, Tel Sheva, and Kadesh-Barnea. Many of these finds were merely dockets of food shipments or copies of orders, but a few have deeper historical, legal, economic, or social significance.

The only Judaean papyrus to have survived from this period is a palimpsest, i.e., a document from the time of the Judaean kingdom overwritten with a much later document. This is a lone fragment from the kingdom's archives. Other fragments of such papyrus documents are the many bullae

I.75 Clay Judaean bullae from the City of David

that sealed them and on which the names and titles of many of the kingdom's officials and administrators occur. Some assemblages of such bullae were discovered during scientific excavations, as at Lachish and the City of David in Jerusalem, but most were found in illicit excavations or are in private collections. Besides the bullae, a number of inscriptions is found in Judaean tombs: in some of the tombs discovered at Silwan in Jerusalem, at the site of Khirbet el-Qom, the Beit-Lei tomb near Lachish, and in a cave in the Judaean desert.

A few hundred seals and seal impressions have been uncovered at Judaean sites, and even more are known from private collections. These are also connected with the administrative apparatus of the state: some were the state's seals, while others belonged to private individuals. There are also many clay vessels on which incised inscriptions indicate contents, volume, or the name of the vessel owner. Some of these are inscribed in a technique peculiar to 7th century BCE Judah. Finally, we should mention the common find of incised inscriptions, seal impressions, and other inscriptions in relation to the new system of weights and measures established at this time by the Judaean kingdom, which may have spread beyond its boundaries into neighboring lands.

We shall deal with all of these in detail below. Quantity in this case also creates a certain quality of data, in terms of evidence about the administrative system and the high educational level attained in Judah during this period. In order to be a part of this bureaucracy, it was necessary to master reading and writing, as well as to be able to make complicated calculations involving quantities of merchandise, services, etc. The Judaean system (and perhaps its predecessor as well) was based on an Egyptian model, from which it borrowed the numerical system and perhaps other features.

The Ostraca

The hundreds of Judaean ostraca found at many of the sites, dated to the later period of the monarchy, enable us to study various aspects of the kingdom's daily life: its history, military organization, administration, cult, and above all, the daily life of its citizens. Some of these aspects (it is impossible to deal with them all here) will be treated below.

One of the most important and often-discussed topics relating to ostraca is the **Judaean army.** Military organization played an important role in the life of the kingdom as well as in that of every citizen, for its service was a continuous and heavy burden for all Judaeans. They were obliged to render service either in the form of annual labor duties or as soldiers in combat units.

The subject of the army and related civil duties is often reflected in discoveries made in recent years, both in written documents and in remains of weapons and other military equipment and installations found at Judaean sites. This should not come as a surprise, for the Judaean army participated in many wars against the country's neighbors, especially against the Edomites but also against the "superpowers" of the period: beginning with Assyria in 701 BCE, later (609 BCE) Egypt, until the final engagement with Babylonia.

Important pertinent archaeological evidence includes, in particular, the Assyrian reliefs from Nineveh dated to the time of Sennacherib, which depict the siege of Lachish (see below). In these reliefs, Judaean soldiers are depicted fighting from atop the city walls and being taken away to captivity. These reliefs also provide a glimpse at their military equipment, which was also taken as spoils: bows and arrows and even a complete war chariot. Remains of similar weapons, mainly arrow and javelin heads, were found in great numbers at Lachish, especially in the small area in which the Assyrian siege rampart meets the city wall at its extreme southern point. In the few squares excavated here, several hundred of these weapons, belonging to both sides, were recovered.

But the military organization of the Judaean kingdom is also reflected in inscriptions and the inscribed seals. Two seal impressions are inscribed with the title "city commander" (sr ha'ir) and depict an officer receiving a bow and arrows from someone who was probably his supreme commander (the king of Judah?), a motif taken from an Assyrian prototype.

An ostracon found at the Judaean fortress of Meẓad Ḥashavyahu, located near Yavneh-Yam and dated to the 7th century BCE, gives the name of its Judaean commander. This fortress was attributed by its excavator, J. Naveh, to King Josiah, who ruled the region for a short time (see below). In this fortress, where Greek mercenaries formed the largest contingent, some Judaean inhabitants recruited for labor duties by the kingdom's authorities were also active. Here, a letter from one of these laborers was found. It was originally sent to the fortress commander, whose title is adoni ha-sr ("my lord the commander"). Among the Lachish Letters, which were written only a few years later, appears a certain Kanyahu whose title, sr haẓavah ("army commander"), is mentioned. One of the Arad Inscriptions mentions adoni sr ("my lord the commander"; cf. 1 Samuel 17:18 sr ha-elef, "commander of a thousand"). Another sr, found in a recently published 7th century BCE ostracon, is again mentioned only by title. This sr is asked by a widow to return to her a wheat field that had belonged to her husband. It is impossible to conclude whether the sr was a military or a civilian authority. Lastly, "Uriyau the sr" is inscribed in the Judaean tomb excavated at Khirbet el-Qom.

Another military title is the *kazin* ("officer"), which appears on an ostracon found in the Judaean fort at **Khirbet ʿUza** in the Arad Valley (cf. Joshua 10:24 *kzinei anshei ha-milḥamah,* "the captains of the men of war"). A large amount of data concerning this has accumulated from excavations at the various Judaean forts in the Beersheba Valley. Some light has been shed upon daily military routine as well as military language and orders, which were short and usually imperative, using a one-word command such as "Send!" "Take!" "Come!" "Bring!" "Hand!" etc., or usage such as *amez zaroa* ("take strength") and "the word of the king is incumbent upon you for your very life! Behold . . . lest Edom should come here," which probably reflect standard military expressions.

As to the army service imposed on the citizens of Judah, two documents are known. One, mentioned above from Meẓad Ḥashavyahu, tells the story of a Judaean recruit summoned for annual labor service in the fort. The other, from the fort of ʿUza, probably includes an order to place three Judaean soldiers to serve in this remote fort against Edom. All three came from settlements located in the center of Judaean territory, such as Moledah and undoubtedly Makkedah (perhaps Khirbet el-Qom). Another recently found ostracon from Tel ʿIra, a Judaean military fort in this region, starts with the word *mifkad* ("census"); its contents contain a list of names of soldiers who were stationed there. Another ostracon, also from ʿUza, probably describes the everyday military routine. It is evidently divided into two identical inscriptions written on the side of a jar in which a certain Elnathan is mentioned whose title is *kazin le-mateh givli* ("officer to the unit of the Givlites"), perhaps a small military unit. Afterward, four names are mentioned giving the order: first, second, third, and fourth. In the opinion of the excavator, I. Beit-Arieh, this inscription was located in the central room in the fort and announced the duty rotation of the unit's members.

A unique description of military activity in time of war has survived in Ostracon No. 4 of the Lachish Letters: "because if in his turning he had inspected, he would know, that for the signal-stations of Lachish we are watching, according to all the signs which my lord gives, because we do not see (the signals of) Azekah." According to the interpretation of this text proposed by Y. Yadin, we have here a description of a battle order involving the commander of the city of Lachish (a certain Hoshayahu) and his superior located in Jerusalem (Yaush, possibly a member of the royal family). The instruction was to light the signals at Lachish only if those of Azekah (which is located closer to Jerusalem) have not been lit or seen in Jerusalem for any reason. We have evidence here of the sophisticated signal system functioning between the border fortresses and the capital of the Judaean kingdom.

THE SEALS

The lmlk *Seal Impressions*

THESE SEAL IMPRESSIONS were dealt with by A. Mazar in his volume in this series, where their two main types are identified: one in the shape of a scarab with the word *lmlk* and the name of one of four towns: *ḥbrn, socoh, zf,* or *mmsht;* the second shows the winged sun disk with identical inscriptions. Both types have been dated by recent excavations at Lachish, where they were found together in one of the gate rooms, destroyed in 701 BCE by Sennacherib, i.e., before the period with which we are dealing here. Therefore, we shall not discuss these two types at all, neither their meaning nor the controversy about who was responsible for them and where they were stamped. In any case, most scholars now agree that the two other symbols depicted on the *lmlk* jar handles, the rosette seal impressions and the concentric circles incised on them, should be limited to a period from the later part of the 7th century BCE until the destruction in 586 BCE. We shall therefore discuss these two types in detail, for their very existence in a given stratum is an accurate criterion for the existence of a settlement in the 7th century BCE within the borders of the Judaean kingdom in its latest stage.

But before discussing the rosette and concentric circle seal impressions, the impressions of the winged sun disk seals should be considered again. We have already mentioned that among the finds at **Ḥorvat Shilḥa** near Jericho, one winged disk impression was uncovered on a handle of a *lmlk* jar. Our interest in this impression lies in the fact that Ḥorvat Shilḥa is a one-period settlement dated by its pottery to the latter part of the 7th and early 6th centuries BCE (see below). However, the stamped handle from Ḥorvat Shilḥa is not unique, for similar winged sun disk seal impressions were found in other one-period settlements in Judah, such as En-Gedi and Khirbet e-Samrah in the Judaean Buqeiah. They are present also in clear stratigraphic contexts at Stratum II at Tel Batash (7th century BCE). From these, one may deduce—following A. Mazar—that their occurrence in this time period indicates their continued use, in limited quantities and one type only, long after Sennacherib's campaign to Judah in 701 BCE. Mazar is nevertheless careful to state that this does not contradict the chronological conclusions of the Lachish excavators for their final use in 701 BCE, for it is possible that several thousand jars of the same type were stored at other Judaean settlements, which were not captured by the Assyrians (as, for instance, Jerusalem itself), and were transferred for various reasons to other sites that had not been destroyed, or were reconstructed during the 7th century BCE. Even so, it is still probable that this one type of the *lmlk* seal impressions was still being produced after 701 BCE, as King Hezekiah himself, the creator of these impressions, continued in power for some years after 701. It is now absolutely clear that the *lmlk* jars impressed and incised with the rosette and concentric circles continued until the destruction of the Judaean kingdom. This means that this royal system endured and only the types of seals changed. Moreover, the same system continued even into the Persian period (see below). Ending debate on this matter is a single find published by

N. Avigad. This is a new type of seal impression on a bulla , which is inscribed "in the year 26th Eltolad *lmlk*." This must be a kind of bulla that sealed goods delivered by the town of Eltolad (a city in the south of Judah; cf. Joshua 15:30; 1 Chronicles 4:28) as tax to the king (the number 26 is written in hieratic). This is not the first evidence of a city tax paid to the king. Especially important here is the date and the terminology. Avigad believed that this was the twenty-sixth year of King Josiah (i.e., 613 BCE), and the terminology is again "to the king." Recently, a second bulla of this type was published with an inscription reading "in the 13th year, the first crop of

I.76 Judaean bulla: "In the 13th year of the first crop of Lachish to the king"

Lachish, to the king." This is a bulla that was stamped on a clay stopper and is said to originate at Eltolad as well. It must therefore be dated to 626 BCE, during the period in which the *lmlk* seal impressions were previously thought to be no longer in use.

Within the territory of Judah were also discovered some large stone and clay seals, some nonepigraphic and others inscribed with personal names (at En-Gedi, Ramat Raḥel, and Arad), all from clear 7th to early 6th century contexts, in which a simple geometric design is depicted. These are heavy seals that were suspended from the neck (each of them is pierced), and they were probably used to mark or seal leather or woven sacks.

The Rosette Impressions

The last of the kingdom's official seals are definitely the rosette seal impressions. Up to now about 250 have turned up at twenty-four sites, all within the territory of Judah. They consist of many variants that differ from each other in shape and number of petals in the rosette. All were found on jar handles of the *lmlk* type, but of taller and narrower derivatives. The one exception was an impression stamped on the handle of a water decanter found in the City of David in Jerusalem. Another was found incised on a Judaean *bqʿ*

I.77 Rosette seal
impressions from
En-Gedi

weight. The archaeological evidence points to the conclusion that the rosette seal impressions on the *lmlk* jar-type handles all date to the last decades of the Judaean monarchy. This evidence comes from clear stratigraphic contexts at sites such as Lachish, where all are assigned to Stratum II, or Tel Batash II. Here we should like to add a unique find from Tel Malḥata in the Beersheba Valley, a complete *lmlk* jar type stamped with a rosette seal impression found within an assemblage of pottery vessels that includes Judaean and Edomite types as well as a complete East Greek jug, dated by J. N. Coldstream to ca. 600 BCE. Additional evidence comes from one-period sites dated to this period alone, such as Vered Jericho, En-Gedi, and Tel 'Ira, where rosette seal impressions were the only kind recovered.

With the rosette seal impressions and in the same stratigraphic contexts appear, on the same type of jar handles, concentric circles incisions with a dot in the center. These were incised after firing, and at one time Y. Yadin expressed the (apparently correct) view that the incisions are a schematic rendering of the rosette emblem. The problem of the change in emblems on the *lmlk* jar handles was indeed a focus of long debate among many scholars. From the evidence at Lachish, we have learned that both the four-winged beetle and the winged sun disk are in fact two variations of the same emblem, for both were uncovered (with identical inscriptions) in the same room. Many authorities, including, recently, J. Cahill, who studied all the rosette seal impressions, suggest that this last emblem was adopted from the Assyrians. There appears, however, to be ample evidence for the interpretation of the rosette sign as related to the sun disk, like the previous scarab and the winged sun disk emblems. Recently, the problem of the interpretation of the concentric circles symbol was also solved: a 7th century BCE decorated limestone "bird nest" cosmetic palette found in eastern Jordan and published by D. Barag portrays a scene depicting two persons kneeling and praying on both sides of a "tree of life." The tree is crowned by a two-winged sun disk symbol. The interesting thing about this motif is that the sun disk itself is executed here as concentric circles, in exactly the same fashion as in the incisions on the jar handles. This may indicate that all four symbols on the jar handles—the winged beetle, the (two-)winged sun disk, the rosette, and the concentric circles—are variations on one and the same motif. Why was it necessary to change them from time to time? The reason may have been practical and simple: the symbol in the impressions and incisions becomes more and more simple and schematic and easier to execute. The remaining question is, why did the Judaean monarchy choose to use this emblem as its symbol in the first place? There is no simple answer, but it should be pointed out that this symbol is by no means unique to Judah. It is shared by many of Palestine's peoples. There are even some authorities who believe that the beetle was first the emblem of the Israelite monarchy and that Judah inherited it. But identical seal impressions have been found in Ammon, too (perhaps one that even belonged to the local royal family), and in Phoenicia. It also frequently appears in personal seals, both in Judah and among other peoples of the region (for example, the winged sun disk in the seal of Nera from En-Gedi). This is undoubtedly a local adaptation of an Egyptian motif that was originally connected with the sun cult and was incorporated into the local Palestinian repertoire in an earlier period. It was also chosen by the royal Judaean house. It is hard to say if it had a cultic meaning beyond its decorative function.

Lastly, it should be pointed out that the distribution of the rosette seal impressions as well as the concentric circles incisions is almost the same as that of the *lmlk* impressions. They were found at all the major sites of Judah, including Tell en-Naṣbeh, Gibeon, Gibeah, Jerusalem, Ramat Raḥel, Nebi Daniel, Beth-Zur, Jericho, Vered Jericho, and En-Gedi, as well as in the west at Gezer, Tel Batash, Socoh, Azekah, Tell eṣ-Ṣafi, Tel Ḥarasim, Tel Burnat, Lachish, and Tel ʿErani, and in the south, too, at Arad, Tel Malḥata, and Tel ʿIra. Therefore, it may be concluded that the overall area of Judah in the late 7th century BCE was the same as it had been prior to 701 BCE and perhaps even greater, as we have already seen, even though the total number of impressions from this period is only 250 (in comparison with more than 1,200 *lmlk* impressions). The one exception is an impression that was found outside Judaea, at Tel Miqneh (Ekron) in Philistia.

In conclusion, we may assume that the rosette emblems and the concentric circles are the symbols of Judaean royalty of late 7th century BCE. We may perhaps also attribute to this period a few two-winged *lmlk* seal impressions that continued in use.

Seals of the Kingdom's Officials

As already observed in relation to the written evidence from this period in general, the phenomenon of seals in Judah during the Assyrian period is unique, though not because of their rich variety of ornamentation or their artistic value; on the contrary, as N. Avigad had already shown, the seals of the kingdom of Israel and Judah prior to the days of Sennacherib are more beautiful and present more pleasant motifs and decorations. The uniqueness of the Judaean seals of this period is related to their enormous quantity: a

I.78 A large Judaean stone seal from En-Gedi: "belonging to Tovshalem"

comparable number of seals in all possible forms—seals, seal impressions on jar handles or other clay vessels and bullae—have not been found in any other state of the region from the 7th and early 6th centuries BCE. Many of these seals and impressions are also characterized by inscriptions. In this period, only a few bear a family emblem or pagan motif.

Many of the seals and impressions of the Judaean kingdom of the 7th century BCE bear the titles of the kingdom's officials. Some of these are mentioned in the Bible, such as "the son of the king," "servant of the king," "who is over the house," "who is over the corvée," "governor of the city," etc. There are also biblical titles that have not yet turned up among the archaeological finds. On the other hand, there are titles of officials on seals that are not mentioned in the Bible. We may also include here titles found in the neighboring states, for there existed a clear similarity among the titles of the officials in all the states of Palestine during this period.

The titles mentioned in the seals and seal impressions, in the bullae, in the ostraca, and in some of the tomb inscriptions of Judah during the 7th to early 6th centuries BCE can be divided into two groups: the first and main group includes the titles of the kingdom's officials; the second declares the occupation of the owner of the seal. Within the first group, there is a separate royal subgroup, which includes the king himself: "belonging to the king" (no name). Others are simply "the son of the king" or "the daughter of the king." The first title, "the son of the king," now occurs in more than a dozen seals and impressions. These people might have indeed been actual sons of kings, as, for example, "Manasseh the son of the king" or "Yeraḥme'el the son of the king," for these names appear as such in the Bible, but others, Neriyahu, Gaddiyahu, Yareyahu, Pedayahu, or Malkiyahu, all with the title "son of the king," were not perhaps always biological sons of the king. We accept N. Avigad's suggestion that this was an administrative title given only to officials who belonged to the royal family, or "the king's children" as mentioned in the Lachish Letters, who fulfilled various functions in the kingdom's hierarchy.

Another seal mentions the title "servant," which appears in two forms: the first refers to the king's name, too, i.e., the name of one of the known Judaean kings, such as "Shebanyahu servant of Uzziyahu" or "Yehozarah son of Hilqiyahu servant of Hizqiyahu"; the other form consists of the official title alone: "servant of the king." This title frequently appears on Judaean seals and bullae, as well as in the ostraca of the period. There are also a few seals with the female title, *amah,* which means "woman servant," and must be the female version of the same title.

Another group of inscribed Judaean seals is those belonging to the officials with the title "who is over." Most of them were "who is over the house," a title mentioned in the Bible and given to a high-ranking state official. Many of these titles were found inscribed on seals and seal impressions, but others appear in ostraca or tomb inscriptions, such as "Adoniyahu who is over the house," "Yiddo who is over the house," etc. Perhaps these officials were in charge of the king's property all over the state. In one of the Judaean seals is also mentioned "Pelayahu who is over the corvée." This person must have been in charge of the forced labor of the kingdom.

It is almost impossible today to understand confidently the exact meaning or function of each of these titles. Some of the people involved were perhaps officials and persons who are actually mentioned in the Bible. For example, the name Gedalyahu found on a Judaean seal is probably Gedalyahu the son of Ahiqam, who was appointed by Nebuchadnezzar king of Babylon over Judah and was killed by Yishmael the son of Nethanya (2 Kings 25:25). Others are Shebnayahu who is over the house and Yeraḥme'el the son of the king, and there are still more.

Other seals and bullae that have recently been found belonged to the military hierarchy of the kingdom, for example, the impression of *lsr* ("to the commander"), which depicts a soldier leading a captive, or the bulla of *sr ha'ir,* "the commander of the city," which depicts bow and arrows being handed to him (by the king?). We pointed out above that the title *sr* is usually connected with army officers, such as the title *sr hazava Kanyahu* ("the army commander or officer Kanyahu"), who is mentioned in the Lachish Letters, or the title *sr* alone, referring to a person who was probably ap-

I.79 Seals of Judaean officials; from left to right: "the daughter of the king"; "servant of the king"; "commander of the city"

pointed over the soldiers of the Judaean fortress of Meẓad Ḥashavyahu and mentioned in its well-known ostracon. Another military title could have been *ha-nasis,* "the standard bearer," which, although not found in Judah itself, could have been used there, too, for as already stated, most of these titles were common to all the states of Palestine.

To an inferior level of the official hierarchy may belong the title *hamazkir* ("the memorist"), which is known only from Moab; or that of the *gnzbar,* "the treasurer," which appears in the Arad Ostraca, and perhaps also the title mentioned in a bulla: "belonging to Azaryahu the porter of the prison."

There are many examples of the title *na'ar* ("steward"), from nearly all the states of Palestine. This title meant—as N. Avigad had shown—the personal steward or clerk of a private person, such as a certain "Netibyahu steward of Mattan" or "Benayahu steward of Haggi" and many other names of unknown persons, meaning that this title was not one of the official titles of the kingdom.

The other group of seals or impressions designates the occupation of the seal owners. Additional occupations are mentioned in the ostraca and inscriptions of this period in Judah. Among the known occupations, that of scribe is the most common in Judah as well as in the other states, and it is not always clear if these people acted on behalf of the kingdom or as private persons, or both. The best known of the Judaean scribes' seals is that of "Berechyahu son of Neriyahu," who was Jeremiah's scribe, a few copies of whose bullae have been found, or those of "Ga'alyahu son of 'Adayahu the scribe," "Ma'ash son of Manoah the scribe," etc.

Other occupations mentioned in the seals are those of priests, such as "Hanan the son of Hilqiyahu the priest," who might be the father of Hilqiyahu, the high priest in the days of Josiah king of Judah. The seal of "Miqnayahu servant of Yahweh" probably means that he had a position among the priests of one of the Yahweh temples. An earlier Israelite seal is inscribed with the title of "the priest of Dor." This man was probably—according to N. Avigad—the chief priest in the Yahweh temple in the city of Dor. Among the Lachish Letters, a person is mentioned whose title is "prophet." Other occupations mentioned in the seals are "Tobshillem son of Zakkur son of Benzakar the Healer" and "Neriyahu the guide"; others have the titles of *rapad* ("upholsterer"), *koves* ("laundryman"), *nosech* ("wine seller"), and *ḥozev* ("quarrier"). It is very probable that in the future other occupations will be found on seals.

Seals with Personal Names

Most of the Judaean seals of the 7th to early 6th centuries BCE are inscribed seals with no decorations or symbols (except for a schematic dividing line that separates the registers). N. Avigad had also observed another difference between the older decorated seals of the 8th century BCE and the later ones: the earlier ones do not usually have the dividing line, while the later examples do; the later seals are also usually less ornamented.

Some of the inscribed seals contain the name of the seal's owner without any addition, such as "Padael" or "Nera"; in others, the letter *lamed* was

I.80 The seal of Uriyahu (the son of) Azariyahu from En-Gedi

added, which means "belonging to," such as "belonging to Putiyahu" or "belonging to Yeqamyahu." The majority of the seals, however, are inscribed with both the name of the owner and the name of his father, divided into two separate lines, such as "belonging to Yeda'yahu son of Karmi" or "belonging to Ya'azanyahu son of Ma'aseyahu," though sometimes the word "son" is divided between the two lines, or sometimes even completely omitted, as "belonging to Neriyahu Adoniyahu," where the relationship between the two names as father and son is clear. There are a few seals in which the names of three generations are mentioned, such as the seal of "Tobshilem son of Benzakar son of Zakkur" or "Yirmiyahu son of Sepanyahu son of Nobai," and one example with four generations: "belonging to Hosea (son of) 'Akhbor (son of) 'Elishama (son of) Hosea." The recurrence of the first name in this family should be noted. Another tradition used by the Judahites was the papponomy, the repetition of names every other generation. A good example for this is the priest family: Hilqiyahu the son of Hanan the son of Hilqiyahu.

Several seals and impressions have been found that belonged to women. Some of these women probably held important positions in the royal administration, such as those women who bear the titles "the daughter of the king" or the *amah* ("maidservant"), which were discussed above and were used in Judah down to the Persian period. But the majority, like the seals belonging to men, bear the owner's name alone, such as "belonging to Hanna," or the woman and her father, such as "belonging to Abigail daugh-

ter of Elhanan." It seems, however, that after her marriage and her transfer
to her husband's house, the woman is related to him: "belonging to Abigail
wife of Asayahu."

The majority of the names mentioned in the seals are well known to us
from the Bible. Moreover, some of these names are identified with particular
biblical persons active in the 7th to 6th centuries BCE, such as "Berechyahu
son of Neriyahu the scribe," who was probably Jeremiah's scribe, and his
brother, "Serayahu son of Neriyahu," or "Yeraḥme'el son of the king" or
"Gemaryahu son of Shaphan," also a scribe in whose office Baruch the son
of Neriah read the scroll dictated to him by Jeremiah (Jeremiah 36:25). But
the biblical list of names has been enlarged by the seals and bullae with
names not previously known, such as "Yahmelyahu," "Nazarel," and
"Ne'ehebet," thereby enriching our knowledge beyond our expectations.
Here, let us mention three hoards of bullae. The first, containing 17 bullae,
was discovered by Y. Aharoni at Lachish in a small juglet. The second, found
by Y. Shiloh in the City of David in Jerusalem, consisted of 51 bullae discovered on the floor of a building destroyed in 586 BCE. The largest hoard of all,
consisting of 210 bullae whose place of origin is not known (but was probably the City of David, too), was recently published by N. Avigad. All three
hoards came from the destruction levels of the Judaean monarchy, and it is
difficult, or even impossible, to estimate their contribution to the study of the
royal administration of Judah in this period.

As to the simple personal names, it is impossible today to discern between
names of private individuals and those of the kingdom's officials. But there
can be no doubt that the majority of the seals belonged to officials, as can be
deduced from the many seal impressions with names found on the *lmlk* jar
handles, or their existence in the Judaean royal palace, fortresses, and estates,
such as Ramat Raḥel, En-Gedi, Arad, etc. But the official roll of the seal owners can also be studied on the basis of their distribution. Y. Garfinkel recently
made a comparative study of these seals and examined the distribution of
seals with identical names at the various Judaean sites, mainly those impressed on *lmlk* jar handles. He concluded that in this specific group most of
the seals seem to have only a limited distribution in the various regions of ancient Judah. The different examples were discovered either at a single site or
at only two or three sites. Such distribution, he believes, points to a hierarchic pattern among the seal owners, indicating the existence of three classes:
interregional, regional, and local. The existence of such a hierarchic pattern
and the geographical distribution of the seal impressions indicate a well-
organized administration. Garfinkel's concept appears to gain support as

more and more impressions are turned up in excavations and in private collections.

Ornamented Personal Seals

In Judah, motifs connected to or depicting animals were very popular, particularly strong and powerful animals—roaring lions, lions attacking various animals, rams, galloping horses, running bulls, bull heads, gazelles, ibexes (running, standing erect, or grazing), grazing does, fighting cocks, various birds, etc.—but sometimes also an animal whose name matches that of the seal owner, such as *shu'al* ("fox"), *ya'el* ("ibex"), *orev* ("raven, crow"), and even *govai* ("locust"). N. Avigad pointed to the connection, in a few cases, between the animal emblem and the personal or family name of the seal owner. In most cases, however, such a connection does not exist, and animals with a name different from that of the seal owner are depicted, such as the fish emblem on the seal of "Menahem the son of Pagi" or a tortoise on that of "Ashyahu the son of *hwyhw*." Anyone who reads the biblical name lists or those mentioned in the ostraca or on seals can see that there are many personal and family names related to animals. These include almost all known animals of the country: besides those mentioned above, *zvi* ("stag, deer"), *gedi* ("kid"), and *shaphan* ("rabbit") occur, as well as animals that today would certainly be regarded as strange names: camel, donkey, owl, mouse, chicken, and even flea and locust. Surprisingly missing are names of well-known local fauna that one would have expected to occur, such as wolf, bear, leopard, and lion. Many plant motifs occur, but these are usually schematic: a tree branch, a palm tree, palmettes, lotus flowers, pomegranates, etc.

Besides the animal seals where both the seal owner's name and his emblem are depicted, there is a small group of nonepigraphic seals and seal impressions that depicts animals alone (a tradition that continues into the Persian period; see below). The motifs represented in these are identical with those appearing in the epigraphic seals. All, like the other material remains of the Judaean monarchy, are derived from the Phoenico-Israelite corpus of motifs. One of the most distinguished examples of this type of seal is the impression of a "galloping horse," three copies of which have been found at different sites in Judah quite distant from one another: one at En-Gedi, one in Jerusalem, and a third at Tel Azekah on the border of Philistia. More nonepigraphic impressions of this type are known in Judah, as, for example, one found in the royal palace of the Judaean kings at Ramat Raḥel, which depicts the old Phoenician motif of a lion jumping on a stag's back, another that de-

I.81 Judaean seals: galloping horse from En-Gedi and a griffin from Jerusalem

picts the figure of an ostrich, or a beautiful seal from Jerusalem engraved with the figure of a bird-head winged griffin. The date of this entire group can be surmised from the impression found at En-Gedi, a single-period settlement dated from the second half of the 7th century BCE until 582 BCE, as well as the one from Ramat Raḥel, dated to the same period. There can be no doubt that the people of Judah in this period were well acquainted with both the names of these seals' owners and their titles and status in the official hierarchy of the monarchy, and could identify them by their emblems alone.

The wide area from which the "galloping horse" impressions have been collected, over almost the entire region of Judah, attests to the importance of its owner. Indeed, a seal was recently published from an unknown site with the same galloping horse motif, which was also engraved "belonging to 'Ashiyahu servant of the king," and thus, perhaps, the identity of the official who utilized the galloping horse emblem has been discovered.

In the course of the 7th century BCE, many Mesopotamian motifs, mainly Assyrian, were added to the nonepigraphic seals, among them pagan motifs such as stars, the moon crescent, the sun disk, etc.

Most of the motifs in the inscribed Judaean seals that are not animals depict various cult emblems and objects; however, it is not clear if they retained their original cultic meanings or were utilized for purely ornamental purposes. Considering the fact that some of them also appear on other objects, it is plausible that here, too, they functioned as religious symbols. In this chapter of the history of Judah, most of the motifs were still derived from Egypt, either from Egyptian mythology itself or indirectly through the Phoenico-Israelite corpus of emblems. This is the same school of art that, in the previous Israelite period, produced the splendid ivory carvings found at Samaria and elsewhere.

These pagan cult emblems not only were clearly used by private owners but were engraved upon the seals of members of the royal family and all ranks of officialdom, including those of "the king's sons," "the king's servants," etc.

Among the Egyptian motifs, the figure of the four-winged beetle is especially common among the seals of Judah in the 7th century BCE, either alone or as a sacred symbol atop "the tree of life." In one case, it is even topped by a human head. The other variations of this motif, such as the winged sun disk or the rosette, also occur beside officials' names. A good example of these is the above-mentioned *ner'a* impression accompanied by the winged disk motif from En-Gedi.

Another common Egyptian pagan motif depicted on seals is the uraeus, or cobra, the emblem of royalty in Egypt. Its Palestinian version is usually depicted with four wings and the double crown. Also common is the ankh emblem, the Egyptian symbol of life, which we have already encountered on Phoenician gravestones. Another common motif depicts the infant-god Horus kneeling upon a lotus or papyrus plant, as well as a motif adopted from the typical headgear of the Egyptian god Amon (recalling that one of Judah's kings of this period was called Amon). Among the Egyptian motifs popular in Judah were the winged sun disk in its Egyptian version, the cow (Hathor-

'Astarte) suckling a calf, the Falcon-Horus wearing the double crown, as well as the figure of a monkey, which may have been connected with the Egyptian god Bes and his apotropaic cult. Others have rather complicated scenes, such as a sun disk with ram's horn pendant, uraei and three Osiris crowns flanked by uraei in the upper register, or a winged sun above the heads of the goddesses Bestet or Sekhmet with a wig. The use of all these motifs in Judah began earlier in the Iron Age, before the Assyrian conquest, when they appear incised on seals and in ivory carvings. Their use in Judah continued until its destruction.

The other major foreign artistic source of this period in Judah is the classic Phoenician "pattern book." These motifs were enormously popular in Judah and were used to decorate objects of art made of other materials, too: stone, shell, and metal (see below). Of these Phoenician motifs, especially numerous are the proto-Aeolic capitals and the "Phoenician palmettes," sometimes separately depicted, but usually one above the other as a schematic rendering of "the tree of life," sometimes with a pair of praying figures flanking the tree. Also common were the sphinxes and the griffins rendered in typical Phoenician fashion: winged and wearing a debased double crown of Egypt. Another motif depicts a hero wearing an Egyptian kilt and hairstyle, thrusting his spear into a griffin's throat; others are four naked winged women and pseudo-hieroglyphs.

Of the Mesopotamian-Assyrian motifs, which penetrated Judah during the Assyrian period, found on both nonepigraphic and inscribed seals alike, especially common was the motif of the winged sun disk in its Mesopotamian rendering; but there are others, such as the hero struggling with one or two lions or with other monsters; a priest standing before a classical Mesopotamian fire altar, stretching forth his hand in blessing; a human-headed legless scorpion with a long tail. Another motif recently found on the bullae of the "commander of the city" type, mentioned above, shows him receiving from his lord a bow and arrows: a local imitation of a well-known Mesopotamian motif.

Hebrew Incised Inscriptions on Judaean Pottery Vessels

The inscribed seals used by the monarchy's officials to impress jar handles (mainly the *lmlk* jars but sometimes other vessel types such as *pithoi*, water decanters, cooking pots, bowls, etc.) were employed at the time of the vessels' production and are all clearly a part of the administrative system of the Judaean kingdom. In contrast, an individual wishing to mark ownership of possessions could usually do so only at a later stage; i.e., after the clay vessel was fired, his name was engraved in the hard material, for rarely was it possible to mark the wet clay. Some of these incisions indicate vessel contents or its measure of volume. These incisions are usually found on water decanters, rarely on other vessels, such as, for example, an "Assyrian" bottle from Tel Batash. The letters incised on the pottery vessels are executed in a unique technique and they are known as "chiseled inscriptions" and are limited to the territory of the kingdom of Judah and perhaps even to the Jerusalem area alone, with perhaps the exception of one site, Tell Keisan east of Acco. There, for some reason, other Judaean finds were also recovered, such as *sheqel* and *nsf* weights. The accepted date for this script is from the late 8th century BCE to the destruction of the monarchy, but its total absence in Lachish III perhaps makes it possible to fix it more accurately to the 7th to early 6th centuries BCE. Sometimes figures such as human beings, birds, stars, and rosettes were added to the inscriptions. These may be interpreted as additional signs of ownership.

The incised texts usually include personal names, such as "belonging to Hanan, to Zidki," etc; but also more composite ones that denote the vessel's contents: *leYehezyahu yyn khl* ("blue-dark wine") or *leNatanyahu yyn nsk rb't* ("a quarter of libation wine"), etc. Other volume measures mentioned in these inscriptions are "half," "half for the king," *bat,* and "*bat* for the king." A recently published *lmlk* jar had a chiseled inscription reading *lmlk shmn shpr* ("to the king good oil").

JUDAEAN WEIGHTS AND MEASURES

IN COMPARISON WITH the Judaean *lmlk* seal impressions, only a small number of which can be attributed to the 7th century BCE, it is now clear that the various weights of the kingdom found at its sites were made and used only in the 7th to 6th centuries BCE, making it necessary to discuss these finds here, as well as new evidence for the kingdom's measures of volume.

In the many excavations conducted at Judaean sites of the 7th to 6th centuries BCE, many weights have been uncovered, mostly incised with numbers but sometimes bearing inscriptions. Most of these were carved from various types of stones (in many instances from a red Jerusalem stone). Their form is usually half-dome-shaped. Perhaps they started out as complete balls and were shaved in order to bring them to the precise weight intended, and thus

I.82 Weight in the form of a turtle

received their flat base. When the correct weight was achieved, the inscription or number, or both, were incised. There are also some bronze weights in the same dome shape, some of which are incised, others not. There are also a few bronze weights (and one of iron!) in the form of a rectangular cube, or even a trapezoid, bearing inscriptions or numbers similar to those on the previously described dome-shaped weights; also bronze weights in the form of various animals, some with incised numbers, others unmarked.

Both the metal dome-shaped weights and the cube-shaped ones were forms imitating Egyptian weights. Of the animal-shaped weights, some were local fauna such as stags, bulls, turtles, and frogs, while others were adopted from the Egyptian realm, including monkeys and water buffalo. It seems, however, that both types were adopted from the Egypto-Phoenician repertoire that was already present in Palestine several centuries earlier. During the 7th century BCE all over Palestine, but especially in Judah, new stone and bronze weights appear in the form of ducks or lions, shapes certainly taken from the weights of Mesopotamia or Assyria. Their weight standard was probably also based on the Mesopotamian one.

There is no doubt, however, that all these various weights were Judaean and were made according to standards fixed by the monarchy's administration. This conclusion is based both on their limited distribution and on the form of the numbers and inscriptions incised upon them. As to their distribution, they are found all over Judah in all its main regions: at Gibeon, Tell en-Naṣbeh in Benjamin; Jerusalem, Ramat Raḥel, and Beth-Zur in the hill country; En-Gedi in the Judaean desert; and in most of the towns on the western boundary of the kingdom, such as Gezer, Nebi Rubin, Meẓad Ḥashavyahu, Beth-Shemesh, Tel Batash, Azekah, Khirbet el-Qom, Tell Judeideh, and Lachish. They are also distributed among the Judaean towns of the Negev: 'Uza, Arad, Tel Malḥata, Aroer, and 'Ira. Their number is especially large in the major towns such as Jerusalem, Lachish, and Arad.

Several Judaean weights (more than twenty!) have also been uncovered in Philistia, five in the provinces of Megiddo, Samaria, and Dor, and three in the Transjordanian states (both Moab and Edom). Though there is no doubt that originally they were Judaean weights, we may perhaps assume, in the absence of other types of inscribed weights from all the rest of the Palestinian kingdoms of the period (i.e., Ammon, Moab, Edom, and Philistia), that during this period the Judaean weight served as the basic unit of measure for trade transactions among all these nations, as well as in trade with Egypt (see below), while trade with Assyria and Babylon was based upon Mesopotamian units of measure.

Indeed, like the "private" impressions of the Judaean officials impressed on the *lmlk* jars, we find, from time to time, personal names incised on various weights, perhaps as marks of ownership by these individuals, or possibly the names of the officials responsible for their accuracy. Of the latter, we shall mention here a weight from Lachish upon which the name Nedabiah was marked, and a weight from Nebi Rubin on which *leBarchi* was incised. One *pym* weight was inscribed *leZecharyahu Yair,* etc.

The Sheqel *Weights*

According to the Bible, the major weight standard in Palestine was based on the *sheqel.* In its entirety, the system included the following weights: the *kikar* or "talent," which was divided into 60 *maneh;* the *maneh* weight, which was divided into 60 *sheqels*; and the *sheqel* weight, which was divided into 24 (or 20) *gerah.*

In addition to the Bible, the *sheqel* weight is also mentioned in the period's ostraca. Based upon the inscribed archaeological finds and the actual weights, the *sheqel* system was indeed the major system of weights in use. At Tell Qasile, an ostracon was found (a surface find), inscribed "the gold of Ophir to Beth-Horon—*sh* 30," where the letter *shin* has been interpreted as *sheqel.* The date of this ostracon may be somewhat earlier than our period, but a recently published 7th century BCE ostracon mentions a donation of "silver of Tarshish—*sh* III" (i.e., three *sheqels*). The question arises whether the terms "gold of Ophir" and "silver of Tarshish" refer to places of origin or perhaps a standard of quality. At Meẓad Ḥashavyahu, two ostraca were found. On one appears the inscription *sh 4;* the other reads *sheq(el).* In the Arad Ostraca, too, the standard weight is the *sheqel,* usually abbreviated by

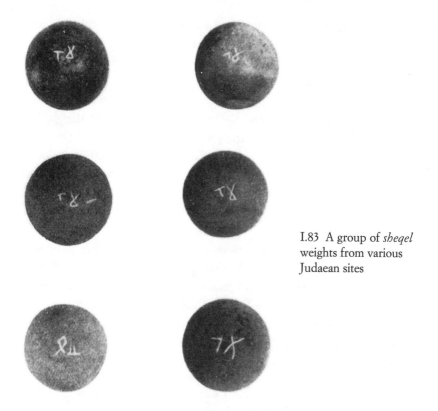

I.83 A group of *sheqel* weights from various Judaean sites

the first letter: *shin.* Also at Kadesh-Barnea the *sheqel* is mentioned on two ostraca with the hieratic sign *(sh).* There are more examples in the period's ostraca. It is noteworthy that in most cases the number of *sheqel*s is given in the ostraca using Egyptian hieratic signs in the same manner as they were incised on the Judaean weights themselves, except for the numbers 1 to 4, which appear as individual strokes.

Recently, new evidence has been found for the early use of a *sheqel* system in Israel even before its use by the Judaean monarchy. A bronze, dome-shaped weight was published with the word *sheqel* inscribed in full beside the number 1. Its weight is entirely different and much heavier from that of the Judaean *sheqel.* In the opinion of its publishers, it should be dated to the 8th century BCE, a period for which the standard weights are not precisely known.

Returning to Judah of the 7th century BCE, there are some weights originating in clear 7th to 6th century BCE contexts, upon which the word *sheqel* is inscribed in full. From the Shephelah region, either in Judah or in Philistia, there is a bronze weight in the form of a turtle. Its back is inscribed *peleg sheqel,* meaning "a fraction of a *sheqel,*" and on its belly appear the words *peleg rb't,* meaning "a fraction of a quarter" of a *sheqel* (it weighs 2.63 g.); such a weight is mentioned in the Bible (1 Samuel 9:8). Another weight from Samaria, also in the form of a turtle, is inscribed with the Hebrew word *ḥamesh* ("five") and should be interpreted as five *gerah,* also equivalent to a quarter of a *sheqel* of twenty *gerah* (2.49 g.). One weight from Samaria in the form of a cube is inscribed on one side "a quarter of a *sheqel*" and on the other "a quarter of *nsf*" (2.54 g.).

The other inscribed *sheqel* weights found in Palestine date, according to their archaeological contexts, from the period of the Assyrian conquest until the destruction of the First Temple, and all are weights issued by the Judaean monarchy. Approximately 170 have been found.

Most of these weights are inscribed with the symbol *(sh)* and with hieratic numbers. The symbol *(sh)* has been interpreted in various ways: Y. Yadin suggested that it is a schematic emblem of the Judaean kingdom. Another scholar, R. B. Y. Scott, believes that it is a symbol representing the Hebrew word *ṣeror* ("bag"); and there have been other proposals. When it became clear that all the numbers inscribed on these weights are Egyptian hieratic numbers, W. F. Albright's view gained acceptance, i.e., that the symbol γ represents the hieratic sign *sh,* a shortened version of the word *sheqel.*

More light has been shed by several inscribed weights: for example, two trapezoid bronze weights, one found at Gezer and the other in a private collection, bear additional inscriptions. On one, in addition to the usual hieratic number 2, the word *lmlk* ("to the king") appears. In the other, the word *lmlk* is incised side by side with the symbol γ. It is therefore possible to interpret the two inscriptions thus: "two *sheqel*s in the 'king's weight'" or in Hebrew, in the "king's stone," i.e., in the royal weight. And because their weight is similar to that of the rest of the regular *sheqel* weights elsewhere, it becomes clear that the rest of the *sheqel* weights, too, were made according to the "king's stone," or standard. Another weight, on which the letters *nun* and *lamed* survived with the number 1, was interpreted by its excavators as including a short version of the inscription "one *nesef lmlk,*" i.e., "one *nesef* of the king." And indeed its weight coincided with the average weight of the regular *nesef.* Another inscribed weight recently published, in the usual form of a domed stone of one *sheqel* weight, had an incised winged sun disk on its flat bottom; above appear the moon crescent and two stars.

As to the numbers inscribed upon the weights, it seems that the first to suggest the use of hieratic numbers in ancient Hebrew inscriptions was A. Noth (1927). But it was Y. Aharoni who first interpreted the numbers on the weights as Egyptian hieratic ones. This suggestion leaves a serious difficulty: for the *sheqel* weight system, as deduced from the weights found to date, is based on the numbers 1, 2, 4, 8, 16, 24, and 40 (all these weights are indeed represented in the finds), while the Egyptian hieratic numbers incised on them reflect a different system: 5, 10, 20, etc. The problem was solved by Scott, who showed that one 8-*sheqel* weight, the basic weight of this system, is equivalent to one Egyptian *deben* weight (subdivided into ten *qedet*), as the following table shows:

4 *sheqels* = 5 *qedet* (or half *deben*)
8 *sheqels* = 1 *deben* = 10 *qedet*
16 *sheqels* = 2 *deben* = 20 *qedet*
40 *sheqels* = 5 *deben* = 50 *qedet*

This adaptation of a local weight system to the Egyptian one encouraged trade, especially with Egypt, but not only with the Egyptians, for they traded in this period with almost all countries of the ancient Levant and their weight system was recognized and used in many other countries, too.

As already shown, the basic weight of the *sheqel* system was the 8-*sheqel* unit. It differed from the Egyptian decimal system and from the Mesopotamian base-6 system. We believe that this basic difference may indicate its origins in a third, Canaanite-Phoenician system, utilized in the region since the late second millennium BCE.

The average weights of the *sheqel* system appear to be as follow: 1 *sheqel* = 11.332 g.; 2 *sheqels* = 22.161 g.; 4 *sheqels* = 45.239 g.; 12 *sheqels* = 129.145 g.; 16 *sheqels* = 184.769 g.; 24 *sheqels* = 274.330 g.; 40 *sheqels* = 454.55 g.

The Gerah *Weights*

In addition to the weights of the *sheqel* system, some dome-shaped or rectangular stone and bronze weights were also found in Judah, upon which only one Egyptian hieratic number appears. These weights are smaller in size and weight than the *sheqel* unit and are—as has been convincingly shown by G. Barkai—fractions of the *sheqel* unit, which the biblical sources called *gerah* (cf. Exodus 30:13; Leviticus 27:25; Ezekiel 45:12). The average weight of one *gerah* is 0.566 g., a weight that fits—according to Barkai—the biblical definition that one *gerah* is the twentieth part of a *sheqel* (according to the weight of 11.39 g. for a *sheqel,* the value of one *gerah* should therefore be 0.569 g.).

I.84 A group of *gerah* weights

This system is now represented by almost seventy weights with the following values: 2, 3, 4, 5, 6, 7, 8, 10, and 11 *gerah* (all stone except for one of bronze), which are also inscribed with hieratic numerals. This system was employed to weigh small amounts of unusually expensive materials, such as incense, spices, or silver and gold. The many weights of this system that have been found do not necessarily lead one to assume a division of the *sheqel* into only twenty *gerah,* for there are some *gerah* weights that may be ¹/24 of the Judaean *sheqel.* This problem has not yet been satisfactorily solved.

Why did the Judaean monarchy adopt Egyptian hieratic letters and numerals on its official weights? The sophisticated Egyptian administrative system always served as an example for the various administrative systems in Palestine, not only in this period but in much earlier ones as well. There are scholars who believe that in this case, too, Egyptian influence continued uninterruptedly from the Late Bronze Age and is reflected in all local weight systems in Palestine until the first millennium BCE. This means that the Judaean system of the 7th century BCE followed a road paved long before.

The Nsf, Pym, *and* Bqʿ *Weights*

Together with the regular system of the *sheqel* and the *gerah,* which allowed weighing down to a fraction of a gram (not a single inscribed weight of the heavier *maneh* or *kikar* units has been found), we find in the various Judaean sites of the 7th century BCE an additional weight system which includes three different weights, the names of which are inscribed in full: *nsf, pym,* and *bqʿ.* This system was perhaps added because the *sheqel* and *gerah* did not answer all needs. This additional system was intended perhaps for other purposes,

I.85 *pym nesef* and *beqʿa* stone weights from Lachish

and may have been exclusively Judaean, not in use, or less connected with the prosperous international trade of the age. In any case, it, too, was developed by the Judaean monarchy at the same time as the *sheqel* and the *gerah* system.

These weights were also made of stone (in many cases, the same red Jerusalem stone), are distributed all over the territory of the Judaean monarchy, and have been found at nearly every site at which weights of the other system were found, both in Judah and in Philistia. Most of them were dome-shaped, but there are a few rectangular bronze weights, too.

The first weight, the *nsf,* is not mentioned in the Bible, but the meaning of the name in many Semitic languages is probably "half." About fifty *nsf* weights are known today and their average weight is 9.659 g. There is also a weight that indicates a fraction of the *nsf,* for it is inscribed with the words *revʿa nsf,* i.e., "a quarter of a *nsf,*" and another one, mentioned above, is incised with the number 1 and the letters *nun* and *lamed.* This inscription has been interpreted by A. Ben-David as "one *nsf lmlk,*" i.e., "one *nsf* of the king," and it weighs 9.515 g., nearly the average weight of other *nsf* weights.

The next, somewhat smaller weight is the *pym.* The average weight of the fifty known examples is 7.815 g. The *pym* is mentioned in the Bible only once (1 Samuel 13:51), in the context of a much earlier period, and the meaning of the name is obscure. There is, however, one *pym* weight with base incised "lZechario Ya'ir," probably the name of its Judaean owner.

The third, and smallest, weight in this system is the *bqʿ*. About thirty examples are known, and weigh an average of 6.003 g. The name *bqʿ* is usually inscribed on the stone weights in full, but sometimes only its first letter appears. The *bqʿ* is the only weight unit of those mentioned in the Bible whose value is given there: half a *sheqel*. But because the known examples range between 6.003 and 6.11 g., they cannot be the half *sheqel* weight described in the Bible. It is most probable that all three weights constitute parts of a separate system. It should be mentioned that one of the *bqʿ* weights had an incised rosette on its base. As already pointed out, this was the last emblem of the Judaean monarchy. This emblem probably replaced the word *lmlk* ("belonging to the king") or the royal emblem engraved on the *sheqel* weights, to indicate a royal guarantee of accuracy. About five of the weights of the *nsf, pym,* and *bqʿ* system were made of bronze in the form of small cubes.

In the excavations at En-Gedi, two round, flat lead weights were uncovered. Their weight was never recorded but they had the rosette emblem engraved on both sides. It is possible that they were one of the first attempts to create weights in the shape of a coin, on which the royal Judaean emblem was stamped for accuracy. Neither of these weights has been published.

There is also some evidence that this royal weight system was continued in name, if not in standard, into the Persian period. At Tel Shuqaf, located in the Shephelah, a large stone weight was found, inscribed *nsf* in square Aramaic letters typical of the Persian period. This weight was many times heavier than the usual *nsf* of the period of the Judaean monarchy. We know nothing about the standard or system to which it belonged.

Many attempts have been made to unify the different Judaean systems into one coherent whole. Recently, R. Kletter claimed that the *nsf, pym,* and *bqʿ* system was issued in order to complete that of the *sheqel* and *gerah*. He suggested that these weights should be placed between the *sheqel* and the *gerah,* for there is not a single *gerah* weight that consists of more than ten or eleven *gerah* units, while at the same time we lack almost entirely weights indicating *sheqel* fractions. Careful examination of these two weight systems and their exact relationships does not—in our opinion—support Kletter's proposal, or any of the many other proposals that reached similar conclusions. Therefore, there must have been two independent systems operating in Judah: (1) the *sheqel* and the *gerah* system, inscribed with hieratic numbers and mentioned in the Bible; (2) the system of weights inscribed *nsf, pym,* and *bqˁ*. In any case, all were utilized in the Judaean monarchy from the 7th century BCE until its destruction.

The Units of Volume

In addition to the inscribed weights, excavations in Judah have uncovered new information about the system of volume measurement practiced in the kingdom during the 7th century BCE.

As described in the Bible, the system of volume measurement was as follows:

Dry measures	Liquid measures
1 *homer*	1 *kur*
2 *lethekh*	10 *bat*
10 *ephah*	60 *hin*
30 *seah*	720 *log*
100 *omer-esaron*	
180 *qav*	

Some of the names of these units are of Mesopotamian origin, while others are Egyptian. There are also a few that must have been of local Palestinian origin. Together, they functioned as a single, compact system. It is quite difficult today to convert the old biblical measures to modern ones. Usually, the complete vessels found have no inscribed volume indications. A few volume names were found either on the walls of jars and jugs, the capacities of which could not be accurately reconstructed, or on ostraca alone.

In the past, various scholars have tried to establish the amounts of ancient Judaean volumes by measuring either the complete *lmlk* jars or jars that were impressed with the royal rosette seals, which they interpreted as the *bat lmlk* ("*bat* of the king") volume. But according to recent finds at Lachish, Tel ʿErani, Tel Batash, Tel Malḥata, and other sites in Judah where complete *lmlk* jars have been uncovered, their exact volumes seem to differ one from the other. Thus, this idea has been generally abandoned.

At the same time, archaeological finds from 7th century BCE Judah do offer the same names of measures that appear in the Bible, while adding a few new ones and enriching the overall picture of the system.

Both the Bible and the archaeological finds provide evidence for the old custom of using volume units based upon "natural" measures. In the Arad

Ostraca, for example, such measures as "2 donkey load" occur. Elsewhere, units of measure reflect the names of various clay vessels: "1 pot of wine." It is not clear if the writers meant here to count fixed units of volume or simply counted the number of vessels. If this is compared to the evidence from Samaria dated to the period in the kingdom of Israel, this custom was in practice there, too, for in the Samaria Ostraca quantities are also listed by units such as "*nevel* ('leather flask') of old wine" or "leather flask of ointment oil." The same custom is also found among the other nations of Palestine: in Phoenician ostraca from Dor, the units are counted by *kadim* ("jugs"), and at other sites, amounts are counted by vessels called *grbn* or *lagin*.

Another custom mentioned in the Bible and reflected in archaeological finds of the 7th century BCE is counting volume units without mentioning the name of the unit itself, a name probably well known to all. This, too, is a custom that continued from a much earlier period. Examples are found in the Bible (1 Samuel 25:18; 2 Samuel 16:1) and in an ostracon found at Tell Qasile, dated to the 8th century BCE, which mentions "a thousand and one hundred oil." In the 7th century BCE, this same custom is represented on a jar found at Kadesh-Barnea which is inscribed "*sh* 5," which was interpreted by the excavator as "5 (units) of *shemen* ('oil')." At Arad, the measure of *hezi* ("half") is mentioned, while at Tel Sheva, that of *hazi lmlk* ("half in the king's measure") appears, while the name of the unit is not mentioned. There are also some clay decanters from Judah on which only numbers are inscribed— 3 or 4—also without mentioning the unit's name. These were interpreted as a third or a quarter of a *hin,* for another decanter from this period carries an inscription that says "libation wine, a quarter."

All other volume measures uncovered in the excavations at Judaean sites reflect the biblical system with some previously unknown additions. In the Arad Ostraca, the units *homer* and *bat* are mentioned, but here the *homer* unit, which was usually used for dry material, is used for wet, as "a full *homer* of wine." The *bat* unit is always mentioned there by its first letter alone: "*b* I III wine" (one *bat* and three *hin* of wine). Among the hieratic letters appearing in the Arad Ostraca are a few interpreted by Y. Aharoni as the units *kur* and *lethekh.* Another Egyptian unit is mentioned there that is not found in the Bible but was frequently used by the local Judaean population: the *hakat,* which is similar to the measure of the local *ephah.* As has already been shown here, Egyptian measures were well known in the Judaean kingdom.

The *bat* also appears inscribed on some shards belonging to this period. One was uncovered at Tell Beit Mirsim, in central Judah, including only the word *bat.* Two additional ones were uncovered at Lachish and Tell en-

Naṣbeh. Here, they are inscribed *bat lmlk* ("*bat* of the king"—or "*bat* in the royal standard"). Among the liquid units, too, the *hin* and the *log* are mentioned in a Hebrew inscription found at Susa in Iran, but this inscription probably originated in Judah.

That this system continued even after the destruction of the Judaean monarchy, at least in the use of the names of the units of measure, can be deduced from ostraca and inscribed jars dated to the Persian period and even later. An Aramaic ostracon from Tell el-Farʿah (S) dated to the Persian period was inscribed with the word *bat*. Others mention the dry units of measure, the *seah* and *qav*, in their usual short formula: *s*1 *q*III, which means: one *seah* and three *qav*. At Arad, some of the Persian-period ostraca record them in a similar way: *s*4 *q*3, i.e., four *seah* and three *qav*.

The Judaean Cult

Introduction

DURING RECENT YEARS, many archaeological finds connected with the everyday cult practiced in Judah during the late 8th century BCE and until its end have been uncovered. We shall base our discussion here on the archaeological finds only and not the biblical examples. The conclusions reached are, in a way, simplified and one-dimensional, for with one or two exceptions, at Kuntillet ʿAjrud and Deir ʿAlla, no religious literature or religious texts have survived. Most of the relevant material encountered in the various excavations in Judah belongs to what may be called Yahwistic paganism. It consisted mainly of the remains of sanctuaries, *bamot* ("open sacred high places"), as well as altars and figurines or other vessels that were in use in those sanctuaries. It is interesting to observe, concerning the use of all of these cultic artifacts, that there was hardly any difference between their function in the cults of the various nations of Palestine, including that of Judah. The major differences between the cults of the various nations of Palestine in this period were expressed mainly in the different names of the chief national gods: Yahweh in Judah, Qos in Edom, Milkom in Ammon, Baʿal in Phoenicia, etc.

In Judah, there was always the monotheistic central cult practiced in the Temple of Jerusalem by its priests and preached by the various prophets, and the kings of Judah made efforts from time to time to centralize worship in Jerusalem. They did it in the days of Hezekiah, perhaps in the early period of Manasseh, and certainly during the reign of Josiah. Regarding the quantity of the remains of the cult objects related to Yahwistic paganism from this period in Judah, it seems that the success of efforts to promote the monotheistic central cult was not very great. This pagan cult was very common in Jerusalem and the rest of Judah during this entire period until the very end of the monarchy, in marked contrast to the impression obtained by reading the Bible alone.

The Sanctuaries

It may be assumed according to recent archaeological finds that in Judah, many sanctuaries dedicated to the national god were erected at various sites. Such a sanctuary was called "the house of Yahweh." The most important among them and the central one was without doubt the one on the Temple Mount in Jerusalem. The Bible itself attests to the existence of additional sanctuaries at Bethel, Shiloh, and Beersheba (1 Samuel 1:24). Another sanctuary was erected during the 7th century BCE in Bethel by one of the surviving priests from the kingdom of Israel who initiated the new deportees into the Yahwistic cult. And as the writer of 2 Kings 17:41 points out, perhaps in irony: "those nations worshiped the Lord, but they also served their idols."

A complete Judaean sanctuary was uncovered by Y. Aharoni at the Judaean fortress of **Arad**. Although erected long before the 7th century BCE, many scholars tend to attribute its last stages (Strata VII–VI) to this period, from the beginning of the 7th century BCE until the destruction of the kingdom, while others tend to believe that it was destroyed earlier. In either case, this temple may serve as an example for all other Judaean temples and sanctuaries of the period. The Arad sanctuary contains three parts—'*ulam,* *hekhal,* and *debir*—and was oriented east-west. From the central unit, the *hekhal,* one stepped up three steps to the holy of holies, to a raised platform, upon which one of its m*azzebot* ("stelae") was found in the destruction level; two additional ones were built into the wall of the holy of holies and were thus not in use during the sanctuary's last period. On the third step, two limestone incense altars were found, on the upper part of which were remains of a burnt material, probably incense. In the courtyard, another large altar was uncovered. Its dimensions were 2.5 x 2.3 m. and it was built of clay bricks and unworked stones and covered with a heavy layer of plaster. On the left side, a small room was excavated, which contained a clay incense stand. Aharoni thought that the plan of the house and its contents make clear that "it was a Yahwistic-Judaean temple."

Besides the Arad sanctuary, some additional cult platforms were uncovered in other Judaean fortresses of the 7th century BCE. I. Beit-Arieh, for example, recently reported the existence of cult platforms approached via several steps near the gates of the Judaean fortresses of 'Uza and Radum. Another *bamah* was previously reported by Y. Aharoni near the gate of the large Judaean fortress of Tel Sheva, where a large four-horned stone altar was found. Recently, a similar installation was uncovered in the Judaean fortress of **Vered Jericho.** The excavator, A. Eitan, claims that it, too, was a cultic *bamah*. Some stone stairs were also found near the gate of the fort of Meẓad Michmash, on the kingdom's north border, which were also thought to lead to a sacred platform, or *bamah*. All these new finds strengthen Aharoni's assumption that all the kingdom's border fortresses had cult places. In a large number of these fortresses, numerous figurines, altars, and other types of cult objects were recovered. Such cultic installations were not unique to Judah, for in the destruction level of the late 8th century BCE caused by Tiglath-pileser III in the Aramaic town of Bethsaida at the northeast corner of the Sea of Galilee, as at Israelite Dan, an identical complete platform and steps were recently uncovered, surmounted by a stone stela.

The existence of a Yahweh sanctuary at Lachish, the second city in importance in Judah, is indicated in the reliefs from Sennacherib's palace: a pair of large cultic stands is shown being removed as war spoils by Sennacherib's soldiers after the city was sacked by them. These stands belong to a type known in smaller examples from many of the country's towns.

Concerning the Judaean cult in the 7th century BCE and during the last stage of the monarchy, the archaeological finds are quite heterogeneous: there are many occurrences of the name Yahweh in the ostraca found at Lachish and Arad, as well as in ostraca from other Judaean sites. It appears in texts of oaths and blessings, such as "I have blessed you to Yahweh"; "May Yahweh let my lord hear tidings of peace"; "May Yahweh bless you in peace"; "May Yahweh give my lord pleasant tidings"; "May Yahweh give you prosperous tidings"; or of a warning (not to open a tomb, etc.). There is also an inscription found at Khirbet el-Qom in Judah from the same period mentioning the name of the divine couple that was worshiped by the locals: Yahweh and Asherah, exactly as they appeared in the earlier Israelite sanctuary at Kuntillet 'Ajrud. This Judaean inscription was found in a tomb at Khirbet el-Qom (perhaps the town of Makkedah in the central Hebron Hills). The inscription says "Blessed will be Ariyahu to Yahweh and his Asherah." At the nearby site of Beth Loyah, another Judaean tomb inscription was uncovered which mentions Yahweh as "the Lord of Jerusalem and the Hills of Judah."

The very existence of sanctuaries dedicated to Yahweh in various towns outside Jerusalem was not peculiar to the 7th century BCE. In addition to the sanctuary at Kuntillet ʿAjrud, dated to the end of the 9th century BCE, in the Mesha Stela, which is even earlier, the Moabite king tells that he had taken (from the city of Nebo) the vessels of Yahweh and had laid them before his own god, Kemosh. This means that in the Judaean city of Nebo, before it was sacked by the Moabites, there was a sanctuary dedicated to Yahweh.

"The house of Yahweh" is also mentioned in many inscriptions of the period; for example, in one of the Arad Ostraca it is said of someone that "he is in the house of Yahweh." A recently published Judaean ostracon reads "pursuant to the order to you of Ashyahu the king to give by the hand of Zecharyahu Silver of Tarshish to the house of Yahweh three *sheqels*"; in an inscription on a small ivory pomegranate, N. Avigad reconstructed the fragmentary inscription: "sacred to the priests of the house of Yahweh." The meaning of the word *qodesh* ("sacred") will be discussed below. As to "the house of Yahweh" mentioned in the two inscriptions, it is true that the scholars who published them believed that the reference is to the Temple in Jerusalem. However, in consideration of the information presented above, this need not be the case. "The house of Yahweh" may be located in any settlement within Judah or anyplace settled by Judaeans. It should be added that in the sanctuary of Arad, the names of two well-known priestly families, Meremoth and Pashhur, were found, who probably served in the local "house of Yahweh."

Generally, the priests who served in the Yahweh sanctuaries traditionally received their posts from previous generations within their families, passed from father to son. Only rarely were they appointed by the ruler. There are a few seals in which only the title *cohen* ("priest") is added. One of them recently published is that of "Hanan the son of Hilqiyahu the priest," who may have been the father of a high priest in Jerusalem. From a somewhat earlier period, the last days of the Israelite kingdom, comes a seal that mentions an Israelite priest who was active in the Yahwistic temple at Dor. It reads: "belonging to Zechario the priest of Dor" (cf. "Amaziah, the priest of Bethel," Amos 7:10). And there is also the seal of "Miqnayahu the servant of Yahweh," who served in the cult of one of the many Yahweh temples.

Cult Objects

In the temples of the Judaean monarchy, as well as in the period's strata and tombs, many cult objects have been uncovered. These can generally be divided into two classes. One, of which there are only a few examples, is com-

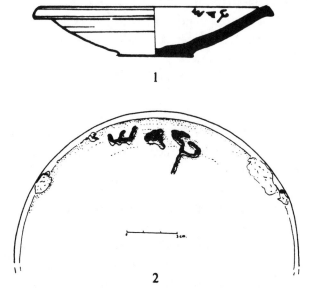

1

I.86 Votive bowl
inscribed with the word
qodesh ("sacred")

2

posed of ordinary clay vessels for daily use which turned into sacred ones after being dedicated with inscriptions incised or written on them. The majority of these is bowls, but there are also a few other vessel types. The other kind of cult objects is vessels that, according to their form and character, are specifically intended for sacral purposes.

Of the vessels of the first type, there are a few bowls and one krater in which the word *qodesh* ("holy") was incised after firing, sometimes in full and sometimes only represented by one or two letters such as *qsh, q,* and *sh.* Such vessels were found in both Israel (Hazor) and Judah (Arad, Tel Sheva, and Tell Beit Mirsim). They date to the late 8th and 7th centuries BCE. The word "holy" indicates that the contents of the vessels were dedicated to the sanctuary at each of these sites. This was probably done by the priests of the various temples.

This hypothesis is now strengthened by the contents of two inscriptions. In Ekron in Philistia, some inscribed jars were found with the words *qodesh le ashtoret* ("sacred to the goddess Ashtoret"). On other jars, the word *lamaqom,* which means "to the temple," is incised. The second inscription is on the ivory pomegranate mentioned above, which was mounted at the end of a short scepter and inscribed with the words "sacred to the priests of the house of Yahweh." Those four words summarize the entire story of all the *qodesh* inscriptions. It should be noted that recently, more dedicatory inscriptions have been found, which have not yet been satisfactorily explained, such as the inscription *le-akhikha* ("for your brother"). Regarding the ivory pomegranate, this fruit became sacred as an emblem of fertility among all the country's nations during the Canaanite period. Many Canaanite cult objects depicting pomegranates have been found in Judah. Their holiness was recognized both in Judah and elsewhere in the country. Many pomegranates of various types have been uncovered in Edomite and Philistine sanctuaries (see below), as well as in those of Judah: they have been found at Jerusalem, Ramat Raḥel, Beth-Shemesh, and elsewhere. The best representation is undoubtedly the pomegranate bowl found in a Judaean tomb of the late 8th century BCE at Tel Ḥalif.

As to the ivory pomegranate with scepter mentioned above, it is a well-known object in the Palestinian cultic repertoire from the Late Bronze Age (examples occur at the Fosse Temple at Lachish and in the tombs of Tel Nami, among others). It passed, virtually without changes, first to the Phoenician cult and later to that of the rest of the Palestinian nations and remained in use until the end of the Iron Age. Such scepters are known from many Judaean sites and are made of ivory, bone, metal, and glass. There is no apparent difference between the Judaean scepters and those found in the sanctuaries of the other nations of the region. There was therefore no particular difficulty in transferring such an object from one sanctuary to another—i.e., from the service of one deity to another—exactly as was done by Mesha king of Moab.

The other type of cult objects that were certainly in use in the Judaean sanctuaries and in those of the other nations of the country was the standard cult objects that included clay figurines, anthropomorphic and zoomorphic vessels, stands, chalices, goblets, and stone altars.

Judaean Clay Figurines

The pagan cult in Judah, whether of foreign (Egyptian or Phoenician) origin or belonging to the local national Judaean cult of Yahweh and 'Astarte, is represented by a rich and heterogeneous body of finds, particularly common during the late 8th to the early 6th centuries BCE.

The clay figurines, which we shall examine below, are found all over Judah: from the Benjamin region in the north at Bethel, Tell en-Naṣbeh, Gibeon, Ramot, Mozah, Jerusalem, Ramat Raḥel, Beth-Zur, and Tell Rabud, to Jericho and En-Gedi in the east and Gezer, Beth-Shemesh, Batash, Azekah, Tell Judeideh, Tel 'Erani, Tel Ḥalif, Lachish, Tell Beit Mirsim, and other sites to the west. In the southern part of the country, they are found at Tel Sheva, Tel Masos, Tel 'Ira, Aroer, and Arad. They are found in large set-

I.87 Judaean clay "pillar figurines" of ʿAstarte from Jerusalem

tlements and in small fortresses such as Khirbet et-Tuwein. In short: at all towns from all parts of Judah.

In Judah, unlike other kingdoms of the period, most of the figurines represent females and are of the type known as "pillar figurines," i.e., figurines whose heads are mold-made, and are all nearly identical, bearing the same somewhat stylized expression. The body is solid and handmade, in the shape of a small column to which exaggerated breasts, supported by the goddess's hands, were added by application. This deity is usually identified with ʿAstarte, the fertility goddess. Sometimes the goddess is depicted playing a tambourine or holding a dove—her traditional symbol in all periods. She is seldom found with a hollow round body made on a wheel in the Phoenician type referred to above as "bell-shaped." Even rarer are those figurines made as flat impressed plaques that represent similar figures.

Another popular type is the 'Astarte figurines with "pinched" heads, sometimes called "bird-headed figurines." In this case, the head is also made by hand rather than formed in a mold. These figurines, too, portray a standing female supporting her breasts with one or both hands.

It should be pointed out that the figurines from Judah, like all the rest, were painted in bold colors: white, black, red, etc. A few figurines have survived with paint intact, showing that eyes and hair were emphasized by painting and that sometimes jewelry was added around the neck. The best examples of painted figurines came from the City of David in Jerusalem. There are also 'Astarte figurines from Judah made of different materials, such as ivory and bone.

As mentioned above, the distribution of the 'Astarte figurines shows that their cult was practiced all over the kingdom. Summarizing his recent comprehensive study of these Judaean figurines, R. Kletter writes: "if we adopt the heartland of Judah concept [i.e., Judah within the borders described above], then 822 figurines (ca. 96%) were found within this area. This number is so high that there is only one possible conclusion: that these pottery figurines are Judaean." It should be noted that out of the 822 figurines found in Judah, at least 405 came from Jerusalem itself, from various excavations there, including those of Kenyon, Y. Shiloh, B. Mazar, and E. Mazar in the City of David, and those of N. Avigad and others in the Upper City. Since Kletter's study (1996), many more figurines from Mesopotamia have been published: female and male, some found a very short distance from the Temple Mount itself.

Though found by the dozens at all the sites of Judah enumerated above, including Gibeon and Jerusalem, the male figurines are not well represented in the reports and literature. Now that we have some statistical data from the cult remains found in other parts of the country representing those of the Phoenicians, Ammonites, Edomites, and Philistines, it seems that there, too, male deities constituted an important part of the assemblage. Here again, Judah did not differ significantly from its neighbors.

The Judaean male figurines here, as those in the other kingdoms, appear in two forms. The more complete figurines depict horsemen who, according to one interpretation, are connected with the cult of "sun chariots" mentioned in the Bible, but according to a more plausible explanation, they represent the figure of the warrior god that appears in the cult of all other nations of the country: Phoenicians, Ammonites, etc. (cf. Isaiah 13:4: "the Lord of hosts is mustering a host for war"). The "Judaean horseman" is stylistically unique: the head is sometimes executed in the "pinched" form of

I.88 Lachish, Judaean male
deity with a "bird face"
riding a horse

the "bird heads," which is also used for some of the heads of the Judaean
'Astartes (see above). The horse, too, has a characteristic head: long and cut
straight at its end, a head with no analogy among the horse figurines of other
nations. The bodies of the Judaean horsemen and horses are solid and handmade.

Another type of male head is one that is covered with a round "turban."
This type is not familiar to us in its entirety, and there are only a few dozen
examples. The turban here is very similar to the one worn by the Judaeans of
Lachish, who are depicted departing the town in Sennacherib's relief. Similar turbans are carried by some of the male Israelite figurines from Megiddo,
as well as some of the Ammonite stone sculptures (see below). If we compare
the Judaean male figurine heads with the more complete Ammonite examples, both were apparently depicted with hands at their sides or with one
hand raised in blessing.

Who were the deities represented by these Judaean clay figurines? We can
only guess. They might represent one of the foreign deities whose cult was
practiced in Jerusalem, perhaps the Phoenician Ba'al. But, more plausibly,
they represent the national Judaean god, Yahweh, and his consort, 'Astarte,
for all these figurines—as we have seen—are Judaean and only Judaean.

The combined archaeological evidence of references to the name of Yah-

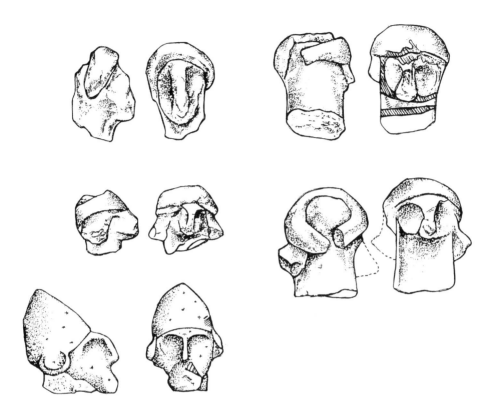

I.89 Heads of Judaean male clay figurines from Jerusalem

weh (and his 'Astarte) in ostraca and other Judaean inscriptions of the period, and the fact that many clay figurines are typical only of Judah, bring us to the inevitable conclusion that between foreign pagan practices and pure monotheism, most of the material collected here belongs to what may be called Yahwistic paganism. It includes remains of sanctuaries, *bamot* ("open sacred high places"), as well as altars and figurines and other vessels in use at these sanctuaries. There appears to be hardly any difference between the function of these artifacts in the Judaean cult and in those of the other Palestinian nations. The only real difference is the name of the chief national god, which was Yahweh in Judah. In the background, there was always the monotheistic central cult practiced in the Temple of Jerusalem in the days of Hezekiah, perhaps in the early days of Manasseh, and certainly during the reign of Josiah. Regarding the distribution of the cult objects of Yahwistic paganism from this period, it seems that those promoting the monotheistic central cult did not really succeed and Yahwistic paganism remained very common in Jerusalem and the rest of Judah throughout the entire period until the end of the monarchy.

It is true, however, that while in most cases it is possible to interpret the Judaean figurines in this manner, there are some figurines of a different nature: for example, a figurine from Beth-Shemesh which carries an open lamp of the late Judaean type on its head. (Figurines of deities, both males and females, carrying lamps on their heads have been found to date to the same period among the Phoenicians as far away as Cyprus and the western colonies, and in the Transjordanian kingdoms.) A molded plaque figurine was found at Tel 'Ira in the Beersheba Valley; it probably represents a hermaphrodite figure, with female breasts and phallus, holding a tambourine. We know of two other hermaphrodite figurines in ancient Palestine. One is Ammonite, its head surmounted by a quadruple spiral symbol, and it is bearded and pregnant. The second one is Edomite, found at a site in Transjordan; it also holds a tambourine and carries a lamp on its head. Although these three figurines represent different formal types, they nevertheless share hermaphroditism and remain a mystery to us.

The last type of Judaean cult objects to be dealt with here is the anthropomorphic and zoomorphic vessels. In addition to the clay figurines described above, and in parallel to the cultic finds among the other nations of Palestine during the 7th century BCE, many clay stands have been uncovered at the various Judaean sites. These, decorated with human figures, are hollow clay vessels made in the shape of regular Judaean vessels but open toward the base or at the top. Usually, bearded males are portrayed, but sometimes female figures are depicted. Unique among these vessels is a published small juglet found in the City of David in Jerusalem. Two sides were impressed in a mold and depict two faces of 'Astarte, with her peculiar Judaean headdress. This juglet is reminiscent of the Phoenician-style "face" vessels. Such anthropomorphic vessels were a permanent feature in the repertoire of cult objects of the period's Judaean sanctuaries, and many have also been uncovered in the cultic centers of neighboring states. Unique anthropomorphic vessels have been found in Judah at Tell en-Naṣbeh, Lachish, Beth-Shemesh, and Tel 'Erani. The tradition of such vessels is an old one in Palestine and was probably derived from the Canaanites.

Many other types of 7th century BCE cult objects found in Judah were also common among the other nations of Palestine, such as clay figurines of animals, especially horned animals such as bulls, stags, and deer, but birds, mainly pigeons, are also portrayed. There are also numerous figurines of

I.90 A clay "face" vase from Jerusalem depicting the head of ʿAstarte

horses (which in some cases may be fragments of figurines depicting mounted horsemen). At Lachish, Tel Sheva, and elsewhere were found small clay models of furniture: sofas, chairs, and stools. These were placed as votives in sanctuaries or graves by the Phoenicians, Ammonites, and Edomites. Among the other clay figurines were also models of sanctuaries and many "shakers," round closed clay vessels in which some small loose stones were sealed. These may have served as musical instruments in cult ceremonies.

Altars

We have already dealt with the large horned stone altar intended for sacrificing animals, and one made of brick from the sanctuary of Arad. In the holy of holies of the Judaean temple at Arad were also found two limestone incense altars and a stone stela. The altars are of the long type, usually equipped with four small horns on the four corners. This type first appeared long before the 7th century BCE, and many have been uncovered in the territory of the kingdom of Israel (Dan, Megiddo, and Tel Qadesh), as well as in ancient Judah (Gezer, Lachish). This type continues in Judah into the 7th century, too, as indicated by finds at Arad and Gezer, and was also found in Jerusalem in the destruction layer attributed to the Babylonians near the

Temple Mount. It is mainly attested, however, by the many altars uncovered at 7th century BCE Philistine Ekron, discussed above. These altars were not always located in sanctuaries but were sometimes left in private houses and workshops. In Judah, as in Edom and other regions, there was a clear change from the use of this type of limestone horned incense altar to smaller altars (of both stone and clay), which resemble a small box standing on four feet. These were probably introduced here by the Assyrians, and Assyrian prototypes exist. They occur at all of the important Judaean sites of the 7th century BCE and come to replace the previous horned type totally during the Persian period (see below).

Additional stone artifacts with a long prior history used in the Judaean cult of the 7th century BCE are the stone stelae (*mazzebot*). At the Arad sanctuary, a large stone stela was found standing in the back of the holy of holies. It was about a meter high and its sides were smooth and painted red. It was found in the last destruction of the sanctuary, generally attributed today to the Babylonians. Beside it were found two more stelae built into the wall of the room, which were probably not in use during this last phase. The use of stelae in Judah and Israel was common during previous periods and undoubtedly continued old Canaanite traditions (an example is the stela found by Y. Aharoni in the temple of Lachish, dated to the 10th century BCE). The line of stelae found at Dan in the temple adjacent to the city gate is also dated to the 7th century BCE. Additional stelae have been found in Aram, Philistia, Edom, and elsewhere.

A unique and surprising find concerning another Judaean religion, the monotheistic religion practiced in the Temple of Jerusalem, was uncovered at Ketef Hinnom in Jerusalem. These were two silver charms inscribed with the text of the Priestly Blessing (Numbers 6:24–26), the oldest existing evidence for the use of this text, which is still recited today by observant Jews. These artifacts also provide proof that the form of the text had already been fixed by this time. There is still some debate concerning the exact date of the find, which was written either in the later part of the Judaean monarchy or somewhat later, during the 6th century BCE, but this issue is not pertinent to our presentation.

THE JUDAEAN POTTERY

THE POTTERY OF Judah in the 7th and early 6th centuries BCE has special characteristics in regard to variety of types.

The typical jar forms are small and elongated holemouth jars with rounded bases, no necks, and no handles. Their rims are either horizontal or turned inward; they are thick, sometimes plain or wavy. Another common type is a jar with short straight neck and sack-shaped body. A third jar type has a narrow elongated body and four handles from the shoulder to its outer wall. This is a late form of the previous *lmlk* jars. Its handles bear only the rosette seal impression, rather than the *lmlk* seal impression, which was the last emblem of the Judaean kingdom and was typical only of the late 7th to early 6th centuries BCE. As has already been pointed out, these impressions have been uncovered at most Judaean sites, and are first-class criteria for the chronology of this period. Some complete jars of this type were unearthed in the south at Tel 'Ira and Tel Malḥata in the Beersheba Valley. At Tel Malḥata, they were found together with an East Greek jug dated by an expert to ca. 600 BCE. In the west, they were found at Lachish as well as in the City of David in Jerusalem. A few original *lmlk* jars also survived into the 7th century BCE (cf. above, the discussion on these seal impressions), and were found together with the rosette ones at the westernmost sites of the Judaean kingdom, including Lachish, Tel Batash, and Tel Sheva. During this period, a type of jar with flat shoulders, most typical of the coastal region, is frequently also found in western Judah. These jars first appeared in an earlier period, but they do not occur in western Judaean towns before the 7th century BCE.

Of the jugs, the regular decanters are very common in this period. These have a carinated shoulder, a sack-shaped body, and a handle from the neck to the shoulder. They appear in a variety of sizes ranging from a wide medium-sized jug to a small, almost bottle-shaped slim one; some are unburnished, while others have a delicate red burnish. That these vessels were used for wine is proved by the inscriptions found on some of them mentioning several kinds of wine: "dark wine," "libation wine," "smoked wine," "black raisin wine," etc.

The cooking pots of Judah in this period differ from their predecessors. They are round with a short neck and with inverted rim. Another type has a long neck with a single ridge at the center.

Bowls and kraters are numerous. Some are small, very flat, and well burnished on their inner side, with regular concentric circles made on the wheel. The kraters are large and deep, usually with four handles.

Most important among Judaean pottery forms to appear in this period is the Judaean high-based lamp, which is unique to the later part of the period. It can be used as a good indication for dating, almost as good as the royal rosette seal impression. It also continues until the early 6th century BCE.

In addition to the vessels peculiar to Judah (though some of them penetrated the eastern Philistine towns), it seems that the typical ceramic assemblage in Judah in this period also included other shapes such as the Pseudo-Assyrian vessels including carinated bowls and various types of bottles, some undecorated East Greek vessels like the flat-based heavy bowl (mortarium), which penetrated into almost all Judaean sites, and the loop-handled amphorae found in its western region. There are also small decorated East Greek ceramic vessels found throughout the kingdom, including Jerusalem, Ramat Raḥel, En-Gedi, and Tel Malḥata. Less frequent are the Cypriot imports of the period, but these occur everywhere in Judah and include the entire large decorated White Painted Cypriot far found in the Judaean fortress of Tel 'Ira, in the Beersheba Valley. In the southern part of Judah, there are also some Edomite pottery vessels as well as late Negebite wares.

This mixed pottery assemblage reflects that during the 7th century BCE, with the development of the Philistine cities, their prosperity, and the growth of trade between them and Judah, the farther west a Judaean site is located, the more obvious the influence of the coastal-Philistine ceramics on it assemblages. A similar influence in the opposite direction is also apparent. In some western border towns of Judah, such as Tel Batash (Timnah) and Tell eṣ-Ṣafi, it is difficult to distinguish between the Philistines and the Judaeans, in making an attribution of their ceramics.

THE GLYPTIC ART OF THE KINGDOM OF JUDAH

AT NEARLY ALL Judaean sites, ivory and bone objects decorated in the familiar Phoenician-Israelite style have been found. Some were certainly engraved during the 8th century BCE and survived into the 7th. One of the best-known objects in this category is the ivory head of 'Astarte in its Judaean version, found in the Bethlehem region. But many artifacts for daily use are also known, such as decorated bone handles rendered in the motif of the "fallen leaves," found at sites such as Tell en-Naṣbeh and Gezer. A bone stopper for a bottle in the form of a stag's head was found at Lachish (resembling another one found at Philistine Ashdod); the decorated ivory "bird nest" vessel depicting a praying male and the ivory depicting a sphinx from Beth-Zur are both noteworthy. At Aroer in the Beersheba Valley, an ivory game board decorated with a proto-Aeolic capital was found, which has a close parallel at Tell Jemmeh in Philistia.

A special find comes from the City of David in Jerusalem, where, in the destruction level of the city caused by the Babylonian army in 586 BCE, a small group of partly charred wood carvings was encountered. Like the more usual ivory carvings, these were used as decorations on wooden furniture. The motifs are identical to those found on the ivories. This find demonstrates that the traditional Phoenico-Israelite style, though its material changed from ivory to wood and bone (perhaps, as we have seen, due to problems in ivory supply), continued in the kingdom of Judah until its end.

In addition to the ivory and bone artifacts unique to this period, and quite common, are engraved shells of the *Tridacna squamosa* type, commonly found in the waters of the Red Sea. Above, we designated them as Phoenician-style cosmetic containers. They have been found at all the important Judaean sites, including Jerusalem, Bethlehem, and Arad.

The third type of engraved cosmetic vessel is the engraved limestone bowl, the rim of which was decorated with geometric designs and painted or filled with small colored stones, in the same tradition as the ivories. These first appeared in the period before the arrival of the Assyrians but continued to the end of the Judaean kingdom. Similar decorations, mainly of concentric circles executed with a drill, were found on simple local round shells and on bone objects. No examples of Ammonite-type large stone sculpture have come to light in Judah.

Assyrian influence in 7th century BCE Judah is attested in only a few finds. The most distinguished one is a small model for a wall painting from the royal Judaean palace of Ramat Raḥel. It depicts a ruler sitting on his throne, imitating a style frequently used in portraying Assyrian kings. Clearer Assyrian influence is visible in the art of seal carving, discussed above. It may also be perceived in pottery production and in the cult. As we have seen, small Assyrian-influenced stone incense altars replaced the old four-horned variety. New types of weights in the shapes of ducks and lions also appear during this period, imitating Assyrian-Mesopotamian prototypes.

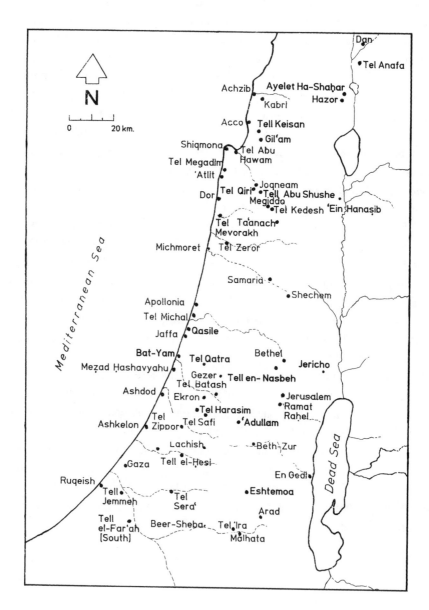

I.91 Sites containing imported Early Greek vessels

· Chapter 7 ·

THE GREEK PENETRATION

THE IMPORT OF GREEK POTTERY

The initial stage of the import of Greek pottery to the Phoenician coast in general and the Palestinian coast in particular began long before the Assyrian conquest and continued through the Assyrian period. The date of the earliest Greek pottery imports is steadily being pushed back by current research (even as far as the late 11th century BCE, when Greek pottery vessels occur at Tyre, at Tel Hadar on the east side of the Sea of Galilee, and recently at Tel Dor), and Greek imports are now well known from the 10th to 8th centuries BCE. We shall not discuss these vessels here.

Large-scale trade between the east coast of the Mediterranean and Greece started only during the late 8th century BCE, close to or immediately after the Assyrian conquest of the Phoenician coast. Many examples of Late Middle Geometric (mid-8th century) and Late Geometric types (760–700 BCE), mostly from Euboea and its major sites, such as Eretrea and Lefkandi, have been found (at Tyre more than twenty-five vessels were recovered). The decorative motifs utilized are adopted from various stages of Corinthian prototypes. At Tel Dor, in the present writer's excavation, a Greek bowl of Late Geometric type was found in clear stratigraphic context on the floor of the city gate of the Israelite kingdom period, destroyed by Tiglath-pileser III in 733/2 BCE. From that time on, many more imported Greek vessels arrived on the Palestinian coast. During the 7th century BCE and somewhat later, Corinthian vessels arrived, too, but the main imported types of that period arrived from the East Greek islands. The vessels are divided into two major types: 1. Decorative vessels, some from mainland Greek sites in Euboea and

I.92 Tel Seraʿ, Corinthian
aryballos from a pit in Stratum V
(7th century BCE)

I.93 An East Greek jug
from Tel Malḥata
(ca. 600 BCE)

from Corinth, but the majority from the East Greek islands, including Samos, Kos, Chios, Knidos, Lesbos, Rhodes, etc., as well as from the coasts of Cilicia and west Anatolia, where some vessels were produced in unique decorated styles such as that of the Wild Goat. This period is known in the history of Greek culture as the "Orientalizing period" (730–630 BCE). 2. Plain vessels for daily use, which include wine amphorae, large jars with basket handles, heavy large bowls (mortaria), and even Greek elongated cooking pots and the first closed lamps.

These vessels had a strong influence on the local east Mediterranean potters. "Greek lines" are characteristic of the local coastal pottery of the 7th and early 6th centuries BCE all along the shores of Phoenicia, Palestine, and Philistia. But their influence expanded far beyond the coastal region, penetrating many inland sites in the 7th to 6th centuries, both Judaean settlements and those of the Transjordanian states. It is today quite impossible to consider Palestinian 7th century BCE pottery assemblages without looking at Greek imports. These East Greek and Corinthian vessels are known today from all coastal sites from north to south, and have been found in particularly large numbers at Phoenician sites, including Al-Mina, Ras el-Basit, Tell Sukas, Byblos, Sidon, Tyre, and Sarepta, and along the Palestinian coast at Kabri, Tell Keisan, Acco, Tell Abu Hawam, Megiddo, Jokneam, Tel Qiri, Dor, Tel Michal, Meẓad Ḥashavyahu, Ekron, Ashdod, Ashkelon, Batash, Haror, Seraʿ, Tell el-Ḥesi, Tell Jemmeh, Ruqeish, and elsewhere. Many have also been found at interior sites in the Galilee (Tel Dan), in the Samaria Hills (the town of Samaria), and in Judah (Tel Malḥata). Many were also, as already pointed out, local imitations that developed from Greek prototypes. Let us take as an example one of the most common types in Palestine: the mortarium bowl. The earlier type with a flat base already occurred in 7th to 6th century BCE contexts, both in Palestine and at sites along the eastern coast of the Mediterranean, and continued to exist until the Persian period. It is noteworthy that in the course of counting all the mortaria finds of the early type, it became clear that most sites from which these vessels originate lie near the East Greek islands of Rhodes and Samos and western Anatolia (sites in Lydia, Caria, and Lycia), whence they spread to Cyprus and the early Greek colonies along the eastern Mediterranean coast: al-Mina, Tell Sukas, Meẓad Ḥashavyahu; and the Greek colonies in Egypt: Daphne and Naukratis. It may be concluded that the origin of this type should be traced to the East Greek sphere. It was later adopted by local potters. The large basket-handle jars, or amphorae, probably had the same history and the same origin, but in their case it is still disputed whether they originated in the East Greek islands or in Cyprus. There are similar disputes concerning other types of Greek-inspired vessels, such as the well-known al-Mina vessels from the Phoenician coast.

The same assemblages often contain other western types, some of quite large dimensions, that no one hesitates to designate as genuine Cypriot imports because of their peculiar texture and painted decoration. Beautiful examples of these vessels are the White Painted Cypriot jar found at Tel 'Ira in a clear 7th century BCE context and the large, richly decorated 7th century BCE Bichrome jug, which was recently found in one of the Achzib tombs.

Ordinarily, Greek pottery vessels constitute only a small part of the large assemblages of local vessels; however, a find at the site of Meẓad Ḥashavyahu on the coast north of Ashdod is an interesting exception. Here was uncovered the richest and most important concentration of East Greek pottery vessels of the late 7th century BCE along the entire Palestinian coast. Included are both fine decorated ware and undecorated vessels for daily use: a consid-

I.94 A Cypriot amphora from Tel 'Ira, late 7th century BCE

erable number of Greek cooking pots (also known from such sites at Batash, Ashkelon, Mikhmoret, Shiqmona, and Kabri as single examples; see below). These finds, combined with literary evidence, indicate that during this early period there were two kinds of Greek inhabitants in the eastern Mediterranean: 1. Greek traders who settled in existing cities. The clearest traces of such settlement have probably been uncovered at Al-Mina, Tell Sukas, and Tabat el-Hamam in Phoenicia and at Acco, Dor, Jaffa, Tell Jemmeh, and Ashkelon in Palestine. 2. The Greek mercenaries who were posted in military forts, such as the Judaean fort at Meẓad Ḥashavyahu mentioned above, or the three fortresses excavated in Egypt: two in the Egyptian Delta (Daphne and Naukratis) and another close to Tell el-Ḥer in northern Sinai, near the Pelusiac branch of the Nile, recently excavated by E. Oren. All these fortresses contained a large variety of Greek vessels.

As to the date of these Greek vessels, recent excavations at Ashkelon, Ekron, and Batash, as well as those at Meẓad Ḥashavyahu, have revealed sealed destruction layers attributable to the Babylonian conquests of the late 7th century BCE (mainly 604–603 BCE). The pottery originating in the destruction debris of the four sites above was recently studied by J. Waldbaum, who found that it included shards of imported East Greek and Corinthian pottery, including Ionian cups, Wild Goat style *oinochoae,* cooking pots, amphorae, and Corinthian vessels. While the Greek vessels from all four sites consist of types generally dated to the 7th century BCE, there has previously been little independent historical evidence to confirm the accuracy of this dating, for the chronology of early Greek pottery is based on its presence at Near Eastern sites with problematic stratigraphy. Some scholars, questioning the traditional chronology for Greek pottery, have tried to lower its dates. The new, securely dated material from Ashkelon, Ekron, and Tel Batash, supported by evidence from Meẓad Ḥashavyahu, Kabri, Tell Keisan, Malḥata, and other sites, assures the earlier old dates.

THE GREEK POPULATION IN 7TH CENTURY BCE PHOENICIA AND PALESTINE

THE ARRIVAL OF Greek traders to the region during the 7th century BCE was first well attested in the excavations of the site of **al-Mina,** located at the mouth of the Orontes River. Prior to World War I, L. Woolley uncovered ten occupation strata that he divided into three major periods. The first, including Strata X–VII, started in the late 9th century BCE and continued to the end of the 8th, i.e., up to the Assyrian occupation. After a short gap, the buildings of Period B, dated to the 7th century BCE, were erected (Strata VI–V). The third period dates to the Persian period. In the strata of the first period were uncovered Greek vessels that were brought from Euboea, the Cyclades, and Cyprus, in addition to local wares. In the second period were found even more Greek vessels, but their place of origin is distinct: the Greek pottery from Euboea virtually disappears and is replaced by East Greek vessels that originated in Rhodes, Lesbos, Chios, and Samos, as well as some Corinthian vessels.

At nearby **Tell Sukas,** which was excavated in the 1960s by P. J. Riis, a similar picture emerged: after a few Phoenician strata that continued until the first quarter of the 7th century BCE, three consecutive building stages were unearthed that the excavator designated as Greek. These contained many pottery vessels and other Greek finds, as well as Greek sanctuaries and cult objects. A Greek cemetery of the same period was also excavated nearby. Riis believed that this settlement existed from 675 to 498 BCE, when it was destroyed by the Persians, perhaps because of its participation in the great Ionian revolt against them.

Similar results were also reported—as far as we are able to understand them today—from the excavations conducted by Braidwood at **Tabat el-Hamam,** another coastal town in this region. New excavations along the Phoenician coast from **Ras Ibn-Hani** and **Ras el-Basit** and south to **Tyre** and **Sarepta,** the finds from which were discussed above, provide further confirmation.

The general impression obtained concerning Greek mercantile settlement during the 7th to 6th centuries BCE along the Phoenician coast, and probably also in Palestine, is of a strong Greek element within the Phoenician towns. In no case did Greeks constitute a majority among the local inhabitants (with a possible short-term exception at Tell Sukas, according to its excavator), as they did in the Greek colonies of the western Mediterranean. Their presence in the eastern Mediterranean had the character of *enoikismos,* i.e., a Greek community within a Phoenician one, or more or less peaceful coexistence with an already existing local population. There now appears to be a solid foundation to W. F. Albright's claim that in the 6th century BCE many trade centers were established along the coasts of Egypt, Palestine, and Syria. We can now add that those centers were established during the 7th century BCE.

The evidence for **Greek military presence** in 7th century BCE Palestine, especially on its southern borders with Egypt, comes from two sources: the results of the excavations at the sites of Meẓad Ḥashavyahu and Migdol; and written evidence.

Meẓad Ḥashavyahu, as was shown above, was a fortress dated to the late 7th century BCE, situated approximately 2 km. south of Yavneh-Yam. The remains of the fortress were first investigated by J. Naveh and later by R. Reich. The fortress covers an area of about 1.5 acres, and its form follows the natural contours of the hill on which it stands. The fortress is L-shaped and composed of two rectangles: a larger rectangle containing a courtyard and rooms adjacent to the wall, and a smaller rectangle consisting of three rows of houses flanking two streets. The wall of the fortress was built of bricks on stone foundations with buttresses along its facade, projecting from the wall. The gate complex, including the guardrooms and towers, were built of dressed stone. Included among the finds was a large amount of East Greek pottery. Much of this pottery was decorated in the Middle Wild Goat style, dated to 630–600 BCE. At Meẓad Ḥashavyahu, it appeared in large quantities. There were also ordinary household wares such as amphorae, cooking pots, lamps, and cups. On the basis of this pottery, the excavator concluded that the site was occupied by soldiers of Greek origin, probably mercenaries, who preferred to use their own pottery, to which they had grown accustomed. Herodotus (2.152,154), relates that Pharaoh Psamtik I (664–610 BCE), founder of the 26th Dynasty, hired Greek and Carian mercenaries. It seems likely that other contemporary rulers used Greek mercenaries as well and that the soldiers stationed at Meẓad Ḥashavyahu were hired by King Josiah of Judah. The fortress was apparently destroyed during Pharaoh Necho's campaign in 609 BCE, the same year that Necho defeated Josiah at Megiddo. While some scholars have suggested that this fort belonged to the Egyptian king and that the Greeks here were in his hire, not a single Egyptian find was uncovered in the two excavations conducted here.

The results of the second excavation, at site T-21 in northern Sinai, conducted by E. Oren, unearthed a similar Greek fort. The site is located in the outskirts of the eastern Delta, between Tell el-Ḥer and Pelusium. Here was uncovered a huge square fort fortified with strong brick walls built in Egyptian style, covering an area of 10 acres. Two types of pottery vessels were recovered here (the excavator counted three, but it has already been pointed out that the mortaria and basket-handle jars are of East Greek origin and not Cypriot): (1) Many Attic vessels and vessels from the East Greek islands of Chios, Samos, and Lesbos, some decorated, as well as many amphorae, basket-handle jars, and mortaria; (2) Egyptian vessels from the period of the

26th Saite Dynasty. The excavator identified the site with biblical Migdol (Jeremiah 46:14; Ezekiel 29:10) and interpreted the finds as the remains of a military fort on the Egyptian border manned by Greek mercenaries (according to Jeremiah, there may have been some Judaean soldiers at this garrison, too). In the same region, several kilometers west of Migdol, a new site was recently excavated by a French-Egyptian team. Called Qedua West, this site also produced much Greek and Egyptian pottery of the same Saite character and was probably a part of the same line of border forts. These forts were conquered in the days of Pharaoh Necho II in 609 BCE, probably during the initial stage of his campaign to Carchemish, and before his arrival at Gaza (Herodotus 2.152).

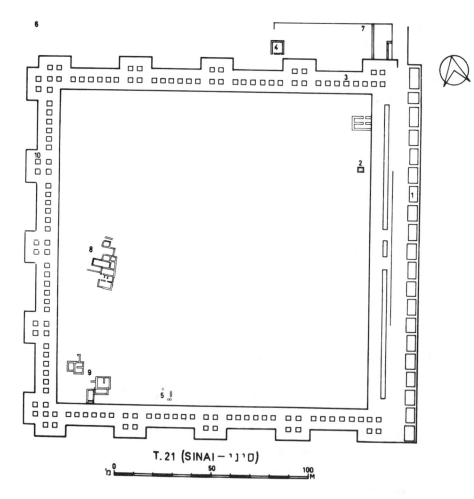

T. 21 (SINAI — סיני)

I.95 Migdol (site 21 in north Sinai), plan of Saitic fortified complex

I.96 Migdol, East Greek amphorae from the islands of Samos and Chios

The findings at Meẓad Ḥashavyahu and Migdol led some scholars to assume the existence of a cluster of fortresses in the Judaean kingdom partly manned by Greeks, especially during the reign of King Josiah. A. Mazar, summing up the results of his excavation at Tel Batash on the western border of Judah (and not far from Meẓad Ḥashavyahu), pointed out that the latest of the Iron Age strata at the site (Stratum II) should, in view of the resemblance of its pottery to that of Meẓad Ḥashavyahu, be regarded as a fort town of Judah related to Josiah's effort to annex parts of the coastal territory with the help of Greek mercenaries.

The other evidence for the presence of Greek mercenaries (mainly from Cyprus and Anatolia) in Judah and Philistia comes from written sources. The story of these mercenaries in the army of Pharaoh Psamtik mentioned in Herodotus was already told above. In the Bible, too, mention is made of the *ludim* who served in the Egyptian army (Jeremiah 46:9). Y. Aharoni, who published the Hebrew ostraca from Arad dated to the same age, pointed out that in many of them, people called *kittiyim* are mentioned as recipients of the supplies. He suggested that these people were probably mercenaries of Aegean origin, from Kition in Cyprus, and this is, so he believed, the first evidence we have that in this period there were Aegean-Greek mercenaries in the service of the kingdom of Judah. At Arad, no decorated Greek pottery was discovered, but a complete vessel dated to 600 BCE was uncovered at nearby Tel Malḥata, and mention was already made of an entire large, decorated, Cypriot White Painted jar unearthed in a Judaean fort near Tel 'Ira. It is natural that this pottery would be more common on the coast than in Judaean Negev fortresses. However, even the ostraca do not necessarily prove that the *kittiyim* lived in Arad, only that they passed by the fortress on their way to more southerly forts, perhaps those lying on the border itself.

Y. Yadin accepted Aharoni's view that the *kittiyim* were Greek soldiers stationed in the garrison at Arad, and suggested that one of the inscribed bowls found at Arad Stratum VI (7th century BCE), in which the name Arad was written eight times, was actually written in Greek. If so, this would be the earliest Greek inscription found in Palestine so far (the other early Greek inscriptions found in the country are not before the Persian period; see below).

Recently, Y. Garfinkel again proposed that the *kittiyim* were indeed Cypriot mercenaries from the city of Kition, for, in addition to Arad, their name also occurs at Kition itself. He also suggested that another people mentioned in the Arad Ostraca, the *krsym,* were also from the west. The information concerning the Kerosites is fragmentary and scattered over some 250 years, and it is not yet clear whether they were autochthonous Cypriots, East Greeks, or of some other origin. Their appearance in the Arad Ostraca dated to the end of the 7th century BCE is the earliest reference to them. Not until the middle of the 5th century BCE do they again appear on an ostracon originating in the Achaemenian military colony of Elephantine in southern Egypt, as well as in an even later graffito found in the temple of Abydos in Egypt. Finally, the Kerosites are mentioned in three inscriptions from Cyprus dated to the first half of the 4th century BCE. It now appears that the very distribution of the two names through Cyprus, Palestine, and Egypt perhaps justifies Garfinkel's suggestion.

Recently, new evidence has come to light that the Greek language might have still been in use among the Philistines of the Late Iron Age until the end of the 7th century BCE. The one example comes from the monumental royal dedication inscription from Ekron, discussed above, in which the title of the goddess is read as *potnia,* which is the common Archaic Greek word for "divine." This new 7th century BCE inscription strengthens the argument for Philistine ties with the Greek world and, in fact, makes it the earliest evidence (besides the Arad bowl) for Greek having been spoken in ancient Palestine. The very existence of the Philistines along the coast during this period encouraged Greek settlement. Another recently published piece of evidence should be mentioned: several ostraca found at Tell Jemmeh published by J. Naveh. In these ostraca, also dated to the 7th century BCE, many non-Semitic names are mentioned, and Naveh points to the fact that they may be the names of either Philistines or other Greek-origin people (Ionians, Carians, Lydians, etc.), who may have been employed either by the Assyrians or even by the king of Gaza himself.

From this combined evidence of both written documents and archaeological remains, it appears that, even before the arrival of the Assyrians, but mainly during and after their period of domination, there was Greek penetration into Palestine by traders and mercenaries. No discussion of the archaeology of Palestine of this period can ignore them, and in any case, their presence here seems to reflect somewhat more than the results of regular trade relations alone, as was recently suggested by J. Waldbaum.

· Chapter 8 ·

EGYPTIANS IN PALESTINE IN THE 7TH CENTURY BCE

INTRODUCTION

A separate chapter should be dedicated to the intensive Egyptian activity in Palestine during the 7th century BCE, especially in Philistia but also in the southern part of Judah.

The story of Egyptian activity in these regions is actually divided into two parts: (1) the period of the Assyrian domination in Philistia (734–640 BCE); (2) the period from the retreat of the Assyrians to the coming of the Babylonians (640–604 BCE).

In the first period, Egypt, led by the Nubian 25th Dynasty, tried at least twice to send its army to Philistine kingdoms to prevent their occupation by the Assyrians. The first time an Egyptian army was sent was in 720 BCE, under the leadership of the Egyptian *tartanu* (so in the Assyrian document) Reʿu to assist Ḥanun the king of Gaza in his war against Sargon. The Assyrians and Egyptians met near Raphia; the Egyptians were defeated and driven away. The city of Raphia was destroyed and its inhabitants were deported. The second time was when the Egyptian army led by Pharaoh Shabtaka came to help Tyre, Judah, Ashkelon, and the rebels of Ekron in 701 BCE. Sennacherib's army engaged the Egyptians near Elthake (Tell e-Shalaf?), defeated them, and pushed them back to Egypt. The story of the relations between the two countries during the climax of the Assyrian empire, the days of Esarhaddon and Ashurbanipal, included the campaigns of the two Assyrian monarchs to Egypt itself and Egypt's occupation (674–663 BCE).

At first, Assyria attempted to rule through its army and the local Egyptian administration, leaving the Egyptian princes on their thrones. Later the Assyrians raised the status of the rulers of Sais, Pharaohs Necho I and Psamtik I, to near independence and even helped them to subdue their rivals. Psamtik became an ally of the Assyrians, who appear to have given up their domination of Egypt.

The second chapter in the relations between the two empires started ca. 640 BCE, with the retreat of the Assyrians, first from Philistia and later from the rest of Palestine. In Egypt, Psamtik I (664–610 BCE) was still their ally. The Assyrian retreat was immediately followed by a massive Egyptian invasion of Philistia, and according to Herodotus (2.157), Psamtik laid siege to Ashdod, which lasted twenty-nine years until he captured the city.

At this time (some believed earlier—for the Saite Dynasty was supported by the Assyrians from the beginning), a treaty was made between Egypt and Assyria. N. Na'aman suspects that the Assyrian retreat from Philistia and the rest of the coastal region of Palestine was the result of an Egyptian-Assyrian agreement, which also brought the Egyptian army to the rescue of the Assyrians twice: first, in 616 BCE under Psamtik, during the war against Babylon, and once again in 609, under Pharaoh Necho II (610–595 BCE), in the same year that Josiah king of Judah opposed him at Megiddo after the annexation of all of Philistia (Herodotus 2.159; Jeremiah 47:1–5). The Egyptian army stayed in Syria till 605 BCE and then, beaten and chased by the Babylonians, retreated to Egypt. Through the years from the death of Josiah until the coming of the Babylonians, Egyptian officials ruled both Philistia and Judah. The first Babylonian army invaded Philistia in 604 BCE and captured Ashkelon. In 603 BCE, the Babylonians conquered the rest of the Philistine cities and destroyed them.

EXCAVATIONS AND STRATIGRAPHY

THE STUDY OF the results of excavations in Philistia shows that the retreat of the Assyrians and their replacement by the Egyptians left clear traces in all major Philistine cities. It seems that even if there was an agreement between the Assyrians and the Egyptians, it was not always accepted by the Philistines themselves.

But before studying the archaeological picture in the Philistine towns, it should be pointed out that some authorities still believe that one of the important pieces of evidence for Egyptian military presence in Philistia is the fortress of Meẓad Ḥashavyahu near Yavneh-Yam, which we previously attributed to Judah. These authorities assume that the Greek mercenaries in the fort served under the Egyptians at the time of the lengthy siege of Ashdod rather than under the Judaeans. But this assumption ignores finds in the fort such as the Hebrew letter and ostraca as well as the Judaean weights, and even more important, the complete lack of any Egyptian finds. Interpretation of these finds clearly supports the fort's attribution to Judah.

At **Ashdod,** Stratum VII (the period of Assyrian domination) came to an abrupt end. This destruction was attributed by the excavator, M. Dothan, to Pharaoh Psamtik. Stratum VI was the period of the Egyptian domination in the city (630–603 BCE), and it was brought to an end by the Babylonians.

At **Ashkelon,** where a well-built and planned city of this period was uncovered (see above), the excavator does not specify whether it existed through the entire 7th century BCE or only its last phase. In any case, all of the numerous finds uncovered there belong to the Babylonian destruction level of 604 BCE. This contained many Egyptian and Greek artifacts (see below).

But most of our information is derived from five recently excavated sites: Ekron, Tel Batash, Tel Haror, Tel Sera', and Ruqeish.

At **Ekron,** two strata of this period were excavated. Stratum IC is the city described above, erected and supported by the Assyrian regime and becoming a flourishing town. The next stratum, IB (630–603 BCE), was rebuilt with no signs of prior destruction and continued its predecessor. The new city is inferior in almost every respect: the city gate is smaller, the various constructions are weaker, the oil production centers in the industrial area shrank in both number and capacity. Among the finds are many Egyptian artifacts (some of them dated much earlier), including an inscribed stone *sistrum,* parts of stone sculptures, jewelry, including a gold uraeus (part of an Egyptian crown), many ivory carvings, some of considerable size, faience, shells, and even a scarab of the 26th Dynasty. Many Greek vessels were included as well. This stratum was destroyed in 603 BCE by the Babylonians.

The period of the Egyptian occupation of nearby **Tel Batash** (Timnah) is not entirely clear. Being a Judaean town on the Philistine border, it was severely damaged by the Assyrian armies headed by Sennacherib in 701 BCE (Stratum III). The next Stratum (II) was a flourishing one that is attributed by the excavators to the entire 7th century BCE, i.e., under both Assyrian and Egyptian domination, without apparent difference between the two. In this period, as we have shown above, the material culture of the city was divided into Judaean and Philistine components. This stratum was also destroyed by the Babylonians in 603 BCE.

Things are different at the three sites excavated by E. Oren in the territory of the kingdom of Gaza: Tel Haror, Tel Sera', and Tel Ruqeish. At **Tel Haror,**

I.97 Ekron, part of carved ivory elephant tusk representing a figure of an Egyptian goddess or princess from Temple Complex 650; 7th century BCE

the Assyrian city was built, as we have seen, by the Assyrian administration on a large scale, surrounded by strong fortifications (Stratum G-4), and in this stratum many Assyrian finds were uncovered. The next stratum, G-3, represents the last fortified city of the Iron Age and is still Assyrian. This settlement was destroyed by conflagration in the mid-7th century BCE and is attributed by the excavator to the Egyptian 26th Dynasty campaigns against Philistia.

Nearly identical stratigraphy was found in **Tel Seraʿ**. Stratum VI was the flourishing Assyrian town discussed above. The date of Seraʿ Stratum V is similar to that of Haror G-3, and was also destroyed in the mid-7th century BCE. The town of **Ruqeish,** erected by the Assyrians as a harbor town (Karu) in the late 8th century BCE, was badly hurt by the Egyptian occupation. The

I.98 Tel Seraʿ, Egyptian statuette of Sekhmet, Stratum V, 7th century BCE

status of this trade center deteriorated and the city's fortifications went out of use.

The overall picture obtained from excavations in Philistia shows that the Egyptian conquest of the region, partly accomplished by force and destruction (Ashdod, Seraʿ, Haror, and later also in the coastal strip held by Judah: Meẓad Ḥashavyahu) and partly by other means (Ashkelon?, Ekron, and Batash), brought about an obvious decline in the economic status and prosperity of Philistia. The final blow and complete destruction of the Philistine cities, including the deportation of its citizens, was carried out by the Babylonians in 604–603 BCE. This destruction is well attested in all excavations (see below).

The Finds

IN ADDITION TO the destruction levels caused by the Egyptian attacks on the Philistine cities and the decline in economic activity in the region, the

Egyptian presence is not clearly reflected by Egyptian pottery vessels in Philistia.

The short Egyptian domination of this part of Palestine, however, is clearly reflected in the relatively rich finds from Ashkelon excavated by L. Stager, and at Ekron. Finds from Ashkelon include many Egyptian clay vessels and even more finds of art and cult objects. These include vessels for daily use, such as alabaster bottles and Nile shells that served as cosmetic containers for women, bronze figurines depicting Egyptian deities (Osiris, Hathor, Horus, Bestet, and many others), and faience beads worn around the neck for apotropaic purposes, many of which depict the figure of Bes. A unique find was the group of seven Egyptian bronze *situlae* (bottles) featuring the Egyptian god Min, found in the remains of a wine shop where an engraved bronze offering table depicting bread and libation flasks was recovered. There can be no doubt that the Egyptian influence on the material culture of Ashkelon at the time of their domination there is clearly visible. At other Philistine sites, too, Egyptian artifacts of this period are quite common: we have already described the assemblage of Egyptian artifacts found at Ekron and a few scarabs belonging to the 26th Saite Dynasty that were found at other coastal sites. In fact, there is only one actual Egyptian monument of the period that survived along the Palestinian-Phoenician coast: this is a part of a stela of Pharaoh Necho found at Sidon. Egyptian military presence in the Palestine coastal region was probably partly represented by various Greek mercenaries.

In addition to Philistia, another Palestinian region in which Egyptian influence is quite visible during the 7th century BCE is the Negev of Judah. Here, it is reflected in the administrative system and particularly in the local system of measures of volume and weights. At Tel Haror, for example, a jar inscribed in the local Philistine script bears the Egyptian ankh with four Egyptian number 8 incisions. This is but one example. Cubic bronze weights from Ashkelon are exact replicas of contemporary Egyptian weights.

In the Negev of Judah at the Judaean fort of Kadesh-Barnea, a few contemporary ostraca were found, the most important of which is inscribed with six lines of hieratic numbers and measures. The numbers are written in lines, from 1 to 10, from 10 to 100 in tens, from 100 to 1,000 in hundreds, and from 1,000 to 10,000 in thousands. The number 10,000 contains the hieratic number 10 and the Hebrew word '*lfm* (thousand), and this is repeated at least twice. Was this a scribal exercise?

The symbol representing the *sheqel* γ appears in this ostracon beside the numbers from 1 to 900 in lines 4 and 5. On the opposite left lower side of the

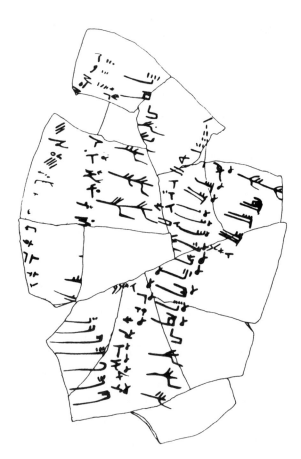

I.99 An Egyptian ostracon from Kadesh-Barnea

ostracon, three numbers—4,000, 5,000, and 6,000—are visible. To the right of these numbers appear illegible numbers. In the upper part of the ostracon, the number 3,000 is visible, beside it a Hebrew word, perhaps 'lf ("a thousand"). An additional ostracon was found at Kadesh-Barnea in which three lines of hieratic numbers and Hebrew letters appear. The third line, the clearest, includes rising numbers up to 800. Near every number the Hebrew word gerah is written, which is the smallest known Judaean weight measure (0.5 g.). The excavator mentions that at Kadesh-Barnea more ostraca with hieratic numbers were found, but these are rather fragmentary. On one of them, the symbol γ representing the sheqel occurs.

In the Judaean fort at **Arad,** two ostraca were found, one containing mixed hieratic and local numbers representing measures of wheat (i.e., with sheqel symbols); the second is inscribed with only the hieratic signs. Y. Aharoni thought that the first was written by a Judaean scribe trained in hieratic and the other by an Egyptian scribe!

In addition to the hieratic ostraca, the numbers incised on the Judaean *sheqel* weights are hieratic, too. Evidently, some of the names of Judaean measures of volume are Egyptian (such as the *hin*). A recent comparative study shows that in this period some of the Judaean clay jars reached the trade centers of Egypt, such as those found at Daphne and Naukratis in the Egyptian Delta.

It should also be mentioned here that the findings of the hieratic ostraca at Kadesh-Barnea led some scholars, including N. Na'aman, followed by D. Ussishkin, to assume that this site was under Egyptian rather than Judaean control in this period. They believe that this was the site of a joint garrison sent by the Assyrians and Egyptians when they became allies, and was later an Egyptian garrison composed of soldiers from several vassal states, including Judaean and Edomite soldiers. This view is difficult to accept, for the Egyptian hieratic numbers here had a Hebrew suffix, and Egyptian hieratic numbers, as well as names of weights and measures, and Egyptian motifs in general, are represented in the traditional material culture of Judah long before the conquest of the region by the Egyptians. These attest only to the fact that Judah borrowed some of the Egyptian administrative conventions.

Even so, the hieratic tradition of the Iron Age in general, and the widespread use of hieratic signs in the late 8th and the 7th centuries BCE in particular, are in fact a puzzling phenomenon. The Egyptian influence on other aspects of the local material culture is not so easily perceived. In any case, the fact that the hieratic numerals appear in both Israel and Judah points to their adoption at an earlier date, i.e., perhaps at the beginning of the monarchy in Israel. In any case, it is also a commonly accepted view that the Hebrew kingdoms borrowed much of their administrative system from Egypt.

Chapter 9

THE GILEAD AND THE
KINGDOM OF AMMON
UNDER ASSYRIAN HEGEMONY

THE GILEAD

As on the west side of the Jordan, on its east side the Assyrian occupation was a gradual process. After conquering Damascus, Tiglath-pileser III created, according to E. Forer, three provinces in the northern part of the region: **Qarninah** in the Bashan and **Galaʿadah** in the Gileʿad, in the former Israelite territory in Transjordan, and **Haurinah** in the Hauran. Regarding this third province, some authorities cast doubt upon its existence. All other assumptions, such as that the kingdoms of Ammon and Moab became Assyrian provinces, or B. Oded's view on the existence of three other provinces—Gidir, Tabʿel, and Hamat—do not have solid basis in fact.

The Assyrian occupation, however, can be clearly traced in all excavations conducted in the region: at **Tell Rumeith,** where the city wall was destroyed in 732, at **Irbid,** at **Tell Abu-Kharaz,** and at the sites along the northern and eastern coasts of the Sea of Galilee, i.e., Aramaic towns of the Land of Geshur: at Tel Chinnereth(?) or at the site of **Bethsaida,** where the huge city gate decorated with an Aramaic orthostat was burned, at **Tel Hadar** and at **Tel ʿEn Gev,** which were not resettled during the Assyrian period. Along the Jordan Valley, too, sites such as Peḥal (Pella) and, in particular, **Tell es-Saʿidiyeh,** where the well-planned Late Israelite period city was burned, including its sanctuary, on the walls of which were inscribed the famous Balaʿam Inscription. This region, which was transferred to direct Assyrian domination, was bordered on its south by the kingdom of Ammon, even though the boundary between the two is not entirely clear. B. Oded even assumed that south of the Galaʿadah province there may have been some additional administrative units under direct rule of the Assyrian regime, such as "the Land of Tabel" and "the Land of Gader."

In the region south of the Assyrian provinces, the three east Jordanian kingdoms—Ammon, Moab, and Edom—continued to exist. They were not hurt by the Assyrian conquest, and this period became one of prosperity for them, for their traditional enemies, the Aramaeans in the north and Israelites in the west, had been defeated and ceased to exist, and even Judah was severely weakened. Moreover, the Assyrians protected them from nomadic attackers who frequently came from the deserts to the east.

THE KINGDOM OF AMMON

THE BORDERS OF the kingdom of Ammon were the Jabbok River (Wadi Zarka) in the north and the Heshbon River in the south. With the destruction of Israel in the days of Tiglath-pileser III (732 BCE) and the occupation of Samaria in 720 BCE, the kingdom of Ammon began to develop. Tiglath-pileser did not wage war on the Ammonites and did not penetrate their territory. An Ammonite king named Sanipu sent him tribute and accepted his sovereignty, which mainly entailed the payment of annual tribute, assistance in construction activities of the empire, and bringing his army under Assyrian command in time of war. Indeed, in 701 BCE, the Ammonite king "Pada'el of the house of Ammon" assisted Sennacherib in his war against Judah during that famous campaign. Again in 677 BCE, Esarhaddon ordered "Pada'el the king of the children of Ammon" to provide assistance in his construction of a palace at Assur (not necessarily the same Pada'el, for the same names often recur among the successive generations within the royal family). The next Assyrian monarch, Ashurbanipal, mentions in 667 BCE an Ammonite king, Aminadabu, who assisted him in his wars against Egypt and also paid him a heavy tribute in gold. This and other evidence add to a general impression of the acceptance of Assyrian domination by the Ammonites. Neither is there evidence for Ammonite participation in any of the rebellions against the Assyrians. Moreover, it seems that the Assyrian regime supplied the Ammonites with necessary defense against neighboring states, and especially against the desert nomads, who periodically invaded the land of the Ammonites. The Assyrian sources themselves describe the wars conducted by Ashurbanipal against the Arabs, and it is logical to assume that the Assyrians established garrisons throughout the entire territory, including the capital city of Rabbath-Ammon, as a part of their imperial defenses. This partnership of interests probably brought both sides to build joint military units with the common task of defending the Ammonite eastern border, which was also that of the empire.

The Assyrian kings indeed helped those local kings who were loyal to them, like the Ammonite kings, annexing to them some small territories or even towns that were taken from the defeated rebellious states (cf. Jeremiah 49:1). In any case, the Assyrian protection of Ammon served as a catalyst for economic prosperity, clearly perceived in the unusual prosperity of the material culture of the Ammonites and of their neighbors during this period. This is apparent in the archaeological remains and in the rapid assimilation of the culture of the Assyrian rulers. This process was already observed many years ago by W. F. Albright, who concluded that "Ammon, which began a rapid rise, became the most important state of Transjordan in the 7th–6th centuries BCE."

THE INSCRIBED AMMONITE FINDS

THE LANGUAGE OF the Ammonites is somewhat similar to Hebrew and Phoenician, but from the beginning of the 8th century BCE, it began—according to F. M. Cross—to develop certain unique characteristics. The similarities are reflected in the language of the inscriptions, including the use of the words *ben, bat, na'ar, amah,* and *'ebed* in the seal inscriptions. Hebrew script was not, however, adopted. They utilized the contemporary lapidary Aramaic script, and later they followed the Aramaic scribal traditions common in the Assyrian empire.

The small assemblage of Ammonite inscriptions uncovered includes fragments of two monumental stone stelae found in Rabbath-Ammon. One is called the Acropolis Inscription and the other the Theater Inscription. Another inscription is incised on a limestone sculpture, and a fourth is incised on a small bronze bottle found at Tell Siran located near the city. There are also reports of several dozen Ammonite ostraca found in excavations at Tell Mazar, Tell es-Sa'idiyeh, Heshbon, and Tell el-'Umeiri and at a few other smaller sites. The rest of the Ammonite inscriptions are inscribed on their seals. This is an important beginning for the study of Ammonite language and history. Comparing these inscriptions with the biblical sources and Assyrian inscriptions, we are able to reconstruct the names of many members of the local royal dynasty.

Of the three stone inscriptions, the Acropolis Inscription is the largest and the most complete. It is a fragment of a stela that one of the Ammonite kings erected in a temple that he built for his god Milkom. The inscription is probably earlier than the period of time with which we are dealing here. Of the second inscription, the Theater Inscription, only two lines are preserved. These mention the erection of a building for the god Ba'al in Rabbath-Ammon. The third is a short dedicatory inscription on the base of a small sculpture depicting a god, in which a certain *zkkur bar SHNB* is mentioned,

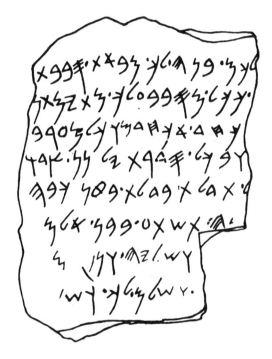

I.100 Rabbath-Ammon, the Acropolis Inscription and the inscription on the Tel Siran bottle

who has been identified by F. Zayadin as Sanipu, the Ammonite king mentioned by Tiglath-pileser III, though this remains uncertain. The most important of all is the fourth inscription, incised on a bronze bottle from Tell
Siran. This is a building inscription dated ca. 600 BCE, reminiscent of those
of the kings of Judah. Many authorities believe that it was taken from a book
chronicling the history of the Ammonite kings. Through it, we can reconstruct three generations of the royal Ammonite family, for it mentions Aminadab I (the contemporary of Ashurbanipal), Hissal'el, and Aminadab II
(whose full title is given: "the king of the children of Ammon"). Adding
names occurring on Ammonite seals, we may reconstruct the Ammonite dynasty of this period as follows: Sanip? (br Shnb) = the reign of Tiglath-pileser
III (735 BCE); Pada'el (701–635 BCE) = the reigns of Sennacherib and
Esarhaddon; Aminadab I (mid-7th century BCE) = the reign of Ashurbanipal.
These are followed by the list inscribed on the Tell Siran bottle: Hissal'el the
son of Aminadab I (625 BCE); Aminadab II the son of Hissal'el I (600 BCE).
The last name appears on a seal from Tell el-'Umeiri (see below), inscribed as
ba'alyasha, which the excavator tends to identify with Baalis the king of Am-
mon mentioned in Jeremiah 40:14. If this list is correct, archaeological research has provided us with no fewer than six of the names of the last
Ammonite kings!

The script of the ostraca from Heshbon, Tell el-'Umeiri, Tell Mazar, and
Tell es-Sa'idiyeh is Ammonite and their contents are administrative: lists of
personal names of people who send or receive various goods, as well as quantities, reflecting administration similar to that of all other Palestinian states.
Ostracon No. 1 from Heshbon, for example, is sent to the king. Among the
many agricultural products mentioned in it are wheat, barley, figs, wine,
goats, and lambs. Most important for this region are the names of some types
of incense such as the *nechot.* Silver is mentioned, too, in various local
weights, and the volume unit of liquid, the *kur.* Even some names of towns in
the region, such as Bozrah and Elath, appear. The majority of the names
mentioned in the ostraca is common names with the component El, and in
one of the ostraca from Mazar, Yahu is a component of a name, though we
may assume that in this case he was an Israelite residing in the region. In the
same ostracon, however, also appear Ammonite names such as Milkomyat
and Hissal'el.

For some reason, tomb inscriptions, common in Judah, have not been
found in Ammon.

Ammonite Seals and Seal Impressions

SEVERAL DOZEN AMMONITE seals and seal impressions have been found in excavations at Rabbath-Ammon, Tell Mazar, Tell el-'Umeiri, and elsewhere. Even more are in private collections. These seals are an important source for the study of the Ammonite culture and its different aspects: script, personal names, the royal Ammonite house and the functionaries around it, cult, and iconography. Their great number and quality are surprising. N. Avigad noted in preparing them for publication that "it is strange how many important seals originated in this small country." All of the known Ammonite seals are dated from the very end of the 8th and the 7th centuries BCE.

At least three of these seals mention the names of Ammonite kings: Pada'el, Aminadab (I), and Ba'alyasha. The first two are also mentioned in the Assyrian records: the first during the reign of Sennacherib and Esarhaddon (701–685 BCE) and the second during the reign of Ashurbanipal (mid-7th century BCE). The third, Ba'alyasha, was interpreted by its publishers as Baalis, mentioned in Jeremiah (40:14; ca. 580 BCE).

The titles of the kingdom's officials appearing on the seals are quite similar to those of the other Palestine kingdoms. There are four *'ebed ha-melekh*

I.101 Drawing of the Baalyasha seal impression

("the king's servant") seals that include the name of the king; two are "the servant of Aminadab," one is "the servant of Pada'el," and the fourth is "the servant of Ba'alyasha." Two more seals are inscribed with the title "the king's servant" with no name of a king, and similarly, two have the title *amah* ("woman servant"). Two additional seals mention the title *na'ar* ("steward"). We also have the titles of several occupations similar to those in Judah and Israel, such as *ha-sofer* ("the scribe") and *ha-kohen* ("the priest"), and others including a new one, *ha-nasis* ("the standard bearer"), which must be a military title, and one that belongs to *ha-zoref* ("the goldsmith"). Another mentions someone who is *koves,* "a laundryman." Six Ammonite seals belonged to women, which may tell us something concerning the status of women in the Ammonite kingdom.

The majority of the Ammonite seals is dated to the late 8th and the 7th centuries BCE based upon correlating the paleography of the seals with historical dates, for example, those seals inscribed with the names of Pada'el, Aminadab, and Ba'alyasha. In most of them, only the name of the owner of the seal and sometimes also the name of the father are mentioned. Most of the names are taken from the standard West Semitic repertoire, and similar names are known in Judah, Israel, and other neighboring nations. There are also some Arabic names.

In addition to these are a few with the theophoric component of the Ammonite national deity, Milkom, or the names of members of the Ammonite royal family. Even so, some names occur more frequently than others, perhaps because of the small number of families that ruled the kingdom or because these were more common among the Ammonites than among their neighbors. The list of names includes Abinadab, Nadab'el, Bd'el, Ami'el, Peda'el, Elnadab, Elhanan, Elibar, Elisha, Adonipelet, Adoninur, Inahem, Shim'az, Tamakh'el, Tenahem, and more. The names of a few animals, such as *shu'al* ("fox") and *kfir* (a young lion), as well as a few Arabic names, such as 'Aliah, 'Anmaut, 'Aw', and Btsh, occur too.

As to the theophoric names, the majority appears to be general titles such as Adon ("Lord") or El. It is surprising how few seals bear the name of the national Ammonite deity Milkom: Milkomur, Milkomgad, *baruch leMilkom* ("blessed to Milkom"), Mlkom'oz, and the title "Belonging to *Tmk'l 'ebed-Milkom* ('the servant of Milkom')," which may refer to a priest of Milkom. None of the known royal Ammonite names mentions the national deity, which is surprising and demands further investigation. Perhaps D. N. Freedman is right in this matter in suggesting that the royal family was not native Ammonite.

During the period of Assyrian domination, some Assyrian names penetrated here. The seal of *Mng'nr baruch leMilkom* should be mentioned in this context, as it is the Aramaic version of the Assyrian *Mannu-Ki-Inurta* ("who can be compared to Inurta"). Among the seals inscribed in Ammonite are some that belonged to foreigners, such as the seal of "Abinadab who vowed to 'Astarte in Sidon." There are also—for reasons unknown—numerous abecedary seals.

I.102 The seal of *Manu-ki-Inurta*

The Motifs

The decorations in the Ammonite seals at first mainly reflect the influence of Phoenician-Israelite art, which includes many Egyptian prototypes. With the introduction of Assyrian influence, many Mesopotamian-Assyrian elements penetrate, becoming more numerous in the course of time, practically displacing their predecessors and even continuing to the following periods. Another of the peculiarities of Ammonite seals is the arrangement in three registers consisting of inscription, motif, and inscription.

Of the first group, the one inspired by Phoenician-Israelite tradition, motifs include sphinxes, griffins, the combination of a monkey and Horus-

Harpokrates sitting on a lotus flower, the four-winged beetle, the two-winged sun disk, human head, nude goddess supporting her breasts or holding a flower staff, the four-winged human monster, the head of Anubis, cow suckling a calf, ram's head, various birds, winged stag and bull, and other imitations of Egyptian motifs.

Seals of the second, Assyrian-inspired group depict mainly the scene of praying figures in front of an altar on which stand the emblems of the sun, the moon crescent, and the stars, or the motif of the moon and the stars alone. Another popular motif is a demonic figure of the guardian of the Assyrian temples, appearing in the form of a bearded and winged bull-man, which is introduced on the seal of Adonipelet the servant of Aminadab; or that of a hero struggling with a lion, a hero raising his hand in blessing, etc. In the tomb of Adoninur, a few uninscribed seals were found depicting various Assyrian deities. One, made of imported chalcedony, depicts a priest standing before an altar on which rests a standard with the emblems of Ishtar and Marduk, i.e., a triangle with crescent above it. One seal, the seal of "Amar'el the son of Inahem," is made in the form of a duck turning its head backward, definitely an imitation of an Assyrian prototype. An Assyrian cylinder seal inscribed with an Assyrian name was also found in Ammon. Typical purely Ammonite motifs are the bull and the strange figure combining a monkey and Horus-Harpokrates. Also Ammonite in nature are the triple-registered seals referred to above.

EXCAVATIONS AND SURVEYS IN AMMON

THE MAJOR EXCAVATIONS in the land of Ammon have been carried out in the city of Rabbath-Ammon itself, in the acropolis-fortress (Jabal al-Qalaʿa), and in the vicinity of the theater. In addition, about a dozen tombs have been excavated, in the fort itself or at sites within its immediate surroundings: at Tell Ṣafut, Tell Siran, Meqabelein, and Tell el-Sahab, in those times, small independent settlements surrounding the Ammonite capital.

Many more excavations have been conducted within a unique fortification system that surrounded the Ammonite state, such as the towers in Rujm el-Malfuf, Umm Uthainah, Khirbet el-Hajar, Khilda, and elsewhere.

Another important group of probable Ammonite sites was excavated in the Sukoth and Jordan valleys, including Tell es-Saʿidiyeh, Tell Deir ʿAlla, Tell Mazar, and Tell Nimrin.

A third group was recently excavated on Ammon's southern border in a region that traditionally belonged to Moab, but which in the 7th century BCE was apparently annexed to Ammon: Tell Heshbon, Tell Jalul, Tell Jawa, and Tell el-ʿUmeiri. Further information has been obtained in the extensive surveys carried out there recently.

At the majority of these settlements, strata and structures of the period of Assyrian domination have been uncovered, revealing a new and interesting picture. In **Rabbath-Ammon,** the capital city, a few excavations have been conducted (and some are still ongoing), which have exposed some of its Ammonite remains. In the city's fortified citadel (the acropolis), a rock-cut water system has been uncovered as well as a system of fortification walls, built of brick on stone foundations, at least part of which is attributed to this period.

In recent years, several missions, British, French, and Jordanian, have uncovered parts of a monumental building in Area A (Stratum 7), which was interpreted as the Ammonite palace. It includes a large paved courtyard and an adjoining system of rooms. The excavators attribute these remains to the 7th century BCE and interpret them as a structure built strictly according to an Assyrian plan, like the palaces at Nimrud and Nineveh. It is clear, however, that this "Assyrian" palace replaced one of the pre-Assyrian period, of which only chance finds have been recovered, such as a few carved ivories of the Samaria ivories type, as well as some architectural ornamentation: two pieces of proto-Aeolic capitals (also found here was a clay figurine that carries a double proto-Aeolic capital on its head; see below). The most significant finds here are clearly the four limestone double-faced Hathor heads, found out of context at the site of the palace. Some remains of paint are preserved on them, as well as depressions (eye sockets, etc.) in which colored stones were inserted, as was done in the carved ivories as well. Their form, dimensions, size, and their double faces indicate that they served as the window balustrades of the palace, large-scale works in the "woman in the window" motif tradition well known among the Phoenician-Israelite ivories. They closely resemble heads common among the Ammonite clay figurines from Rabbath-Ammon (see below). The four heads are not identical and were probably executed by different artisans. They also bear some mason's marks, similar to the markings found on the ivories. In some later building remains on the citadel, such as the Umayyad palace, other decorated stones from this Ammonite palace were reused. One large piece was clearly part of a curved monumental door lintel.

All this attests, no doubt, that the pre-Assyrian Ammonite royal palace was built in the Phoenician-Israelite style, like those of the kings of Israel, Judah, and other states. The "Assyrian" palace that replaced it (a full plan of which has not yet been published) was built in different proportions and with distinct ornamentation.

A similar picture emerges from the excavations of **Tell el-Mazar,** located in the Ammonite portion of the Jordan Valley. Here, Strata IV and III contained a large structure built in the site's center in a spot overlooking the entire town. This structure is called "the palace-fort" by the excavators. It, too, contained rooms arranged around a paved open courtyard, and presents some Assyrian characteristics, including several architectural details. The excavators assumed that the building served as an administrative center and the place of an Ammonite garrison, perhaps that of Hiṣal'el the king of the Ammonites whose name is mentioned in one of the ostraca discovered at the site. In an earlier stratum of this fort, another palace was uncovered (Stratum V), which was much larger and was destroyed close to the Assyrian conquest. Of this palace only a few details are yet known.

At **Tell Jawa,** some settlement phases of this period were uncovered. It was a fortified city. Residential houses have also been uncovered at **Tell Jalul.**

These three excavations clearly show that the Assyrian conquest of Ammon brought with it quite a considerable change in the local architecture. The change is from buildings in a Phoenico-Israelite style previously adopted by all independent states in Palestine, to structures built as Assyrian-Mesopotamian open-court buildings. The signs of this change are clearly visible in all other aspects of Ammonite material culture (see below).

The excavators of **Tel eṣ-Ṣafut** have reported the existence of a building that may be "the regional Residence of the government," and point out that in a later stage of the town, still within our period, the city became larger in area and received larger fortifications.

A unique phenomenon in Rabbath-Ammon and its surroundings, almost unknown in other parts of Palestine, is the surviving remains of the many fortress towers around the city built from massive stone blocks. The largest and most prominent among these, excavated several times, is the fortress tower of **Rujm el-Malfuf (N).** Many others were discovered in the various surveys conducted in the region, showing that they encircled the capital, but mainly protected its western side. These tower forts are mainly round, with a diameter of ca. 20 m. The width of their megalithic stone walls is about 3 m. A few have a different, square or rectangular plan. Rarely, a few residential dwellings stand near them. In the latest studies of these forts, some thirty have been recorded. It now appears that all were built at the same time by one authority for the defense of the city of Rabbath-Ammon and its surroundings. The towers were usually two stories high and stood on a strong, elevated podium. Entrance into them may have required ladders.

In addition to the two Rujm el-Malfuf forts, the major sites where these fortresses have been uncovered are Rujm el-Kursi, Umm Uthainah, Abu Nuseir, Rujm el-Henu, Khilda, and Khirbet el-Hajar. Some of these have recently been excavated. From the results of excavations in the forts and in the tombs attached to them, it is evident that they were built during the late Ammonite period as units composing a single defensive array. This system probably encompassed the entire rural area of the kingdom and functioned as an alarm for the inhabitants of the capital. New studies indicate that this system functioned for a considerable period of time, from the Assyrian to the Persian periods, perhaps including the Babylonian period in between (see below). We should remember that a similar defensive and alarm system was recently found in Moab. A somewhat different system existed in Judah.

Remains of residential dwellings are relatively scarce in Ammon. Part of a residential quarter was found at **Tell es-Saʿidiyeh,** which was probably destroyed by the Assyrians, and a house has been excavated at **Sahab.** In both cases, they are variations of the "four-room" house plans, probably the main plan here as elsewhere in the Palestinian states until the Assyrian occupation. It was gradually replaced by the "Assyrian open-courtyard" house plan (though, in some cases, as in Tell el-ʿUmeiri, the "four-room" plan continued to the end of the Iron Age).

AMMONITE CULT AND CULT OBJECTS

THE OFFICIAL AMMONITE cult, like that of the other Palestine peoples in this period, was generally based upon a divine couple: a male and a female deity. We know only the name of the male god, Milkom (probably: "the King"), who is mentioned in the Bible (1 Kings 11:5, 33). The name also appears in the form Molekh (1 Kings 11:7), and in Ammonite inscriptions and seals. The Citadel Inscription from Rabbath-Ammon starts with the words "and so told me Milkom," and later tells about the construction of the temple dedicated to Milkom by one of the Ammonite kings, whose name or the name of whose father includes the component Milkom, too. There are also two seals inscribed *baruch le Milkom* ("blessed to Milkom") and several seals in which this name is a component in the Ammonite personal names, such as Milkom-or, Milkomgad, Milkomyat, Milkomoz, etc.

Other titles that probably served as honorific epithets for the same deity are Adon ("Lord"), which appears in the Ammonite names such as Adoninur and Adonipelet, and El, which here is a generic term for divinity, and the commonest of them all, used in every possible compound among the personal Ammonite names, both those of the kings (Pada'el and Hissal'el) and those of private individuals: Bid'el, Haza'el, Hanan'el, Nedab'el, Noam'el, Abad'el, Azar'el; or as El'amas, Eliram, Elior, Elinor, Elnadab, etc. This title is also mentioned in the Bala'am Inscription from Tell Deir 'Alla. Another deity's name that is mentioned in the Ammonite inscriptions is that of the Phoenician god Ba'al. In the Theater Inscription from Rabbath-Ammon, the building of the sanctuary of "the house of Ba'al" is mentioned. This is not surprising, for the influence of Phoenician culture on the Ammonites until the Assyrian occupation, as already pointed out, was very strong. The Ba'al name is also used as a regular component among the Ammonite personal names: Ba'alyasha, Ba'alnatan, or Ba'aly'.

The name of the female deity should therefore be 'Astarte (or perhaps Ishtar-Milkom, like the Moabite goddesses Ishtar-Kemosh; see below). But she is not mentioned at all in the biblical sources or in the Ammonite ones (in the Bala'am Inscription, however, appears the form "Shagar and Ishtar," which may be another local variation). The major evidence for her existence comes from her many statuettes and clay figurines and her depictions on Ammonite seals, where she is portrayed in the usual form of a naked woman supporting her breasts, the standard depiction in all other Palestinian states.

In Ammonite glyptic also appears the figure of the child-god known only from archaeological evidence, mainly in the form of the Egyptian deity Horus-Harpokrates, on both carved ivories and seals. Unknown among the Phoenicians, Israelites, and Judaeans, his name is not recorded in the Ammonite sources.

In addition to the appearance of the deity's names in inscriptions and seals, the study of the Ammonite cult of this period relies mainly on the relatively rich finds of statuettes and clay figurines.

Thus far, no Ammonite temple has been excavated, but recently M. Najjar, the present excavator of the Rabbath-Ammon citadel, has reported the discovery of the remains of a structure that he interprets as an Ammonite sanctuary, found below a late Roman temple dedicated to Hercules. The major reason for this identification is the building's location below a later temple, as well as the character of the finds, which included many late Ammonite vessels and a whole *Tridacna* shell. The other archaeological finds related to

Ammonite sanctuaries are the stone fragment inscribed with the Theater Inscription, a stela erected by an Ammonite king in the main temple of the city dedicated to Milkom, the reference to "the House of Ba'al" in the Citadel Inscription, and a few clay models of sanctuaries that will be discussed below. At Tell el-'Umeiri, an ostracon was found which is probably inscribed with the word *qdsh* ("holy"), in the same manner as on the cultic clay vessels found at Hazor (Israel), Ekron (Philistia), and Arad, Tel Sheva, and Tell Beit Mirsim (Judah), discussed above.

There are more than thirty Ammonite limestone statuettes as well as many stone and clay figurines from excavations in Ammon, which are or should be attributed to this period. The majority of the stone statuettes were found in clear stratigraphic contexts.

The appearance of these stone sculptures, some life-sized, originally painted with bright colors, red, black, and blue, is a phenomenon unique to Ammon. These statues can be compared only with Cypriot limestone examples, which first appear in Palestine slightly later and became common in the cult centers of the Phoenicians and Idumaeans in the coastal region of Palestine during the Persian period (see below), possibly continuing to the early 5th century BCE.

The stone sculptures (mostly made of limestone with a few of basalt) are divided into two types: most of these statues portray males; some females are also depicted. One of them, the first to be found, has a dedicatory inscription on its base in which some personal names are included (one of these names is supposed to be that of a king; see above). All are executed in a characteristic and easily identifiable style, which differs from that of all other Levantine sculpture. There is little doubt that this reflects the development of a local school of sculpture. Most of the statues are sculpted in the round and stand on a base. Others lack certain details and may be incomplete.

Most of the males are depicted wearing a long dress. Their bearded heads, large in proportion to the rest of the body, are covered with an elongated headdress, in which G. M. Landes saw Assyrian-Syrian influence. But it now seems more plausible that it is a local imitation of the crown of the Egyptian god Osiris with an addition of two volutes on both sides, resembling those of the proto-Aeolic capitals. Indeed, the long debate over whether we should interpret these sculptures as deities or as Ammonite kings recently came to an end with the discovery of clay male figurines in the citadel of Rabbath-Ammon, Tell el-'Umeiri, and Tell Jawa, with features almost identical to those of the stone male statuettes, particularly the shape of their headdress.

I.103 The Ammonite
divine couple

We do not know of clay figurines of kings in this region, and it is logical to assume that these statuettes with the Osirian headdress represent the local national god, Milkom.

Some of the male statuettes wear a different type of headdress, a kind of round "turban," while their beard and hair are in long locks in almost Assyrian fashion, but with a stylistic uniqueness. These must have been the later products of the group, i.e., after the Assyrian occupation. They usually stand with their hands next to the body, but sometimes hold lotus flowers: since Canaanite times, the emblem of divinity among the Egyptians, Canaanites, and Phoenicians, later adopted by the Cypriots and others. In this connection, it should again be remembered that clay figurines with almost the same headdress have been found in other Palestinian sites of the same period, and even in Israel and Judah. This means that this headdress, although appearing here in Ammonite statuettes, may generally be interpreted as that of a divinity.

Depictions of females among the Ammonite stone statuettes are relatively rare. Generally, these wear an Egyptian-style wig. Their role as fertility goddesses is represented by the gesture of holding the breasts, but there are a few (broken) examples in which they are shown holding the lotus flower. There is a unique, fragmentary statue of a goddess wearing Egyptian wig and jewelry, including a medallion in the shape of the Horus eye, around her neck.

No Ammonite statuettes depicting children are known, but the image of Horus appears on some Ammonite seals. The stone sculptures, like the other cult objects (clay and stone figurines), as well as all architectural ornamentation, were painted in bright colors and sometimes decorated with colored stones (instead of painting), a technique well known to us from ivory carving. Remains of paint have survived on some of the stone statuettes. Most beautiful are a pair of Ammonite life-sized divinities from the collection of M. Dayan, now in the Israel Museum. The male head is made in Assyrian fashion, but his headdress remains the Osirian hat; the female, wearing a long robe, supports her breasts with her hands.

In Ammon, some of the small figurines were also made of stone. Two of these, from Rabbath-Ammon, are executed in the local style observed in the large sculptures. Another is reminiscent of an Egyptian statuette.

Clay figurines are more common and also have easily recognizable Ammonite features. Most of them were recovered in tombs, but others have been found in excavations at sites such as Rabbath-Ammon, Tell Mazar, Tell Deir 'Alla, Tell el-'Umeiri, etc. The figurines from both sources are identical.

I.104 Clay head of the
Ammonite god Milkom

I.105 Clay figurine of
the Ammonite god
Milkom as a horse rider

The bodies of most of the figurines are handmade and only the head was pressed in a mold, i.e., in the technique of the Judaean "pillar figurines." Their shape, however, is distinct: the head is very flat. Here, as in other Palestinian states, there are more female clay figurines than males, and there are also many animals, especially horses.

Among the figurines of the male gods, there are almost no representations of "the ruling god" depicted in the form of a male sitting on his throne, but only of "the warrior god" who is riding his horse. Some of these were found intact, others only in fragments (either horses or the riders' heads). G. M. Landes regarded their pointed hats as indicating that they represent actual riders wearing Assyrian-style helmets, and interpreted them as members of an Assyrian-Ammonite cavalry unit. But there can be no doubt today that this is the local schematic version of the pointed Egyptian Osiris hat, identical to the pointed hat on the stone sculptures. Some of these figurines were extensively painted, mainly with black.

In addition to the male horsemen were discovered some additional male figurines wearing strange headdresses that are difficult to explain and have no analogies among the rest of the Palestinian figurines. This fits well with our observation that every nation in Palestine found a different way to depict its own god. A peculiar example was found in a tomb at Rabbath-Ammon. Though it depicts a pregnant woman (her hands are touching her belly), she also has a black-painted beard. On her head she carries a proto-Aeolic capital with four corners, a kind of caryatid, the significance of which is not known.

The heads of the female figurines are usually covered with Egyptian wigs, reminiscent of the Judaean "pillar figurines," and they are divided into two types: one (from Rabbath-Ammon) is common to all the Palestinian nations in the previous period and in this period as well. This type originates in the sophisticated ivory carving art forms, as can be detected in the small details of the hairdressing and jewelry, already encountered in Israel, Judah, and Philistia. In Ammon, mainly molds have been found, but also some figurine fragments. This group appears to have been produced in the period antedating the Assyrian occupation, when the major influence came from Phoenicia and Israel. The body of the female figurine is made in the "pillar figurine" technique, the head is flattened, and the hat almost as pointed as that of the male gods. Mainly heads and body parts have survived, and many are holding tambourines. Others are depicted supporting their breasts (this female fertility figure is also found on Ammonite seals carrying personal names; one appears on the seal of one of the "king's servants").

A typical assemblage of Ammonite figurines is one unearthed recently in the excavations of Tell el-ʿUmeiri. It included many female figurines in the classic attitude, supporting their breasts or nursing a baby. Their head-dresses, too, are of the type common among all Palestinian nations, the Egyptian wig; but some had a local one with pointed edges. The male figurines in this assemblage usually wear the pointed hat of Osiris. There are also some figurines of horsemen. The peculiarity of the Tell el-ʿUmeiri assemblage is in its many animal figurines in general, and those of lions in particular (one mold of which was recovered). In the course of the 7th and the early 6th centuries BCE, new types of deities began to appear in the Mesopotamian-Assyrian style commonly found all over the empire, mostly on seals but also as figurines.

It should be pointed out that all the Ammonite clay figurines—males, females, and animals—were painted in a particular fashion. On many, the paint is perfectly preserved. They appear to have been painted in black and white; the hole of the eye sockets was intentionally exaggerated.

The metal cultic objects. In addition to the figurines, some of the other types of cult objects found here are of clear Phoenician origin, a source of influence observed in architecture and all the other aspects of Ammonite culture prior to the Assyrian occupation. One of the best examples is a bronze caryatid censer, uncovered in one of the Ammonite tombs at Umm Uthainah near Rabbath-Ammon, which contained finds dated from the Assyrian to the Persian periods. In addition to the censer, the seal of "Palti the son of *Maʿas ha mazkir* ('the memorist')" was found here. The censer depicts a female figure standing on a tripod. Above her is a tall cover pierced with many holes. There is no doubt that the entire concept is borrowed from the Phoenician cult, for similar bronze tripods are well known in the 7th century BCE—as has been shown by P. R. S. Moorey—from other sites along the Phoenician coast. The difference is in the details and execution: for here we are in the late Assyrian period and the bowl is therefore executed in pure Assyrian style. The figure of the goddess holding the lotus flower here wears Ammonite clothing closely resembling that of some of the Ammonite stone statuettes discussed above.

THE AMMONITE POPULAR CULT

AS IN ALL other Palestinian states of this age, in Ammon a popular cult developed beside the official one of Milkom and his consort. This popular cult was apotropaic, the function of which was to defend its users from bad luck, death, and other troubles. The cult was demonic in character and involved mainly imported common Egyptian apotropaic emblems, such as faience amulets depicting the eye of Horus, figures of Bes, Ptah, Pataikos, etc. In Ammon, a unique clay figurine pertaining to this cult depicts a frightening-looking monkey-monster, which may be connected with the monkey-like Horus depicted on Ammonite seals (see above).

It is impossible to discuss the Ammonite cult without mentioning the surprising discovery of the text of the inscription of Bal'am son of Be'or at Tell Deir 'Alla, which, according to one view, may have been an Ammonite site. It is written in black and red ink on white plaster covering a stela found fallen on the floor. In addition to the inscription, a drawing of a griffin was found. There is currently a dispute among scholars as to whether its language is Ammonite, Midianite, Aramaic, or even "Gileadite" (the script is Aramaic but the language is local). Others suggest that it pertained to the Aramaean deportees brought here after the Assyrian occupation. Its date, too, is disputed: some believe that it was written shortly before the Assyrian occupation of the region, and others claim it was somewhat after the Assyrian occupation. In any case, it is a composition attributed to a biblical personality and reflects a pagan world rich in mythic component, themes, and vocabulary. It mentions some deities, including Shagar and Ishtar.

AMMONITE BURIAL CUSTOMS

TYPICAL AMMONITE TOMBS are much the same as those in other regions of Palestine in the 7th and 6th centuries BCE, i.e., bench or shelf tombs. As we have already pointed out, these were family rock-cut tombs. At the entrance of the tomb, which was closed with a cover stone, there was sometimes a shaft or a flight of steps. From the entrance, more steps descend into the chamber. From the central chamber, there are openings to a few side chambers. Around the walls are cut shelves on which the deceased were laid. The tombs vary in size and the number of chambers but share the basic features of shaft and chamber with shelves. Frequently, a deep pit was dug in the floor of the room in which the remains of previous burials were deposited when the tomb was filled. Sometimes walls were erected around this pit in order to create more space for the bones. In one of the tombs, some animal bones were found together with clay vessels in a depression, perhaps attesting to a custom of bringing offerings to the dead. The form of the tomb is usually regular, but often natural caves were also used and the shape of the tomb was adapted accordingly. All the tombs were cut in the slopes of hills around the outskirts of cities, either scattered (Rabbath-Ammon) or concentrated in a central cemetery (Tell Mazar).

Among the Ammonite tombs of the Assyrian period, one group of about a dozen graves is well known. These were uncovered on the slopes of the local citadel and the hills around it, as well as at Sahab and Meqabelein. These are simply designated as "Ammonite tombs" and differ from the tombs of this period in other regions of Palestine mainly in their rich contents, which included clay coffins, pottery vessels, figurines, metal objects, alabaster vessels, and other finds attesting to the wealth of the kingdom in this period. Male and female burials contain distinct grave offerings: female burials are accompanied by jewelry and many cosmetic utensils, while male burials contain pottery vessels and weapons. A particularly significant example of the latter is the tomb of Adoninur the servant of Aminadab, discussed above.

Prior to examining the contents of the Ammonite tombs, let us point out that in burial customs, as in other aspects of Ammonite culture, a distinction must be drawn between the period preceding and that following the Assyrian occupation. In the former, the Ammonites buried their dead according to their own tradition in a standard burial (as explained above) or in anthropoid sarcophagi. After the arrival of the Assyrians, they began to bury in Assyrian-type clay coffins, which we dealt with earlier in our discussion of the territories of the provinces of Megiddo, Samaria, and Dor.

The anthropoid clay coffins uncovered in the Ammonite tombs (only a few have been found in scientific excavations) differ in form from the Philistine anthropoid coffins of Iron Age I, but both types were presumably influenced by Egyptian prototypes, as reflected in the "Osirian beard" and general appearance. The Ammonite sarcophagi also bear a resemblance to the faces of the Ammonite statues discussed above. Only a few of the published coffins in fact have human faces, and many lack such details. Another peculiar aspect is the many handles (up to sixteen!).

Although the imitation of an Egyptian custom is clear, it is surprising that the Ammonites would adopt it at this particular time. During the 26th Dynasty in Egypt, the custom of burial in stone anthropoid coffins was introduced. It is possible that following this, some of the Palestinian nations gradually began to adopt it, too (as did the Moabites and the Phoenicians; see below). At the same time, it is clear that later, when Assyrian influence became stronger, the anthropoid coffins disappeared and were replaced by Assyrian clay coffins.

Burial in such coffins was a privilege of the rich. The majority of the Ammonite tombs are the ordinary shelf tombs. No visible change occurred in their form before and after the arrival of the Assyrians. There was, however, a significant change in tomb contents, reflecting the transition from the Phoenician sphere of influence to the Assyrian.

THE AMMONITE POTTERY

MOST OF THE Ammonite pottery has been collected from about a dozen tombs in Rabbath-Ammon and its immediate surroundings and in excavations near some of the round towers, such as Khilda. Other rich assemblages were found in the excavations of some of the major Ammonite sites, such as the citadel of Rabbath-Ammon itself, as well as Tell Ṣafut, Heshbon, Tell Jawa, Tell el-ʿUmeiri, Tell Mazar, Tell Deir ʿAlla, Tell es-Saʿdiyeh, etc.

Chronologically, Ammonite clay vessels of this period may be divided into two groups. The first one belongs to the period just prior to the Assyrian occupation of the Israelite kingdom and the kingdoms of Transjordan. The other group belongs to the period following this occupation. In both groups, some pottery types appear, which are common to all the Transjordanian kingdoms, such as the three-legged cups, water decanters with sharply carinated shoulders, lamps pinched on four sides, and other forms. But there are also some types peculiar to the land of Ammon alone. Moreover, some have a decoration in the form of painted steps, usually executed in black and white paint. Some of the Ammonite pottery has also been influenced by other neighboring traditions. It has already been said that the earlier Ammonite group is influenced by the Phoenician-Israelite tradition that was present in Ammon after the destruction of Samaria (visible mainly in the bowls, jugs, and juglets). Among the later Ammonite groups, the Phoenician-Israelite vessels are few, and they are replaced in part by Judaean prototypes (such as the high-base lamp) but mainly by vessels in the Assyrian tradition. One can get a sense of the progress of Assyrian cultural influence on Ammon by looking at the sequence of Ammonite pottery during the 7th century BCE. In the recent excavations at Tell el-ʿUmeiri, this pottery was found stratigraphically together with Attic pottery and cylinder seals attributed by experts to the late 6th to early 5th centuries BCE. This, together with Attic pottery found in a few typical Ammonite tombs, strengthens a previous suggestion by W. F. Albright and J. Sauer that these wares continued to be produced into the Persian period (see below).

Ammonite Cosmetic Utensils

MANY COSMETIC PALETTES and vessels made of limestone, alabaster, and *Tridacna* shell have been found in the Ammonite tombs and at several sites, including the citadel of Rabbath-Ammon. They seem to be—in the early part of the period—a part of the Phoenician *koine* that dominated all of Phoenicia and Palestine. Similar finds have been collected from Phoenicia itself, in the Assyrian provinces in the north of Palestine, Judah, Philistia, and throughout the Transjordanian kingdoms. These finds do not reflect any change resulting from Assyrian influence. These objects are the same in Ammon as in the other local states, and the reader is referred to the relevant sections above.

Ammon: Summary and Conclusions

THE PROSPEROUS AND flourishing Ammonite material culture from the late 8th century BCE until the Babylonian conquest deserves special attention, not so much for the quantity of artifacts found as for its uniqueness. Remains encompass almost all components of material culture: language, script, religion, cult and burial customs, architecture, glyptic and carving art, as well as everyday vessels of all materials: pottery, stone, metal, shell, etc.

Ammon and its unique cultural revival of the age deserve more attention. This small kingdom with a very limited area was also a branch of the Phoenician-Israelite *koine* that spread all over Palestine. The surprising fact about it is that its real uniqueness only emerged at the time of the Assyrian occupation. It would appear that under the security guaranteed by the Assyrians, Ammonite culture in general, and art in particular, prospered. The Ammonite material culture of the Late Iron Age is characterized, therefore, by two criteria: on the one hand, a typical Assyrian influence that may have been willingly adopted; on the other, the growth of an individual Ammonite style based upon earlier local traditions.

· Chapter 10 ·

The Moabites

Introduction

The original territory of Moab lies between the Heshbon and the Arnon rivers. Following the campaigns conducted by Tiglath-pileser III to Syria and Palestine, Moab, like all other small kingdoms of the region, came under the domination of the Assyrian empire. As far as we can judge from our written sources, the Moabites were usually loyal to the Assyrian regime and did not participate in the rebellions that erupted from time to time in the western part of the empire. There may be two reasons for this. One is that Moab—like Ammon—was under the constant pressure of various Arab tribes roaming in the Syrian-Arabian desert. Defended by the Assyrian army, it gained security and prosperity. The second is that Moab was situated far from the centers of rebellion.

In the Assyrian lists of tribute-bearers to Tiglath-pileser III are mentioned a few kings from Palestine, among them Salamanu of Moab. The land of Moab is also mentioned in Assyrian texts from Nimrud, approximately of the same date, from which we may assume that Moab was closely connected with Assyria. In one document, we are told that Moab, together with other states, sent horses to Assyria. Another document, a letter sent by an Assyrian official to his king, tells about the people of the land of Gader, who penetrated Moab and killed some of its citizens. Later Moab is mentioned among the states that paid tribute to Assyria in the days of Sargon II; and as a border state of the empire in a "geographical" document dated to the same king.

Among the kings who accepted the Assyrian yoke at the time of Sennacherib's campaign against Judah in 701 BCE was Kammushu-Nadabi of Moab. Among the kings that Esarhaddon king of Assyria summoned to his palace in Nineveh was Musuri the king of Moab. From the same time, there is an Assyrian tax document in which we are informed about a tribute of gold accepted from Ammon, Moab, and Judah. While the tribute of Ammon was two *mina* of gold, that of Moab was only one. The king of Moab is also mentioned among those who paid taxes to Ashurbanipal king of Assyria (652–650 BCE) during his first campaign against Egypt (667 BCE).

During the days of Ashurbanipal, the pressure of the Arabian tribes of the Syrian desert on the region's borders was increasing, and finally, they rebelled against him. They penetrated Moab and clashed with the Assyrians there. The Moabites also took an active role in these wars. According to the Assyrian sources, the Moabite king Kamashkhalta defeated the Qedarite king Ammuladi, who invaded the land of Moab, took him captive, and brought him to Nineveh to the king of Assyria.

THE MOABITE WRITTEN EVIDENCE

THE MOABITE LANGUAGE, like that of the Ammonites, belongs to the Canaanite branch of the West Semitic languages. It is similar to Hebrew, but there are certain peculiarities that characterize the Moabite script. At the end of the 8th century BCE, with the end of the Israelite-Judaean influence, the Aramaic language and script were introduced. In the Moabite seals of the 7th to 6th centuries BCE, there is therefore a mixture of Hebrew-Aramaic letters as well as local Moabite ones.

With the exception of the two well-known Moabite stelae of Mesha and Kemoshyt, kings of Moab in the 9th century BCE, no important written material has been unearthed in Moab. All that is available is a group of seals, none of which were found in excavations. Most were purchased from antiquity dealers. The reason for regarding them as Moabite is their script or the personal names mentioned in them. Among the seals classified as Moabite are a few that bear the names of officials of the kingdom, as was the custom in all of Palestine's states. Among these, there is the seal of "Manasseh the king's son," one seal of a *na'ar* ("steward"), that of "Palti the son of *Ma'as ha mazkir*" ("the memorist," a title also mentioned in the Bible, the meaning of which is not clear), and no fewer than four seals of scribes: "Amos the scribe," "Kemosh'am the son of Kemoshel the scribe," "Kemoshhasid the scribe," and a bulla of "Kemosh'oz the scribe," which shows—in N. Avigad's opinion—that this profession was popular among the Moabites.

The rest of the seals include personal names, which incorporate the

Moabite divine name Kemosh, in the same forms used by the other peoples of the country, such as Kemoshur ("Kemosh is light"), Kemosh Yehi ("May/Let Kemosh live"), Kemosh Natan ("Kemosh has given"), Kemosh Dan ("Kemosh has judged"), etc. However, in comparison with the Ammonite and Edomite seals, many of which have been uncovered in excavations, the Moabite group is small and most of the names are simple. Most of the Moabite seals contain short names, without the addition of the father's name, such as *leYahun* ("belonging to Yahun"), or *leYira,* and sometimes even without the "belonging to": Yish'a, Shaḥar. Moreover, it seems that a small number of the Moabite seals was executed before the Assyrian conquest, for they contain the familiar Phoenician-inspired scenes of worshipers dressed in Egyptian kilts, winged griffins and sphinxes, or a four-winged male monster with debased Egyptian double crown. But most of the motifs on the known Moabite seals fall within the sphere of Assyrian influence from the start of the Assyrian domination. The seal of "Amos the scribe," for example, depicts the king of Assyria standing before the god Assur, whose emblem is located above the altar between them. Without the Moabite inscription, one might have suspected that this was an Assyrian seal. Most of the other seals are decorated with the moon crescent and the star, or with the winged sun disk, which were also adopted from the Assyrian repertoire. The Mesopotamian influence is also visible in the conical form of some of the seals.

In summary, we may conclude again that we know of no Moabite seal that includes a motif that can be interpreted as typically Moabite. This absence, together with the absence of typically Moabite figurines (see below), is in complete contrast with the situation at that time in Ammon and Edom, the two immediate neighbors of the Moabites.

Within this discussion of the written Moabite sources, let us note a surprising discovery published recently. It is a small piece of papyrus (17.5 x 2 cm.) that contains two complete lines. The papyrus was sealed with a bulla bearing the title "The king of EQT[]." Its publishers, P. Bordreuil and D. Pardee, believe that this is the name of a town preserved in that of present-day Tell Iqtanu, located in the center of Moab. The contents of the document concern a structure and its contents, which include millstones and *marzeaḥ* (the same obscure word that we have already encountered in a Phoenician cult inscription dealt with above). The two written lines are: "So said the gods to Sarah: yours are the *marzeaḥ,* the millstones and the house." The date of the papyrus, which is written in Aramaic mixed with Moabite expressions, is, according to its publishers, probably the late 7th or early 6th century BCE.

Its importance lies in the light that it sheds on the script and language of Moab in this period.

THE EXCAVATIONS IN MOAB AND THEIR RESULTS

THE EXCAVATIONS CONDUCTED in the area of Moab have been few. In fact, we may exclude from Moab those conducted at Jawa, Tell el-ʿUmeiri, Heshbon, and perhaps Tell Jalul. These should have been Moabite, but the results indicate that all were part of Ammon during this period (see above). We are left, in the vast Moabite territory between the rivers Heshbon and Arnon, with only six sites: Mount Nebo, Madeba, Dibon, Khirbet el-Mudayna, and Aroer. Only at Dibon and Mudayna have some building remains of this period been uncovered. From the rest, there are mostly small finds. In the southern part of the country, three more sites were excavated and surveyed: Baluʿa, Ader, and Kerak (biblical Kir-Moab). Here, too, only one yielded some building remains, while the other two provided only small finds. Of all the Moabite towns, only Dibon, the country's capital, has been systematically excavated.

The excavators of **Dibon** found three strata of the period of the Moabite kingdom, two of which, Strata 2 and 3, are of interest to us. It should be pointed out that they claim that there was nothing to indicate any violent destruction caused by the Assyrian occupation. They concluded, therefore, that the city fell to the Assyrians without war. Stratum 2 of the kingdom-era construction was dated by them to 713–712 BCE, the days in which the Moabite kingdom tried to join the rebellion of Ashdod; Stratum 3 is dated to the days of Moabite king Kammashaltu, who assisted Ashurbanipal in his campaigns. But these dates are not clearly supported by the finds. In the slope outside and opposite the city, eight tombs of these periods were also found (see below). Of the building remains attributed to the 7th century BCE, parts of city walls attest that Dibon was a fortified city. Some huge heaps of earth and stones covering large areas point—in their view—to the fact that some large public structures of that period may have been located there, but the buildings themselves were not found.

In recent years, new excavations have been conducted at the site of **Baluʿa** in Moab's southern region. The excavations, directed by V. Worschech, showed that during the Assyrian period this town was extended far to the east. This new quarter was enclosed within a casemate wall, and the few houses uncovered here were built according to the new plan of the Assyrian "open-court" house. The finds here include local as well as "Assyrian" pottery bowls.

At **Aroer,** as far as we can judge from the excavation's results, a fortress was destroyed even before the Assyrian occupation and not subsequently rebuilt. The rest of the excavations and surveys conducted in Moab revealed only a few building remains that are relatively uninformative. More important are groups of tombs excavated at Dibon and Mount Nebo.

In Moab, as in Ammon, there was, in addition to the regular settlement, a system of fortresses erected along the eastern border of the country against the desert nomads. Such fortresses are known at Lehun and Qasr el-ʿAl. The problem in the case of the Moabite fortresses is that they served intermittently over long periods, and the archaeological research here has not yet succeeded in separating those that existed during the period of interest to us and those of other periods. In any case, the Moabite fortresses are different in form from others we have examined. The circular Ammonite type is not known here.

Our knowledge of building practices in Moab comes from an insignificant, desolate, and distant site located on the southeastern border of Moab. The name of the site is **el-Mudeibia** (or **el-Mudayna**). It was probably connected with the Moabite defensive system on the eastern frontier. Here stand to this day the remains of a large fortress (this is the only structure of its kind that has been preserved above foundation level). The fortress is built of local

I.106 Moabite proto-Aeolic capital from Mudeibia

basalt stones, with the exception of two (perhaps four) of its monumental gates, which are made of limestone. The fortress, built in the 8th century BCE, continued to exist for a long period of time, perhaps because of its remote location, until it was finally destroyed, probably by an earthquake, during the Hellenistic period. In the area of one of its gates, on the surface, a few proto-Aeolic capitals survive, as well as the huge stone lintels of the monumental gate. These capitals, executed in a typical Phoenician style, reflect the southern variant, which was thought to be found only in Judah, and there, only at Jerusalem and Ramat Raḥel. At Kerak (biblical Kir-Moab), another proto-Aeolic capital, which probably belonged to the biblical town, was found built into the wall of a Crusader-period fort.

These exceptional finds indicate two things: first, in Moab, as in Rabbath-Ammon (and the rest of the Palestinian states), the architectural style in the period before the arrival of the Assyrians was Phoenician; second, this style in Moab was influenced by the Judaean variant. The strong influence of Judah on Moab, both in the period before the Assyrians and after their arrival, is well attested in many other components of Moabite material culture, especially the clay vessels (see below). One more conclusion that can be drawn from these excavations is that here, too, during the Assyrian period the new buildings were erected according to Assyrian models.

THE MOABITE BURIAL CUSTOMS

MOABITE TOMBS OF the Iron Age have been uncovered mainly at Dibon and Mount Nebo (the tombs from Madeba are dated to the first part of the Iron Age). Generally, they resemble the other tombs of the 7th century BCE in other parts of the country, i.e., they are family bench tombs. The tombs found at Dibon were dug in a long line into a rock step. The grave openings were strengthened and narrowed by stone construction, as were those at Nebo. From the opening, some steps descended to the tomb chamber, which sometimes had a few benches. Most of the rooms are irregular and carelessly cut and the corners are usually rounded. They were cut very close to one another. The burial custom in these graves was the same as in the bench tombs encountered elsewhere. First, there was burial on the bench, followed by the transfer of the bones to a pit and the introduction of a new burial on the bench.

The one exception to this custom was found in one of the Dibon tombs, where an anthropoid clay coffin was uncovered, different from the Ammonite type. The coffin, found entire but empty and broken, attests to the acceptance of this new tradition among some of the Moabites. These coffins were probably replaced after the Assyrian conquest by the simple Mesopotamian ones, as in Ammon. Indeed, fragments of such Assyrian clay coffins were found in two of the tombs at Mount Nebo. In one of these tombs, an Assyrian-style cylinder seal was also uncovered.

THE MOABITE CULT

IT COULD HAVE been expected that at least in their national cult the Moabites would exhibit some unique system or tradition. For the Moabites had their own national deity, Kemosh (and are even called "the people of Kemosh"), who is mentioned both in the Bible and in Moabite inscriptions and seals in various forms. Even among the Moabite kings, the name was popular, as: Kemoshyt, Kemosh-Nadab, Kemoshshaltu, etc. It was also popular as a component in other Moabite personal names: Kemosh-el, Kemosh-am, Kemosh-zedek, and others. The name of his consort is known from the Mesha Stela: Ishtar-Kemosh, which should be interpreted as Ishtar (or ʿAstarte) of Kemosh (this combination of two names is also known from the Phoenician realm, as in Baʿalat-Gebal from Byblos, Tanit-Ashtoret from Sarepta, and mainly Tanit the face of Baʿal from Carthage). According to the Mesha Stela, there was a temple to this god in his capital at Dibon, which was known as Beth-Kemosh ("the house of Kemosh," just like "the house of Yahweh" in Judaean inscriptions), and he had some *bamot* ("open cult places") in the city fortress. But not a single Moabite cult place has been uncovered, not from the earlier part of the Iron Age nor from the 7th century BCE. Numbers 22:41 mentions a place called Bamot Baal and another called Beth Baal Meon, which may refer to the cult of a local or Phoenician Baʿal, but it seems more likely that these are cult places for Kemosh, to whose name Baʿal was added, as noted among the Ammonites.

Among the Judaeans who dwelled in the Moabite land, as at the town of Nebo, the cult of Yahweh was in practice, as we are told in the text of the Mesha Stela.

As to the cult objects, no large stone sculptures of the Ammonite type have been found at any of the Moabite sites. The few figurines recovered in excavations, especially in the Moabite tombs, are almost without exception of the types common in Judah, and lack any unique characteristics. Most of them are of the "pillar figurine" type, with molded face and solid, handmade bodies, or "bell-shaped" figurines produced according to the Phoenician technique. They depict the usual tambourine players etc., and it is impossible to detect any special Moabite features. Some clay models of sanctuaries have also been found in the Moabite tombs, where they were placed as votives. It may be deduced from these that in form, the Moabite sanctuaries resembled those of Judah and the rest of the Palestinian states.

THE MOABITE POTTERY

EXCAVATIONS AT MOABITE sites such as Dibon, Madeba, Mount Nebo, Ader, Balu'a, Kerak, and elsewhere, and especially the tombs mentioned above, have produced a few assemblages of clay vessels dated to the 7th century BCE. Moabite clay vessels have not been studied as thoroughly as those of Ammon and Edom. It seems that part of this pottery exhibits typical Transjordanian features. In the Moabite pottery assemblages, however, the influence of the Judaean pottery tradition is especially strong, and so far as can be judged, much stronger than the latter's influence on Ammonite and Edomite wares. Perhaps this is due to the existence of a large group of Judaean inhabitants in Moab, living separately or together with the native Moabite population.

Recently, as more Moabite material has become available, it has become possible to identify a few types of exclusively Moabite vessels: these are mainly deep bowls with three loop feet, as well as a few types of jugs and juglets discovered in the Mount Nebo and Dibon tombs. Some of them are decorated with broad painted strips (sometimes even bichrome), with triangle patterns in between. But further research and study will be required for verification. W. F. Albright also designated certain pottery types, which he collected in his survey in the region of Kerak, as Moabite vessels.

It may be concluded that the influence of Assyrian pottery on the region's vessels is rather small. Most of the vessels discovered here are local imitations of bottles and "carrot vessels." This may indicate a relatively early date for the pottery discovered in Moab, just prior to the Assyrian conquest, or perhaps there are other unknown reasons, but in the matter of relatively minor Assyrian influence, Moabite pottery also differs from that of the two neighboring provinces.

MOAB: SUMMARY AND CONCLUSIONS

IT IS ALMOST impossible to define a separate and independent Moabite material culture. This may be due to the small number of systematic excavations conducted in the land of Moab, or other reasons, such as the incorporation of a large Judaean-Israelite population, the loss of important northern regions during this period to the Ammonites, as the excavations at Heshbon, Tell el-'Umeiri, and Tell Jalul have shown, the possible loss of land in the south to the Edomites, or all of these. This holds true for both the period around the Assyrian conquest and the period of Assyrian domination. This is in marked contrast to the other two Transjordanian kingdoms, Ammon and Edom, for which this period was a time of prosperity and a period during which distinct, independent cultures developed. This situation affects almost every aspect of material culture: architecture, burial customs, cult, glyptic art, and even pottery. There are no clear archaeological signs that this period was even a prosperous one for the Moabites. This is peculiar and stands in contrast to the few known written sources, both biblical and Assyrian, that point to this small country as very active, with a considerable military capability and successes to its credit in clashes against Judah and the Arabs (naturally assisted by the Assyrian units stationed in its territory). It should also be pointed out that the Assyrian conquest and presence did not, for some reason, leave clear traces here (except, perhaps, for some structures at Balu'a or a few seals). Until more centers of this land are excavated or more finds emerge, the existence of a separate "Moabite culture" remains more fantasy than reality.

· Chapter 11 ·

THE EDOMITES

INTRODUCTION

Following Tiglath-pileser III's campaigns in Palestine in 734 BCE, Edom, too, came under Assyrian domination. Some of the Assyrian sources deal with the kingdom of Edom, and mention the names of some of its kings and their achievements: for example, the building inscription of Tiglath-pileser III refers to Qosmalku of Edom as one of the kings from whom he received tribute. One of the Nimrud letters tells of a coalition of Palestinian states, led by Ashdod, among which Edom is listed. The letter dates from the time of Sargon II's campaign in 712 BCE. Aiarammu king of Edom was one of the kings who brought gifts to Sennacherib in 701 BCE. Qosga, a later king of Edom, was one of the twelve kings compelled to furnish supplies for the construction of Esarhaddon's palace at Nineveh. That same king offered gifts and submitted to Ashurbanipal, who, in his ninth campaign (against the Arabs), pursued his quarry into Moab and Edom.

The seal impression of one of these Edomite kings, Qosgabru, was found in the excavations of Umm el-Biyara (later Petra) on a bulla, with his full title: "king of Edom." A second seal was found in the German excavations in Babylon!

The traditional territory of the Edomites was in the southern part of the Transjordan, and there they dwelled until the coming of the Assyrians, after which they started to expand, first into the Aravah and later into the southernmost part of Judah. It is now clear from the results of excavations in Edom, as well as from the biblical and Assyrian references to Edom, that the Assyrian period was the period of Edom's greatest prosperity and a time of economic expansion, as it was for the other main Transjordanian kingdom, Ammon, and—to a lesser degree—Moab.

In 734 BCE, Edom (if the reading Edom for Aram be allowed in 2 Kings 16:6) seized Elath on the Gulf of Aqabah; according to 2 Chronicles 28:17, the Edomites "had again invaded and defeated Judah and carried away captives." Edom's interest in southern Judah may be further attested by the fragmentary Ostracon No. 40 from Arad Stratum VIII (destroyed, according to Y. Aharoni, in 701 BCE). This ostracon appears to refer to some diplomatic activity between Edom and Judah. Among a second group of ostraca from Arad, Ostracon 24, dated by Aharoni to 598/7 BCE, contains an order that troops be sent from Arad and Qinah to Ramot Negev "lest anything should happen to the city" and "lest Edom should come there."

The westward expansion of the Edomites in this period—archaeological evidence for which will be discussed below in detail—occurred for the following two reasons: 1. Edomites and Judaeans were engaged in a struggle for control over copper sources, both on the eastern side of the Aravah, i.e., Khirbet Naḥas and Funon, and in the region of Timnah. The importance of these copper sources was immense, for these were the only metal sources in the area. 2. The importance of the Aravah was even more prominent as the major highway between the shores of the Red Sea and the Arabian trade routes and the roads leading to the Transjordanian plateau and on to Syria, or to the Palestinian Mediterranean coasts. There was a short route through Kadesh-Barnea to Gaza (and from there to Egypt) and a longer (but much more comfortable) one, through the Aravah, the Beersheba Valley, and the western Negev to Gaza.

From a military standpoint, the Edomites did not encounter any difficulty in holding the Aravah, for it was an open, flat, desert area, close to the rocky mountains where they dwelled, and the approach to it from the various parts of Edom was quite short and easy. The Edomites were therefore able, as long as they were independent, to hold with small effort the various oases and the copper mines along the Aravah and to defend them against raiding nomads from the east and against the Judaeans from the west. At the same time, the Aravah with its mines was somewhat remote from the center of Judaean settlement, separated from them by wide desert areas difficult to cross.

After the Edomite conquest of the Judaean settlements and fortresses along the Aravah, i.e., at Tell el-Kheleifeh and Meẓad Ḥaẓeva, during the Assyrian period, the Edomites took control over the entire area south of the Beersheba Valley. Here, they even gained control over the southern side of the valley itself, from which they dominated the copper, incense, and spice trade toward Gaza and the Mediterranean coast, destined for the Greek and the Egyptian markets.

An echo to the bitter struggle taking place between the Edomites and the Judaeans as well as the Judaean retreat before the Edomites is found in the bitter accusations against the Edomites pronounced in the Bible and in the two Arad Ostraca mentioned above, especially no. 40, which tells about "the evil that Edom has done."

The Edomite language, like that of the Ammonites and the Moabites, also belongs to the Canaanite branch of the West Semitic languages and is also close to Hebrew. It, too, at the end of the 8th century BCE with the cessation of Judaean influence, passed to Aramaic script while maintaining a separate local dialect.

All of the inscribed Edomite sources from the Iron Age date to the 7th to 6th centuries BCE and no earlier ones are known. On the other hand, there are many later Edomite inscriptions down to the Hellenistic period. From the Assyrian period, two ostraca in particular stand out. One is from Tell el-Kheleifeh, in the Edomite-Assyrian Stratum IV, which is a list of names, three of which have the component Qos (the name of the Edomite national god,

I.107 An Edomite ostracon from Ḥorvat ʿUza

I.108 An Edomite bronze seal from Qitmit in the form of a human head

not mentioned at all in the Bible): Qosbaneh, Qosnadab, and Pegaqos. The second ostracon was found in the fortress of 'Uza, south of Arad, in which an order is given to bring some food to an altar. Here, the writer of the ostracon blesses the man to whom he is writing in the name of Qos. In a nearby Edomite sanctuary at Qitmit, a few fragmentary ostraca were recovered, which also mention the name Qos. West of here, at Aroer, another small Edomite ostracon fragment was recovered.

The rest of the Edomite inscribed material was found incised on seals or on seal impressions. We have already mentioned the bulla with the impression of "Qosgabar the king of Edom" found at Umm el-Biyara (and a second seal of his that turned up in the excavations at Babylon). These are until now the only seals containing a Palestinian king's name and title to have been found in excavations (Qosgabaru himself, the king of Edom, is mentioned, as was pointed out, in the Assyrian records of Esarhaddon and Ashurbanipal). Another seal found at Buṣeirah, the capital of Edom, belonged to "*mlklb*' servant of the king." At Tell el-Kheleifeh, a few seal impressions were found on jars in which "Qos'anali servant of the king" is mentioned. These last two impressions attest that in Edom, too, the administrative hierarchy was the same as in all the other Palestinian states of the period. In this connection, a

I.109 An Edomite seal from Tel Malḥata depicting a stag

I.110 An Edomite seal from Ḥazeva in an Assyrian style

stone seal found in Aroer in the Beersheba Valley is inscribed with an Edomite name, "belonging to Qosa." In the Edomite fort of Meẓad Ḥazeva, another stone seal was found inscribed with the name *mskt bn mhzn* (Mskt the son of Mhzn). An additional seal of bronze from the Edomite sanctuary at Qitmit is in the form of double human heads. An inscription incised on its base reads *shuvnqos* ("Qos come back"). The shape of this seal is rare among the Palestinian finds, but we do have similar Phoenician clay vessels, and this form probably originated there.

While two of the motifs depicted in the Edomite seals, the one of the king of Edom and another inscribed with the name Qosa, are taken from the Phoenico-Israelite repertoire of figures (both depict sphinxes), all the other seals, among them those found at Meẓad Ḥazeva and Qitmit, display purely Assyrian scenes such as two bearded figures standing in front of an altar on which the moon crescent, the sun disk, and stars can be observed. These were probably the seals of the priests who served in these two sanctuaries. Most of the other Edomite seals, such as that of *qos'dry* ("Qos is my help"), are also engraved with Mesopotamian motifs. In the Hecht collection, there is another priestly Edomite seal inscribed with the words "the seal of Qos." But there is at least one Edomite seal with the title "servant of Ba'al." Among the Edomite pottery vessels is a group with stamped decorations, the motifs of which are also purely Phoenician ones, such as the cow suckling a calf, a grazing stag, etc. We did not find among the Edomite glyptic art any Assyrian-influenced objects, except for the above-mentioned late seals from Ḥazeva and Qitmit. We may therefore assume that the Assyrian influence in Edom was mainly limited to pottery shapes and forms, many of which were direct copies of Assyrian Palace ware. These are quite common in the Edomite settlements of the period (see below).

EXCAVATIONS AND SURVEYS

Eastern Edom

OUR KNOWLEDGE OF the sites and settlements of eastern Edom (located on the east side of the Aravah, i.e., the original Edomite homeland) came in the past mainly from the excavations conducted by C. Bennett at three of its major cities—Buṣeirah, Umm el-Biyara, and Tawilan—as well as from some small excavations at other sites, or from a few extensive surveys conducted in the region. Buṣeirah (biblical Bozrah) was the state's capital and proved to be a large fortified city in the north of Edom. The other two excavated cities were smaller and are just south of Petra. Tawilan was identified with the biblical Edomite city of Teiman and Umm el-Biyara with Edomite Sela. Both were found to have been unfortified settlements, built according to a symmetrical plan. Recently, a fourth Edomite site was excavated at Ghrareh, which resembles the others in both date and character. This site is located farther to the south.

In the main excavation at **Buṣeirah,** the capital of Edom, an interesting administrative center was unearthed. The town was fortified by a wall and was evidently divided into two parts: an upper and a lower town (a similar division, also based on the natural morphology of the area, was also observed in another capital city: Rabbath-Ammon). In the center of the upper town (Area A) were discovered some public buildings. In the area between the upper and lower towns, the city fortifications were uncovered, while in the lower town (Areas B+D), remains of domestic dwellings were found. Here, too, it became clear through the excavations that all the architectural remains and all the finds date to the Late Iron Age alone, i.e., from the Assyrian conquest and later. Some date to the Persian period.

The public buildings unearthed at Buṣeirah were built according to a plan that had some of the characteristics of Assyrian architecture discussed above. In the acropolis of the city, two buildings were uncovered which were built one above the other. The lower one had large dimensions (77 x 38 m.) and was composed of two wide courtyards surrounded by rows of rooms. In the line of rooms that separated the two courtyards, one room served as a sanctuary. The structure of the upper stratum is smaller than the lower (48 x 36 m.). Here was found only one courtyard surrounded by rooms. In all the structures of Buṣeirah, only a small amount of dated finds was recovered, but the very fact that the upper building was built on a structure that was already planned as an Assyrian "open-court" house makes it clear that it should be dated to the late 7th and early 6th centuries BCE.

From the third public building (its estimated dimensions are 105 x 67 m.), only a small part was uncovered in Area C. The remains were part of a large hall, about 6.5 m. wide with an estimated length of 14 m. An interesting element that connects it to the Assyrian world, according to R. Reich, is a wide and shallow depression into which the thick plaster floor that covers the hall did not extend. This was interpreted as having held a stone platform: a common feature in Assyrian reception rooms. The stone was missing. In another part of the building, the remains of toilet installations were found, also of a type common in Assyrian palaces. The two buildings—the lower one in Area A and the one that was partly excavated in Area C, the largest structures in Buṣeirah—must therefore have been built after the city was taken by the Assyrians. One perhaps served as an administrative center and the other was probably a sanctuary.

At **Tawilan,** a small unfortified agricultural settlement, were uncovered five phases, all dated to the 7th century BCE. The town probably continued, however, into the Persian period, as attested by a cuneiform tablet found there dated to the days of one of the three kings of Persia named Darius. The same is true of **Umm el-Biyara,** an unfortified settlement atop a rock overlooking Petra. Within its houses were found many loom weights. It is a single-period settlement from the first half of the 7th century BCE, according to the bulla found there, and belonging to Qosgabar king of Edom, who is mentioned in the Assyrian records dating to the days of Esarhaddon (673 BCE) and Ashurbanipal (667 BCE).

In recent years, several small Edomite fortresses and settlements have been excavated by M. Lindner. These belong to a chain of Edomite settlements built on mountain tops or spurs in a straight line, forming a clear defensive line toward the west. The sites contained Edomite vessels of the 7th century BCE (including imitations of Assyrian vessels). These settlements were uncovered at the following sites (from north to south): Ba'ja III, Kutle II, Jabal al-Khubtha, Jabal al-Qseir, Es-Sudeh, and at **Ghrareh**. The results of the excavations here, as well as the results of extensive regional surveys, clearly showed that all the rural settlements here were likewise erected in the 7th century and later. It should be added that, as in Ammon and Moab, a network of roads and border forts was discovered in the east, the most prominent example being the fortress at **Khirbet esh-Shudigia**.

The results of the excavations and surveys in eastern Edom bring us two important pieces of information:

1. There are no clear Edomite remains from the Late Iron Age that are earlier than the Assyrian conquest of the country, and there is no doubt that the Assyrian domination of the region was the major factor contributing to the new wave of construction and prosperity, especially in the southern part of the country.

2. Because all the remains that have been uncovered here were constructed after the Assyrian conquest, it is clear that most of the houses that have been cleared were built following the Assyrian "open-court" model, for here, too, the few examples of previous construction encountered followed the Phoenician-Israelite plan in its Transjordanian version: adjacent three-room structures.

Results of the various excavations and surveys conducted recently in the **Wadi Feinan** (biblical Funon) large copper mines also point to the new prosperity of the region in the 7th century BCE during a renewed period of copper extraction from these mines. This could only have been achieved, as some scholars have suggested, with the help of the Assyrians. The Assyrians must have been interested in the region's prosperity for the benefit of the trade crossing it. During this period, the Edomites already dominated the entire Aravah, including the copper mines of Timnah.

Western Edom

Parallel to the intensive construction of settlements in their original homeland in the east with Assyrian encouragement, recent archaeological discoveries have shown that the Edomites made an enormous effort to expand their territory into the Aravah and the Negev. In so doing, they had to fight against the Judaean kingdom into whose territory they were penetrating, destroying its fortresses and settlements and pushing its population northward. It is now clear that there are more Edomite finds from this region than we have from the original eastern Edomite territory, due to the many excavations that have been carried out in this area.

Tell el-Kheleifeh, the first Edomite settlement in the Aravah, was found by N. Glueck. Within the remains of the excavated site, he noted five different strata, correctly attributed Stratum IV to the Edomites, and dated it to the late 8th to early 6th centuries BCE. Among the finds of the stratum, he published Edomite ostraca and clay vessels, plain and decorated; local imitations of Assyrian Palace ware vessels; and Edomite seal impressions, including that of "Qosanal servant of the king." These were found in a fortress that during this period was almost square, with a strong gate of four-chambered plan. This Edomite fortress, built upon the remains of a previous Judaean one, served as an Edomite administrative center and fort on the highway from the Red Sea shore that crossed the southern part of the Aravah.

The northern part of the Aravah was dominated by the Edomites from their fort at **Meẓad Ḥaẓeva.** This fort (identified by its present excavator, R. Cohen, with biblical Tamar; cf. Ezekiel 47:19) is built close to the northern side of the Ḥaẓeva River. Like Tell el-Kheleifeh, it was located on an important crossroads along the Aravah highway, as well as at an important source of water, much needed by the caravans passing there. Before it came under Edomite domination, it served, like the site of Tell el-Kheleifeh, as a Judaean fort, perhaps the largest in the region (it was four times larger than the fort of Arad). The Edomite fortress established here was much smaller than the Judaean one. It was included here in Stratum IV, also dated to the 7th and early 6th centuries BCE. Of the walls were preserved here only the lowest courses of the foundation, and the complete plan was not established. In the excavations, mainly the eastern side was exposed, the width of which was about 2.5 m. There were also remains of two towers 14 m. apart, each measuring 11 x 11 m. On the floors of the towers were unearthed a few local Edomite and Assyrianized vessels dated to the 7th to 6th centuries BCE, as well as an Edomite seal inscribed "belonging to Maskit the son of Whazim." Outside the fort, an Edomite sanctuary containing a rich assemblage of cult objects was found.

Edomite pottery, Edomite cult objects, and Edomite ostraca and seals were found, outside the Aravah (i.e., Tell el-Kheleifeh and Ḥazeva) in the southern part of the Negev on the border of the Sinai, along the road leading from Elath to Kadesh-Barnea and Egypt. Along this road, Edomite material was recovered in the fort of Kadesh-Barnea and in the fortresses of Ḥorvat La'ana and Ḥorvat Rogem, but most of the finds come from the settlements along the southern side of the Beersheba Valley: from the forts and settlements of 'Uza, Qitmit, Tel Malḥata, and Aroer, with some of Tel 'Ira and Tel Masos. The rest of the Edomite artifacts (again, small quantities) come from the settlements of the western Negev, such as Tel Sera', Tel Haror, and Tell Jemmeh, and perhaps also from Tel Qatif (Ruqeish), all of which were also Assyrian strongholds.

There are two possible roads connecting Elath on the Red Sea coast with Gaza on the Mediterranean coast. One follows the Aravah to Ḥazeva, then turns into the Beersheba Valley and passes through the western Negev to the coast (to this road were possibly connected the short east-west routes that led from eastern Edom to the sea). This is the route crossing from Ḥazeva through 'Uza and Malḥata (with its sanctuary at Qitmit), along the south side of the Beersheba Valley outside the Judaean territory, and through Aroer, 'Ira, and Masos to Tel Sera', Tel Haror, Gaza, or the Assyrian-built harbor at Tel Qatif (Ruqeish).

The shorter but much more difficult route is the one that led from Elath to Kadesh-Barnea, where it split in two: one branch leading to Gaza and the countries in the west and the other to Egypt.

Anyone who follows the Edomite finds of this period in the area can see that their settlements were established along these two roads, along which they transported the costly Arabian merchandise to destinations in Egypt and lands farther west. One cannot understand the tremendous development of this desert border region, which over a period of fewer than a hundred years was dotted by so many Judaean settlements and fortresses, then replaced in part by Edomite ones, without understanding the renewal of the Arabian trade with the west and with Egypt. Edomite pressure to break through Judaean territory to the coast was entirely motivated by the will to control this trade. The echo of this pressure is found in the biblical narratives that condemn "wicked Edom" for its evil deeds, accusations more numerous than against all the other neighbors of Judah combined. We shall again mention Ostraca Nos. 24 and 40 from the Judaean fort of Arad, which also warn against the Edomites or complain about "the evil that Edom has done." The question remaining is, which of the Judaean forts and settlements were captured and occupied by the Edomites? The answer becomes clearer from one excavation to the next, and there is little doubt that in the struggle over the domination of the road along the Beersheba Valley, Judah lost to Edom. There were two reasons for this loss, both results of Assyrian intervention in favor of the Edomites. One relates to the Assyrian military campaigns to the region and especially that of Sennacherib in 701 BCE, in which he destroyed forty-six Judaean settlements, among them probably many of the Judaean forts on the kingdom's southern border, such as Arad and Tel Sheva (which never recovered). In this manner, the Assyrians opened the way for the Edomites. It took some time before the Judaean kingdom recovered during the days of Manasseh and again rebuilt its southern line of fortresses, and as has already been shown, added many new ones. It seems that at this time the Edomites were already well established in the region and may even have settled some of the destroyed sites.

The second factor that acted in the Edomites' favor is the constant Assyrian support they received through the entire Assyrian period, promoting their expansion, both because they were considered better and more reliable allies than the Judaeans (they supported the Assyrian army in its campaign to Egypt) and because in southern Philistia the Assyrians had built large civilian and military administrative centers on the way to Egypt, the remains of which were discovered in the excavations at Tell Jemmeh, Sera', Haror, Anthedon (Sheikh Zuweid), and in the new harbor site that they built at Qatif (Ruqeish). There can be no doubt that this large construction effort was intended, besides protecting the road to Egypt, to reap some of the benefits of Arabian trade, and for this, Arabs and Edomites were the perfect partners.

The archaeological evidence for this development is clear. We have seen that the Edomites captured and destroyed the two large Judaean forts along the Aravah at Tell el-Kheleifeh and Hazeva. Next came the Judaean fort of 'Uza, the easternmost fort in the Beersheba Valley, which was also probably the first of the Judaean fortresses in the valley to fall to the Edomites. Here, the Edomites perhaps first served as mercenaries in the army of the Judaean kingdom. Somewhat later, perhaps in the mid-7th century BCE, they captured the fort of 'Uza, according to the evidence of the Edomite ostracon found here, which indicates that at that time the fort had an Edomite commander. The Edomite finds at Malhata, Qitmit, and Aroer also show that this line of Judaean defense fell to them. The Judaean borderline was pushed back in the course of the 7th century BCE to the northern part of the Beersheba Valley, to Arad, the defenders of which and of the neighboring forts were told: "and the word of the king is incumbent upon you for your very life! Behold, I have sent to warn you today lest Edom should come there." In the same ostracon, two more unidentified Judaean forts are mentioned: Qinah and Ramot Negev. But the same line included—according to recent investigations—the forts at Radum, 'Ira, and Masos and approached the Judaean settlement that today lies under modern Beersheba (for at Tel Sheva itself, the Judaean fort had been destroyed long before, in 701 BCE).

In the western Negev, Edomite remains are less numerous and probably were left by their convoys on their way to the Mediterranean coast. It is impossible that sites such as Tel Haror, Tel Sera', Sheikh Zuweid, and Tell Jemmeh, at this time, as was shown above, strong Assyrian fortresses, were captured by the Edomites. On the other hand, the southernmost road, which passed through Kadesh-Barnea, La'ana, and Rogem, must have been under Edomite control, for it is difficult to believe that Judaean control was maintained here after the area to the north of it had already fallen into Edomite hands.

It was during the late 7th and early 6th centuries BCE that "greater Edom" was established on both sides of the Aravah and in the southern Negev, the first step in the creation of the later Persian-period "Idumaea."

THE EDOMITE CULT

ANOTHER AREA IN the study of the Edomite material culture in which there has been great progress is the Edomite cult and its cult objects. It was already mentioned above that the name of the Edomite national deity was Qos (a name not mentioned in the Bible) and that the name of his consort was not preserved, but it can be reconstructed perhaps as Ishtar-Qos (on the basis of the Moabite Ishtar-Kemosh mentioned in the Mesha Stela). But the name Qos appears frequently both in the Assyrian documents and on Edomite seals and ostraca (inscribed also on clay vessels found in the Edomite sanctuary at Qitmit). In the last two sources, it appears frequently in the personal names of the Edomite kings, high-ranking officials of the kingdom, and its citizens, such as Qosgabar the king of Edom, who is also mentioned in the Assyrian records, Qos'anal the king's servant, Qosa, Pegaqos, Qosnaqam, etc., and mainly in the opening blessings in the Edomite texts, such as the ostracon from ʿUza, which starts with the words "and I shall bless you to Qos." But virtually no actual Edomite cultic remains were known until recently.

For many years, only a handful of Edomite clay figurines was known from a site by the name of ʿAin Jenin near Buṣeirah, found by G. Lankester-Harding. They are figurines and anthropomorphic vessels very peculiar in form, the structure of their bodies, and especially the morphology of their faces: they have unusually large applied eyes and sharp noses. One of these probably represents a hermaphrodite, for it has both beard and breasts. It also has a headdress in the shape of a lamp and holds a tambourine (which we already saw to be one of the four standard musical instruments in all Palestinian cults). The second find looked like a female anthropomorphic vessel. A similar anthropomorphic vessel depicting a bearded male was found in the Judaean site of Tel ʿErani west of Lachish, far north of Edom.

Until recently, no Edomite sanctuaries were known at all. At Buṣeirah, the Edomite capital, a structure was excavated between two courtyards, which was interpreted by R. Reich as a temple on the basis of the following characteristics: A wide flight of steps extends across the entire width of the room and leads to a higher floor. These steps are flanked by two stone bases that supported either sculptures or other large cult objects (and not columns as the excavators believed). The steps led to a smaller rectangular room, on the other side of which were three small cell-like rooms, very similar to the cells of the Edomite temple at Qitmit (see below). Reich believes that the plan of this entrance is identical to that of Assyrian temples in the central part of the Assyrian empire (at Khorsabad, for example), as well as to some Syrian temples in regions under Assyrian domination (Tel Halaf), or the Assyrian temple at Sheikh Zuweid near Gaza.

The major Edomite cult finds came again from the region of west Edom. They were uncovered at two sites: **Qitmit** in the Arad Valley and **ʿEn Ḥazeva** in the Aravah.

At **Qitmit,** the remains of a single-period temple (dated to the late 7th to early 6th centuries BCE) were found atop a rocky hill covering an area of about half an acre. The temple is composed of two building groups. The major part of the local cult was practiced in a three-room structure and at a platform erected nearby, which was surrounded by a stone wall. Nearby were also found an altar and a basin. At the site were also found many Edomite clay vessels. In the area around the platform, a few dozen broken clay figurines, large clay sculptures, and anthropomorphic vessels, as well as stands, chalices, and small incense altars, were found. The plan of this temple at Qit-

I.111 Qitmit, aerial view and view of the Edomite sanctuary

mit was quite different from all other contemporary Judaean sanctuaries, including the one at nearby Arad, and so were all its finds.

It is true that among the many finds discovered here, a few resembled those found elsewhere, such as female figurines supporting their breasts, with mold-made heads and handmade bodies, but this type of Judaean figurine formed a small minority of the finds. The majority of the finds was composed of figurines of males and females, of animals such as bulls, lions, stags, and birds, including a cock, ostriches, and perhaps also doves, and pomegranates. All were executed in the peculiar Edomite style, which differs from all other styles in the other states of Palestine. It is distinguished in particular by the features of the faces: large eyes, long nose. On some were preserved some red and black paint. Based upon some of the preserved body parts, hands, and even weapons, some of them would have been almost lifelike in size and shape, like a human body, and would compare in size with Ammonite stone sculptures discussed above. Another peculiarity is the crosshatch painted garments with dotted borderlines.

Among the finds here were also many hollow anthropomorphic vessels, some made on the potter's wheel, which mainly depict bearded males. Another common type was the open cylindrical stands, also wheel-thrown; their lower part was open without a base, and they were surrounded by human and animal figurines, creating a composite scene. The animal figurines were also hollow. They were sometimes made by hand and were attached to the stand's walls, or were placed on narrow shelves. Among them is the figure of a winged sphinx. This, together with some pottery lotus buds, undoubtedly harks back to Phoenician prototypes. Another group of cult objects included clay chalices standing on a tall base, which were surrounded by lines of pomegranates hanging on their sides. Some of the clay vessels here also had incised dedications to Qos.

The Edomite sanctuary uncovered at ʿEn Ḥaẓeva in 1993 is north of the fort, outside its defensive wall. It was a long and narrow structure divided into a few rooms that were not very well preserved above the foundation. In a pit within the enclosure of the sanctuary, which probably served as a *favissa,* a large assemblage of various cult objects was uncovered. Many of them were broken by large stones, which were part of the sanctuary before its destruction. This peculiar assemblage included sixty-seven clay objects and seven stone incense altars in various sizes. Among the clay objects, nine different types were observed. Some of these are as follows: (1) three stands in the shape of human figures, among them one that holds a cultic bowl, similar to one of the Qitmit figures; (2) eight cylindrical clay stands surrounded

I.112 Edomite clay figurines from Qitmit

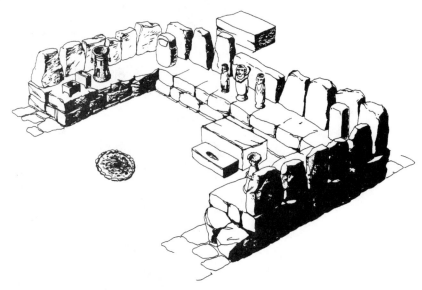

I.113 Reconstruction of the Edomite sanctuary at Ḥazeva

by applied figurines; (3) fifteen clay incense burners, which were shaped as chalices with windows; (4) eleven small chalices decorated with applied projections, one incised with the image of a bull; (5) five small cups, five small bowls; (6) two incense ladles with projecting handles shaped as pomegranates of two types: three very small complete pomegranates and three large ones. Among the most impressive finds were the three human stands. Their heads and bodies were wheel-thrown; the other parts were applied later by

I.114 Edomite clay stands from Ḥazeva

hand: hands and legs, various face parts (noses, ears, mouth, etc.), and especially the locks of hair. Here, too, remains of brown-red paint are preserved. The date of this assemblage, according to its excavator, R. Cohen, is in the late 7th century BCE or the early 6th. The concentration of the vessels in one location, their deliberate breakage, and their deposition in a pit show that this pit was a *favissa* that belonged to the Edomite temple. Nor is there doubt

I.115 Tel Malḥata, Edomite clay figurine of a male god playing a double flute

concerning the clear resemblance between the assemblages from Qitmit and Ḥazeva, as well as between the plan of the two sanctuaries; both differ from all known Judaean sanctuaries elsewhere. Evidently, the distance between the two is about 50 km., and both are outside the main settlement (the sanctuary at Ḥazeva is outside the fort, and the Qitmit sanctuary is located on a hill a very short distance from Tel Malḥata, the major Edomite town in the area). Establishment of cult centers along trade routes is a custom well known in other regions and periods. In one of the buildings of the large Edomite settlement that survived at Tel Malḥata, more Edomite cult vessels were recently recovered. The most distinctive of them is a painted clay figurine depicting a bearded male playing a double flute. The excavator, I. Beit-Arieh, also pointed out that "the geographical proximity of Qitmit to the sizable settlement at Tel Malḥata, 5 kms. away, and the similarity in the material culture of the two sites leads one to believe that the Qitmit shrine must have served the population of the town."

The Edomite sanctuaries and cult objects are unique only in their plan and forms, not in content, for they clearly continue old Palestinian traditions in the figurines, sculptures, anthropomorphic vessels, stands, and chalices that were long established in the country's cult. The one innovation that can be observed here is the cessation of the typical Iron Age four-horned stone altars, which were popular before the Assyrian conquest all over the country. These are replaced (both at Ḥazeva and Qitmit) by the small cubic stone (sometimes clay) incense altars. This change was accepted within a short time in other Palestinian states, too, including Judah.

The deities that were worshiped in the Edomite sanctuaries were evidently Qos and his consort. The male god is depicted in the two usual forms: the ruling god and the armed fighting god. P. Beck also recently pointed to the frequent appearance of the figure of the "goring bull" at the two sanctuaries: clay bull figurines at Qitmit and an incised goring bull on a clay stand from Ḥazeva, as well as two bull horns incised on the top of an altar depicted on a seal from Ḥazeva; and most important, the bull horns engraved on a

I.116 Edomite clay figurine of a lamp-bearer deity

stone slab-stela, also from Ḥazeva. She suggested identifying the bull as a representation of the Edomite god Qos in the form of a weather god.

The consort of Qos usually appears as a fertility goddess who supports her breasts, but there might be a version that portrays her as a fighting goddess, for one of the prominent finds at Qitmit depicts a clay goddess head crowned with three horns. Similar complete figurines from elsewhere depict such goddesses as carrying weapons. The horns point to her divinity. One group among the female figurines may represent what we have called hermaphrodites, similar to the type that we have already seen among the cults of other nations such as Ishtar-Kemosh in Moab, or Tanit the face of Baʿal among the Phoenicians, which may be interpreted as the goddess representing her husband. The other finds, the birds and the pomegranates, may also pertain to her cult, for they are well-known symbols of fertility. The figurines depicting the double-flute, lyre, or tambourine players, as well as a figurine of a dancer, should be compared with those common in most other Palestinian cults. They also have many analogies, even among the artifacts of the Canaanite cult. The same is true of some of the products of the apotropaic cult, such as the clay masks, some of which were found at Qitmit. To summarize, the uniqueness of the Edomite cult lies in its form and style rather than its content.

THE EDOMITE POTTERY

MOST OF THE Edomite settlements produced a peculiar pottery called "Edomite," all of which is dated to the 7th to early 6th centuries BCE. This pottery is composed of two different groups: one is characterized by typical forms and is undecorated; the other is decorated, sometimes with red burnish, but usually with schematic geometric patterns painted in brown, black, red, and white in broad and narrow stripes. Frequent motifs here are the "ladder" design, triangles, triglyphs, and metopes. For this ware, the latter group is dominant. S. Hart recently suggested that the painted decorations on Edomite pottery did not become common until after the Umm el-Biyara settlement had ended, possibly around the mid-7th century BCE, because no Edomite wares were found there.

As to the forms of these Edomite vessels, it seems that because of the Assyrian influence, the Edomite potters incorporated mainly the forms of the Assyrian Palace ware as their prototypes. Archaeometric examination of this pottery showed that the vessels were produced at the sites where found. It should be pointed out, however, that the decorated Edomite pottery is but a small portion of the overall finds, and some authorities believe that the origin of the painted decorations must be in northern Arabia.

The three east Edomite sites excavated by C. Bennett all produced Edomite ceramics. The first is **Umm el-Biyara,** located on a rock overlooking Petra. This is a single-period site dated by the seal of "Qosgabar the king of Edom," who is mentioned in the annals of Esarhaddon and Ashurbanipal the kings of Assur, in the first half of the 7th century BCE. The local assemblage consists of plain Edomite vessels and does not contain any of the decorated Edomite ware, probably because it is earlier. The second site, somewhat north of Biyara, is **Tawilan,** which is a large settlement from the end of the 8th to the early 6th centuries BCE. Here, Edomite pottery vessels of the two main kinds were uncovered, some plain and others decorated with typical Edomite motifs.

The major assemblage of Edomite ware in east Edom was found at the third site: during the four seasons of excavations at **Buṣeirah,** which was constructed on a rock cliff close to the major highway, a few kilometers north of Tawilan. This site can be used as a key to understanding the development of Edomite pottery in its homeland, for Buṣeirah is the only Edomite site that included more than one stratum. According to all signs here, Strata 6–5 were of the late 8th century BCE, i.e., just prior to the Assyrian occupation, when the Phoenician-Israelite material culture was still a major influence. While Strata 4–3 were already Edomite in character, decorated pottery is still rare. Strata 2–1, from the later part of the 7th century BCE, have a high percentage of typically decorated Edomite ware, unique both in the use of the peculiar colors and motifs and in its plastic decoration. On one of the kraters was found an Edomite inscription.

There is another decorated family in Edomite pottery and other south Transjordan pottery, which is characterized by stamped decorations executed in the style of cylinder seals. These are applied to the vessel in the leather-hard stage. The motifs of this group are borrowed from old Israelite-Phoenician repertoire and include a cow suckling a calf, roaring lions, a stag grazing in the field, and a deity seated on a throne. Such motifs clearly antedate Assyrian influence, but nevertheless they continued through the 7th century BCE. They were found in Buṣeirah in Edom, En-Gedi in Judah, and recently at Tell Nimrin in Ammon. The vessel from Nimrin is the only complete one and the most important in the group. It is a handless krater encircled by a stamped frieze depicting animals (grazing stags and roaring lions), palm trees, and incense altars. There are in addition human figures: naked

I.117 En-Gedi, a stamped Edomite vessel

men carrying boars on the shoulders, naked men praying, and figures of the Egyptian-Phoenician god Bes, which had an important apotropaic role among all Palestinian nations of the period (see above).

In this period and following, the Edomite expansion to the west took place. This expansion created a region under their control from the coasts of the Red Sea through the southern part of the Beersheba Valley via the Mediterranean coast (see above). It seems that more Edomite settlements have been excavated in west Edom than in the east. At two of the Edomite sites along the Aravah, Edomite pottery was uncovered at **Tell el-Kheleifeh.** N. Glueck first identified Period IV as an Edomite settlement and pointed out the importance of the Edomites' westward penetration. Here, many Edomite vessels were found together with Assyrian types. At the second site, **'En Ḥaẓeva,** pottery vessels of these two types—decorated Edomite and Assyrian—were uncovered in the Edomite fort (Stratum 4) and in the fort's sanctuary, where an important group of painted Edomite clay figurines and stands was recovered (see above).

At the first site located in the Beersheba Valley, **Aroer,** the Edomite pottery found was divided, according to the excavators, into two types: the undecorated vessels already appeared in Stratum III, and the decorated only in

Stratum II. Even though the chronological difference between the two strata is not great, it definitely shows the trend. More than seventy vessels were found here, the largest existing Edomite pottery assemblage in the Beersheba Valley. At this site were also found an Edomite seal and ostracon.

Farther to the west, at **Tel Malḥata,** in its first excavations by M. Kochavi, a large pottery assemblage was found in one of the casemate rooms of the city wall, which was destroyed by the Babylonians in 582 BCE. The assemblage consisted of both Judaean and Edomite (undecorated) pottery vessels, as well as one complete East Greek jug, which was dated by J. Coldstream to ca. 600 BCE. Also a few painted shards were found in the Iron Age level of the 7th to 6th centuries BCE, revealed in a section cut through the northern slope of the mound. In the recent excavations of this site by I. Beit-Arieh, painted Edomite figurines were found, as well as cosmetic stone palettes of the same

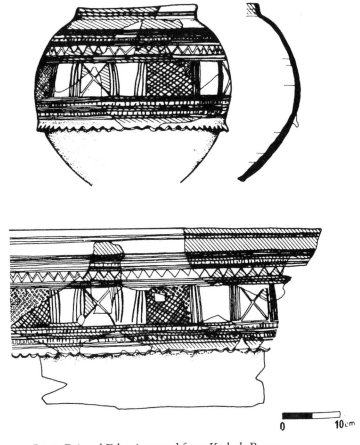

I.118 Painted Edomite vessel from Kadesh-Barnea

date, and a great quantity of Edomite pottery, which may point to the relative importance of this site among the Edomite settlements. Further, at **Qitmit,** the Edomite sanctuary located above Malḥata, a large assemblage of Edomite pottery, as well as many Edomite clay figurines, was recovered. Two phases of the 7th century were discerned in the excavations of **Tel 'Ira,** where only five painted Edomite shards were found, all belonging to the latest phase. At **Tel Masos,** four phases dated to the 7th century were exposed in Area G, but only a single decorated shard was found in the latest level (Phase 1). At **Tel Haror,** located in the western Negev, two decorated shards occurred in the 7th century locus. Two additional Edomite decorated shards were found in Stratum 4 at **Tel Sera',** in the same locus where an East Greek vessel dated to 610 BCE was also found. Finally, at **Kadesh-Barnea,** a relatively large amount of painted Edomite ware was found in the destruction level of the uppermost fort dated to the Babylonian conquest, and more were found in the small forts of La'ana and Rogem. At all the sites listed above, denticulate projecting fringes applied as decoration and bar handles appear together with the painted pottery. The painted pottery was found in minuscule quantities—one to five examples at each site—except at Aroer and Kadesh-Barnea. Even at these sites, the concentrations of decorated Edomite pottery constitute only a tiny proportion of the total pottery assemblages, but undecorated Edomite pottery was more common. Neutron activation analysis of Edomite pottery shows that most of it was made locally in the Judaean Negev, probably by Edomite potters, except perhaps for the cooking pots that are assumed to have been made in Transjordan.

EDOMITE ART OBJECTS

AT THE VARIOUS Edomite sites—Buṣeirah, Tawilan, Umm el-Biyara, as well as those of western Edom—in addition to the seals, ostraca, cult objects, and pottery vessels discussed above, were also found some engraved stone and shell artifacts. The stone and shell vessels are of the cosmetic-palette types, already dealt with above among the Phoenician finds. This industry originated in Phoenicia, from which it spread to other regions of the country. To these finds we should add a few engraved bone and ivory artifacts that were also made under Phoenician inspiration, probably in the period before the arrival of the Assyrians or immediately afterward. These include regular engraved stone cosmetic bowls, some rounded and others in "bird nest" shape; alabaster palettes engraved in the form of women; similarly engraved

Tridacna shells; and recently, a few engraved ivories, such as the head of a roaring lion from Buṣeirah, and two thin ivory plaques depicting human figures in a style similar to that of the *Tridacna* shells, which were recently found out of context at Aila, a late settlement on the Red Sea coast.

EDOM: SUMMARY AND CONCLUSIONS

RECENT EVIDENCE FROM excavation and exploration in eastern Edom suggests that the bulk of the settlement sites there do not predate the 7th century BCE, and perhaps only at this point may we speak confidently of an Edomite state (Bienkowski). The factors leading to Edomite statehood were the stability of Assyrian control and improved economic opportunities, for it should be remembered that the Assyrian system of vassaldom also prevented fighting between and among the vassal states. The economic opportunities were the resumption of mining in Feinan and the Arabian trade in luxury goods, particularly frankincense and other kinds of incense as well as various spices. Nevertheless, eastern Edom never became fully urban. The only site that might be called "urban" is Buṣeirah, probably the Edomite capital. The remainder of the settlements in eastern Edom, which date to the 7th and the early 6th centuries BCE, were mostly open villages, small towns or fortresses, sometimes located on almost inaccessible mountaintops. These were long ago identified by N. Glueck as "border forts." Apart from Buṣeirah and Tawilan, this ring of forts includes the sites of Sela and Umm el-Biyara as front forts and the forts at Kutle II, Baʾja III, Jabal el-Khubtha, Jabal al-Qseir, Es-Sudeh, and Ghrareh, all recently excavated. Although many details of the plans are different, there are some common characteristics in the architecture of these sites: the environmental setting of the Edomite sites lends itself to building in stone rather than mud brick. Pillars were occasionally used (for example at Tawilan and Ghrareh) as roof supports. Building plans were generally rectangular, sometimes with long corridor-like rooms with smaller rooms adjoining.

The Edomite expansion to the west during the 7th century BCE was characterized not only by the destruction of the Judaean forts and settlements in the region but by their replacement with a new Edomite system of road-fortresses. This probably began with Tell el-Kheleifeh and Ḥazeva along the Aravah. The Edomite fort at Ḥazeva was much smaller than the last Judaean one. Perhaps the new Edomite settlements at Malḥata and Aroer were somewhat larger, and Malḥata perhaps served (with Qitmit) as their central site. It is logical to speak about an expansion executed in two waves. The first was accomplished by Edomite traders and perhaps also some mercenaries. The second occurred when the Assyrian domination was well established both in Transjordan on one side and in Philistia on the other. This was mainly during the forty years when Esarhaddon and Ashurbanipal were active in Palestine (680–640 BCE), and especially during the fifteen years when they campaigned against Egypt and therefore were acquainted with what was happening in southern Palestine. The Assyrian domination no doubt much improved the status of Edom, in its traditional land, in which we are able to detect large-scale building activity, the renewal of copper production, and Assyrian support for the Edomites and the Arabian traders in the area between the desert and the Mediterranean coast. This trade began to develop in the late 8th century BCE with the renewal of old ties with the west in general and with Greece in particular, and encouraged the movement of Greek and Phoenician traders to settle even in this remote region.

It even seems probable that the struggle between Judaeans and Edomites was renewed, with all its strength, during the period starting with the Assyrians' retreat from the country until the coming of the Babylonians (640–604 BCE), who conquered and destroyed both countries (586–582 BCE).

There is some analogy between the picture that has been drawn here about the relations between the Edomites and the Assyrians and what occurred in this region later, during the Persian period, between the Persians and the Qedarite tribes who inherited the Edomites' role in the Arabian trade, and the Nabataeans in the Hellenistic and early Roman periods. For, from the time of the renewal of the Arabian trade with the west by the Edomites and Assyrians (and by the Greeks and the Phoenicians on the western end), it continued almost uninterruptedly (except for a short time in the Babylonian period) in all the following periods. The main change was in the peoples who conducted this trade across the desert to the Mediterranean ports.

Chapter 12

THE ARABIAN TRADE

INTRODUCTION

We shall now discuss the appearance of the nomadic tribes in the desert border regions of Palestine and northern Sinai during the Assyrian period, reflected in the written documents of the archaeological finds.

I. Eph'al's recent extensive study serves as the basis for our discussion of the historical background of these tribes. He claims that the nomadic tribes in the Syrian-Arabian desert and northern Sinai are already known from the biblical and Assyrian sources as 'arabya or 'aribi and that they should be considered an independent factor in the political and administrative fabric of the Assyrian empire. These nomads had a permanent need for grazing pastures and water sources located along the border of the settled country, especially in years of drought. They must have profited from the services they provided for the convoys passing through their territories (supplying them with water and protection), convoys that carried incense and spices and other luxurious merchandise from southern Arabia. The establishment of Assyrian domination over the entire western part of the Fertile Crescent, including the road system of the North Arabian trade, brought the nomads under effective if indirect Assyrian rule from the days of Tiglath-pileser III and on. The formal relation between the leaders of the nomads and the kings of Assyria—according to the Assyrian kings' inscriptions—was that of a vassal to his lord, and found formal expression by the payment of tribute in fixed amounts and periods, as well as by oath of obedience that all the Arab leaders had to take before the Assyrian kings. We have the most information about the military campaigns of Tiglath-pileser III against the Meonites roaming along the

Egyptian border, and the campaign of 733/2 BCE, at the end of which he appointed the people of the Idib'el tribe as "the guards to the gates of Egypt." Additional lists of nomadic tribes on the North Arabian border from the days of Tiglath-pileser III and Sargon II, as compared with the biblical sources, indicate the following tribes: the Meonites and the Masa children, Tema, Sheba, Eipha, Dedan, Heth, Idib'el, and Qedar. But one should not exaggerate the extent of active Assyrian domination over the desert people.

Eph'al also believes that the relatively small size of the Assyrian professional army as compared to the huge dimensions of its defense obligations all over the vast border areas of the Assyrian empire, as well as the growing tendency to take a more active role in the Arabian trade and increase its profit for the empire, brought the Assyrian kings also to include some Arabian units within the administrative and military organization of the western part of their empire. In the days of Tiglath-pileser III and Sargon II, some of these tribes were allowed to graze in the border area of the settled lands or even within them (especially within the territories of the directly ruled provinces). Official recognition was granted to their leaders. In the days of Sargon II, some nomadic units originating in northern Arabia were even brought to settle in Samaria, and perhaps also in the el-'Arish region on the Egyptian border. This act should be explained by the desire of Sargon to benefit from their good relations with the other tribes who were involved in the international trade of incense, spices, and perhaps also of gold, through territories ruled by Assyria.

Eph'al points to other important, even decisive roles of the Arabs in other activities of the Assyrian empire. When the Assyrian military campaigns against Egypt began and large contingents of soldiers were transferred through the Sinai desert, it became necessary to supply huge quantities of water and food, for which the Assyrian army, like other large imperial armies of the ancient periods, lacked the means of transport and the know-how. Only the Arabs with their many battalions of camels could handle such matters. In this way, they became an essential factor in the success of the Assyrian campaigns into Egypt, and there is no doubt that they were granted a favorable position within the Assyrian administrative and military organization in the days of Esarhaddon and Ashurbanipal.

The Arabs, the desert dwellers, were divided in the Assyrian period into many tribes widely dispersed geographically. Their policy toward the Assyrians differed from region to region. In some cases, they cooperated with the Assyrian authorities, while in others they were hostile, forcing the Assyrians to campaign against them, or at least to remain militarily alert on the desert borders to defend the settled lands. It seems, however, that the Assyrians were successful through most of this period, and the convoys and the desert trade continued to move.

THE ARCHAEOLOGICAL FINDS

OUR PROBLEM WITH this historical reconstruction is that it lacks substantial supporting evidence in the archaeological finds. The "evidence" consists largely of several short Arabian inscriptions that contained some personal names or ligatures and monograms, as well as one inscribed seal.

This list actually contains two South Arabian objects found in archaeological excavations in Palestine, one from Tell el-Kheleifeh and the other from Bethel. In 1938, N. Glueck found at Tell el-Kheleifeh a South Arabian monogram inscribed, after firing, on the shoulder of a jar. Glueck and G. Ryckmans suggested various readings for the Arabic name that appeared in the inscription. The jar was found in Stratum IV, dated to the early 6th century BCE. The discovery of the first South Arabian inscription at a Palestinian site, located in the Edomite sphere of influence, opened the way for various speculations regarding the substance of the trade relations and the cultural connections between this area near the Gulf of Eilat and South Arabia.

In 1957, the second find was discovered by J. L. Kelso in his excavations at Bethel. This was a broken clay seal inscribed with a South Arabian name written in South Arabic letters. According to A. Jamme, it should be read ". . . Hamiyan the delegate."

In addition to these two inscriptions, Y. Shiloh found three South Arabian ostraca in his excavations in the City of David in Jerusalem. Two of these

I.119 Bethel, an inscribed South Arabian clay seal

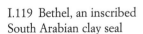

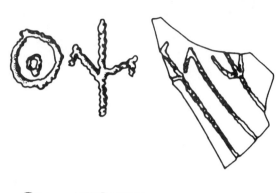

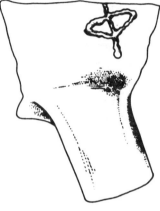

I.120 South Arabian letters incised on pottery shards from Jerusalem

were uncovered in Stratum 10, dated from the end of the 7th century BCE until the destruction of 586 BCE; the third was a surface find. They include Arabic names such as Hallal, Hali, and Dad. But all three were incised on the pottery vessels after their firing by chisel, imprinting a zigzag line, i.e., a method that we treated as "Judaean" or even "Jerusalemite" and only found on local ware. From these facts, Shiloh concluded that "these South Arabian names were inscribed in the City of David, in a Jerusalemite method on local ware at the end of the 7th century BCE."

Shiloh also asked if these finds provided proof of a direct connection with South Arabia, or perhaps pertained to Arabian elements closer to Judah that served as intermediary links between Transjordan and faraway South Arabia. Corroboration, Shiloh believed, could be found in the above-mentioned deportations of Arab tribes by Sargon II to Samaria after its conquest by the Assyrians. It could be that these people carried South Arabian culture into Palestine in this period. Due to their presence, the South Arabian clay seal reached Bethel, and it is to them that the South Arabian names found on objects in Jerusalem relate. This theory does not explain, however, the South

Arabian find at Tell el-Kheleifeh, located on the Red Sea far from Samaria or Judah.

As to other archaeological finds that may have been influenced by the Arabs, E. Mazar has explained the decorated Edomite ware as pottery that originated in Arabia and was used by the local Edomite population, but clear supporting evidence for this interpretation is lacking.

Another proposal was the attribution to South Arabians of the coarse, handmade vessels called Negevite ware, with a geographical distribution limited to the southern part of the Negev, the Aravah, and north Sinai (their northern limit is in the Beersheba Valley). It is true that, as long as this ware was wholly dated to the 10th century BCE, we could not have treated them here at all. In recent excavations at Kadesh-Barnea, this ware evidently continued to the 7th century BCE, where it appears side by side with decorated Edomite pottery, as well as with Assyrian and East Greek material. In Ruth Amiran's discussion of this ware, which was first discovered in N. Glueck's excavation at Tell el-Kheleifeh, she claimed that it is representative of a local nomadic element (perhaps the local Arab tribes of the Meonites or Idib'el), who dwelled close to the Judaean forts during the later period of this kingdom and occupied them after the decline of Judaean domination here in the late 7th century BCE. This is clearly the case at Tell el-Kheleifeh and Ḥazeva and perhaps also at Kadesh-Barnea, even though some of these vessels, even at this relatively late period, reflect Judaean prototypes.

An additional find that perhaps originated with the nomads and the period of their domination of the trade routes between the Red Sea and the Mediterranean are the *Tridacna* shells from the Red Sea, which have been found in all Palestinian regions east and west of the Jordan, and which were engraved by the Phoenicians during the period of 630–580 BCE. It now seems that the raw material, found only in the Red Sea, was supplied to the engravers by the Arabian tribes. Y. Shiloh connected these artifacts with the Arabian trade and pointed out: "It can be assumed that the finished [engraved] objects were imported to Judah from Phoenicia, but it is the less worked fragments or those unworked at all which provide additional evidence of the relation between Palestine and the Gulf of Eilat and the Red Sea, which were the only source of these shells." "We find in this fact," he added, "further evidence for the conclusions made from the discovery of the South Arabian inscriptions in the City of David, concerning the connection and trade relations between Palestine and the Gulf of Eilat and South Arabia in the 7th–6th centuries BCE."

Although the archaeological finds are scanty, the combination of the archaeological discoveries and the historical documentation of this subject suggests the strengthening of an Arabian element in the southern part of Palestine at the end of the Iron Age, a phenomenon that finds more solid evidence in the coming periods. Further support is provided by the occurrence of many Arabic names in contemporary ostraca and seals found in Transjordan and in the Arad Ostraca.

BOOK TWO

THE BABYLONIAN PERIOD

(604–539 BCE)

INTRODUCTION:
THE HISTORY OF PALESTINE
IN THE BABYLONIAN PERIOD

THE LITERARY EVIDENCE

The Babylonians waged far fewer military campaigns for the domination of Palestine than the Assyrians, and the number of the written sources at our disposal describing these is likewise much smaller. However, the results of the Babylonian conquest were, by all measures, far more destructive, and brought the once-flourishing country to one of the lowest ebbs in its long history. Unlike the previous Assyrian imperial system, which strived to create a network of semi-independent provinces, the Babylonian concept was quite different: their entire focus was on the welfare of the city of Babylon and its immediate surroundings, while the periphery was largely neglected, with negative consequences for those living in those territories.

In the first stage of Babylonian expansion, i.e., the actual conquest of Palestine, there are certain similarities to the Assyrian period. However, the few reliable Babylonian sources do not cover the entire Babylonian period. The *Babylonian Chronicle,* our main source of information, covers only the end of the 7th and the beginning of the 6th centuries BCE (from 627 to 594 BCE). Thus, historical information for the greater part of the period is absent.

We learn from the *Chronicle* that Nabopolassar became king in Babylon in 626 BCE and immediately rebelled against the Assyrians. After a few years, Babylon emerged victorious. In 615 BCE, Assur was besieged by a combined Babylonian-Median army. Assyria was defeated in 612 BCE, but the government persisted in control in Haran for a few years. During this period, Egypt extended its assistance to Assyria and sent its forces several times, once in 609 BCE when they clashed with King Josiah near Megiddo. In 606 BCE, immediately after succeeding to the throne, Nebuchadnezzar II king of Babylon (605–562 BCE) defeated the Egyptian army stationed at Carchemish and gained another victory over the Egyptians a short time later, near the city of Hammat. This time the Babylonians drove the Egyptian army out of Syria and built their own headquarters at Rivla, the seat of authority of the defeated Egyptian governor. From here, the Babylonian monarch sent his troops to chase the retreating Egyptians farther south.

In 604 BCE, the Babylonians arrived in Philistia. Within a short time, they conquered Ashkelon, took its king captive, destroyed the city, and deported all its inhabitants. Results of the latest extensive excavations conducted in this region (see below) appear to indicate that at that time, almost all of the other important Philistine towns were completely destroyed and razed and did not recover until the start of the Persian period, i.e., when a new imperial policy was implemented. According to a citation from Berosos preserved by Josephus Flavius (*Against Apion* 1.19), during the same campaigns the Babylonian army almost reached the Egyptian border.

An Aramaic letter found at Saqqara in Egypt, written on a papyrus from the time of these campaigns, was sent to "our lord, king pharaoh," perhaps even Pharaoh Necho himself, by a certain "King Adon," whose name and city are not preserved. He requested help against the approaching Babylonian army. The letter was perhaps sent by the king of Ashkelon, or perhaps by some other Philistine king (the king of Ekron?), whose city was captured and destroyed some time later.

In the same year, Judah was subjugated and King Jehoiakim transferred his allegiance from Egypt and became a vassal of the Babylonian king (Jeremiah 31:9).

In the following years, the Babylonian armies returned to "the land of Hatti" (west of the Euphrates). One campaign was conducted in 603 BCE, perhaps resulting in the capture and destruction of the city of Gaza.

In 601 BCE, the Babylonians returned to Palestine. This time they tried unsuccessfully to conquer Egypt. They suffered great losses and returned to Babylon. This event perhaps encouraged King Jehoiakim of Judah to rebel against them. In 599 BCE, a stronger Babylonian army was sent to the region. This force assaulted first the Arabs (Jeremiah 49:28–33), forcing them to change their trade route so that it would pass through Babylonian-governed territory; at that time they encouraged all east Jordanian peoples—the Ammonites, the Moabites, and the Edomites—to wage war against King Jehoiakim of Judah (2 Kings 24:4). Immediately afterward (598 BCE), the Babylonian king himself arrived to suppress the rebellion in Judah. In 597

BCE, Jehoiakim died and his son Jehoiachin succeeded him as a king. Judah surrendered: King Jehoiachin and his officers were exiled to Babylon, and Zedekiah, Jehoiakim's younger brother and the uncle of the present king Jehoiachin, was appointed by the Babylonians in his place (according to Jeremiah 52:28, the Babylonians also deported 3,023 people from Judah at the end of this episode).

In 594/3 BCE, King Zedekiah started preparations for the final Judaean revolt against Babylon, probably with the encouragement of Pharaoh Psamtik II king of Egypt (595–589 BCE). Zedekiah was soon ordered to come to Babylon (Jeremiah 27:2). On the death of Psamtik in 589 BCE, Pharaoh Hophra (Apries) came to power and spent his entire reign continuously fighting against the Babylonians.

In 588 BCE, with Egyptian support, the final rebellion erupted in Judah. Nebuchadnezzar returned to Jerusalem and laid siege to the city. He was forced to abandon the siege for a short time in order to engage an Egyptian force sent to Judah's rescue (Jeremiah 37:5). The Egyptians were again defeated and soon retreated, leaving the Judaeans to fight alone, and the Babylonians resumed the siege.

In 586 BCE, Jerusalem was captured by the Babylonians. The city and the temple were destroyed, and subsequently, an important part of its population was deported (2 Kings 25:12; Jeremiah 39:9–10; 52:15–16). The Babylonians appear to have exiled only members of the upper classes at this time. Additional deportations took place in later years: in the twenty-third year of Nebuchadnezzar (582/1 BCE), carried out by his general Nebuzaradan, probably at the time when Nebuchadnezzar himself campaigned against the peoples east of the Jordan, especially Moab and Edom.

In contrast to the Assyrians, the Babylonians never exiled any peoples from the other lands under their control to Palestine. The story recorded by Josephus Flavius on a lengthy siege laid by Nebuchadnezzar against Tyre, which lasted thirteen years, perhaps fits within this context (*Against Apion* 1.21; cf. Ezekiel 29:17–18). Because the *Babylonian Chronicle* covers only the first eleven years of Nebuchadnezzar's reign (605–594 BCE) and does not include the siege of Tyre, it seems probable that it began later, perhaps in 587 BCE (Ezekiel 26:7–14) or 570 BCE (Ezekiel 29:17–20), during the height of Babylonian military activity in the region. In any case, a Babylonian administrative document dating to the 560s mentions the existence of a Babylonian army unit at Tyre, under a Babylonian procurator. Some additional details about Nebuchadnezzar's campaigns in Syria are inscribed in his stela carved on the rocks overlooking the Nahr el-Kalb River, near Tyre.

Concerning Palestine, there are almost no biblical sources for the period of Babylonian domination except, perhaps, for a short period after the fall of Jerusalem, when Gedaliah the son of Ahikam, a pro-Babylonian minister of Zedekiah, the last of the Judaean kings, tried to establish an autonomous government at Mizpah (Tell en-Naṣbeh), before being killed by Ishmael, a member of the Judaean royal family.

Another source of information concerning the Babylonian administrative system and the maintenance of the exiles in the land of Babylon itself is the records found in the excavations of the city of Babylon. These documents shed some light on the administrative system of this huge empire. From these documents, published mainly by E. Weidner, it is clear that many of the deportees who were settled in Babylon, including Jehoiachin king of Judah and his sons, as well as the sons of Aga' the last king of Ashkelon and their companions (who had probably been exiled earlier, in 604 BCE), received fixed rations from the Babylonian royal treasury. These exiles apparently had a special status in Babylon. It also seems that Nebuchadnezzar held all members of royal families of conquered lands in Babylon, either as hostages or as candidates to replace the active kings of subject lands if the latter misbehaved. Concerning the establishment of the new system of appointment of rulers from among the members of these royal houses, or from the ranks of the previous high administration officials in the rebellious countries, we learn from the appointment of Zedekiah as king and, later, of Gedaliah son of Ahikam as governor in Judah (cf. *Against Apion* 1.21, concerning appointments in Tyre).

Deportees who were not members of the royal houses were organized in numerous settlements established in the vicinity of Nippur: Philistines lived in communities named after their hometowns, such as "Ashkelon" and "Gaza"; Phoenicians lived in "the house of the Tyrians" and in "Arvad," clearly named after the towns from which they were exiled. As for the deportees from Judah, we find a similar pattern, though with a significant variation: the Judaeans were settled in the Nippur area, on the Kebar River, but the names of their settlements were of a different character: they were local names such as Tel Aviv (Til-Abubu), Tel Melah, etc.

The Babylonian kings who came to power after Nebuchadnezzar, Amel Marduk (562–560 BCE) and Nergal Shar Usur (560–556 BCE), reigned for too short a time to influence the remote regions of the empire. After them, Nabonidus, last of the Babylonian kings (556–539 BCE), was enthroned. He was a rather unusual character, who left his land for many years to live at the remote site of Tema in Arabia, leaving imperial matters to his son Belshazzar. Economic, religious, military, and even medical reasons have been offered to explain his behavior, but available data, though enriched within the last twenty-five years by new sources, which have sparked renewed scholarly debate, are too meager to permit a decisive conclusion to be reached. It is, however, almost a common opinion that Nabonidus was mentally unbalanced. We know nothing about events in Palestine during his reign, except perhaps for one large rock inscription incised on the cliffs overlooking the Edomite town of Sela located along the King's Highway. This inscription, only recently discovered, depicts the image of the standing king. Nabonidus had been identified mainly by his peculiar headdress and the accompanying Babylonian divine symbols, for the text is completely erased.

Following the large-scale destruction of Palestine that followed the Babylonian conquest, all the royal families that existed during Assyrian rule were eliminated; not only the royal Judaean house but those of Philistia as well: the kings of Ashdod, Ashkelon, Gaza, and Ekron; and those east of the Jordan: Ammon, Moab, and Edom. All disappear from the Palestinian stage at this time.

During the Babylonian period, power appears to have been transferred for the first time, in the southern and eastern parts of the country as well, from the hands of the kings to the empire's administrators, whether local officials (as, for example, Gedaliah the son of Ahikam in Judah) or unknown imperial Babylonian officials. In the north, in the province of Samaria, the house of Sanballat appears to have continued to provide provincial governors during this period and down to the Persian period (see below).

In 538 BCE, the Babylonian empire was defeated by Cyrus king of the Achaemenian Persians, and the entire area west of the Euphrates was transferred without a battle to the winner, who, in turn, adopted an entirely different policy toward Palestine, as we shall see below.

THE CHARACTER OF THE BABYLONIAN REGIME

BABYLONIAN DOMINATION OF Palestine lasted for approximately seventy years (604–538 BCE), a period of time roughly equal to that of Assyrian rule. A clear distinction must be made between the influence of Babylonian occupation on the country and its material culture and that of their Assyrian predecessors and the Persians after them. Although the Babylo-

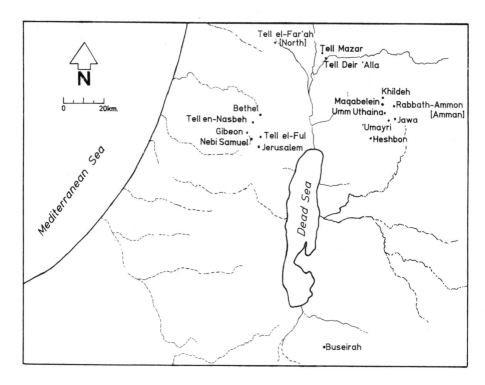

II.1 Excavated sites of the Babylonian period

nians created a new administrative organization, different from that of their predecessors, this did not leave any clear traces in the country's archaeological record. The reasons for this unique situation will now be examined.

During the Babylonian period, the main foreign influence in Palestine remained Mesopotamian culture. In many cases, this makes it almost impossible to determine if a certain artifact with Babylonian parallels should be dated to the late Assyrian period, to the Babylonian period, or even to the early Persian period. During all three periods, Palestine absorbed influences from the same remote Mesopotamian center.

Another, more important factor lies in the character of Babylonian domination itself as noted above: it was an extremely centralized regime, interested only in the welfare of the capital city of Babylon and its immediate surroundings, and completely neglected the periphery. This policy had devastating results for Palestine.

Subsequently, the most prominent feature left by seventy years of Babylonian domination in Palestine was the total destruction and devastation of all the main cities that had flourished during the Assyrian period, even those fortresses established by the Assyrian authorities themselves. A survey of the results of all the archaeological excavations conducted in Palestine (minus regions of Phoenicia, Benjamin, and Transjordan) reveals that all its cities lay in ruins by the end of the Babylonian period. This has produced an almost complete gap in the archaeology-history of Palestine, a view strengthened from one excavation to the next.

Archaeological findings for the Babylonian period throughout Palestine include massive destruction levels, a few weapons (arrow- and lanceheads), and some seals and seal impressions (a large number of which may actually belong to the Persian period). The only two Neo-Babylonian clay tablets found in Palestine are also dated to the Persian period. A few tombs appear to date from the end of the Judaean monarchy and to continue into the Babylonian period, but each of them also contained Persian-period finds, and it is still impossible to establish if Persian burials did not follow Judaean ones, with a gap in between. Even with great effort, no more than one or two types of clay vessels can be found that may be safely attributed to this period alone.

The Babylonian army and its military system were probably similar to the Assyrian, as were its equipment, its siege techniques, systems of deportation, and other aspects of its military machine. Thus far, however, no major Babylonian military remains similar to the numerous ones left by the Assyrians during their siege of Lachish have been found, although Babylonian destruction layers are known throughout Judah and elsewhere. It seems that the major Babylonian effort in Judah was concentrated in the siege of Jerusalem. Here, in his excavations of the Upper City, N. Avigad uncovered the remains of a gate and a small section of the attached city wall, which were destroyed by the Babylonians. He found there a layer of ash at the foot of the fortifications, which contained typical Judaean arrowheads together with Babylonian ones. These unique remains of the Babylonian devastation of Jerusalem in 586 BCE are a clear reflection of the biblical sources (2 Kings 25:8; 2 Chronicles 36:18–19) describing the destruction, burning, and collapse of houses and walls. The archaeological evidence for this phase in Jerusalem's history in the rest of the city's excavated areas, especially in the City of David, can be counted among the most dramatic at any biblical site. Many of the buildings excavated by Y. Shiloh in the City of David were also destroyed by a fierce conflagration: namely, the so-called Ashlar House, House of Ahiel, Burnt Room, and House of the Bullae. Their walls collapsed and buried abundant finds, including large quantities of pottery vessels, dozens of metal and stone artifacts, bone implements, and considerable epigraphic material. The dozens of flat iron arrowheads of a local type and triangular bronze arrowheads of the so-called Scythian type found in these houses bear mute witness to the battle for the city on the eve of its destruction, as its inhabitants amassed ammunition in their homes. The destruction of this residential quarter, which resembles the one excavated by N. Avigad on the Western Hill, as well as the large building called the House of Millo cleared by E. Mazar north of the City of David, was total. The destruction layer was preserved in some of the buildings to the height of their first-story ceilings. Perhaps the most vivid description of Jerusalem's destruction by the Babylonians remains Nehemiah's account of the ruins of the City of David as he saw them during his tour of the city some 140 years later (Nehemiah 2:13–14).

Another site at which the activity of the Babylonian army was detected is the Judaean settlement in the oasis of En-Gedi on the western shore of the Dead Sea. Here, too, a group of typical triangular Babylonian arrowheads was found stuck in one of the walls of a house that was destroyed and burned

II.2 En-Gedi, destruction layer, caused by the Babylonian army, covering the floor of a Judaean house

in 582 BCE in the course of the Babylonian campaign in Transjordan. Other identical Babylonian arrowheads were found among the remains of the burnt wooden palm tree beams that once supported the ceiling of one of the En-Gedi houses and collapsed into it. These arrows were probably shot with small torches tied to them. It was even possible to surmise the direction from which the Babylonian soldiers' fire emanated.

· Chapter 1 ·

EXCAVATIONS AND SURVEYS

THE PROVINCE OF MEGIDDO

Although the Babylonians inherited two previous Assyrian provinces, Megiddo and Samaria, in which the new population brought by the Assyrians should, by then, have been established and prosperous, the results of several excavations conducted there do not support this supposition. We should distinguish, however, between the province of Megiddo and that of Samaria: i.e., between the Galilee and the Jezreel Valley and Samaria Hills, which present a different picture.

In the Megiddo province, major excavations have been conducted at Dan, Hazor, Tel Chinnereth, Beth-Shean, Tel Kedesh, Megiddo, Tel Qiri, and Jokneam. We have already mentioned that some of these sites, including Tel Dan, Tel Hadar, 'En Gev, Beth-Shean, Tel Kedesh, and many other sites, were previously destroyed by the Assyrians and their settlements not renewed until the Persian period. The comprehensive Galilee survey conducted recently by Z. Gal clearly showed that settlements throughout the Galilee were destroyed by the Assyrians and later became much smaller, if they recovered at all. Those that did recover did not do so before the Persian period. Only a few finds have been attributed in this region to the Babylonian period, and even these are questionable.

At **Hazor,** at the close of Y. Yadin's excavations it became clear that after the destruction of Stratum IV (Assyrian), only one building survived (in Area B), which was assigned to Stratum III. It was situated on the highest part of the mound, identified as the city's citadel. Two construction phases were identified in this building. In the first phase (Stratum III), it was constructed as a fortress (30 x 26 m.), consisting of a large open courtyard, surrounded on three sides by a single row of rooms and halls and by two rows of rooms on the south side. North of the citadel stood a tower composed of two large rooms. The finds in Stratum III were very meager, and the building itself was found to contain no primary artifacts. This, together with the fact that no traces of fire or serious destruction were found in the building, allows for a hypothesis that the building was destroyed by natural causes after it had been abandoned and not as a result of its capture by an enemy.

The date of this large structure was not clearly established, for lack of artifacts. The excavators did not exclude the possibility that it might date to the initial phase of the Persian period, while the Stratum II fortress should clearly be dated to the late Persian period. In Stratum II were found coins of the Persian monarch Artaxerxes III (358/9–337/8 BCE). It is highly probable, therefore, that the two fortresses, i.e., both the Stratum III fortress and that of Stratum II, date to the Persian period. This assumption is further strengthened by the fact that it was not necessary for the Stratum III fortress to be reconstructed by the occupants of Stratum II, who only had to clear its debris. The walls of the citadel remained standing, and it is not likely that they would have remained in this state after a very long abandonment. It seems, therefore, that during the Babylonian period the city of Hazor was deserted.

A similar picture emerged at Tel Chinnereth: this mound was also completely destroyed by the Assyrians. Only in one excavated area was a large structure found, probably a fortress or administrative center of the Persian period. In any case, this structure dated to a single phase and was almost devoid of finds, making exact dating impossible.

The provincial capital, the city of **Megiddo,** which the Assyrians carefully rebuilt and fortified (Stratum III; see above), was destroyed at the end of the 7th century BCE, and in its place—as at Hazor and Chinnereth—one large fortress was erected over it, similar in plan to those of Hazor and Chinnereth, i.e., an open-courtyard house in Mesopotamian style. This building, too, was almost completely devoid of finds. The few loci that could be attributed with certainty to the building contained Persian-period pottery only. A small residential quarter composed of similar smaller open-court houses was uncovered beside it. In this fortress, too, two different strata, II and I, were noted. Stratum I, from which most of the finds came, is securely dated to the Persian period. As to Stratum II, as early as 1928 C. Fisher attributed it to the last decades of the 7th century BCE. This proposed date became the source of the numerous hypotheses associating this stratum and its destruction with the dramatic events of 640–605 BCE, in which the Egyptian armies of Psamtik

I and Necho replaced the Assyrians in Syria-Palestine. The first idea was to attribute the fortress and the Stratum II city to the expanding kingdom of Judah under Josiah. The historical reconstruction of some scholars (in particular, A. Malamat) identifies the Judaeans as the builders of the fortress, soon after the reforms of 628 BCE. It explains why Josiah chose to stop Necho in 609, here at the strategic site of Megiddo (2 Kings 23:20–29 and 2 Chronicles 35:20–24). In a study on Stratum II and the battle of Megiddo, Malamat suggested that Megiddo may have been delivered into the hands of the Egyptians by the Assyrians on their retreat from Palestine, as part of the general process during which Egyptians replaced the Assyrians in Syro-Palestine (see above); thus, Megiddo's Stratum II fortress would be Egyptian. This, Malamat believes, is reflected in Herodotus (2.157), who recorded Psamtik's conquest of Ashdod, and by a stela dating to 612 BCE, which mentions the princes of Lebanon paying tribute to the pharaoh. According to Malamat's historical reconstruction, it was here, near the Stratum II Egyptian forces' base, that Josiah tried to stop them on their march toward Carchemish.

But all these historical theories lack any archaeological basis: Stratum II at Megiddo produced almost no finds, and there is no Judaean material anywhere at Megiddo dated to this period, or even any East Greek ware of the type common to the late 7th century BCE, not to mention Egyptian remains, which are virtually nonexistent.

The solution to the problem of the chronology of Megiddo II is similar, in our opinion, to one we have offered concerning the fortresses of Hazor and Chinnereth: i.e., that both the Megiddo fortresses of Strata II and I date to the Persian period. This dating is now supported by recent finds at Dor (see below). Therefore, the last offset-inset city wall and its two-chambered gate dating to the Assyrian Stratum III must have remained in use to the end of the 7th century BCE and the Babylonian conquest, whether the city fell into the hands of the Egyptians or Josiah, or not. During the Babylonian conquest, the city was completely destroyed. The two last strata, II and I, in which one large fortress of Mesopotamian open-court plan replaced the fortified town of the previous period, were both built during the Persian period. Both are just two short living-floor phases of one structure. It has been shown that Megiddo was settled through the entire Persian period.

The evidence gathered from two sites in the vicinity of Megiddo, Tel Qiri, and Jokneam is similar to that at Megiddo. Qiri Stratum V, which consisted of a large building and parts of a residential quarter, was destroyed at the end of the 7th century BCE. The next phase is dated to the Persian period, and no

Babylonian-period remains were identified. At Jokneam, an Assyrian-period stratum has been identified, following the destruction of which a new Persian-period settlement was constructed. A similar picture emerges from the results of the various surveys recently conducted in the western part of the Jezreel Valley.

Summing up the picture emerging from the Megiddo province, it seems that despite the major destruction caused here by the Assyrian army, and the deportation of its inhabitants, new settlements were rebuilt by the Assyrians at some of the more important sites, such as Ayelet ha-Shaḥar, Hazor, Megiddo, Qiri, and Jokneam. These were destroyed, in turn, by the Babylonians at the end of the century. All these towns and many more were rebuilt, but not before the Persian period. Thus, during the Babylonian period there were but few settlements in existence in the entire area of the Megiddo province.

PHOENICIA AND THE PROVINCE OF DOR

IT HAS ALREADY been pointed out that when the Babylonian army first came to this region, it laid a lengthy siege against Tyre and some other Phoenician cities until they were conquered and destroyed. Some of the north Palestinian harbor towns dominated by the Tyrians were also destroyed. While some traces of occupation during the Babylonian period have been found here, mainly in the cities along the coast of the western Galilee, these are quite insignificant.

The excavator of **Acco** claimed that after the destruction of the last Iron Age settlement "of the Babylonian period only scanty remains survived after which it entered—in the Persian period—into a period of prosperity."

In the large Phoenician settlement to the east of Acco at **Tell Keisan,** Stratum 4, the latest Iron Age town, was destroyed, according to the excavators, in the mid-7th century BCE (in the year 643 during a campaign conducted by Ashurbanipal king of Assyria against Acco). But the reassessment of the material published for this site clearly indicates that among the imported Greek vessels, many should be dated to the last part of the 7th century BCE, meaning that this city was probably destroyed by the Babylonians (perhaps during their long siege against Tyre and its dependencies). The next settlement, Stratum 3, dates to the Persian period. Thus, there is no evidence for a Babylonian-period settlement at Tell Keisan. As at Acco, the Persian-period stratum there reflects a flourishing town.

At **Tell Abu Hawam,** at the southern end of the Acco Valley, no strata of the Late Iron Age survived, and the prosperous settlement that arose in the Persian period (Stratum II) is the first after a long gap. At **Shiqmona** on the Carmel coast, no clear evidence for a Babylonian-period stratum survived. On the contrary, it seems that this period falls into a gap between the Late Iron Age and the Persian period. If there were any Babylonian remains here, they were not detected in the course of years of excavation.

From here we come to Dor, where extensive excavations did not uncover a clear Babylonian-period phase. The only (doubtful) evidence for a Babylonian phase here is the continuous use of the city fortifications (a two-chambered gate and an offset-inset city wall) from the Assyrian to the Persian periods. But this is merely hypothetical, for these fortifications could have also been reconstructed during the Persian period, after a relatively short gap. The few artifacts under Babylonian influence found here may also be attributed to the Persian period, as well as the handful of Greek pottery imports.

The same picture emerges from the sites along the coast south of Dor: **Tel Mevorakh, Mikhmoret, Tel Michal, Tel Ḥefer, Apollonia,** and **Tell Qasile,** all coastal towns of the Sharon Plain, which either had no Late Iron Age strata at all or at which a new settlement was built during the late 7th century BCE (Qasile). No Babylonian period remains have been uncovered at any of these sites. *All* these towns were resettled at the same time, in the beginning of the Persian period. At that time—not earlier—settlement of all parts of the Sharon Plain occurred. From this period on, it grew very quickly and a dense new net of settlements spread from one end to the other (cf. Book Three).

PHILISTIA

THE BABYLONIAN campaign of 603 BCE was a disastrous one for Philistia as well. All the excavations in this region provide clear indications of the total destruction in the 7th century BCE of all the prosperous Philistine cities of Assyrian and Egyptian times. In their stead were built, during the Babylonian period, only a few unfortified, small, poor settlements—so poor that archaeologists find it difficult to detect them.

Excavations have been conducted in all the major towns of Philistia. We have already followed their results relating to the Assyrian period at Ashdod, Ashkelon, Ekron, Tel Batash, Tell el Ḥesi, Tel Seraʿ, Tel Haror, Tell Jemmeh, and Ruqeish.

We shall begin our survey in the northernmost Philistine city, **Ashdod.** Here, the last town of the 7th century BCE (Stratum VI = 630–604 BCE) was destroyed by the Babylonian army. Whether it was already an Egyptian-ruled town or was still an autonomous Philistine city, no remains of the Babylonian period were found during the extensive excavations conducted at the site. The next stratum (V) is dated to the Persian period.

The same is true concerning three fortresses uncovered along the Via Maris (Way of the Sea), to the north near Ashdod. The first is Meẓad Ḥashavyahu, located north of Ashdod and close to Yavneh-Yam, which, as we have already seen, was erected ca. 630 BCE and was probably destroyed in the campaign of Pharaoh Necho in 609 BCE, or a few years later in 604 by the Babylonians. Scholars are divided between those who believe that the fortress was held by Greek mercenaries brought by the Judaean king Josiah and destroyed by Necho and those who claim that the Greeks were mercenaries sent here by Necho and that the fortress was captured by the Babylonians. The latter view has been strengthened by the find of another Greek fortress in the Sinai, on the way to Egypt, identified by its excavator, E. Oren, with ancient Migdol, which was also destroyed in 604 BCE.

The second fortress is at Ashdod-Yam, excavated by J. Kaplan. This fort contained two phases, one Assyrian and one Egyptian, both dated to the 7th century BCE. It, too, was destroyed in 604 BCE and never rebuilt.

The third fortress, located west of Rishon le-Zion, southeast of Ashdod, and also erected in the Assyrian period, was recently uncovered. It had two clear Assyrian phases and a later, Persian-period phase, with a gap in between.

A similar picture emerges from all the excavations in Philistia: it seems that the disastrous destructions brought upon the entire region by the Babylonians razed all its cities until the Persian period.

The second Philistine city after Ashdod, **Ekron,** has recently been extensively excavated. At the end of the 7th century BCE, this city appears to have been destroyed, probably in 603 BCE as part of Nebuchadnezzar II's campaign. This dating is supported by a rich assemblage of entire ceramic forms from Stratum Ib (7th century BCE), sealed by three feet of destruction debris. These forms are known to have first appeared in the last quarter of the 7th century BCE. After this complete destruction of the prosperous Assyrian-period town comes Stratum Ia, which was rebuilt at the very beginning of the 6th century BCE, perhaps by the few people who survived in the site. According to the excavator, S. Gitin, this was "a random, unfortified settlement in the lower city." It contained at least one structure of open-court plan. Following this short-living settlement, the site was, according to its excavators, abandoned until the Roman period.

As for **Timnah** (Tel Batash), which is close to Ekron, and was previously a Judaean town, here, too, it is clear that there was a gap in settlement after the destruction of Stratum II by the Babylonian army (whether in 605 BCE or 603 BCE or even at the time of the great war between Egypt and Babylon in 601 BCE). B. Porten recently suggested that the Aramaic letter from Saqqara, mentioned above, telling about the approach of the Babylonians perhaps originated in Ekron, and may indicate severe tension in the region during the Babylonian invasion. Timnah and Ekron were probably destroyed during the campaigns of 605–601 BCE. Both were conquered and destroyed by the Babylonian armies in a massive conflagration. At Timnah, slight traces of a squatters' settlement existed above the destruction debris. An industrial installation, probably a winepress, was constructed on the remains of the previous stratum. This phase (IIa) included some very late Iron Age vessels. This installation, as well as some additional walls, perhaps attests to some activity at the site after the city's destruction in the beginning of the 6th century BCE.

The same is true of **Ashkelon,** which was also destroyed by the Babylonians in 603 BCE. This impressive destruction stratum has been described above. The majority of scholars believes that the events mentioned in the Saqqara papyrus are connected with this city rather than Ekron. In any case, the next settlement built at Ashkelon, also constructed on a large scale and based upon careful city planning, began in the Persian period. According to Ashkelon excavator L. Stager, no traceable settlement existed here during the Babylonian period.

Southward, in the new excavations at **Tell el-Ḥesi,** the same massive destruction layer left by the Babylonian armies, composed of a heavy layer of ash and destruction debris, was uncovered (Stratum VII). Stratum VI consisted of a poorly built mud-brick house dated to the late 6th century BCE, i.e., perhaps to the beginning of the Persian-period resettlement. The later Stratum, Vd, appears to have been a flourishing Persian-period center.

At **Tel Seraʿ,** south of Tell el-Ḥesi, it was concluded that after the destruction of the Assyrian fortresses built here during the 7th century BCE (Stratum IV), destroyed either by invading Egyptians or, more probably, by the Babylonians, no new settlement was built until the Persian period (Stratum III). The same state of affairs had been revealed in the nearby mound of **Tel Haror,** where the Stratum G2 was destroyed in the late 7th century BCE or at the very beginning of the 6th century BCE. The next stratum, G1, is Persian. This picture is again repeated at **Tell Jemmeh,** where only a few scattered walls were attributed by the excavator, G. Van Beek, to the Babylonian period, stuck between two large, flourishing towns: one Assyrian and the other Persian. The same is true of a recently excavated site on the Gaza coast.

At **Ruqeish,** too, the results of extensive excavations by E. Oren clearly showed that this important southern harbor, first erected by the Assyrians on the Philistine coast, declined considerably in significance at the end of the 7th century BCE and that its strong fortification system went out of use. Here, too, the excavations indicate that during the Persian period a new and prosperous settlement was established.

Summing up the results of archaeological excavations in Philistia, we find a relatively clear and uniform picture of thorough destruction of Iron Age towns at the hands of the Babylonians; a gap during the subsequent Babylonian period, during which the region's inhabitants were deported to Babylon (or, at some sites, evidence for small, poorly built settlements); and the large-scale reconstruction of carefully planned, prosperous towns during the Persian period and their settlement by a new Phoenician population (see below).

THE PROVINCE OF SAMARIA

THE ASSYRIAN PROVINCE of Samaria may have remained in existence even after the conquest of the region by the Babylonians (it was restored during the Persian period), but evidence for this is poor and scanty. The governors of the province, on behalf of the Assyrian authorities, appear to have transferred their loyalty from the Assyrians to the Babylonians without resistance. Therefore, no conquest or destruction remains have been observed, and consequently, no conflagration levels, such as those found in the coastal region, have been detected. It also seems that if they did exist at all during the Babylonian period, their material culture was almost identical to that of the 7th century to early 6th centuries BCE. It is also possible that the later intensive building activity in the province's settlements removed most of the remains of this period. The main sites excavated in this region are Tel Dothan, Samaria (city), Shechem, Tell el-Farʿah (N), and Gezer. However, none of these produced any clear Babylonian-period remains. The results of the various surveys conducted here will be discussed below.

At **Dothan,** after the destruction of Stratum I, dated to the Assyrian period, no subsequent settlement was built on the site until much later periods.

At **Samaria,** a few poorly constructed walls found below the Persian-period stratum were attributed to Stratum VIIA, which may date to this period. But the fact that the fortifications of the Israelite city remained in use in later periods (perhaps even down to Hellenistic times) makes it appear probable that the Assyrian, and perhaps even the Babylonian, cities used them, too. Some Babylonian finds were recorded among the excavation's finds, a few Babylonian seals were recorded, and one cuneiform tablet written in a Neo-Babylonian script, a letter to a local person whose name is Avi-Ahe. There are also a few local ostraca with Babylonian names. But, as at other sites, even if these finds originated in Babylon, we have no assurance that they do not date to the Persian period, as is the case with most Babylonian finds in Palestine. In any case, it is possible that this city did exist during the Babylonian period. As to **Shechem,** according to the conclusions of its excavators, Stratum VI attests to limited occupation of the site in the Assyrian period, but Stratum V is dated to the Persian period. Being unable to find anything dating to the Babylonian period, the excavators decided to attribute the remains of this period to the same Stratum V, and have dated it to the period 600–475 BCE, i.e., to both the Babylonian period and the beginning of the Persian period. This date, however, had no solid basis in the finds themselves. Similarly at **Tell el-Farʿah (N),** the excavators attributed a separate stratum (VIIe1) to the period *after* the Assyrian settlement. While in the Assyrian stratum they discovered a palace and a cultic center that contained some *mazzebot* ("sacred stelae"), their conclusion regarding the stratum that followed was that "the palace was subdivided by poorly built partitions and the cultic place was abandoned. A small farming community occupied the site. This was also gradually abandoned during the 6th century BCE."

The excavations of **Gezer** showed that the important Assyrian center built here (Stratum V), including the city's fortifications, was completely destroyed by the Babylonians when they seized the town in 586 BCE and left it in ruins. The excavators also concluded that during the Babylonian period there existed a gap in settlement at Gezer and that the town was rebuilt (Stratum IV) only in the Persian period.

Lastly, the results of the many surveys recently conducted here show that the region was rebuilt after the Assyrian conquest and included new ethnic elements brought in by the Assyrians, including people from Assyria and Babylon. Many settlements previously destroyed were erected again in this period. During the Persian period, the overall number of settlements increased considerably, and the surveyors found it almost impossible to distinguish Babylonian-period remains.

JUDAH AND IDUMAEA

HERE WE SHALL first deal with the region of Benjamin. No fewer than six of the excavated settlements in this small region include remains attributed to the Babylonian period. This indicates that, in contrast to all other regions west of the Jordan that had been conquered by the Babylonians, the settlements of Benjamin were not destroyed, continued to exist during the Babylonian period, and may even have prospered. According to the biblical text (Jeremiah 41), the town of Mizpah (Tel en-Naṣbeh), located in this region, was designated by the Babylonians as the seat of Gedaliah son of Ahikam, the new governor of the state of Judah, who was appointed by them after the destruction of Jerusalem. Mizpah probably continued to function in this capacity for a certain period of time after Gedaliah's murder. There can be little doubt that this region served as a temporary refuge for "the rest of Judah," which included all the other destroyed settlements located south of Jerusalem. It seems that this was Mizpah's position, at least until the beginning of the Persian period, i.e., until the return from Babylon, the rebuilding of the deserted settlements, and especially, the reconstruction of the city of Jerusalem and its Temple.

Sites that have been excavated in the Benjamin region are Bethel, Gibeon, Tell el-Ful (Gibeah), Tell en-Naṣbeh (Mizpah), Mozah, and a settlement atop the hill of Nebi Samuel (probably ha-Ramah). Findings from the latter two recently excavated sites have not yet been published. We shall therefore discuss results from the other four. A few tombs in this region contained finds that may also attest to continued population during the entire 6th century BCE, this including some that should probably be dated to the Babylonian period. These tombs have been uncovered at Ḥorvat 'Almit, Tell en-Naṣbeh, Tell el-Ful, Abu Ghosh, and elsewhere (see below).

At **Bethel** toward the close of the 7th century BCE, the city and its shrine were rebuilt. It seems that the city did not suffer any major destruction at the time of the Babylonian campaign of 586 BCE. On the contrary, the excavators pointed out that its prosperity continued until the end of the Babylonian period, or even until the early Persian period. The city of **Gibeon** apparently also reached the peak of its prosperity in the 7th century BCE, when buildings crowned most of its enclosed area, and the Gibeonites busily engaged in producing and trading wine. If the many Gibeonite inscriptions found here, including those inscribed on wine-jar handles, are indeed from the Babylonian period, as most scholars believe (and see below), then this city, too, continued to prosper during the Babylonian period. **Tell el-Ful** (Gibeah) has been excavated many times. The most recent excavation demonstrated that Period III consisted of two phases: IIIA=650–586 BCE and IIIB=586–538 BCE. This is the same picture we have already seen of a prosperous town during the final phase of the Judaean kingdom, where settlement did not end in destruction in 586 BCE, but continued through the end of the Babylonian period. There is no Persian-period layer at this site.

The picture emerging from the results of the excavations in Benjamin is repeated by the results of excavations at the major site and capital of this region, **Tell en-Naṣbeh** (biblical Mizpah). As pointed out above, this site served as the temporary capital of Judah following the destruction of Jerusalem and was the seat of Gedaliah son of Ahikam, for a short time the governor of Judah on behalf of the Babylonians. Gedaliah must have had a small Babylonian garrison at his disposal, as well as some of the Judaean army officers who survived the war; but he was soon assassinated by Ishmael, son of Nathaniah, a member of the Judaean royal family, who came from Ammon. After the assassination, Ishmael, together with most of the Judaean officers and their men, fled to Egypt. It is possible that the important position that the city of Mizpah enjoyed until this assassination was maintained through the rest of the Babylonian period, for an examination of the results of the excavation here shows that Stratum 2 should be dated to this period. Attributed to Stratum 2 are a few large "four-room" structures in the city center and in the gate area, a palace in the northern part of the site (perhaps the seat of the governor), and an area assigned to storehouses. The plan of the city in this period is entirely different from that during the previous Judaean kingdom. Among the important Babylonian-period finds are the *mwṣh* seal impressions uncovered here (see below) and a fragment of a bronze bracelet bearing a cuneiform dedicatory inscription in a probable Neo-Babylonian script.

These finds allow us to assume that the region of Benjamin, with all its major towns, even if partly ruined by the Babylonians in 586 BCE, was quickly reconstructed, probably becoming a haven for some of the refugees from other parts of Judah. Its major town, Mizpah, even became the temporary capital of the destroyed Judaean state. At other towns, particularly Gibeon and Mozah, wine production either continued or was resumed. All these Benjaminite settlements continued to exist during the rest of the Babylonian period. Some, such as Mozah and Mizpah, even continued into the Persian period. The archaeological evidence shows, however, that all these cities in the territory of Benjamin were laid waste in approximately 480 BCE. This date is virtually certain, and is based on the date of the Attic pottery uncovered in the excavations of Mizpah, Bethel, Tell el-Ful, and Gibeon. There is no known historical event that can count for this destruction. Perhaps these towns were only abandoned for various unknown internal reasons. In any case, it is interesting to note that this small region continued to function and even prosper during the Babylonian period.

A review of the archaeological evidence from 6th century BCE Judah clearly reflects the literary evidence for the complete destruction of all the settlements and fortified towns by Nebuchadnezzar II's armies in 586 BCE, a decrease in population due to slaughter, deportation, pestilence, flight, and resultant total economic collapse, which persisted despite the efforts of those who remained behind and those who slowly drifted back. So rudimentary must this existence have been that it has proved extremely difficult to find its traces in the material remains. Of the destroyed cities and towns, many ceased to exist entirely; others were inhabited by poorer elements, who must have salvaged material for their shelters from the rubble. Of hundreds of sites examined in Judah, many were newly established. Most of these were villages or small settlements, largely nameless and therefore not of the type that has hitherto attracted the archaeologist interested in biblical sites. A number of these has yielded material believed to date to the 6th century BCE. It now appears that some of the remaining inhabitants of Judah lived at such sites after the more important centers were destroyed by the Babylonians.

The Babylonian conquest clearly brought total destruction to Jerusalem and the Judaean Hill sites to the south of Jerusalem. It is impossible to describe here in detail the remains associated with this destruction, uncovered in several excavations conducted in Jerusalem at the City of David and upon the Western Hill (the Upper City). We shall confine ourselves to two examples. One is in the City of David, where remains of a huge destruction level in the residential quarter on the eastern slope (including Area G) were uncovered. This level contained many dozens of clay vessels, found together with about fifty bullae. It was possible to date the bullae accurately, which included the names of Gemariah son of Shaphan and Berachiah son of Neriah the scribe, contemporaries of Jeremiah (see above). Another large building of this period, which also contained a large quantity of pottery vessels dated to the last decade of the Judaean monarchy, was uncovered in the upper part of the City of David, where it adjoins the Temple Mount (the *milo*). The second example is the impressive remains uncovered in the Upper City (on the Western Hill). Here, a well-preserved tower was excavated, which was incorporated in the city's fortifications destroyed by the Babylonians. At the foot of this tower, some weapons from the Babylonian siege were found, including Babylonian arrowheads mixed with local ones utilized by the defenders.

An important question is, was Jerusalem settled during the Babylonian period? According to Jeremiah 41:5, settlement here may have continued in some fashion. But the results of the excavations conducted here do not supply a definitive answer. It seems more probable that the city remained in ruins until the Persian period. Some tombs outside and close to the town may have belonged to this period, such as the tomb uncovered by G. Barkai at Ketef Hinnom, which he attributed in part to the Babylonian period. But even these scanty remains are questionable, for this tomb may also have had two different phases with an intervening gap: the earlier one from the last stage of the Judaean monarchy, and the second from the beginning of the Persian period. If so, burial in this tomb was resumed after a hiatus during the Babylonian period.

A more definitive answer emerges at sites excavated in the extensive Judaean territory east and south of Jerusalem: here, all excavations attest to a complete destruction and gap in the history of the vast majority of the settlements. This gap lasted from the end of the Judaean monarchy until the Persian period. Even here, however, at some sites there are scanty remains reflecting renewal of settlements on a minor scale.

On the eastern side of Judah, sites such as **Jericho** and **En-Gedi** prospered during the last phase of the Judaean kingdom (see above), but did not recover from their destruction by the Babylonians until the Persian period.

Among the sites situated in the higher parts of the Judaean Hills is **Ramat Raḥel.** Stratum Va here was the final stratum dated to the Judaean monarchy. The following stratum, Vb, was attributed by Y. Aharoni to the Persian-Hellenistic periods (5th to 3rd centuries BCE). A similar picture emerged from excavations at **Beth-Zur,** just a few kilometers south of Ramat Raḥel. At the site of **Khirbet el-Qom** (Makkedah), it became evident by the end of the excavation that the city was destroyed in 586 BCE. Settlement here was not renewed even as late as the Hellenistic period. Only at the site of **Khirbet Abu Tuwein,** excavated by A. Mazar, did results indicate continuity following the destruction of the settlement during the downfall of the Judaean kingdom. Mazar claims that "its central building continued in use from the Babylonian period to the beginning of the postexilic period, and this may reflect the continuity of the Jewish population here. In any case it served as a fortress for a small garrison." A complete and final destruction in 586 BCE was also observed at **Tell Beit Mirsim.** The same situation becomes more and more apparent in the region of the southern part of the Judaean Hills, which was resettled in the Persian period by the Edomites. No remains from the Babylonian period were found here. According to all indications and the results of many excavations conducted here, the Babylonian destruction was complete, and the resettlement, if there was one, did not occur before the Persian period. For example, at the site of **Tel Ḥalif,** the last Judaean city came to an end during the Assyrian period (650 BCE). Only after a long gap (650–500 BCE) was settlement renewed.

To summarize: among the many sites located in the region of the Judaean Hills south of Jerusalem, only at three did the excavators report on some measure of continuity into the Babylonian period: the fortress of Khirbet Abu Tuwein, Beth-Shemesh, and **Tell Rabud,** south of Hebron. The excavator of Tell Rabud, M. Kochavi, claims that after the Babylonian destruction "only a few buildings, not enclosed by a wall, could be attributed to the post exilic period" (Stratum AI). These are rather unimpressive results for such a long list of excavated sites. The overall picture emerging from the hilly part of the former Judaean kingdom is of almost complete destruction followed by the erection of small, poor villages without central towns.

The major towns in western Judah, with **Lachish** topping the list (concerning its last days before the Babylonian conquest, we learn from the ostraca found there; see above), were all totally destroyed. There is a long list of excavated sites, which includes **Maresha, Tell Judeideh, Tell Burnat, Tel ʿErani, Azekah, Tell eṣ-Ṣafi, Tel Ḥarasim,** and **Tel Batash.** Settlement was not renewed before the Persian period at any of these sites. As for **Beth-Shemesh,** not much of the last stage of the Judaean monarchy period was found there in recent excavations. Only one tomb that may have contained some Babylonian-period remains was found (Tomb 14).

Turning to the southern part of Judah, to the **Beersheba Valley,** here, too, all the many sites excavated appear to have been utterly destroyed by the Babylonians (if not in 586 BCE then in 582). These include the towns and fortresses located at **Arad, Ḥorvat ʿUza, Ḥorvat Radum, Tel Malḥata, Qitmit, Aroer, Tel ʿIra, Tel Masos, Tel Sheva,** and even the remote Judaean fortress of Kadesh-Barnea. All these sites were totally destroyed. Their settlement was renewed, if at all, only in the second part of the Persian period, i.e., during the 4th century BCE. This date is based upon the dates for the many ostraca found at these sites. After the renewal of settlement, their population consisted mainly of Edomites and Arabs. Even the Edomite fortresses along the Aravah at Ḥazeva and Tell el-Kheleifeh were destroyed. Of these two sites, only the second was rebuilt in the Persian period, a station along the prosperous new trade route passing through the region. In it were already settled, besides the Edomites, the new merchants of the period: the Phoenicians and the Greeks (see below).

While Edomite settlements were destroyed by the Babylonians in the same manner as the Judaean settlements in this region, it seems that Edom itself continued to exist. Sometime after the deportation of the Jewish population from this region, the Edomites returned here alone, as well as to the now empty southern part of the Hebron Hills as far as Beth-Zur. This region will henceforth be referred to as Idumaea. As more sites are excavated here, it appears increasingly probable that this process began during the Persian period.

The bottom line in this discussion is that after the Babylonian conquest of Judah, only in the small region of Benjamin did some sites continue to exist or were rebuilt, while the rest of the country remained in a state of total destruction and near abandonment.

II.3 Tel Malḥata, a heap of slingstones shot by the Babylonian army during the siege of the town

THE EASTERN SIDE OF THE JORDAN

THE TRANSITION FROM Assyrian to Babylonian hegemony was not followed by a radical change in the status of the kingdoms east of the Jordan. Josephus Flavius tells us about captives taken by Nebuchadnezzar from among the Judaeans, Phoenicians, Syrians, and Egyptians during his campaign to Egypt in the last year of his father's reign (605 BCE), but he does not mention the peoples to the east of the Jordan (*Against Apion* 1.19). The kings of Ammon, Moab, and Edom were probably included with "all the kings of the land of Hatti" who brought tribute to Nebuchadnezzar when he fought against Ashkelon (604/3 BCE). Moabite, Ammonite, and perhaps also Edomite battalions served under the Babylonian king and helped him to suppress the rebellion of Jehoiakim king of Judah (2 Kings 24:12).

A few years later the kingdoms east of the Jordan changed their policy toward Babylon and made alliances with other countries to remove the Babylonian yoke. In the fourth year of King Zedekiah (594 BCE), these kings sent messengers to encourage him to join forces against the Babylonians (Jeremiah 27:2). We do not know why this change of policy occurred. Perhaps the Babylonians took some harsh measures against them, or perhaps they were influenced by the Egyptians (cf. Jeremiah 37:5). There is no clear evidence for their actual participation in this rebellion, and it seems that after it started, they stood aside, showing their sympathy by helping the Judaean refugees find shelter in their land (Jeremiah 40:11–12).

A Babylonian campaign to punish the rebellious states, including the kingdoms east of the Jordan, followed within a few years. Josephus Flavius tells (*Antiquities* 10.9.7) that in the fifth year after the destruction of Jerusalem, i.e., the twenty-third year of Nebuchadnezzar (582 BCE), the Babylonian monarch set out against Syria and conquered it. He also campaigned against the Moabites and the Ammonites, and after defeating them continued to Egypt. There is no clear evidence that the Babylonians changed their status and turned them into Babylonian provinces at this time. Despite the lack of clear information concerning the status of these kingdoms from this point on, the reference to "the governor of *(paḥat)* Moab" (Ezra 2:6) and Tobiah "the Ammonite servant" (Nehemiah 2:10), as well as the seal impressions of the province of Ammon from the Persian period, may point to the fact that they became Babylonian provinces, after all. Most important is the lack of the names of any of their kings (see below).

From the following period, there is only sparse information indicating that the last Babylonian king, Nebonidus, laid siege to "the city of Edom," and probably captured it in the second half of the third year of his reign. This city was most probably the Edomite capital of Bozrah, even though his monumental relief and erased inscription had been recently found on a cliff overlooking another Edomite town, Sela. It is not clear what moved Nabonidus to undertake this measure, nor can we draw any conclusions about the fate of the states east of the Jordan during the subsequent, final years of the Neo-Babylonian empire.

The archaeological picture east of the Jordan differs from one region to the next. While settlements north of the Jabbok River in the **Gilead, Golan,** and the **Bashan,** at least those that have been excavated, were already destroyed in large part during the Assyrian conquest and not subsequently rebuilt (e.g., Bethsaida, Tel Soreg, Tel Hadar, and 'En Gev), others, such as Pella, which were rebuilt during the Assyrian period, were utterly destroyed by the Babylonians. Later, some of these settlements were reestablished, but not earlier than the Persian period. Some were rebuilt only in the Hellenistic period.

The archaeological remains present a different picture within the territory of **Ammon.** Here, as in the region of Benjamin in Judah, settlement continued under Babylonian rule. Evidence for this comes from a few excavations, mostly ones conducted recently. Some tombs have also be excavated, both in the highlands of Ammon and in the lowlands along the Jordan Valley, which may also have been under Ammonite hegemony.

In the Ammonite capital, **Rabbath-Ammon,** nothing has come to light from this period except a few tombs. One of these is the tomb at **Meqabelein.** This is one of the well-known "Ammonite tombs" found near the city. Most of these tombs are dated to the 7th century BCE (see above). This particular tomb, although a regular rock-cut bench tomb similar to all other Ammonite tombs, had distinct contents in terms of pottery types and the metal vessels that accompanied them. W. F. Albright, followed by other scholars, pointed out that the Meqabelein tomb is later in date than all other Ammonite tombs. Albright tended to date it to the Persian period, but it seems that it was somewhat earlier: not later than the mid-6th century BCE (and see below). Near the two "Ammonite fortresses" that defended Rabbath-Ammon (see above), at **Umm Uthainah** and **Khilda,** other tombs of the same plan and with contents similar to those at Meqabelein have been excavated. Moreover, these tombs clearly remained in use until the end of the 6th century BCE and into the Persian period (as Albright thought), as attested by a few Attic vessels. We must therefore assume, as K. Yassine has stated, that use of some of the so-called Ammonite tombs continued throughout the entire Babylonian period, at least into the early Persian period.

A large cemetery (Cemetery A), the larger part of which is dated by its excavator to the Babylonian period, was uncovered at **Tell Mazar** in the Jordan Valley. This area was probably under Ammonite control. This cemetery contained finds similar to those discovered in the city of el-Mazar. In Area I of that settlement, the excavator attributed the finds from Stratum III to the 7th to 6th centuries BCE (including the Babylonian period). This stratum contained a large, impressive structure (Building 300), located at the acropolis of the town, which was probably erected by the Assyrians and later captured by the Babylonians. It seems that the Babylonian phase of the building, based upon the published artifacts, should be attributed to the latest phase at the site, i.e., that of Building 200, which is of Mesopotamian open-court plan. Finds from this stage of the building are identical to those found in the cemetery. In both cases, it is clear that the Babylonian period is well represented in the artifacts from Tell Mazar. It is peculiar, however, that at the other two major excavated sites situated close to Tell Mazar, Tell Deir ʿAlla, and Tell es Saʿidiyeh, no remains of this period appeared at all, and the excavators claim that there was a gap between the Late Iron Age and the Persian period. The same is true of another site recently excavated south of Tell Mazar, **Tell Nimrin.** No Babylonian-period stratum was recorded there.

Turning back to the hilly part of Ammon south of the capital city of Rabbath-Ammon, excavations have brought remains of the Babylonian period to light. At **Tell el-ʿUmeiri,** recent excavations proved to be important for the understanding of the end of the Iron Age (see above). This is one of the sites where Babylonian-period remains have been found. On the western side of the town, two public buildings and one domestic dwelling were uncovered. The width of the walls of the public buildings is more than a meter, and they were preserved to the height of two stories. The walls must have been but part of the cellars, which were dug deep into the previous strata. The date of the structures was fixed by two inscriptions found in a pit below the foundations of the buildings. One is an ostracon that contains a list of names. Its cursive Ammonite script was dated to the mid-6th century BCE. The other inscription is a bulla found in Building A. This bulla belonged to a person whose name is "Malkior the servant of Baʿal Yasha," whom the excavator, L. Herr, identifies with Baalis the last king of Ammon (Jeremiah 41). Herr believes that the structures described above were built after the reign of Baalis and continued through the Babylonian period and into the Persian period.

Other settlements with the same history as Tell el-ʿUmeiri were found, according to Herr, at **Tell Jawa** and at the important town of **Heshbon,** according to the results of recent excavations there. At Heshbon, too, Ammonite settlement continued from the Late Iron Age through the Babylonian period and down to the Persian period. During that time, according to Herr, "the town at Heshbon is characterized by a central government planning including a huge water reservoir which supplied the convoys passing through the King's highway."

The major excavations conducted at **Moab** were disappointing. For both **Dibon** and **Madeba,** we lack information about the Babylonian period. The extensive surveys conducted in this region by M. Miller did not uncover clear evidence concerning the period. We thus lack archaeological evidence for the Babylonian period in Moab.

As for **Edom,** three major excavations were conducted in this region by C. Bennett at **Umm el-Biyara,** Buṣeirah, and Tawilan. Umm el-Biyara is a single-period site, dated to the 7th century BCE, which was permanently abandoned at the end of this century. Another Edomite site close to Biyara and south of it is the recently excavated site of **Ghrareh.** This site, too, is from a single period and dates to the 7th to early 6th centuries BCE. At **Tawilan,** north of Biyara, results of the excavation attest to a similar situation, but this short period was divided here into no fewer than five phases, after which the site is said to have been abandoned until the Hellenistic period. At this site, two important Babylonian finds were recovered: one is a cuneiform tablet dated to the Persian monarch Darius; the other is a jewelry assemblage, also dated to the Persian period. Of the Babylonian-period remains, only one find is reported: a typical Neo-Babylonian seal, which may have also belonged to the Persian-period remains. Otherwise, no Babylonian-period remains are reported.

Only at **Buṣeirah,** the capital of Edom, in which the major stratum was dated to the 7th century BCE (see above), did the excavator, C. Bennett, attribute one clear phase to the Babylonian period, intermediate between the Iron and Persian periods. The existence of the town during this period is supported in the Babylonian sources, which tell about the conquest of the city by Nabonidus.

The last Edomite site to be discussed here is **Tell el-Kheleifeh** on the coast of the Red Sea, excavated by N. Glueck. This site did not produce any Babylonian stratum either, though there were clear Late Iron Age Edomite and Persian-period strata. Recent examination of the use of the copper mines at **Feinan,** one of the major foundations of the Edomite economy during this period, shows that it particularly flourished during the 7th and beginning of the 6th centuries BCE. There were no Babylonian-period remains of any kind.

Summing up the findings from the Babylonian period east of the Jordan, it seems that while Ammon, or at least some parts of it, continued to exist during this period, most of the other regions, Gilead and Golan in the north and Moab and Edom in the south (except for the capital, Buṣeirah), did not survive. Ammon may have been rescued from the Babylonian destruction, like Benjamin, because the Babylonians chose it as the seat of the Babylonian governor of the region, who might have replaced the kings of all three kingdoms (for, from this conquest on, there are, according to historical sources, no kings reigning east of the Jordan). We may also assume, based upon archaeological evidence, that during the period of Babylonian hegemony, the defensive line constructed by the Assyrians on the eastern border against the desert tribes was breached as a result of neglect by the authorities at this time. The destruction of most of the Moabite and Edomite towns was a result of this neglect, which enabled the desert nomads to penetrate into the settled areas and stop also the major trade along the King's Highway.

Chapter 2

SEALS AND SEAL IMPRESSIONS

BABYLONIAN SEALS

Of the finds of the Babylonian period, Neo-Babylonian inscriptions and Babylonian seals and seal impressions should provide the clearest evidence for Babylonian domination. Theoretically, these finds should also have been one of the safest criteria for the existence of a Babylonian stratum at a site. But, in reality, this is not the case.

Until now, only two Neo-Babylonian cuneiform tablets had been found in excavations in Palestine—one at Tawilan in Edom; the other at Mikhmoret on the Sharon coast—but both belong to the time of Persian-Achaemenian monarchs and are dated by their regnal years. A third Babylonian inscription was found long ago at Tell en-Nasbeh in Benjamin, i.e., the site that may have served as the provisional capital of Judah during the Babylonian period. It is inscribed on a bronze strip and is a dedicatory inscription that unfortunately was found out of context. We are therefore uncertain regarding its attribution to the Babylonian period.

Other Babylonian inscriptions found in Palestine are from two Babylonian seals: finds include a cylinder seal from Samaria belonging to a scribe by the name of Nabu Zabil. This seal was also found out of context. The other find is a votive cylinder seal found at Tel Sheva in a *favissa* of the Persian period, and is inscribed "to Apil-Addu, the great lord, His lord Rimut-ilani son of Hadad-'idri made and donated."

All the rest of the Babylonian seals found in Palestine are nonepigraphic. It is a curious fact that of the Babylonian cylinder seals that were so widespread at that time, and uncovered in great numbers in Egypt, Syria, and

Anatolia, only two examples (besides the inscribed ones mentioned above) have been found thus far in Palestine. One is from Tell Jemmeh in Philistia, located on the Way of the Sea (Via Maris). It is dated by its stratigraphic context to the end of the 6th century BCE, i.e., the beginning of the Persian period. This seal, which is of chalcedony (and thus, imported), shows on the right side a bird-man with a scorpion tail, standing on a low platform facing the fish-goat emblem of the god Ea, who stands on an altar. In the area between are depicted the moon crescent and a common Babylonian motif called "the eye." The other cylinder seal, also of chalcedony, was found at the Ammonite cemetery of Tell el-Mazar in the Jordan Valley. It depicts a rider shooting a gazelle. This seal may be of either the Babylonian or the Persian period.

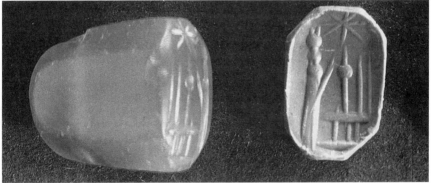

II.4 Babylonian cylinder seal and a stamp seal from Tell Jemmeh and En-Gedi

All other nonepigraphic imported Babylonian seals are conical chalcedony stamp seals with octagonal base, except for one duck-shaped example. In Babylon, northern Mesopotamia, and Persia, many such seals were uncovered in clear Neo-Babylonian-period contexts. In Palestine, too, several seals were discovered, which apparently date to the Babylonian period, but the majority of these was evidently in use during the Persian period (see below). Most of these seals were not uncovered in clear enough contexts to enable us to decide confidently to which of the two periods they should be attributed. The Babylonian stamp seals were uncovered at numerous sites all over the country, both in Palestine itself, such as Tel ʿAmal, Taanach, Tell Keisan, Samaria, Bethel, En-Gedi, and Tell eṣ-Ṣafi, and in large numbers all over Transjordan. They also turned up in Edom (at Tawilan) and in Moab, though they were especially common in Ammon, where they were uncovered in two concentrations. One of these was found around the capital city of Rabbath-Ammon, which included one seal found in the acropolis of the city itself (this one also included two Neo-Babylonian letters), one near Tell Ṣafut, and the rest in the Ammonite tombs excavated around the city, such as the tomb of Adoninur, the tomb at Meqabelein, the tomb of Umm Uthainah, and one of the Khilda tombs. Use of the last two tombs ended in the Persian period (see above).

The second group of Babylonian seals was found in the Ammonite cemetery of Tell Mazar in the Jordan Valley. Here, too, they have been uncovered in two different groups: one in the tombs, which was dated by the excavator to the Babylonian period (they were placed on the chests of the deceased or hung on their belts), and the others at the settlement, the majority in a structure dated to the Babylonian and Persian periods. The tombs of Umm Uthainah, Khilda, and Tell Mazar contained many seals clearly imported from Babylon, for all are of chalcedony, except for a single example in agate, also a stone not native to Palestine. The majority of these seals depicts Babylonian priests, praying before an altar upon which were set the emblems of the gods Nabu and Marduk (a spear, a stylus, and a spade). Some also contain representations of the crescent and the sun, while on others, these symbols appear alone. At times, individual motifs, which form but a part of the above scene, are depicted. In others, we find a composite scene, such as the palm-and-ibex motif; a hero struggling with ibexes with heads turned back; a wheel from which the winged *protomai* (busts) of a lion, ibex, and mountain goat project; a bird; a scorpion; and seals depicting simple geometric motifs. All of these are well-known motifs among the Neo-Babylonian seals found elsewhere.

Among the Babylonian seals is a small group in which Babylonian names are inscribed in alphabetical, usually Aramaic, script, though other West Semitic scripts also occur. Good examples for these are the seals of "Nergal Sallim son of Ahhe-eresh," "Manku-ki Inruta blessed by Milkom," and "Yehoyishmaʿ daughter of Shamash-shur-usur." These are local imitations of Babylonian seals. Here, too, we cannot be sure if they were made in the Babylonian or the Persian periods.

From the discussion above, it can be concluded that Babylonian seals, both epigraphic and nonepigraphic, began to arrive in Palestine in the late 7th and early 6th centuries BCE; however, the majority of the Palestine finds dates to the Persian period. Also interesting are the large concentrations of these seals in Ammon, where at least some may be dated to the Babylonian period.

Another conclusion is that along with the imported Babylonian seals appeared many local imitations. These imitations of Mesopotamian seals first appear during the Assyrian period. Above, we mentioned the appearance of seals with Babylonian names, but many are also nonepigraphic seals made of local stone with Babylonian motifs, such as the popular one of the altar with the emblems of Nabu and Marduk, or the moon crescent, reported from sites all over the country. Good examples of this type include a bulla found at the Judaean city of Ḥorvat ʿUza in the Beersheba Valley and one found at the Edomite site of Qitmit. Others are known from Ammon, Philistia, and Phoenicia (Dor and Tell Keisan). It is possible that the symbols in these imitations lack the original cultic meanings they had in the Babylonian setting.

Hebrew Seals and Inscriptions

TO THE BABYLONIAN PERIOD should also be attributed a group of seal impressions and incisions, with script dated on paleographic grounds to this period, and with distribution limited to the region of Benjamin, the only relatively prosperous region in Palestine during the Babylonian period.

The first group includes the seal impressions stamped on clay jars with the name of the town Mozah. These impressions can be divided mainly into two types: one is round with the legend *moṣah* inscribed in plene spelling on the body of the vessel; the second is the abbreviated form *mṣh,* written in a single line on the jar handle. N. Avigad interpreted the seals as representing the name of the town of Mozah, in Benjamin, on the basis of the impressions of the first type. As for their purpose, he suggested three possibilities: (1) the

II.5 A *moṣah* seal impression

city Mozah served as a center of tax collection, similar to the position held by the four cities inscribed on the *lmlk* seals (see above); (2) the seals represented the trademark of a special wine produced in the town; and (3) Mozah was a royal estate. It is important to recall here, once again, that these impressions, unlike the *yehud* seal impressions of the Persian period, have been found only in the small region of Benjamin, north of Jerusalem. About thirty of them came from Tell en-Naṣbeh (Mizpah), which was probably the seat of the governor of Judah during the Babylonian period, one from near Bit Hanina, four from Gibeon, and one from Zobah. Four more came from Jerusalem and one from Ramat Raḥel. This limited distribution recently persuaded J. Zorn that they should be dated to the Babylonian period alone. This idea is not new. In the past, it was held by a few scholars on the basis of paleographic considerations. This view is also supported by the stratigraphy of Gibeon, as described above, which also points to a gap in settlement from the beginning of the 5th century to the Hellenistic age. The fact that the Mozah seals were discovered at this site may again indicate an early (Babylonian) date for the Mozah impressions.

At **Gibeon,** about sixty incised jar handles similar to those of the Mozah jars were found. The inscriptions mention the town's name, *gbʿn,* as well as another site in Benjamin, *gdr,* and some personal names such as *ʾznyahu,*

II.6 Seal impression of a monogram in the form of a cross

II.7 Gibeon, incision of the
city's name on a jar handle

'mryahu, hnnyahu, nr', and dml', probably names of families in Benjamin. The date of these inscriptions was not clear from the archaeological contexts. The excavator, J. B. Pritchard, was of the opinion that they dated to the last days of the Judaean kingdom, but many others, including F. M. Cross and N. Avigad, dated them to the later part of the 6th century BCE, probably during the Babylonian period. In the same way, another inscription, in which the name of the town of *hamosah* is again mentioned, but also with a name of a Benjaminite family, *shu'al* ("fox"), was also dated to the Babylonian period. It now seems, therefore, that this entire group of Mozah impressions, the *mosah shu'al,* and the Gibeon incised jar handles probably date to the Babylonian period. Their limited regional distribution within Benjamin and their paleography and archaeological context all place them within a relatively short period during which this region enjoyed particular importance. This also strengthens the assumption that in the Babylonian period these seals were trademarks of wine produced in the tax-exempt governors' estates, including Mozah. Later in the Bible, Gibeon is explicitly mentioned as an estate of the governor of the Abar Nahara satrapy (Nehemiah) 3:7.

· Chapter 3 ·
_____

Tombs and Burial Customs

The survey of burials in Palestine, and their classification according to form and, especially, content, enable us to attribute some of them to different phases of the 6th century BCE, perhaps within the Babylonian period. In many respects, they are transitional types between tombs of the last stage of the Iron Age and the earliest tombs of the Persian period. Tombs of this type are represented along the Palestinian coast (at Achzib, Mount Carmel, 'Atlit, and Azor), but they are mainly concentrated in the land of Benjamin and the environs of Jerusalem, at sites such as Ḥorvat 'Almit, Tell en-Naṣbeh, Tell el-Ful, Ketef Hinnom in Jerusalem, Abu Ghosh, and Tomb 14 at Beth-Shemesh west of Jerusalem. The others were found in the land of Ammon at Meqabelein, Umm Uthainah, Khilda, and in the large Cemetery A at Tell Mazar in Ammonite territory near the Jordan River, attributed by its excavator in its entirety to the Babylonian period. It seems that in most of these cases the burials continued the older Iron Age tradition of using rock-cut bench tombs.

These tombs share several common features:

1. At sites where their plans could be ascertained, such as Beth-Shemesh, Abu Ghosh, Ketef Hinnom, and 'Almit, they were seen to be a direct continuation of tombs from the end of the Iron Age. They consist of a straight entrance and an irregularly shaped burial chamber with a pit in the center and benches along the walls. This is the common tomb type in many parts of Palestine at the end of the Iron Age.

2. The pottery and other finds discovered in these tombs were mostly of the types common at the end of the Iron Age.

3. All these tombs were parts of cemeteries, mostly from the end of the Iron Age, in which they appear to represent the latest burials.

4. Against this background of the continuation of form and contents of the Iron Age, each of these tombs usually contains one or more innovative objects. This is generally a vessel not found in typical Iron Age tombs, but which becomes widespread during the Persian period. There are no typical Babylonian finds in any of them.

It is also possible that some of the tombs (Beth-Shemesh, Tell el-Ful, Ketef Hinnom, and the Ammonite tombs at Meqabelein, Tell Mazar, Umm Uthainah, and Khilda) contain mixed assemblages, part of which date to the end of the Iron Age and part to the beginning of the Persian period. There is, however, no way of showing this conclusively. Other tombs, on the other hand, are definitely homogeneous. In the light of the similarity of the problems of the group as a whole, it seems likely that all these tombs are contemporaneous.

Neither the layout of the tombs nor the bulk of their finds will be discussed here, for they are typical of the tombs and vessels common in the Iron Age. We will confine ourselves to those exceptional features that in our opinion necessitate lowering the date of the tomb assemblages. These fall into three main categories:

1. Vessels that first appear at the end of the Iron Age but are also characteristic of the Persian period

2. Vessels that are absent in the Iron Age and common in the Persian period

3. Metal and stone burial offerings of various types, which suddenly appear in large quantities. These include bowls, mirrors, kohl utensils, strainers, dippers, bracelets and anklets, and numerous cosmetic containers of alabaster, especially alabastra and small bowls.

Even so, it is very difficult to point to those elements that are unique to the Babylonian period alone. For the majority of these tombs, in particular the richest ones, such as the tombs of Ketef Hinnom in Jerusalem, or Meqabelein, Umm Uthainah, and Khilda in the land of Ammon, there can be no doubt that they were also in use during the Persian period, for they contained some Attic pottery vessels and Achaemenian jewelry. In this connection, in the Ketef Hinnom tombs, a unique East Greek coin from the island of Kos (the earliest coin found in Palestine) was dated to 570 BCE. This strengthens the dating of at least part of the assemblage to the Babylonian period. The excavator, G. Barkai, believes, on the basis of this evidence, that there was a settlement in Jerusalem during this period.

In Benjamin and in the land of Ammon, where these rock-cut tombs of the Babylonian period are located, were found some clay coffins of Mesopotamian type, which we already encountered in connection with the previous Assyrian hegemony in Palestine (see above). Clay coffins of this type attributed to the Babylonian period have been uncovered at Tell en-Naṣbeh, i.e., the Judaean provisional capital of the period located in Benjamin, as well as in two peripheral parts of Jerusalem: at Ketef Hinnom and at Malḥah. In Ammon, one complete clay coffin was found in Cemetery A at Tell Mazar, also dated by its excavator to the Babylonian period. It now appears most probable that high-ranking Babylonian officials, and perhaps even the local ones of this period, continued to practice this Mesopotamian custom of burial in clay coffins during the Babylonian period.

As to the large cemetery at Tell Mazar, located in the probable Ammonite territory of the Jordan Valley, although its excavator is certain that it was utilized over a relatively short period, the finds published from it closely resemble those in the other Ammonite tombs. They also contained some Persian-period artifacts and may have continued down to the Persian period, as the tombs around Jerusalem and in Benjamin, discussed above. Here, in addition to the heterogeneous finds uncovered, it should be pointed out that types of burials are also diverse. Out of eighty-four tombs, most (seventy-one) were simple cist graves in which the deceased was laid covered with a piece of cloth or by a mat. Others (three) were lined with bricks. Still others (six) were built and covered with stones. There was one infant jar burial and one burial in a Mesopotamian clay coffin. In the tombs were found all the known 6th century BCE pottery-vessel types, as well as many metal vessels, including bowls, strainers, *thymiateria,* decanters, and a bottle. Also recovered here were various weapons, such as arrowheads, spearheads, swords, daggers, etc., as well as bronze, silver, and gold jewelry, stone and glass perfume containers, and a few Babylonian and Persian seals.

To sum up, we conclude that the majority of the tombs of the Babylonian period in Palestine bridge between types common in the Late Iron Age and those typical of the Persian period, and contain finds from both periods. Another important conclusion of this short discussion is that they are concentrated in the region of Benjamin and in the periphery of Jerusalem in the west, and around Rabbath-Ammon east of the Jordan.

· Chapter 4 ·

POTTERY VESSELS

There are almost no pottery vessels from Palestine that may be exclusively attributed to the Babylonian period. A few scholars, among them P. W. Lapp, have tried to separate the 6th century BCE Babylonian pottery from the rest on the basis of the assemblages found in strata excavated at Bethel, Tell el-Ful, and Tell en-Naṣbeh (see above), but this has proved unsuccessful, as the greater part of these vessels appears at the turn of the century (mostly in the late 7th century BCE), a period belonging to the time of the Judaean kingdom rather than that of Babylonian domination, while the rest may be dated to the beginning of the Persian period. Another problem stems from the fact that almost all the material comes from two small regions: Benjamin and Ammon.

The short period (586–538 BCE) of Babylonian domination in Palestine is thus devoid of clear characteristics in comparison with other periods, even ones almost equal in length (such as the Assyrian period). In general, we may conclude that the closer in time the assemblage is to the early part of the 6th century BCE, the more vessels continuing the regional pottery of the Late Iron Age it contains. The closer an assemblage is to the mid-6th century BCE, the more new types there are, which will continue later into the Persian period, especially its initial phase. It should also be taken into consideration that most of the assemblages of this type originate in tombs that enjoyed long periods of use, and that have not always fallen into the framework of our historical division of Judaean, Babylonian, and Persian periods. Some continued uninterruptedly from one period to the other. We have already seen that the most prominent evidence for the existence of the 6th century BCE pottery comes from a small number of tombs at Tell en-Naṣbeh, Tell el-Ful, Abu

Ghosh, and especially from Tomb 14 at Beth-Shemesh. In Tomb 14, for example, three types of clay lamps were found together. One is the Judaean high-footed lamp, typical of the last stage of the Judaean monarchy, which perhaps continued to the mid-6th century BCE. The second type is the closed Babylonian lamp with a long nozzle, which in Mesopotamia was the emblem of the god of light Nusku. It is very rare in Palestine. This lamp appears here for the first time, but continues down to the early part of the Persian period (in assemblages found in the Judaean Hills). The third lamp type is the large flat open lamp, which later becomes the most common type in the Persian period. Here, it makes perhaps its earliest appearance. This mixture of three types could occur only in mid-6th century BCE.

Other vessels, which on statistical grounds achieve wide distribution during the 6th century (but which begin to appear earlier and continue to the Persian period), are the "carrot-shaped" bottles, clay alabastra, round black *pixides,* and decanters with sack-shaped shoulders. Large assemblages of vessels similar to that of Beth-Shemesh Tomb 14 were also found in the tombs of Tell en-Naṣbeh, Tell el-Ful, Abu Ghosh, and ʿAlmit.

The difficulty in tracing the pottery of the Babylonian period is clearly exhibited in the large assemblage of pottery vessels found at Ketef Hinnom (a total of ca. 250 complete vessels). Here, the excavator dated the earliest to the Late Iron Age and the latest to the Persian period. Most were, in his opinion, from the Babylonian period; i.e., the tomb was in use all through the 6th century BCE. Here, at least, one piece of evidence missing in all other cases was found: a coin from the island of Kos dating to 570 BCE, well within the Babylonian period. Here, too, the pottery assemblage included carrot-shaped bottles, clay alabastra, flasks, round black *pixides,* flat open large lamps, and sack-shaped decanters. With these 6th century vessels were also found many other types characteristic of the last stage of the Judaean monarchy, such as the high-footed lamps, the latest types of Cypro-Phoenician juglets, etc. The main importance of this large assemblage is therefore the appearance of those types that are particularly common after the destruction of Judah by the Babylonians, and before the Persian period.

The same is true of the finds from the Babylonian-period tombs in the land of Ammon, such as the cemetery at Tell Mazar, the tomb in Meqabelein, and especially those at Umm Uthainah and Khilda, which cover the entire 6th century BCE; i.e., the start in the last period of the Ammonite kingdom, and their major period of use covers the Babylonian period. They cease to appear in the initial stage of the Persian period, based upon the occurrence of Attic vessels in the latter two. The characteristic features of the Babylonian-period pottery in Ammon are almost identical to those of the types of the last stage of the Ammonite kingdom during the 7th century BCE, as described above. Only a few new pottery types appear, but in addition, many metal artifacts and the ubiquitous Babylonian seals, along with local imitations, are frequently found. At the end of the century, in the beginning of the Persian period, some Achaemenian seals, Attic ware, jewelry, and coins are added. Thus, distinguishing among tombs dated to the late Ammonite kingdom, the Babylonian period, and those of the early Persian period is difficult on the basis of local pottery alone, and is almost impossible without the help of the Greek material. For example, a Persian-period tomb from Shechem, recently published, included all the typical vessels of the Babylonian period— clay alabastra, sack-shaped decanters, a rich assemblage of metal artifacts, one of these shaped like the closed Babylonian lamp—but the date was securely fixed by the presence of three Attic *lekythoi* (bottles), dated to the beginning of the 5th century BCE (see below).

From the rest of the country's regions, there are virtually no tombs that can be confidently dated to this period. It is even possible now to challenge some excavators' conclusions attributing some of their finds to a Babylonian-period stratum, as at Tell Keisan in the Acco Valley and elsewhere.

Surprisingly, a similar gap exists for Greek imports of the 6th century BCE. The well-known scholar S. S. Weinberg summed up this peculiar situation by writing that "in Palestine we are left with a gap of almost a century for which we have so little imported Greek pottery, that is of no help just when it is most needed." This gap occurred, as we have seen, as the result of the complete devastation of the Palestinian coastal harbor towns by the Babylonians in 604–603 BCE.

· Chapter 5 ·

METAL AND STONE ARTIFACTS

Much of what has been said above about the clay vessels is also applicable, with certain modifications, to the period's other finds. During the last decades of the Iron Age, and more often, in the Babylonian period, many new metal vessels begin to appear quite suddenly. Some of these are utensils that originated in Mesopotamia, but the majority was imitated en masse in Palestine. They were found in great numbers in all of the tombs of this period: Tomb 14 at Beth-Shemesh, the Ketef Hinnom tombs, all the Ammonite tombs at Tell Mazar, Meqabelein, Umm Uthainah, and Khilda. These artifacts include bowls, some plain, others with leaf decoration, and strainers and dippers, sometimes equipped with handles decorated with animal heads: ducks, snakes, and stags. These will be dealt with in detail in the next major section, for the majority is dated to the Persian period.

With these utensils are found many other metal artifacts, which were mainly used by women, such as mirrors, typical jewelry, toggle pins, and toilet vessels (alabastra and small bowls made of alabaster), kohl sticks, glass and bronze bottles. Weapons were found in the men's tombs: local arrowheads and Babylonian arrowheads (of the Irano-Scythian type), many of which have also been found on the battlegrounds and in the destruction levels associated with the Babylonian conquest at such sites as the City of David in Jerusalem, the Upper City of Jerusalem, En-Gedi, Ashkelon, Ekron, and Batash.

All these vessels are dated to the Babylonian period, but some, such as the alabaster vessels and the glass bottles, first occur in late 7th century BCE contexts, or from the very beginning of the 6th century BCE, i.e., during the age of the kingdoms. Their main distribution, however, is the 6th century BCE up to the initial stage of the Persian period. Others, mainly the various types of metal vessels, jewelry, and weapons, only begin to appear in the Babylonian period, but their main period of distribution is during the Persian period. As already stated, there is not even one type that can unequivocally be attributed to the Babylonian period alone.

· Chapter 6 ·

CULT OBJECTS

With the exception of one structure at Bethel, which was interpreted as a continuation of a previous sanctuary on the site, and the date and function of which must await further clarification, there are no sanctuaries or cult objects that can securely be attributed to the Babylonian period. Moreover, we may assume that the Babylonian period, especially in Judah and Samaria, is characterized by the complete disappearance of the clay figurines that were so common in the last phase of the Iron Age, and that this disappearance, in Judah and Samaria, will continue into the Persian period. This topic will be discussed below in detail. Pagan emblems are found only on imported objects, which perhaps date to the Babylonian period, such as a handful of coins or Babylonian seals. As we have seen, only a few really belong to this period, and some local seals are imitations. In the Persian period, for which more material is available for study, the cult objects, and especially the clay figurines, continue, manufactured by a different technique than previously, except in Judah and Samaria. This fact is of great importance for the study of Jewish and Samaritan religion (and see below).

Among the finds that may be attributed to the Babylonian period are those found in the Umm Uthainah tomb in the land of Ammon, dated from the early 7th century BCE to the Persian period. These include one bronze *thymiaterion* (lamp) of standard Phoenician type, which included a cover. It perhaps originated somewhere on the Phoenician coast and was sent from there to Ammon, either in the Babylonian period or, more plausibly, later, in the Persian period.

THE BABYLONIAN PERIOD: SUMMARY AND CONCLUSIONS

OUR SURVEY OF the results of excavations at each of the sites in Palestine indicates that the vast majority of the towns, which were resettled after being destroyed by the Babylonians, was rebuilt during the Persian period. To name a few in Philistia: Ekron, Ashkelon, Tel Batash, Tell Jemmeh, Ruqeish, and Tel Seraʿ. The Assyrian fortresses along the Way of the Sea (Via Maris), such as the recently excavated fort at Rishon le-Zion, were also reoccupied only in the Persian period. The same is true throughout the Beersheba Valley, destroyed by the Babylonians and resettled, according to the date assigned to the ostraca found at Tel Sheva and Arad, only in the 4th century BCE. The same results were obtained in regard to the settlements along the Aravah and the Jordan Valley, from Tell el-Kheleifeh on the coast of the Red Sea, through En-Gedi and north to Dan. Similar results were obtained in excavations at Hazor, Megiddo, Dor, and central Judah: Jerusalem, Ramat Raḥel, Lachish, and other sites.

This vacuum during the Babylonian period is also reflected in a different way: the length of the Babylonian domination in some regions of Palestine was sixty-six years (from 604 to 538 BCE), a considerable period of time. From this period, no document connected to the Babylonian administration of the country has been found. Up to now, the Babylonian remains consist of a few dozen Neo-Babylonian seals and seal impressions, some imported and some local imitations. Even a superficial examination of their stratigraphic contexts shows that a minority originated in assemblages dating to the end of the 7th and beginning of the 6th centuries BCE, i.e., prior to the Babylonian period. The overwhelming majority is dated to the Persian period, and very few can be safely attributed to the Babylonian period.

Three Neo-Babylonian cuneiform inscriptions have been recovered in Palestine, but two of these, both clay tablets, one from Mikhmoret on the Sharon coast and the other from Buṣeirah in Edom, which might have provided evidence for the renewal of international trade along the two major highways, are dated to Persian-Achaemenian monarchs rather than the Neo-Babylonian period. Only the third one, a dedicatory inscription from Tell en-Naṣbeh in Benjamin, may perhaps belong to that age, but it came from a doubtful context. Other evidence for international trade of any kind is definitely lacking.

In order to understand the archaeological vacuum of the Babylonian period in Palestine, we must compare it to the previous Assyrian age (especially beginning with the establishment of the Assyrian provinces in Palestine; see above), which is only somewhat longer in time to the Babylonian period, dating from around the middle of Sargon's reign, following the occupation of Samaria, to the Assyrian retreat from all their estates in Palestine, from 715 to 640 BCE.

We have already discussed the major remains from the Assyrian period in detail in the previous section. There are four stone memorial stelae left by the Assyrian kings, at Samaria, Ashdod, Ben-Shemen, and Kakun. There are Assyrian administrative cuneiform tablets from Tell Keisan, Samaria, Gezer, and Hadid, as well as the Lamashtu tablet from the vicinity of Lachish. Assyrian structures were found at Ayelet ha-Shaḥar, Gezer, Tell Jemmeh, Tel Seraʿ, Tel Haror, and elsewhere, as well as the line of Assyrian fortresses of the types that was recently uncovered at Rishon le-Zion. Fortifications and gates and even the general replacement of the local "four-chambered" house with the Mesopotamian "open-court house" plan provide further evidence. The Assyrian siege ramp at Lachish, weapons, military equipment, etc., provide insight concerning Assyrian military practice. Assyrian burial customs reflected in the form of clay coffins are known in Palestine from all the territories under direct Assyrian domination in the northern part of the country: at Dor, Megiddo, Tell el-Qitaf near Beth-Shean, at Dothan, Samaria, and Tell el-Farʿah (N), and recently also at Jezreel.

There is also Assyrian "Palace ware" and its local imitations, Assyrian stone vessels, metal artifacts, and Assyrian reliefs, as well as dozens of imported Assyrian seals, some of which are inscribed with official titles. The appearance of the Assyrian glyptic style in Palestine appears to have revolutionized local glyptic art, which was previously based on Phoenician-Israelite archetypes.

Returning to the Babylonian period, no such rich material culture has survived. The only traces of Babylonian presence are the massive destruction levels that they left behind, which are indeed impressive. These have been uncovered at Ashkelon, Ekron, and Tel Batash; in Jerusalem, both in the excavations of Y. Shiloh and E. Mazar in the City of David and in those of N. Avigad in the Upper City, near the remains of the Judaean tower; at En-Gedi; and elsewhere. But there is *nothing* above these levels that can be attributed to the Babylonian period.

Why is there such a great difference between two periods of almost equal duration? This is clearly not a result of chance. The reason appears to be a difference in the policies of the two empires. While the Assyrians at first adopted a policy of destruction and deportation, this changed, for some reason, and after a short time, was almost entirely reversed. They rebuilt every destroyed town, sending in large numbers of new people from other lands, on a scale not often seen in the long history of Palestine. This is a phenomenon still awaiting proper study. The rebuilding of Megiddo Stratum III, Dor, Dothan, and many other towns in a relatively short time completely changed the character of the desolated country. The Babylonians, on the contrary, left the country as it was during the initial phase of their domination, after they deliberately destroyed, burned, and robbed all the settlements they occupied. They also deported those not killed to Babylon. The Babylonian authorities never built anything. It was mainly the destruction of the country's major harbor towns along the coast that immediately affected international trade relations and the economic situation of the rest of the country in general, including the previous Assyrian provinces, which were probably under their direct rule, reducing them to poverty.

The major conclusion of this discussion is that in the archaeology of Palestine, there is virtually no clearly defined period that may be called "Babylonian," for it was a time from which almost no material finds remain. This means that the country was populated, and there were settlements, but that the population was very small in number, and that large parts of the towns and villages were either completely or partly destroyed, and the rest were poorly functioning. International trade virtually ceased. Only two regions appear to have been spared this fate: the northern part of Judah, i.e., the region of Benjamin, which did not suffer terribly from the Babylonians and exhibits signs of relative prosperity; and probably the land of Ammon, a region that still awaits further investigation.

· BOOK THREE ·

THE
PERSIAN
PERIOD

(539–332 BCE)

INTRODUCTION:
THE HISTORY OF PALESTINE
IN THE PERSIAN PERIOD

When in 539 BCE Babylon fell to Cyrus, the Achaemenid king of Persia (559–530 BCE), Persia was raised to the status of an empire comprising the entire Near East. In contrast to the Babylonians, whose rule had been based upon large-scale deportations of people and a reign of fear, Cyrus, from the outset, adopted a much more lenient policy. This included resettling exiles in their homelands, reconstructing their temples, and fostering the image of a liberator. This policy gained him the goodwill of most of the subject peoples in his empire.

Within the framework of this policy, Cyrus issued a proclamation to the Jewish exiles in Babylon urging them to return to Jerusalem and rebuild their Temple there. The first Jews to return from Babylon, headed by Sheshbazzar "the prince of Judah" (apparently Shenazzar the son of Jehoiachin, the former king of Judah), encountered numerous difficulties in their attempt to reestablish the national and religious center of the Jewish people. On arrival they found, on the outskirts of the ruined city, a small community that had continued to dwell in the largely desolate land after the destruction of the First Temple. This remnant and the neighboring Samaritans, Ashdodites, Edomites, and Arabs did not view the repatriates with favor and used all means in their power to obstruct them. They finally succeeded in putting an end to their building activities in Jerusalem.

Throughout this period, Cyrus was engaged in military expeditions in order to consolidate the borders of his new empire. He fell in battle in 530 BCE in the area east of the Caspian Sea.

Cyrus was succeeded by his son Cambyses II (530–522 BCE), whose chief accomplishment was his conquest of Egypt and its annexation to the

Achaemenid empire in 525 BCE. He assembled his troops in Acco and achieved victory with the help of Arabian-Qedarite tribes, which supplied the Persian army with water during its advance across the Sinai desert. In 522 BCE, when Cambyses was still in Egypt, a revolt broke out in Persia. The king set out to suppress it but died on the way home.

The death of Cambyses was followed by a series of revolts in Persia and a power struggle for the throne which was finally won by Darius I (522–486 BCE), also a member of the Achaemenid royal family, even though of a collateral line, and not a direct descendant of Cyrus. His assumption of the kingship provoked widespread rebellions throughout the vast empire. The first uprising took place in Elam and was swiftly quelled. Another rebellion broke out in Babylon, led by Nebuchadnezzar III the son of Nabonidus, last of the Babylonian kings (see above). Darius quelled this rebellion as well, and by 519 BCE he seems to have pacified the entire kingdom, strengthened his rule, and even extended his empire to hitherto unknown frontiers by annexing parts of India and eastern Europe. During the rest of his reign, he waged wars mainly on the western border, in Anatolia and in Greece. In 512 BCE, he crossed the Bosphorus and conquered Thrace. According to Herodotus, he also engaged the Scythians in battle at the mouth of the Danube.

Of major importance for the future of the Persian Empire was the rebellion of the Greek cities of Anatolia and Cyprus in 499 BCE. Although it was put down harshly, it brought about a major confrontation between the Persians and the Athenians. The hostilities continued over a long period of time and ended in the complete rout of the Persian army at the battle of Marathon in 490 BCE. This was the Persians' first serious defeat. According to Herodotus, Darius intended to wage a further war against Greece, but in 486 BCE an uprising led by the Egyptian ruler Khabasha took place in Egypt and Darius died during the preparations for a campaign against the Egyptians.

The main accomplishments of Darius' reign were in the realm of imperial administration. He consolidated the empire, which during his lifetime reached the largest extent ever attained by any empire in the Near East. He organized it into twenty satrapies, and, in order to maintain efficient control over even the most remote governors in the realm, he developed a sophisticated road and postal system. He also exercised control over the activities of the governors and took the Persian armies out of their jurisdiction. Darius carried out a reform of the laws in the different satrapies and initiated a new system of tax collection and also an efficient administrative organization. His name is likewise connected with the new imperial monetary unit—the daric.

The king also devoted much effort to large-scale building projects. The main palaces in the capitals of the empire are attributed to his reign.

In the early days of Darius' reign, there was a steady increase in the stream of refugees returning to Palestine from the Babylonian exile. Some historians regard the great turmoil in Babylon caused by the revolts of Nebuchadnezzar III (522 BCE) and Nebuchadnezzar IV (521 BCE), descendants of the royal Babylonian family, which were suppressed with great cruelty, as one of the reasons for the large number of returning exiles. Another possible factor was the economic crisis that followed in the wake of the revolts. The repatriates may also have been encouraged by Darius' new imperial organization. Judah appears to have been constituted as an independent "state" (Heb. *medinah*) for the short period during which Zerubbabel the son of Shealtiel and grandson of Jehoiachin served as a governor *(peḥa)* of the province by Darius' appointment. In any event, the Bible records that 42,360 persons returned to Judah from Babylon in those days. They included a large number of priests headed by Jeshua son of Jozadak, high priest of the house of Zadok. Darius ordered removal of all obstacles placed in the way of the returning exiles by the enemies of Judah. The king reaffirmed Cyrus' edict in a letter to Tattenai, the governor of the Abar Nahara (Beyond the River) satrapy. In the second year of Darius' reign, Zerubbabel began to rebuild the Temple in Jerusalem with the support of the prophets Haggai and Zechariah. Zerubbabel developed commercial relations with the Phoenicians, who, through the port of Jaffa, supplied him—as they had Solomon—with cedars of Lebanon for the reconstruction of the Temple.

For some unknown reason, perhaps because Darius suspected that Zerubbabel was plotting an uprising, the governor—last heir of the Davidic line—disappeared suddenly, only a short time after construction work began. How the Jewish community was governed thereafter is unknown. N. Avigad may be correct in suggesting that another Jewish governor—Elnathan—replaced Zerubbabel. In the opinion of the present writer, however, the province may have been ruled by Persian governors from their seat in Samaria. A third possibility is that the leadership of the community passed to the priests and the landed oligarchy. Nevertheless, by 515 BCE the reconstruction of the Temple was complete and Jerusalem again assumed its position as the sacred center.

In 486 BCE, the year of the death of Darius I and the accession to the throne of his son Xerxes I (486–465 BCE), another revolt broke out in Egypt, led by the same Egyptian ruler, Khabasha. The revolt was crushed with difficulty and after heavy fighting in 483 BCE. Some authorities believe that the letter of "accusation against the inhabitants of Judah and Jerusalem" (Ezra 4:6) was written at this time and that it was in some way connected with the Egyptian insurrection. At the end of the same year, another revolt broke out in Babylon in which the Persian satrap of Babylon and Abar Nahara, Zopyrus, was killed. Xerxes suppressed the rebellion and severely punished the rebels. Babylon was henceforth separated from the Abar Nahara satrapy, which then appears as an independent unit.

In 480 BCE, Xerxes undertook an expedition against the Greeks and suffered major defeats in the famous battles of Salamis and Mycale. The Greek campaign ended when the Persian fleet was totally destroyed in the battle of Eurymedon, and the Persians appear to have been driven out of the Aegean basin.

After his defeat, Xerxes retired to his palace and was murdered several years later by his vizier, Artabanus. Xerxes' son Artaxerxes I Longimanus (465/4–424/3 BCE) succeeded him on the throne after a short struggle with other candidates of the royal family. As a result, the Egyptians again rose in rebellion, this time led by Inaros the son of Psamtik, aided by an Athenian fleet. Only after a prolonged effort were Megabyzus, satrap of Abar Nahara, and Arsames, satrap of Egypt, able to crush the rebellion (455 BCE). They also destroyed the Athenian army, which had failed in its siege of Kition in Cyprus. In 448 BCE, Megabyzus himself rebelled against the Persian king with the support of his two sons, Zopyrus and Artyphius. Although Megabyzus later expressed regret for his action, he was nevertheless removed from his post.

In Judah, the time from the death of Darius I to the death of Artaxerxes I may be characterized as a period of expansion and population growth. Owing to the lack of strong leadership, the national and religious laws were no longer observed: intermarriage undermined the religious and national uniqueness of the Jewish community, and farmers were harshly oppressed by the landed oligarchy. Conditions changed when Artaxerxes I attained the throne. A new wave of Jews from Babylon left to resettle in Palestine, this time headed by a strong religious and political leadership. According to the biblical sources, Ezra, the priest and scribe, left Babylon in the seventh year of the reign of Artaxerxes (458 BCE). Artaxerxes had appointed him to repair the Temple and to establish the laws of the Torah as the religious and social authority of the Jewish community. His plans collapsed, however, when confronted with the problem of intermarriage and the enmity of the local Jews and their neighbors. Lacking political power, Ezra failed to achieve his aims.

Some time later, Artaxerxes accepted the appeal of a court official, Nehemiah the son of Hachaliah, and appointed him governor of Jerusalem. Despite the hostility of Judah's neighbors, Nehemiah immediately undertook the rebuilding of the walls of the city. He also strengthened the town by increasing its population. He enacted new social and economic laws beneficial to the priests and the oppressed farmers, who had suffered both from the former governors and from the Jewish landlords. In this religious sphere, Nehemiah and Ezra forbade further acts of intermarriage and strengthened the observance of the Sabbath.

During this period, Nehemiah appears to have reestablished "the State of Judah" (*yehud medintha*) as an independent political unit, after a long period—since the days of Zerubbabel—during which the governors of Samaria had ruled the province.

By these actions, Ezra and Nehemiah laid the foundation for the future way of life of the Jewish people. However, they also provoked the final division between the Jews and the Samaritans. The latter abandoned the center at Jerusalem and established a separate temple on Mount Gerizim.

Thereafter, the Bible and other Jewish sources make almost no mention of the Judaean province. Only Greek sources and archaeological finds throw light on its history. The history of the Persian Empire is also known largely from the Greek writers' descriptions of the Persian-Greek wars, whereas Persian and Babylonian sources are scarce.

On the death of Artaxerxes I, a crisis arose within the empire, which ended when his son Darius II seized the throne (423–404 BCE). During his reign, new revolts erupted in Media, Anatolia, and Syria. The satrap of Egypt, Arsames, was sent to pacify these regions, but during his absence from Egypt serious disturbances broke out there as well. From this period, there are two extant letters from the year 408 BCE, which were sent by the Jewish mercenaries in the Persian-Jewish garrison at Elephantine (Yeb). They wrote to Bagohi governor of Judah and to Delaiah and Shelemiah the sons of Sanballat governor of Samaria to complain of the destruction of their Temple by the Egyptian rebels. From this time, there is also evidence of a similar military colony of Qedarite Arabs at Tell el-Maskhuta in the eastern Nile Delta. At this site, an inscription was found on a silver bowl belonging to "Qainu Bar Gashmu king of Qedar," i.e., the son of "Geshem the Arabian," one of Nehemiah's rivals.

The Persians met with success when the satraps Tissaphernes and Pharnabazus and Darius II's younger son Cyrus gave assistance to the victorious Spartans against Athens during the Peloponnesian War.

Artaxerxes II Memnon (404–358 BCE) succeeded to the throne after the death of Darius II. His rule was challenged by his younger brother Cyrus, who raised an army and marched to Babylon. There they met in battle at Cunaxa and Cyrus was killed. The war is described vividly in the *Anabasis* of the Athenian historian Xenophon.

During the reign of Artaxerxes II, the process of disintegration of the Persian Empire began. During the war between the two brothers, the Egyptians again arose in rebellion, headed by Pharaoh Amyrteus (404–399 BCE) of the 28th Dynasty from Sais. This time they succeeded in throwing off the Persian yoke for some sixty years (until 343 BCE). During their revolt, the Egyptians destroyed the Jewish-Persian military colony at Elephantine and the Arab colony at Tell el-Maskhuta.

Shortly after their successful rebellion, the Egyptians set out on an expedition against the Persians. The route of their campaign was through the Sinai desert into the coastal plain of Palestine. They appear to have occupied this territory gradually. At Gezer were found a seal impression and a broken inscribed stone bearing the name of Pharaoh Nepherites I (399–393 BCE), the last king mentioned in the Elephantine records and the first king of the 29th Dynasty from Mendes. This inscription indicates that Nepherites conquered at least the southern part of the Palestinian coastal region. His advance was apparently made possible by the war between the two brothers, which continued until 396 BCE. Nepherites successor, Achoris, formed alliances with the Cypriot king of Salamis Evagoras I and with the Athenians. They seized the northern part of the coastal plain of Palestine and for a brief period also held Tyre and Sidon. Two inscriptions of Achoris have been discovered, one at Acco and one at Sidon. The presence of the Cypriots in this region is attested by a few other contemporary inscriptions written in the Cypro-Archaic Syllabic script found at Sidon, Sarepta, Kabri, Acco, and Dor.

In 385 BCE, when Abrocamus became the satrap of Abar Nahara, peace was concluded with Athens and the Athenians withdrew their armies. Abrocamus joined forces with the satraps Pharnabazus and Tithraustes and together they expelled the Egyptians and Cypriots from Phoenicia and Palestine. By 380 BCE, they had completed the task.

One year later Pharnabazus, satrap of Cilicia, began mustering mercenaries in Acco for a fresh attack on Egypt. By 375 BCE, he had assembled three hundred ships, some twelve thousand Greek mercenaries, and a large number of native soldiers. But even before it engaged in its first battle, logistic problems and disease had decimated the force and it was thoroughly routed by the Egyptians.

From 366 to 360 BCE, the whole of the Persian Empire was endangered by what is generally known as "the revolt of the satraps." In 360 BCE, when Pharaoh Tachos came to the throne, he assembled a large Egyptian army, as well as Greek mercenaries, and renewed the Egyptian occupation of the coastal plain of Palestine and Phoenicia. During the campaign, the Egyptians were actually assisted by the Phoenicians. As Tachos was marching to join the revolting satraps, his own nephew Nekht-har-hebi rebelled against him in the camp and Tachos was forced to surrender to the crown prince Artaxerxes III at his headquarters in Sidon. After a short time, Nekht-har-hebi himself was forced to return to Egypt because of an internal crisis and Persian rule was gradually restored to Abar Nahara as, one by one, the rebels were captured or surrendered.

In 358 BCE, Artaxerxes II died and the throne passed to Artaxerxes III Ochus (who reigned until 336). After successfully putting down the satraps' revolt, the new king set out to reconquer Egypt. After a full year of hard fighting (351–350 BCE), he abandoned the attempt. This failure was the signal for the rebellion of the towns of Phoenicia led by Tennes king of Sidon with the aid of Pharaoh Nectanebo II (359–341 BCE). The uprising encompassed a large area and caused turmoil in the empire in the west. Belysses and Mazeus, the satraps of Abar Nahara and Cilicia respectively, tried in vain to reconquer the Phoenician towns.

At the beginning of 345 BCE, Artaxerxes himself assembled a huge army in Babylon and marched against Sidon. The inhabitants of the town made preparations for a lengthy siege, but their leaders betrayed them to the enemy and the whole town was razed to the ground. The Persians then directed the satrap Bagoas to continue the pursuit into Egypt itself. In 343 BCE, Bagoas finally succeeded in restoring Egypt to the Persian yoke. Shortly after the end of the Phoenician revolt, Mazeus was appointed satrap of Abar Nahara, a post he held until the satrapy was conquered in 332 BCE by Alexander the Great.

Did Judah take part in the revolt of the Phoenician cities? According to Eusebius and Josephus Flavius (*Against Apion* 2.134), there was a rebellion in this province in the days of Artaxerxes III, and in a punitive action, many Jews were exiled to Hyrcania on the coast of the Caspian Sea. A reference to the destruction of Jericho by Diodorus Siculus should perhaps be attributed to this period, and this is perhaps supported by contemporary papyri recently found in a cave east of the town (see below). Some historians believe that an extensive wave of destruction swept through the whole of Palestine. Others see a connection with the story related in the book of Judith. In the opinion of the present writer, however, recent archaeological discoveries indicate that the main Palestinian towns were only destroyed some years later by Alexander and his successors (see below).

In 338 BCE, the satrap Bagoas, the conqueror of Egypt, poisoned Artaxerxes III. The brief reign of Arses (337–336 BCE) ensued, followed by Darius III Kodomanus, the last king of the Achaemenid dynasty (336–330 BCE). Darius was defeated by Alexander at the battle of Issus and fled to the eastern part of his realm, where he was killed. The whole of the Persian Empire was annexed to Alexander's kingdom.

In Phoenicia and Palestine, Alexander met fierce resistance at Tyre and Gaza before continuing into Egypt. Later, in 332 BCE, he also had to put down a Samaritan revolt, traces of which have been found recently in the Wadi ed-Daliyeh cave, where the Samaritan rebels found refuge.

As mentioned above, there are almost no literary references to Judah and Samaria in the 4th century BCE (apart from the possible allusion to a revolt in the days of Artaxerxes III). Records found at Wadi ed-Daliyeh and Samaria indicate that all the governors of Samaria belonged to the same family. These provinces do not appear to have suffered damage in the continuous warfare that took place in the coastal plain throughout this century and possibly took no part whatsoever in such hostilities.

THE LITERARY AND EPIGRAPHIC EVIDENCE

ALTHOUGH THE PERSIAN period is relatively late from the archaeological standpoint, it is one of the most obscure eras in Palestine and its history remains practically unknown. The Bible, the chief source for the history of the Israelite period, is almost silent concerning the Persian period. Any references it does contain are applicable only prior to the mid-5th century BCE. Among the books of the Bible ascribed to this period are Isaiah, from chapter 40 onward, Haggai, Zechariah 1–8, Malachi, Ezra, Nehemiah, several chapters of Chronicles, and the book of Esther. The books of Ezra and Nehemiah in particular present an account of the fortunes of Judah midway through the period of Persian rule. Our knowledge is supplemented by references in the Apocryphal literature: 1 Esdras, Tobit, Susanna, and Judith, works that were either composed in the Persian period or describe events said to have occurred at that time. Brief references are also contained in the works of Josephus. Further information, mainly descriptions of the coastal area of Palestine, is derived from contemporary Greek writers such as Herodotus (mid-5th century BCE) and pseudo-Scylax (probably mid-4th century BCE). Occasional references to the history of Palestine in the 4th century BCE can also be found in the writings of Diodorus Siculus, and events from the days of Alexander the Great are mentioned by Arrian.

Throughout the years, our understanding of the period has been enriched substantially by the discovery of epigraphic documents that have either a direct or an indirect bearing on the history of Palestine. At Behistun, Persepolis, and Susa in the eastern part of the Persian Empire, inscriptions of Darius I have been discovered, which shed light on the administrative organization of the kingdom in his days. In Phoenicia, inscriptions of the Sidonian kings have been found, an outstanding example of which is the epitaph on the sarcophagus of Eshmun'ezer (end of the 6th century BCE), which speaks of this king's rule over the coast of the Sharon. Another inscription generally assigned to the Persian period is that of Yahumelekh king of Byblos.

Egyptian sources include the important archive of the Jewish military colony at Elephantine (5th century BCE), which comprises some one hundred papyri and numerous ostraca, among which are several duplicates of documents sent to the governors of Judah and Samaria. Another Egyptian archive contains papyri attributed to the satrap Arsames, who ruled Egypt at the end of the 5th century BCE. Although these make no direct reference to the history of Palestine, they furnish illuminating details on the form of organization and administration of the provinces of the empire. Similar information is also provided by the archive from Hermopolis, which contains some Aramaic documents of the 5th century BCE. Also of interest are inscriptions on silver bowls discovered at Tell el-Maskhuta east of the Nile Delta, one of which reads "Qainu son of Geshem king of Qedar," and several Aramaic inscriptions on stone stelae from Aswan and Saqqara.

In Palestine, many written documents of a heterogeneous nature have been uncovered. It is true, however, that not even one of them is written in the Persian language and script, but two clay tablets written in the Babylonian cuneiform script have been found, both dated to the Persian period. These were inscribed in Babylon and were brought to the west by traders who traveled between the two regions.

One of the Babylonian clay tablets was found at Mikhmoret along the main coastal highway on the Sharon coast. This contains an account of the merits of a slave girl brought from Babylon. The other tablet was recovered at Tawilan in Edom, i.e., along the Transjordanian trade route, and is dated to the reign of one of the three Achaemenid kings named Darius (probably the third). This is a legal document concerning a disputed sale of livestock, drawn up in Haran in upper Mesopotamia.

Two more inscriptions written in Egyptian were found. These are important documents of the Egyptian king Pharaoh Nepherites I (399–393 BCE), found at Gezer, and that of Pharaoh Achoris (393–380 BCE), found at Acco. Both belong to the period of the rule of these two kings over the Palestinian coast.

All the rest of the written material found here is written in local scripts: Phoenician, Hebrew, etc. The overwhelming majority, however, is written in Aramaic, the *lingua franca* of the age. We shall include here the Aramaic papyri found at two sites. One is the archive of papyri discovered in a cave in Wadi ed-Daliyeh, about ten miles north of Jericho. This archive belonged to refugees who fled from the city of Samaria. The documents, dating to the

III.1 Memorial stone from Acco which mentions the name of Pharaoh Achoris of the 26th Dynasty (393–380 BCE)

III.2 The inscribed papyrus from Ketef Jericho, 4th century BCE

years 375–335 BCE, shed light on the dynasty of governors of the province of Samaria. A few more papyri of the same period (late 4th century BCE) were recently found in a cave at Ketef Jericho, about one mile east of the town of Jericho. These may be connected with the same events as the Wadi ed-Daliyeh documents, but may, as their excavator believes, be somewhat earlier—dating to the time of a Jewish rebellion against the Persians centered at Jericho.

Other valuable epigraphic sources for the study of the daily life of the Persian period are the dozens of ostraca, written mainly in Aramaic but also in Phoenician and other local dialects, that have been discovered all over the country. Few of these originate at northern sites such as Dan, Mizpe Yammim, Jokneam, and Tel Qiri. More come from sites along the north coast from Achzib, Kabri, Acco, Shiqmona, Dor, Eliachin, Tel Michal, Apollonia, Tell Abu Zeitun, and Jaffa, and down to the Philistine coastal region: Tel

III.3 A Phoenician inscription on a jar from Shiqmona

Taoz, Nebi Yunis, Ashdod, Ashkelon, Tell el-Ḥesi, Tell Jemmeh, Tel Seraʿ, Tell el-Farʿah (S), Tell Abu Salima, and elsewhere. Others have been recovered in Samaria and Judah: in the city of Samaria, at Gezer, Kirbet el-Qom, Yatir, En-Gedi, Lachish, and Maresha, among other sites.

Even more important are the large Persian-period ostraca assemblages found in west Idumaea at Tel Sheva and Arad, and also at Tell el-Kheleifeh on the Red Sea coast. But the largest group of all, which contains more than four hundred ostraca purchased from a Jerusalemite antiquity dealer, was recently published by I. Ephʿal, J. Naveh, and A. Lemaire. The exact site in Idumaea from which these originate is not yet known. Nearly all the texts in this collection deal with the cultivation of fields and orchards. They consist of dockets that provide the names of the parties and commodities involved in the transactions. One of them, however, was a legal document, apparently reporting a court decision concerning a loan. The texts are dated according to the regnal years of Persian and Greek kings, and range from 363 to 311 BCE.

From Transjordan, we now have some Aramaic ostraca, mainly from Heshbon and Tell el-ʿUmeiri in Ammon and from Tell es-Saʿidyieh in the Jordan Valley.

Even more important are the inscribed seal impressions belonging to the officials of the local Persian provincial administration. These have been found on jar handles as well as on bullae. A few bullae assemblages have been found; the most important of these, the hoard of bullae from a post-exilic Judaean archive near Jerusalem, was published by N. Avigad.

More bullae were found during the excavations of the City of David in Jerusalem. The largest bullae group originated in the city of Samaria and was discovered at the cave in Wadi ed-Daliyeh. Most of these were not epigraphic, but some carried the names of provincial officials and governors such as Sanballat and Delaiah.

Both inscribed seals and seal impressions mention the names of two of the provinces: Judah and Ammon. On the Judaean seals, the names of some of the rulers of the province appear, sometimes with their title, such as "governor" *(peḥa):* Yehoʿezer, Ahzai, and Elnathan, in addition to Bagohi, who is mentioned in the Elephantine papyri. Some seal impressions provide important information on the administrative organization of the provinces and the names of their officials, such as the Judaean seal bearing the inscription "Shelomith maidservant of Elnathan the *peḥa*" or a Phoenician seal from Tell Qasile belonging to a certain "servant of the king."

III.4 Aramaic ostracon from Tell el-Farʿah

Finally, let us mention the hundreds of numismatic finds, coins struck by the governments of different Palestinian provinces. Thus far, coins of the Persian period have been found with the names of Judah, Samaria and Ashdod, Ashkelon and Gaza. Other coins bear the names of governors, such as "Yehezqiah the *peḥa*" among the Judaean coins and Sanballat among the Samaritan ones. Others carry the titles of priests, such as "Yohanan the *kohen*" ("priest"). But most bear names without titles and appear to have been the property of lower-level officials.

All these rich new finds contribute much to our understanding of the period's history, providing information about political organization, names of the previously unknown governors and officials, the composition of the population in different regions, cult, daily life, and diverse cultural influences.

It is interesting to note that among all the assemblages of Persian-period inscriptions from Palestine, almost none are written in Greek. One inscription from Tell el-Ḥesi is in Greek characters but contains a Phoenician personal name. Another, from Dor, consists of only a few letters. Individual Greek letters are sometimes found incised on pottery vessels.

The only archaeological evidence thus far for the use of the Greek language here during the Persian period is from sites along the north coast: Sidon, Sarepta, Kabri, Acco, and Dor, where Greek-language inscriptions written in the Cypro-Archaic script were found. Most are dedications to various local deities. The first traders and soldiers who reached Palestine in the Persian period may have utilized this script.

Another script rarely encountered in this country from Persian-period contexts is Arabic. On the southern coast, near el-ʿArish, a cultic vessel bearing a Thamudic-Arabic dedicatory inscription was found.

THE GEOGRAPHICAL-HISTORICAL BACKGROUND

PALESTINE IN THE Persian period formed part of the satrapy called "Beyond the River"—Hebrew: *eber hanahar* (Ezra 8:36; Nehemiah 2:7, 9; Aramaic: *abar nahara* (Ezra 4:10–11, 16, 20; 4:3, 6)—a term derived from Assyrian administration usage *(ebir-nari),* known from the time of Esarhaddon and perhaps even much earlier (1 Kings 5:4). In the list of towns in the *Periplus* of pseudo-Scylax, the region was still known as Coele-Syria, which is a translation of the name and sound of the Aramaic *kol-syria* ("all of Syria"), an ancient term that also apparently designates the Syrian hinterland.

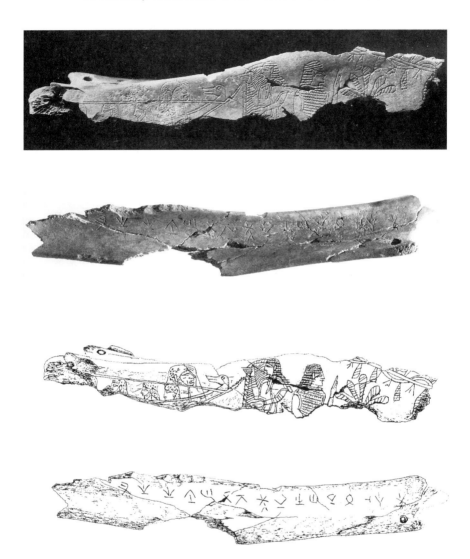

III.5 A Cypro-Archaic inscription and a Phoenician maritime scene carved on a cow scapula from Dor

Although the boundaries of the satrapy correspond with those delimited in the Assyrian period (see above), they passed through a number of transformations before becoming fixed. During the reign of Cyrus, all of the conquered Babylonian territories (including Babylon itself) and the Babylonian Abar Nahara region were apparently absorbed into one satrapy that was placed under the rule of the satrap Gabaru. At the beginning of the reign of

Darius I (522–486 BCE), a far-reaching reorganization of the Persian imperial administration was carried out. According to Herodotus (3.88–95), the empire was subdivided during the reign of Darius into twenty satrapies. Babylon was severed from Abar Nahara and annexed to Assyria to form a single satrapy (no. 9 in the list), while Abar Nahara, which was the fifth satrapy, included Syria, Phoenicia, Palestine, and Cyprus (3.91). This division is not, however, confirmed by the epigraphic sources from the time of Darius I. Three inscriptions of Darius I, which contain the names of the satrapies he established, omit the satrapy of Abar Nahara. Thus, it seems that during his reign, the satrapy of Abar Nahara was still included within the larger unit of Babylon and it is clear that the list of satrapies appearing in Herodotus—despite its attribution to Darius—is later and dates to the reign of Xerxes I (486–465 BCE). Babylon was surely detached from the satrapy of Abar Nahara only after its rebellion against the Persians and its destruction in 482 BCE. Its mention in the Bible in the days of Ezra and Nehemiah does not date prior to this time. At any rate, its boundaries remained more or less as Herodotus described them until the end of the Persian period. In almost all the contemporary sources in which the boundaries of the satrapy are mentioned, only the sites along the coast appear, and we lack a description of the eastern boundary. According to Herodotus (3.91), the northern frontier extended from Poseidium on the border between Cilicia and Syria (probably the modern site of Ras el-Basit) and in the south as far as Egypt. The southernmost border site is also given by Herodotus in two additional passages, and in both cases it is situated at Lake Sirbonis (Sabhat Bardawil): "near which stretches Mt. Casius" (3.5; 2.6).

In the *Periplus* of Scylax (pseudo-Scylax), which dates about a century later, the boundaries of the satrapy are recorded at distances of stadia from Thapsacus in the north "to the city of Ashkelon" in the south. Though K. Galling maintained that Thapsacus was located in the area of the Orontes (since he was of the opinion that Scylax included only coastal cities), it has a close resemblance to 1 Kings 5:4. In both cases, it seems that the reference is apparently to a city on the banks of the Euphrates. It is strange that the southernmost border point terminates at Ashkelon, and not, as in the time of Herodotus, at Lake Sirbonis. Scylax seems to have omitted the entire area under Arabian rule. On the coins of his reign, the satrap Mazdi, one of the last rulers of this satrapy, is given the title "ruler of Abar Nahara and Cilicia." The Cilician coastal plain may also have been annexed to this satrapy at the end of the Persian period.

The internal administrative division of the satrapy is not described in the

Greek sources, though Herodotus mentions four regions on the coast, which were occupied by three different nations. In the north (apparently extending from Poseidium) was Phoenicia, whose southern boundary is not mentioned. From Phoenicia "to the boundaries of the city of Cadytis [Gaza], the country belonged to the Syrians, who are known as Palestinians. From Cadytis to Ienysus [el-'Arish?], the seaports on the coast belong to the king of Arabia and the land from Ienysus to the Sirbonis Lake is Syrian territory" (3.5 and cf. on the Syrians and the Phoenicians: 2.104, 116; and on the Arabs: 3.88, 91, 97). The subdivision of the area between Syria and Phoenicia is also recorded, as was noted, in the *Periplus* of Scylax. He omits all mention of the Arabs, perhaps because he located the satrapy's southern border at Ashkelon. In contrast, he mentions in detail the specific Phoenician ownership (Tyrian and Sidonian; see below) of the various coastal cities of Palestine. He apparently employed the term Syrian to designate the inland population.

The picture presented by the Greek sources is not an accurate representation (except for the coastal area) of the administrative division of Palestine in the Persian period, which must be learned from the contemporary biblical sources and from what is known of the Assyrian administrative system. It is the consensus that the Persians did not alter the internal administrative division of Palestine, which was established under Assyrian and Babylonian rule. From the time of Sargon II (715 BCE) on, the Assyrian administration system in the north of the country consisted of the provinces of Megiddo, Samaria, and Dor and another province in the Gilead. In the Babylonian period, when the southern part of Palestine was also subjugated and the remnants of formerly independent states were eradicated, new provinces were, perhaps, annexed: Judah, Ashdod, and Idumaea (the southern Judaean Hills) in the west and Ammon and Moab in Transjordan (see above). Farther south, the Qedarite Arabs ruled Gaza, the Negev, and apparently also Edom. Since conclusive contemporary evidence is lacking, the organization of these provinces by the Babylonians is a matter of conjecture, though the existence of the northern provinces in Transjordan during the Babylonian period may perhaps also be indicated by the reference to Hauran and Gilead in Ezekiel 47:8. Some of the above-mentioned provinces may have been created only at the beginning of the Persian period. In the time of Ezra and Nehemiah, mention is made of the provinces of Samaria in the north, Ashdod in the west, and Ammon in the east. The southern region was occupied by Geshem the Arabian. The existence of a province in Moab may be indicated by the biblical reference to "the children of the Pahath-Moab" (Ezra 2:6; 8:4; 10:30; Nehemiah 7:1). No reference to Edom is found and it is possible that during this period it was annexed to the Arabian territory. Further contemporary evidence for the existence of the provinces of Samaria and Judah can be found in the Elephantine papyri and in the documents from Wadi ed-Daliyeh. The names of the provinces of Samaria, Judah, and Ammon also appear on coins, seals, and seal impressions that have been uncovered in several excavations, sometimes in addition to the term *phwh* ("province"), meaning an area under the rule of a *phh* (no distinction is made between the larger unit, the satrapy, and the secondary division, the province, just as the titles of the governor and satrap are interchangeable). The smaller unit of the satrapy of Abar Nahara is also called *medintha* ("state"). Proof that these terms are identical is provided by the name of the province of Judah, which also appears in the form *yehud medintha* (Ezra 5:8). This name is also taken from Persian administrative usage and it is merely the Aramaic equivalent of the Persian-Assyrian name (cf. also Esther 1:1, where the whole territory of the Persian Empire is divided into 127 *medinoth* and not, as was customary, into satrapies; and cf. also 3 Esdras 3:2).

The subdivision of a *medinah* ("province") is described in chapter 3 of Nehemiah, which mentions the rulers of the *pelekh* ("district" or "part" [Nehemiah 3:14–15]). The *pelekh* is further divided into a half-district (Nehemiah 3:9, 12, 16–18). According to the roster, Judah was organized into at least five districts (see below for details).

Whereas the administrative division into provinces (*medinoth*) apparently existed in Transjordan and was also employed as the political framework in Samaria, Judah, and Ammon, i.e., in each area occupied by distinct national groups, some scholars have expressed doubts that this framework also applied to the other parts of Palestine. Phoenician organization, for example, was essentially urban, while the Arabs dwelled in a tribal framework. Thus, in the view of M. Avi-Yonah, the Persian administrative structure west of the Jordan was adapted wholly to the heterogeneous nature of the population, and in fact included three types of political units: province (*phwh* or *medinah*), autonomous cities, and tribal areas. In the first category, he included the Galilee (the province of Megiddo), Samaria, Idumaea, and Ashdod. The second category is represented by the coastal cities that the Persians granted to the jurisdiction of Tyre and Sidon (see below, with the exception of Acco and Gaza, which, in Avi-Yonah's opinion, were under direct Persian rule). The Negev and southern Transjordan belonged to the Arab tribes.

Avi-Yonah's theory is impossible to prove on the basis of known sources, and in our view it is doubtful. Though according to pseudo-Scylax' list of cities it can be assumed that all the coastal cities were in the possession of one or another of the Phoenician kings, this document, by its very nature, does not mention any of the larger units, the provinces. We have already seen in the previous chapters that it was very likely, according to the results of recent excavations at Dor, as well as new Assyrian documents, that already in the Assyrian period Dor became a separate province. This province should have continued in existence, like all the others, into the Persian period. In any case, in another contemporary Persian-period source, the Eshmunʿezer Inscription, the area described also bears an amazing resemblance to the territory of the province of Dor. Another possible hint of the existence of a provincial framework in the northern coastal plain as well may be found in Herodotus' account, which, as was noted, distinguishes between the areas held by Phoenicians, Syria-Palestinians, Arabians, and, again, Syrians. This can be translated in accordance with the provinces known to us as Dor (Phoenician), Ashdod (Syro-Palestinian), the Gaza region (Arabian territory), and another unknown province also belonging to the Syro-Palestinians, which was situated in this period to the south of modern el-ʿArish.

The existence of large administrative units in the coastal plain is also attested by the numerous remnants of forts, royal granaries, etc., along the entire coastal Via Maris (Way of the Sea). Many of these were initially erected in the Assyrian age, destroyed by the Babylonians, and then rebuilt by the Persians. We shall mention here the Persian-period forts at Shiqmona, Tell Kudadi, Tell Qasile, Rishon le-Zion, Ashdod, Tell Jemmeh, Tell el-Farʿah (S), Tel Seraʿ, Tel Haror, Ruqeish, Sheikh Zuweid, etc. Pseudo-Scylax also mentions a "king's palace" at Ashkelon, and since in Avi-Yonah's view as well, Ashkelon belonged to the province of Ashdod, this palace may well have been the seat of a governor. It is possible that this line of forts along the coastal plain formed a part of the excellent network of roads and communication constructed by the Persians in all the lands under their rule. Such large-scale projects entailed employment of royal officials who could deal with large areas and not merely with isolated cities. It therefore seems that the "ownership" and rights granted to the various Phoenician kings in the coastal cities by the Persians involved such matters as tax concessions and other economic advantages, though not necessarily political rights. It thus seems more probable that the southern coastal plain was organized only in a network of "autonomous" cities. On the other hand, in the Negev and Sinai, i.e., in sparsely populated areas that were not occupied by sedentary peoples, Persian rule aimed at preserving the goodwill of the Arab tribes who received payments for protecting the remote areas inaccessible to the Persian army. This area, however, by its very nature, was never organized into clear administrative units. Nevertheless, excavations here, too, have uncovered evidence of a network of permanent fortresses that contained Persian garrison troops, as, for example, at Tel Sheva, Arad, Ḥorvat Ritma, Tell el-Kheleifeh, and Kadesh-Barnea. According to an ostracon of the Persian period found at Arad, the fortress at this site was manned by a military unit that was designated as a *degel* ("standard"), a large Persian unit also known from the Elephantine documents.

In summing up, it appears that in Persian-period Palestine the administrative structure retained the basic divisions established during the Assyrian age, but in a more developed form. This period also witnessed the loss of a modicum of autonomy enjoyed by the inhabitants of the south, both east and west of the Jordan, at the end of the Assyrian period. This process may have already begun in the Babylonian age.

Below we shall present a detailed description of the settlements of Palestine in the Persian period based on a summary of the evidence from excavations and surveys as well as epigraphic finds and historical sources.

· Chapter 1 ·

EXCAVATIONS AND SURVEYS

THE PROVINCE OF MEGIDDO

N one of the historical sources known to us from the Persian period
mention any cities in Galilee, the Jordan Valley, or the Jezreel Valley.
As we have seen, according to the Assyrian administrative system, the entire
northern part of Palestine was incorporated into the province of Megiddo. It
is generally agreed that this division continued into the Babylonian and Persian periods and that the provincial capital in the Assyrian and Babylonian
periods was located at Megiddo. With the discovery of a large urban settlement in the excavations at Hazor, M. Avi-Yonah proposed it as the site of the
provincial capital. There is, however, no conclusive proof at present to substantiate this view. On the contrary, a detailed examination of the finds from
Megiddo may provide indications that this city continued to serve as an important urban center down to the end of the Persian period. Hazor in that
period may have been the site of a district *(pelekh)* capital, though no written
sources substantiate this, either. Another opinion holds that in a later phase
of the Persian period Acco replaced Megiddo as the capital of Galilee. This
view is based—like that of Avi-Yonah—on the assumption that Megiddo's
position deteriorated during the Persian period. It is nevertheless clear that
Acco's political status underwent a change in this period and it was very
likely under the suzerainty of Tyre, which had been given control of the
northern coastal plain from Achzib to Carmel.

Except for a few ostraca, epigraphic material has not been uncovered in
the Galilee. We consequently lack information on the character of the local
population from written sources. However, the pottery and other finds dis-

covered throughout this area, from the coast to Dan, Hazor, and Beth Yeraḥ in the east, are identical for the most part with those uncovered at sites along the coastal plain. These differ from the finds from the mountain regions of Samaria and Judah. We may thus conclude that the population of the Galilee in this period was largely composed of Phoenicians, or at least, that this area was strongly influenced by Phoenician culture. Indeed, judging by its finds and especially the contents of an inscription discovered there, the sanctuary recently found at Miẓpe Yammim, located in the center of Galilee, was clearly Phoenician (see below).

In the excavations conducted in the provincial territory of Megiddo, remains of Persian-period settlements were uncovered at a significant number of sites, including Tel Dan, Tel Anafa, Hazor, Ayelet ha-Shaḥar, Tel Chinnereth, and Beth Yeraḥ, all located along the Jordan Valley. Some fortresses were located in the mountainous region of the Galilee at Saʾsaʾ and Gush-Halav, and there is the unique Phoenician sanctuary at Miẓpe Yammim mentioned above. Pottery and other Persian-period finds have also been uncovered at other sites discovered in the many archaeological surveys carried out in this region. For example, the extensive survey carried out by N. Zori in the area of the Beth-Shean Valley found Persian-period pottery at forty-four sites, while the Issachar region survey uncovered Persian-period artifacts at seventy-three sites. Zori concluded on the basis of his surveys that during the Persian period the population density in the area he explored equaled that of the Israelite period before the coming of the Assyrians.

Results of excavations at the major sites of the Megiddo province give us the following picture: At **Hazor,** building remains from the Persian period were discovered both on the mound and to the east of it in separate excavation areas. When the citadel on the acropolis of the mound was first unearthed, the excavators believed it to be an isolated structure. After the discovery of a farmhouse at the other end of the mound, it became evident that a small rural settlement on the slopes of the mound had been attached to the citadel.

The building excavated and identified as a citadel was located on the highest point of the mound. Two construction phases were identified. During the first phase (Stratum III), it was constructed as a fortress (30 x 26 m.), consisting of a large open courtyard surrounded on three sides by a single row of rooms and halls with two rows of rooms on the south side. Part of a wall running parallel to the fortress may have enclosed it on the south side. North of the citadel stood a tower composed of two large rooms. The finds in Stratum III were very meager, and the building itself

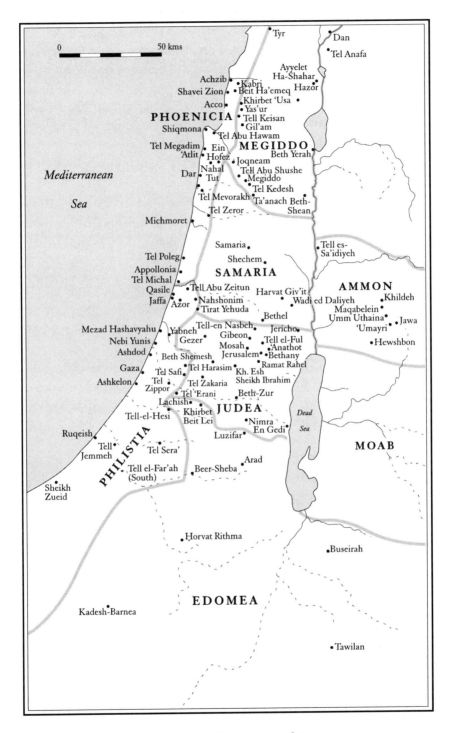

III.6 Excavated Persian-period sites

was found to contain none of its primary objects. This, together with the fact that no traces of fire or serious destruction were found in the building, perhaps supports the hypothesis that the building was destroyed by the forces of nature after it had been abandoned, rather than being violently destroyed by an enemy. The citadel of Stratum II continued the earlier plan almost unchanged, except for minor alterations, which seem to indicate that only a functional change occurred, namely, the large citadel was transformed into two separate dwellings. This may also be reflected in the reduction in the size of the rooms.

The date of Fortress III could not be established, since it yielded no datable remains. The date of Building II is fixed by coins of the 4th century BCE to the reign of Artaxerxes III (359–338 BCE). It was probably destroyed during the campaign of Alexander the Great in 332 BCE.

The excavations in the center of the mound of Hazor by Y. Yadin revealed that this part of the site was uninhabited during the Persian period and was used as a burial ground. The same conclusions concerning this area were reached in the recent work at the site conducted by A. Ben-Tor, during which more tombs were uncovered.

The building on the eastern slope of the site was defined as a farmhouse. In any event, it was not the type of house generally encountered in a densely populated town. The house plan consists of a central courtyard with rows of rooms attached to it on three sides. Y. Yadin noted that "the people of this period carried out some extensive building work on the terrace."

Beth-Shean. No levels of settlement were attributed to the Persian period during the excavations conducted there. However, a study of the published finds confirms the presence of Persian-period figurines, which in turn attest the existence of a temple on the mound during this period. Some Persian-period pottery vessels likewise appear to have been included in the published material. It is possible that the occupation level of this period was overlooked, both by the excavators and by writers.

In the excavations conducted by P. W. Lapp at **Taanach**, the Persian period was represented by "part of a substantial building and quite a number of stone-lined pits scattered throughout the excavation." The vessels published so far include two Attic *lekythoi*, among the finest yet discovered in Palestine, and two assemblages of local pottery.

Megiddo. Remains of the Persian period at this probable capital city of the province are represented by the topmost building level (Stratum I), which was attributed by the excavators to the years 600–300 BCE. These remains were found scattered in three separate excavation areas on the mound:

Area C in the east, the area of the "fortress"; Area D in the north near the gates; and Area A in the south, the "residential quarter."

Remains of a massive structure were uncovered in Area C and identified as a fortress. Two separate building phases were distinguished: the building was first constructed in Stratum II and continued in use with slight modification in Stratum I. From the description, the later phase seems to have consisted of the addition of a number of poor-quality walls, using walls of the earlier phase as their foundations. The plan of the building consists of an open central courtyard enclosed on three sides by a row of roofed rooms. There may also have been a row of rooms on the fourth side, remains of which collapsed down the slope. The walls were about 2 m. thick, constructed of two large, straight stone faces, the gap formed between them filled with unhewn stones. The great width of the walls plus the fact that they extended above the city wall, putting it out of commission, made the excavators conclude that this was the fortress of an unwalled settlement.

In the northern part of the mound, the excavators attributed a building consisting of three very long and narrow rooms (nos. 634, 635, 576) to Stratum I. It was defined as a barracks. The rooms were empty. A long wall (1045) was attached to this structure. Also assigned to this stratum were two large rectangular rooms (nos. 603, 604) that were identical in shape and size and stood facing one another opposite the site of the main city gate of the previous periods. The excavators maintained that these rooms marked the site of the main entrance to the city in Stratum I (although no actual gate was found). The passage between them marked the beginning of a street that led to the higher residential quarter in the southern part of the mound. The floors of these rooms were not found, perhaps, because they lay too close to the surface level and did not survive. Another building attributed to Stratum I and similarly consisting of three long narrow rooms (nos. 1346–1348) was also designated a barracks. All these structures were attributed to Stratum I on the basis of stratigraphy alone, for no finds could be safely connected to them.

The excavations of a residential quarter in the southern part of the mound failed to isolate architectural elements that belonged with certainty to Stratum I. The multiplicity of wall sections in the plan of this stratum makes it appear as though the excavators inserted here all of the walls and rooms that remained unaccounted for in the plans of the earlier strata. In many cases, walls extend above other walls assigned to the same stratum. Two principal buildings appear in the plan: 736 and 1295. Building 736, with a plan strongly reminiscent of the fortress in Area C, consists of an open central courtyard flanked by rooms on three sides. Attached to this building on the west side are sections of another building (1295), apparently constructed following the same plan. Based upon a restored plan of Stratum I in the southern field at Media, one may conclude that Building 736 represents the only complete dwelling unit in the area, which dates to the Persian period. In addition, the remains of seven other buildings from this period have been noted in the area. They seem to have been built according to a plan identical to that of Building 736. All these remains were concentrated along the two sides of the excavated area, the majority on the east and one house on the west. There seems to be no reason to doubt that this entire area was originally a residential quarter of Hippodamian type consisting of *insulae* with "open-court" plan.

To sum up, Megiddo Stratum I appears to have included the following remains: during the earlier part of the Persian period, a wall and a gate; in the later part of the period, two stages of a fortress of "open-court" plan. A residential quarter in the south is indicative of a large and extensive city during this period. Stratum I at Megiddo apparently lasted from the end of the 6th century BCE or the beginning of the 5th to the year 332 BCE. It thus represents an occupation that continued throughout the entire Persian period and consisted of several phases.

Based upon the above, the main outline of the site's history may be sketched as follows: In Stratum III (the Assyrian stratum), the city's offset-inset wall was repaired and a two-chambered gate was constructed (see above). This fortification, together with the residential quarter, was again reconstructed with many repairs in the Persian period. During the *early* Persian period, several fundamental changes were made in the gate area as a result of new requirements (for example, long narrow barracks to house the local garrison replaced the Stratum III Assyrian-style public buildings located there). The city wall and gate and the settlement at Megiddo were destroyed around 350 BCE by the Persian army, probably during the great revolt of the Phoenicians. The fortress in Area C was built *above* the offset-inset wall and replaced it. At the time, it was the only fortification at the site. This fortification was built after the Phoenician rebellion and continued to exist until the city's final destruction by the Greek army and its abandonment.

West of Megiddo three other excavated sites produced important Persian-period remains and attest to the rapid growth and substantial recovery of the settlements in this region during the Persian period. These sites are **Tel Abu Shusha** (Mishmar ha-ʿEmek), **Tel Qiri**, and **Jokneam**. All three are located along the highway leading from Megiddo to Jokneam. In Jokneam,

III.7 Jokneam, a Persian-period storeroom

a Persian-period settlement has been found, which was presumably unfortified. Its buildings, mostly storehouses, were built on a steep slope. In one of these, an astracon bearing Hebrew and Phoenician names was recovered.

PHOENICIA AND THE COAST OF GALILEE

THE CLASSIC REGION of Phoenician settlement in Persian-period Palestine consists of two areas of the Mediterranean coast: the northern area includes the coast of Galilee and the Acco plain from Achzib to Shiqmona, which was under the domination of Tyre; the southern area consists of the Carmel coast and the Sharon Plain, "from Dor to Jaffa," which, according to the Eshmun'ezer Inscription, was ruled by Sidon.

In both regions, settlements were densely built. Excavations in the northern region have revealed Persian-period remains at Achzib, Kabri, Nahariya, Acco, Khirbet Uṣa, Tell Bireh, Tell Keisan, Gil'am, Tell Abu Hawam, and Shiqmona. Surveys conducted in the Acco plain revealed Persian-period remains in many smaller sites. These generally conform with literary evidence referring to the three important coastal settlements—Achzib, Acco, and

Shiqmona—which in this period were apparently detached from Galilee and under the authority of the Tyrian kings. From this area, pseudo-Scylax listed (from north to south after Tyre), "the city of Ecdippa [Achzib] and its river" (K. Galling identified the river as the Keren), followed by the "city of Acco." In the list, both of these sites lack the usual designation of Tyrian or Sidonian possession, and M. Avi-Yonah consequently deduced that they were independent cities, but that Achzib was very likely dependent on Acco, which, in his opinion, had a special status as a port and a Persian military base. However, since Acco's fate was bound up with that of Tyre to such a great extent, and given the marked Tyrian influence on the coinage of Acco, it would seem that Acco, too, was under Tyrian jurisdiction. At any rate, there is no doubt that the southern part of this area was dependent upon Tyre.

The next name mentioned in the list of pseudo-Scylax is corrupted. K. Galling suggested that it should be read "beyond the bay the city of Shiqmona" or alternatively "Haifa, the city of the Tyrians." Galling himself preferred the first reading, and this also seems to be confirmed by the results of the excavations at Shiqmona. The following name in the list is "the sacred mountain of Zeus," which both Galling and M. Avi-Yonah complete as "Carmel the sacred mountain of Zeus." It is not clear from the text whether an actual settlement existed at the site (apart from the temple), or whether it was important only for seafarers, for Carmel at this point is a very prominent topographical landmark. In any event, this area was definitely within the Tyrian sphere of influence, as Achzib and Acco may also have been. Thus, there was a continuous Tyrian strip from Tyre to Shiqmona, paralleling the Sidonian one from Dor to Jaffa.

Another reference to the cities of Achzib and Acco in the book of Judith (3:1, "settlers of Achzib and 'Ukina") may also reflect the situation in this period.

The results of the excavations and surveys undertaken in this area not only emphasize and reconfirm the importance of the three major cities mentioned in the historical sources. They also add to our information on the smaller settlements. Thus, there existed a dense network of rural settlements in the hinterland of the large seaports, in the eastern and southern parts of the Acco plain as well as in the narrow coastal strip adjoining Achzib and Shiqmona, such as Kabri in the north and Tell Abu Hawam at the mouth of the Kishon River.

At **Achzib,** a Persian-period settlement stratum was uncovered in the excavations on the mound. Two areas were opened on the mound within the walls: one area in the south and the other in the north. The stratum attrib-

uted to the Persian period appeared only in the south. It continued to exist
throughout the period. Among the finds from this stratum are imported Attic vessels and a number of figurines. The excavator also assigned a layer of
floors and pits found outside the walls to the 6th to 5th centuries BCE.

Around the mound, several important large cemeteries of the period have
been cleared (see chapter 3).

South of Achzib, the remains of two more Phoenician coastal towns have
recently been uncovered. The first is at **Tel Nahariya,** where two strata of the
Persian period have been excavated. Stratum III (early 4th century BCE) was
erected over the dune on a thin layer of silt. It contains sections of walls built
in a technique that combines ashlar piers and rubble. The earliest stage of
this stratum may have begun as early as the end of the 5th century BCE; it
ended at the beginning of the 4th century BCE. Stratum II (mid-4th century
BCE) produced the first signs of a definite town plan, consisting of a central
street running north-south. Flanking the street are public buildings including an administrative structure, storehouses, and workshops. Among the
finds were local pottery typical of the end of the Persian period and imported
Attic ware, metal implements of copper, bronze, and iron, and large quantities of iron slag, mainly in the storehouses. Numismatic finds include Tyrian-
Phoenician coins and three coins of Alexander the Great, which date the
destruction of the Persian city to the time of the Hellenistic conquest. In a
recent (1995) excavation conducted on the western side of the site, two
Persian-period strata were once more uncovered. The upper stratum consists of the remains of a large, central-courtyard house. Finds include local
and imported Attic ware and about ten different 4th century BCE coins.

The second site in this region is **Tel Kabri** (Rehob?), which was fortified
by a wall. Details of the Persian city here have not yet been published, except
for the fact that the Persian-period city was larger than that of the Late Iron
Age.

Other unique Persian-period finds along this coast are the remains of two
boats, one of which was discovered off the coast of **Shavei Zion.** Here, during an underwater survey, some of the cargo of a 5th century BCE shipwreck
was located and exposed; the remains were found scattered over a large area.
The principal finds were hundreds of clay figurines of various sizes, all depicting a female with her right arm raised in a gesture of blessing, her left arm
folded below her chest. Many of the figurines bear the sign of the Phoenician-Punic goddess Tanit on their base; others bear Phoenician-Punic symbols such as dolphins, stelae, and other ritual motifs common in the
iconography of Carthage and the Punic colonies. Among the other finds

were an African elephant tusk, amphorae, bowls, and other small pottery vessels. Laboratory tests, using neutron activation analysis to assess the source of the clay from which the figurines were made, show that the cargo originated along the southern Phoenician coast between Sidon and Achzib and not in Carthage.

The second wreck was found about 1.5 km. from the shore of the Philadelphia Youth Village, north of Acco. Here, remains of cargo mainly included wine amphorae with flat rims, wide angular shoulders, and conical bodies. This type of amphora is known from Phoenician sites throughout the Mediterranean and is most commonly found along the coast of the Phoenician heartland and Cyprus. Laboratory tests of the amphorae indicate that they were also made from clay originating in the area between Tyre and Sidon. The jars contained raisin wine. Solitary examples of Etruscan, Italian, and Aegean amphorae suggest the lands visited during this wrecked ship's final voyage. The typological range of the assemblage allows for a date around 500 BCE or slightly later. The finds from these two boats are an indication of the extensive international maritime trade conducted by the Phoenicians during the Persian period between the Phoenician and Palestinian coasts and the west.

Acco. Even before the start of excavations at the mound, the importance of this site during the Persian period was well documented in historical sources (see above). A great number of important surface finds were made here. The local museum contains a large collection of Attic ware. Another significant find is a fragment of a granite pedestal bearing the cartouche of Pharaoh Achoris of the 28th Dynasty (393–380 BCE). The pedestal was found in the city of Acco in a Turkish building. On the mound of Tell Fukhar itself, many Persian-period coins from Sidon, Tyre, and Arvad, as well as a number from Cilicia, have been discovered, including a hoard of twenty-five Tyrian coins dated by A. Kindler to 364–332 BCE.

The results of the excavations on the mound of Acco clearly illustrate the city's prosperity during the Persian period. At least two Persian-period occupation strata have been found. During this period, Acco's commercial and administrative center moved closer to the coastal and port area. A large public building was constructed, partly of hewn stones, containing a courtyard and a large complex of rooms. This building apparently functioned as a Persian administrative center. Its contents, which included imported pottery, mainly Attic ware, are attributed to the time of Cambyses II (530–522 BCE). A building to its north may have been in use throughout the Persian period. One of its rooms was bisected by a row of four columns; a pit discovered in its floor contained cult objects—zoomorphic and anthropomorphic statuettes and a fragment of a bowl with a Phoenician inscription on both sides. The seven-line inscription refers to an order according to which votive offerings were to be brought to the temple of Asherah. This building was most likely the administrative center of the nearby temple, which was almost entirely destroyed in the Hellenistic period. In addition to the wealth of Phoenician finds in the Persian strata, including a fragment of an incised lapidary script inscription on stone, the buildings and installations contained Greek, mainly Attic, pottery: a complete krater, numerous shards of *skyphoi, lekythoi,* and other vessels that attest to a strong Greek influence on the material culture of Acco in the 5th to 4th centuries BCE. This influence is especially marked in the buildings and installations situated opposite the sea. Near one of the buildings, constructed in the Phoenician style of alternating headers and stretchers and fieldstones, was a kind of stone-built *bothros (favissa).* It had a round, flat stone slab at its base on which a large number of vessels was found. One of them was an Attic red-figured bell krater, almost intact, decorated with a depiction of Hercules. The architectural remains uncovered in the residential areas bear clear signs of city planning. The houses, courtyards, numerous silos and ovens, continued in use into later periods. Also dated to the Persian period were the remains of the first city's port, uncovered in the southern bay of the town.

A few miles to the east of Acco, another Phoenician town of the Persian period located at the center of the Acco plain was excavated at **Tell Keisan.** These excavations were conducted on behalf of the French expedition of the Ecole Biblique. In Stratum 3A+B, not much architecture was found; however, there was a wealth of finds from the Persian period: local pottery, figurines, seals, and coins, which also attest to established ties with the Greek world through maritime trade.

More excavations in the Acco region have been conducted at **Beth ha-'Emek** and **Yas'our,** which yielded Persian-period tombs. Remains of Persian-period settlements have been found at a few other nearby sites, including **Khirbet Uşa, Gil'am,** and **Tell Bireh.** These contribute to the accumulating evidence for the existence of a dense net of Persian-period towns and villages in the plain in general and along the highway crossing it in particular.

The major Persian-period port town in the southern part of the Acco plain is **Tell Abu Hawam,** situated at the mouth of the Kishon River. In excavations carried out at this site by R. W. Hamilton, two building phases of the Persian period were identified. As no building remains of the lower stratum

have been preserved and as the excavator could not distinguish any differences between the pottery of the two strata, he included them in one stratigraphic unit that was designated "Stratum II Persian-Greek period" and
dated from the end of the 6th to the beginning of the 4th centuries BCE. Of
the lower phase (A), only a thick ash layer survived, and part of a building
constructed of a row of long stones. Several pits were also attributed to this
phase. One pit, which contained local pottery of the Persian period, was
blocked by a wall of a Phase B building constructed above it. All the other
structures presented in the plan of Stratum II were assigned to the upper
phase. Most of them were built according to the standard Phoenician
method: the walls of unhewn stone were strengthened at 2-to-3-m. intervals
by ashlar piers constructed of one stretcher and two headers. The buildings
in this phase show some degree of planning according to the Hippodamian
scheme: i.e., straight streets intersecting each other. In the center of the
mound was found a facade of a building almost 30 m. long, which faced the
street. Although this facade was not entirely straight, it ran more or less parallel to the longitudinal axis of the city. A wall, partially cleared on the south
and the east, surrounded the town in this phase.

Later research by E. Stern has shown that Hamilton's dates for his two
stages should be reevaluated as follows: Phase A starts—after a long gap—at
the end of the 6th century BCE and continues to the beginning of the 4th
(500–385 BCE). Phase B ranges from this time to 333/2 BCE, when Tyre and
her vassal towns were occupied by Alexander the Great, as is clearly attested
by a large hoard of coins unearthed here that date to 364–332 BCE.

New evidence was uncovered in the later excavations at the site conducted by a French mission. This presented a more complicated picture of
the Persian-period levels. The city was shown to have been much larger than
had previously been imagined and to have played an important role in
Phoenician maritime trade. The destruction of Phase A, attested by large
numbers of broken jars, might very well have been a result of the Phoenician
revolt and Persian reaction to it. On the basis of architectural remains, G.
Finkielsztejn, however, refined Phase A into IIA1 (ca. 500–450 BCE) and
IIA2 (540–380 BCE) and Phase B into IIB1 (380–350 BCE), IIB2 (350 BCE),
and IIB3 (350–335 BCE). According to Finkielsztejn, Phase IIA marks a reoccupation of the site utilizing previous structures. Another feature of this
phase is refuse pits, indicative of the Persian economic exploitation of the
coastal region. The walls of this phase are built of monolithic pillars distinct
from the ashlar-pillar technique. Phase IIB1 shows a slow reoccupation. In
Phase IIB2, the site was realigned east-west, north-south. This points to a

well-designed rebuilding program in the mid-4th century BCE. The finds of this period suggest renewed commercial activity. In conclusion, Tell Abu Hawam was apparently reestablished in the same period and under the same conditions as the other Phoenician sites in the northern coastal region, but received its regular plan only after the destruction of 380 BCE.

The surveys of the Acco plain concentrated mainly in its southern part, again showing that the region was densely inhabited and settled during the Persian period. Pottery and other remains of this period were found in a dozen or more sites in this relatively small area.

Similarly, the survey recently conducted in the mountainous part of the Galilee by Z. Gal showed that this area was also covered by a dense net of small rural settlements, first established at the end of the 6th or beginning of the 5th centuries BCE. These served as the agricultural hinterland for the large coastal towns. Many of these settlements were established at sites never previously occupied.

THE PROVINCE OF DOR AND THE SHARON PLAIN

THE PROVINCE OF Dor, which extends down the coastal plain from Shiqmona to the vicinity of Jaffa and includes the adjoining Shephelah, contains, besides Shiqmona itself, some thirteen excavated sites with Persian-period settlement strata (Tel Megadim, 'Atlit, Dor, Tel Mevorakh, Mikhmoret, Tel Poleg, Tel Michal, Apollonia, Tell Abu Zeitun, Tell Qasile, Meẓad ha-Yarkon [Tell Kudadi], Jaffa, and Bir es-Saba'). Five or six other sites were discovered by the Israel Survey in western Haifa (the major ones are sites at the mouth of the Galim River: Tell Hurreis and Tell 'Akra) and about twelve more in the 'Atlit area. Farther south, the Sharon Survey uncovered several more settlements (Tel Taninim, Tell Ahdar, Tel Gedor, Tel Asor, and Khirbet Zuriqiyeh). One site was exposed in the Tel Aviv area itself. Thus, a total of thirty-seven large and small settlements has been discovered along this short coastal strip. There was probably little unoccupied space between these coastal settlements, which were within sight of one another. The situation inland is less clear, but that area seems to have been more sparsely populated. These inland sites include el-Mazar, Naḥal Tut, 'En Ḥofez, Tel Zeror, Eliakhin, Tel Ḥefer, Aphek, Tirat Yehudah, Jaljulia, Tel Qaneh, and many more.

Adjoining the mouth of every river lay a settlement that exploited it for anchorage, beginning with the rivers Galim, Megadim, Taninim, Haderah,

Alexander, Poleg, and the Yarkon. The same is true of the few bays, such as the bay of 'Atlit. Its port apparently served a densely populated settlement, and the bays of Dor, Mikhmoret, Apollonia, and Jaffa. Thus, the possibilities of anchorage were fully exploited. The coastal settlements in the Sharon Plain seem to have gained an ascendancy over the inland towns during the Persian period.

Historical sources containing references to this area are quite scarce. Pseudo-Scylax mentions only four settlements here (after Shiqmona): Arados "the Sidonian city," which K. Galling read as Adaros, maintaining that it represented the Hebrew name Adar or Migdal-Adar. In his view, the reference is to 'Atlit, since Eusebius (*Onomasticon* 130.21) mentions the settlement Magdiel at this spot. Pseudo-Scylax then lists "the river of the Tyrians." Galling suggested that the name of the city was missing here and he identified it with the name of the river—"the city and the river of the Tyrians"—and equated it with Crocodilopolis, referred to by Strabo (17.758), and the "Crocodile River" in Pliny (5.19). He identified this city with Tel Malat and the river with the el-Zarqa. But since this identification disrupts the north-south sequence of the sites, he proposed placing the following name, Doros (whose equation with Dor is certain), before Crocodilopolis. The complete verse should then read: Adaros, "city of the Sidonians, Doros, city of the Sidonians, and Crocodilopolis, city and river of the Tyrians." The "city of Jaffa" also appears in Scylax' list, but without being ascribed to a specific Phoenician ownership and with only a parenthetical remark on its mythology: "It is the city where, they say, Andromeda was abandoned to the sea monster."

Dor and Jaffa also appear on the well-known sarcophagus inscription of the Sidonian king Eshmun'ezer, which confirms that Dor, and probably Jaffa as well, belonged to Sidon. Although the latter is referred to in the Bible as "the sea of Joppa" (Ezra 3:7) where Sidonians and Tyrians worked together, a dedicatory inscription on a stone slab found in the city mentions the erection of a temple to Eshmun, the chief god of Sidon. Ostraca found at Tel Dor, Tel Michal, and Apollonia also attest to Eshmun as the chief deity in this region.

The sum total of settlements listed in the historical sources does not, therefore, exceed four. The most prominent are Dor and Jaffa, which recur in all the lists and were probably the principal cities of the province. According to Galling, 'Atlit and Crocodilopolis are also mentioned. In comparison with the almost forty sites known through excavations, the historical sources are a disappointment. Of the two major documents from this period relating to the province of Dor—the Eshmunʿezer Inscription and the *Periplus* of pseudo-Scylax—the first was dated to the end of the 6th to the beginning of the 5th centuries BCE and the second was dated by K. Galling to the mid-4th centuries BCE. The concurrence of both sources in stating that the two major cities of Dor and Jaffa were under Sidonian control enables us to assume that their control over this area persisted throughout the Persian period.

The organization of the Phoenician settlements is of interest. According to the *Periplus,* a Tyrian settlement, of uncertain identity (Crocodilopolis), was situated inside Sidonian territory, and we have already noted that according to Ezra 3:7 Tyrians and Sidonians worked together in the sea of Joppa. Galling has suggested two reasons for this: (1) the Tyrian city was founded later (i.e., it was not in existence in the time of Eshmunʿezer); (2) there was no hostility or competition among the Phoenician cities in relation to their colonies, giving the king of Sidon no reason to oppose the presence of a Tyrian colony in his territory.

A possible explanation is perhaps found in Diodorus' description (26.41) of the city of Tripolis in Phoenicia. According to Diodorus, the city received its name from the fact that it was divided into three sections, located at a distance of one stadium from one another. People of Arvad dwelled in one section, Sidonians and Tyrians in the other two. This city, with its tripartite division, seems to have been a kind of jointly established colony of people from various Phoenician cities on Phoenician land (similar to the Greek settlement in the pan-Greek colonies of Daphne and Naukratis in Egypt). In our view, the same situation is encountered in the administration of the Phoenician towns in the Sharon and in Palestine in general. Thus, administrative authority (mainly in matters of ordinary daily life, tax collection, commerce, etc.) was largely in the hands of the Phoenician king, whose citizens constituted the majority of the population, or who had been granted this right, for some reason, by the king of Persia. Citizens of other Phoenician cities dwelled in the same city, perhaps in separate residential quarters. This would explain the complete absence of cities in the possession of Arvad and Byblos in Palestine. Inhabitants from these cities, few in number, dwelled among the populations of the towns controlled by Tyre and Sidon and did not enjoy the direct economic protection of their own kings.

These coastal cities were clearly not occupied exclusively by Phoenicians. There is also evidence for Greek merchants—for example, at Acco, Dor, and Jaffa (see below).

A still unanswered question is, in whose possession was the Sharon after

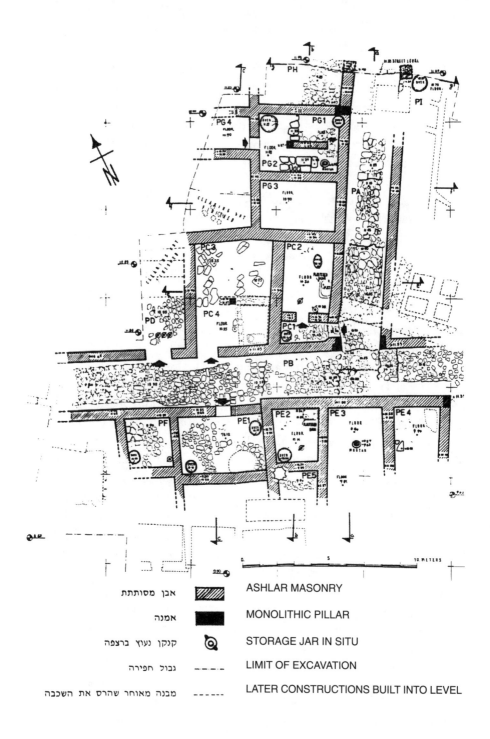

אבן מסותתת   ASHLAR MASONRY

אמנה   MONOLITHIC PILLAR

קנקן נעוץ ברצפה   STORAGE JAR IN SITU

גבול חפירה   LIMIT OF EXCAVATION

מבנה מאוחר שהרס את השכבה   LATER CONSTRUCTIONS BUILT INTO LEVEL

III.8 Shiqmona, general plan of the Persian-period stratum

the Persian destruction of Sidon in 348 BCE? According to D. Barag, most of the coastal cities were completely destroyed in this period and were rebuilt only in the Hellenistic period. However, one of the following two possibilities appears more likely: either the Persians, still interested in the maritime services of the Phoenicians, gave this area to the kings of Tyre, or they restored it to direct Persian control. There are grounds, however, for assuming that Sidonian suzerainty was reinstated in this area a short time after the revolt. According to the consensus, the city of Migdal Sharshon (later Caesarea) was named after the Sidonian king Straton I (the "philhellene"), who was killed in 361 BCE. Since this city is not mentioned by Scylax, it was apparently established only after 350 BCE (the latest possible date for the composition of the *Periplus*). The city does, however, appear as a seaport in the Zenon Papyri (259 BCE). For this reason, Galling assumed that its founder was Straton II (343–332 BCE), who erected the city a short while after the suppression of the revolt at Sidon. If this assumption is true, the area of the Sharon would appear to have been returned to its Sidonian owners shortly after the revolt.

The northernmost settlement of the Persian period along the Carmel coast was **Shiqmona.** In excavations carried out at this site by J. Elgavish, two strata of great interest from the Persian period were uncovered. The lower stratum was dated by the excavator on the basis of Attic pottery from the end of the 6th to the first third of the 5th centuries BCE. A well-planned residential quarter was excavated in this stratum, with two paved streets intersecting at right angles. On either side of the street stood two blocks of houses, courtyards, and rooms of which little was cleared. Although the plan of a complete dwelling unit was not ascertained, it seems that the houses were generally composed of a courtyard (which formed the entrance from the street) and a group of rooms around it or arranged in a row at its rear. Most of the courtyards contained ovens and the rooms yielded rich assemblages of local pottery. Of special interest is the large number of juglets. In one room alone, about eighty juglets were uncovered. In several rooms were found vats plastered with fine cement for collecting liquids. The impression is thus of a well-planned city roughly following along Hippodamian lines. Judging from the position of the remains, the city also extended down the slope of the mound in terraces cut one above the other. In the opinion of the excavator, the city in this period also spread into the plain surrounding the mound, but this hypothesis must await further investigation.

Overlying this stratum were the remains of a large public building attributed by Elgavish to the mid-4th century BCE. Its plan could not be determined, as only the floors had survived. One room was a subterranean store-room that contained scores of vessels of various types, including four storage jars bearing two-line royal Phoenician inscriptions in ink, relating to the delivery of wine from a settlement called Gat Carmel. The excavator concluded that the building was a fortress or large (royal) storehouse. It was apparently destroyed—according to numismatic evidence—at the end of the 4th century BCE in the days of Alexander the Great or shortly thereafter. In both strata, rich pottery finds were uncovered, which exhibit a particularly strong Cypriot influence. The pottery is important for two reasons: first, several of the vessels are unique in Palestine; second, it enables us to distinguish between pottery of the 5th and the 4th centuries BCE in this region divided between the two strata.

South of Shiqmona, at the mouth of the Megadim River, is another Persian period site, **Tel Megadim,** which was excavated twice. In the first excavation, three Persian-period settlement strata (I-III) were uncovered. Stratum I was occupied for only a short time. Its buildings were of poor quality. This uppermost stratum was severely damaged and only a few walls survived. Stratum II—the main level—contained the remains of a well-preserved and well-planned city. It was rectangular in plan with streets running

III.9 Tel Megadim, storehouse with cache of jars and jugs, and part of the western casemate wall

parallel to the wall. Of the city's fortifications, the entire western wall (170 m. in length) and portions of the northern and southern walls were cleared. For most of its length, the wall was of casemate type. Eleven casemate rooms were uncovered in the northern part of the western wall. They were symmetrically arranged with large rooms flanked by smaller ones. A street (90 m. long) parallel to the wall was cleared. Two blocks of buildings were uncovered to the west of it and parts of buildings to the east. These blocks were cut by narrow lanes that intersect them at right angles to the main street. They were divided into smaller units, apparently following a precise plan. One such unit, excavated in its entirety, consisted of an open courtyard flanked by rooms on both sides, similar in plan to the buildings of the Persian period in the lower stratum at Shiqmona. The excavator also attributed the city wall described above to this stratum. In one completely excavated building, a large number of jars stood along two of its walls. The majority was jars with basket handles but there were also jars of other types, as well as bowls, jugs, stands, juglets, etc. The finds included Attic ware, East Greek imported ware, figurines, arrowheads, etc. Stratum III contained remains of well-constructed buildings; however, the plan of that settlement has not been established.

In the later excavation conducted by S. Wolf at the eastern side of the site, more of the Persian-period city came to light, including large numbers of local and imported pottery vessels and a rich assemblage of figurines, masks, etc. In the opinion of the excavator, Stratum I dates to the second quarter of the 4th century BCE; Stratum II dates from the end of the 5th to the beginning of the 4th centuries BCE; and Stratum III dates to the 5th century BCE. The impression conveyed by the Stratum II city remains at Tel Megadim is of a well-planned commercial harbor town that was entirely erected at one time. The large number of jars found in every room seems to indicate that the area excavated consisted of storehouses in the harbor.

A few kilometers south of Tel Megadim another important harbor city of the period was discovered at 'Atlit, a rocky projection into the sea. The settlement itself has not yet been uncovered. It is now partly covered by a large Crusader castle built over it and by large salt pools. The major remains belong to the harbor itself, revealed by undersea research, and to a huge cemetery.

The Phoenician harbor in the northern bay is, according to its excavator, A. Raban, the only one along the coast of Israel with sufficient remains to permit an investigation of pre-Hellenistic Phoenician building methods and harbor engineering. This harbor was connected to the southern settlement, located between the water and the cemetery (see below). The general plan of the harbor shows that it is composed of two similar, but separate, wings. Each wing has a quay with a mole perpendicular to one side. The moles acted as breakwaters but are constructed so that cargo ships could anchor along both their sides and could use their surface to load and unload goods. The moles are similar in construction to those in the southern (Egyptian) harbor of Tyre, the southern breakwater of the Acco harbor, and the ancient mole discovered at Tabat el-Hamam (Ṣumur?) on the Phoenician coast. The ʿAtlit harbor is dated to the late 6th century BCE. The separation of the harbor into two wings enabled a distinction to be made between the "home quays" for Sidonian or other Phoenician ships, and the "free quay" or emporium for foreign vessels, which transshipped using lighters, as at the harbors of Sidon and Acco.

The undersea project here (like the projects at Shavei Zion and Philadelphia, the two settlements on the northern coast [see above]) revealed remains attesting to the intensity of maritime trade along the Mediterranean coast during the Persian period. Ship remains and cargoes were found on the inner side of the northern mole. These were composed of concentrations of broken amphorae and groups of basalt stones that had been used as ships' ballast. Among the concentrations it was possible to distinguish two principal groups containing typical Phoenician biconical amphorae. The amphorae originated in the area of Tyre and Sidon and date to the end of the 5th century BCE. A third concentration was a cargo of large, basket-handled amphorae of the mid-5th century BCE, whose apparent origin was the Syrian coast or Cyprus. Another cargo contained 5th century BCE wine amphorae from the East Greek islands of Samos, Chios, and Cnidus. The fact that these concentrations date to the same period and are the latest finds suggests that the harbor was abandoned at the time that these cargoes were lost. Many three-holed stone anchors were found at the foot of or in the vicinity of the moles. In one case, the wooden stakes (cypress) of an anchor were found in the lower holes. This type of anchor was very common at the Phoenician ports of Tyre, Arados, and Kition in Cyprus.

The other impressive Persian-period remains at ʿAtlit belong to the cemetery, which was first excavated by C. N. Johns in the 1930s. The grave types and date of the cemetery will be discussed below. The survey of the site revealed extensive Persian-period cemetery remains covered by the Crusader fort, near the present salt pools, on the shore and on the hills to the east. It is thus very likely that this was the central cemetery serving a dense network of small settlements that dotted the entire area.

To the south of ʿAtlit we come upon **Tel Dor,** excavated by the present

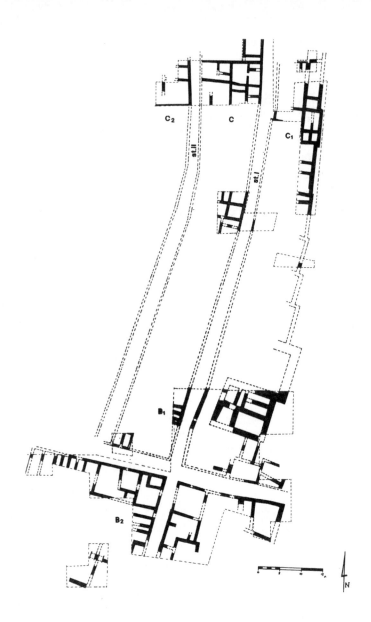

III.10 Tel Dor, plan of the eastern residential quarter of the city in the Persian period

writer, and also located on a small rocky peninsula. This site is undoubtedly the most important port city of the Persian period along the Carmel coast and the Sharon Plain. It was the regional and provincial capital. It is a key site for the study of the various elements of the material culture of all the coastal cities, following their transformation from an oriental to a western-Greek model.

Persian-period remains were discovered in two main strata. During this period, the entire eastern part of the mound was a residential district, laid out meticulously according to a Hippodamian plan. The closest parallels to the town plan of Persian-period Dor are found at Berytus in Phoenicia, Olynthus in Macedonia, and Monte Sirai in Sardinia. This type of orthogonal plan probably originated in the late 6th century BCE and continued nearly unchanged until the early Roman period. In it, residential quarters are divided into long narrow blocks *(insulae),* approximately 15 m. wide, separated by streets intersecting at right angles. The city's two eastern blocks and its two easternmost streets, running from north to south, parallel to the city wall, were excavated in Area C.

The continuation of these *insulae* and of the easternmost street was exposed in Areas A and B, and the residential buildings probably extended to the vicinity of the city gate. In Area B, the lengthwise street is intersected by a street running east to west, from the city-gate piazza to the city's public buildings and down to the harbor. Additional transverse streets probably existed beyond the excavated area. Some of the walls are preserved to a considerable height, mainly in the western part of Area C, where they still stand about 3 m. high. Internal walls divided the *insulae* into residential units consisting mainly of long narrow rooms. Both the internal and the external walls of the buildings are constructed in what is termed the Phoenician style: alternating ashlar pillars and a fieldstone fill. Some walls are built entirely of ashlars. The local *kurkar* (sandstone) was quarried for building. The standard of workmanship in the construction of the *insulae* was higher in the Persian period than during the Hellenistic period. This is especially noticeable in the facades of the buildings facing the streets.

Buildings uncovered in Area D, on the southern slope of the mound, had partitions that divided them into long narrow rooms. The long walls of one of these buildings were built in the characteristic Phoenician manner, while the short walls were built of fieldstones. Numerous storage jars were recovered in these rooms, some of which may have served as storehouses for the commercial activities carried out in Dor's southern harbor. Recent excavations have revealed that in this area, too, the Persian-period buildings followed an orthogonal plan. Evidence uncovered in Area D—hearths full of ash, bronze and iron slag, and perhaps glass waste—is indicative of an extensive industrial quarter. Some dog burials were also found in this area. A more monumental structure, containing what may have been a tower with a staircase, was excavated in the western part of Area D. The distinctive technique used to construct its walls consisted of separating sections of fieldstone

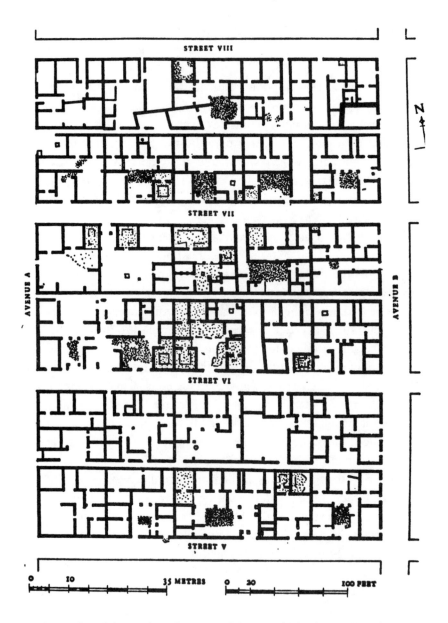

III.11 Plan of the residential quarter of the city of Olynthus in Macedonia

masonry at regular intervals with roughly dressed monolithic pillars. This building technique is closely related to the method called *a telaio,* commonly found in Phoenician colonies in the west. This is the only example of this technique known on the eastern shore of the Mediterranean. The plan of the building (not yet fully excavated) consists of three long halls and a fourth along their narrow side (a typical "four-room" plan).

To the south of this structure (which had two clear Persian-period phases), an installation related to the purple dye manufacturing process was excavated. It consists of two pits: one is stone-lined and was full of crushed shells of the murex snail, which produces the dye; a lime-plastered channel led to the second pit (not plastered), which contained a large quantity of purple dye residue mixed with ash.

Persian-period remains were also found in the areas on the west side of the mound (E and F) as well as in the mound's center (G). They included several pits with additional evidence of purple dye manufacturing. The pits contained many clay storage jars, both Greek and Phoenician, as well as heaps of

III.12 Tel Dor, aerial view of the Persian-period strata on the eastern side of the mound

II.13 Tel Dor, view of the Persian-period public building on the mound's acropolis (Area D)

crushed murex shells. In Area G, monumental walls reflect a number of ashlar construction methods. In the Persian-period strata, large quantities of both local and imported pottery were found, especially Attic ware, including many fragments of painted vessels, and East Greek and Corinthian pottery. Hundreds of vessels have been recorded, perhaps the largest assemblage of Greek pottery found to date at any site in Israel; some are rare types. Of special interest are large wine amphorae not previously found in Israel's coastal region. In addition to pottery vessels, there were scores of figurines and statuettes and a relatively large number of seals, some recovered *in situ*. Particularly important is a conical glass seal carved with the figure of a Phoenician sphinx. The majority of the seals is scarab-shaped. Two glass scaraboids are outstanding: on one, the king of Persia is depicted in his chariot; on the other, he fights two griffins or lions. Undoubtedly, these seals, whose motifs often appear on Sidonian and Tyrian coins, belonged to local officials. In addition, many coins of all the known types—Greek, Phoenician, and local—have been recovered.

Several ostraca found in the recent excavations were written in Phoenician, in ink (one was incised). They have been deciphered by J. Naveh. Other ostraca bear incised inscriptions in Greek (one is in the Cypro-Archaic script) and are the first Greek inscriptions to have been found in Israel in Persian-period strata. Many Persian-period cult objects have also been recovered. These mainly include clay figurines, stone statuettes, and faience amulets that reflect the Phoenician cult, both official and popular, and the various foreign influences it absorbed. Two bronze censers, also used in cult and ritual, have been found. Some of the seals may have had a cultic function as well. Most of the figurines were discovered in two large groups in *favissae,* one in Area B and the other in Area C, on the eastern side of the mound. These pits were probably situated close to temples of which no trace survives. Objects of a similar nature were scattered throughout the other excavated areas.

Four kinds of cult objects were found in the Area B *favissa:* (1) clay figurines in the eastern style, (2) clay figurines in the western, mainly Greek, style, (3) limestone statuettes from Cyprus, and (4) a necklace of faience beads. The first three categories represent the official cult of Ba'al and 'Astarte. It was customary at the time that the iconography of the deities was either Phoenician or assumed the form of deities already worshiped in the region—Egyptian, Persian, and even western. The faience beads, also found in other areas, were similarly connected with popular beliefs and were used mainly as amulets to protect their wearers. The necklace consisted of three pairs of Horus eyes and the head of Bes, a god who was originally Egyptian but whose main function in the Phoenician popular cult was to stave off evil spirits and bad luck. Such necklaces were worn by young girls. Sometimes the necklaces included grotesque heads of colored glass or faience. The many clay masks found here, some of which were painted, as well as the "Bes vase," also belonged to the sphere of the Phoenician popular cult.

The nature of the objects found in the *favissa* excavated in Area C at Dor differs considerably from that of the objects in the one previously described. In fact, the assemblage in this *favissa* differs from that of all other *favissae* known in Israel. All the figurines recovered were fashioned in unmistakable Archaic Greek style and thus far constitute the only examples of this style found in Israel. Most of the shards found are also Greek, either Attic or East Greek. These are probably the remains of a Greek temple that can be dated precisely to the second half of the 4th century BCE. It may well be that this was the temple used by the Greek inhabitants of this Phoenician city. They may even have had their own residential quarter. This evidence corresponds to the many discoveries, both past and recent, at sites along the eastern Mediterranean.

The fortifications of Persian-period Dor were in the first phase, the same wall and gate described above, already erected in the Assyrian period. These consisted of an offset-inset wall and a two-chambered gate. This complex was probably destroyed in the mid-4th century BCE. Pottery from that period covered the gate pavement and the road that led into the city. It is likely that these were the vessels used at the end of thestratum's existence. The destruction of this system may have occurred at the time of the Sidonian revolt against the Persians in 348 BCE. This revolt ended in the destruction of many Phoenician cities along the coast of Phoenicia and northern Palestine, probably including Dor, which at that time was ruled by Sidon.

According to the archaeological evidence, which is supported by historical records, Sidon and its territories in Palestine recovered in a short time, probably with Persian assistance. The Dor excavations have shown that during this period a new fortification system was erected. This is of interest because of the building methods employed, which faithfully follow Phoenician techniques. A long stretch of this fortification has been uncovered in all excavated areas on the eastern side of the city, where parts of the gateway were also found. The outer line of this wall rested almost directly on the earlier offset-inset wall, but it ran in a nearly straight line with the exception of some small projections. Thus, at times, it climbed over an offset and at others it descended from it to the plaster glacis that ran up to the offset-inset wall and stopped a short distance from the inset. At first sight, the wall looks like a casemate wall, and it may indeed have functioned as such. However, it is more likely that the "casemates" were in fact the eastern ends of rooms in structures abutting the inner north-south street that runs parallel to the outer line of the fortifications, 6 to 7 m. from it. These rooms form part of a row of typical contiguous structures extending from the inner street to the outer line of the wall. Their western end has not been exposed, but it is clear that their outer walls, more than 1 m. wide, formed part of the city's fortification system.

In the 4th century BCE, these city fortifications were still in existence. They were replaced by entirely different Greek fortifications only at the beginning of the 3rd century BCE, under Ptolemy II.

Close to and east of Dor, along the road leading to Jokneam, at a site called **Naḥal Tut**, a large fort, ca. 55 x 55m., was uncovered. This fort was built on the plan of a courtyard building, with casemate wall surrounding all four sides of a large open courtyard. The inner and outer casemate walls are about 5 m. apart, and cross walls, built at varying distances, created rooms of different sizes between them. On the northwestern corner, a finely built tower was excavated in its entirety. Two additional similar towers were traced in other corners. The ceramic repertoire includes, in addition to the large quantities of storage jars, various types of local Persian-period pottery. Many well-preserved iron agricultural implements were found in the destruction layer on the floors. This assemblage includes a plowshare, pickaxes, scythes, sickles, shearing scissors, and a fishing hook. A few iron weapons include a spearhead, an arrowhead, and a possible catapult head. The pottery group dates from the beginning of the third quarter of the 4th century BCE. A single coin minted by Alexander the Great in the early period of his reign points to a final destruction in 332 BCE. The excavator believes that this fort belonged to the central Persian authorities and that it had strategic, administrative, and perhaps also agricultural functions.

A few kilometers east of the Naḥal Tut fort, another Persian-period site has been recently excavated at ʿEn Ḥofez. Here, another massive structure has been uncovered. The complex is characterized by a single orientation and a unity of plan and building techniques. An outer enclosure wall 1.2 m. wide incorporated several large rooms roofed with the support of two pillars, smaller rooms, open courtyards, and small storage rooms. In the course of its existence, possibly about 150 to 180 years, the building underwent some changes, but there was no change in its basic functional concept. A rich assemblage of local and imported Greek pottery has been uncovered here, along with well-preserved metal objects. A complete range of iron agricultural tools was found: plowshare, adzes, and sickles. Bronze objects include a mirror, a ladle, bowls, pins, needles, the nozzles of six bronze lamps, and a bronze weight in the form of an eagle. The final phase of occupation produced two coins of Alexander the Great. Like the fort at Naḥal Tut, this site was also a stronghold and administrative center of the Persian authorities on the highway, as well as an agricultural settlement. It, too, was destroyed by the armies of Alexander the Great.

Off the coast of **Maʿagan Mikhaʾel,** a site located a few kilometers south of Dor, the remains of a Persian-period cargo ship were uncovered by E. Linder and his colleagues. This is the best-preserved boat of this period to have been found along the eastern Mediterranean coast. It provides more than a mere glimpse at maritime trade and important information concerning the art of shipbuilding during this period. The preserved part of the hull is 13 m. long and about 4 m. wide. The vessel's estimated displacement was 25 tons and the ballast stones it carried weigh over 12 tons. A rich assortment of artifacts was retrieved from the hull and its immediate vicinity: a total of seventy ceramic items included a dozen basket-handle storage jars and everyday utensils used by the crew, such as cooking pots, mortaria, oil lamps, and jugs.

Personal articles included juglets, black-glazed miniature cups, and carved wooden boxes, one of which was heart- or leaf-shaped, the other violin-shaped. The boxes may have been used for cosmetics or jewelry. The shipwright's tool kit included a carpenter's square, handles or mallets, bow drills, spare tenons and treenails, and a whetstone. Among the organic materials found in a fairly good state of preservation were a woven basket and a large quantity of rope of different diameters ranging from 2 to 40 mm. thick. There were also food remains: grapes, olives, and barley. A large quantity of dunnage was uncovered, which had protected the hull timbers from possible

IIII.14 Tel Mevorakh, general view of the Persian-period stratum

damage from the heavy ballast. Metal objects include a copper incense scoop, copper nails, and iron nails used to fasten the ship's frames to the hull structure. This latter feature is uncommon in ship construction of such early date, when copper was generally used. One single rectangular ingot of 95 percent pure tin raised questions about its possible use on board. The exceptionally heavy load of ballast, composed of seven lithic types with schist stones predominating, was the subject of a twofold investigation: of the origin of the stones, a clue to the ship's home port and sailing route; and of their function, as they left limited space on board for normal cargo. The results of these investigations, as well as the character of the pottery, which seems to originate in its majority in the East Greek islands (except for a few Cypriot and Phoenician wares), lead the present writer to the conclusion that the ship, its ballast, and most of its contents came from one of these islands.

South of Maʿagan Mikhaʾel, the next excavated Persian-period site was **Tel Mevorakh.** This mound was also excavated by the present writer in 1973–1976. Three Persian-period strata were uncovered. The earliest (Stratum VI) dates from approximately the middle of the 5th century BCE and consisted mainly of a large rubbish pit that covered a considerable part of the excavated area. It was filled with ash, pottery, and other objects. Stratum V, from the end of the 5th or beginning of the 4th century BCE, was represented by a single large building that occupied most of the area of the mound, but was preserved mainly on the west side, where a row of long and narrow rooms was cleared. Part of a spacious central courtyard containing numerous storage pits was also preserved. The building was apparently constructed following the open-courtyard plan, with rows of rooms surrounding the courtyard. In Stratum IV (4th century BCE), a large new building was erected over the entire area of the site. It consisted of a series of rooms and open courtyards set close together, with a tower on one side. Outside the building was a casemate wall. Its inner wall was built of ashlar piers alternating with a fill of fieldstones; its outer wall consisted entirely of ashlars laid in alternating header-stretcher fashion. The two buildings of Strata V and IV can be interpreted as agricultural estates. In all three strata, a large quantity of local ware of diverse types, Attic pottery, a considerable amount of East Greek pottery, as well as a group of terra-cotta figurines, a *rhyton* in Achaemenian style, and a Bes vase, was uncovered.

A short distance south of Tel Mevorakh, another Phoenician port town of the Persian period was uncovered at the mouth of the Alexander River, on the coast of the natural bay of **Mikhmoret.** The mound was subjected to a few excavations. The first excavation uncovered some wall segments displaying Phoenician construction technique. In the same area, the first excavator, B. Isserlin, discovered storage yards that were destroyed at the end of the Persian period. There was also evidence of a burnt, ashy deposit on the floor of a public building. The excavator interpreted the destruction as indicating that the Persian-period settlement was overrun in about 345 BCE, in the aftermath of the revolt against Persian rule by the Sidonian king Tennes. The shards associated with Isserlin's excavations included Phoenician and Greek vessel fragments. Indeed, quantities of imported Attic ware of Persian-period date were found all over the site, indicating that the harbor was used extensively for trade during this time.

In the new excavations conducted at the site in the 1980s, a large public building was unearthed, this time on the southwestern side of the bay. Its walls and foundations, preserved in some sections to the height of over 2 m., were built of a mixture of fieldstones and large dressed *kurkar* blocks. The foundations were set on bedrock. A floor dated to the 5th or early 4th century BCE on the basis of finds, including a few fragments of Attic ware, was discovered below an ash deposit. This building, with an excavated area of over 150 sq. m., was apparently a fort overlooking the harbor. Along with the many Attic shards that pepper the site, the head of an 'Astarte figurine was found. Numerous murex shells were also discovered, as well as a fragment of a Babylonian cuneiform tablet. The text records the sale of a slave girl for fifteen silver *sheqels*. All the names preserved are Babylonian and the tablet is dated to the tenth of the month Ab, year 5 of the Persian monarch Cambyses (530–522 BCE), the year of his campaign to Egypt. Since the tablet was baked, it probably originated in Babylon. It seems to have been connected either with the activities of Babylonian traders passing through the province of Dor or with the campaign of Cambyses to Egypt.

Another major Phoenician port town was uncovered a few kilometers to the south of Mikhmoret at **Tel Michal** (Makmish). About 400 m. north of the mound, N. Avigad found the remains of a Persian-period sanctuary containing two phases and a cemetery of the same age farther to the north (see below). During later excavations, directed by Z. Herzog at the mound itself, it became clear that at the end of the 6th century BCE Tel Michal served as a way station and trading post and continued to develop for the next two hundred years. Six settlement phases from this period of prosperity were uncovered. Remains of a fort dating to the earliest phase (Stratum XI) were found at the northern edge of the high mound. The rest of the mound was covered with silos and ash pits, with cooking ovens next to the silos. These remains indicate that the site was used as a garrison headquarters. South of the fort was the camp of the soldiers, who were probably responsible for guarding the food stored in the silos. This stratum is characterized by pottery decorated with geometric and floral motifs in the East Greek style. The finds from Stratum XI date to the late 6th and early 5th centuries BCE. The military and administrative headquarters continued to exist at the northern edge of the high mound in the subsequent phases of the Persian period. Each phase saw new buildings erected, differing from their predecessors. Houses built in the southern part of the mound from the second phase (Stratum X) onward indicate the beginnings of a permanent settlement. The houses all face in the same direction but no traces of intersecting streets were found. The foundations of the house walls were built of rocks from the beach and *kurkar* stones, while the superstructure was of sun-dried clay bricks. Stratum X is assigned to the first half of the 5th century BCE. The stratum attributed to the third phase of the Persian period (Stratum IX) contained an extremely large quantity of black-figured Attic ware. The fourth phase (Stratum VIII) yielded a room at the south edge of the high mound, which, judging from the twenty storage jars found in it, was probably used as a wine cellar. Several of the jars were made of yellowish clay and appear to have been produced locally, having been fired in the kilns discovered on the north hill. Both phases (Strata IX–VIII) have been dated to the second half of the 5th century BCE. The fifth phase (Stratum VII) is characterized by the higher standard of buildings to the south of the northern fortress. A large structure with thick mud-brick walls was erected in the center of the mound. This building contained a round room, the walls of which were sunk approximately 3 m. into the ground. The upper part of the walls sloped inward, and the room seems to have been a silo with a domed ceiling. In light of the finds here, especially coins of 'ebed-'astarte, namely Straton I king of Sidon, Stratum VII has been dated to the first half of the 4th century BCE.

The final phase of the Persian period (Stratum VI) is characterized by a functional division of the high mound: the northern edge was occupied by a fort (first erected in Stratum XI); the center was used for dwellings; and the south area was left empty—apart from several silos. The settlement was not destroyed when Alexander the Great conquered the country but continued to exist until the end of the 4th century BCE. Toward the end of the 5th and especially in the 4th centuries BCE, the settlement reached its zenith. In addition to the temple uncovered by N. Avigad on the northeastern hillock, another temple, including a structure with benches and *favissa* nearby, is situated on the eastern hillock. The *favissa* yielded unused lamps and a bronze signet ring. The northern hill showed the first signs of dense occupation in this period. The houses and workshops built on the northern hill were bordered on the east by a common wall, indicating the careful planning of the settlement, which covered about 1.5 to 2.5 hectares. To the south and west of the structures was an industrial quarter that included the remains of several kilns. One of the kilns, which had collapsed, was undoubtedly used for firing pottery, as five storage jars were found in the debris. Two wine-presses dating to the Persian period were found near the settlement remains. A Persian-period cemetery was also found on the northern slope. A section covering less than a tenth of the cemetery's estimated area revealed 120 graves of men, women, and children (see below).

Farther to the south, extensive remains of the Persian period have been uncovered at many other sites, such as Apollonia and Meẓad ha-Yarkon (Tell Kudadi), which were also harbor settlements. Others were discovered along the brook of the Yarkon River at Tell Qasile and Tell Abu Zeitun.

The most important site in the southern part of the region was undoubt-edly the city of **Jaffa,** where Persian-period remains were uncovered throughout almost the entire excavated area (Levels III–I). These remains were attributed by the excavator, J. Kaplan, to the period during which the Sidonians held Jaffa. Several building stages of this period were discovered, notably sections of walls of a large storage building (Building M) for im-ported goods. This building extended from east to west across the entire ex-cavated area. Fragments of its mud-brick floor were found in its western part. The entrance was paved with large stones. The walls were built of reg-ularly spaced ashlar piers with a stone fill between them in which several coins dated to Stratum I were found. Great heaps of blacksmith's waste were discovered in various locations, apparently above the Persian levels; this waste was also found in the subsequent excavations along with part of a forge. The earliest Persian level (III) was dated by the excavator to the end of the 6th to the beginning of the 5th centuries BCE; Phase II was dated to the period between 385 and 372 BCE; and Phase I to 371–332 BCE.

In one room of the large storehouse (Building M), an extensive assem-blage of Greek *lekanides* (bowls) was uncovered. All were of the same fabric and ornamentation and presumably were imports from the same Athenian workshop. Another Athenian pottery vessel assemblage was found at **Bir es-Saba'** just south of Jaffa's port.

The two surveys carried out along this coastal area in the 1960s also re-vealed that it was densely populated during the Persian period. We have no statistical data on the ratio between the settlements of this period and those of other periods, but it is difficult to imagine this area being more densely populated. The Sharon Survey indicated a major flowering of settlement during this period. Later surveys conducted in this region during the 1980s and 1990s added to the number of known settlements and support the general picture obtained from prior surveys.

PHILISTIA

Ashdod and Ashkelon

THE SOUTHERN COASTAL region from south of Jaffa to el-ʿArish was inhabited by the Philistines before the Babylonian conquest. During the Persian period, it remained divided among four of the cities of the Philistine Pentapolis: Ashdod, Ashkelon, Gat (probably Tell eṣ-Ṣafi), which replaced Ekron, never resettled after being destroyed by the Babylonians in 604 BCE, and Gaza, which became the most important city of the region during this period. The region appears to have been predominantly inhabited by Phoenicians, who replaced the Philistines. Nevertheless, it remained known as Philistia.

Intensive excavations and surveys conducted throughout Philistia have contributed considerably to our knowledge of both its history and its material culture during the Persian period. The results of this work shall be presented from north to south:

At **Ashdod**, a Persian-period occupation level (Stratum V) was uncovered in two separate areas. This stratum was almost totally destroyed by Hellenistic buildings, but in one area, remains of a large structure, possibly a public building, were discovered. It was built in brick on stone foundations. Despite the meager architectural remains, the excavator, M. Dothan, succeeded in distinguishing three superimposed Persian-period phases dating from the end of the 6th to the 4th centuries BCE. The two areas yielded many finds associated with this period, including an ostracon that mentions a shipment of wine.

Just north of Ashdod, on a sandstone ridge some 400 m. from the coast, a square (29 x 29 m.) fortress of the Persian period was unearthed. In its center was a large open courtyard surrounded by rooms on all sides. The length of the rooms varies, but they are all of uniform width. The walls were constructed of bricks on stone foundations. No other remains were discovered either above or below the fortress. This structure appears to have guarded the section of the coast between Yavneh-Yam and Naḥal Lachish.

Also within the territory of the city of Ashdod, at **Nebi Yunis** remains of a *favissa* were found, probably belonging to a temple dedicated to the Phoenician god Ba'al, as indicated by an ostracon found there. Other nearby sites of the Persian period include those found along the Sorek River: Yavneh-Yam, Tel Ya'oz (Ghazza), and others. A few more, including Yavneh itself, were found in the area of the inner Shephelah that was attached to Ashdod.

Farther south along the coast are the remains of the fort at **Rishon le-Zion,** which was originally erected by the Assyrians (see above). The remains of the collapsed mud-brick building were leveled and another kind of fortress was built on this platform, which probably included watchtowers. The architecture of this phase suffered significant destruction. Little can be said about the end of the Persian-period occupation here. A destruction layer found close to the surface in all excavated areas contained Persian pottery, including Greek imports.

Of the two eastern ex-Philistine cities, **Ekron** and **Gat,** the first, a prosperous town under Assyrian and Egyptian domination (see above), was apparently never resettled after its destruction by the Babylonians in 603 BCE. But at Gat (Tell eṣ-Ṣafi), excavated in 1888, many objects of the Persian period were found. They are included in the excavation report under a broad "Jewish stratum." The finds came mainly from a large rubbish dump on the east side of the mound. It contained four types of objects from the Persian period: local vessels; imported Greek (mainly Attic) vessels; some seals; and a large group of stone statuettes in Cypriot style and clay figurines and masks in various styles, which probably represent the remains of a temple *favissa.* No building remains of the period had been found yet on the mound.

Close to Tell eṣ-Ṣafi, and within the territory of Gat, are two more sites. One is **Tel Zippor,** where a large cache of clay figurines and stone statuettes was found in a *favissa.* The other is **Tel 'Erani,** where a hoard of stone statuettes and clay figurines was discovered. It seems that in all of the three cities within Gat's territory, all the finds, by chance, belonged to sanctuaries existing there in the Persian period.

As to the region of **Ashkelon:** in the Persian period, it perhaps included, besides the city itself, the town located at Tell el-Ḥesi, which is situated closer to the eastern part of the Shephelah.

The city of Ashkelon itself was excavated in 1921 by W. J. Phythian-Adams. It is almost impossible to obtain any clear picture of the stratigraphy of the site from his report, and the existence of a Persian-period level is indicated mainly by the imported Greek pottery. Another important find from Ashkelon was a cache of bronze figurines uncovered in 1930 in a room that also contained Persian-period Attic pottery. All these finds were assumed to originate in a local metal workshop.

The renewed excavations at the site headed by L. Stager completely changed the picture: it became clear that, after Ashkelon was destroyed in 603 by the Babylonians, it did not recover for a considerable time and was rebuilt only at the beginning of the Persian period on a quite impressive scale. In one area, Stager observed a deposit 2 to 3 m. thick representing several phases of architecture and including a large repertoire of imports, which made the Persian period one of the richest at the site, especially on the south mound. On the north side of this mound, 3 m. of Persian-period strata overlay the 7th century BCE strata discussed above. The Persian-period sequence began with monumental ashlar buildings and continued with at least four more phases of architecture, culminating in a major destruction in about 300 BCE. Rooms in the destroyed building were filled with burnt debris from the collapsed mud-brick superstructures, which buried basket-handled amphorae and many other items, including a linen bag filled with several Phoenician silver coins from the 4th century BCE. In another area, the same evidence for a citywide conflagration emerged. Here, five phases of Persian occupation marked the period, beginning with a monumental building, dated about 500 BCE (Phase 6). It was followed by a dozen dog burials (Phase 5) and three phases of architecture of workshops fronting the street (Phases 4a-c), which again ended in massive destruction. Shortly before the destruction, the inhabitants of one of the buildings hid a hoard of silver coins (tetradrachmas of Alexander the Great) and silver bracelets. Several late-type basket-handled amphorae stored on the second floor of one of the buildings collapsed onto the first story; the basement was filled with burnt brick, rubble, and pottery from the late 4th century BCE.

Perhaps the best evidence indicating that Ashkelon was a major port throughout the period was the series of warehouses in another area. The earliest of them here (Phase 9) was an impressive building with at least six almost identical magazines, each with about 30 sq. m. of storage space on the ground floor. Most of the magazines had been emptied, but one still contained several Phoenician amphorae, undecorated Attic black-glazed ceramics, as well as red- and black-figured wares. Also found in the same magazines were a camel scapula and the imprint of a basket that had contained red ocher and brown umber from Cyprus.

At some time in the first half of the 5th century BCE, the use of this part of the port city changed dramatically. Because the large warehouse had been raised toward the sea, the stone foundations of the western half of the building lay at a lower level than those of the eastern half. Before the next warehouse (Phase 6) was constructed, the western half of the old warehouse was gradually leveled with a series of rubbish-laden fills. This seaside area was then converted into the largest dog cemetery known in antiquity. Of more than eight hundred dog burials excavated, most (80 percent) were concentrated in this area. The dog cemetery probably extended to the south for at least another 100 m., where another dozen intact dog burials and forty-six partial ones were found in similar fills. In the late 4th century BCE, some dogs were still buried here. Each dog was carefully placed on its side in a shallow pit. Its legs were flexed and its tail tucked in around the hind legs. The dog was then covered with earth taken from the fills, which contained a mixture of cultural debris. Both males and females are present: the high proportion of puppies (ca. 62 percent) in comparison with young and mature dogs suggests a mortality profile similar to that of modern urban dog populations. This profile, the care with which the dogs were interred, and the lack of butchering marks suggest that the dogs died of natural causes, rather than epidemic or as a result of human intervention. The Ashkelon dogs were of medium height and build and there is no evidence for selective breeding. The prime location of their burial ground inside the city and the careful attention given to the interment of newborn puppies as well as of mature dogs express a human concern beyond that of mere companionship: the dogs were probably regarded as sacred animals. Of the several plausible cultural links that could be made with the variety of peoples who lived in Ashkelon in the 5th century BCE—Greeks, Egyptians, Persians, and Phoenicians— Phoenician culture was predominant and constitutes the likely source for this phenomenon. A contemporary Phoenician text from Kition, Cyprus, refers to dogs and puppies performing some unstated services in Phoenician temples there. The excavator suggests that the sacred dogs and puppies buried at Ashkelon may have been part of a healing cult connected with a Phoenician deity.

Greek material culture is also well represented in Persian-period Ashkelon. Sixth century BCE deposits have yielded a few Corinthian imports and Ionian cups. A Greek Chalcidian war helmet was retrieved from the sea at Ashkelon. In the 5th century, Attic imports predominate. Italic red-figured imports arrive in the 4th century BCE and later still, West Slope ware. Other imports come from Cyprus (stone statuettes and clay vessels), Egypt (bronze figurines, scarabs), and from Persia (a few rare objects, such as a 5th century BCE scale weight consisting of a lead filling encased in decorated bone and weighing one *karsha,* a Persian unit of weight, and a carved ivory comb with Achaemenian hunting scenes).

In the other settlement within the territory of Ashkelon, at **Tell el-Ḥesi,** a few excavations have been conducted, first by Bliss and Petrie and recently by a large American expedition. It now seems that during the Persian period Ḥesi became a military or governmental center in the first half of the 5th century BCE. As a result, a massive building project was initiated. A huge platform was constructed on which a citadel was built (Stratum V-d). The citadel was formed by casemate walls surrounding a central courtyard with hard-packed earthen floor. No residential dwellings were found in the excavation area, although there were some signs of domestic activities, including the production of flour from grain. In Stratum V-d, as well as in the later Persian-period phases, there were significant quantities of imported Attic vessels, which aided in dating the stratum. On this basis, Stratum V-d may be dated to 500 to 460 BCE. The excavators concluded that the citadel of this stratum functioned as a governmental grain storehouse. In the mid-5th century BCE, Stratum V-c was occupied for a short time. A building of simpler construction than that of V-d was located roughly above the V-d citadel. Again, a hard-packed earthen floor covered much of the excavation area. The ceramics and artifacts strongly resembled those from Stratum V-d, with the exception of the high proportion of transport jars. Transport jars were less common in Stratum V-b, while the architectural evidence showed fragmentary walls of several buildings. The Greek pottery from Stratum V-b indicates occupation over several years in the last third of the 5th century BCE. A small cemetery from the Persian period was found on the southern slope of the acropolis and it is probably contemporary with Strata V-c and V-b. This cemetery contained simple graves of men, women, and children, which suggests that some people remained at the site year-round to oversee the grain business. Stratum V-a, dated to the end of the 5th century BCE, was structurally a renovation of the preceding phase. Characteristic of this phase were large, brick-lined pits 1 to 2 m. wide and up to 2 m. deep. These pits were probably used as grain silos. They were a rich source of broken pottery, seeds, bones, and a variety of implements and weapons. The botanical evidence indicates a preponderance of wheat over barley within the pits. The general absence of 4th century Greek pottery suggests that the Stratum V-a occupation probably did not continue into the 4th century BCE. Among the finds in the mound dating to the Persian period were a ram-shaped clay *rhyton,* a Bes vase, figurines and statuettes made of clay and stone, limestone incense altars, and an Aramaic ostracon.

The Gaza Region and Northern Sinai

Although the two most important sites of the Persian period in this region, the city of Gaza itself and the one located at Tell el-ʿAjjul, have not yet been excavated, we are able to draw a reliable and comprehensive picture of the Persian period in this region from the many other sites already excavated on the northern side of the Besor River. These are Tell Jemmeh and Tell el-Farʿah (S) and the two sites located at the region's eastern side and recently excavated by E. Oren: Tel Haror and Tel Seraʿ.

In his excavation report of the site of **Tell Jemmeh,** W. M. F. Petrie attributed the topmost and latest stratum to the Persian period. This stratum contained a storehouse consisting of five rectangular-shaped rooms with mud-brick walls plastered with mud. A similar, badly eroded building was also found on the southeastern side. Aside from these groups of storehouses, Petrie also assigned to this stratum some ten round granaries (silos) found on the surface. Another granary was uncovered in the plain to the west and many more were visible in the unexcavated area. One granary contained a large amount of charred grain. In several of the silos, staircases were still preserved. The sloping sides of the granaries suggest that the roofs were conical in shape. Petrie found parallels for these in descriptions of Assyrian granaries. By means of complicated calculations of their volume, he concluded that they could hold food for an army numbering approximately seventy thousand men. The buildings of this stratum were dated on the basis of an Attic *lekythos* to "as early as 460 BCE," and because he regarded the granaries as a storage depot for the Persian army while preparing to attack Egypt, he maintained that they were constructed in 457 BCE, about one year before the Persian attempt to invade Egypt.

Underlying this stratum was Stratum A-B. In it were uncovered two large buildings. Building A, in the east, is square in plan and of very large dimensions with thick brick walls. It consisted of an open central courtyard surrounded by rooms on three sides. According to Petrie, there was no space on the east side for another row of rooms. The stone-paved area in the center of this side was interpreted by him as the threshold of the entrance gate. He regarded this building as a fortress similar to the ones he excavated at Dephene and Naukratis in Egypt. The remains represent the bottom floor, which supported the upper stories. West of the fortress, on the same level, stood another large building (B), which Petrie called a palace. It consisted of two separate units, each with central courtyard enclosed by rooms. According to Petrie, Buildings A and B were contemporaneous, and because of their resemblance to the fortresses of Dephene and Naukratis and the presence of jars with basket handles, which he also found in the fortress in Egypt, he dated them to the 26th Dynasty (mainly to Psamtik I, 664–610 BCE). He considered these buildings to have been part of the fortifications erected to protect Egypt from Assyrian invasions. He also attributed to this stratum part of a storehouse uncovered on the south side of the excavated area, which resembled storehouses of the "Persian" stratum. Petrie's dating of Stratum A-B was challenged by many scholars. This stratum was re-excavated by G. W. Van Beek, who came to the conclusion held by many, that this large complex dates to the late 6th to 5th centuries BCE. It now appears that there are not two stratigraphic phases here, one earlier and the other dating to the Persian period, as Petrie assumed. Instead, there are three phases, all of which were in existence during the Persian period. In the first phase, the fortress (Building A) was the central structure on the mound. In the second phase, after the destruction of the fortress, Building B was erected (both units), together with the adjacent large storehouse (with three units). It is thus clear why: (1) Building B stood at an angle to Building A; (2) the round granaries were also dug into the fortress, Building B, and the storehouses (all of them preceded the construction of the granaries). In the third phase, the round granaries were built all over the area of the mound. There is no doubt that the urban settlement on the mound had ceased to exist, for the builders of the granaries ignored it altogether. The site in this phase apparently served as a supply depot. The time range indicated by the Attic pottery (i.e., from the late 6th to the 4th centuries BCE) is wide enough to accommodate three separate destructions within its two hundred years.

New parts of the upper level with two additional round granaries were excavated by G. W. Van Beek. According to his report, ostraca within the granaries indicated that grain, collected through government taxation, was stored there, while another and smaller granary on the east slope stored wine. The local pottery was dated to the late Persian or early Hellenistic period, and it included several new forms, especially a storage jar with a hollow, cuplike base, the most common storage-jar form in the granary. One of these jars bears a South Arabian monogram reading ʿabum, a name known in both Sabaean and Minaean inscriptions. This suggests that South Arabian caravans also stopped at Tell Jemmeh, probably bringing cargoes of frankincense and myrrh on their long journey from Yemen to the Mediterranean port of Gaza (Pliny *NH* 32.63–64).

The second important site in this region is **Tell el-Far'ah (S).** This site was initially excavated in 1929–30 by Petrie and later by J. L. Starkey and G. Lankester-Harding. Petrie claimed that no Persian-period building of importance was uncovered. Starkey and Harding, on the other hand, later published a plan of the area excavated in the south part of the mound, which shows a large area occupied by a big building with thick walls. The fragmentary plan seems to indicate that this was a fortress of the open-courtyard type, similar to that of Tell Jemmeh. It appears also that the site was occupied by a very large settlement that extended over the entire mound, protected by the above-mentioned fortress on the south. The data are very fragmentary and thus misleading, but are supplemented to some extent by the important tombs found in the vicinity (see below). Among the finds from the Persian period, two Aramaic ostraca and a fragment of a limestone altar with incised decorations are noteworthy.

Two more sites located in the southeastern part of the kingdom of Gaza were recently excavated by E. Oren. At **Tel Haror,** following the destruction of the Late Iron Age fortified town by the Babylonians, the site was occupied again in the 5th to 4th centuries BCE by one or two settlement phases (Stratum G1) represented in Area G by a large building, cobbled floors, and grain and refuse pits. The finds included Greek and Cypriot imports, clay figurines, bone spatulas, and an Aramaic ostracon. Excavations in Area D exposed the remains of a large structure based on stone foundations and attached to a courtyard paved with stone slabs. As in Area G, the construction of the Persian-period settlement involved a large-scale leveling of the Iron Age site. In another area, a cemetery was found with Egyptian pottery and a Greek fibula. According to its excavator, the settlement at Tel Haror is in line with the densely populated western Negev of the Persian period.

The second site in this region is **Tel Sera'.** Stratum III here was attributed to the Persian period. As at the other sites in the southern Shephelah and the northern Negev, it consists of numerous built silos and grain pits. A large brick-lined granary with brick floor was excavated. The floor was covered by a thick layer of organic matter, probably remains of cereals, as well as diagnostic Persian-period pottery. In Area D, above the ruins of the "Assyrian" citadel (see above), were the remains of a citadel and courtyard building similar in plan to structures at Ashdod. Stratum III yielded a large collection of imported Attic wares, Greek figurines, Aramaic ostraca, and a fine limestone incense altar decorated with incised proto-Aeolic capitals. In conclusion, it seems that here, as in all other sites in Philistia, after a short period of abandonment following the Babylonian conquest, the site was resettled from the beginning of the Persian period and remained settled to the end of that period.

We now turn to the results of the recent research in **northern Sinai** along the Mediterranean coast directed by E. Oren. Here, Cambyses' conquest of Egypt in 525 BCE was an important landmark in the history of the region. Henceforth, the history of the northern Sinai and Egypt was linked to that of the great powers that successively controlled the entire region.

Herodotus (3.5) remarked that "the only entrance into Egypt is through its desert. From Phoenicia to the boundaries of Kaditis [Gaza]; the country belongs to the Syrians known as Palestinians. From Kad'tis—a town not much smaller than Sardis—the emporia [seaports of trade centers], as far as Ienysus [el-'Arish], belong to the kings of Arabia; from there as far as Lake Sirbonis near Mount Casius and running down to the sea, it is once more Syrian territory." The seaport emporia were apparently the termini of the Arabian trade, and the entire spice-trade route in the desert was controlled by the Arabs. Two principal changes occurred in the northern Sinai in the Persian period: the first was the reestablishment of the major road along the shore of the Mediterranean partly abandoned before, and across the sandbar of the Bardawil lagoon, and consequently, the establishment of a series of permanent settlements, forts, and fishing villages on the coastline.

In the course of the northern Sinai survey, an expedition headed by E. Oren, nearly two hundred Persian period settlement sites between the Suez Canal and Gaza, including towns, villages, forts and cemeteries, and numerous seasonal encampments were documented. The settlement map shows large concentrations of sites in northwestern Sinai, on the shores of the Bardawil lagoon and along the coast between el-'Arish and Gaza. Of special consequence is the considerable volume of Greek pottery recorded at almost every site, a clear testimony to the major role that Greek trade played in the economy of north Sinai.

At the coastal site of **Ruqeish,** near Deir el-Balah, established in the Assyrian period (see above), survey and excavations recorded impressive remains of a large Persian-period town, probably an administrative and commercial center and a major trading station for maritime and land traffic. The location and nature of the rich archaeological remains at Ruqeish in the Persian period support its identification as one of Herodotus' coastal emporia south of Gaza. Also at **Tel Qatif,** on the coastal ridge about 2 km. west of Ruqeish, the remains of a small fort and observation post were excavated. It guarded the traffic in this section of the coastal highway. Excavations exposed a section of a massive mud-brick structure of the "courtyard fort" type that was enclosed by a 5-m.-wide defensive wall, and a sizable tower overlooking the sea at the northwestern corner. The fort of Tel Qatif probably belongs to a network of military installations constructed by the Persian administration along the coastal highway of North Sinai, between Gaza and Pelusium (Tell Farama). Remains of similar fortified sites were encountered near Sheikh Zuweid, Rumani, and Tell el-Ḥer (Migdol).

A few kilometers to the south, at the site of **Tell Raphia** (Tell Abu-Salima), sections of walls, floors, and installations were recorded with quantities of imported Greek pottery. This combined evidence suggests that the Persian-period town at Raphia was rather extensive and probably unfortified. At a distance of about 1 km. west of Tell Raphia, the badly damaged remains of a small cult site (R-26, according to the expedition registration)—perhaps a wayside shrine—which included sections of a small two-room structure with two spacious courtyards and a narrow enclosure wall, were explored. The larger courtyard was occupied by various installations such as a plastered basin for liquids and two *favissae* full of ash and charcoal intermixed with animal bones. Many fragmentary clay and faience figurines of different styles were collected: Greek, Phoenician, Cypriot, and Egyptian. The associated pottery indicated that the site functioned over a relatively long period, from the 7th to the 3rd centuries BCE, reaching its zenith in the Persian period.

One of the more important stations along the coast of Sinai is located in the center of the Bardawil lagoon sandbar near Katib el-Gals, almost universally identified as ancient **Kasion.** In the classical sources, Kasion is known as an important way station on the coastal road, as well as an industrial center that specialized in shipbuilding and for which a particular type of seagoing vessel was named. The prominent ridge nearby, Ras Qasrun, is generally considered the location of the temple of Zeus Kasios, the patron god of ships and seafarers. The site of Kasion gained further importance because of the commonly accepted identification of biblical Baal-Zephon with Mount Casius (Exodus 14:2, 9). In twenty-two of the forty-three sites that were systematically surveyed in the region of Katib el-Gals, rich occupational evidence for the Persian period, including much Greek pottery, was recorded.

Philistia: Summary and Conclusions

The picture that emerges from the excavations and surveys conducted throughout Philistia shows that during the Persian period this area was divided into two main parts: the northern part that included the territories around Ashdod, Ashkelon, and Gath; and the southern part, the region of Gaza, which continued south along the coastal highway through north Sinai toward Egypt. The northern part, where the major town in the beginning of the period was Ashdod and later became Ashkelon, included, in addition to these major cities, the town of Gath (Tell eṣ-Ṣafi) located at its eastern side and a long list of other settlements, in both the western and the eastern parts of the region: a fortress north of Ashdod and a fortress west of Rishon le-Zion, which guarded the coastal highway in this section, continuing the system already formed in the Assyrian age (see above). Here, we have counted also a temple at Nebi Yunis and some settlements on the eastern side such as Yavneh, Tel Zippor, Tel 'Erani, and Tell el-Ḥesi. Dozens of additional settlements were uncovered in the territories of these three towns in the various surveys or small excavations, such as those conducted at the coastal settlements of Yavneh-Yam, Tell Ghazza (Ya'oz), Ashdod-Yam, and settlements in the eastern Shephelah, such as Tell Kidna, Tell e-Shalaf, Tel Shafir, etc.

The results of the combined excavations and surveys confirm our previous observations on the density of settlement in the coastal plain of the north with certain differences dictated here by the topography. The coastal strip at this point is straight. Nevertheless, the few possibilities were exploited to their maximum potential. Due to the broad strip of shifting dunes which in this area divides the coastal plain from the fertile inner Shephelah, an unusual phenomenon was produced in which the major cities were separated from their ports (Yavneh—Yavneh-Yam; Ashdod—Ashdod-Yam). These two cities must consequently be treated as if they lay on the coast. Thus in all, there are at least five harbor towns, four of which may be considered large: Tell Ghazza, Yavneh, Ashdod, and Ashkelon. At the same time, since this region has not yet been properly surveyed, we lack information about the network of smaller settlements that surely existed here. This may be hinted at by M. Dothan, who noted that in the territory he explored (the lower Rubin River), "the results of our survey show clearly the development of settlement in the Persian period, in the hills along the coast," though he does not specify their locations.

The picture of settlement in the inland Shephelah is much clearer than that of the Shephelah adjoining the coastal strip of the Sharon. These differences seem to be less the result of objective data, i.e., sparser occupation in the Sharon hinterland in comparison with the Ashdod hinterland, but are rather due to the difference in the scope of the surveys carried out in the two areas. From the list above, it is evident that this area was very densely populated in the Persian period. In all, some dozen settlements have been uncovered, some of considerable size.

The history of this area in the Persian period is shrouded in obscurity and can be reconstructed only by conjecture, since the historical and epigraphic sources are scanty. We shall start with the city of **Ashdod.** In the Bible, its inhabitants are called "Ashdodites" and they spoke in a special dialect known as "the speech of Ashdod" (Nehemiah 4:1; 13:23–24). Since no names of the rulers of the city are mentioned, it can be assumed that the form of government in the city itself, and its neighboring port cities, was identical with that in the other coastal cities in the Persian period, i.e., it enjoyed partial autonomy and in the course of time may have been handed over to one of the Phoenician kingdoms, either Tyre or Sidon. At all events, aside from the book of Judith (3:1), in which Ashdod, Ashkelon, and Yavneh are referred to as the main cities in the region, Ashdod does not appear in any other contemporary documents (in Herodotus, too, it appears only in connection with an earlier event). All the other nonbiblical sources mention only **Ashkelon.** In the *Periplus,* Ashkelon is described as a "city of the Tyrians and royal palace." Not only does this designation substantiate our remarks as to the form of government of the port cities of the region, it also seems to indicate that during this period Ashdod lost much of its prominence and Ashkelon acquired importance in its place. The "royal palace" in Scylax may have been the residence of the local governor, who moved his seat there during the fourth century BCE. Ashkelon is also mentioned by Diodorus (3.4.2), as containing a great temple. Ashkelon's attribution to Tyre also attests to the presence there of a large Phoenician population that may have become dominant in the 4th century BCE, as indicated by the character of the material culture discovered in all the ex-Philistine sites, as well as the numismatic and epigraphic finds. We have already mentioned the ostracon, found at Nebi Yunis near Ashdod, that is dedicated to the "lord of Tyre" and the emblem of the Phoenician goddess Tanit-Pane-Ba'al recovered at both Ashdod-Yam and Ashkelon. Indirect confirmation of the immigration of Phoenicians to this region in the Persian period may be found also in the Phoenician cult objects uncovered in all *favissae* belonging to the temples that once existed at Tell eṣ-Ṣafi, Tel 'Erani, Yavneh, and Tel Zippor. Also of significance in this connection are the early Hellenistic Sidonian inscriptions from the tombs of Marissa, as well as the recently published large inscription on a tombstone dating to 163 BCE, which is a petition made to Antiochus V Eupator from the Sidonians in the harbor of Yavneh, who supplied him with maritime services. A Greek inscription from the Persian period from Tell el-Ḥesi also bears a

Phoenician name. The penetration and settlement of the Phoenicians into previously Philistine territories in the Persian period is evident at almost every new excavation: At Ashkelon, for example, L. Stager came to the conclusion that:

> The predominance of Phoenician Material Culture at Ashkelon in the Persian period is evident from the Phoenician inscriptions found: several ostraca bearing Phoenician personal names, and an East Greek Bowl incised in Phoenician script with 'gm, or "cakes." Again, religious insignia, the sign of Tanit in the form of three bronze and two bone pendants attests to the presence of her cult here. Later, in the Roman period, the goddess appears on coins, minted exclusively at Ashkelon, as Phanebalos (pane baal). The iconography of these Phanebalos coins suggests that an impressive temple to Tanit still stood in Ashkelon in the Roman period. From the 4th century BCE Sidonian coins of 'Ebed ashtart I (Straton I, 375–361 BCE) reached the warehouse of the age. At the same time, Ashkelon was minting its own coins if, as seems likely, those bearing the abbreviation aleph-nun refer to Ashkelon [similar to the coins of the same Phoenician type and script which are inscribed with the full name of Ashdod; see below]. Also Phoenician amphorae dominate the ceramic repertoire. (*Ashkelon III,* pp. 108–109)

All the other cultural influences such as Greek, Cypriot, Egyptian, Achaemenian, or Arabian are much scantier.

Now we come to the kingdom of **Gaza.** The southernmost part of the ex-Philistine territory, the Gaza region, was evidently the largest of the four in the Persian period as well. Here, besides the large Phoenician component there was also strong Arabic influence, for this city was again the terminal port of all Arabian trade. The extent of the area under this influence in the Persian period can be established by the biblical sources, other written sources, and new epigraphic finds.

In the Bible, Geshem the Arabian appears among Nehemiah's enemies (Nehemiah 2:19; 6:1, 2, 6). The area under his rule is not defined, but it was evidently situated in the southern part of the country. Herodotus, on the other hand, located the territory of the Arabs, who were "exempt from taxes," on the coast between Gaza and Ienysus (el-'Arish?). The Arabs were freed from paying taxes for aiding Cambyses to pass through the desert on his way to Egypt (525 BCE). The Arabs had lived in the area in an earlier period, but they apparently became important after the Persians conquered Gaza and stationed garrison troops here (Polybius 16.40). Handing over a city to friendly inhabitants was an accepted custom, and in Gaza it was repeated when Alexander the Great captured it. The Arab role in the city apparently continued until the end of the period, as is attested in the description of the siege of the city by Alexander (see below).

Though neither the Bible nor Herodotus mentions the tribal affiliation of the "Arabians" who inhabited the Gaza region, this is revealed in the epigraphic finds: the inscriptions of Geshem and of Qainu the son of Geshem. The former was discovered at Dedan (el-'Oula) in North Arabia and the latter at Tell el-Maskhuta in the Egyptian Delta. Aside from indicating the vast territorial expansion of these tribes, these inscriptions also designate Qainu the son of Geshem as a "Qedarite." It thus appears that Geshem, who is mentioned in Nehemiah, was also the head of the Qedarite federation and not of the Nabataeans, as was widely believed in the past. The Qedarite tribes are already known from documents dating to the time of Ashurbanipal (see above), and their penetration into the southern border area of Palestine probably began in this period, was intensified in the Babylonian period, and reached its zenith in the Persian period. At this time, they supported the Persian domination of the parts of the desert under their control. The assistance they extended to the Persians was similar in many ways to the maritime aid extended to the Persians by the Phoenicians. Consequently, they were granted similar privileges.

We have already noted above that despite the "autonomy" and tax exemptions granted to the Arabs, the administration of their affairs was in the hands of a Persian ruler who was also in charge of everyday matters. We also maintained that the "autonomy," which is generally attributed to the area and its possession by the Arabs, consisted in reality of economic concessions, such as exemptions from certain taxes (though the Arabs did in fact pay taxes in kind), the free passage of trade to and from Gaza, and perhaps also payment for guaranteeing peace and security in those far-flung areas that were inaccessible to the Persians. The rest of the area was governed in the 5th century BCE by means of a network of fortresses and permanent garrison troops, such as the fortresses at Tel Sheva, Arad, and Tell el-Kheleifeh, where the soldiers were mainly Arabs, Edomites, and Persians. It can be assumed that beginning with the year 400 BCE, when the Egyptians liberated themselves from Persian subjugation and the whole area became a border region, Persian rule was undoubtedly strengthened, troops were dispatched to the area in large numbers, and numerous fortresses were erected. Only thus can we explain the remains in the upper stratum at Tell Jemmeh, which consisted entirely of storehouses containing food supplies for the army (cf. also the finds from Tell el-Far'ah (S), Tell el-Ḥesi, Tel Sera', Tel Haror, Tel Qatif, etc., and the smaller fortresses along the highway, such as those discovered at Rishon le-Zion, the one north of Ashdod, etc.). Arrian as well noted that Gaza served as a Persian military base and fortress (2.25.4). Much important information is also revealed in Arrian's detailed description of the siege of Gaza by Alexander (2.26–27; and cf. Diodorus 17.48.7), which relates that Gaza at that time was a large, well-fortified town, which was ruled by a Persian governor called Batis (Babymasis in Josephus *Antiquities* 11.8.3). The town was taken only after a lengthy siege lasting two months in which Alexander was wounded and some ten thousand Persian and Arab soldiers met their death. Much booty was captured, including large amounts of costly metals and spices. After Gaza's conquest, it was given to other Arab tribes.

The area of Gaza itself stretched from a point between Ashkelon and Gaza (for according to Scylax, the border of "Coele-Syria" ended at Ashkelon, and Herodotus stated that the territory of the Arabs began at Gaza). It can be assumed that this area undoubtedly lay between the Gerar and the el-'Arish rivers and also included an adjacent strip of the inner Shephelah.

Excavations in this area uncovered important strata of the Persian period at Tell Jemmeh, Tell el-Far'ah (S), Tel Sera', Ruqeish, Sheikh Zuweid, and elsewhere. The results of the various surveys of the area as well as chance finds indicate that settlements from this period also existed along the southern coastal strip at Tell Raphia, Tell Abu Salima, and Mount Casius, which, according to Herodotus, formed the southern frontier of Palestine (see above). In the excavations and surveys conducted by E. Oren in the area of Pelusium, a large number of flourishing settlements from this period was revealed, among them a Persian military fortress (Migdol).

The various literary sources, on the other hand, mention two cities that have not yet been excavated. Herodotus (3.5) speaks of Kaditis (Gaza) and Ienysus (el-'Arish?), and Gaza is again referred to by Arrian (2.26–27), who describes its siege by Alexander.

The evidence derived from the archaeological and historical sources is thus complementary but not identical, since the two cities mentioned in the documents remain unexcavated, while the sites that have been investigated do not appear in the sources. At all events, the two types of evidence indicate that, as on the other parts of the coast, the cities from Gaza to Ruqeish and in the inner Shephelah were Tell el-Ḥesi, Tel Nagila, Tell Jemmeh, Tell el-

Far'ah (S), Tel Ḥaror, and Tel Sera'. Gaza was the principal city of this region and perhaps also of the entire Qedarite zone; according to Herodotus, Gaza "was not much smaller than Sardis" (3.5), i.e., the major capital of Anatolia. The excavation results reveal that some of the other sites were also quite large. We have, as yet, no evidence that can throw light on the string of small villages that undoubtedly encircled these cities. The population of the Gaza region that is mentioned in the various records consists mainly of Persians and Qedarites, but, according to the archaeological results, it seems that the major ethnic element in this area during the entire Persian period is Phoenician. E. Oren's conclusions after his excavation at Persian-period Ruqeish are almost identical to those of L. Stager. Concerning the results of his own excavation at Ashkelon (see above), Stager speaks about the distinctive Phoenician orientation of the material culture of this flourishing Phoenician settlement at Ashkelon in the Persian period. Second in importance are the Greek and Cypriot remains found at every excavation in the region, as in the other coastal regions of the country, which points to the fact that these people, too, were important components in the region's population. To this, one may add some Egyptians, who left only a modest mark on the region's remains.

The Province of Samaria

Introduction

INFORMATION ON THE province of Samaria as an administrative unit in the Persian period is contained in (1) the Bible, where Sanballat the governor of Samaria appears among the enemies of Nehemiah (Nehemiah 2:10, 19; 4:1); (2) a letter of Elephantine from 408 BCE, which mentions "Delaiah and Shelemiah, sons of Sanballat governor of Samaria" (Cowley, nos. 30:1, 29); (3) Josephus' account of the continuous strife between Judah and Samaria (*Antiquities* 11.7.2); and (4) the Wadi ed-Daliyeh papyri, bullae, and coins from 375–335 BCE, which contain the names of the above and additional governors of the dynasty of Sanballat; and perhaps also the Ketef Jericho papyri (see below).

Several ostraca written in Aramaic script were uncovered in two campaigns of excavations at Samaria, but they are mostly receipts for shipments of dates, oil, and wine with the addition of a date, and their historical importance is therefore marginal. In all the written sources cited, only two cities from this area are mentioned: Samaria and Shechem (*Antiquities* 11.8.6). No names of other settlements appear, and it is thus difficult to determine the boundaries of the province and especially its internal structure. M. Avi-Yonah assumed that the Persians retained the same boundaries they inherited from the Assyrians and that they included only the mountainous part of Mount Ephraim to the Yarkon River and the Sharon coastal plain on the west, the mountains of Gilboa and the Jezreel Valley in the north, the Jordan on the east. He equated the southern boundary with the northern boundary of the province of Judah. As to the internal division of the province into districts, Avi-Yonah lists the following: Aphaerema, Acraba, Shechem, Samaria, and Aruboth (Narbata). Samaria and Shechem undoubtedly served as the district capitals. The city of Aphaerema is attested in this period by later references (1 Maccabees 11:28; Josephus *Antiquities* 13.5.9), which relate that it was annexed to the Hasmonaean kingdom in 145 BCE when the majority of its population was already Jewish. The district of Acraba and Nabrakhta (Narbata) are mentioned in the book of Judith. If this book was indeed composed between 366 and 360 BCE, as maintained by M. Grintz, it can provide contemporary proof of their existence. Furthermore, according to the book of Judith, the Narbata district was already inhabited by Jews in the Persian period, and formed a kind of northern enclave, like the one in the south of Judah (see below). The boundaries of this district, as described by the book of Judith, included the Dothan Valley to the west, the Jezreel Valley in the north, the Beth-Shean Valley and the Jordan River in the east, and the area of Tubas in the south. These boundaries in the west, north, and east were proposed by M. Avi-Yonah for the whole province of Samaria. A number of settlements is also mentioned in the book of Judith. Grintz suggested identifications for them, but only some of these are certain: Jezreel, Koaman (Khirbet Kumiya), Bel'am (Khirbet Bel'ame), Betuliah (Kubatiya?), Beth-Homotayim?, Dothan, Hobah (Khirbet Mukhubi), Asher (Tayasir), Abel-Mayim (Tell el-Maliḥ), and Holah ('Ain Hilweh), at the southern end of the Beth-Shean Valley.

The major source for our knowledge of the population of Samaria during the Persian period is presumably Ezra 4:8–10, where "The men of Erech and Babylon and of Susa—that is the Elamites" are mentioned. H. Tadmor noted that these deportees from Erech, Babylon, and Susa regarded themselves as being of a superior rank; Elamite Susa was one of the capitals of Persia, and the cities of Babylon and Erech were highly esteemed in the Persian kingdom. Thus, this document constitutes instructive evidence of the social distinctions existing within the population of Samaria, some of whom bore with pride the appellation of their city of origin, although two hundred years had passed since they were exiled. It would also appear that these inhabitants of Samaria had no qualms about writing directly to the king and that they received direct replies.

Additional sources for the composition of the population at Samaria are the documents from Wadi ed-Daliyeh. They seem to show that Samaria contained a more varied population at this time. Apart from the usual Yahwistic names, F. M. Cross noted names with the components Qos (Edomite), Sahar (Aramaic), Kemosh (Moabite), Ba'al (Phoenician), and Nabu (Babylonian; mentioned also in one of the ostraca found in the city). Josephus, on the other hand, speaks of a Sidonian colony at Shechem (*Antiquities* 11.8.6), and in M. Avi-Yonah's opinion, it already existed in the Persian period.

Excavations and Surveys

In this area, excavations have revealed Persian-period strata only at the two principal cities of Samaria and Shechem, and additional information on the Samaritan population has been provided by the excavation of Wadi ed-Daliyeh. It is strange that the other two large sites excavated in this region, Tel Dothan and Tell el-Far'ah (N), have thus far yielded no Persian-period levels. On the other hand, new light has been shed on the settlement in this region by the results of the many surveys conducted there in recent years. We shall now describe these results, starting with the region's capital, the city of Samaria, as well as results of the excavation at Wadi ed-Daliyeh, to which area some of the inhabitants of the city of Samaria fled.

The destruction wrought upon the city of **Samaria** by Alexander the Great, precipitated by the revolt of its inhabitants at the end of the Persian period, and the population exchange in which Samaritans were replaced by Macedonians, who dwelled in its ruins and undertook restoration work, brought about the total obliteration of all Persian-period building remains. Whatever survived was apparently razed by the intensive building activities in the Herodian and Roman periods. For this reason, the two large-scale excavations at the site succeeded in uncovering only slight traces of the city, which at that time was one of the most important in Palestine. All the finds attributed to the Persian period came from pits or unstratified assemblages, preserved here and there. None of this evidence was sufficient to throw light on the city of Samaria during the Persian period. A very important find from the city was, however, uncovered in the Wadi ed-Daliyeh cave, north of Jericho, and in the Ketef Jericho cave (see below). Due to the lack of a building stratum, the first excavations in Samaria—a Harvard University expedition—established the existence of a Persian-period settlement on the basis of finds alone. It is possible that this is why they attributed those remains to such a broad time span (700–330 BCE), which they designated as the "Babylonian-Greek period." Despite this, the excavators state that the main indicator for fixing the date of these finds was provided from the outset by Greek pottery. Its date is much more limited, and a considerable amount was found in the excavations. The main find from the period uncovered by the Harvard expedition was the contents of a square rock-cut pit filled with debris and "sealed by Greek and Herodian building." Aside from stratigraphic evidence, the attribution to the "Babylonian-Greek period" was based mainly on the eight Aramaic ostraca found there and a red-figured Attic vessel. The Aramaic ostraca were shards of jars on which the jars' contents were written (in two cases "wine"). Since some of them also bear dates, it is possible that they are receipts of deliveries, in accordance with the widespread custom in the Israelite period. The excavation report also includes isolated Persian-period finds. The most important of these are a seal impression in the Achaemenian style, of which many others were later found in Wadi ed-Daliyeh, a Neo-Babylonian seal, and an Athenian coin of the 5th century BCE.

The second joint expedition to Samaria also had difficulty in locating building remains from this period. On the summit, however, a layer of fertile brown earth was found covering an area of about 50 x 50 m. Beneath this layer, all the walls and floors of the late Israelite stratum were torn down and the debris carefully cleared of stones. The whole area was filled at that time. The layer of fill and the brown earth both contained Attic potshards from the 6th to 5th centuries BCE. Kathleen Kenyon maintained that this layer was agricultural soil that was artificially piled up to form a garden or grove around the palace of the Persian governor. In her opinion, the palace was located on the eastern side, outside the excavated area.

All the remains of the Persian period were assigned within the framework of Stratum VIII. The finds from this stratum included a clay cup that Kenyon considered a direct Achaemenian import. Several unstratified Aramaic ostraca were also found, one dated to the 6th and five others to the 4th century BCE. Each is inscribed with a single word or separate letters, and their contents cannot be deciphered. Together with the ostraca found in the first excavation, a total of fourteen was found. Also found were three local coins, probably Samarian, three Sidonian coins that were dated to the reign of Straton I (370–358 BCE), and a large amount of Attic ware from the end of the 6th to the end of the 4th centuries BCE. In a small salvage excavation conducted in Samaria during the 1950s, another coin, at the time the only Achaemenian coin found in Palestine, was uncovered. It is dated to the reign of Darius III, the last of the Achaemenian kings. More important finds were the bronze parts of a throne of one of Samaria's governors.

A hoard of coins, said to have been found in the city and called "the Samarian hoard," was recently purchased with its clay juglet. It contained 334 silver coins. Thirty-two of them were Tyrian, 43 Sidonian, 11 from Arwad, 66 local Palestinian imitations of Attic prototypes, and 182 of the city of Samaria. Because no coins of the satrap Mazday were found in the hoard, and because the Tyrian coins were dated to the years 1–14 of Artaxerxes III (358–345 BCE), Y. Meshorer and S. Qedar concluded that the hoard's date is 345 BCE, the time when the Phoenician revolt was suppressed and Mazday became the satrap of Abar Nahara.

The most important find from Samaria, however, was discovered outside the city, in a cave in Wadi ed-Daliyeh north of Jericho, where it is assumed that some of the inhabitants of the city (in all, some three hundred men, women, and children) took refuge after revolting against Alexander's governor in 331 BCE. Finds included about forty papyrus fragments, 130 bullae, two gold signet rings, jewelry, pottery vessels, and coins, including a Macedonian coin from the time of Philip (Alexander's father), a Persian coin struck by the governor Mazaeus, and other local and Phoenician coins of the period. Some of these artifacts were found in the excavation, while others were purchased from the Bedouins who first discovered the cave. The documents, which were written in Samaria, are dated according to the era of the Persian kings. They were later published separately. The earliest document is dated to 375 and the latest to 335 BCE. Several governors and high officials of Samaria are mentioned on the papyri and the bullae (see below).

Later the cave was identified and excavated by P. W. Lapp, and additional finds similar to those described above came to light. Especially important was the pottery assemblage, which was soon published. In recent years, a few hundred Samarian coins as well as additional bullae, all dating to the same period and coming from either the Bedouin excavations at the Wadi ed-Daliyeh cave or the city of Samaria, have been purchased from various antiquities dealers. Many of them depict local, Persian-Babylonian, and a surprisingly high proportion of Greek motifs. Others are inscribed with the city's name or the names of its governors, some of whom were previously unknown. Both the bullae and the coins were published separately. This rich, well-dated find is of unusual importance for establishing the dates of the pottery and of other finds from other sites.

The combined Persian-period finds from Samaria and Wadi ed-Daliyeh are thus extremely rich and important. Together they serve as an indicator of the prosperity of the city of Samaria in the Persian period, corroborating the historical sources. It is regrettable that so little of the city itself came to light during the course of numerous excavations.

The second important site in the Samaria province was **Shechem,** excavated by G. E. Wright. Wright distinguished remains of the Persian period in two areas. In Field VII, a few remains of an intermediate stratum that was apparently totally destroyed (Stratum V) were found in a fill between the latest Israelite stratum and the early Samaritan stratum from the beginning of the Hellenistic period. In Field IX, the remains of this stratum were noted on the surface. The date of this stratum was fixed by the discovery of Attic pottery that was assigned by Nancy Lapp to 525–480 BCE. Wright therefore maintained that the city was destroyed in about 475 BCE, but he could offer no explanation for the cause of this destruction. In conclusion it seems that Wright thought that the site was deserted during the 6th century BCE. Also after 475 BCE it was abandoned for about 150 years, until it was resettled as a Samaritan center during the time of Alexander to replace Samaria, which was now occupied by Macedonians. But this date (475 BCE) should now be lowered for two reasons: the first is the find of an Achaemenid tomb and a clay coffin that included Attic vessels of 475–450 BCE; the second is the recent finds in the central Samaritan sanctuary on Mount Gerizim, established at the beginning of the 4th century BCE if not earlier (see below). Among the finds of the Persian period in Stratum V of Schechem is a large assemblage of Attic ware, a late 6th century BCE electrum coin from the island of Thasos, and an Achaemenian bulla depicting the Persian king as an archer with the emblem of Ahura-Mazda behind him. Also of extreme importance is the coin hoard purchased in 1968 in Shechem (called "the Shechem hoard"), which contains 965 silver coins. Among these coins were 131 Tyrian coins, 206 local Palestinian imitations of Attic ones, 625 coins of the city of Samaria, and 3 from north Anatolia! (2 from Sinope and 1 from Amisos). On the basis of the Tyrian coins, which are not later than 332 BCE, and those bearing the name of the satrap Mazday, it is now agreed that the hoard was hidden in 332 BCE (see below).

This rather fragmentary picture of the Samaria provincial towns in the Persian period is supplemented by the many intensive surveys conducted in the region. The first survey was by the Joint Expedition to Shechem under the direction of E. Campbell, who worked mainly in the outskirts of the city. Of the 41 sites investigated, only 5 contained any remains of the Persian period, but the brief report does not give the names of the sites. Different results were obtained in a much more extensive survey made by R. Gophna and Y. Porath in 1968. This survey encompassed some 250 sites, and of these, 81 were settled in the Persian period. Z. Kallai surveyed the area south of Samaria and found an additional 15 sites. The later surveys, from the 1980s on, were much more sophisticated and detailed. Their results clearly show that settlement in this period was concentrated mainly in the northern and western parts of the province. The survey showed that 247 settlements of the Persian period were in existence in the northern part of Samaria, more than during the period of the Israelite monarchy (238). The southern survey reached different results. I. Finkelstein came to the conclusion that there was a sharp decline in the number of settlements in this area during the Persian period. Only about 90 such settlements were recorded and most of them were smaller than those of the preceding Iron Age. This decline was probably due to the destruction of the kingdom of Israel. The bulk of settlement activity shifted to the western part of this area, probably within the framework of the development taking place on the coastal plain. Indeed, the survey of Samaria conducted by S. Dar, focusing on this western zone, encountered a dense network of settlements there in the Persian period. The villages were usually small, seldom exceeding 2.5 hectares in area.

One of the west Samaritan settlements was excavated by Y. Magen at Qedumim. Here, no building remains from the Persian period were uncovered, but many finds came from the cisterns. Cistern A, for example, a bell-shaped installation coated with a thick layer of plaster, contained hundreds of potshards, copper needles, and loom weights from the Persian period. The pottery included imported vessels from Greece and a unique, large holemouth jar, decorated with faunal and floral designs and an Aramaic inscription (*mtr'*) that probably relates to a local industry.

The Province of Judah

Introduction

OUR KNOWLEDGE OF the settlements of the province of Judah from the biblical records is much more extensive than that concerning other provinces. The major sources of information are five rosters of place-names appearing in the books of Ezra and Nehemiah. The first two rosters are of the returnees from the Babylonian Exile (Ezra 2:21–35; Nehemiah 7:25–38). These two lists are identical and contain the same place-names with one exception that appears in Ezra as Gibbar and in Nehemiah as Gibeon. The first seems to be a corrupt version. These lists contain place-names in four regions: (1) settlements south of Jerusalem: Bethlehem and Netofah; (2) two settlements in the Jericho Valley: Jericho and Senaah; (3) twelve settlements north of Jerusalem: Nob, Anathoth, Azmaveth, Ramah, Gaba, Michmas, Ai, Bethel, and the four Gibeonite cities, Gibeon, Chephirah, Beeroth, and Kirjatharim (Jerusalem is not mentioned, nor are the other district capitals: Keilah, Beth-Zur, Beth-Haccerem, and Mizpah); and (4) three settlements in the northwestern Shephelah: Lod, Hadid, and Ono.

The third roster, that of the families settled in Jerusalem (Nehemiah 11:25–35), completely omits the area south of Jerusalem and the Jericho area. But in contrast, many settlements from the Negev, outside the borders of the province, are mentioned (see below). From the area north of Jerusalem, seven of the place-names in the list of the returnees are contained here (Nob, Anathoth, Ramah, Gaba, Michmas, Bethel, Aija), while Azmaveth and the four Gibeonite cities are deleted and Ananiah and Hazor are added. From the area of the northwest Shephelah, the three place-names, Lod, Hadid, and Ono, are repeated, and four others are added: Neballat, Zeboim, Gai ha-Harashim, and Gittaim (Ras Abu-Hamid). Other new place-names from the area of the southwestern Shephelah not included in the list of returnees are Zareah, Jarmuth, Azekah, Zanoah, and Adullam. It is curious that no mention is made of the capital of the district, Keilah, but this roster as a rule does not include district capitals, not even Jerusalem.

The fourth roster (Nehemiah 3:1–22), that of the people who helped rebuild the wall of Jerusalem, contains mainly the names of district capitals. Cities explicitly designated as capitals include Beth-Zur, Beth-Haccerem, Keilah, Jerusalem, and Mizpah. Also mentioned in this list are the inhabitants of Jericho, Hassenaah, Tekoa, Gibeon, Zanoah, and "the priests, the men of the plain *(kikkar)."*

The fifth roster, that of the singers, is brief, and contains only Jerusalem and Netophah in the Judaean Hills and Azmaveth and Gaba in the territory of Benjamin, as well as two place-names whose location is not certain: Beth-ha-gilgal and the *Kikkar,* which may represent additional sites in the Jericho area.

From the above, it is evident that only the two rosters of the returnees are identical in contents. The others show marked differences from them and from each other. It is therefore not surprising that scholars disagree concerning the date of the composition of the lists and the periods of settlement reflected in them, as well as the boundaries of the province in the

Persian period. There are no other contemporary sources that would allow a comparison of the boundaries and the settlements of the province. The sources closest in date are from the Hellenistic period. Because of this gap in time, each scholarly authority determined the sequence and dates of these lists according to his own interpretation. Most assumed, on the basis of the absence of place-names in one list and their appearance in another, that the documents date from different periods and reflect the development of Jewish settlement through time. The main controversy revolves around the dates of the first three lists (those of the returnees and of the families settled in Jerusalem), which have been dated from the end of the Israelite period to the Hellenistic period. The fourth list, that of the builders of the wall of Jerusalem, on the other hand, is generally agreed by all to be a contemporary document and to reflect the area of the province during the days of Ezra and Nehemiah. Without entering into details of the different views on this matter, all the lists must be regarded as tendentious. The beginning of each list contains a statement of its subject, whether it lists the returnees, builders of the wall, settlers in Jerusalem, etc. All of them are definitely related to the days of Ezra and Nehemiah, i.e., the second half of the 5th century BCE. In our opinion, the particular purpose of each roster holds the clue to the different nuances of its contents. Only thus can we explain the absence of a particular site in one list and its appearance in another.

We have already noted the main distinction between the roster of the builders of the wall and the other three: the latter lists systematically omit the district capitals, even though most of them are located in the heart of the areas described, while the former specifically enumerates them. The ordinary place-names recur, for the most part, in all the lists and the omissions are generally of entire regions. Thus, the entire southeast Shephelah (Keilah district) is missing from the roster of the returnees, while areas of the Judaean Hills and Jericho are excluded from the list of the families settled in Jerusalem. The northwest Shephelah (Lod area), which appears in the first three lists, is omitted from the roster of the builders of the wall.

According to Nehemiah 3 (the list of the builders of the wall), Judah was subdivided into five districts: (1) Mizpah, (2) Jerusalem, (3) Beth-Haccerem, (4) Beth-Zur, and (5) Keilah. Many attempts have been made to include in these districts settlements mentioned in the other lists in Ezra and Nehemiah and thereby to delimit clearer borders for these districts. The following subdivision of the province conforms better, in our opinion, to the natural features of the area:

Capital   District
Mizpah—the territory of Benjamin
Gezer—the northwest Shephelah
Jerusalem—Jerusalem and surroundings
Beth-Zur—the hilly area south of Jerusalem
Keilah—the southwest Shephelah
Jericho—the Jericho Plain

Only the district of Beth-Haccerem ('En Karem) seems at first glance to be superfluous, but it is possible that the vicinity of the provincial capital of Jerusalem was divided into districts of smaller size. Though it is possible to attempt to establish more exact boundaries for each of these districts, we lack information necessary for such an undertaking. We have no evidence, for example, for the boundaries of the Jerusalem district nor for its division into two subdistricts. For the same reason, there is no way of proving the theory that each district contained both a district capital and a subdistrict capital, for the two rulers of the subdistricts are always assigned to the district capital alone. In any case, we can now examine these boundaries according to two *archaeological* criteria: one is the line of border fortresses that encircled the province of Judah in the west and south and that have been uncovered in excavations and surveys; even more important is the area of distribution of the seal impressions and coins inscribed with the name of the province Yehud. Based upon the latter, the southern border of this area of distribution would appear to be at Beth-Zur; the northern limit is at Tell en-Naṣbeh; the eastern limit is a line extending from Jericho to En-Gedi; in the west, some seal impressions were recovered at Gezer, which is definitely located in the district of Lod, and at Tel Ḥarasim, which belonged to the Keilah district. Thus, the distribution of coins and impressions of the Judaean province encompasses the entire area mentioned in the Bible.

The Region of Benjamin

We will now turn to discuss in detail the results of the excavations of the Persian-period sites conducted in the territory of Judah, starting at the district of Benjamin north of Jerusalem, the same region that, as shown above, was the only one not destroyed during the Babylonian period. The major excavations in this region have been conducted at Bethel, Tell en-Naṣbeh (Mizpah), tell el-Ful (Gibeah), Gibeon, and Nebi Samuel. All these excavations showed that here the settlements were not destroyed in the general destruction of the First Temple and that the remains from the Persian period were the latest in a chain that creates a direct continuation from the Iron Age and on.

The site of **Bethel** was excavated by two expeditions, the first in 1934 by W. F. Albright and the second in the 1960s by J. L. Kelso. In the preliminary reports published by Albright at the conclusion of the first season of excavation, he distinguished two strata of settlement from the Persian period. The first settlement was founded during the 6th century BCE and extended over only part of the site. It was built in a primitive fashion, mostly of reused materials. In a second area of excavation, a level of settlement from the 4th century BCE was also found, built in a manner superior to its predecessors. Albright does not assign a date to the destruction of the early settlement, stating only that it existed during the 6th century BCE, following the destruction of the First Temple.

The final combined excavation report was published only in 1968. Here, the excavators reiterate the main points of the preliminary reports, namely, that the destruction of Bethel took place in the transition period between Babylonian and Persian rule and that it was resettled after a time (at the end of the Persian period). A special chapter is devoted to a study of the 6th century BCE. Among the important finds here are an Attic *lekythos* dated by J. H. Iliffe to the second half of the 5th century BCE and a conical agate seal of the 6th to 5th centuries BCE in the Babylonian style.

Persian-period remains were also uncovered at **Tell en-Naṣbeh.** The building remains are meager and are confined to several rooms built above the city walls of the Israelite period and a few walls near the surface that were visible in various places on the mound. The excavators also attributed a modest attempt at defense to this day, i.e., a thin wall erected above the ruined Iron Age wall. From the description, it is evident that the remains were assigned to the Persian period mainly on the basis of their stratigraphy—they lay above the ruins of the last Israelite stratum—and to some extent based upon the pottery found in the walls, which the excavators state is not earlier than the 6th century BCE. The existence of a Persian-period settlement at Tell en-Naṣbeh is indeed attested by the finds. A small amount of pottery from this period was uncovered on the mound, but more came from pits scattered over the site. About thirty shards of Attic vessels of different types dating to 540–420 BCE were found on the mound and in the pits. A bronze coin, an imitation of an Athenian tetradrachma dating to 406–393 BCE and seal impressions of various types, including thirty-five *yehud* seals and impressions of animals and a limestone incense altar, are among the other finds.

In a reassessment of the Naṣbeh finds recently conducted by J. Zorn, besides strengthening the role of the site during the Babylonian period (see above), he also claims that the city certainly existed during the Persian period, too. He assigns some additional walls, installations, pits, etc., to this period.

As to **Gibeon,** excavated by J. B. Pritchard, the excavator assumed that all the remains he found there dated exclusively from the Iron Age to the destruction of the monarchy. But some of the finds he reported, even some written ones—the inscribed jar handles, seals, and seal impressions—were attributed, by such authorities as Albright, Wright, Cross, Lapp, and others, to the 6th century BCE, *after* the fall of the kingdom, i.e., to the Babylonian period (see above). It seems, however, that some of the finds, including pottery and seal impressions, may even belong to the Persian period, perhaps to its earlier part. In this regard we note Nehemiah 3:7–8, where the Gibeonites are mentioned among the builders of the Jerusalem wall.

The fourth major site excavated in the territory of Benjamin is **Tell el-Ful.** Here, too, a Persian-period settlement stratum was uncovered; however, as at Gibeon, its phases and nature were long a matter of dispute and were interpreted in a variety of ways. The first excavators, W. F. Albright (1922) and L. A. Sinclair (1933), dated Stratum IV to "no later than the Persian period"; but in 1964, when excavation on the mound was resumed by P. W. Lapp, as a result of his conclusions (see below) and on the basis of a comparison of the finds with those from Bethel, Shechem, and Gibeon, Sinclair retracted his previous dating of Stratum IV. In a brief article, he suggested dividing it into two phases. The first phase, IVA, he dated from the end of the 6th and the early 5th centuries BCE. To this phase he assigned Fortress IV and part of the houses on the mound's eastern slope. This was followed by an interruption in settlement, which was renewed at the end of the 3rd century and ceased in the 2nd century BCE (Phase IVB).

In a short report of the results of his excavations at Tell el-Ful, P. W. Lapp stated that the site was resettled after the destruction of the First Temple, in the middle of the 6th century BCE. This conclusion was based mainly on the contents of a large plastered pit, from which about one hundred baskets of potshards were removed. Half of them were from the lower level, which was "a homogeneous group to be assigned to the last half of the 6th century BCE." Among the finds he mentioned was a large number of *yehud* seal impressions. Similar ceramic finds were also made on the western side of the mound. It is evident from the report that the area of the city increased during this time and that peaceful conditions made it possible to build houses outside the Iron Age wall. P. W. Lapp dated the end of this settlement, like those at Gibeon, Bethel, and Shechem, to about 500 BCE, but neither he nor Wright could offer an explanation for the cause of the destruction. He dated the renewal of the settlement at the site to the end of the 3rd century BCE. In the final discussion of the site's pottery (1981), N. Lapp suggested the following new subdivision: IIIA=late period of the Judaean kingdom; IIIB=exilic (Babylonian) period, 586–538 BCE, based upon comparison to similar pottery groups from Bethel, Gibeon, Tell en-Naṣbeh, and Tomb 14 at Beth-Shemesh (see below).

Another major site in this region that was recently excavated is **Nebi Samuel,** which proved to be an important town in the Persian period. The pottery is not published or even treated yet, but among the finds recorded is a group of *yehud* seal impressions and a lion seal impression typical of the province of Judah in the Persian period (see below).

More information on this region came to light in excavations conducted at some smaller sites such as Ras el-Haruba, Bethany, and Mozah, which contribute to the general picture drawn above. It is the continuation of the settlements from the end of the kingdom of Judah into the Babylonian age without interruption and later into the Persian period.

Jerusalem and the Highlands

In the area of Judah, the main excavations of Persian-period settlements have been conducted at Jerusalem, Ramat Raḥel, and Beth-Zur, located in the highlands; at Jericho; and at En-Gedi in the east; and Gezer in the western foothills. The rest of the sites situated along the western Shephelah such as Beth-Shemesh, Tel Batash, and Azekah produced few finds from the Persian period. One must bear in mind that large parts of the territory of the previous Judaean monarchy, including cities such as Lachish and Maresha, not to mention the southern sites in the Beersheba Valley such as Tel Sheva and Arad, were annexed to Idumaea during this phase (see below).

We shall start our detailed discussion of the Judaean cities in this area during the Persian period with the capital—**Jerusalem.** Persian-period Jerusalem was bounded by walls erected by Nehemiah. Despite the relatively detailed description in the Bible (Nehemiah 2:13–15; 3:1–32; 12:31–40), the location of these walls has been a matter of controversy for many years, similar to the controversy surrounding the extent of the city during the First Temple period. The maximalist school, whose main proponents were J. Simons and L. H. Vincent, maintained that the borders of the city extended to the western hill, while the minimalists claimed that Jerusalem in this period was confined to the southeastern hill, the Ophel and the Temple Mount, as proposed by M. Avi-Yonah.

In the various excavations that took place at sites on the eastern hill at the beginning of the present century, finds from the Persian period have been made—a small amount of pottery and numerous seal impressions of the *yehud* types—but none of these excavators have succeeded in connecting them with a level of buildings. In 1961–1967, excavations were carried out in Jerusalem by Kathleen Kenyon in which it was established that in the Persian period Jerusalem occupied the eastern hill alone; i.e., the wall surrounding the summit of the eastern hill, which was previously considered to be Jebusite, or dating from the Israelite period, was in fact from the Persian period (the days of Nehemiah). To this wall were added a tower and other structures in the Hasmonaean period. A section of the wall—on the east side—was erected directly over the quarried rock. Against it lay a rubbish dump that contained pottery from the 5th to 4th centuries BCE.

The latest excavations at the site of the City of David directed by Y. Shiloh strengthened these conclusions. They showed again that the Persian stratum in Jerusalem was less preserved because it was nearly obliterated between the destruction of the Israelite city and the extensive construction in the Hasmonaean and Herodian periods. The eastern slope of the eastern hill was in such a ruinous condition, so covered with rubble from its buildings and retaining walls, that for the first time in its history no attempt was made to build and resettle it. The city developed on the crest of the narrow spur of the City of David, over a small area. The fortified area no longer included the eastern slope. Only a few traces have survived of the city wall of Nehemiah along the course described in the Bible (Nehemiah 3:1–32). A segment of a wall excavated by Macalister on the summit of the eastern slope, reexamined by Kenyon and Shiloh at the higher, western edge of Kenyon's Site A and Shiloh's Area G, should, however, be assigned to this period. For the first time, in several places on the eastern slope, the Shiloh expedition was able to locate layers of Persian-period Stratum 9 in a clear stratigraphic context. Only a few building remains were found, but there was a large quantity of small finds, mainly assemblages of pottery and seal impressions on jar handles, representing the whole range of known types of such impressions: *yehud* impressions of various kinds, names of satraps such as Ahazai and Hananiah, a seal featuring the figure of a standing animal, and a Lycian silver coin from the 5th century BCE. It follows, therefore, that in the Persian period the City of David spur was again the center of Jerusalem's settled area.

No remains from the Persian period were uncovered in the Jewish Quarter excavations on the western hill. Directly overlying the remains of the First Temple period are Hellenistic strata. This gap in occupation after the Babylonian destruction of Jerusalem in 586 BCE and the deportation of its inhabitants indicates that the Mishneh on the western hill also remained abandoned. Support for these conclusions now comes from the excavations conducted in Jerusalem since 1967: in the Armenian Quarter, on Mount Zion, and in the citadel. In none of these has a settlement stratum or any Persian-period objects of significance been uncovered. As the excavated areas increase and cover more of the western hill, it can be stated today with almost complete certainty that no urban settlement existed in this period in Jerusalem outside the southeastern hill.

A few kilometers south of Jerusalem another important Persian-period site was excavated in the 1960s by Y. Aharoni. This is the site of **Ramat Raḥel.** In the first three seasons, the Persian-period remains were included within a very broad chronological framework (Stratum IV), which encompassed the Persian, Hellenistic, and Herodian periods. In the fourth season, this stratum was subdivided into IVB for the 5th to 3rd centuries BCE and IVA for the later periods. The building remains attributed to Stratum IVB are meager and consist mainly of the remains of a massive wall on the east side of the excavated area, which is about 1.2 m. wide and is oriented roughly along the course of the outer wall of the Judaean citadel (see above). Its foundation trench contained pottery of the Persian-Hellenistic periods. Some 25 m. of the wall were cleared without hitting any lateral walls, and in the opinion of the excavator this was a defensive wall enclosing a large courtyard. A rubbish dump (no. 484) on the east side contained pottery and seal impressions from the Israelite, Persian, and Hellenistic periods. Other buildings from this stratum were found in the southern part of the excavations, about 2 to 3 m. south of the Judaean citadel. The whole area was badly damaged by Byzantine construction and only a complex of a few rooms was uncovered. It should be pointed out that the built walls were constructed of large trimmed stones set alternately in headers and stretchers. The finds from the Persian period at Ramat Raḥel are unique. Some of the local pottery was found scattered over the entire excavated area, but the bulk of it was found in a number of assemblages, one in the foundation trench of a long wall on the west side (Loci 429, 430) and especially in the large rubbish dump on the east side of the wall (484). Other pottery assemblages also came from rooms of this period (439, 457). Attic ware and a few East Greek shards were found scattered in various places on the mound.

The outstanding feature of the Persian-period finds at Ramat Raḥel is the large number of seal impressions of almost all known types and also some new ones. They constitute, for the time being, the largest and most varied group of impressions found in one place from this period. Some are inscribed with the names of the province's governors or high officials in its administration. The impressions came from all areas of the excavation but the largest groups were uncovered in the courtyard of the Judaean palace or citadel and rubbish dump 484. The great number of the impressions prompted the excavator to suggest that in the Persian period the seat of the governor of the province was located in the Ramat Raḥel citadel, as it used to be in the last days of the Judaean monarchy (see above).

The next important Persian-period site in the Judaean province was unearthed at **Beth-Zur**. In excavations carried out here in 1931 by O. R. Sellers, a Persian-period settlement stratum was discovered. The excavator did not succeed in separating it from the later phases and included it within a wide chronological range (from Late Iron Age to the Roman period) and designated it as "Hellenistic." The building remains from this stratum included a citadel on the north side of the excavated area and parts of houses surrounding it on the east and south sides. Three phases of construction were distinguished in the citadel. Sellers dated the earliest phase to the time of Judas Maccabeus (165–163 BCE) and the second phase to the time of Bacchides (161 BCE). C. Watzinger, on the other hand, stated that Citadel II was built on an oriental plan and therefore attributed it to Judas, assigning the third citadel to Bacchides. W. F. Albright accepted these corrections and accordingly changed the date of Citadel I (of which only fragments that do not fit into a coherent plan were preserved) to the Persian period. In his opinion, the citadel was built facing the border of Idumaea. The existence of a Persian-period phase in Beth-Zur is also clearly attested by the finds. As was mentioned, Sellers almost completely failed to distinguish between the remains of the Persian and the Hellenistic periods. But in one place, where the conditions were somewhat better, he managed to isolate them. In Loci 58–62, beneath a pavement containing Hellenistic pottery, Sellers noted clear traces of Persian-period remains, especially in Locus 59, where seven jars were found *in situ*. One jar contained an Attic tetradrachma, dated to 450 BCE. Examination of the plates of finds published in his report shows more Persian-period finds. Aside from the Attic coin, six more coins of other types were recovered, of Sidonian, Tyrian, and the generally nonepigraphic "Palestinian" type, from the 5th to 4th centuries BCE, and one Judaean coin inscribed *hezekiah hpḥ* ("Hezekiah the governor"), which dates to the end of the Persian period. The latest excavations at the site (1957), by P. W. Lapp, shed little new light on the Persian-period settlement of Beth-Zur. Several new finds were made but none were stratified.

Recently, R. Reich has urged that the Beth-Zur Citadel II is the one that should be dated to the Persian period. He based his assumption mainly on the resemblance of its plan with that of the Persian-period Lachish Residency (see below), as well as the attribution of some of the above-mentioned finds to this stratum.

Judah's Eastern and Western Boundaries

Along the **eastern** boundary of the province of Judah in the Persian period, two main settlements have been excavated: **Jericho** and **En-Gedi**. In **Jericho**, the remains of a small settlement were uncovered. Most of it was excavated by E. Sellin and C. Watzinger in 1908–1909. They cleared unconnected remains of several structures in the northern part of the mound and attributed them to the "late Jewish period," which according to them was the last period of occupation on the mound. The existence of a Persian-period town was also indicated by the finds in their excavation which included local and Attic pottery of the 5th to 4th centuries BCE and about ten *yehud* seal impressions and one "lion impression." In Kathleen Kenyon's excavations at Jericho, only one more seal impression of the Persian period was found. It was unstratified and bore the legend *yehud 'wryw*. Later a few coins of the *yehud* type were also reported from the site. On the basis of these finds, it appears that the Persian-period settlement at Jericho dates to the 5th to 4th centuries BCE. It is impossible to assign a more precise chronological framework.

A unique find was recently made at **Ketef Jericho** in a cave located in the mountain, about 3 km. west of the mound of Jericho. This is a papyrus document containing a list of Jewish names and is dated to the second half of the 4th century BCE. This document was attributed by its publisher, H. Eshel, to the period of a rebellion against Persia in the days of Artaxerxes III (344–343 BCE), mentioned by Solinus, who also claimed that Jericho was destroyed and its Jewish inhabitants exiled.

The second important site on the eastern border of the province of Judah in the Persian period was **En-Gedi**. Here, in five seasons of excavations, the remains of a stratum of a Persian-period settlement were uncovered (Stratum IV). Fragmentary building remains were first encountered on the southern slope of the mound and several plastered pools on the western slope. The principal structure from this period was cleared on the northern slope. This large house (234) was built of rough stones and divided into three wings erected on three terraces, following the terrain of the site. The floors and walls of the building were thickly plastered. Trunks of palm trees were used for the construction of the roof and the steps. One room (231) contained a plastered pool, loom weights, bottles, and various stone implements. It was apparently a workshop. This building extended beyond the built-up area of the Iron Age (see above). It was not an isolated structure, for sections of walls of buildings lay on its west, south, and east sides, with only a narrow lane separating them. Nearby, to the south, on the slope, stood another large building, perhaps a public one. The residential quarter of Persian-period En-Gedi thus seems to have stretched over the entire area of the summit and even beyond it.

The Persian-period settlement at En-Gedi was apparently renewed at the site at the beginning of the period, after having been abandoned following its destruction by the Babylonian army in 582 BCE. The duration of the settlement was established on the basis of the Attic pottery found there. Most of the Attic vessels date from the last three quarters of the 5th and the early 4th centuries BCE, and a small amount dates to the remainder of the 4th century BCE. All the 4th century shards were found on the floors of the western wing. The excavators therefore concluded that the building contained two phases. The first phase, when the entire building was in use, dates from the beginning of the 5th to the beginning of the 4th centuries BCE. In the second phase, only the western wing was restored to use. The final destruction of the Persian-period stratum at En-Gedi occurred—according to B. Mazar—in the period 350–340 BCE.

The finds uncovered in Stratum IV at En-Gedi are rich and varied. Aside from the Attic ware mentioned above, there was also a great quantity of local ware, including "Persian" bowls, ordinary bowls, deep bowls, cooking pots, a diverse collection of vessels decorated with wedge and reed impressions, jars, flasks, lamps, bottles, jugs, and juglets. Most of these are known from other assemblages in the Judaean Hills. Since at En-Gedi these vessels were uncovered in clear stratigraphic contexts, they were of considerable help in fixing the date for similar unstratified vessels from other sites. Various types of *yehud* seal impressions were also uncovered, as well as lion seal impressions, Aramaic ostraca that apparently dealt with the processing of leather, two Babylonian-type seals, and two Phoenician glass pendants.

Of the **western** boundary concerning the province of Judah, we shall discuss here mainly the results of the excavations at **Gezer**. Here, many objects

III.15 En-Gedi, Building 234 of the Persian period, looking south

from the Persian period were found in the excavations carried out by R. A. S. Macalister in 1907–1910. Like many other excavators of that time, Macalister included these finds within an all-inclusive stratum, which he dated to 500–100 BCE and designated "Persian-Hellenistic." Nevertheless, in his discussion of the pottery groups and other finds, he succeeded in separating the vessels from this period. No building remains from the Persian period were uncovered by him, and most of the finds come from a number of pits and tombs, while others were found here and there on the mound. Aside from the so-called Philistine tombs and an additional tomb from the Persian period (to be discussed below), an important pottery assemblage from this period was discovered at the opening of a pit where almost all the vessels were found broken and were correctly assigned by the excavator to the Persian pe-

riod. Other objects of great interest from this period include the fragment of
a stone slab and a scaraboid seal bearing the name of Pharaoh Nepherites,
the first ruler of the independent 29th Dynasty (399–393 BCE), several *yehud*
seal impressions of various types, a group of limestone incense altars,
weapons, and other finds. Large amounts of Attic ware were discovered,
later studied by C. Clermont-Ganneau, who dated all of it to the 5th century
BCE. The rich and varied finds from Gezer excavated by Macalister already
attested to the existence of the city during the Persian period, even though
the excavator did not succeed in locating any clear building remains of it.

In the latest excavations at Tel Gezer carried out in 1964–1970 and directed by G. Ernest Wright, S. Gitin, W. G. Dever, and others, the excavators discovered a stratum from the Persian period. This stratum (IV) was

encountered in two fields, in each of which two phases were identified. The stratum was found totally destroyed and no building remains had survived, but pottery and other finds of the period were uncovered, among them an Aramaic ostracon. These have been treated in detail by S. Gitin.

South of Gezer some few scattered remains of the Persian period were discovered at the site of **Timnah** (Tel Batash). These finds, recovered from the mound's surface, suggested the presence of a modest settlement on the tell during the 5th to 4th centuries BCE. The gate area of the previous Judaean city here also provided evidence of the reuse of the gate passage during this period. A drainage trench cut through the gate area probably drained an area in the center of the site, where more substantial buildings might have existed. Several refuse pits were cut into earlier Iron Age occupation layers during the Persian period.

Excavations at other sites along the western frontier of the province of Judah in the Persian period, at Beth-Shemesh, Azekah, and Tel Ḥarasim, produced scanty evidence. These sites were inhabited during the period but were small settlements. They reflect an effort to resettle the region on a small scale after their long abandonment following total destruction by the Babylonians.

The territory of the province of Judah has been examined in several **surveys**. The first, conducted by L. A. Rahmani in the western part of the Judaean Hills, in the Adullam region, on the Azekah–Beth-Govrin line, was followed later by an intensive survey directed by Y. Dagan. Another survey was directed by M. Kochavi in the central Judaean Hills. In the Adullam region, for example, a settlement dated to the Persian period was Khirbet Rasm el-Seba, where remains of a fort were uncovered. It consisted of a square tower, each side 9 m. long, and a network of walls protected by towers surrounding the fort. Farther south, at Khirbet er-Rasm, were found remains of walls and towers built of unhewn stones from this period. Scanty remains were also revealed to the south, at Khirbet Rafiaʿ, Khirbet Umm Razak, and Khirbet Sabia. To the east, Persian-period pottery was found at two more sites (Khirbet Drusiye and Khirbet Hauran). According to Rahmani, these settlements should be interpreted as *ḥazerim* ("daughters" or "fenced villages") of Azekah and Adullam (Nehemiah 11:30).

In the survey of Judah carried out by M. Kochavi in 1968, the fort at Khirbet er-Rasm was again investigated. Four more settlements were found in the Shephelah near Adullam, and Persian-period pottery was also found at Khirbet Kilah (biblical Keilah). In the main survey of the Judaean central hills, twenty-eight settlements contained Persian-period pottery (roughly equal to the number of settlements from the end of the Iron Age). According to Kochavi, these settlements are of two types: (1) unwalled sites from the late 6th century BCE (his nos. 14, 27, 39), which he identified as Jewish settlements that continued to exist after the destruction of the Judaean monarchy; and (2) fortresses from the 5th century BCE, such as Khirbet el-Qatt (79) and Khirbet ez-Zawiyye (85), which in his opinion form a continuous defensive line along the southern border of the province of Judah. These fortresses are of equal dimensions and uniform in plan. To this list of fortresses we may add the one at Khirbet Abu Tuwein excavated by A. Mazar, which contained a Persian-period stratum and finds. It seems that there was quite a dense network of rural villages in the Persian period, but we still lack clear information on the nature of the urban settlements of the region, such as Adullam, Keilah, and Yarmuth.

IDUMAEA AND MOUNT HEBRON

Introduction

THIS REGION SHOULD be divided into two parts in the Persian period as we have done in the previous period: the traditional **Edom** on the eastern side of the Jordan, to be discussed with the rest of the Transjordanian provinces, and a western part that shall be dealt with here and that is known by its later name **Idumaea.** This is the territory in the Negev that had been captured from Judah, partly during the Assyrian age and completely in the Persian period, when Idumaea encompassed the entire region of southern Judah from Lachish and Marissa almost up to Beth-Zur. The sites that produced Persian-period finds are Lachish and Marissa as well as Tel Ḥalif, which are located in the northwest of the region. A survey of the region uncovered pottery of the Persian period at eight sites on the mountain ridge: Khirbet Canaan, Khirbet El-Marjum, Khirbet Tarma, el-Hadab, Khirbet Nimra, Tel Zif, Tell Rabud, and Khirbet Luzifar. Other finds were recovered at Eshtemoa and ʿAin ʿArrub.

Because of the scanty, sometimes contradictory evidence, the nature of the administrative organization of this area in the southern Judaean Hills south of Beth-Zur in the Persian period has not yet been satisfactorily established. The only biblical reference to this region is contained in the list of families settled in Jerusalem (Nehemiah 11) which enumerates twelve Jewish settlements, ten of them in the vicinity of Beersheba. These include Dibon, Jekabzeel, Jeshua, Moledah, Beth-Pelet, Hazar-Shuʿal, Beersheba, Ziklag,

Mekonah, and En-Rimmon. Hebron is also mentioned by its former name, Kirjath-Arba, as the only town in the southern Judaean Hills, as well as Lachish on the northwest border of the area. The date of this list is a subject of controversy. In the opinion of the majority of scholars, however, it refers to the settlement at the beginning of the period of the Exile, and perhaps even earlier (see below). However, even if the situation existing at the beginning of the Persian period is represented here, there seems to be evidence supporting the theory proposed by Z. Kallai, Y. Aharoni, and others that the list contains names of the Jewish villages whose inhabitants were not exiled, and that there is no question here of renewal of settlements. At all events, it is generally agreed that they were located outside the territory of the Judaean province. A. Alt also maintained that the northern border of this province passed through two stages. At the beginning of Babylonian rule in the area, the whole region of the southern Judaean Hills was separated from the land of Judah at the Bethlehem-Netophah line and was created as an independent southern zone, while the area to its north was annexed at first to the province of Samaria. In his opinion, this situation is still reflected in the rosters of the returnees, which list villages just up to this line. In the days of Nehemiah, when the province of Judah was detached from Samaria, the southern frontier line was removed to Beth-Zur, and it is this boundary that appears in the list of the builders of the Jerusalem wall. However, Alt made no attempt to define the other boundaries of this "southern region" or to determine its name and owner in this period.

The historical sources dealing with this region are either earlier or later than the Persian period. Various hints in the Bible (Jeremiah 13:19; 49:7–22; Ezekiel 35; Obadiah; Malachi 1:14; and perhaps also 3 Esdras 4:50) and other sources indicate that at the end of the 6th century BCE and perhaps earlier, Arabs began to expel the Edomites from their traditional dwelling places in Transjordan and forced them to migrate to the north and west, to the northern Negev and southern Judaean Hills. They were aided in their attempts at resettlement by the collapse of the Jewish settlement and its final destruction by the Babylonians (see above). Clear evidence of the Edomite occupation of the northern Negev in the Persian period is now provided by the Edomite (and Arab) personal names appearing in ostraca from Arad and Tel Sheva and especially from a hoard of about two hundred additional ostraca from an unknown site within Idumaea. Others have been found in the mountainous part of the region at sites such as Maresha, Lachish, Khirbet el-Qom, and Yata. Only from the Hellenistic period do we have clear information on the boundaries of Edomite settlement. In this period, the hyparchy

Idumaea came into existence and the Edomite population lived in the whole area stretching between Judah and Beersheba (Diodorus 19.25.2; 98.1). They continued to inhabit the same region in the days of the Hasmonaeans. Judah fortified Beth-Zur as a fortress "against the Edomites" (1 Maccabees 4:60), i.e., at the former boundary on the Judaean Hills. In the northern part of the region at that time were situated Hebron (ibid., 5:65), Adoraim and Maresha (Josephus *Antiquities* 13.9.1; *Wars* 1.2.6). Maresha is also mentioned as an Edomite city in one of the Zenon papyri (258 BCE), and in the book of *Jubilees* (38:8) it is stated that Esau was buried in Adoraim. Thus, the situation that began in the 7th century BCE continued in the Hasmonaean period. It is very likely that Edomite settlement was a gradual process that occurred in waves. At the beginning of the Persian period, Jewish villages may still have existed alongside Edomite ones, with Edomites gaining possession of them only later. However, this is a matter of speculation. Recent archaeological survey has revealed that the defense line at Beth-Zur formed a fortified frontier in the Persian period, a fact that W. F. Albright had earlier deduced on the basis of the excavations at Beth-Zur. It is therefore even stranger that the Edomites are not mentioned as Judah's southern neighbors in the Persian period, but only Geshem the Arabian. A possible explanation for this is that in this period Edomite settlement had not yet become consolidated into an independent administrative unit, and at the beginning of the period the inhabitants of the area were not among the enemies of Judah. A second possibility, proposed by F. M. Cross on the basis of the finds at Tell el-Maskhuta, is that this region, together with the Negev, is represented in the Bible by Geshem the Arabian, who in the beginning of the period ruled over it (see below).

The identity of the capital of this region is another unsolved problem. Hebron and Lachish appear as the only large cities in the list of Nehemiah 11, whereas in the Hellenistic period, the principal cities were Maresha and Adoraim. The name Batanei (Hebron) appearing in the book of Judith (1:9) is explained by M. Grintz by the fact that this city still served as a regional capital in the Persian period and that Batanei was its Edomite name. At the end of this period or at the start of the Hellenistic period, this city lost its position and was replaced by Maresha and Adoraim. M. Avi-Yonah, on the other hand, maintained, on the basis of the excavations at Lachish and the discovery of a palace there, that Lachish was the capital of the region in the Persian period.

If we turn back to the archaeological sources, in addition to the results of the excavations conducted at Lachish, Maresha, and Tel Ḥalif in the Judaean

Hills, and at Tel Sheva, Arad, Kadesh-Barnea, and Tell el-Kheleifeh in the Negev and the Aravah, and at a few more fortresses uncovered in the two regions, there is now a large number of *written* documents from this particular region. There are many ostraca that survived here because of the dry climate: few have been found at sites in the Judaean Hills, including Yata, Khirbet el-Qom, Maresha, and Lachish. About a hundred were found in two large hoards: one at Tel Sheva and the other at Arad. The two groups were published by J. Naveh, who dated them to the 4th century BCE. A few others came from Tel 'Ira in the Beersheba Valley, and from Tell el-Kheleifeh in the Aravah. Recently, a third large group, which contained about 300 ostraca, turned up on the antiquities market, about 220 of which have been published: one group by J. Naveh and I. Eph'al and the other by A. Lemaire.

Nearly all the texts in these ostraca deal with the cultivation of fields and orchards. They consist of dockets that provide the names of the parties and list the commodities involved in the transaction. The ostraca also shed more light on the various components of the region's population, such as the Phoenicians, who had penetrated to this region (see above). According to the **Tel Sheva** ostraca, which were the first to be published, it seems that the personal names of their owners are divided between Edomite names with the divine component Qos (Qosgabar, Qoshanan, Qosbarech), as well as Qosadar, which according to Naveh also has an Aramaic component. Naveh points out that more important are the mixed names, such as Qosot or Qosvaheb, in which the Edomite theophoric element Qos is compounded with Arabic verbal elements. Other ostraca indicate that both Arabic and West Semitic dialect were used contemporaneously at this time. Some of the names could have been used either by Arabic-speaking Edomites or by Arabs who worshiped the Edomite god Qos. Thus, the Aramaic ostraca from the Persian period found at Tel Sheva reflect the character of the settlement in Idumaea. The ostraca from Tel Sheva also indicate that there was an administrative center here to which grain was brought as taxes.

The **Arad** Ostraca also portray its existence as a way station where barley was supplied to horsemen, horses, and donkeys. The personal names here likewise mirror the makeup of the population in the southern part of the country.

The third hoard of ostraca, which is also the largest, is dated precisely to the days of the Persian king Artaxerxes III (Ochus), as well as to those of Philip and Alexander, i.e., from 363 to 311 BCE. Particularly important among the ostraca is a legal document that seems to report a court decision concerning a loan. According to Naveh and Eph'al, who published the largest group, out of fifty-seven names mentioned in them, Qos appears in seventeen, the Phoenician Baʿal in sixteen, El in fifteen, and Yahu in three. There are also a few Babylonian and Egyptian names. The Egyptians are in the mixed form that we met previously among the Phoenicians (see above), such as *ʿebedosiri* ("the servant of Osiris") or *ʿebedisi* ("the servant of Isis"). The Babylonian names are *ʿebed-shamash* or *natan-sin*, who were among the local Persian army commanders (the same as *ʿebed-nanai*, the commander of a *degel* army unit mentioned in the ostracon found at Arad), or various officials and administrators. About twenty of the names here end with the letter *u*, which is frequently found as a suffix in Arabic names, while fifteen others are clearly Arabic.

From a somewhat later period (late 4th or early 3rd century BCE) comes a bilingual ostracon, Aramaic-Greek, from Khirbet el-Qom in the Judaean Hills, but here, too, the name mentioned in it is Edomite: *qosyadaʿ*. More Edomite documents from this region dating to the early Hellenistic period, some of them unique, are now also known from the recent excavations conducted at the large site of Maresha. From the Hellenistic age, an Aramaic ostracon containing an Edomite marriage contract attests to the already well-established Edomite population in this region.

The combined evidence from all this rich written documentation therefore testifies to the fact that a large proportion of the population in this part of Palestine was already Edomite in the 4th century BCE, thus completing a long process that began during the Assyrian period.

Excavations and Surveys

The sites excavated in Idumaea in which Persian-period levels were uncovered are mainly Lachish, Maresha, and Tel Ḥalif in the north part of the region and Tel Sheva, Arad, Tell el-Kheleifeh, and Kadesh-Barnea in the Negev and Aravah. Many other sites, especially fortresses, have been uncovered in smaller excavations and surveys. These were located along the desert ways.

In the summary of the excavation results at **Lachish,** O. Tufnell assigned the finds from the Persian period to a broad stratum (I), which in fact comprised all the remains later than the Judaean monarchic period. It covered a very wide chronological range, from 450 to 150 BCE. A few structures in Lachish were then attributed to Stratum I. They were (1) a gate and sections of the wall on the west side, (2) two houses on the west: one near the gate (G-18 is the gatehouse) and the other a short distance to the north (G-12/13), (3) the Residency on the summit of the mound and rock-cut pits adjoining it on the east, and

(4) two structures on the east, one a house (RQS-15/16) and the second a temple (the solar shrine). Several tombs and assemblages uncovered in Cemeteries 500 and 1000 were also assigned to the Persian period.

The city-gate complex assigned to Stratum I at Lachish includes the approach road ascending to the outer gate, the lower wall, the outer gate, the tower, the inner gate, and the upper wall. The road leading to the outer gate followed the same course as that of a similar road from the Judaean period, but at a higher level. The road was supported below by a wall that was built along the line of an earlier retaining wall of the Judaean period. About 20 m. north of the outer gate a square structure was defined as a temple or the base of a statue. Of the outer gate, little survived, but in the opinion of the British excavators, it was in use during the existence of the Residency (see below). The tower (bastion) of this period was also largely destroyed. It could not be related directly to any remains in the inner gate or upper walls. In this period, the inner gate was narrowed from 4 to 3.6 m. and its threshold was rebuilt at a higher level. Two lintels of the gate were now enlarged and widened and in fact turned into towers. According to the excavators, the area inside the gate was empty, except for one structure—the gatehouse, which was attached to the gate on the south side. The date of these remains was determined by their high level in relation to Stratum I.

The other major structure of the period was the Residency or the palace. It was erected on the summit of the mound, on a raised podium, which was preserved from the Judaean period. According to the excavators, the Residency of the Persian period was set directly above the remains of Stratum III and no traces of Stratum II were encountered here. The size and plan attest to its having been a public building, a palace or residency according to them. The plan of the building is quite clear. It was divided into two principal parts. In the north stretched a large square courtyard (P), which was surrounded on the north and east by a row of rooms. On the west a staircase led to a double row of rooms. The steps were divided by two columns, both bases of which were found *in situ* together with one of the bottom drums. Column drums were also found scattered in the courtyard and in one of the side rooms (in a secondary use), and the form of the entire column could therefore be reconstructed. The southern part of the Residency was entered through another staircase, which was also flanked by two columns. On this side, the entire width of the building was occupied by two long and narrow rooms set one behind the other. A third row of rooms in the south was divided into small rooms. Rooms A-B were lavatories, as was evidenced by their finely plastered floors that sloped down to a drainage canal. The walls of the building were constructed of small, semidressed stones bonded with clay and plastered on the outside. The column bases were similarly plastered. Collapsed stones from the upper parts of the walls, however, showed that they were more carefully dressed. From the position of the fallen stones, the excavators concluded that the ceiling was supported by arches that sloped toward the walls. The ceilings themselves were made of plastered stone slabs and the floors were of beaten lime, of the same type used in plastering the walls. During the course of excavations, J. L. Starkey was of the opinion that the building was in use during one main period and a secondary one. In several rooms, he distinguished two floor levels. Starkey assigned the building in its entirety to the "postexilic" period, with the second and the last phase of its use occurring in the period 475–425 BCE (corresponding to J. H. Iliffe's date for the Attic pottery). When the finds were later studied by O. Tufnell, she reached the conclusion that the Attic pottery found on the two floor levels displayed no differences and that the existence of a later phase is therefore doubtful. In the meanwhile, the Attic ware has been newly assigned by J. D. Beazley and Joan du Plat-Taylor to the mid-5th and beginning of the 4th centuries BCE. In the final report, the date of the Residency was accordingly set at 450–350 BCE. The local pottery from the Residency was composed of vessels typical of the Persian period, but some Hellenistic pottery was also found. Near the Residency a few pits were uncovered, which contained Persian material, too. They must have been storage pits of the Residency inhabitants. Another building was uncovered about a hundred meters east of the Residency; it consists of an open courtyard surrounded by a row of rooms on three sides. Also attributed to Stratum I is the building excavated east of the Residency, the so-called solar shrine (see below).

The data presented by the excavators on the settlement in the Persian period can therefore be summed up as follows: In the first phase, i.e., from the end of the 6th and the beginning of the 5th centuries BCE, the gatehouse and building G-12/13 were erected and some of the pits were dug. Later the Residency was built (450–350 BCE), more pits were cut, and the fortifications near the gate were constructed. This interpretation is fraught with difficulties. In several cases, the excavators clearly differentiated between two building phases, but no date was assigned to the later phase. There is no possibility of reexamining the chronological data today, since the excavators recorded neither the elevations of the finds nor their relationship to the floors. Nevertheless, the attempt to limit the western buildings to the early part of the Persian period is surprising, for in this stratum the excavators did not even succeed for the most part in distinguishing between the levels of two separate periods—the Persian and the Hellenistic.

The new excavations at Lachish, headed by D. Ussishkin, almost did not touch upon Stratum I. A few probes dug in the Residency area brought the excavator to the same chronological conclusions expressed above, including that of the solar shrine.

The second major site in Idumaea in which substantive remains of the Persian period have come to light is **Maresha.** Here the first excavations at the site, conducted in 1898–1890, failed to uncover a clear Persian-period stratum. Nevertheless, isolated finds from this period at the site (mainly figurines and pottery) attest to its occupation at that time. In the recent large-scale excavations conducted by A. Kloner, a Persian-period stratum was indeed found below the huge Hellenistic tower at the northwest corner of the town. This stratum was uncovered mainly by sections, but it had more than one stage and it might even have been fortified. Except for the Persian-period pottery, some clay figurines were also uncovered, as well as a few ostraca in which the name Qos, the national Edomite deity, is mentioned; however, most of the Edomite ostraca found here are of the later Hellenistic period.

South of here, **Tel Ḥalif** is the next excavated site with a Persian-period stratum. At this site, Stratum V of the Persian-period occupation was encountered in a number of pits and bins in two fields. In one of them, substantial architectural remains were uncovered. There, excavations revealed elements of a large building, directly overlying the latest Iron Age structures. The surfaces associated with the Stratum V walls were generally sterile, but clear evidence of a late Persian-period date was recovered from foundation trenches. The substantial size of the walls suggests that they may have been part of a large storehouse, barracks, or military building erected on the summit of the tell during the Persian administration of the region.

Recently, two more important Persian-period remains have been uncovered in the Judaean highlands: one is **Khirbet Nimra,** just north of Hebron, and the other is **Khirbet Luzifar,** on the southeast point of the Hebron Hills overlooking the Beersheba Valley. Both sites are located on the north-south highway. At Khirbet Nimra, a large structure (25 x 12m.) was uncovered. It was probably an administrative center. The finds here included local vessels (including a complete animal-shaped *rhyton*), a unique, large stone seal engraved in a local imitation of Achaemenian style of the type that was worn around the neck, a Palestinian silver coin, a basalt incense altar, and many loom weights. At the second site, Khirbet Luzifar, a large fort was excavated, which also contained local Persian-period pottery and imported Attic ware, as well as another local Palestinian silver coin.

All other Persian-period sites in Idumaea are located either in the Beersheba Valley or in the Aravah. They include Tel Sheva itself, as well as Tel Arad and Tell el-Kheleifeh, with the one exception of Kadesh-Barnea, situated in the northern Sinai. This list has its closest analogy to those parts of the Judaean kingdom that in the 7th century BCE had already been captured by the Edomites (see above).

At **Tel Sheva,** no settlement stratum was exposed in the excavation carried out by Y. Aharoni. However, the existence of such a stratum was confirmed by the contents of some rubbish pits in the area on the summit of the mound. The pits contained local pottery, Attic ware, Aramaic ostraca, and limestone incense altars. One pit, which yielded a number of bronze figurines and glass pendants, was probably a *favissa* of a small nearby temple (see below). In the report, the level of these finds is designated as H-3 and was dated to the 4th to 3rd centuries BCE (Persian and Hellenistic periods). The excavators also assumed that a military fortress and several houses were situated on the site at this time. In any case, the most important evidence of the Persian-period occupation came from the Aramaic ostraca that were published by J. Naveh. About fifty-four ostraca were discovered and were dated to the middle of the 4th century BCE. According to Naveh, they provide us with quite important data on the history of the Beersheba region in the Persian period. The dockets mention exact dates, specific amounts of barley or wheat, and names of persons who supplied these provisions. They seem to be descriptions of produce brought to Tel Sheva as tax payments. Most of the ostraca were found in pits, presumably because they were used as labels for the barley and wheat stored in them. Most of them consist of personal names, about thirty or more, which can be divided into three groups: a third are compounded with the Edomite theophoric element Qos; another third are clearly Arabic; and most of the remaining names are common Semitic. In this group there is only one Iranian name. Between Tel Sheva and Arad, recent excavations at Tel 'Ira also revealed a small Persian-period settlement (Stratum V).

At **Arad,** on the eastern side of the Beersheba Valley, are similar finds: remains from the Persian period were discovered in excavations conducted here by Y. Aharoni. The Persian-period remains were included in Stratum V. Only a few walls were attributed to this period, and the excavator assumed that the buildings of this period stood in the center of the mound and were demolished during the construction of a Hellenistic tower. Persian-period pottery was found in a disturbed stratigraphical context, but mainly in twenty pits containing ash, bones, pottery vessels, and ostraca. The pits also contained Attic ware of the 5th to 4th centuries BCE. The principal find from this period consists of some eighty-five Aramaic ostraca. Their script was dated by J. Naveh to the middle of the 4th century BCE, like that of the ostraca from Tel Sheva and Tell el-Kheleifeh. All ostraca from Arad date to the same generation, since they are all signed by the same official (probably the commander of Arad), called Yido'a. The ostraca are receipts of confirming the delivery of various types of food for men and animals (horses, donkeys, and camels). The food mentioned includes flour, barley, grain, oil, and wine (*ḥmr*). Also included are the names of those who received the supplies and their function. In Naveh's opinion, at least part of this food was intended for soldiers, for one of the ostraca mentions a certain person who belonged to the *degel* of 'Ebed-nanai, i.e., a soldier belonging to a military regiment headed by 'Ebed-nanai (a Babylonian deity's name). This was apparently the Persian military division known from the Elephantine papyri. Also mentioned are three men who held the title "commander of ten" (a cavalry unit). Other officials are the *ganzabar* ("treasurer"), 'Aqabiah, who was in charge of ten donkey drivers, and 'Anani, who owned a storehouse or was in charge of a granary. It is interesting that most of the functionaries at Arad were Jews, except for the Babylonian commander of the *degel* ("regiment"). The personal names on the Arad ostraca, on the other hand, are mostly Arab and some are Edomite. These names undoubtedly reflect the population of Arad and the ethnic composition of those serving there. Y. Aharoni originally suggested that there was a direct relationship between the Arad ostraca and Tell el-Kheleifeh and that the fortresses at these two sites guarded the main route descending from Arad through the Aravah to Eilat. Naveh maintained that because of its geographic position, Arad served as a link between the cities of Judah and the Negev, the Aravah, Edom, and Philistia and that the horsemen and donkey drivers mentioned in the ostraca, in addition to belonging to the garrison force that defended the fort and the roads, may also have operated a wide range of communication and mail services, including the transport of various merchandise and food to the military units and royal officials stationed at distant posts in the Negev and the desert.

At the southern end of the Aravah, excavations conducted by N. Glueck at **Tell el-Kheleifeh** revealed a Persian-period stratum of occupation (Stratum V). In his survey of the excavation results (which were not altered later by G. D. Pratico in his comprehensive reappraisal), it was stated that an "industrial settlement" located here in this period was constructed on a new plan which bore no resemblance to that of the previous phases dating from the end of the 6th or beginning of the 5th to the 4th centuries BCE. A few Attic potsherds mentioned in the report were dated by the excavator mainly to the 5th century BCE. Also found in Stratum V was a number of ostraca, the majority being lists of names. Several were receipts of wine deliveries. In N. Glueck's opinion, these ostraca were written in Aramaic and dated to the 5th to 4th centuries BCE. Two of the ostraca were later discussed by J. Naveh, who attributed the Edomite ostracon to the 7th to 6th centuries BCE (see above), while, in his view, the other ostracon was written in Phoenician (and not Aramaic) and contained a Phoenician onomasticon. Three other Aramaic ostraca published earlier by Glueck were assigned by him to the beginning of the 4th century BCE. Thus, of the five published ostraca, four have been dated by consensus to the Persian period.

Much farther along the road to Egypt lies another Persian-period fortress at **Kadesh-Barnea.** Here, in a brief excavation conducted by M. Dothan in 1956, the third and uppermost stratum was attributed to the Persian period. The walls of the previous Judaean fort lay in ruins at this time, but its inner space was used as a dwelling and new structures were also built. Among the finds from this stratum, the excavator mentions local and imported Greek ware from the 5th century BCE. The beginning of the settlement of the Persian period at Kadesh-Barnea was dated by the excavator to the end of the 6th or beginning of the 5th century BCE. The date of its destruction was not ascertained, however; since no Hellenistic remains were found, it was assumed to have come to an end during the Persian period.

The site was re-excavated in the 1970s by R. Cohen. His results indicate, too, that in the 5th and 4th centuries BCE an unfortified settlement was established at the site on the remains of the upper Judaean fort. Several of the early casemate rooms, primarily those on the eastern side of the fort, were used as temporary dwellings. In the northern part of the site, a small room of the "postexilic" period was uncovered; a similar room was found on the southern part of the mound. However, most of the finds from this period were discovered in pits dug into the earlier levels. These again included local wares and Greek imports. Another important find was a *yehud* seal impression, common in Persian-period Judah, but never before found outside the boundaries of the Judaean province. It is possible that the fort at Kadesh-Barnea was on the road used mainly by Jews who made their way between Judah and their settlements in Egypt, thus continuing a long tradition (see above). An ostracon inscribed with the words '*skr tb* was also found here. The meaning of these Hebrew words is "offering" or "merchandise" (cf. Psalm 72:10 and Ezekiel 27:15).

In a survey conducted in the **Hebron Hills** by S. Gutman and M. Kochavi in 1968, pottery of the Persian period was uncovered at six sites (Khirbet

Canaan, Khirbet El-Marjim, Khirbet Tarma, Khirbet el-Hadav, Tel Zif, and Tell Rabud). Three of these sites were founded in the Persian period. Two tombs of this period were discovered by chance, one at Eshtemoa and the other at 'Ain 'Arrub (see below).

More surveys were conducted in the 1980s and 1990s by A. Ofer and Y. Baruch, followed by some excavations that uncovered a few additional Persian-period sites. Baruch came to the conclusion that during the Persian period settlements on the Hebron Hills ridge were nearly as numerous as at the end of the period of the Judaean monarchy and included mainly small settlements defended by a few central fortresses.

In the numerous surveys carried out throughout the **Negev,** no Persian-period settlement has been found, with the exception of Ḥorvat Ritma, near Sede Boqer. This site was excavated by Z. Meshel, who was of the opinion that it was not an actual settlement, rather, a way station that was located on the spice-trade route crossing the Negev Hills, which connected to roads leading to Arabia. R. Cohen later conducted more surveys, followed by test probes in this region and in the southern Negev. He found four more Persian-period fortresses at Ḥorvat Masorah, Naḥal Ro'ah, Yatir, and Be'erotaim. All were constructed according to the same plan: they measure approximately 21 sq. m. each and consist of nine rooms surrounding a square central courtyard. Cohen thought that they had been erected during the 7th century BCE during the period of the Judaean monarchy and were renewed and continued in use within the framework of Persian imperial administration. The road along which they were erected led from Arad to Kadesh-Barnea and on to Egypt. This view is shared by Z. Meshel, who has pointed out that despite the scarcity of Persian-period sites, their distribution closely parallels that of sites during the Judaean monarchy, along the route that crosses the central Negev highlands to the west, through Kadesh-Barnea. This road is still known today in Arabic as Darb al-Ghazza (the road to Gaza), and it still connects the southern Mediterranean coastal cities of Palestine with Elath and Ezion-Geber on the Red Sea. The settlements along the route should all be interpreted as centers of supply and way stations for the small army garrisons that kept the roads to Gaza and Egypt open for traders and travelers.

THE TRANSJORDANIAN PROVINCES

IN TRANSJORDAN, MOST of the excavations in which Persian-period remains have been uncovered are situated around Rabbath-Ammon, primarily in the line of fortresses that surrounded the capital city during the period of the Ammonite kingdom or among the towns on its southern boundary, including Heshbon and Tell el-ʿUmeiri. A second group was uncovered in the Ammonite part of the central Jordan Valley at Tell es-Saʿidiyeh, Tell el-Mazar, and Tell Nimrin. The situation in Moab and Edom remains unclear.

We shall begin our discussion with the Jordan Valley sites. At **Tell es-Saʿidiyeh,** remains of a "palace" were discovered in excavations carried out by J. B. Pritchard on the summit of the mound, beneath a large Hellenistic building of the 2nd century BCE. The structure is square in plan, each side 24 m. long, with an open central court surrounded by rooms on all sides, constructed of mud bricks on a stone foundation. Tiles found in several rooms attest to the manner in which the palace was roofed. On the floor of one of the rooms was found a limestone incense altar decorated with incised geometric designs, a horseman, and the name *yknw,* apparently the name of the altar's owner. The finds also included a common Persian-period clay figurine of a pregnant woman.

More Persian-period remains have been uncovered at **Tell el-Mazar.** The finds from a large cemetery (Cemetery A) at this site have been published (see below). On the mound itself, two Persian-period strata were found. Stratum I dates to the 4th century BCE and was probably destroyed by Alexander the Great. It included mainly rounded storage pits. In several cases, these cut through Strata II, III, and IV walls and deposits. Some of the pits were over 2 m. in diameter and more than 4 m. deep. Some had a brick lining preserved up to 3 m. The floors of the pits were of bricks, stone, or clay. The round shape of these granaries suggests that they had conical roofs. Similar pits or granaries were also found at Tell es-Saʿidiyeh and Deir ʿAlla. In shape and function, they closely resemble the round granaries of Philistia (see above) and may have served as supply centers for the army units stationed in the region.

Stratum II at Tell el-Mazar (5th century BCE) was composed of parts of three buildings. These were private dwellings, for they contained domestic utensils. Each building consists of a central open courtyard enclosed on three or four sides by architectural units. The excavators also point to the fact that this stratum was built above a thick destruction deposit dated to the end of the Iron Age.

Farther south in the Jordan Valley is the recently excavated site of **Tell Nimrin,** which also had two Persian-period strata. Following its destruction in the 7th century BCE and a 50–100-year period of abandonment, the site was resettled. In both strata, clay vessels and other Persian-period finds were encountered. Most important was the find of an Aramaic ostracon in the up-per stratum dating to the late 5th or early 4th century BCE, which mentions the delivery of one and a half *garev* ("jar"), sent by two locals. The name of one is 'Abd-'ate; the second is 'Aqqub, the slave of Bgwp, perhaps a Persian dignitary or official.

In addition to these sites in the Jordan Valley, more sites were excavated in the Rabbath-Ammon region. Among these is **Heshbon,** where a Persian-period stratum was uncovered. Outstanding among the remains is a section of the acropolis wall, which was preserved to a height of 3 to 5 m. At the east side of this wall, remains of a tower were cleared, which the excavator con-sidered to be part of a gate. A few Aramaic ostraca were also discovered. The other site in this region is **Tell el-'Umeiri,** where, again, two relevant oc-cupation strata were encountered. In the earlier of the two (Stratum V), a structure was uncovered, which was interpreted as an administrative center in the service of the Persian provincial administration. Here were found two stamped jar handles, each bearing the same inscription: *shuba Ammon,* i.e., the name of the province of Ammon. These are the first known examples of Persian seals of the province of Ammon. The upper stratum included re-mains of Persian-period dwellings. It seems that another Persian-period stratum was also uncovered recently at nearby **Tell Ṣafut,** but we still lack details.

Most important were the excavations conducted within the "Ammonite towers" encircling the capital city of Rabbath-Ammon (see above), in some of which Persian-period remains were recovered. One of these was the tower at **Khirbet el-Hajar** that had been destroyed in 580 BCE and was reused in the Persian period, as shown by a Sidonian coin of 400 BCE found in it. Another excavated tower is at **Tell el-Dreijat,** also destroyed in 580 BCE. Its excavator claims that it was reused in the Persian period.

Also important are the tombs from this period found near Rabbath-Ammon many years after W. F. Albright concluded that one of the "Am-monite tombs" near the capital city at the site of **Meqabelein** dates to the Persian period. The Meqabelein tomb was rich with metal objects of types later encountered at Tell el-Mazar (see below). In recent years, more tombs of this type have been excavated very close to the "Ammonite towers." At the site of **Khilda,** two tombs were found about 75 m. from the tower. Both were rich with imported Babylonian-Persian seals and metal vessels. In one of them, a complete 5th century BCE Attic *lekythos* was found. It is noteworthy that most of the pottery found here was clearly Ammonite and bore a close resemblance to Ammonite pottery of the 7th century BCE, though typologically late and reminiscent of the finds from the Meqabelein tomb. These finds probably testify to the renewal of the settlements here in the Persian period by the original local population. A similar find was uncovered in the Ammonite tower at **Umm Uthainah,** which also included a mix of Ammonite pottery, metal vessels, seals, and a few Attic vessels. This peculiar assemblage of finds has occurred again and again in recent excavations (another group is known from **Abu Nuseir**), and probably attests to the continuation of Ammonite pottery into the Persian period, as Albright suggested many years ago. It also points to the reuse of "Ammonite towers" by the Persian administration in order to defend the capital city of Rabbath-Ammon, as was done previously by the Assyrians (see above). L. Herr recently reported that in his excavations at Tell el-'Umeiri, Ammonite pottery types usually dated to the Late Iron Age were found in a stratigraphic context with Attic shards and cylinder seals attributed by the experts to the late 6th and the 5th centuries BCE.

In **Moab,** we lack, for the time being, excavations that will contribute to our knowledge of the Persian period. In any case, during the excavations of the capital city of **Dibon,** no Persian-period remains were recovered. The only major find was the chance discovery of an Aramaic dedicatory inscription at **Kerak** (biblical Kir-Moab), assigned by J. T. Milik to the end of the Persian period. This is an inscription dedicated to the Moabite deity Kemosh and his consort, Sara, by a certain Hillel bar 'Ama. Despite the Aramaic script and the dedication to Kemosh, Milik interpreted the donor's name as Arabic and claimed that he was a member of the Qedarite Arabs; however, this hardly seems plausible.

The situation in **Edom** is quite different. Persian-period remains were uncovered at two of the three major Edomite cities excavated by C. M. Bennett, i.e., Tawilan and Buseirah. (At the third, Umm el-Biyara, no Persian-period remains were found. It was destroyed in 580 BCE and never rebuilt.) At **Tawilan,** a Neo-Babylonian cuneiform tablet was found, which dates to the accession year of an Achaemenid king named Darius: i.e., Darius I (521 BCE, the most likely candidate), Darius II (423 BCE), or Darius III (335 BCE). The tablet could have given us a date for the occupation level at Tawilan, but was unfortunately found in a deposit postdating the end of Edomite monarchy, which cannot be definitively linked to any clear stratum. In any case, besides providing absolute evidence for the existence of the site in the Persian period, it attests to the importance of the trade route that passed there to Haran and Babylon. It is also interesting to note that among its inhabitants were a few able to read this cuneiform script. Also discovered here was a hoard of jewelry dated to the 6th to 5th centuries BCE, further attesting to the site's connections with other parts of the Achaemenid empire.

At the capital of Edom, **Buṣeirah** (Bozrah), according to C. M. Bennett and P. Bienkowski, one of the largest administrative buildings of the Late Iron Age discovered in this country, the so-called Winged Building (Building A), which replaced an earlier building of the Edomite period there (see above), may conceivably be dated as late as the Persian period. This suggestion is based on the similarity in plan of Building A to that of a building in another area (C), which contained Persian pottery. Following the Persian-period occupation, the site was abandoned.

From the southern part of Edom, recent surveys and excavations in the copper mines of **Feinan** provide evidence for the renewal of work there during the Persian period, continuing to ca. 400 BCE. An interesting assemblage of the period's pottery also came from a nearby site called **Khirbet el-Jariyeh.** Similar results were also obtained from the various surveys conducted in this region and especially the one recently conducted by S. Hart, who, however, reached the conclusion that civilization on the Edomite plateau collapsed sometime in the 5th century BCE and did not emerge again until the Nabataean period.

This state of affairs, however, was not confirmed by the results of the excavation at **Tell el-Kheleifeh** on the Red Sea coast at the southern end of the Aravah. The Period V settlement there is dated to the Persian period, though its population at this time was no longer Edomite. According to the evidence of the ostraca and pottery found in this stratum, its population consisted of Phoenicians and Greeks! Here, too, the site was totally abandoned after the Persian period and was not resettled even by the Nabataeans. An interesting question is, what were Phoenicians and Greeks, usually located along the Mediterranean coast, doing in such a remote site? In fact, we should not be surprised to find them at any site that served as a trading post. Besides the many Attic vases and Greek wine amphorae, Greek presence is also attested by Greek coins and their local imitations, as well as the use of Greek words and titles in the Persian-period ostraca found here. As to the Phoenicians, evidence for their presence here is more direct. Among the ostraca found in Period V, one contains a list of Phoenician names. Among these is Ebed-Ashmun, i.e., a Sidonian (for Ashmun was the god of the city of Sidon). This is not surprising, for as we have already seen, the Phoenicians settled along the southern coast of Philistia and along the coasts of northern Sinai during the Persian period (see above).

Summing up the archaeological-historical picture of Transjordan that emerges in the Persian period, our knowledge of settlements and population there does not exceed what we know of the Negev and other semidesert areas. Initially, results of the extensive surveys conducted in this region by N. Glueck revealed that the kingdoms of Transjordan suffered total destruction in the 6th century BCE, leaving the area without permanent population for a considerable period of time. More recently, surveys and excavations have changed this picture considerably, providing results that could have been anticipated on the basis of the historical records alone. The books of Ezra and Nehemiah refer to Persian provinces in this area. In the book of Nehemiah, Tobiah is several times called "the Ammonite servant" (2:19; 4:1; 6:1), which is usually interpreted as "servant of the king," i.e., an official in the service of the king of Persia. Tobiah himself may have belonged to a family that ruled the entire province from his capital (the Tyre of the Tobiads).

Like Ammon, Moab, too, probably became a province during the Persian period. At any rate, at the time of the first wave of repatriates, Jewish families of the "province of Moab" are mentioned (Ezra 2:6; 8:4; 10:30; Nehemiah 7:1). The existence of Ammon and Moab as national entities in the 5th century BCE is indicated by the fact that foreign women who married Jews at that time included the "wives of Ammon and Moab" (Nehemiah 13:23). J. M. Grintz even interpreted the phrase "those who dwell in Moab and the Ammonites" in Judith 1:2 as the author's reference to actual Ammonites and Moabites who still occupied the area in the 4th century BCE. Confirmation may be contained in the Wadi ed-Daliyeh papyri of the 4th century, which mention inhabitants of Samaria bearing names with components such as Kemosh and Qos.

The **archaeological** evidence of the above-mentioned seal impressions from Tell el-ʿUmeiri, in which the Persian-period province of "Ammon" is named, clearly indicates Ammon's existence as a separate province during the Persian period. The many excavations and surveys conducted in these regions indicate that this was a flourishing and prosperous period in Ammon and Moab. We may also assume that during the Persian period—as in the Assyrian period—this coincided with the renewal of international trade along the King's Highway, which crossed Transjordan from south to north and continued on to Syria and Mesopotamia. Evidence for this includes the rich finds in silos, fortresses, administrative centers, and dwellings in sites along the Jordan Valley, as well as at Rabbath-Ammon and its surroundings. Most important was the reconstruction of the previous defensive system around the capital city of Ammon, i.e., the line of "Ammonite towers," the rebuilding of the settlements at Heshbon and Tell el-ʿUmeiri, etc. The same is true of the many tombs uncovered in Ammon, which included rich finds from the Persian period, around Rabbath-Ammon and in the Jordan Valley. In Edom, too (we still lack evidence from Moab), we witness the rebuilding of large public structures in its capital city of Bozrah (Buṣeirah) and in neighboring towns. Even more important is the renewal of work at the Feinan mines and the revival of international trade, which was probably badly hurt during the Babylonian period, with Phoenician, Greek, and probably also Edomite and Arab help. This trade, via the Red Sea (Tell el-Kheleifeh), linked the Arabian peninsula with the Mediterranean coast. It also carried merchandise along the King's Highway across the Transjordanian plateau, as indicated in the Neo-Babylonian tablet from Tawilan, dated to the reign of Darius II.

· Chapter 2 ·

ARCHITECTURE

TOWN PLANNING

In spite of the large number of sites in Palestine yielding Persian-period artifacts, not many building remains have been uncovered, and even less evidence has been preserved permitting reconstruction of city plans. The paucity of architectural remains recovered during decades of archaeological investigation is surprising, particularly in view of the fact that this is a relatively late period during which here, as in Persia and Greece, high building standards were achieved. This period also witnessed the development of the Hippodamian plan (named for the 5th century BCE Greek architect from Miletus who was the first to write about the "correct" principles of town planning), in which the streets of the city were laid out on a grid, an arrangement that became common practice in subsequent periods. The scarcity of finds from this period is regarded by some scholars as a peculiarity of Palestine, reflecting widespread destruction at the end of the First Temple period. Theories put forward by W. F. Albright, K. M. Kenyon, and others concerning "a cessation of town life in the Persian period" and "concentration of the population in villages" appear to have less to do with the actual situation at that time than with the incomplete nature of the archaeological data. Three characteristic features of the Persian-period strata contributed to the creation of this picture: 1. In the Persian period, numerous mounds were abandoned and never resettled. Since the stratum from this period was the uppermost on the site, it was exposed to erosion and other depredations. 2. At those sites in which settlement continued, the Persian-period occupation levels were severely damaged by intensive building activities conducted during the Hellenistic-Roman periods. 3. At most of the large excavated sites of this period, the mound was occupied by a palace-fort or other building. These three factors can explain the relatively disappointing results of the excavations at the major mounds. During the past decades, this overall picture has changed as a result of new excavations, particularly that at Dor, which revealed well-planned towns. The results of surveys and excavations in settlements of the Persian period throughout Palestine also reveal a different picture of urban life in different regions. We lack a full account of the cities in the hill country. The coastal plain, on the other hand (and perhaps Galilee as well), was very densely populated in this period and, without doubt, the scene of active urban life. It is sufficient in this matter to recall Herodotus' description of Gaza (3.5). Indeed, examination of the building remains in this region reveals several examples of well-planned settlements: careful study of the plans of cities outside Palestine shows that most were built according to the Hippodamian plan, i.e., dividing the residential areas into symmetrical blocks, separated by streets that cross each other at right angles. It is important to note that this plan assigned different functions to different parts of the town: there were residential, public, cultic, sport, and other zones. The clearest examples of a classical Hippodamian plan can be seen at Olynthus in Macedonia and at Berytus in Phoenicia.

In the coastal region of Palestine, there are several examples of well-planned towns. A certain amount of planning may be observed in the cities excavated at Tel Nahariya and Acco as well as the latest city at Abu Hawam. Here, the front of a building facing a main road that ran roughly parallel to the longitudinal axis of the city was uncovered. At Shiqmona, a residential quarter consisting of two streets set at right angles to one another contained houses constructed with considerable symmetry. A similar discovery was made in the excavations at neighboring Tel Megadim, where a built-up quarter intersected by a broad straight thoroughfare was excavated. The large blocks of buildings on either side of the road were separated by lanes crossing the main road at right angles. The houses themselves are divided into a number of smaller units of similar plan.

Remains of well-planned cities of the Persian period were also uncovered along the southern coast at Ashdod, Tell el-Ḥesi, and Ashkelon. At the last site, an impressive ashlar-built emporium has been uncovered, with six rectangular rooms.

But the major example of Hippodamian plan in a Persian-period town in Palestine is the city uncovered at **Tel Dor.** The closest parallel to the plan of

Persian-period Dor is Olynthus in Macedonia. Even a superficial glance at the plans of these two cities shows this very clearly.

The picture emerging from the investigations at Dor presents us with a long row of stores and workshops along the entire length of the inner face of the city wall. The doors of the shops opened onto a ruler-straight street, running parallel to the wall from north to south. On the opposite side of the street, which is approximately 2 m. wide, was found the fine facade of a long narrow block of residential buildings. The eastern doors of each unit of houses open onto the street, opposite the row of shops. The building is about 20 m. wide. Its western side, which faces another street, parallel to that on its east, was also uncovered. This elongated block of buildings, preserved to a height of over 2 m. and traced for tens of meters, was probably crossed by passages leading from one street to the other, but these seem to fall outside the areas thus far excavated. Another, identical building or block of houses existed to the west of this second street. The block was divided lengthwise and widthwise by partition walls into smaller units or "apartments," the doors of which opened onto the closest street. It is reasonable to assume that while only the ground floor remains today, another story rose above it. The easternmost street, between the residences and the stores, appears to have originally been roofed to provide an overhang for pedestrians.

On the basis of the finds, the structure described above was in use throughout the Persian and Hellenistic periods. It seems not to have been violently destroyed, at least not until the days of Alexander Jannaeus, but was rebuilt from time to time. With each reconstruction, the floor was raised, resulting in as many as two Persian and three Hellenistic floor levels; the openings were blocked and the walls rebuilt on a higher level. In this way, from one phase to the next, the inner divisions of the building and the function of its rooms varied; for example, in one stage, two plastered storage pools for water were added. However, none of the alterations changed the external walls. Many coins were found on the different floors, as well as stamped handles from Greek wine amphorae, yielding reliable dates for the different stages. The outer walls of the building were constructed in the usual style of the period, mostly of well-hewn hard sandstone ashlars laid as headers. The inner walls and partitions, however, were built in typical Phoenician style of ashlar piers with rubble fill.

The surprising fact about these town plans is that, while Olynthus appears to have been laid out in the 4th century BCE, i.e., *after* the time of Hippodamus and the publication of his writings, Dor was probably laid out in its earliest form in the late 6th century BCE, *before* Hippodamus, and may have even served as one of the examples that inspired his theories.

FORTIFICATIONS

DEFENSIVE WALLS ASSIGNED by their excavators to the Persian period have been uncovered at a few sites, such as Acco, Tell Abu Hawam, Gilʻam, Megiddo, Tel Megadim, Tel Mevorakh, Dor, Mikhmoret, Tell Abu Zeitun, Jaffa, Tell el-Ḥesi, Ruqeish, and elsewhere. All these towns are located along the coast and in the nearby Shephelah. Remains of walls have also been cleared at Samaria, Jerusalem, Tell en-Naṣbeh, and Lachish, and at Heshbon in Transjordan. Some of the walls, especially those that continued the earlier defense systems, such as the walls of Megiddo, Dor, and Ruqeish, were thick, usually of offset-inset type; others were of casemate type. These were usually built in Phoenician style. By far the best preserved fortifications of the period have been uncovered at Tel Dor. These prove a good source of information for a renewed study of the process of Hellenization that took place in Palestine in the 4th to 3rd centuries BCE. For most of the Persian period, Dor's fortifications remained the same as those of the preceding period, i.e., the last city wall built in the Iron Age, which was actually the Assyrian wall, with offsets and insets and a two-chambered gate. We can say that this wall protected the city for almost the entire Persian period (the same is true at Megiddo and Ruqeish). This massive and sophisticated fortification system was destroyed by the Persians when they suppressed the great Phoenician revolt against Persian rule in the mid-4th century BCE (see above).

Judging from the archaeological evidence revealed in the excavations, a new fortification system was built at Dor very soon afterward—still in the 4th century BCE. The outer line of this city wall was built almost directly above the line of the earlier offset-inset one, though this time it ran along a straight line, apart from a few small projections. This line was formed of buildings constructed close together in the space between the city wall and the inner street. Their outer walls, over a meter thick, formed the external defensive line. The interesting feature of this fortification system is its method of construction: it is quite clear that the Phoenician tradition of building was still employed here in the mid-4th century BCE. The outer wall and all the inner dividing walls were built in the style characteristic of this tradition: ashlar piers laid in header-and-stretcher fashion, i.e., with one stone lengthwise and two widthwise across the pier, with fieldstone fill between them. As far as we know, all the city walls of coastal Palestine and Phoenicia were built in this way during the Persian period. Up to now, this construction method has been observed at Persian Acco, Tell Abu Hawam, Megadim, Tel Mevorakh, Mikhmoret, Jaffa, and elsewhere. At Dor, however, another construction method was also observed in a public building on the southern coast of the city. The walls were built with fieldstone filling set between large stone monoliths instead of the usual built piers. This construction technique is, along the Palestinian and Phoenician coasts, unique to Dor. It was, however, the most commonly used Punic construction technique in the western Mediterranean. Some parts of these Phoenician walls have been preserved to a height of over 2 m. and are among the most impressive of their kind yet found in Palestine.

During the 3rd century BCE, when this last Phoenician wall of the 4th century BCE and associated buildings were apparently still standing, the city received a new fortification system. The wall was built in a totally Greek style previously encountered only rarely at other sites in Palestine, in particular at Berytus, Acco, Samaria, and Maresha, which became Greek settlements at the very beginning of the Macedonian conquest.

During the 4th century BCE, as we have already seen, many city fortifications of the old offset-inset style were destroyed. They were soon replaced by fortresses that were built on the higher parts of many of the mounds of the country. These were constructed following the traditional Mesopotamian plan, which had penetrated into Palestine during the Assyrian period (see above). The plan consisted of a large open court surrounded by rooms on all sides. Such fortresses have been found in the north on the mounds of Hazor, Tel Chinnereth, Megiddo, Acco, and Gilʿam. Along the coast they were encountered at Shiqmona, Megadim, Dor, Tel Mevorakh, Mikhmoret, Tel Michal, and Tell Qasile, and along the southern coast and in Philistia at Ashdod, Tell Jemmeh, Tell el-Farʿah (S), Tel Seraʿ, Tel Haror, and other sites. One is known from Transjordan at Tell es-Saʿidiyeh. In the mountainous region of Judah, some old forts utilized during the Late Iron Age were rebuilt and reused, as at Khirbet Abu Tuwein and elsewhere. It is significant that several forts of nearly identical plan were built along the major highways, some replacing earlier Assyrian ones. These include one rebuilt at Rishon le-Zion and another at a site north of Ashdod, which guarded the Via Maris to Egypt. Others were newly added to the previous line in this period, such as the fort recently found at Naḥal Tut along the road leading through Wadi

Milek from Dor to Jokneam, or the nearby fort at 'En Ḥofez, or Khirbet Luzifar in the Hebron mountains. These are but a few examples.

In addition to the city walls and forts described above, there are also remains of several city gates, though such evidence remains scant.

The most important of the Persian-period gates discovered to date is at Dor. It is a two-chambered gate attached to the offset-inset wall described above. The entire fortification system was first built by the Assyrians and remained in use through the mid-4th century BCE. The same appears to hold true as regards the city wall and gate of Megiddo, which shares a similar history to that of Dor during this period (see above), as well as other settlements where Assyrian fortifications had remained intact. At Dor, the two-chambered gate was replaced in the early Hellenistic period by a new gate, built according to newly introduced Greek concepts.

In the hill country, however, with the exception of the Valley Gate in Jerusalem, which Kathleen Kenyon assigned to the Persian period (though its final dating must await a more thorough investigation), a gate complex of the Persian period has been discovered only at Lachish. According to Olga Tufnell, this gate was poorly constructed above the last Judaean gate of Stratum II and following the same plan. It included an outer gate (which continued from Stratum II), only the threshold of which has survived, and an inner

III.16 The Persian residency at Lachish: plan and reconstruction

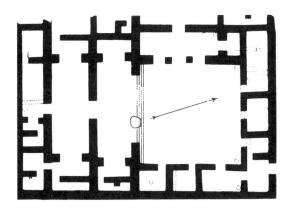

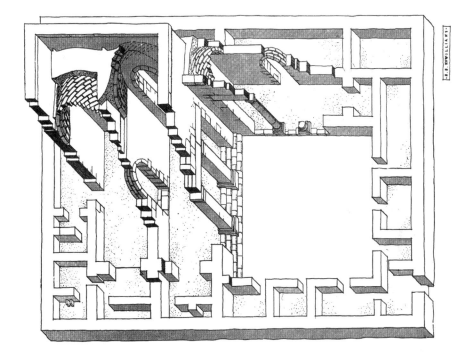

gate. The walls connecting the inner and outer gates were also destroyed. The inner gate again followed the plan of the Stratum II gate, but its entrance was narrowed from 4 m. to 3.6 m. A threshold of undressed stones replaced an earlier one of well-dressed stones. Both sides of the gate were enlarged, forming two towers with steps leading up to them. Remains of a building interpreted as a gatehouse were attached to the gate on the inside. The rest of the area was occupied by an open square. The approach to the gate and its inner area were plastered with clay and soft chalk, which was laid on a gravel base and packed hard by treading and ordinary use. A drain ran out of the square.

RESIDENTIAL STRUCTURES

AN EXAMINATION OF Persian-period buildings indicates that most followed a surprisingly uniform plan, regardless of whether they were for private or public use. As previously mentioned, this building type is known as the "open-court house." It consists of an open courtyard surrounded by rooms on several or on all sides. It was introduced to Palestine during the Assyrian period and continued without modification into the Babylonian and Persian periods. The first to recognize the Mesopotamian origins of this plan were R. Amiran and I. Dunayevsky, as a result of the excavation of such a structure at Hazor. But they wrongly assumed that one may differentiate between the Assyrian and Persian variants. It now appears that while they were right about the Mesopotamian origin of such structures, all such buildings in both Assyrian and Persian periods follow the same plan.

The only exception to the uniformity in plan noted up to now is the Residency at Lachish. Its main divergence from the standard plan is its two wings of *hilani* type, which are not found elsewhere in Palestine during this period. Following her thorough investigation, O. Tufnell concurred with C. Watzinger's interpretation that the building follows a Syro-Hittite plan. Both, however, encountered difficulties in locating appropriate parallels. The closest parallel presented by Tufnell is the palace of the Assyrian governor at Arslan Tash, which is hardly identical in plan. The difficulty in finding examples similar to the Lachish Residency led W. F. Albright to a far-fetched comparison: he likened it to the early Parthian palaces, such as the small palace at Nippur in Babylon. The latter, however, is of later date and could not therefore have served as a source of inspiration for the builders of the palace at Lachish. In a later study, Y. Aharoni defined the plan of the Residency as a combination of a Syrian *hilani* building and an Assyrian open-court house. This last interpretation accurately conveys the essence of the building, which represents a fusion of two different building styles. For this reason, early scholars found it difficult to draw comparisons. Moreover, the combination of two separate plans in a single building is one of the characteristics of provincial Persian palaces. The Lachish Residency, therefore, seems to have been constructed under Achaemenid influence. Its appearance among the buildings of the Persian period in Palestine can be explained by the fact that it is the only building that was undoubtedly a palace; the others may have served different purposes. In a recent study, R. Reich has urged that the Beth-Zur Phase II citadel, which resembles the Lachish Residency in plan, should also be regarded as a Persian residency. Even if the details of its plan are agreed upon, it lacks many features of the Lachish Residency. Up to now, however, no true Achaemenian palace structure has been unearthed in Palestine. The closest example so far is the palace excavated at Sidon. It appears to be the only one discovered in the entire area of the Abar Nahara satrapy.

· Chapter 3 ·

BURIAL CUSTOMS

Burials of the Persian period have been found in all parts of Palestine. Several have been excavated in the Galilee and the Jezreel Valley: at Hazor (in both Y. Yadin's and A. Ben-Tor's excavations), at Khirbet Ibsan, at 'En ha-Naẓiv, and at Mishmar ha-'Emeq. Most, however, have been discovered along the coast: a large group from three cemeteries at Achzib, Shavei Ẓion, a large cemetery north of Acco, Beth ha-'Emeq, Loḥamei ha-Geta'ot, and Yas'our. Farther to the south along the Carmel coast and in the Sharon Plain, Persian-period burials have been found at 'Atlit (a large cemetery, rich in artifacts), at Dor, and at Tel Michal. In the southern part of the coast, they are known from Azor, Bat-Yam, Ashkelon, Tell el-Ḥesi, Tell el-Far'ah (S), and from Gaza itself. From the Samaria Hills comes an important tomb, discovered at Shechem. In Judah, too, a few Persian-period tombs have been excavated: some from Benjamin at sites including Naḥshonim, Tell el-Ful, and Abu Ghosh, and others from Jerusalem and its surroundings, Beth-Shemesh, and Gezer. In Idumaea, tombs have been found at Lachish, Horvat Beth Loyah, Eshtemoa, and 'Ain 'Arrub near Hebron. Some tombs are also known east of the Jordan River, all from the vicinity of Rabbath-Ammon, where settlement started in the Late Iron Age and continued almost uninterrupted through the Persian period. Finds here have included some Attic vases. Tombs have been excavated at Meqabelein, Umm Uthainah, and Khilda. A large cemetery recently excavated at Tell el-Mazar in the Jordan Valley is mainly attributed to the Babylonian period (see above). Finds there included clay coffins of Mesopotamian type, which may also date to the Persian period. The monumental rock-cut tombs of the Tobiad family at 'Iraq el-Emir should be mentioned in this context. To this list should now be added the two "tumulus" tombs found in the Jordan Valley (at Yafit), attributed by Y. Magen to the Persian period.

This constitutes a large enough group to enable us to create a typology and to draw conclusions regarding style. Significantly, all the tombs in Palestine from this period have close parallels in neighboring lands, many of which are dated. During this period, Palestine was but one small part of a huge empire.

A survey of all the Persian-period tombs in Palestine clearly shows that most belong to two distinctive types: **cist graves** and **shaft tombs.** The two types are distinct in almost every aspect: shape, content, and distribution. In addition to these two types, some simple, rectangular pit graves have also been unearthed. These can be divided, on the basis of their contents, into the cist and shaft categories.

The **cist graves** are usually rectangular rock-cut tombs in mountain regions. In sandy areas, they are built tombs surrounded by stone walls with stone floor and a cover. Sometimes they contain clay coffins in Mesopotamian style, inserted into a rectangular pit. Typically, they contain large assemblages of metal vessels in a characteristic Achaemenian style that will be described below. The clay vessels and other finds likewise reflect Achaemenian influence.

The most distinctive example of this type of burial is the "Achaemenian" tomb discovered at Shechem, dated to the second quarter of the 5th century BCE. This is a rock-cut tomb. Inside it was placed a clay coffin of

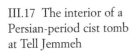

III.17 The interior of a Persian-period cist tomb at Tell Jemmeh

Mesopotamian type, decorated with a rope relief with numerous handles (utilized to lower the coffin into place) on both of its narrow sides.

The use of Mesopotamian-type clay coffins in Palestine began—as we have already seen—during the Assyrian period, when most coffins were small urns utilized for secondary burial rather than sarcophagi. They remained in use during the Babylonian period, but a larger type was then introduced, which could accommodate complete skeletons. One of these coffins, found in the large cemetery of Tell el-Mazar, where three cist tombs lined with bricks were also found, contained an assemblage of metal vessels and seals in Mesopotamian style. The coffin was dated by its excavator to the Babylonian period. Similar coffins discovered in Jerusalem and Tell en-Naṣbeh have likewise been attributed to the Babylonian period (see above), though it remains unclear whether they date to the middle of the 6th century BCE (Babylonian period) or to the late 6th century BCE (Persian period). They clearly reflect a Mesopotamian custom to be associated with the burial customs of the overlords of the country during these periods: Assyrians, Babylonians, or Persians. This practice was apparently introduced by the local administrators, some of whom were definitely outsiders posted in Palestine.

The rich metal assemblage found in the tomb at Shechem both inside and outside of the clay coffin was, in part—as proved by metallurgical analysis—imported from Iran, but partly produced in Palestine. Even the local pottery vessels found in this tomb differ from those found in the shaft tombs (see below).

In addition to those found at Shechem and Tell el-Mazar, cist tombs have also been discovered at Khilda in Jordan, Khirbet Ibsan in the Lower Galilee, in the Beth-Shean region, at Gezer, Lachish, Tell el-Far'ah (S), and elsewhere. Outside Palestine they occur in Syria, Anatolia, Mesopotamia, and Iran at sites including Ugarit, Deveh-Huyuk, Til Barsip, Babylon, Nippur, Kish, Ur, Susa, and Persepolis. Not a single example of this type of tomb has been discovered in the lands to the west of Syria and Palestine. The contents of all of the known tombs of this type found in Iran, Mesopotamia, Anatolia, Syria, and Palestine are remarkably uniform. For example, the finds from the Deveh-Huyuk tombs in Anatolia and those from the tomb at Gezer are quite similar. At all of the above-mentioned sites, such tombs are referred to as "Persian," "Achaemenian," or "Iranian" by the excavators. They should probably be attributed to Persian soldiers serving in the garrisons of the various provinces, or to the imperial civil administrators. In some cases, they may have belonged to local administrators or dignitaries who adopted the customs of the overlords, as a considerable portion of the

III.18 The Shechem tomb and the clay coffin found in it.

"Achaemenian" metal vessels were locally produced in Palestine, or by artisans working along the Phoenician coast.

The **shaft graves** are all distributed along the Palestinian coastal region and the Shephelah, from Achzib through Shavei Zion, Beth ha-ʿEmek, Acco,

Yasʿour, ʿAtlit, Dor, Mikhmoret, Bat-Yam, Ashkelon, and Gaza and certainly also along the Phoenician coast. There are no shaft tombs of this type in the eastern parts of Palestine or in neighboring lands. The shaft tombs are of two distinct types: rock-cut shaft tombs and built tombs. There is also an inter-mediate type, half rock-cut and half built. They differ from the cist tombs not only in shape but in content as well: Achaemenian vessels are not found in them, while many Phoenician and Greek vessels and other artifacts are. Out-side Palestine, they are found in Phoenicia, Cyprus, and the western Phoeni-cian colonies. Unlike the Palestinian examples, which are usually either individual burials or small groups of tombs, the typology of the Phoenician shaft tombs is substantiated by their large number, which permits statistical generalization. We assume that no marked difference will be observed in the development of the tomb types in Palestine and elsewhere. In Persian-period Palestine, all tombs of this type were concentrated in the coastal plain and in the Shephelah. They were apparently built by Phoenicians, as in Cyprus and Phoenicia, or under Phoenician influence. Typological comparison of the shaft tombs of Palestine and those of Cyprus and Phoenicia produces similar results. Within the Cypro-Phoenician sequence of development, the earliest Palestinian types appear to date to the 5th century and the latest to the 4th century BCE.

Two stone anthropoid sarcophagi have been found in shaft tombs in Palestine. This burial practice was very widespread on the Phoenician coast in the Persian period. The first sarcophagus was found many years ago at Gaza, and the fragment of a second was discovered at Shavei Ẓion, north of Acco. As it happened, the two sarcophagi represent two different styles. The coffin from Gaza is a fine example depicting the head of a woman in purely Greek style. Many very close parallels are known from Sidon. The fragment from Shavei Ẓion, portraying the head of a man in a local style, imitates an Egyptian prototype of a man wearing a wig and a false Osiris beard. It like-wise has parallels in Sidon. These coffins are assigned to the 5th or 4th cen-tury BCE. It is generally accepted that the origin of these sarcophagi was in Egypt. The earliest examples found on the Phoenician coast, made of stone imported from Egypt, are the coffins of the Sidonian kings Eshmunʿezer and Tabnit. An Egyptian inscription in hieroglyphics from the original burial is preserved on the coffin of the latter. These coffins were manufactured in Egypt at the end of the 26th Dynasty (i.e., from the 6th to the 4th centuries BCE). This form of burial was connected with the practice of embalming the dead. In later times, Phoenician artisans imitated the Egyptian sarcophagi using local basalt or limestone and occasionally pottery. The earliest imita-

III.19 Phoenician anthropoid sarcophagus from Gaza

tions preserved the original Egyptian motifs, and their heads bore additional features, such as the Egyptian headdress, the false beard, etc. This type of sarcophagus has been dated to the 5th century BCE. Toward the end of the century and especially in the 4th century BCE, Greek influence became stronger and the latest sarcophagi are rendered in a purely Greek style. The anthropoid coffins were very widely distributed in Phoenicia: at Sidon and its surroundings (Sarepta, 'Ain Ḥilweh, 'Ein Zeitun, Meimiyeh, el-Mahrah, Barami), Beirut, Byblos, Tripoli, and Arwad. None were found at Tyre itself, for this was probably a Sidonian burial custom. Other coffins have been found at Tarsus and Soloi on the Cilician coast, and in Cyprus, where several were uncovered at Amathus and Kition. This custom subsequently spread across the western Mediterranean to almost every large Phoenician settlement, especially those inhabited by Sidonians.

The **pit graves** constitute a third type of tombs during this period. These were the simplest form of burial and it is therefore not surprising to find them beyond Palestine, throughout the neighboring countries (both east and west) during the Persian period. The form of the grave itself is insignificant in this type of burial. In some cases, however, close parallels in content exist (local and Attic ware, typical jewelry, figurines, and Phoenician coins) be-

III.20 Persian-period pit graves from Tel Michal

tween these and the shaft tombs of Hazor, ʿAtlit, Tel Michal, and other sites, indicating burials of the same population. Other burials that contained "Persian" metal objects, such as the tomb at Khirbet Ibsan, should be related to the cist group.

To summarize, Persian-period tombs, like other aspects of Persian-period material culture in Palestine, may be classified into "eastern" and "western" types on the basis of form and content. While the shaft tombs contain an abundance of Greek and Phoenician pottery and Greek and Phoenician coins, jewelry, and cosmetic utensils, the cist tombs are characterized by metal objects and weapons in Achaemenid style. Aside from local pottery, there is marked similarity in the contents of the "eastern" tombs in all the lands from Persia to Palestine. Shaft tomb contents at all the sites are likewise similar.

As to the tombs that are neither "Achaemenian" nor "Phoenician," we know of only a few, mainly in the hill country and at Transjordanian sites. These include the tombs at Ketef Hinnom in Jerusalem, the tombs of the Tobiads, and tombs at Khilda, Amman, and Naḥshonim. This type appears to have continued the old burial tradition of rock-cut-bench rooms, either reused or newly dug in the Persian period. These tombs may have belonged to the old local population. It is noteworthy that from this period we sometimes find (as at Tel Michal in the Sharon Plain or at Tell el-Mazar in the Jordan River) infant burials in storage jars.

Another possible Persian-period tomb type is represented by the "tumuli" tombs of the Jordan Valley, which may also reflect a continuation of old local traditions. It remains impossible to attribute them to any specific ethnic group.

· Chapter 4 ·

TEMPLES AND CULT OBJECTS

THE TEMPLES

Only a few complete Persian-period sanctuaries have survived in Palestine or along the Phoenician coast. We shall describe most of these here. During this period, as in previous ones, they are divided into three types that are continuations of old local tradition: 1. Large, central, city temples, the most distinctive example of which is the so-called solar shrine at Lachish. 2. Medium-sized sanctuaries that have been uncovered at many sites, sometimes (as at Dor) with more than one at a given site. Some fine examples of this type are the sanctuary at Sarepta on the Phoenician coast and those at Mizpe Yammim in the Galilee and at Tel Michal (Makmish) in the Sharon Plain. 3. Small (ca. 1 sq. m.) chapels in which a sacred object stood: an idol or a *mazzebah* ("stela") stone, sometimes a few stelae together. It was impossible to enter such a chapel and worshipers remained outside, leaving their offerings near the entrance.

Each of these three types has close analogies, in both plan and dimensions, in previous periods. There can be no doubt that they perpetuate older traditions, not only in their plans but also as regards their contents and cult objects. There is, however, one major difference between the Persian-period temples and those of the Assyrian period: this is the surprising homogeneity of the finds. While during the Assyrian period, Phoenician, Philistine, Judaean, Edomite, and Ammonite cults are distinguishable because each ethnos had its own specific cult objects, during the Persian period this is no longer true. All finds at all sites throughout the country are nearly similar. It is impossible to say if a certain find comes from Idumaea, Philistia, Galilee, or even Phoenicia, although the chief deities of each people remained distinct: Qos in Idumaea, Baʿal in Phoenicia, etc. Another difference is, perhaps, even more meaningful: since the beginning of the Persian period, in all the territories of Judah and Samaria, there is not a single piece of evidence for any pagan cults! There are no sanctuaries (except, of course, for the Jewish one in Jerusalem and the Samaritan one on Mount Gerizim), no figurines, and no remains of any other pagan cultic objects. This is in sharp contrast to the late Judaean monarchic period. The only possible exception is the continuation of apotropaic cults intended to ward off evil spirits, bad luck, or disease. Such cults, however, are found almost uninterruptedly among all ethnic groups in the country in all periods. Some pagan motifs are depicted on the coins of Judah and Samaria. It is unclear, however, if they had any cultic significance or were merely copies of motifs borrowed from the coins of neighboring provinces of the empire (see below).

We shall now turn to a discussion of the period's **sanctuaries.** It has already been mentioned that of the Type A sanctuaries in Palestine, i.e., large central temples, only one clear example, the solar shrine at Lachish, is known. Of the medium-sized sanctuaries, we have three examples: at Sarepta, Tel Michal (Makmish), and Miẓpe Yammim. Of the third type, the small chapel, there are several examples, including the chapels at Tel Dan and Tel Michal. In Phoenicia, we find more sanctuaries, some of the large type and the rest of the medium size, which can serve as comparisons to Palestinian examples. One group, excavated on the Phoenician coast, includes examples at ʿAmrit, Tell Sukas, Byblos, Sidon, Kharayeb, and Umm el-Amed. Others are known from Cyprus. There remain some complex chronological problems connected with the temples at Lachish, Miẓpe Yammim, ʿAmrit, Sidon, Kharayeb, and Umm el-ʿAmed. According to the consensus, these continued to function during the Hellenistic period. Moreover, in most cases, the excavators did not isolate the architectural features peculiar to the Persian period. Even assuming that all these temples date to the Persian period alone, it remains very difficult to determine the typical plan of most because of their small number and their poor state of preservation. In addition to the actual remains of temples, there are some inscriptions from Persian-period sites, which attest to central sanctuaries at Acco, Dor, Jaffa, Ashkelon, and elsewhere (see below).

We shall now examine these remains individually. The **large temple** uncovered at **Lachish** was called the "solar shrine" by its excavator, J. L. Starkey. This building measured 27 x 17 m., had plastered walls and a vaulted roof, and was oriented east-west. It consisted of a square courtyard with a row of small chambers, probably storerooms, to the east of it. The main rooms lay on the west. A stairway of five steps, apparently set along the entire width of the courtyard, led to a rectangular antechamber. Behind it was the holy of holies, raised above the service rooms at its sides. Because of its large size, distinctive layout, and the presence of incense altars and other cultic vessels, Starkey concluded that "it seems certain that this room was the sanctuary of a building dedicated to one of the later intrusive cults introduced during the Persian regime. The eastern orientation of the building and the position of the libation altar on the open axis suggest a solar cult." Two phases of use were noted in the building. The earlier stratum dates to the Persian period and a later stratum is Hellenistic. Excavations at the site by Y. Aharoni in 1966–1968 showed that a late-Judaean-period layer lay directly below the floor of the temple. Aharoni also found conclusive evidence that the main entrance to the temple was in the east, i.e., at its narrow side, as is usual in this type of temple, and not in the north as claimed by Starkey.

We have three examples of **medium-sized sanctuaries.** One was uncovered at Sarepta along the Phoenician coast between Tyre and Sidon. It is situated in the midst of a potters' quarter, and we have already dealt with its

III.21 Lachish, general view of the "solar shrine"

previous phase above. The Persian-period phase does not differ much from its predecessor: it is a rectangular structure (6.5 x 2.5 m.), oriented east-west. Along its walls were plastered fieldstone benches. The benches were 20 cm. high and 30 to 40 cm. wide. They were intended for placement of votive objects rather than as seating. In the center of the western wall stood a small, raised platform, probably the focal point of the temple on which sculptures and figurines of the deities were placed. The opening in the narrow wall was in the east, opposite the platform. The plan of this temple reflects very old traditions dating as far back as the Late Bronze Age. It is identical, for example, with the plan of the Late Bronze Age Fosse Temple at Lachish, the Late Bronze Age temple at Tel Mevorakh, and some of the Late Bronze Age temples at Beth-Shean, among others.

Approximately nineteen Phoenician **inscriptions** were found in the sanctuary at Sarepta. The personal names mentioned in them are typically Phoenician. The most important among these is one incised on a small ivory plaque which says that "Shillem son of Mapaʿal son of ʿIzai made a statue" (presumably, the plaque was attached to this statue) for Tanit-Ashtart. Although it is remotely possible that this votive object was brought from elsewhere and deposited in the shrine, it is probable that the shrine was dedicated to a goddess called Tanit-Ashtart, and that both names pertain to one deity. Previously, the name Tanit was mostly known from the Punic settlements in the western Mediterranean. This is the first time it has been encountered in the east. It should also be pointed out that the emblem of Tanit was also found at Sarepta, incised on a glass seal.

A medium-sized shrine of a different type is the one uncovered at **Tel Michal** (Makmish) by N. Avigad in the 1950s. The shrine stands some 400 m. north of the mound. Two phases of construction, both dated to the Persian period, were encountered in the building. The plan of the shrines was not established in its entirety but seems to have consisted of two rooms in its upper phase, a long room in the south and a small chamber attached to the north side. The total length of the shrine was 15 m. and its width was assumed to be 5 to 6 m. The building was oriented south-north. Dating to the first phase are the east wall and the southeast corner of the large room. The wall was preserved to a height of one or more courses above floor level and contained the entrance. East of the entrance stood a spacious courtyard, the limits of which were not ascertained. Its floor was 1 m. below that of the room. A pavement of stone slabs was found near the entrance. In the second phase, the building was enlarged on the north side, the east wall was diagonally lengthened by 2.5 m., and the north room was added at a

III.22 Persian-period sanctuary at Makmish

lower level. The floor of the east court was raised 17 cm., and two round plastered basins were sunk into it, one north of the entrance, the second, slightly projecting above the floor in the south. An open drain, preserved to the length of 5.2 m., ran from the east in the direction of a basin in the courtyard. Near the basin lay a carved basalt column base, no longer *in situ*. Inside the building and outside it on the northern slope of the podium, upon which it was built, were found numerous clay figurines and a few of stone. The majority of the clay figurines is hollow, mold-made representations of seated men wearing high-pointed headgear and fondling the end of a long beard; pregnant women; or women with children in their arms or supporting their breasts with their hands. Among the stone statuettes is a distinctive type made in Cypro-Classic style of the 5th century BCE.

Statuettes in Egyptian, Persian, and Greek styles were also discovered. Other finds included several small sculpted limestone incense altars, beads, many faience and colored glass amulets and pendants, and bronze bracelets. These objects were all presumably offerings brought to the place of worship, which was probably dedicated to a fertility cult. The figurines, other finds, and historical considerations indicate, according to the excavator, that this cult was practiced by Phoenician inhabitants of the nearby settlement on the mound during the Persian period.

During excavations at Tel Michal conducted by Z. Herzog in the 1980s, another structure interpreted as a shrine was uncovered on the east side of the mound. This building had benches and probably resembled the shrine at Sarepta. A bronze seal and other objects were uncovered in a nearby *favissa.*

The third medium-sized shrine excavated in Palestine was found at **Miẓpe Yammim.** In plan, this shrine resembles the one from Makmish described above—i.e., it is a broad shrine—but here it was changed to fit the specific local setting. It is constructed on the southern side of a large fortified structure in Upper Galilee, atop a high mountain overlooking all of Lower Galilee. On one side, the Sea of Galilee is visible and on the other, the Mediterranean. The temple is entered from the north and is a broadhouse structure consisting of two rooms: the main room on the west (6 x 13.7 m.) and a secondary room (4.8 x 10.4 m.). The walls reveal two distinct phases; in the later stage, large stones were carelessly laid. The walls in this phase probably surrounded an open courtyard. Along the east, south, and north walls of the main room were benches. The north wall was partly founded on bedrock and stands approximately 1.7 m. above floor level. Several of the benches and the northwest corner of the building were hewn from bedrock. The main room, paved with stone slabs, contained three column bases and two platforms, one standing against the south wall, the second in the northwest corner of the temple. A stone slab, probably used as a cover for the *bamah* in its second phase, was found resting against it. The *bamah* appears to have served a cultic function in the temple during its original phase and was used as an altar in an open enclosure in its later phase.

The Miẓpe Yammim temple yielded many juglets and bottles as well as storage jars from the Persian period. Some of the jars are of types known throughout the country, but the majority is of the coarse ware typical of the Upper Galilee. Other finds included a Tyrian silver coin of the 4th century BCE; a bronze *sheqel* weight; fibulae and arrowheads. A large quantity of animal bones was also found. The upper strata of the temple area yielded Hellenistic pottery. On the uppermost step of the western *bamah* was a Seleucid Tyrian coin from the second half of the 2nd century BCE. Before the excavations, four bronze objects were found in a survey conducted at the site. They seem to have come from the bedrock, against which the western *bamah* was built. The objects were figurines of a young lion, a crouching ram, an Apis bull, and a *situla* (a cultic vessel used for libation). During the excavations, a slate statuette depicting three Egyptian gods, Osiris, Horus, and Isis in the

III.23 Persian-period sanctuary at Miẓpe Yammim

form of the goddess Hathor, was found near the *bamah.* The bronze *situla* was decorated with typical Egyptian motifs arranged in four registers. It is Egyptian in character and origin, but used by Phoenicians in their own cult, for it bears two Phoenician inscriptions that were clearly added later. One is a dedication to the goddess Astarte by a person whose name is Akhbor Bdashmun, i.e., a Sidonian!

To sum up: The building complex, which dates to the Persian period, appears to have been a cultic enclosure that included a temple, courtyard, and fortress. The site was undoubtedly related to the special location of Mount Miẓpe Yammim. The Phoenician inscription and Egyptian objects found here indicate the existence of a Phoenician cult, probably devoted to the goddess ʿAstarte. However, the unusual ceramic finds reflect a local assemblage different from that commonly found along the Phoenician coast. The sanctuary probably continued down to the Hellenistic period and ended in the 2nd century BCE.

The third type of Persian-period sanctuary is the chapel, i.e., a small, square structure measuring approximately 1 x 1 m. which housed a sacred object: a statuette or a stone stela (sometimes more than one such object). Visitors to this type of sanctuary prayed outside and laid their votive offerings beside it. This type of shrine has been found at Dan (there are several there), Tel Michal, and in the northern cemetery at Achzib. These chapels were in use during the entire Iron Age. They continued so without modification through the Persian period, at which time they became even more popular. It should be pointed out that such chapels perpetuate older Canaanite traditions going back to the Late Bronze Age, as, for example, the stela sanctuary at Area C at Hazor. Many similar chapels have been uncovered along the Phoenician coast, where a few, such as the chapel at 'Amrit, cut into a single rock formation, are entirely preserved. From here, they spread to the Phoenician settlements of Cyprus and later to the western Mediterranean. Of their existence in Persian-period Palestine, we also learn from miniature stone stelae (models) depicting such chapels. One good example is the miniature stone model from Achzib, which depicts a goddess standing in the entrance of a facade of such a chapel. Another example is a stone stela from Dor, which depicts a chapel facade. Many clay models of chapels from different parts of Palestine range in date from the Late Bronze Age through the entire Iron Age, and become most popular during the Persian period. They are mainly found in the northern Phoenician part of the country at sites such as Achzib, Tell Keisan, Acco, Tel Megadim, and Dor.

Remains of other Persian-period shrines have also been found at other sites in Palestine; however, not enough has been preserved to make their plans intelligible. At other sites, inscriptions mentioning the existence of such shrines have been recovered. Such remains provide data for study of the distribution of these shrines and the character of the cult in different parts of the country. Some of these remains will now be described.

At Dan, minor remains of a Persian-period cultic structure have been found. They formed part of the cultic center of previous periods. In the courtyard of this building, two 4th century BCE Macedonian coins were found. A number of small cult objects were uncovered, including a clay figurine of the god Bes, a goddess carrying a child, a horse and rider, a figurine of a "temple boy," and two bronze representations of Osiris. All these objects and other fragments were uncovered in a temple repository *(favissa)*.

At Acco, a structure was uncovered in the Persian-period stratum that was probably used for an administrative purpose. Nearby, a well-constructed wall was apparently all that remained of the Phoenician shrine in which an ostracon with a long inscription was found. The ostracon attests to the function of the building: it was an order issued by the high authority, perhaps even the office of the governor of the city. According to the order, the local guild of metalworkers was to give the man in charge of the 'Astarte temple an expensive basin *('agan)*. He is also ordered to donate more metal vessels, some of which were probably of silver or gold. Nearby, in a pit that was also

assigned to the same Persian stratum, were found another Phoenician ostracon inscribed with numbers only, male and female clay figurines, and animal
figurines. Another important find was the feet of a broken stone statuette,
probably the part of a seated goddess, inscribed with a Cypro-Syllabic sign.
These and other cultic objects clearly indicate that this building functioned
as a shrine.

In addition to the Acco ostracon, a few other dedicatory inscriptions mentioning the existence of local temples have been recovered at other Persian-
period sites in Palestine. Most come from coastal sites. An inscription from
Dor indicates the existence of a central temple in the city, which probably
also served pilgrims from distant lands. It is an inscribed cow scapula found
in a Persian-period pit, from which a Phoenician ostracon was also recovered. The scapula is decorated on one side with a sophisticated maritime
scene, while the other side bears a Cypro-Syllabic inscription in Greek. It is
probably a dedicatory inscription to the local temple of the goddess 'Astarte
by a Greek-speaking Cypriot pilgrim visiting Dor. This is one of the first
Greek inscriptions found in Palestine in a script resembling the letter found
on the base of the Acco statuette (see above). Recently, O. Masson published
two more similar inscriptions: one from Sarepta and the other from Sidon,
inscribed on the bases of stone altars. Masson interprets them as dedicatory
inscriptions of Phoenician pilgrims to central Phoenician shrines: one was
dedicated to Ba'al-Ashmun (Asclepius at Sarepta) and the other to 'Astarte
at Sidon.

A few kilometers south of Dor, at the site of Eliachin, a large limestone
statuette was found together with Persian and Hellenistic-period pottery
near the remains of a building interpreted as a temple. Later, some bronze
bowls and one bronze cymbal, all inscribed with dedicatory inscriptions in
Phoenician and Aramaic, were found at the same site. These have recently
been published. The inscriptions mention the deity's name, l'strm or l'strm zy
dsrn ("to the 'Ashtorim of the Sharon"), meaning that the dedication was intended for a local Sharon Plain deity. There is no doubt now that the site was
an important cult center from the second half of the 5th century BCE. Among
those presenting the dedicatory offerings is an individual with a Persian
name, bgwy, perhaps one of the Persian provincial officials.

Two other dedicatory inscriptions related to shrines are a monumental
building inscription, found in Jaffa at the beginning of the 20th century,
which tells about the erection of a temple to Ba'al-Ashmun in Jaffa, and an
ostracon that was uncovered within the remains of a structure in Nebi Yunis
on the coast, south of Ashdod, which mentions a donation of silver for Ba'al-

Tyre (Baʿal Melqart), whose shrine was probably there. This structure has not been properly excavated.

In recent years, a new cultic practice dating to the Persian period was encountered: sacred dog burials. Some were found recently at Berytus on the Phoenician coast. At Dor, too, a few graves of dogs have been uncovered. Others (about seven) were found at Ashdod. At Ashkelon, however, a whole cemetery was excavated, which included several thousand dog burials. The skeletons examined from Ashkelon were mostly puppies. They were laid on their side, tail folded, without burial offerings. The excavator, L. Stager, assumed that they belonged to the Phoenician population of the city. The Ashkelon dogs appear to have been revered as sacred animals and were probably associated with a particular deity and with that deity's sacred precinct. Although no actual remains of a temple were found there, Stager suggested that there was a sanctuary related to matters of healing. The cemetery existed for only a short period, above a previous Persian-period storehouse. Later the area was returned to commercial activity. As regards Persian-period cultic objects found at Ashkelon, metal and stone medallions in the shape of the emblem of the goddess Tanit, bronze figurines of Horus, as well as various clay figurines, and Cypriot stone statuettes reflect the usual Phoenician repertoire.

In addition to the Persian-period shrines mentioned above at Dan, Miẓpe Yammim, Achzib, Acco, Dor, Eliachin, Tel Michal, Jaffa, Nebi Yunis, Ashkelon, and Lachish, several dozen temple *favissae,* i.e., refuse pits into which cult objects from nearby sanctuaries were dumped, have been uncovered. These pits can be used as indicators of the existence of sanctuaries at those sites. Some were found at the sites mentioned above, while others have been discovered at other settlements, the most important of these being Beth-Shean, Megiddo, Shiqmona, Dor, Tel Mevorakh, Apollonia, and in particular, the large assemblages (many dozens of clay figurines, stone statuettes, and masks) in the Philistine Shephelah, the Negev, and Idumaea at Yavneh, Tel Ẓippor, Tell eṣ-Ṣafi, Lachish, Maresha, Tell ʿErani, Tell Jemmeh, Tel Sheva, and elsewhere.

Many cult objects have also been found in dwellings and in graves: at the cemeteries uncovered at Achzib, at the large Persian-period cemetery discovered just north of Acco, and in cemeteries at ʿAtlit, Tel Megadim, Tel Michal, Ashkelon, and other sites. These provide quite a detailed map of their distribution. To this evidence we may add the hundreds of figurines recovered from the sea, particularly from the wreck found off the coast of Shavei Ẓion, which was entirely devoted to trade in such artifacts.

The interesting fact about the distribution of temples, tombs, and *favissae* containing cult objects in the Persian period is that they are found throughout the Galilee, in the major valleys, and along the coast from the north to the extreme south, in the Shephelah, and also in Idumaea. Up to now, no pagan cult remains have been encountered in Judah or in Samaria; this totally contradicts our observation concerning the final stage of the Judaean monarchy (see above). Judging exclusively from this archaeological evidence, Jews and Samaritans in Palestine underwent a complete revolution in their attitude toward the cult practices of the preceding period.

CULT AND CULT OBJECTS

WE HAVE ALREADY examined the specific character of the Phoenician cult during the Late Iron Age (see above). All finds, including written material from the Persian period, merely strengthened the observation that it continues in the same manner into the Persian period. The Persian-period shrines excavated thus far indeed reflect the continuation of old Canaanite-Phoenician traditions. Most of the names of deities encountered in excavated artifacts or mentioned in written sources are purely Phoenician. This certainly indicates that the Phoenician population was expanding during this period, not only in Galilee but also to the southern part of the coast, which was previously held by the Philistines.

The major goddess in the Palestinian cult during the Persian period is ʿAstarte, called Tanit-ʿAstarte in the Sarepta inscription and ʿAstarte on a stone throne found at a nearby site, on the *situla* from Miẓpe Yammim, and in Cypriot dedicatory inscriptions from Sarepta and Dor. Another variant is "ʿAshtorim" or "ʿAshtorim of the Sharon" at Eliachin (but this form may refer to the male god Baʿal). In the Yehumelekh stela, a Persian-period royal stela from Byblos, she is called "the Lady of Gebal," i.e., the ʿAstarte of Byblos.

Her other name is Tanit (usually connected with the western Phoenician deity) or Tanit-ʿAstarte; the emblem of Tanit appears all over the Phoenician and Palestinian coasts: on a glass seal from Sarepta, impressed on jars from Acco, on lead weights from Umm el-ʿAmed and Ashdod, on bronze and stone amulets from Ashkelon, and on dozens of clay figurines rescued from shipwrecks off the coast of Shavei Zion and Tyre. On these figurines, her second emblem, the dolphin, is sometimes also present.

The name of the male god is also mentioned quite often, in several variants, both in written documents or as a component in personal names. The name Ba'al appears in a few ostraca from Dan and Dor (Ba'al-Palet, Ebed-Ba'al); Ba'al-Ashmun (at Miẓpe Yammim, Dor, Apollonia, and Jaffa); Ba'al Melqart at Sarepta and Tel Anafa; and Ba'al-Tyre at Nebi Yunis. Other variations of the name are Ba'al-Shamem at Tel Michal and Ba'al-Shelama at Tell Jemmeh. In the new hoard of ostraca from the region of Idumaea, the name "Ba'al" is also quite popular.

In addition to the usual pair of Phoenician deities, the Phoenicians appear to have frequently worshiped Egyptian deities, too. Evidence for this is found in imported Egyptian figurines and statuettes or their imitations. Examples are the stone statuette from Miẓpe Yammim, which depicts the figures of Horus, Isis, and Hathor; the common use of the figures of Isis and Horus at Dor, Tel Michal, and elsewhere; and bronze figurines of Osiris and Horus from Dan, Ashkelon, and Tel Sheva. There are many other Egyptian figurines from Persian-period contexts in Palestine, in particular, deities connected with the popular apotropaic cult. The reverence for Egyptian deities among the Phoenicians is further reflected in the incorporation of names of Egyptian deities in Phoenician personal names of the period, such as the name 'Ebed Isi ("the servant of Isis") on an ostracon from Dor; Ebed Osiri and 'Ebed Isi on ostraca from Idumaea; a Phoenician inscription on a bronze *situla* from Miẓpe Yammim which reads: "May Isis grant favor and life to Abdi-Ptah son of Abdo." Mention should also be made of the dedicatory inscription on the stone throne of 'Astarte, which was dedicated by 'Ebed Ubasti the son of Bodba'al. This name indicates a devotee of the Egyptian goddess Bastet, while the patronymic shows that the father was a Ba'al worshiper. This apparently reflects the adoption of an Egyptian cult by a Phoenician family, which seems to be a pervasive custom: the Phoenician goddess Ba'alat-Gebal from Byblos, for example, is depicted on the Yehumelekh stela in the shape of and with the attributes of the Egyptian goddess Hathor.

In Idumaea, the national god Qos remains dominant during this period. His name appears there frequently, especially as a component in personal names, as in the Persian-period ostraca from Arad and Tel Sheva, as well as in a recently published ostraca group that also originated somewhere in Idumaea, and ones found in recent excavations at Maresha. This name is also mentioned in the Wadi ed-Daliyeh papyri. But as already pointed out, in the Persian period all the characteristic Idumaean clay figurines, so common in the 7th century BCE, disappeared entirely. In their place, the *favissae* found in this region all contain the usual mix of artifacts, most of eastern origin (mainly Phoenician), with some western Greek types. There is absolutely no distinction evident between the cult of Qos and that of Baʿal. The Moabite god Kemosh is also mentioned in a Persian-period inscription uncovered in the Moabite town of Kir-Moab (Kerak), as well as in the Wadi ed-Daliyeh papyri, but no Persian-period figurines representing the god have been found.

To complete the picture, let us note the existence of some foreign cults in Persian-period Palestine, some of Mesopotamian (mainly Babylonian) origin, found as components in local names, such as ʿEbed Nanai (at Arad) or ʿEbed Shamash, Shamashdan, or Natansin in the recently published assemblage of ostraca from Idumaea. A Phoenician inscription on a bronze bowl dated to the 4th century BCE includes the words *marzeaḥ shamash,* a reference to a god of Babylonian origin. It is indeed possible that some of these cults were also adopted by the locals, with a change of meaning and character, or that we have here cultic remains of peoples brought from Mesopotamia, who maintained their cultic traditions as best they could.

A Thamudian (North Arabian) inscription found in the vicinity of el-ʿArish is inscribed on a limestone bowl supported by a winged figurine of a boy, which originated in the East Greek world (late 6th or early 5th century BCE). It is a dedication to an Arabian god: "say Hadad the son of Masik, may Ma(rna) bless him." J. Naveh claims that the use of a native Thamudic script here, instead of the international Aramaic script, points to a relatively early date within the Persian period. In any case this is a prayer to an Arabian god.

Clay Figurines

Many hundreds of clay figurines have been found in Persian-period temples, *favissae,* buildings, and graves. While occurring in large numbers, their geographical distribution is limited to the Galilee and the large valleys, the coastal region and the Shephelah, and Idumaea, which in this period included the southern part of Hebron Hills (from Lachish and Maresha to Beth-Zur). None, as was already noted, have been found in Judah and Samaria.

Most figurines were uncovered in *favissae,* pits into which clay figurines and stone statuettes had been deposited. The figurines were placed in the sanctuary by worshipers, who dedicated them to various deities. After a time, they were deliberately broken and thrown into a pit dug nearby, apparently in ceremonial fashion, thereby making room on the sanctuary's benches for new votive offerings. The practice of depositing religious objects in special repository pits is fortunate for archaeologists. Such pits are frequently the only cultic remains of the shrines encountered.

III.24 Limestone vessel in Archaic Greek style from the region of el-ʿArish with Arabic Thamudian inscription

The clay figurines are made—like the pottery of the Persian period—in two shades: greenish-white and pinkish-red. In some examples, a thin white slip is applied to the reddish clay. Traces of red and black paint have survived on some of them. They were made—according to N. Avigad and A. Ciasca—using two techniques: hollow mold-made and solid handmade. Among the wealth of finds at Tel Zippor, O. Negbi also identified: 1. Hollow terra-cottas consisting mainly of figurines, plaques, or masks. All are molded in front; backs are sealed with smooth strips of clay. The backs of the masks are open. 2. Solid terra-cottas consisting of figurines and plaques. The figurines are handmade and the plaques were cast in molds. 3. Partly hollow and partly solid terra-cottas, usually consisting of two sections. The solid part is either handmade or molded, while the hollow part is either molded or wheel-made. Stylistically, the figurines fall into two main classes, representing men and women in eastern- or western-style dress. The eastern class of figurines is characterized by varied styles of dress, subdivided into Phoenician, Egyptian, Persian, and Babylonian dress, with a large group of nude female figurines, a direct continuation of figurines depicting the Iron Age fertility goddess 'Astarte. The second, western group includes men, women, youth, and children in Greek dress.

As a whole, the distinctive feature of the figurines of the Persian period in Palestine and on the Phoenician coast is the heterogeneous nature of assemblages found together in the same pit. One may distinguish in these figurines traces of Phoenician, Persian, Egyptian, Canaanite, Cypriot, and Greek influences. The diversity of styles is perhaps characteristic of the Phoenician seafarers, who acted as intermediaries among several cultures.

Generally, these heterogeneous assemblages are divided into two main groups: the eastern group and the western one.

The eastern group. Aside from the Egyptian figurines and statuettes, which will be dealt with separately, this group includes several styles. Among those depicting male figurines, a very common type represents a bearded man with a large mustache. He is seated on a throne, wrapped in a cloak, and fondles his beard. In a variation, the figure appears in identical dress but stands with arms crossed on his breast. A distinctive feature of this type is the round flat headdress, which occurs frequently on Phoenician reliefs of the Persian period and probably represents the typical Phoenician headdress of the period. Accompanying this type and almost as common is the figure of a bearded man with mustache seated on a throne and clasping his beard. It differs from the preceding figures, however, in the long pointed hat in Egyptian style (known as the "Osiris" hat). Despite the different headdress in the two types, they apparently represent the same god. This is indicated by the identical beard and mustache and especially by the seated attitude. In distribution, the scores of figurines of these two types are confined to the Phoenician-Palestinian coast, suggesting that both derived from a single source and Phoenician creations. This assumption is supported by the distinctive headdress of figurines of the first type. There is no doubt, however, that the figurines with the Osiris hat do not represent Osiris, because the beard and mustache are absent in the original Egyptian depictions. A possible explanation for the frequent appearance of these figurines is that the two represent the figure of a god common in the cult of Phoenicia and Palestine, perhaps the god Ba'al. Their different dress may attest to "Ba'als" of different localities, a characteristic of the Canaanite-Phoenician cult. A further possibility is that they represent two separate gods of unknown identity.

Another, less common male figurine depicts the head of a man wearing a pointed cloth hat, also covering his chin and cheeks. This hat appears at times on Achaemenid reliefs at Persepolis and is also worn by Persians depicted on the well-known sarcophagi from Sidon. This was apparently the national headdress of the Persians. Figurines of this type were also widely distributed. Aside from Palestine, they are known from Egypt, Phoenicia, north Syria, Mesopotamia, and Persia, i.e., throughout the Persian Empire. Hats of this type are also worn by the figures of riders (who are even called "Persian" riders). Two groups of riders occur. The first group is solid and handmade. This rider is bearded and wears a peaked cloth cap that also covers the chin and a heavy cloak thrown over the shoulders. A breastplate appears on the horse. The second group resembles the first in its details but was produced by a different technique. The horse is solid and handmade, while the rider is hollow and molded in the front. The rider is clothed similarly to that of the first group, but the horse is clumsy and lacks the breastplate. In a number of variations, the lower part of the rider's body is missing and seems to be attached to the horse's body. The "Persian" rider figurines were also widely distributed throughout the Persian Empire.

Of the female figurines in eastern style, a few are depicted fully clothed and are also characterized by different styles of dress. The bulk of these figurines, however, are nudes, apparently representing a fertility deity. The figures of these women are standing, and the genital region is enlarged and emphasized; hands support the breasts or hang at the sides, following a tradition already well known in Palestine in the Bronze and Iron ages. These figurines appear to represent the continuation of a native popular art that persisted despite periodic changes in style. The large group of fertility god-

III.25 Persian-period male deities with oriental (Phoenician and Egyptian) headdresses from Tel Dor

dess figurines, nevertheless, seems to bear typical Persian-period features. They differ from their predecessors in the great variety of types and in the new, completely mold-made and hollow production technique. The variety of types is not manifested in new attitudes of the body—in these they follow their predecessors—but is evident in the facial expressions, which become more vividly naturalistic, apparently through the influence of the western-type figurines (see below). This is in sharp contrast to the previous "pillar fig-urines," the faces of which present a frozen demeanor. Another class of female figurines popular in the Persian period is the seated or standing preg-nant woman and the woman holding a child on her shoulders or in her arms. These figurines usually wear the Egyptian wig, but their distribution is restricted to Palestine, Phoenicia, and Cyprus, which indicates, like the eastern group of male figurines that wear the Osiris hat, that these, too, were produced by Phoenicians. Support for the view can also be found in the hoard of figurines from the wrecked ship at Shavei Zion, which are largely identical to some of the female figurines from Dor, Makmish, and other sites, and bear the stamped emblem of the Phoenician-Punic goddess Tanit-Pane-Baʿal, a round head above a body shaped as a triangle with two uplifted hands.

Animal figurines were also found in the excavations. In addition to horses

III.26 Clay figurine of a "Persian" rider from Beersheba region

III.27 Oriental 'Astarte clay figurines from Tel Dor

with and without riders, we have dogs, camels, rams, felines, lions, bears, cats, and monkeys. One figurine from Tell Deir 'Alla even depicts the ancient Phoenician-Israelite motif of a cow suckling a calf. Some are made of clay but others are carved in limestone. These figurines may be interpreted as accompanying animals of Ba'al and 'Astarte; others, such as dogs, were venerated instead of being sacrificed to the gods.

The influence of the Egyptian cult on that of Palestine during the Persian period is clearly apparent. Many of the clay figurines are made in the form of Egyptian deities or possess Egyptian elements. These were undoubtedly adopted by the Palestinian cult in previous periods. During the Persian period, they underwent certain changes. They also exerted considerable influence on glass and faience pendants and other objects utilized in the popular cult. Some of the glass objects uncovered in Palestine and on the Phoenician coast, such as the "Nile water bottles" and faience figurines in the shape of deities (e.g., that depicting Isis and Horus from Dor), may have originated in Egypt. Egyptian influence is also recognizable in some of the stone cultic objects, such as the small incense altar from Makmish to which a monkey figurine is attached. But the majority of Egyptianizing finds consists of stone statuettes and bronze figurines.

The stone statuettes uncovered at Makmish, for example, are purely Egyptian in style and were apparently imported from Egypt. Most were made of limestone, but one was made of polished black stone and depicts the goddess Isis holding the child Horus on her lap. On the back of this statuette, there is also a dedicatory hieroglyphic inscription that probably mentions the name of the votary. Another example is the stone statuette from Mizpe Yammim, which depicts the images of Horus between Isis and Hathor. Most of the Persian-period bronze figurines in the Egyptian style were found in the *favissa* at Ashkelon. One bears traces of gold leaf, which

III.28 Dor, a faience figurine of Isis and Horus

III.29 Dor, a clay figurine
of the child Horus

originally covered it, and the excavator believes that all were originally
gilded. A few stood on square stands but were also equipped with loops for
hanging. Others stood on a projecting peg suitable for insertion into the
ground or being mounted upon a wooden pole. The figurines from the
favissa at Ashkelon depict Horus (Harpokrates), Osiris, the bull Apis, Isis
nursing the child Horus, Anubis, Bastet, Ra, and Ibis. There is also the figure
of a kneeling Egyptian priest with a hieroglyphic inscription on its back,
which includes the name of the votary. In the *favissa* of Tel Sheva were found
bronze figurines of the bull Apis, the goddess Neith, and the bird Ba.

Recent excavations at Ashkelon yielded two more bronze figurines of
Osiris, at least one in a clear late 7th century BCE context. This led the excavator to assign the entire Ashkelon assemblage to this period, including the
hoard from the *favissa.* It is indeed possible that some of these bronze Osiris
figurines, like those from Tel Dan or Gibeon, antedate the Persian period,
but most, including those from the Ashkelon *favissa,* date to the Persian period. This dating also applies to the other Egyptian bronze cult objects found
in Palestine. At Ashkelon, some seven imported Egyptian bronze *situlae*
were recovered in the same late 7th century BCE stratum in which the Horus
figurine was found. Two almost identical bronze *situlae* bear Phoenician in-

III.30 Bronze figurines from Ashkelon depicting various Egyptian deities

scriptions and are dated to the Persian period. One, dedicated to ʿAstarte, was found in the Phoenician sanctuary at Miẓpe Yammim in the Upper Galilee. The second, of unknown provenience, bears a dedicatory inscription mentioning Isis. The complete inscription reads: "May Isis grant favor and life to Abdi-Ptah son of Abdo." As already mentioned, many Phoenicians in the Persian period were given names of Egyptian deities, such as ʿEbed Ptah, ʿEbed Osiris, ʿEbed Isis. Does this reflect a true Egyptian cult or merely a symbiosis, i.e., the adoption of Egyptian motifs, emblems, and the use of the names of Egyptian deities identified with local gods by a local cult? Two factors favor the latter hypothesis: The Phoenician goddess Baʿalat-Gebal depicted on the stela of the Phoenician king Yehumelekh is equipped with all the attributes of the Egyptian goddess Hathor. At the same time, the Egyptian triad of Osiris, Isis, and Hathor, as well as the bull Apis from Miẓpe Yammim, was found in a shrine dedicated to the goddess ʿAstarte by a Phoenician from Sidon. Egyptian figurines, mainly those of Isis and Horus from Makmish, were uncovered in a purely Phoenician sanctuary. At all these sites, not a single Egyptian deity's name is ever mentioned!

The western group. The western group of figurines comprises an entirely different repertoire. All of these figurines are rendered in a purely Greek style. Their subjects are also generally taken from the realm of Greek religion. All have close, and even identical, parallels in Cyprus, Rhodes, eastern Greek islands, and mainland Greece. The Cypriot group will be dealt with separately. Among the Greek male figurines, especially popular is the nude youth, known as the "Apollo type," which in Greece was considered as a votive of this god. It appears in several variations. Unusual figurines include a pair of young boys embracing and a pair of wrestling youths from Tell eṣ-Ṣafi. All the figurines of this type are hollow, while another type is mounted in the form of plaques. Several figurines were uncovered, which have been identified as representing Hercules. One comes from Lachish and is more readily identifiable because the head is covered with a lion mane, Hercules' customary attribute. Others had been found at Makmish. At Tel Ẓippor, a male head wearing a conical hat, identified as Hermes, based upon parallels from Rhodes and Greece, was found. A very significant find was made at Tel Dor, where a *favissa* was uncovered with contents distinct from those in all other *favissae* excavated in Palestine till now. Most of the figurines in it are obviously Greek in style, in marked contrast to the Phoenician items in all other *favissae.* It also included vessels that were almost exclusively of East Greek or Athenian origin. One of the figurines found there depicts the head of a bearded man. A second is similar but wears a Greek helmet. Another wears

III.31 Mizpe Yammim, an Egyptian bronze *situla* with a Phoenician dedicatory inscription and other bronze figurines

III.32 Tel Dor, an assemblage of western- (Greek) style male deities heads

a wide-brimmed hat. The fourth depicts a young girl with long braids and the characteristic Archaic smile. The three male heads also feature the Archaic smile, and all have the pointed beards typical of early Greek sculpture. The quality of the modeling puts this group among the finest of such work from this period. Unlike most of the mass-produced and rather crudely made Greek figurines previously discovered in Palestine, these date to the second half of the 5th century BCE. The uniformity of this entirely Greek assemblage at Dor attests to the *favissa* having been attached to a temple that served the Greek segment of the city's population, which probably occupied one of Dor's quarters or was connected with a Greek trading post located there. In later excavation seasons, many similar figurines were encountered in buildings in all excavation areas. These were generally variations on the same Greek warrior heads. When one of the bearded heads was found missing part of its helmet, it became clear that the technique by which these figurines were made was pressing the faces into molds, which explains their uniformity, and adding hand-fashioned headgear. One of the Greek types is the "temple boy." The usual interpretation of this type of figurine is that it represents a boy dedicated by his parents to serve his entire life in the sanctuary, recalling the biblical story of Hannah and Samuel. Another, probably more credible, explanation regards this figure as representing the child-god Horus, the son of Ba'al and 'Astarte, like the infants held by the goddess in the figurines described above. This view is now supported by other finds, including a figurine discovered in the Beth-Shean Valley, which depicts a similar boy with a finger in his mouth, a common posture for Horus.

Of the female figurines in western style, a prominent group is of a mature, fully clothed woman seated on a chair. In Palestine, two types are found, which are differentiated by the form of the chair and the headdress. The first type depicts a woman seated on a chair with a backrest with two armlike projections at the top. She wears a long dress and her hair is curled and topped by a diadem. The other type shows a woman seated on a low chair without a prominent backrest. She wears a very high, round hat. These two types represent unidentified goddesses. The other female figurines represent standing women. These are of a great variety of types and differ from one another in dress and hairstyle. Figurines of both mature women and maidens are found. Several female heads have been found in various parts of Palestine. A few of these definitely belong to the standing women type.

An outstanding example of the standing female figurine is dressed in a long *chiton* (robe) with a *haemation* (overcoat) over her shoulder. Her left arm is bent backward and holds the edge of the *haemation*, while the right arm is bent at the breast and the hand holds an unidentified object. The hair is long and curly. She wears a wide flat hat. Another type, several examples of which were found at Tel Zippor, represents a standing woman dressed in belted *chiton* and *haemation*. Her hair falls to her shoulders in two long plaits, her arms hang at the sides of the body, and she displays the well-known Archaic smile. Most of the clothed women, both sitting and standing, were considered to be votives of Aphrodite in Greece.

III.33 Clay heads of western-style goddesses

The last group of figurines in western style to be discussed here shares a common feature: in Greece all examples are associated with the cult of Dionysus. They include male and female figurines, reclining on their sides as if preparing to partake of a feast; grotesque figures of big-bellied, squatting nude pygmies with exposed genitals, bent legs, and hands holding their stomachs; figures of satyrs; and terra-cotta masks depicting faces of men and women in both eastern and western styles.

The significance of this entire category of finds can only be partially understood, since we know very little of official Phoenician ritual as practiced in the coastal cities of the eastern Mediterranean and have but few references from Greek literary sources. Most of our information comes from brief Phoenician texts, uncovered throughout Phoenicia and its dependencies, which include dedications to the various gods. From these we learn that each city had its own chief god. All of these deities had the name Baʿal in common, but in each location another distinguishing name was added; sometimes it was a geographical name such as Baʿal-Lebanon or Baʿal-Tzaphon. We know of Baʿal Melqart of Tyre, Baʿal-Eshmun of Sidon, Baʿal-Gebal of Byblos, and from the west we know of the Adon ("Lord") Baʿal-Hamman. The same applies to the chief goddess 'Astarte or Ashtoret. One of the inscriptions from Byblos refers to her as Ba'alat-Gebal. The most common goddess in the west is Tanit-Pane-Ba'al. Thus, it seems that the statuettes and figurines from dwellings and repositories of the Persian period are representative of three primary deities that appear simultaneously, in either oriental- or western-style attire: an adult, bearded man seated on a throne, or as a warrior; a woman representing the fertility goddess in various stances, sometimes holding babies; and young boys alone. There appears to be no special significance to the form of the figures or their attire, which may be Persian, Egyptian, Phoenician, Greek, or composite. This is well summarized by Italian scholar S. Moscati: "It seems evident that a triad of deities is common to all Phoenicia. This triad is composed of a protective god of the city, a goddess often his wife or companion who symbolizes the fertile earth, and a young god, somehow connected with the goddess, usually her son, whose resurrection expresses the annual cycle of vegetation. Within these limits the names and functions of the gods vary, and the fluidity of this pantheon, where the common name prevails over the proper name, and the function over the personality, is characteristic. Another characteristic of the Phoenician triad is its flexibility from town to town."

The Cypriot Cult

It has already been pointed out in the preceding discussion that a few dedicatory inscriptions to 'Astarte and to Ba'al Eshmun uncovered at Sidon, Sarepta, and Dor were inscribed in Greek using Cypro-Syllabic script. Besides being the earliest Greek inscriptions in Phoenicia and Palestine, they attest to the existence of Cypriot pilgrims or soldiers here. Perhaps they were the source of the many Cypriot limestone statuettes found in Palestine. But these statuettes may also have been intended for the cult of the local population. Their distribution covers the entire Phoenician and Palestinian coastal region from 'Amrit to Dor through Eliachin and Tel Michal in the north down to Ashkelon and Gaza in the south, and at Tel 'Erani, Tell eṣ-Ṣafi, and Tel Ẓippor in the Shephelah.

The Cypriot limestone statuettes were made in various dimensions: from almost life-sized to miniature (none of the very large sculptures common in Cyprus have been found in Palestine to date). In Palestine, they are a permanent part of the assemblages uncovered in the various *favissae* of Persian-period shrines. According to the attached inscriptions, these were dedicated to local deities. Examples include Eliachin, where a limestone goddess stat-

III.34 Limestone Cypriot statuettes from Tel Dor and Makmish

uette was found and where dedicatory inscriptions to the "Ashtorim of the Sharon" were also uncovered; they were found in the Phoenician temple at Tel Michal; and the *favissa* at Dor, where, recently, many Phoenician and Greek figurines were recovered. These finds indicate that the figurines of Cypriot deities were adopted by the local population as their own. The frequent occurrence of Hercules, identified with Ba'al Melqart, among the Cypriot statuettes found here attests to this assumption. This also appears to be true of other figurines depicting males, females, and youths.

Because the stone statuettes were individually hand-carved, rather than mass-produced like the clay figurines, they may be divided into several local Cypriot styles. The Swedish Cyprus Expedition proposes dividing the statuettes into four stylistic groups: (1) Archaic Cypro-Greek style, (2) Sub-Archaic Cypro-Greek style 1, (3) Sub-Archaic Cypro-Greek style 2, (4) Classical Cypro-Greek style.

The chronology of the site of Vouni in Cyprus serves as the basis for the chronological division of the groups. Accordingly, styles 1 and 2 date to

500–450 BCE; style 3 to 450–400 BCE; style 4, the Classical Cypro-Greek style, of which only scanty and sporadic examples have been found, is dated to the latter part of the 4th century BCE (until 325 BCE). Therefore, the presence of hand-carved stone figurines among the mass-produced clay figurines in the assemblages creates a firm chronological framework for the rest of the finds.

The Popular Apotropaic Cult

Besides the official cult described above, a popular apotropaic cult existed in Palestine during the Persian period, primarily aimed at warding off bad luck, evil spirits, etc. This cult was as common as that practiced in the shrines, and perhaps even more popular. It had its own traditions and cultic objects, partly made of clay, such as masks, "Bes" vases and "face" vases, Bes, Ptah, and Pataikos figurines, and grotesque figurines in the form of birds with huge eyes; but the majority of the finds connected with it is faience or colored glass beads, pendants, and amulets, sometimes also made of bronze, which were arranged on necklaces commonly placed on children. This popular cult had no territorial borders within Palestine. Unlike the official cult, its re-

III.35 A Phoenician clay mask from Tel Dor

mains have been encountered all over the country, including Judah and Samaria.

Numerous masks have been found at Persian-period sites in the Galilee and in the coastal region. Especially large assemblages were found at Tel Dor on the Carmel coast and at Tell eṣ-Ṣafi in Philistia. Such masks first appear in the Late Bronze Age cult and are not unique to the Persian period. Examples have been found in nearly all Iron Age strata. They became increasingly common in the late 7th century BCE, peaking during the Persian period, from which we possess dozens of masks. Like the rest of the cult objects of the period, the clay masks are made in two distinct styles: an oriental style depicting the heads of male and female deities (to some of which, magic symbols have been added in the center of the forehead) and a West Greek style. Most of the masks discovered here belong to a third, grotesque type, intended to ward off evil spirits. They usually present an old and beardless face with heavily lined forehead and cheeks, crescent-shaped eye sockets, and a large hole for the mouth, turned up high on both sides in a frightening manner. Some are also characterized by an oval crease surrounding the mouth, which is often unnaturally small. Another group has a skull-like appearance.

The major role in this apotropaic cult is played by the Egyptian-Phoenician god Bes, usually depicted naked, wearing a feathered crown, sometimes with devil's horns. There were also pottery jugs or juglets with his face incised or executed in relief upon their sides, known as "Bes" vases. These were found in domestic dwellings, shrines, and even in graves. Bes was indeed the best figure to carry on the war against all kinds of evils. The Bes vases were originally Egyptian products but were adopted in the Persian period in Palestine and have already been found at many sites in Galilee and the coastal region, as well as at inland sites such as Samaria. Beside them are also found the "face" vases that were made in the shape of "Janus heads," i.e., double faces usually depicting the heads of male and female deities. Clay figurines of Bes, Pataikos, or Ptah, and mainly the whole class of grotesque clay figurines, some in the shape of strange birds, had a similar apotropaic function. But the principal finds in the field of popular apotropaic cult, intended to ward off all evil spirits, were the necklaces of faience beads and amulets worn mainly by children. These again included images of Egyptian deities, or Egyptian emblems that had a similar role in their country of origin and were adopted in Palestine by the locals. Hundreds of similar beads and amulets have been found at all coastal sites. At Dor, two nearly complete necklaces were found depicting images of Bes, Ptah, and Pataikos, in Egyptian as well

III.36 Clay "Bes"
vase from Dor

as Phoenician rendition (in the case of Bes, a pair of horns was added). Other images included those of Taueret, Neith, and Bastet. Of the other emblems, the "eye of Horus" was the most popular.

Besides the variety of faience amulets, there are also glass pendants and beads. The beads are covered with little dots within circles that look like many eyes—no doubt intended, like the eye of Horus, to keep the evil eye at a distance. In the glass necklaces, the pendant in the center, usually made of glass in bold colors—black, red, and yellow—depicts a god or goddess (Ba'al or 'Astarte?), who is supposed to protect the bearer. Alternately, they sometimes depict a frightening, grotesque image whose role is similar to that of the masks, i.e., to frighten off the various harmful forces. Here, too, some are depicted in the shape of strange birds. The distribution of the glass amulets encompassed the entire country; some were found in Jerusalem and En-Gedi from the late 6th century but mainly from the 5th century BCE. Large, supernatural eyes and the twisted mouth are common to all these amulets. We may assume that both the faience and the glass amulets functioned as the clay masks to protect their owners from major disasters.

Amulets of another type, made in the form of the symbols of local deities, such as the bronze and stone amulets recently found at Ashkelon representing the emblem of the Phoenician goddess Tanit-'Astarte, were probably also intended to protect their bearers.

Cultic Incense Vessels of Bronze and Stone

Another kind of cult object is the incense stand. These are usually divided into two major types: bronze and clay incense vessels and limestone incense altars.

Some of the bronze vessels are composite ones known by their Greek name *thymiateria.* The typical *thymiaterion* of the Persian period is made in human form, i.e., depicts the god or goddess standing on a tripod with open bowl above the head in which the incense was burned. Sometimes there is also a cover above the bowl, pierced by many holes to allow the incense to burn while dispersing its smoke. This type of incense burner has, like many other artifacts, an ancient Canaanite prototype, examples of which were recently found at Tel Nami, north of Dor. A bronze *thymiaterion* discovered in a Persian-period tomb at Shechem was decorated with the "fallen leaves" motif borrowed from Phoenician architectural ornamentation, rather than with the image of a god. Other vessels of bronze or bone, also standing on tripods, had three arms on the upper part to support the incense bowl. These vessels were found at sites along the Phoenician coast and in Cyprus and were probably in use in Palestine, too. We also possess some small bronze and clay chalice-shaped incense vessels. At Dor and Khirbet Ibsan in Lower Galilee, bronze incense shovels with rounded handles and flat bases were found. During the Persian period, the handles of these implements were usually zoomorphic in form, representing the head of a bull, calf, ibex, lion, or other animal. Others, with smooth handles, were probably intended for use in domestic rituals. Among the bronze vessels were lamps from various sites, including one found in a cave above Jericho and another in the Hebron Hills.

Some of the bronze incense vessels found in Palestine clearly originated in Mesopotamia. One of these is a bronze *thymiaterion* found in a tomb at Shechem, the upper part of which has the form of the lamp of the Babylonian god of light, Nusku. A bronze chalice of unusual form, filled with natural asphalt as a combustible material, was also found in this tomb.

III.37 A bronze *thymiaterion* from Shechem

The second widespread incense burner found in Palestine in the Persian period is the limestone or clay altar. The altars of the Persian period differ in shape from the altars of the Iron Age, which were larger and had four horns at the corners. In the Persian period, they are small chests of limestone or clay, standing on four legs. This change, a result of Assyrian influence, was introduced at the end of the Iron Age and became most popular during the Persian period (see above). The appearance of these altars is not limited to Palestine. Large assemblages have also been uncovered in three other areas of the Near East: South Arabia, Mesopotamia, and Cyprus. Various attempts have been made to associate the Palestinian altars with each of the other groups and they were attributed to the Mesopotamian-Assyrian sphere of in-

II.38 Limestone incense
altars from Tel Sheva
and Tel Seraʿ

fluence in Book One above. During the Assyrian period, such altars were found in all parts of the country; in Israel, Phoenicia, and Judah, especially in those areas of Judah that were captured by the Idumaeans (including Tell el-Kheleifeh, Ḥaẓeva in the Aravah, and Qitmit and Tel Malḥata in the Arad Valley).

In the Persian period, they became extremely popular and are found all over the country. They became the only form of incense burner during the period. They have been found at sites including Megiddo and Samaria in the northern provinces; Shiqmona and Makmish in the Sharon; Ashdod, Tell Jemmeh, Tel Seraʿ, and Tell el-Farʿah (S) in Philistia; Tell en-Naṣbeh and Gezer in Judah; Lachish and Tel Sheva in Idumaea; and Tell es-Saʿidiyeh east of the Jordan. Concerning their use, we learn from the South Arabian inscriptions on some of them that list the names of various types of incense. On one of the Lachish altars, an incised Aramaic inscription mentions *levonta*, also the name of a type of incense. Some of these altars are decorated with geometric designs imitating Assyrian motifs. Others are ornamented with figures of plants, animals, and even humans, in a popular and simple local artistic tradition. It seems, therefore, that these altars, whether of limestone or clay, were introduced to Palestine under the influence of the Assyrian cult, and remained in use here until the Hellenistic period.

Decorated stone cultic artifacts of another type are the gravestones or stelae decorated with motifs and symbols such as heads of deities, the Egyptian ankh emblem, the proto-Aeolic capital, such as an altar from Tel Seraʿ upon which a proto-Aeolic capital topped with lotus leaves, an old Phoenician emblem, is incised.

Another type of stone cultic object, uncovered at sites along the Phoenician coast dating to the Persian and Hellenistic periods, is the carved stone throne that carried the statuette of the local deity. This probably also belonged to the Phoenician sanctuaries on the Palestinian coast. One such throne was found in 1907 at Khirbet et-Tayibeh, just a few kilometers south of Tyre. The two sides of the throne were decorated with the figures of two sphinxes. On its back were carved the emblem consisting of the moon crescent between two lotus flowers and a Phoenician inscription: "To my lady, to Ashtoret (ʿAstarte) who is . . . which belongs to her, I am ʿAbdubasti son of BodBaʿal." Ubasti should be identified with the Egyptian cat-goddess Bastet, many figurines of whom have been found along the coast from Sarepta through Dor as far as Ashkelon. This type of throne was commonly utilized in Phoenician and Palestinian sanctuaries.

· Chapter 5 ·

POTTERY VESSELS

LOCAL POTTERY

Local pottery of the Persian period was made for the most part from three different clays, two of which were common to the coastal plain and the Galilee and the third prevalent in the mountain regions of Judah and Samaria. The first two types are a light greenish-yellow clay and a red clay. There seems to be no special significance attached to the difference in colors (which is also found in pottery of later periods), for in many cases two vessels of the same type, which may even have been discovered together in a single locus, were produced from the two different types of clay (e.g., the "Persian" bowls and the jars with basket handles). Vessels of these clays are usually very coarsely made and the clay is not well levigated. Another quite typical feature of these vessels is that the material is often very brittle as a result of poor firing. Air bubbles are present in most of these vessels. Some were trapped inside the coating, while others burst, leaving holes in the sides. A characteristic feature of the larger vessels of this type is insufficient smoothing of the sides, which present a great many bulges and dents. The outline of the vessels, furthermore, is asymmetrical and gives the impression that they were produced carelessly and in haste. Most of the pottery produced in the mountain regions of Judah and Samaria, in contrast, is of a brown-gray clay that clearly continues Iron Age pottery-making traditions. These vessels are better fired and are of pleasing proportions.

The pottery of the Persian period seldom was decorated. Some of the vessels from the first phase of the period retain the Iron Age burnish decoration, though in a slightly different form and in varied hues. The burnished bands are broader and have a very light reddish hue. Painted decoration is rare and is confined to a number of types of jugs, juglets, and bottles, in a quite monotonous technique consisting of several horizontal bands painted in a reddish-brown color.

Several vessels (open lamps and "carrot-shaped" bottles) have a knife-shaved surface. A new development in vessels of this period is the appearance of ribbing (in jars, jugs, juglets, "Persian" bowls, etc.). This is not yet the sharp ribbing common from the Hellenistic period onward, but a broad, flat ribbing. Another class of Persian-period pottery has wedge-shaped and reed-impressed decoration. Such decoration, already encountered in the Late Iron Age in a variety of types, is now, for the most part, poor and quite rare. The demand for high-quality vessels appears to have been met by foreign imports, especially Greek pottery, which was immeasurably superior to all local products.

The local pottery repertoire in the Persian period consists of various types of bowls (including mortaria or "Persian" bowls), holemouth jars, kraters, cooking pots, a great variety of jars and amphorae needed for the growing international, and particularly maritime, trade. Large jars with basket handles, of East Greek origin, were imitated here. Smaller vessels include flasks, dipper juglets, perfume juglets and cups, *amphoriskoi* (small juglets with two handles), as well as the many types of bottles. Other small vessels intended for other uses are the closed lamps, which occur for the first time, in imita-

III.39 Jokneam, local Persian-period jars found in one room in a storehouse

tion of the Greek prototypes, stands, cult vessels such as *kernoi* (hollow vases in the shape of a round ring), chalices, and "Bes" vases found in many Persian-period coastal sites, as well as "face" vases depicting the head of the goddess ʿAstarte looking in both directions. Peculiar to this period are also the many *rhyta* (drinking vases in the shape of horns), imitating Achaemenian prototypes and depicting various animals such as bulls, rams, fish, and even horses and eagles, and in one case also a female deity head. All these pottery finds are divided between the mountainous inner areas and the coastal region. There are also types that are peculiar to a smaller area, such as the northern part of the coast, where they were probably produced. An example is a certain type of jar fired in a kiln uncovered at Tel Michal.

In general, the local pottery types of the Persian period can be divided into three major groups: (1) local pottery that continues the ceramic tradition of the Late Iron Age, (2) local imitations of imported pottery of eastern origin, and (3) local imitations of "western" prototypes.

The first group comprises most of the bowls, cooking pots, holemouth jars (an important jar family, especially the jar type continuing the *lmlk* type), most of the flasks, certain types of jugs and juglets, flat open lamps, twin vases, funnels, and stands. Since these vessels were generally confined to the areas of Judah and Samaria, it is evident that Israelite ceramic traditions persisted there longer than in other parts of Palestine.

Vessels of the second group, the imitations of eastern prototypes, exhibit Assyrian, Persian, Phoenician, and Egyptian influences. The Assyrian pottery, especially the Palace ware from the close of the 7th century BCE, was well known by now and became a constant feature of the local pottery repertoire. The continuous Assyrian influence is evident in the Persian period mainly in the ceramic and metallic carinated bowls and in most of the bottles. In their cruder shapes and especially in their lack of the typical painted decoration, the vessels of the Persian period are, moreover, far inferior to both the Assyrian originals and their Iron Age imitations. No attempts were made in Palestine to duplicate the Achaemenid pottery, for it was generally of very poor quality and was not common outside the borders of Persia. Among all the pottery finds in Palestine, only two or three vessels can be designated with certainty as direct Persian imports. The magnificent Achaemenid metalware, in contrast, was a significant source of inspiration for Palestinian potters who imitated it in clay. The most outstanding imitations are the *rhytas*. It is also possible that the impressed wedge-and-reed decoration of the Persian period draws its inspiration from Achaemenian metalware. Other Palestinian vessels can be assigned to a Phoenician origin by analogy with earlier

III.40 Local Achaemenian-style clay *rhyta*

Phoenician vessels of the Late Iron Age and their discovery in Phoenician tombs and sites. The Phoenician influence is particularly marked in the jugs and juglets, "face" vases and "Bes" vases, several types of jars, and lamps. Egyptian influence, on the other hand, can be observed only in the alabastra, apparent copies of alabaster originals.

The pottery imported from the west was widely imitated, especially vessel forms, but the Palestinian potters did not succeed in duplicating the excellent quality and exquisite decoration. We may assume that the East Greek bowls served as the models for the small bowls and kraters with horizontal handles, which were widespread in Persian-period Palestine. The locally produced closed lamps, made of coarse clay without the typical burnish, were certainly patterned after Greek lamps. A juglet found at Tel Megadim bears a close resemblance to an Attic *lekythos;* another from Tel Mevorakh imitates a *laginos.*

In most cases, the difference between the imported ware and the Palestinian imitations can be readily distinguished, as can the source of the originals. At the same time, there is a large group of plain ware, which is nearly identical in form with the imported western groups. Since it lacks distinctive decoration, however, it is impossible to determine whether it is imported or locally produced. This group includes the "Persian" bowls with flat base, a large group of straight-shouldered jars, jars with basket handles, and amphorae of the type that served as the prototype of the Rhodian amphorae of the Hellenistic age. These vessels were all used in transporting goods by sea and are widely dispersed along the eastern coast of the Mediterranean. Only mineralogical and petrographical analyses can pinpoint their place of origin. Nevertheless, it is clear that even if the majority of these jars, bowls, and amphorae were indeed locally manufactured, their origins must be sought in the East Greek islands and in Cyprus. In any event, their appearance in the eastern Mediterranean is connected with the establishment of early Greek colonies such as al-Mina and Tell Sukas on the Phoenician coast, Meẓad Ḥashavyahu in Palestine, Migdol in Sinai, and Daphne and Naukratis in Egypt.

IMPORTED POTTERY

THE MAJOR SOURCE for pottery imported to Palestine in the Persian period was Greece. The earliest Greek pottery found in Palestine dates back (as we have seen) to the 10th century BCE and arrived from Euboea. Later, in the 9th to 8th centuries BCE, Geometric and Proto-Geometric pottery came from the same source. Later Greek vessels came from different regions. During the Assyrian period, most came from Corinth and the various eastern Greek islands, which then held the mastery of the seas. These ceramic vessels were still rare in Palestine and only a few have been found. Only from the end of the 6th century BCE onward did imports from the eastern Greek islands increase—from Rhodes, Kos, Knidos, Chios, Samos, Lesbos, etc., as well as from the Greek settlements along the northeastern Mediterranean coast, such as al-Mina. These East Greek wares included bowls with painted bands and horizontal handles, jugs with black-painted decoration or geometric designs on the upper part, and vessels in the Wild Goat style. During the late 6th century BCE, Greek wares from Athens began to arrive. Though imported initially in small numbers, they quickly became an integral part of the repertory of vessels utilized in Palestine. The first Athenian vessels to arrive were painted in black on red background (black-figured ware); later the colors were reversed and the figures were painted in red on black (red-figured ware); finally, the plain black-glazed types arrived. In the beginning, most of the fine imported Greek pottery in Palestine and Phoenicia fell into two categories: perfumed oil flasks such as *lekythoi* and *amphoriskoi* and vessels appropriate for wine service: cups, *skyphoi*, bowls for drinking, and kraters for mixing wine. This trade was practiced simultaneously by Greeks and Phoenicians.

Changes in the sources of imported Greek ware and the absolute dominance of Attic pottery through the Persian period in Palestine are paralleled by finds in neighboring lands and, in fact, all around the Mediterranean, including its islands. The influx of Greek goods to the eastern Mediterranean coast was simultaneous with the Greek colonization on the coasts of Phoenicia and Palestine. Clear evidence for this process has been found at al-Mina, Tell Sukas, Tabat el-Hamam, and elsewhere along the Phoenician coast. Evidence for the settlement of Greek merchants has also been discovered in Palestine. We shall examine several examples. At Acco, a rich assemblage of Greek pottery was discovered in buildings on the northwestern part of the mound. The excavator, M. Dothan, interpreted these finds as evidence for a merchants' quarter occupied mainly by Greeks in one section of the town. In the excavations at Jaffa, the floor of one of the rooms of a large Persian-period warehouse, with close affinities in plan to those at al-Mina, yielded a considerable quantity of a single type of red-figured ware. The excavator found parallels with similar finds at al-Mina. As in that northern Phoenician port city, it is very likely that a group of Greek merchants likewise resided in

III.41 Greek Attic vases from various sites

Jaffa during this period and engaged in the wholesale trade of products from Athenian workshops. In the same manner, Athenian pottery was also apparently imported to Tell Jemmeh. According to one account, the discoveries there included about a dozen red-figured cups, apparently produced by one painter, which may have been purchased at the same time in Athens and carried over on the same vessel to an eastern Mediterranean port, whence they were distributed to several merchants. The best examples of the phenomenon of Greek settlement come from al-Mina, Tell Sukas, and Ras el-Basit in Phoenicia and from Tel Dor, Meẓad Ḥashavyahu, and Migdol in Palestine. At two other sites in Palestine, 'Atlit and Tell el-Ḥesi, the excavators identified Greek tombs. The general impression obtained of Greek settlement during the 7th to 4th centuries BCE in Phoenicia and, apparently, in Palestine as well, is of Phoenician cities containing a strong Greek element. The Greek population in these cities did not constitute a majority of the inhabitants. Rather, they reflect the quality of *enoikismos*—settlement of Greeks among the Phoenicians, or the more or less peaceful coexistence of a foreign, Greek element in a city with a predominantly native Phoenician population. No matter which of those alternatives is applicable, there now appears to be a more solid archaeological basis for a statement W. F. Albright made many years ago: "In the 6th century BCE numerous Greek trading posts were established on the coasts of Egypt, Palestine and Syria." It now appears, however, that the overall amount of imported Greek vessels in Persian-period Palestine points to something that is much more than just a result of regular trade, as has recently been suggested by J. Waldbaum.

In addition to the decorated Greek pottery discussed above, plain ware from Greece also began to appear in Palestine during the Persian period and even earlier (see above). These included heavy bowls, cooking pots, etc. Prominent among them are wine amphorae from various eastern Greek islands. It seems that even though Palestine produced large quantities of excellent wine, considerable amounts of wine were imported from abroad, perhaps intended for consumption by the increasing numbers of Greeks who had settled in Palestine. The importation of Greek wine gradually increased in volume until it became a veritable flood in the 4th to 3rd centuries BCE. The wine was brought from many of the Greek islands, each with its distinctive jar type. Most jars had stamped handles designating the producers and the official under whose jurisdiction the wine was produced. Most jars came from the eastern Greek islands of Rhodes, Knidos, Samos, Kos, etc. Others were imported from the Greek mainland.

Our knowledge of the extent of Greek commercial ties has been enhanced by a recently published palimpsest from Egypt on which the *Words of Aḥiqar* are written. This is a list of customs duties levied for the royal treasury in the year 11, dated on the basis of paleographic considerations to the reign of Xerxes, or 475 BCE. The list is dated by the days and months of a single year. It records the arrival of forty-two ships at a certain Egyptian port and the customs (duty, tithe) collected from each. Of these craft, nineteen large ships and seventeen of another type, a total of thirty-six out of forty-two, are identified by the nature of their cargo and the names of their Greek owners. A duty of some 20 percent was levied, and the owners were required to pay "silver of men" and "a portion of oil." The tax was paid in kind from the cargoes: gold staters, silver, wine, oil, and a certain kind of wood. The sailing season of the Greek ships lasted approximately ten months. All ships carried natron on their return from Egypt and, of course, paid a tax on departure as well. This information illustrates—if only partially—the vigor of Greek maritime activity in the first half of the 5th century BCE along the shores of the eastern Mediterranean, of which Palestine accounts for a considerable part. The rest of the ships in the list were Sidonian and carried Sidonian wine, cedar wood, iron, wool, copper, tin, and clay.

From the discussion above, we may conclude that in the Persian period, and even earlier, Greek pottery became prominent in the Palestinian repertoire, imported both by local traders and by Greek settlers, soldiers, and merchants. Thus, about two hundred years before its actual conquest by Alexander's armies, Palestine was already under strong, direct Greek influence.

In addition to Greek pottery, Palestine in the Persian period also witnessed the renewed appearance of Cypriot wares. Cypriot ships arrived in relatively small quantities and included both decorated and undecorated wares. Among the first group are usually small vessels such as jugs, juglets, and *amphoriskoi*. The undecorated ware consisted mainly of jars and amphorae used for storing oil, wine, and even fish.

As for imports from the east, almost no Egyptian vessels are noted in excavation reports of Persian-period sites. Egyptian imports tend to be artifacts other than pottery, such as alabaster, faience, etc. (see below). Persian-Achaemenian imports are represented by only a handful of finds, mainly some cups from Samaria made of a light greenish clay with high-ribbed sides. Though direct imports of Achaemenian ware was nonexistent, the indirect influence of Achaemenian vessels on several types of local pottery is obvious, and especially that of metal vessels, as, for example, on *rhyta* and on the group decorated by wedge-shaped impressions. In this regard, W. Culican claimed that Achaemenid pottery was almost uniformly dull, and that its finest examples were a continuation of the shapes of Assyrian metalware. The advent of the Persian period did not alter local pottery styles in the Near East, perhaps because the Persians did not establish colonies.

· Chapter 6 ·

METAL, STONE, BONE,
AND GLASS ARTIFACTS

L arge assemblages of metalware, alabaster, bone, and glass have been
found in Persian-period strata and tombs in Palestine. The favorable
trade conditions seem to have provided a stimulus for the sudden increase of
luxury articles from various sources. These objects of commerce clearly reflect the standard of living, the technical capacity, and the artistic level of the
period, as well as contemporary foreign influences in Palestine. They are
therefore of the utmost significance.

Most of the imported objects found in Palestine came from Persia,
Phoenicia, Egypt, and Greece. The contribution of each of these was generally in the particular sphere in which they had reached a high level of production in their native lands. Accordingly, the Egyptian imports consisted
mainly of alabaster, faience, mirrors, and cosmetic utensils. Cypriot imports
are represented by jewelry, Greek items include cosmetic articles, and
Phoenician wares include furniture, decorated metal vessels, and bone objects. The import of luxury items seems to have been detrimental to local
production and to have stifled its growth. Only a small number of the objects
discussed below can be attributed to Palestinian sources. These were of inferior quality and workmanship, except for some exact imitations of foreign
originals.

Because of the number and diversity of these objects, it is possible to include only a representative selection here, emphasizing those types that best
reflect the finds as a whole. Our choice here is based upon the prevalence of
a given artifact in Palestine, on the one hand, and its representing a well-
known craft in the country of origin, on the other. The finds are presented in

functional groups rather than on the basis of the type of material: household artifacts, cosmetic utensils, and jewelry.

FURNITURE

FURNITURE WAS FOUND in a tomb at Tell el-Farʿah (S), which also contained a great deal of metalware. The bronze joints of a couch and a stool were preserved in this tomb. These objects were cleaned and restored. During the cleaning, a number of Phoenician letters were found incised on some of the joints, one in each corner. These were apparently intended as aids in assembling the parts (like mason's marks). It was correctly observed that this type of furniture is also indicative of Greek origin. However, because of the Phoenician letters, it can be assumed that the furniture was produced in Phoenician workshops that specialized in imitations of foreign luxury articles. The remains of other furniture discovered in Palestine and Phoenicia

III.42 Tell Jemmeh, a Persian-period stool reconstructed according to its bronze joints

can be ascribed to a similar source. Especially outstanding are the fragments of an Achaemenid throne from Samaria. Despite its Achaemenid style, it was considered by M. Tadmor to have been produced in Samaria. Recently, seven parts of another "Achaemenian" throne, almost identical to the one from Samaria, were salvaged from a Phoenician shipwreck near the quay of the 'Atlit harbor. The ship also contained many other metal parts and was probably the property of a metalworker who utilized them as scrap for the production of metal vessels. This is further evidence that the so-called Achaemenian furniture was locally made. In the same shipwreck, other metal components of "Achaemenian" furniture were retrieved.

In the tomb of the Sidonian king Tabnit, a pair of bronze candelabra was found. They are some 1.5 m. high and are fashioned in typical Phoenician style, which continues the candelabra types in bronze and ivory found in Iron Age graves in the Phoenician cemetery of Salamis in Cyprus. More Phoenician candelabra, very similar to those of the Sidonian king's tomb and those from Salamis, were also found in the 'Atlit shipwreck. Additional metal candelabra of various types have been found at many Persian-period sites in Palestine. A 1-m.-long iron candelabrum found in a tomb at Samaria may be dated to the Late Iron Age, as may two bronze *thymiateria* that were found in a Persian-period tomb at Shechem.

These finds indicate that Phoenician workshops located along the Phoenician-Palestinian coast were the source of production of the local furniture and other metal household artifacts, whether in "Achaemenian," "Egyptian," "Greek," or any other foreign style.

HOUSEHOLD UTENSILS

SMALL METAL UTENSILS such as bowls, jugs, chalices, ladles, and strainers suddenly appear at the same time during the Persian period and soon became standard equipment in tombs, temples, and houses.

Metal bowls have been found in many Palestinian tombs and in occupation strata. This reflects a Mesopotamian custom that became common in the Assyrian period and reached its zenith in the Persian period, when it spread throughout the ancient world, both east and west. The common bowl of the Persian period is round (or moderately carinated) and deep. The base is convex with an *omphalos* (round projection) in the center. Another distinctive feature of these bowls is a floral (usually lotus) relief decoration at the bottom of the bowl. These bowls were copied in pottery and glass. This bowl type

III.43 Metalware of the Persian period from various sites

has been studied at length, and an extensive literature exists on the subject. Their place of manufacture is a matter of controversy. Syria, Urartu, Armenia, and Greece have been proposed as the place of origin, but because of their widespread distribution, their source has not been established thus far. They were probably manufactured in several centers simultaneously. Whereas the Palestinian and Syrian bowls closely resemble the Persian and Mesopotamian examples in shape, many of the decorative motifs (the lotus, for example) are copies of Egyptian designs. The Palestinian and Syrian bowls appear, therefore, to be Phoenician creations in which Mesopotamian, Persian, and Egyptian motifs were fused in typical Phoenician fashion. The bowls were also used as votive offerings in temples: a group of inscribed bowls from a Phoenician temple at Eliachin in the Sharon Plain is now known. More inscribed bowls have been found in other temples (see above).

A similar source of production can also be assumed for three types of metalware for daily use—jugs, dippers, and strainers—as well as bronze caldrons, some of which are decorated with animal-shaped handles (lions, ducks, etc.) in traditional "Achaemenian" style. A silver jug from Gezer and the lion-shaped handle from 'Atlit represent this category.

The many bronze dippers and strainers also had handles terminating in animal heads: bulls, calves, ibexes, ducks, etc. Others continued old local Phoenician-Egyptian traditions. The best example is the silver dipper from Tell el-Farʿah (S) in the form of a swimming girl, a motif that goes back to the Late Bronze and Iron ages. Like the bowls, the dippers have also been found throughout the Near East, as well as in Cyprus and Greece. They share a similar history and origin with the bowls and the metal cult objects treated above.

Cosmetic Vessels and Jewelry

IN ADDITION TO the sudden increase in household vessels in metalware, cosmetic articles of various types also began to appear in large numbers. An important group of these objects is the mirrors. These were widespread in the Late Bronze Age, disappeared almost completely in the Iron Age, and became common again at the end of this period. They were most popular during the Persian period. In the same tombs containing the mirrors, kohl tubes and sticks were often found. Complete sets of these cosmetic utensils were discovered in some tombs, but usually only the kohl sticks were found. The tubes were of various materials—bronze, alabaster, bone, and paste—of varied shape, usually flat on one side and slightly twisted on the other. One found at ʿAtlit consisted of four containers around a central support. A tube from Tell el-Farʿah (S) had only two containers attached to a central rod, while bone tubes from Hazor and al-Mina consisted of a single container. The manufacture of kohl utensils has a long tradition in Egypt, which apparently served as the main source for such items in the Persian period.

Two other types of alabaster cosmetic articles were common in Palestine in the Persian period: alabastron-shaped vessels and small bowls. The alabastron-shaped body has two round or rectangular knob handles. The rim is wide and flaring and the base is convex to flat. Body dimensions vary. Such vessels were very widely distributed in Palestine and other countries of the ancient east. Alabastra were likewise very popular in Greece, where they were also manufactured from materials other than alabaster. The Greek alabastron lacks the knob handles of the eastern type. In Palestine, the earliest alabastra appear at the end of the 7th century BCE, but they were most common in the 6th to 4th centuries BCE. Support for this dating is provided by comparison with finds from neighboring lands. In his presentation, I. Ben-Dor distinguished between two types of Palestinian alabastra: (1) Egyptian imports, which were made of alabaster imported from Egypt and are identical to the Egyptian vessels; (2) locally produced, which were made of local alabaster and differ from the originals in details, such as a band added to the neck, flat base, conical shoulders, and knob handles of different shape. In his view, the production of alabaster vessels was revived in Palestine, after a complete cessation at the end of the Iron Age, during the Babylonian-Persian periods as a result of the Egyptian imports. The alabastra of alabaster apparently contained a costly perfume in liquid form, which was measured in minute quantities. The differences in vessel dimensions (from very large to very small) appear to indicate that they held precisely fixed quantities. Some of these vessels may also have served as kohl containers. In a tomb at 'Ain Arrub near Hebron, for example, an isolated alabastron was found with a bronze kohl stick.

The small bowl is the second most common type of alabaster vessel in Palestine. The bowl is flattened and has a wide flat rim. Some also have four knob handles projecting from the rim. Small bowls vary in size. Most were discovered together with alabastra and are identical in origin and date. These bowls were used for crushing tiny quantities of fine aromatic powders. In Palestine, such alabaster bowls replaced the local limestone vessels decorated with geometric designs, discussed above. The hard alabaster was apparently better suited for this purpose than limestone. In addition, we also possess a few small faience bowls from this period, some of Egyptian origin. Others are probably local imitations.

All the cosmetic articles described above, the mirrors, kohl implements, bottles of fragrant oils, and small bowls for crushing kohl, were found primarily in women's tombs, except for one type of mirror, which may be considered a Cypriot import. All these vessels were imported from Egypt or were local imitations of Egyptian products.

As to the bone and ivory cosmetic implements, a few are attributed to the Persian period. Most of these were artifacts for daily use, such as handles of vessels of various materials as well as knife and dagger handles. These are in two prevailing styles. Some are in the local style imitating the Phoenico-Egyptian. One such example is a handle from Dor in the shape of a crouching lioness. Another, from Ashkelon, depicts a crouching bull. Others are in the new Achaemenian style, such as a decorated comb from Ashkelon, which depicts in two registers a Persian rider chasing various animals; another portrays the head of a Persian monarch with a typical Achaemenian crown.

An important artifact is a cow scapula from Dor decorated with an incised maritime scene depicting a Phoenician ship sailing from a harbor. The artifact was discovered in a *favissa* of a local sanctuary, as indicated by a Cypriot dedicatory inscription, added somewhat later. This artifact provides a rare view of the daily life of Phoenician sailors in the Persian period.

A considerable amount of jewelry has been found among the burial offerings in Persian-period women's graves and settlement strata. The majority of the jewelry consists of earrings, rings, bracelets, and anklets of bronze and iron, round in shape and simple and undecorated in form. All of these pieces were undoubtedly produced locally and continued an unbroken, very old tradition devoid of specific elements typical of the Persian period. Nevertheless, a number of pieces was imported from a variety of sources: Achaemenian, Cypriot, Greek, and a few Phoenician examples have survived.

Jewelry inspired by Achaemenian prototypes includes earrings and

III.44 Ashdod, part of an Achaemenian-style gold earring depicting an ibex

bracelets found in Jerusalem, Ashdod, and Gezer. All belong to a ramified class of jewelry in true Achaemenian style. The earrings from Jerusalem and Ashdod are of gold and silver and are made in the form of a ram or ibex. More typical of the Achaemenian jewelry and much more common is a find from Gezer consisting of a pair of silver bracelets in the form of full circles with the ends terminating in the heads of rams or ibexes. Similar bracelets are very well known at Persian-period sites throughout the Near East, including Cyprus. They are especially widespread in Persia. Achaemenian jewelry has been the subject of numerous studies. H. Kantor defined Achaemenian jewelry in general as an "animal style" produced in typical Persian manner: it was a composite style and a modification of earlier motifs from Assyria, Urartu, and Luristan. In her opinion, two classes of jewelry can be defined: that produced by royal metalworkers in the "Palace Style"; and all the other jewelry, produced in the countries where found, inspired by Achaemenian art and attempting to copy it. Support for this view is found in two stone molds, one from Byblos and another from Egypt, incised with designs typical of Achaemenian jewelry.

Cypriot and Greek-style jewelry has been found at 'Atlit and Tell Jemmeh in Persian-period tombs and settlement strata. It consists of coiled wires in the form of springs, of bronze or of gold-and-silver-plated bronze. A study of the distribution of these ornaments shows that they appear mainly in Greece, Rhodes and western Asia Minor, Cyprus, and the coast of Palestine. Of all these places, Cyprus is the only country with an unbroken tradition of the production of similar ornaments. Also in Greek style are some bronze fibulae, used to fasten garments. These were composed of two parts, the back in the form of a bow and the front in the form of a straight pin. Fibulae were common in Palestine from the Iron Age and earlier and continued with minor changes to the Persian period. Here, very thick heavy pins usually found in great numbers only in Greece, the Aegean islands, and Cyprus replaced the old ones, and there can be no doubt as to their Greek origin.

Glass and faience amulets and even whole necklaces have also been found in large numbers in many Persian-period sites. These mainly depict grotesque heads and belong to the apotropaic cult discussed above.

WEAPONS

PALESTINE REMAINED IN a state of desolation following the Babylonian conquest and was captured by the Persians without a war. There are therefore no remains of siege ramps or destruction strata associated with the Persians' conquest comparable to the Assyrian and Babylonian conquests. The onset of the Persian period is marked by a wave of intensive construction. There are, however, some written sources that indicate the existence of military garrisons in a few key sites in the country. The Bible refers, for example, to "the army of Samaria," which was present when Sanballat mocked Nehemiah and the "Jews" (i.e., the people of the province of Yehud) who were building the walls of Jerusalem (Nehemiah 3:34).

It was only in the 4th century BCE that fighting took place in the coastal region following a brief period of domination by the Egyptians, or following the rebellions of Phoenicians and the satraps. At that time, large armies crossed the region, dominated by Greek mercenaries. Some artifacts remaining from these conflicts have been uncovered in the region.

Written evidence from this period, in the form of ostraca, also reflects presence of the military in Idumaea, the southern part of Palestine, during the Persian period. Two ostraca from the fortress of Arad mention a military unit called *degel* ("standard"), namely, a soldier belonging to *degel 'ebed nanai* is mentioned. Thus, a military unit was stationed at Arad, presumably of the same size as the *degel* unit that formed the Jewish garrison on the Egyptian island of Elephantine. Interestingly, the Arad *degel* is named after its Babylonian commander who was "the servant of the (Babylonian) goddess Nanai." The same Arad ostraca also mention units of horsemen who, judging by their names, were mainly Arabs and Edomites, but also included several Jews.

A few weapons of Irano-Persian origin have come to light in excavations in Palestine. More common are remains of weapons from various Greek sources. The remainder, found mostly in tombs of the period, were made according to local tradition and technique.

Our discussion of weapons will be confined mainly to arrowheads, since these are the only weapons of the Persian period found in Palestine in well-defined assemblages and contexts. Other weapons may date to this period (swords, javelins, and spearheads), but they have not been assigned to this period with certainty in the excavation reports. Excavations outside Palestine, however, have yielded a large number of weapons in clear contexts, which provide indirect information on all Palestinian weapons. Other important sources for the study of weapons are the Achaemenian reliefs from Persepolis, Greek reliefs of various kinds, and literary accounts of battles.

Arrowheads, like all other types of weapons of the period, may be divided

III.45 Bronze arrowheads in Irano-Scythian style from Tel Megadim

into three typological classes, each from a different source: Irano-Scythian, Greek, and local.

1. Irano-Scythian arrowheads: (a) A bronze arrowhead with a side barb is found in two forms: socketed and tanged. The arrowheads with sockets are subdivided into three-winged or two-winged types. Most of these arrowheads are bronze, though some are iron. Apart from Palestine, they occur in all other parts of the Persian Empire. No examples have been found farther west, neither in Cyprus nor in Greece. (b) A bronze socketed arrowhead, the blade in the form of a leaf or triangle with three wings. This class is divided into two main subtypes: with flat socket and with prominent socket. The two types already appeared in Palestine at the beginning of the Babylonian period and have been found in the destruction levels at Jerusalem and En-Gedi from the time of the Babylonian conquest in 586 BCE. During the Persian period, however, they became more common.

Also of Irano-Scythian (i.e., Persian) origin are bronze horse bits. Some have been found at Gezer, while others were recently recovered from the sea near 'Atlit.

2. Greek-type arrowheads found in Persian-period contexts are also di-

vided into two types: (a) Bronze arrowheads with sockets and a blade, consisting of three wings separated from the body of the blade. (b) Bronze arrowheads with long tangs and flat blades with central midribs. These are triangular in shape and have two barbs on their bases. A round projection sometimes appears at the point of attachment of the tang and the blade. Examples from the east are few. Only four examples were found at Persepolis and a few in Palestine. At Olynthus, on the other hand, they are abundant, and the excavators seem to be correct in concluding that they are of Macedonian origin. The arrowheads from Olynthus are well dated (479–348 BCE), and the contexts of their occurrence in Persia and Palestine further indicate that this type already appeared in the 5th century BCE and certainly continued into later periods. This type of arrowhead is predominant in the Hellenistic and Roman periods, too.

Greek helmets of the 5th to 4th centuries BCE have been found, mostly in underwater exploration off the coasts of Dor, Ashdod, and Ashkelon. Such helmets constitute important artifacts attesting to the numerous Greek mercenaries who passed through the coastal region of Palestine. Heavily armed

III.46 Bronze Greek helmet of the Persian period found in the sea near Ashkelon

Greek soldiers (hoplites) are depicted on Persian-period seals and bullae found at Dor and other sites.

3. The third weapon category of this period consists of local production. The local arrowheads were mainly of iron. Examples have been found at many sites in Palestine. These are fewer in number than the bronze arrowheads. Most are tanged (rounded or square tang). The blades are flat and foliate. Some have midribs, but the bulk of the iron arrowheads is simple in form. In most places, including Palestine, they were made by local metalworkers who were specialists in the ancient metallurgical tradition, while the bronze arrowheads were probably produced in imperial government or military workshops. A few local iron daggers and swords have also been found at several Palestinian sites.

· Chapter 7 ·

SEALS AND SEAL IMPRESSIONS

The seals and seal impressions found in Persian-period strata and tombs in Palestine fall into three general groups: (1) imported seals: Babylonian, Achaemenian, Egyptian, and Greek; (2) local seals of mixed style, which in form or in motif imitate imported seals from one of the four sources in (1) above; and (3) official seals connected with the administration of the provinces of Judah, Samaria, and Ammon, and possibly also of Phoenicia. Seals and seal impressions have been recovered from many Palestinian sites in all regions.

BABYLONIAN SEALS

THE IMPORTED BABYLONIAN seals are conical chalcedony or agate stamp seals with octagonal face. The majority depicts Babylonian priests worshiping before an altar on which are set the spade emblem of the god Marduk and the stylus emblem of Nabu. Some also contain representations of the crescent and the sun, while on others, the symbols appear alone. In Babylon itself, and in northern Mesopotamia as well as in Persia, many such seals have been uncovered in clear Late Assyrian and Neo-Babylonian contexts. In Palestine, too, several seals have been discovered, which apparently date to the same period (604–539 BCE or even earlier; see above). The majority, however, was undoubtedly found in clear Persian-period contexts. Two of the latter seals come, for example, from En-Gedi. One was found there on a floor upon which was found Attic pottery dating to the 5th and the beginning of the 4th centuries BCE. The other was uncovered on the southern slope of the tell, near a Persian-period house. Other seals dating to the Persian period were discovered in a rubbish dump at Tel eṣ-Ṣafi together with Attic pottery and Cypriot limestone statuettes dating to the 5th century BCE. Similar seals have been found at Taanach, where no Neo-Babylonian-period stratum was encountered. However, their overall number in the Megiddo province (Taanach) or Samaria (the city of Samaria) is small. In Judah, some turned up at Bethel and En-Gedi, and one was found in Philistia (at Tell Jemmeh). Recently, many have been found in Transjordan in the territory of Ammon: assemblages are known from the tombs of Tell Mazar, the tomb of Adoninur, and Meqabelein, as well as tombs at Umm Uthainah and, notably, at Khilda, which also contained Attic vases. Others were found in the excavations conducted at Tell Ṣafut south of Rabbath-Ammon.

In addition to the stereotypical Babylonian seals described above, there is also a small group that includes Babylonian names incised in alphabetic characters, mainly in an Aramaic script, but in other West Semitic scripts as well. Examples include the seal of "Nergal-Sallim son of Ahhe-ers" and the seal of "Mannu-ki-Innurta blessed by Milkom" and that of "Yehoyishma daughter

III.47 A Babylonian seal

of Shamah-Shar-Usur." These also date mainly to the Babylonian period, but some are associated with Persian-period contexts. A similar mixed-style seal was found among those encountered at Tell Mazar. It is an imported agate conical seal, which depicts the usual scene of a priest standing in front of an altar, above which are a stand and a lamp—the emblems of the god of light Nusku—and also an inscribed name in alphabetic characters. In the Tell Mazar assemblage were found, in addition to the regular scenes of priests before altars, other heterogeneous motifs, such as a wheel from which project the *protomai* (busts) of a winged lion, a stag, a mountain goat, a bird, and a hero struggling with two horned animals. All of these motifs are well known among Neo-Babylonian seals, with many parallels in Babylon and elsewhere. It should be pointed out that one of the Tell Mazar agate seals was executed in the shape of a duck rather than in the usual conical form.

It is a curious fact that only two examples of Babylonian cylinder seals, which were widespread at that time and have been uncovered in large numbers in Egypt, Syria, and Anatolia, have thus far been found in Palestine: one at Tell Jemmeh, dated to the beginning of the Persian period, and the other at Tell Mazar. This latter depicts a horseman shooting a gazelle. Both are of chalcedony.

PERSIAN SEALS

BOTH CYLINDER AND stamp seals were employed by the Persians in approximately equal numbers. Achaemenian seal impressions of both types have been found in considerable quantity in Egypt, Phoenicia, Anatolia, and Mesopotamia . . . as well as in Persia. They have been interpreted as remains of the archives of high officials in the Persian administration. A few are thought to have belonged to governors. A number of seals was even engraved with the name of the king. All the impressions of this type were stamped on bullae. In Palestine, a large assemblage of similar bullae was uncovered in the Wadi ed-Daliyeh cave, several still attached to the rolled papyri. It seems certain that these papyri originated in the official archive of the province of Samaria. It should be noted that at all of the above-mentioned sites, Achaemenian-type seals formed only part of the total bullae assemblages, which included others of different styles, though all, as has been noted, belonged to royal archives and directly relate to Persian administration. The hoard from Memphis, Egypt, for example, included Egyptian seal impressions of different types and periods alongside Achaemenian seal impressions,

III.48 A bulla from Shechem

III.48a A cylinder seal from Tell el-Ḥer in Achaemenian style

as well as examples in a markedly Archaic Greek style. The same is true of the bullae that sealed the papyri from Elephantine; these, too, were of Achaemenian and Egyptian styles. The bullae from Dascylium in Anatolia, probably the largest hoard of bullae of this type, with more than three hundred specimens, also included bullae from both Achaemenian and Greek sources inscribed in either Persian or Aramaic script. Another assemblage of stamped bullae found at Ur in Babylon included such a diversity of styles (Achaemenian, Babylonian, Greek, Phoenician, and Egyptian) that L. Woolley, who published them, called it "a collector's treasure." In light of the other finds of bullae, however, these, too, should be regarded as seal impressions that were in use in a single administrative office located at Ur.

In addition to the Wadi ed-Daliyeh bullae mentioned above, bullae have been found at many other sites in Palestine, including the cities of Samaria, Shechem, Dor, and Ashkelon. Some were executed in a purely Achaemenian style, though the execution of some of the seals in either glass or faience makes it highly probable that they are local imitations.

Like the Babylonian cylinder seals described above, Persian cylinder seals are almost totally absent in Palestine. In both cases, this may be explained by the fact that they were used to seal clay cuneiform documents rather than papyrus ones. On the other hand, their absence may be merely a matter of chance. A single Achaemenian cylinder seal was found at Tell el-Her, located in northern Sinai near Pelusium. Found in a Persian-period military fort, it depicts the Persian king in combat with two winged lions.

EGYPTIAN SEALS

SEVERAL SITES IN Palestine have yielded Egyptian seals from the period of the 26th to 29th dynasties. They were rendered in the conventional Egyptian scarab style, and most were interpreted as Egyptian imports. Some were inscribed with the names of various pharaohs of the Persian period, who annexed the coastal region of Palestine, as, for example, the scarab of Pharaoh Nepherites I, of the 29th Dynasty, found at Gezer. A unique group consists of scarabs found in Persian-period contexts inscribed with the names of very ancient Egyptian pharaohs, such as Men-Ka-Ra of the Old Kingdom and Thutmose III of the 18th Dynasty, found at Gezer, Tel Mevorakh, and Tel Dor. These were probably copied during the Persian period by local engravers.

III.49 Egyptian-style seals from 'Atlit and Tel Megadim

Some uninscribed Egyptian scarabs have also been found in Palestine in Persian-period contexts. These depict typical Egyptian motifs, such as Re holding his scepter, Isis suckling Horus, and Isis and Horus among the lotus blossoms. These were partly imported from Egypt, but were undoubtedly also locally made. It is easier to identify local production in the scarabs inscribed with hieroglyphs as mere decorative motifs (see below), as well as in scarabs that depict "Egyptian" figures in non-Egyptian attitudes: the figure of the god Bes struggling with two lions or holding two monsters by their hind legs, for example, combining Egyptian and Mesopotamian motifs and scenes.

LOCAL AND IMPORTED NONEPIGRAPHIC SEALS

DURING THE PERSIAN period, there is a steady proliferation of nonepigraphic seals, found from now on in large numbers at nearly all sites of the period. Finds include seals, seal impressions on pottery vessels, and especially bullae that sealed written papyri. These seals were also made in the three common styles: a local style, a Persian style, and a Greek one. Nevertheless, several are executed in a mixed style, combining Egyptian and Greek motifs, or Greek and Persian ones. Simultaneously, small silver and bronze coins were minted in different parts of the country and have been found in large quantities, in these same styles employing the same motifs. Some direct connection between the two phenomena, bullae and coins, is therefore possible (see below). Many (more than 170) bullae of this type were found in the Wadi ed-Daliyeh cave, where the inhabitants of Samaria sought refuge from Alexander the Great's army. The papyri that these sealed, as we have already seen, date between 375 and 335 BCE. Some were discovered by P. L. Lapp, who excavated the cave. Others were found by local Bedouins, who sold them to collectors. A few of the bullae were found still sealing papyrus documents and are certainly impressions of seals that belonged to witnesses who signed the documents. Only a few were inscribed with the names and titles of high-ranking officials, such as "Sanballat the governor of Samaria" and "Yoḥanan," whose title is *sagna,* an important official in the Persian administration (cf. Nehemiah 2:16). These also sealed the papyri documents with their personal seals. One of the papyri, for example, is signed and sealed by "Sanballat the governor of Samaria"; another bulla is inscribed with the name Ishmael. Many names also appear on the Samaritan coins of the period (see below). It is noteworthy that although the few names mentioned on the bullae and inside the documents are all local individuals, the bullae attached to the majority of the documents were nonepigraphic and their motifs are executed in the following three styles:

1. Local motifs that continue old Phoenician-Israelite traditions: sphinxes

and griffins of various types and in various attitudes. Examples include heads of birds, heads of bulls and rams, griffins attacking bulls; various standing or sitting animals, such as walking lions, lions attacking bulls, *protomai* of lions, horses, horses and riders in many variations; birds, such as eagles and falcons, but also small birds; rosettes; lotus flowers; etc. We are familiar with such motifs on 7th century BCE seals.

2. Babylonian-Persian motifs, which usually depict the Persian monarch in diverse activities, but also certain well-known Mesopotamian cult symbols. Such motifs include the "king-scorpion," the winged sun disk from which emerges the figure of a god, and the moon crescent. Others depict the familiar motif of the Persian king struggling with a lion, lifting a pair of lions or other monsters by their hind legs, or struggling with a griffin or other monster, such as a winged bull. Another common Persian motif is the king shooting his bow, hunting wild animals, riding his chariot or standing before his god. In Judah, a group of nonepigraphic seal impressions has been assembled from various sites: Tell en-Naṣbeh, Gibeon, Mozah, Nebi Samuel, Jerusalem, Ramat Raḥel, Jericho, and En-Gedi, all in clear Persian-period contexts, depicting only some of these Achaemenian motifs. These Judaean seal impressions were engraved mainly with lions—walking and roaring, lion *protomai*—and one or two bulls. A small group of impressions within this category, from Gibeon, Nebi Samuel, and Ramat Raḥel, shows the lion rampant with paws outstretched to the sides. This is but a part of a well-known Achaemenian motif describing a lion wounded by arrows shot by the Persian king, and conveys the lion's agony. The Judaean engraver thus borrowed a popular Achaemenian glyptic motif and selected part of it. Recently, a few locally made cylinder seals reflecting Persian and Babylonian influences have been recovered in eastern Jordan. One, depicting the Persian monarch riding a horse and chasing a wild animal, was found at Tell el-Mazar. Two others dated by E. Porada to the late 6th and 5th centuries BCE were uncovered in the Ammonite town at Tell el-ʿUmeiri.

3. About half of the Wadi ed-Daliyeh nonepigraphic bullae, as well as many of the seal impressions from the other Palestinian sites, are engraved in a markedly Greek style. Their large number caused F. M. Cross, who first publicized them, to note that "one is particularly struck with the vivacity of Attic-Greek influences in the glyptic art of Samaria in the era before the coming of Alexander." The main motifs are the hippocamp (a winged sea horse), the triton (half a man and half a fish), the owl of Athena, the quadriga of Athena, and the figures of Zeus and Hermes with their specific attributes. Many also depict warriors, including a hoplite phalanx equipped with heavy

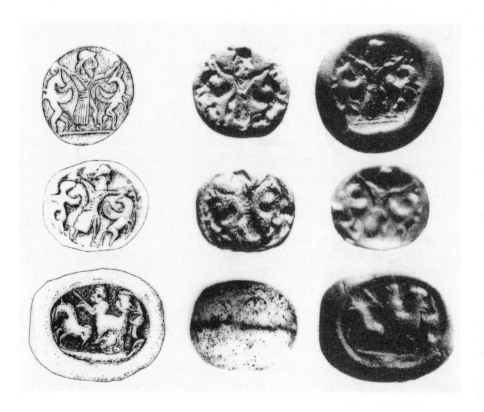

III.50 Dor, local seals in Phoenico-Persian style

armor and metal helmets, individual soldiers with their military equipment, or naked youths standing, sitting, or wrestling. Particularly popular was the figure of Hercules, both because he was identified with the god Baʿal Melqart of Tyre (his famed labors gained him a local following), who replaced the Assyrian or Persian kings, or even older Mesopotamian heroes. Like them, he is depicted raising his club, shooting his bow, struggling with monsters, etc. This hybrid style is often called "Greco-Persian."

In addition to the Greek male figures, there are females, some of whom may be identified as Athena, Aphrodite, and Nike. Other females have not been identified. These seal impressions depict seated and standing women. One is shown seated on a chair and holding a bird, in the same position as the satrap on Cilician coins (see below).

Close examination of the finds from the city of Samaria clearly shows that the same three styles exist among its bullae: local, Achaemenian, and Greek.

One interesting conclusion, at this point, is that there is a direct correspondence between the motifs engraved on both the bullae and the coins of Samaria, as well as on the local nonepigraphic coins from the other Palestinian sites, and the inscribed local coins issued in Judah, Ashkelon, Ashdod, and Gaza (see below). In some cases, this analogy also applies to the motifs depicted on the coins of Phoenicia, Cyprus, and Cilicia.

In addition to the finds from Samaria and Wadi ed-Daliyeh, many other nonepigraphic seal impressions in Greek style have been found at other Palestinian sites, some on bullae and others on clay jar handles or stoppers. The finds from Tell Keisan, ʿAtlit, Dor, Tel Michal, Shechem, Khirbet el-Bira, Gibeon, Ramat Raḥel, Beth-Zur, and En-Gedi all have Greek-style motifs. In certain examples from Atlit and Dor, Shiqmona, Samaria, Tel Michal, Gibeon, and elsewhere, the seals were made of various metals: gold and silver, bronze, and even iron. Others were of precious stones, but the majority is molded in faience and glass. Their shapes, like the motifs engraved upon them, fall into three types: local scaraboid seals, conical seals in Mesopotamian style, and oval seals in Greek style.

THE INSCRIBED SEALS FROM THE PROVINCES OF JUDAH, SAMARIA, AND AMMON

THE GROUPS OF inscribed seal impressions examined here are not personal seals, but relics of the administrative systems of the provinces of Judah, Samaria, and Ammon.

III.51 Seals from 'Atlit in a Perso-Greek style

Dating to the Persian period and belonging to the province of **Judah** are most of the impressions engraved with the name of the province, Yehud (one of these types—inscribed in Hebrew letters—dates to the Hellenistic period), sometimes with the names of its governors and their official titles. Most of these were stamped on bullae or jar handles, but there is now also an actual limestone conical seal of the *yehud* type, and a black-stone seal bearing the name and title of "Shelomit the maidservant of Elnathan the governor." The name of the province as well as the names of more governors and officials of the province of Judah, is also inscribed on some of its coins (see below).

From the province of **Samaria,** there are also some bullae mentioning the names of the provincial governors and officials with their titles. More names of the Samaria province's governors are mentioned in papyri and coins discovered within the city itself and in the Wadi ed-Daliyeh cave.

The names of the province of **Ammon** and of one of its officials are stamped on two jar handles recently uncovered at Tell el-'Umeiri, south of the city of Rabbath-Ammon.

In addition to the official inscribed seals, there are some seal impressions and bullae on which personal names are impressed. The practice of employing seals inscribed with personal names to designate ownership or office is thus known in the Persian period. They are less numerous, however, than in the Judaean monarchic period. Their frequency is illustrated by the assemblage from Wadi ed-Daliyeh: out of 128 seal impressions found there, only two bore a legend reading *(lys')yhw bn (sn')blt pht smr(n),* ("[belonging to Is]aiah son of [Sana]ballat governor of Samaria"). The other name mentioned in the Samaritan bullae is Ishmael. But many additional names are depicted on provincial coins (see below). In the opinion of F. M. Cross, Persian custom prescribed that only officials holding high rank possessed inscribed seals.

In **Judah,** however, the number of seals bearing both the name of a provincial official and the name of the province, Yehud, is greater (see below). For example, in the assemblage of sixty-five Persian-period bullae from Judah published by N. Avigad, stamped from twelve different seals, *all* were inscribed, some with the name of the provincial official and his title, but most with personal name alone, that of the seal owner himself, such as "belonging to El'azar," or his name and patronymic, for example, "belonging to Baruch son of Shim'i." (The latter belongs to the group of large stone seals usually worn suspended from the neck, already in use during the period of the Judaean monarchy. We have pointed out that such seals were used to seal tags on clay and hide jars, etc.) In addition to the Baruch seal, another example, a nonepigraphic limestone seal, was recently discovered in a Persian-period fort at Khirbet Nimra, not far from Hebron, which depicts a bull surrounded by cultic emblems. In the Persian period, some new names that did not occur previously appear, such as *secvi* ("cock"), from Tel Michal and Arad.

Many of the personal names of the period are written not in Palaeo-Hebrew but in Aramaic script such as a 5th century BCE bronze ring from Gibeon inscribed with the words *marat shamen.* Some of these, although found in Palestine, possibly originated in Syria. Many included, besides names, various motifs belonging to all the styles described above, such as the hero struggling with monsters, Hercules lifting his club, etc. A fine example of this type is a 5th century BCE seal found in Rishon le-Zion in Philistia, inscribed with the name *tyln* in lapidary Aramaic script and decorated with the scene of the Persian king chasing a lion.

Personal seals of this type, which are dated to the Persian period, were also found in a few sites in Judah. From these, we learn that the tradition of stating the seal owner's occupation continued. Examples include the seal of "Yermi the scribe," a Judaean coin of this period, which belonged to a certain "Yohanan the priest," and a soapstone seal equipped with a handle inscribed "belonging to Shelomy the notary." Some of the official titles in use during the Judaean monarchy appear to continue into the Persian period. A square limestone seal found at Tell Qasile is engraved with a figure of a bearded man holding a hawk in his outstretched hand, and according to B. Mazar, bears the legend "Ashanyahu servant of the king," thus continuing a common title in Israel and Judah of the previous period. It should be recalled that Tobiah, the Ammonite ruler in the Persian period, is called "the Ammonite servant."

III.52 Assemblage of Persian-period bullae from a Judaean archive

The title *amah* ("maidservant"), too, continued to be used, now by women who had a role in the administrative system of the new state. However, instead of the old title "maidservant of the king," it is now "maidservant of the state governor" *(peḥa)*. Examples include the scaraboid black-stone seal mentioned above of "Shelomith the maidservant of Elnathan the governor," published by N. Avigad, who accepted W. F. Albright's original proposal that the title corresponds to *ʿebed*. In any case, Shelomit was clearly a woman of high rank and was probably the daughter of Zerubbabel (1 Chronicles 3:19). On the Judaean coins appears also the titles "Yeḥezqiyah the governor" and "Yoḥanan the priest" (see below). Other names of Judaean governors appear on seal impressions, bullae, and jar handles of the period.

Some impressions found in Judah include individual letters or even ligatures that cannot be identified. For example, a rectangular-shaped seal impression found at En-Gedi on the body of a jar consisted of only two characters: *b'*. It may represent a personal name or that of a city. Other seals of this type were uncovered in various other regions of the country, for example, a seal found at Beth Yeraḥ, which also contains a ligature of two letters.

In addition to the various types of *yehud* seals, and in many cases together with those bearing Palaeo-Hebrew inscriptions, appear round seal impressions also inscribed in Palaeo-Hebrew script (mostly in retrograde), with the legend *yršlm* ("Jerusalem") set in the spaces between the ends of a five-pointed star (Solomon's shield). E. Sukenik's reading of this legend is widely accepted. Seals of this type have been uncovered thus far at the same Judaean sites as those where the *yehud* seals were recovered, with two exceptions: they were also found at Tel Azekah and Tel Jarmuth on the western border of the Shephelah. They are absent at sites in the eastern part of Judah, at sites such as Jericho and En-Gedi. All the impressions were stamped on jar handles, except for one from Tel Jarmuth, which was impressed on a cooking pot, and another from Jerusalem stamped on a jug. The controversy over the date of this type of seal is similar to that over the date of the *yehud* seals with Palaeo-Hebrew inscriptions. In the past, scholars maintained that they dated to the Persian period, whereas more recent investigators ascribe them to the 3rd to 2nd centuries BCE. Recently, the later date has been widely adopted, as it has for the Hebrew *yehud* seals that N. Avigad's excavations in the Jewish Quarter in Jerusalem uncovered in clear Hellenistic contexts. These seals must therefore be removed from the repertoire of the Persian period.

At the same time, recent works have demonstrated that the so-called *moṣah* seals, which in the past were also attributed to the Persian period, should now be dated exclusively to the Babylonian period (see above).

III.53 The seal of "Ashaniahu, servant of the king"

Coming back to the Aramaic *yehud* seals, these are seal impressions in Aramaic script that bear the legend *yehud,* i.e., the Aramaic name of the province of Judah, written in full or in various abbreviated formulae. Seals of this type have been discovered at the following sites: Gezer, Mozah, Nebi Samuel, Tell en-Naṣbeh, Tell el-Ful, Jerusalem, Ramat Raḥel, Ḥusan, Bethany, Jericho, En-Gedi, and in the above-mentioned postexilic archive, published by N. Avigad, which contained one actual limestone seal. All of these sites are located in Benjamin and Judah, i.e., within the territory of the Yehud province of the Persian period. The one exception to this is the find of one impression in the Persian-period stratum at Kadesh-Barnea in northern Sinai, which served in this period as a caravansary on the main road from Judah to Egypt. Recently, another example came from the site of Tel Ḥarasim, near Tell eṣ-Ṣafi, with a surprising parallel from the German excavations at the city of Babylon, probably belonging to one of the Judaean deportees and clearly indicating contacts of trade or tax payments of oil or wine brought from the province of Yehud. This class of seal impressions may be divided into two main types:

1. Seal impressions on which *yehud* appears written in plene spelling *(yhwd),* or is abbreviated to three letters *(yhd),* two *(yh),* or even a single letter *(h).* A subtype of this seal also has an additional symbol=a monogram. Another subtype is the one to which the title of an official of the province is added, such as *yhwd phwh,* i.e., "Yehud the province."

2. Seals that contain, in addition to the legend *yhwd,* either a personal name or the personal name with the title *peḥa* ("governor"). Some of these types can be divided into subtypes. All of these seals are written in Aramaic with the exception of one subtype with the above-mentioned monogram, the majority of which is written in Hebrew script. Only a few examples are written in Aramaic script. So far, the only seal discovered from which some of these impressions were made is a conical seal, 36 mm. long, of reddish limestone with a rounded top perforated for suspension around the neck. At Ramat Raḥel, the excavators succeeded in reconstructing a whole store-jar with a *yhwd* impression, which very closely resembled the *lmlk* jars of the previous period. No other complete vessels with impressions have been discovered.

The *yhwd* seals of all types have been the subject of numerous studies and we shall not summarize here the results. Suffice it to note that the excavations at Ramat Raḥel, where the greatest typological diversity of these seal impressions occurred, served as a stimulus to their investigation. The new types, on the one hand, made it possible to solve a number of problems dealt with by scholars in the past, and on the other hand, they raised new problems. Further progress in the investigation of these impressions was made by the discovery of the bullae in the Jewish Quarter of Jerusalem by N. Avigad.

It is now the consensus that these seals should be read *yhwd,* as should the various abbreviated forms. And that the title *peḥa* added to some of them means "the governor." The question of the date and relative sequence of these impressions has been a matter of extensive debate. Owing to the lack of convincing archaeological evidence and the difficulties in determining their date on paleographic grounds, the various chronologies proposed extend over a very long period: from the 6th to the 2nd centuries BCE. In general, it may be stated that the earliest investigators relied mainly on the date supplied by the seals themselves, i.e., the resemblance between the monograms appearing on some of the seals and those depicted on vessels from Elephantine, which are securely dated to the 5th century BCE, or, on the other hand, they identified names engraved on the seals with biblical figures and related to the paleographic evidence only as a secondary criterion, which they believed was insufficient for establishing exact dates. Later investigators, however, considered paleography as the main criterion, based on the difference between Hebrew and Aramaic script. In this, all followed F. M.

III.54 *Yehud* seal impressions

Cross, who set the date of the introduction of the Palaeo-Hebrew script at the beginning of the Hellenistic age. This problem has recently been resolved with the discovery of Hebrew *yhwd* seal impressions on vessel shards discovered in N. Avigad's excavations in the Upper City of Jerusalem. From the standpoint of stratigraphy and typology, these can be dated with certainty to the 2nd century BCE.

As to the date of the Persian-period Aramaic seals of the same type, these are attributed to the 4th century BCE. The debate in essence has thus concentrated on the *yhwd* seals in Aramaic. N. Avigad suggested raising their date to the end of the 6th to beginning of the 5th centuries BCE, in opposition to the majority opinion, which maintains that they should be assigned to the end of the 5th and 4th centuries alone. For the *yhwd* impressions in general, the following interpretations have been proposed: that they represent (a) the seal of the official in charge of tax collection on behalf of the Persian authorities; (b) the seal of the treasurer of the Temple of the autonomous province of Judah; (c) the seal of the high priest, who in this period also functioned as governor. Y. Aharoni distinguished between two types of seals: 1. Those that mention the title *peḥa* ("governor") or contain the royal monogram represent seals of the Jewish governors (such as Yeho'ezer and Ahzay). 2. Others that mention only the province name and personal names belonged to the minor officials in the provincial administration (such as Hanana, Uriyau, or Malkiyau), as well as the new type of *yhwd* seal impressions "of Hannuna Yehud" found at Tel Ḥarasim located on the western border of the province, and again in the German excavations at Babylon, in which the personal name comes before the name of the province. Presumably, Hannuna and Hanana are the same person. The finds of seals and bullae in the postexilic archive and in the City of David and the coins inscribed "Yehezqiau the governor" (see below) seem to have also finally resolved the argument: the names of three Jewish governors appear to be mentioned on the seals with their titles—Elnathan, Yeho'ezer, and Ahzay; a fourth governor, Yehezqiyau, appears on the coins. It is agreed by all that the governor Yehezqiyau must have ruled at the very end of the Persian period (and see below). The question of the date of the other three governors mentioned in the seal impressions, Yeho'ezer, Ahzay, and Elnathan, remains open: there are some who believe that they ruled in Jerusalem before Nehemiah and Bagohi, i.e., before 445 BCE, while others believe that they ruled later (i.e., after 408 BCE).

With the *yhwd* seals appear, occasionally, three different types of monograms. One is in the form of the Hebrew letter *'ayin,* similar to the monogram on the Judaean *sheqel* weights of the 7th century BCE (see above). The second monogram has the form of the number 8 lying on its side with open ends. The third is round or lozenge-shaped and either plain or divided by a crossbar or dot. The last is the *tet* symbol. A number of impressions bearing monograms alone have been attributed to the Persian period.

The monogram in the form of the letter *'ayin,* which was common on *sheqel* weights of the Judaean period, was interpreted by Y. Yadin as a conventional sign representing the royal *sheqel* on the *lmlk* seals. Yadin based his opinion on a weight from Gezer, which bears the legend *lmlk* instead of this symbol. He similarly argued that the *tet* symbol, found on vessels from Elephantine together with the word *lmlk,* is also a schematic sign standing for the royal standard. Confirmation of this view has been provided by the discovery of storage jars dating to the 4th century BCE at Shiqmona, which are also inscribed with the legend *lmlk* and the *tet* symbol. In the opinion of F. M. Cross, who published them, the *tet* symbol designates measures of volume "according to the royal standard."

A similar interpretation was advanced on the basis of Egyptian parallels by O. Goldwasser and J. Naveh. The two suggested that, like the letter *'ayin,* it represents the Egyptian demotic sign understood by the Phoenicians and the Judaeans as a determinative meaning "royal." If this is true, it means that Egyptian administration continued to influence the local one, as it did from the Assyrian to the Persian periods.

Several rosette seal impressions from Gibeon and Ramat Raḥel were also ascribed to the Persian period. They are somewhat different in detail from those belonging to the previous monarchic period, but undoubtedly continue the same tradition, i.e., serving as one of the official designations of state measures.

Other seal impressions, found at **Shechem**, were also assigned to the Persian period. They bear only monograms in the form of an oval divided by a horizontal bar with two additional horizontal bars in the upper part. Below this are six upright lines and to the left is another symbol interpreted as a numeral. There can be no doubt that this monogram represents another variant of the royal *tet* symbol and that the number 26 specifies the units of vessel capacity.

The appearance of the *tet* symbol in the region of Samaria and other provinces in addition to Judah, as well as in Egypt (Elephantine), points perhaps to a royal-imperial measure of volume used throughout the Persian Empire.

From the province of **Samaria**, we do not have a single seal or seal impression with the province name impressed on a jar handle. Instead, we have some bullae (mentioned above), one of which is inscribed with the legend "belonging to Isaiah son of Sanballat *peḥa* ('governor') of Samaria." Many additional names of governors of this province appear on the local coins (see below). Names of some of its officials also appear on coins as well as in the Wadi ed-Daliyeh papyri.

From the province of **Ammon** come two seal impressions on clay jar handles. They were found in the excavations of Tell el-ʿUmeiri, south of Rabbath-Ammon, and are impressions of two distinct seals inscribed in an Aramaic script typical of the 6th to 5th centuries BCE. According to the reading by L. G. Herr, excavator of the site, both are inscribed with the words *ʿamn sbʾ,* i.e., the name of the province Ammon and a name of one of its officials, perhaps "shwb." Herr believes that these are the first two examples of official seals of the Persian-period province of Ammon. These seals are similar in content to the Judaean ones, one of which is inscribed *yhwd ʿwryw : yehud uriyo,* i.e., the name of the province of Judah and the name of a governor (or at least one of the provincial officials. These two seals attest to the separate existence of an Ammonite province in the Persian period. We may eventually find impressions from the other provinces in Palestine during the Persian period, such as Edom, Moab, and perhaps also Megiddo and Dor.

INSCRIBED PHOENICIAN AND GREEK SEALS

IN ADDITION TO the inscribed seals connected with the administration of the provinces of Judah, Samaria, and Ammon, there are also a few impressions that pertain to the Phoenician administration over those parts of the Palestinian coast that were handed over to the kings of Sidon and Tyre. These include four impressions, identical in content, each consisting of four lines. In the first line, the word *ʿsr,* i.e., "ten," is mentioned, which probably means "one-tenth." In the second line, one of the four Phoenician cities is mentioned: Sarepta, Achshaf, Beth Zayit, and Labat. Sarepta and Beth Zayit are located in the area between Sidon and Tyre. Achshaf, which is also mentioned in the Bible, is perhaps Tell Keisan in the Acco Valley, and Labat is unidentified. In the third line, the regnal year of Azmilk the king of Tyre (347–332 BCE) is mentioned, and in the fourth, the name of an unknown king, which starts with the letter *B,* is inscribed. He might be one of the

Sidonian monarchs: Baʻna (400–386 BCE) or Baʻalusalim II (386–372 BCE). From a somewhat later period (early Hellenistic), we have other similar Phoenician administrative seal impressions from the site of Kabri (north of Acco). They are inscribed with five lines, in the first of which an unclear name is mentioned (a place-name or a personal one). Then comes a personal name "Ashmun . . . ," the contents (honey), and then a date (according to the Tyrian or Seleucid calendar), which proves that the Phoenician administrative system did not change much.

Probably also connected with the Phoenician administration are the seal and seal impressions on clay jar handles or on the sides of jars depicting the image and emblem of the Phoenician goddess Tanit or her other emblem, the dolphin. These were uncovered at Sarepta and Acco. It is possible that this goddess (identical, according to the Sarepta inscription, with the goddess ʻAstarte), whose cult was also common along the Phoenician-Palestinian coast, was, among other things, responsible for the accuracy of weights and measures, for her image also appears on the lead weights of this period. It is possible, however, that these impressions are connected with the administration of the goddess temples and not with that of the kingdom.

III.55 Phoenician "city" seals

In some Palestinian coastal sites, such as Shiqmona, Dor, and Jaffa, another class of imported seals was found in Persian-period contexts: these are 4th century BCE Greek seal impressions, which were stamped on amphora handles and contain ligatures of Greek letters. In one or two cases, Cypriot seal impressions in Greek, inscribed in Cypro-Archaic script, were also recovered (Kabri and Acco).

Chapter 8

COINS

Our best evidence for the rapid growth of international commerce in the Persian period is the introduction of coins. The use of coins in Palestine began in the first half of the 6th century BCE (i.e., in the Babylonian period; see above). Very few coins are extant from this early period or from the first half of the 5th century BCE. We assume that the use of coins became common only from the end of the 5th and mainly during the 4th centuries BCE.

Owing to the lack of contemporary written sources on the subject, it is difficult to ascertain whether coins circulated widely among the populace in the first century of Persian rule in Palestine or were restricted to a small minority (such as merchants, officials, soldiers, etc.). A most revealing piece of evidence is contained in one of the Wadi ed-Daliyeh papyri. According to F. M. Cross, who published this document, it mentions the sale of a slave by the name of Yehohanan to a Samaritan dignitary called Yehonur, for the price of thirty *sheqels* of silver. The weight of the silver in *mina* is mentioned in the same document. Silver in weight is also mentioned in one of the Arad ostraca of the Persian period. Thus, even in the 4th century BCE, under certain circumstances, it was customary to pay in measured quantities of silver rather than coins.

Comparison with the Elephantine documents presents a close parallel. As in Palestine, so in Egypt, Greek coins were in use, and were apparently very common as early as the end of the 6th century BCE. Nevertheless, a study of the papyri from Elephantine, which deal with commerce, reveals that throughout the 5th century BCE, mercantile transactions in this city were carried out using measured quantities of silver. The earliest document mentioning coins as the means of payment dates from 400 BCE. However, this document still employs the formula according to which coins are equated with the old standard, thus: "the sum of 2 sheqels, that is, the sum of 1 stater." In another document, from 402 BCE, the stater is explicitly described as "money of Greece." These two statements (and they are by no means unique) confirm that metal ingots were still being used by weight as currency in business transactions in the 5th and 4th centuries, though coins were already in everyday use. It should be noted that a number of coin hoards dating from this period, uncovered at various sites in the region, contained both coins and metal ingots.

The coins in circulation in Palestine in the Persian period included (1) the royal Persian coins, (2) Greek coins, (3) coins of Phoenician cities, and (4) local coins minted in Palestine. At the same time, other coins were probably also in use, such as coins of the various cities of Cyprus, Syria, and Anatolia, and possibly also coins from the Egyptian royal mint, which were all in general use in this period in the neighboring lands. However, no examples of coins of these countries have been found so far in Palestine in excavations.

Each of the above-mentioned groups comprised several types. Greek coins are represented mainly by Attic, East Greek, and several Thraco-Macedonian examples. The coins of the Phoenician cities include, for the most part, Tyrian and Sidonian coins and a number from Arwad; none have been reported yet from Byblos. The coins minted in Palestine are generally divided into Philisto-Arabian, Egypto-Arabian, Persian-Greek, etc., all non-epigraphic coins. But among them are also the *yehud* and Samaritan types as well as those issued by the southern harbor towns of the country, such as Ashdod, Ashkelon, and Gaza. Some of these coins are also believed to have been minted by the Persian satraps. All of these types have been found in great numbers and include many subtypes.

All coins were generally minted according to one of three weight standards: Persian, Phoenician, or Athenian. The Persian standard was based on the daric (gold) of 8.4 g., which was divided into 20 *sigloi (sheqels)* of silver, each weighing 5.6 g. Phoenician coinage was based on the stater (silver) of 13.9 g. This coin was divided into 24 parts of which the main unit was the half-stater of 6.5 g. The Athenian weight standard was based on the tetradrachm (silver) of 17.5 g., which was divided into drachms of 4.2 g. each. The Palestinian currency generally followed one of the two principal standards: the Phoenician or the Athenian, and especially the latter. In the Persian period, the Athenian standard was the most stable, for different weights were used by the Phoenician cities for their coins: Arwad at first followed the Persian standard and later changed over to the Athenian, while the coinage of Tyre was at first based on the Phoenician standard but later changed to the Athenian. The same is true of the cities of Cyprus, which began minting according to the Persian standard and later also followed the Athenian.

PERSIAN COINS

THE PERSIAN IMPERIAL coins were of two principal types: the daric, a gold coin weighing 8.4 g., which was subdivided into 20 *sigloi (sheqels),* a silver coin of 5.6 g. Throughout the Persian period, the right to mint gold coins was the sole prerogative of the kings of Persia. The minting of silver coins was also forbidden, except in special circumstances. The Persian governor of Egypt Ariendas was put to death for striking gold coins without authorization (Herodotus 4. 166).

Though there is no doubt that the Persian imperial gold coins were in circulation in Palestine during the period of Persian hegemony there, only two such coins have come to light in archaeological contexts: one at the city of Samaria and the other in Transjordan. Curiously, both belong to its last king, Darius III. The reason for their scarcity may be that, because they were minted in either gold or silver, their material was reused in succeeding peri-

III.56 Persian coins

ods (gold coins are rare in any period). In any case, a few more said to originate in Palestine are known to be in private collections, as well as some in hoards uncovered in neighboring countries.

The fact that the darics were in circulation in Palestine is further supported by biblical evidence. Two verses in the Bible (1 Chronicles 29:7; Ezra 8:27) mention *adarkonim,* a word generally considered to be derived from "daric." In the former reference, offerings given "for the service of the house of God" in the time of David are enumerated in gold *adarkonim,* which is undoubtedly an anachronism. According to the context, these are gold *sheqels,* but the author translated them into the contemporary currency. Similarly, the reference in Ezra is also to gold, which is equivalent to 1,000 *adarkonim,* and not coins. The *darkemonim* mentioned in Ezra 2:69 and Nehemiah 7:70–71 are also of gold, and thus the usual equation of *darkemon* with drachm is without basis, since drachms are known to have been silver coins. It is possible that the author intended to write "daric" and simply confused *adarkonim* with *darkemonim.*

GREEK COINS

THOUGH ACCORDING TO the consensus Greek coins were widely distributed in Palestine in the Persian period, a summary of these coins found in published excavations reveals their scarcity: no more than a few dozen are known. The earliest Greek coin found in Palestine, minted on the island of Kos, dates to ca. 570 BCE and was found in Jerusalem at the site of Ketef Hin-

III.57 Greek coins

nom (only sixteen years after the destruction of the First Temple in 586 BCE!). The second dates to the period 555–545 BCE and was minted at Athens. It was also found in Jerusalem at Givʿat-Ram. A third, from approximately the same period, minted on the island of Aegina, was found in the excavations at Shechem. In addition to Greek coins found in excavations, several hundred in local private collections are said to originate from Palestinian sites. Needless to say, these finds scarcely reflect the true situation, for Greek city coins were as popular in Palestine as they were in neighboring lands. Thus, for example, a single hoard of twelve thousand Athenian coins from the end of the 5th century BCE was discovered at the temple at Tell el-Maskhuta in the Egyptian Delta. This popularity of the Greek coins during the Persian period is likewise attested by the discovery of a large number of local coins imitating the design and standard of many kinds of Greek coins (see below). The Greek coins found in Palestine originated in cities at considerable distances: mainland Greece, various East Greek islands, and all over Anatolia.

PHOENICIAN COINS

FOUR PHOENICIAN CITIES were granted the right to mint coins (of silver and bronze only) by the kings of Persia: Arwad, Byblos, Sidon, and Tyre. As yet, no coins of Byblos discovered in Palestine have been published. Coins of Arwad are also relatively rare in Palestine, whereas Tyrian and Sidonian coins have been found in Palestine in great numbers. This situation is supported by historical facts, for, as is well known, extensive areas of the coastal plain and the Shephelah of Palestine were under the suzerainty of the kings of Tyre and Sidon. Their coins are particularly common at sites of the northern coastal region, such as Acco, Tell Keisan, Tell Abu Hawam, ʿAtlit, Dor, and Tel Michal, but several have also been found on the southern coast, at Ashkelon and elsewhere, as well as in undersea projects. But they are also distributed at inland sites such as Hazor, Dalton, Beth Yeraḥ, Megiddo, Samaria, Shechem and Gezer, Beth-Zur, Lachish, and Jerusalem in Judah, as well as at some sites east of the Jordan, where their number is considerably smaller. There can be no doubt that these coins, more than anything else, symbolize the growing influence of Phoenicia as the central mercantile power throughout the entire country during the Persian period.

The earliest Phoenician coin discovered here is a Tyrian coin from Tell Keisan, dated to 450–440 BCE, i.e., later than the earliest Greek coins. A few others date to the 5th century BCE, but the great majority is dated to the 4th

III.58 Various Phoenician coins

century BCE, fitting well with historical considerations regarding Phoenician expansion in Palestine.

The number of Phoenician coins uncovered in excavations is somewhat over fifty. This is further proof of the uncertain and chance nature of excavated finds. Such meager finds are, furthermore, entirely out or proportion with the number of Phoenician coins present in eight coin hoards. At Beth Yerah, a hoard containing 64 Sidonian coins and 1 Tyrian coin was found. Another cache of 119 coins, all Tyrian, was found at Tell Abu Hawam. Three Tyrian and 17 Sidonian coins are contained in a hoard from Gezer. A fourth cache, with several Tyrian coins and 1 Sidonian coin, comes from the cave at Wadi ed-Daliyeh. A fifth cache of 25 Tyrian coins was uncovered at Acco, where several coins of Sidon, Arwad, and Cilicia (Anatolia) were also found. A sixth cache, containing 15 Tyrian coins and 1 Greek (Athenian) coin, was found near Moshav Dalton in Upper Galilee. Of 965 coins in the Shechem hoard, 131 were Tyrian, while the Samaria hoard, which contained 334 coins, had 32 Tyrian, 43 Sidonian, and 11 Arwad coins. Thus, the number of the Phoenician coins in these eight hoards alone (and there are others) amounts to a few hundred. Many more Phoenician coins of the period said to come from Palestine are found in numerous collections.

Cypriot, Anatolian, and Egyptian Coins

IN ADDITION TO the coins listed above, there were also coins that had been brought from Cyprus in circulation in Palestine, even though only a few have been recovered: for many of the local Palestinian coins of the period adopted many motifs from them and tried to imitate them. It should also be remembered that the Cypriot king Evagoras I of Salamis ruled the northern coast of Palestine from 400 to 380 BCE.

In the same way, **Cilician** coins were used here, probably minted by the Persian satraps of the Abar-Nahara satrapy. A few of them were actually discovered in the hoard from Acco, while more are found in the Shechem hoard. As to **Egyptian** coins, these were probably also used, for Egypt minted many coins of its own during nearly sixty years of independence (400–343 BCE). It is natural to assume that its coins, too, were in circulation here during the time of Egyptian rule over parts of the coast of Palestine. The Egyptian coins of the period, however, were minted in gold and silver, and thus far only isolated examples have been found, even in Egypt itself. Other recently discovered coins minted in Egypt, but from the time of its reconquest by the Persians, have been published. These are clear imitations of Athenian coins. A standard feature is that they contain the legend "Pharaoh Artaxerxes" in demotic. The reference is probably to Artaxerxes III (359/8–338/7 BCE), but no example has been found in Palestine.

PALESTINIAN COINS

THIS TERM ENCOMPASSES a large group of silver coins of small denominations minted in Palestine, mainly during the 4th century BCE. In the past, they were designated by G. F. Hill as "Philisto-Arabian" or "Egypto-Arabian." Hill himself was not wholly satisfied with these designations and other names were subsequently proposed for them. A. Kindler tends to call them "Greco-Phoenician" by analogy with a seal type, and Y. Meshorer initially called them "Greco-Persian" and more recently, simply "Palestinian" coins of the Persian period, a name that has been accepted by many.

These coins, distributed in all the regions of Palestine, are found mainly in sites along the coast, but also in the interior and even in Transjordan. Most of these coins are nonepigraphic and it is difficult to establish with precision where they were minted. There are, however, some large groups with a place-name inscribed on them either in full or in abbreviation. Thus far, the coins of three cities have been identified with certainty, all large harbor towns along the southern coast, Ashdod, Ashkelon, and Gaza; the names of the two major provinces of Palestine, Judah and Samaria, have also been identified. But clearly, other mints existed and may well be identified in the future. This large group of coins, which flooded Palestine in the 4th century BCE, both nonepigraphic and inscribed, is characterized by a diversity of types and motifs: it is difficult to find two completely identical coins.

III.59 A Palestinian coin

In the following list, which is far from complete, we have grouped together some of the motifs appearing on the coins that have been published so far.

Heads: of Athena, bearded or clean-shaven males with or without a helmet or other type of headgear, females of various types, Janus, Zeus, Hercules, satyr, Bes, the king of Persia and other monarchs

Lions: heads of lions, singly or in pairs, standing erect or rampant, crouching, attacking a griffin, a ram, or a bull, eating

Horses: protomai (busts) of horses of different types, riders, riders chasing various animals, horses with quadriga, mad saddling a horse, an Arab riding a camel

Other animals: owls in different variations, goats, wild boars, hippopotami, dolphins, turtles, elephants, cow suckling a calf

Mythological figures: sphinxes of various kinds, winged demons sometimes with heads in the form of a bull or a ram, fighting one another, Bes standing and holding two lions, sea horse, snail

Buildings: a fort with towers, owl in front of a fort

Ships: of various types, both warships and merchant vessels

Kings and rulers, both males and females (deities?): sitting on their thrones holding birds, various royal instruments (Greeks, Persians, and even Egyptians), shooting their bows or holding a lance, stabbing lions and other monsters, handling cult ceremonies, being led into their chariots, playing musical instruments

This diversity, as was noted above, makes typological classification difficult, even though it is generally agreed that these coins constitute a homogeneous group of uniform style. A. Kindler tried to classify them according to their principal motifs thus: (a) Athenian types, with the owl or the head of Athena appearing on at least one of the sides. The other classes were grouped according to a single common motif, such as (b) female heads, (c) *protomai* of horses, (d) male heads, (e) Bes heads, and (f) miscellaneous. A close analogy for each motif is presented from various city coins from Anatolia, Cyprus, and Phoenicia, in Kindler's opinion, their source. But even his detailed classification fails to include all the variations of the motifs.

The date of this heterogeneous minting has been fixed by almost all authorities to the 4th century BCE alone. Support for this relatively late date is supplied by the hoard found long ago at Gezer, in which a few coins of Alexander the Great occur. Further support is provided by the coins from the Wadi ed-Daliyeh cave, dated on the basis of the papyrus documents to the period between 345 and 335 BCE; and the Shechem and Samaria hoards, which included many Palestinian, Samaritan, Greek, and Phoenician coins, dated on the basis of the latest dated coins in the hoard to between 345 and 332 BCE.

The multiplicity of types and of motifs depicted in these coins undoubtedly originates with the many minting authorities (beyond the five already pointed out—Judah, Samaria, Ashdod, Ashkelon, and Gaza—there must have been many others, such as the satrap, the *peḥa,* some other provinces such as Ammon, the high priest or priests, etc.). It appears that aside from the many authorities, this situation also reflects the numerous officials who placed their own seal motifs on their coins. Indeed, among the coins of Samaria, many have motifs almost identical to those on the bullae, with which papyrus documents were sealed and in which the names of the seal owners are recorded. Many personal names appear on the coins as well.

Of the Palestinian coins, we shall first deal with the city coins, of **Gaza, Ashdod,** and **Ashkelon.** Of these inscribed coins, there are many on which the Greek name *athe* (Athens) is depicted. This is an imitation of the Athenian prototypes that these coins copy. On some of them are remains of Phoenician or Aramaic letters that are still hard to interpret, and it remains unclear if they are place- or personal names. Only on a few coins is it possible to read names in full or in abbreviated form. Others may be identified on the basis of the close analogy between them and the fully inscribed examples. It is now clear that some of them were minted in the three southern harbor

III.60 A Palestinian coin struck in the city of Ashdod

towns of Gaza, Ashkelon, and Ashdod in the 4th century BCE under the patronage of the kings of Tyre and Sidon, who granted them permission to mint small silver coins.

The coins of **Gaza,** whether with the city's full name, *'za,* or in short *'z* or *'*, have been known for years; in recent years, some of the coins of **Ashdod** have been found with the full name, *ashdd,* or *ash.* The third town must be **Ashkelon.** No coin with its full name has been found, but usually the letters *an* appear. There can be no doubt, however, that among the uninscribed coins or those not yet deciphered, some other important towns will be represented. For example, a few identical Palestinian coins of types that have never been found at any other site have been found at **Dor.** Y. Meshorer has expressed the view that these may have been minted there.

COINS OF THE PROVINCE OF JUDAH

A SEPARATE GROUP among the Palestinian coins are ones bearing the legend *yehud* or *yhd,* the Aramaic name for the province of Judah in the Persian period, in the Palaeo-Hebrew or Aramaic script. This group now includes several dozen coins of various types on which—as on all other Palestinian coins—numerous motifs are depicted: bearded male heads with various types of helmets, crowns, or turbans; women's heads; falcons; the lily flower; or motifs such as the "the god's ear" (a depiction of a large ear explained by Y. Meshorer as a symbol of the ear of a god); and perhaps also the shofar. In most cases, however, the motifs are borrowed from Athenian coins, for reasons of reliability: the owl and the olive branch. Most examples of known provenience were found at Judaean sites: at Jerusalem, Ramat Raḥel, Beth-Zur, and Jericho, and they were clearly minted in Judah (even though examples have been found at sites such as Tell Jemmeh in Philistia and Mount Gerizim in Samaria). The *yehud* coins are dated, by consensus, in the 4th century BCE, though some numismatists tend to limit them to the second third of this century. The one exception is a rather large coin, unusually inscribed in Aramaic, that appears to be somewhat earlier than the others (see below). The main grounds for establishing their date is a small group of coins that, in addition to the usual *yehud* inscription, includes the personal name *yḥzqyh,* alone or with the title *peḥa* ("governor"). These coins generally depict the Athenian owl on one side and the head of the Greek goddess Arethusa on the other. In recent years, many coins have been found with motifs of various griffin *protomai,* the head of a young man, or the crowned head of the Persian king.

III.61 Various *yehud* coins

Such a coin was first found in the 1930s, in the excavations at Beth-Zur. W. F. Albright attributed it to the high priest *yḥzqyh,* concerning whom Josephus Flavius tells (*Against Apion* I. 187–189) that he was a friend of King Ptolemy I of Egypt and Palestine and even settled in Egypt around 282 BCE. Further evidence for this late date now comes from another group of recently published coins, where besides the usual Aramaic name of the province, *yehud* or *yhd,* the Hebrew name *yhdh* also occurs. There are two types. In one, the Ptolemaic eagle appears on one side; on the others is the head of Ptolemy I (305–286 BCE) or that of Ptolemy II (285–246 BCE). The other type depicts the head of Ptolemy on one side, and that of his wife, Berenice, on the other. Most of these coins were also found within the borders of Judah in the region between Bethlehem and Beth-Zur. These coins prove that at the end of the Persian period, the province of Judah enjoyed sufficient autonomy to mint coins with the province name. They also show that at the beginning of the Hellenistic period (until the days of Ptolemy II), there was no change in this status.

On one recently published coin appear both the Aramic *yehud* and the Hebrew *yhdh*. This may indicate either the name of the province in both languages; or one of these (perhaps *yhdh*) was the personal name of one of the province's officials.

But recent discoveries and surprises have not ceased with the discovery of *yehud, yhdh,* and *yhzqyh* coins. Several coins of priests have also been found. Although *yhzqyh* was indeed the *peha* of Judah in the Persian period, at least one coin depicting identical emblems, as the coins bearing his name and title, bore a different inscription: *yehohanan hakohen,* i.e., "the priest." The fact that the Yehohanan coin is identical to those of the governor may indicate that he, too, was an important person in the Yehud province, perhaps even the high priest. In Nehemiah 12:22, the names of four priests are mentioned: Elyashiv, Yoyada, Yehohanan, and Yadoa. D. Barag, who published the Yehohanan coin, claims that he should not be identified with the high priest Yehohanan mentioned in Nehemiah's list, but with a later one who lived in the same time as *yhzqyh* the governor, from whom he copied the motifs for his coins.

Another coin that has been attributed to a high priest bears the name *yadoa,* last of the high priests mentioned in Nehemiah's list. D. Barag suggests here, too, that he should be identified with Yadoa II, father of Yehohanan II, or perhaps his son (i.e., Yadoa III), who was a high priest when Alexander the Great conquered the country in 333/2 BCE.

The coins of these priests, whether high priests or priests who were appointed to mint the coins, attest to the existence of a mint that was probably connected with the Jerusalem Temple and was active alongside that of the governor.

The last coin connected with Judah to be discussed here was perhaps issued by none other than the satrap of Abar Nahara himself. This is a silver coin, of exceptional size and weight, bearing unusual motifs on obverse and reverse. This coin, the first of the *yehud* coins every found, was initially considered to have been minted by a higher authority than the governor of Judah. On one side is a bearded male wearing a Corinthian helmet, and on the other, a bearded male riding a winged chariot and holding a falcon in his outstretched left hand. Above his head is the legend *yhd* and to his right, a mask. This coin weighs 3.29 g. and measures 15 mm. in diameter. In at-

III.62 The coin of "Yehohanan the Priest"

tempting to interpret this coin, numismatists have emphasized the resemblance between the helmeted head depicted here and that shown on the silver coins issued by the Persian satraps Farnabazus and Datames during the period of their preparation for war against rebellious Egypt between 378 and 373 BCE. Many are convinced that this coin was also minted by one of these two satraps, who in their coins bear the title "the one who is over Abar Nahara and Cilicia," i.e., also over Palestine and Jordan. The coin was probably intended to pay the salaries of Judaean mercenaries active in the Persian army. D. Barag tries to explain the legend *yhd* on the satrap coin by connecting it to the story in Josephus' *Antiquities* 11.297–301, which tells about a Persian general by the name of Bagohi who arrived in Jerusalem to maintain law and order there after a conflict that erupted between two brothers of the high priestly family during the years 345–343 BCE. Barag suggests that Bagohi minted this coin.

In any case, in a province that did not, according to the consensus, have temples or pagan figurines, there is some interest in the appearance of pagan motifs depicted on its coins, mainly those motifs taken from the Greek world.

COINS OF THE SAMARIA PROVINCE

THE LAST PALESTINIAN group of small silver coins of the 4th century BCE to be discussed here comprises the Samaritan coins. This is a most surprising group. A few hundred such coins have been found in the city of Samaria and its surroundings and in the cave of Wadi ed-Daliyeh. These were minted in the province of Samaria during the 4th century BCE. Many have recently been published by Y. Meshorer and S. Qedar. The Shechem hoard consists of 965 coins of which 625 are coins of the city of Samaria; the Samaria hoard contains 334 coins of which 182 are Samaritan. More Samaritan coins have come to light in recent years, and new types and motifs will probably continue to be found.

The Samaritan group is very similar to the other groups of Palestinian coins in that it contains many types and motifs, some identical to those we have already encountered in our discussion of the seal impressions on bullae from Samaria or those from Wadi ed-Daliyeh. In many cases, there exists a complete identity between the motifs appearing on the bullae and on the coins.

The assemblage of motifs on the Samaritan coins is divided here, as in the other Palestinian coin groups, into three different categories. Some of them are executed under Greek (mainly Athenian) influence—the head of Athena, the owl, etc.—but also include many other motifs, some adopted from the satrap coins of Cilicia, such as heads of Greek warriors, armed Greek soldiers, heads of gazelles, Aphrodite and Erathusa, and a king sitting on his throne holding a bird. The second group, the largest, is based on Babylonian-Persian motifs: "the king-scorpion," a head of a Persian ruler, the enthroned Persian king, the king riding his horse, emerging from a winged sun disk, standing in his chariot, struggling with lions, bulls, and various monsters and shooting his bow, frequently draped with the traditional Persian garments and wearing the well-known Achaemenian crown.

The third group consists of motifs derived from the Phoenician-Israelite horizon: a man playing a harp, ships on sea waves, sea horses, sphinxes, griffins, lions in various positions, horses, bulls, stags, as well as the old motif of the ibexes and the palm tree. These motifs are identical to those on the nonepigraphic coins of Ashdod, Ashkelon, Gaza, and Judah. In the Samaritan coins, however, inscriptions appear, including the name of the province *Shmrn* (also abbreviated forms such as *Shmr* or *Shn* or even *Sh* alone) and the names of the known governors of the province, such as Sanballat, Delaya, and Hananya. There are also names unknown from other sources, such as *Yrbʿm, Hym, Yhwʾnh,* and *Abdʾl;* Phoenician names, such as *Bdyhbl;* and even Persian names, such as *Bgbt* and *Mazdy,* who may have also served as officials of this province during the Persian period. To these must be added the names appearing on the Wadi ed-Daliyeh bullae, such as *Snblt pht Shmrn* and *Ishmaʿʾel.*

Study of these coins is only as its initial stage. They will undoubtedly be an extremely important new source for the future study of the archaeology of 4th century BCE Palestine.

In Samaria, no pagan temple has been uncovered. The remains of the central Samaritan temple on Mount Gerizim dedicated to Yahweh is the only known cultic site, though—as in Judah—there are many pagan motifs de-

III.63 A coin inscribed with the name of Samaria

picted on Samaritan coins, adopted from the coins of neighboring lands. On one of these coins depicting an enthroned god holding a flower, a Greek inscription mentioning the name Zeus appears; it may be interpreted as the Greek equivalent of the name of the Samaritan god (cf. Josephus *Antiquities* 12.257–263).

· Chapter 9 ·

WEIGHTS AND MEASURES

MEASURES OF VOLUME

The many Persian-period ostraca found at numerous Palestinian sites in all regions provide sufficient evidence for the study of the system for measurement of volume. In the previous chapter, we saw that volume measures in 7th century BCE Judah were similar to those used in the Bible:

dry measures	liquid measures
1 *homer*	1 *kur*
10 *epha*	10 *bat*
30 *seah*	60 *hin*
180 *qav*	720 *log*

These volumes are frequently indicated (as in the period of the monarchy) by using only the first letter of the word, thus: *s = seah; q = qav; p = peleg* ("half"); *r = reva'* ("quarter"), etc. Sometimes the full name appears.

The names of other measures of volume are mentioned in the Bible, such as the *letech,* which is half a *homer,* and *omer-esron,* which is one-hundredth of a *homer,* but these measures are not reflected in the archaeological finds of the 7th century BCE or of the Persian period.

In Persian-period Aramaic ostraca discovered at Arad, Tel-Sheva, and Tel 'Ira in Judah, at Tell el-Far'ah (S) in Philistia, and in the recently published hoard of more than two hundred ostraca from Idumaea, two units of liquid measure, the *kur* and the *bat,* and two units of dry measure, the *seah* and the *qav,* occur. But somehow in these ostraca the *kur* designates only dry measure, in most cases barley and wheat, while in 7th century Arad the *homer* was a unit of liquid measure (*"homer* of wine") and the *hin* and *epha* are not mentioned at all. There are also some characters, the meaning of which is obscure. It is not known if these are identical to volumes with the same names used in the Judaean monarchy. Perhaps they reflect only the preservation of the names in a different system of measurement.

There is also evidence for the use of "natural" measures during the Persian period, mainly jars, which during this period have the Aramaic name *garban.* These are usually wine jars listed with numbers in the Idumaean Tell el-Kheleifeh ostraca and the ostraca from Tell Nimrin in Ammon. It is unclear whether a quantity of jars or fixed jar volumes are intended here. Favoring the second alternative is one of the inscriptions from Tell Nimrin where a *"garban* and a half" is mentioned. Other "natural" volumes that appear in Persian-period ostraca are "a camel load," "a barrel," and "a basket."

WEIGHTS

IN CONTRAST TO measures of volume, which preserve the names, if not the systems, of measurement used in the kingdom of Judah, all the Judaean weights completely disappear upon the kingdom's destruction.

A weight discovered at Tell el-Shuqaf in the Shephelah may point to the existence of a Judaean system of weights. It is a smooth, rectangular piece of limestone with a depression on the back. It also bears the old Judaean inscription *pym* in the standard Aramaic script of the Persian period. The weight of the stone (112 g.) is several times that of the *pim* weights of the Judaean period (7.8 g.). Though we know nothing of the system of weights to which it belonged, it is nevertheless of great interest because of the survival of the early name. It may be concluded that a local weight system existed in Judah, which preserved ancient Hebrew names, though it was based on a different standard. The same is perhaps true of the biblical *kikar* (talent) mentioned in Ezra 8:26, which may have had a different value during this period.

Some indication of the standard system of weights utilized in Palestine during the Persian period may be derived from the names of weights mentioned in the Elephantine papyri, which are of Babylonian and Egyptian origin.

It is very likely that a standard, uniform system of weights was employed by the Persian government during this period throughout the Persian realm, including Palestine. According to A. Cowley, the value of the Persian weights was 1 *karash* =10 *sheqels;* 1 *sheqel* =4 r; 1 r=10 *hallurin.*

Cowley maintained that the letter "r" represented one-quarter (of a *sheqel*). The name *karash* is Persian, whereas *sheqel* and *hallur* are Babylonian terms. The value of these weights may also be attested by a trilingual weight in the British Museum (inscribed in Persian, Elamite, and Babylonian), which contains the following equation: *2 kerashin* (Persian) = 1 and one-third *mina* (Babylonian). It appears that in Elephantine the *mina* was equivalent to *60 sheqels* and the value of the weights in whole units was *1 mina = 6 kerashin = 60 sheqels.* Two other weights, also trilingual, from Persepolis contain similar formulae: *120 kerashin = 20 mina* and *60 kerashin = 10 mina.*

As stated above, the names of the weights recorded in the Elephantine documents from Egypt are identical to those found in Persia and Babylonia. It seems very likely that one system of weights with standard names was adopted throughout the area located between these two centers, including Palestine.

The actual evidence from Palestine for the existence of this system is quite meager. In document no. 1 from Wadi ed-Daliyeh from the year 335 BCE, a slave is sold for the sum of 35 silver *sheqels*; the fine to be imposed for failure to fulfill the agreement is 7 *mina* of silver. The weights in use are therefore the *mina* and *sheqel.* A Persian-period ostracon discovered at Raphia and published by J. Naveh contains a list of names and numbers with the letter *mem* next to each number. Naveh believes that this represents *maneh;* or perhaps it stands for *ma'ot* (coins). In a group of ostraca from Idumaea, six ostraca mention silver units in *sheqels* and again *ma'ot.* Usually the weights are registered in abbreviated versions as follows: *sh=sheqels; r=reva; m=mane* (or *ma'ot*).

Recently, in the Persian-period level (5th century BCE) at Ashkelon, a Persian scale weight was found consisting of an incised bone case with a lead filling. It weighs 1 *karsha,* i.e., 10 *sheqels.* In a shipwreck of the Persian period found off the shore of 'Atlit, two Mesopotamian-type bronze weights in the form of a duck with head turned were found. They weigh 136 and 228 g., according to the report, 10 *sheqels* (one-fifth of a *maneh*) and 20 *sheqels* (two-fifths of a *maneh*). A similar weight said to have been found in Palestine is exhibited in the Hecht Museum.

There are also several trapezoid-shaped bronze weights from Ashkelon and 'Atlit, of either Egyptian or Phoenician origin, of an unknown standard. A clearer Phoenician origin can be attributed to a lead weight from Ashdod-

III.64 A Phoenician lead weight from Ashdod-Yam depicting the emblem of Tanit-Pane-Ba'al and local weights in the form of various animals

Yam and Umm el-'Amed on the southern Lebanese coast, where the emblem of the Phoenician goddess Tanit-Ashtoret is depicted; another example is the dome-shaped weight from the shipwreck of 'Atlit, engraved in Phoenician script. From Ashkelon come bronze weights representing animals (ram, donkey, calf, etc.) rendered in the finest Canaanite-Phoenician tradition, with many parallels in Palestine and Syria.

THE PERSIAN PERIOD:
SUMMARY AND CONCLUSIONS

A rchaeological excavations in Palestine have been of great value in shed-
ding new light on the history of the country during the Persian period.
A review of the results of excavations at the sites examined above enables us
to state with considerable confidence that the majority of these settlements
was destroyed one or more times during this period. Two settlement phases
assigned to the Persian period have been uncovered at many sites along the
entire coast and in the Shephelah, as well as in the southern part of the country and in Transjordan. Three or more occupation phases have been distinguished at others. A number of towns in the southern part of Samaria and in
the territory of Benjamin was also destroyed during the Persian period.
Though some sites were resettled during this period, others remained abandoned until the Hellenistic period. Some sites were occupied for only part of
the Persian period. At other sites, however, where the Persian-period strata
were in too poor a state of preservation for it to be possible to distinguish between the different stages, the date of the final destruction could be established. Contemporary documents mention the destruction of only two cities:
Gaza was razed by Alexander the Great during his campaign against Egypt
in 333/2 BCE (but has never been excavated). Samaria was also destroyed by
Alexander. Echoes of the latter destruction can be found in historical sources
as well as in the Wadi ed-Daliyeh papyri and, perhaps, Ketef Jericho.

According to the above sources, the cities in the territory of Benjamin and
in the southern part of Samaria appear to have been destroyed in approximately 475 BCE. This date is based on the Attic pottery uncovered during the
excavations at Shechem, Tell en-Naṣbeh, Bethel, Tell el-Ful, and Gibeon.
There is no known historical event that can account for this destruction,

though it was a period of turbulence in the history of the Persian Empire. During the years between 492 and 479 BCE, the Persians were engaged in numerous wars. This was one of the most crucial periods in the empire's history. The long-standing revolts in Ionia and Cyprus were put down (492 BCE); the battle of Marathon took place (490 BCE); and the first revolt in Egypt broke out (488 BCE) and was finally suppressed only in 484 BCE. In 482 BCE, the Babylonians rose in rebellion. Its suppression terminated in the destruction of their city, which, as surmised above, was detached at this time from the "Beyond the River" satrapy. In 480–479 BCE, fierce battles with the Greeks ended in the total defeat of the Persians. It seems clear that the group of Palestinian cities, which were destroyed or whose occupation ceased at this time, is situated in a limited area in the center of Palestine. We have no way of connecting their destruction with any known event, and can only assume that it was a partial destruction that took place during a war between neighboring provinces, such as the one threatened by Judah's neighbors in the days of Nehemiah, or a local rebellion suppressed by the Persian authorities. Though this period is still covered by biblical sources, no possible explanation has been found here for the apparent hiatus in settlement.

This is not the case for the second wave of destruction that struck the areas of the Shephelah and the Negev, according to all evidence, around 380 BCE, which corresponds with the information supplied by historical sources and with several important archaeological finds from Palestine. During the transition between the 5th and the 4th centuries BCE, after repeated and unsuccessful attempts to free themselves from the Persian yoke, the Egyptians again revolted, following the early attempts in 488–484 and 459–454 and 411 BCE, when the temple of the Elephantine Jews was set on fire. In 400 BCE, the Egyptians finally liberated themselves from Persian subjugation, preserving their independence until 343 BCE. During their uprising, the Egyptians also laid waste the Jewish-Persian military colony at Elephantine. It has been revealed that an Arab colony at Tel el-Maskhuta in the eastern Delta was demolished at the same time. External events as well played a part in the success of the Egyptian rebellion. At this time, a war broke out between the brothers Cyrus, satrap of Asia Minor, and Artaxerxes II. Henceforth, the Palestine coastal region underwent a fundamental change: it ceased being an internal passage within the empire and became an arena of extensive battles between the Egyptians and their allies (Cypriots, Athenians, Spartans, and later, Phoenicians) and the Persians. The series of destructions that struck the cities of the Shephelah and the Negev in rapid succession seem to have been closely connected with these events. Immediately after the Egyptians gained independence, they took up arms against the Persians outside the borders of their homeland. The natural route for their advance was through the Negev and the coastal plain of Palestine, where they seem to have proceeded by stages. In Gezer were found a seal and a fragmentary stone plaque bearing the name of Pharaoh Nepherites I (the last of the Egyptian kings mentioned in the Elephantine papyri and the first pharaoh of the 29th Dynasty from Mendes), who reigned during the years 399–393 BCE. These documents indicate that he conquered at least the southern Shephelah. It is very likely that his advance was facilitated by the fact that the Persians were preoccupied with their civil war until 393 BCE. Nepherites' successor, Achoris (393–380 BCE), formed an alliance with Evagoras king of Salamis in Cyprus and with the Athenians, and this league conquered the northern coast of Palestine. For a time, they also held sway in Tyre and Sidon. Two monumental inscriptions of Pharaoh Achoris have been uncovered in this region: one at Acco and another at Sidon. To this short period we may perhaps also attribute three Cypriot dedicatory inscriptions in Greek, written in Cypro-Archaic script, found at Sidon, Sarepta, and Dor (see above).

In 380 BCE, the Persians succeeded in wresting control of the Shephelah from the Egyptians and their allies. We attribute the Greek shipwreck found off the coast of Ma'agan Mikha'el (see above) to this event. In 373 BCE, they took the offensive and attacked Egypt itself (in this year Pharnabazus and Iphicrates made an abortive attempt to invade Egypt). Thus, the wave of destruction in the Shephelah took place in the two decades between the beginning of the Egyptian conquest and its end (399–380 BCE). Which of the two sides was responsible for the destruction of each site remains a matter of conjecture. It may be assumed that much of the destruction was wrought by the Persians, in their campaign to suppress the rebellious cities.

We have no information on events in Judah and Samaria in this period. It can only be assumed on the basis of the continuity of the governors ruling both provinces in the 4th century BCE, as attested in recently discovered Judaean and Samaritan documents, that these provinces were not affected by the conflict between Egypt and Persia. Nevertheless, it appears that the weakening of Persian rule in the border area between Palestine and Egypt led to attempts by Arab tribes, whose regular trade routes to Gaza were disrupted in this period, to seize control of desert fortresses and settlements within this region. The destruction perceived in the excavations at Kadesh-Barnea (where no finds later than the 5th century BCE have come to light) and at the end of the first phases at Tell el-Kheleifeh and En-Gedi is, perhaps, suggestive of the situation. The renewal of settlement in the southern region, as attested by the ostraca assemblages from Arad, Tel Sheva, and the other Idumaean settlements, is thus assigned to the period during which the Persians regained control over the area up to the borders of Egypt, i.e., 380 BCE.

This is the extent of our knowledge concerning the destruction of the cities of the Shephelah and the Negev at the beginning of the 4th century BCE. As for the final destruction of Palestinian cities at the end of the Persian period, the second Persian attempt to reconquer Egypt in 353 BCE also failed, and was followed by a general Phoenician rebellion under Sidonian leadership. A late chronicle relates that in the days of Artaxerxes III Ochus (359/8–338/7 BCE), the Jewish population of Jericho was exiled to Horkania on the coast of the Caspian Sea. J. Klausner and other authorities consequently concluded that the Jews in Palestine were active participants in the revolt, and D. Barag, following them, attempted to attribute the destruction of many Palestinian cities to the suppression of the revolt in 345 BCE. Recently, H. Eshel has also attributed the papyrus he found at Ketef Jericho to this event.

Though a number of cities under Sidonian rule in the province of Dor may have been razed because they joined the rebellion of the mother city, it is not likely that this brief rebellion reached such large proportions. The fact that only Jews from Jericho were banished may point to a local disturbance during the reign of Artaxerxes III, for the majority of the Jewish population was concentrated in the Judaean Hills. The archaeological evidence proposed for such a destruction is also inadequate, in part because it is impossible to distinguish pottery of 345 BCE from that of 332 BCE, but also because it is based on a misinterpretation. In earlier chapters, we discussed the hoard of Tyrian coins of Attic standard found at Wadi ed-Daliyeh together with documents dated up to 332 BCE, the year in which Samaria fell and its survivors fled to the caves. The discovery of similar hoards of coins at Megiddo, Acco, Tell Abu Hawam, Shechem, and probably Samaria itself, as well as the coins of Alexander the Great in the destruction levels of the Persian fortresses along Wadi Milek, in Naḥal Tut and at 'En Ḥofez, indicates that Samaria and the whole northern region, which were closely linked with Tyre in the 4th century BCE, were razed during the long siege laid by Alexander on Tyre. According to its description in the historical sources, Gaza was also destroyed in the time of Alexander. It is logical to assume that he may also have been responsible for the final collapse of the Persian-period settlements in the adjacent region: at Ashkelon, Ruqeish, Tell el-Ḥesi, Tell Jemmeh, Tel Sera', etc., as well as the line of the Persian military fortresses along the coast, which served as supply depots and strongholds for the Persian army during the latest phase of Alexander's campaign. Though major devastation was caused during the conquest of Palestine by the armies of Alexander, it now appears that several additional towns, such as Shiqmona, Tel Zippor, and others, were laid waste several years later, during the wars of the Diadochi, as attested by; coins uncovered in Persian-period levels at these sites.

Now we come to the question of the exact time during the Persian period in which the Judaean state was reestablished after its destruction by the Babylonians in 586 BCE. In our summary of the Babylonian period (above), we stated that during this period, Judah, as well as the rest of the country, was devasted, making its reestablishment during the Babylonian period virtually impossible.

The question of the date of reestablishment of Judah as a formal province or a state is a topic that many generations of scholars have debated and continue debating. No consensus has been reached. The problem can be summarized by two major positions. The one adopted by N. Avigad supports an earlier date, claiming that the Yehud province was already established at the end of the 6th century BCE, in the days of Sheshbazzar and Zerubbabel. Avigad's main supporting evidence for this date was paleographic: this was the date to which he had assigned the hoard of the bullae he published, which included both the province name Yehud and the names of some of its governors with their titles (see above). He claimed that all the bullae belong, on paleographic grounds, to the first ninety years of Persian hegemony, i.e., between the time of Zerubbabel and of Ezra and Nehemiah (540–450 BCE).

The later date, which now seems more plausible, is based on the idea that the independent administrative unit of the province of Judah was established by Ezra and Nehemiah themselves only in the mid-5th century BCE, and therefore, that all archaeological finds attributed to this province date from 450 BCE through the Hellenistic period. There is also a third possibility: that the formal establishment of the province was indeed in the beginning of this period, but that it actually began functioning actively only in the days of Nehemiah.

The reasons for favoring the later date are that when the Persian domination replaced the Babylonian one, the whole of Palestine, and in particular the regions of Judah and the coast, were in a difficult economic and social situation. The Persians—in order to overcome the consequences of the Babylonian occupation—apparently utilized different methods from those employed by the Assyrians and the Babylonians. They did not destroy everything and remove the booty to Babylon, as did the Babylonians, nor did they bring new settlers to the desolate land, as the Assyrians had done. They simply allowed people from surrounding areas who were up to it to settle the half-empty regions. Our impression is that this was accomplished by various extant local authorities (as an almost private initiative), such as the kings of Tyre and Sidon. The coastal region of Palestine indeed appears, for the most part, to have been populated from the beginning of the Persian period by Phoenicians from these two cities. This had been clearly shown by the excavations at coastal towns: Acco, Dor, Jaffa, Ashkelon, Gaza, and Ruqeish. The same conclusion is valid in regard to the Galilee. Here and there, some new elements, such as Greeks and Arabs, also settled, in particular in the south and in Gaza.

It should be assumed that in the beginning the coastal settlements were renewed. Only later did the new prosperity reach the inland mountainous region, too. This process was slow at first, but gradually gained momentum. Despite its slowness, its aim was clear: the erection of settlements of various sizes on a massive scale throughout the country, but mainly along the coastal strip; the renewal of international trade on a large scale; and successful development of the country's economy.

The general picture emerging from the results of the many excavations of Persian-period sites in Palestine has a direct bearing on the date of the renewal of the Judaean state. For, even if there was a formal intent to create it as early as the beginning of the Persian period, with the authorization of the imperial authorities, the country lacked the proper conditions: population was insufficient, the number of settlements to support it economically, no city adequate to serve as its capital existed, and there was no proper administrative infrastructure. Another fifty to sixty years of slow change were required to achieve conditions conducive to creation of the Judaean state.

That is why when Ezra and Nehemiah arrived in Jerusalem, the city remained virtually desolate despite construction of the Temple. Its wall had to be rebuilt and its population had to be recruited from the surrounding villages. The three major excavations conducted in Jerusalem by Y. Shiloh, N. Avigad, and B. Mazar clearly established that until the end of the Persian period, the borders of Persian-period Jerusalem never exceeded the limited area of the City of David!

This situation is by no means peculiar to Judah alone; the new prosperity reached all other provinces of the country rather late in the Persian period. In Samaria, for example, significant remains, including their central temple on Mount Gerizim, now being excavated, are clearly dated to the 4th century

BCE. This state of affairs probably also applies to Dor, Ashdod, Ashkelon, Gaza, and the other coastal cities.

This geographical-historical background favors a late date for the establishment of the Judaean state, as well as that of Samaria and the coastal towns during the Persian period. Other evidence leads to the same conclusion: The artifactual evidence for the Judaean state is mainly in the form of seals and coins. The study of recently found seals shows that the various *yehud* seals and impressions fall into two types: one in Aramaic script attributed to the Persian period; the other, identical to the first but written in Hebrew script, is dated to the Hellenistic period. Ironically, it was N. Avigad himself who finally proved this in his dig in the Upper City of Jerusalem, where only Hebrew seal impressions were found in an area that had only been reoccupied during the Hellenistic period. It is unlikely that a long period of time passed between the appearance of the two nearly identical types of seals. More plausibly, they were produced continuously, from the late Persian period to the beginning of the Hellenistic period.

As regards Judaean coinage, the situation is even more clear. There is a consensus among numismatists that all the Palestinian coins were minted in the 4th century BCE and that not a single example dates to the late 6th or the beginning of the 5th centuries BCE. It has already been pointed out that this date is based on the many hoards that included coins of Alexander the Great, coins of *yhzqyh* the *peha* and coins of the priests, all dated to the 4th century BCE, as well as Hebrew seals inscribed *yhdh,* which depict the head of Ptolemy.

The same is true as regards the relatively rich finds of Shamrine Medinta, official papyri, bullae, and coins of which were recently discussed by Y. Meshorer, S. Qedar, F. M. Cross, D. M. Gropp, M. J. Leith, and E. Stern, who all date the finds to the 4th century BCE. The same date should be assigned to the reconstruction of other parts of Palestine, too. For the date of all Idumaean ostraca is also considered to be in the 4th century.

In conclusion, it is most plausible that the state of Judah and the rest of the country's provinces and major administrative units were established and became functional largely during the latter part of the Persian period.

BIBLIOGRAPHY

BIBLIOGRAPHY FOR BOOK ONE:
THE ASSYRIAN PERIOD

General

E. Stern, Israel at the Close of the Period of the Monarchy: An Archaeological Survey, *BA* 38/2 (1975), 26–54.

Mazar [1990], 403–549.

G. Barkai, The Iron Age II–III, in: A. Ben-Tor (ed.), *The Archaeology of Ancient Israel in the Biblical Period,* New Haven 1992, 302–373.

G. W. Ahlstrom, *The History of Ancient Palestine from the Paleolithic Period to Alexander's Conquest,* Sheffield 1993.

L. G. Herr, Archaeological Sources for the History of Palestine in the Iron Age II Period: Emerging Nations, *BA* 60/3 (1997), 151–183.

E. M. Meyers (ed.), *The Oxford Encyclopedia of Archaeology in the Near-East,* New York and Oxford 1997.

Chapter One: The Assyrian Conquest and Domination of Palestine

History of the Assyrian Empire

A. T. E. Olmstead, *History of Assyria,* Chicago 1923.

D. D. Luckenbill, *Ancient Records of Assyria and Babylon,* London 1927.

J. Oates, Assyrian Chronology 631–612 B.C., *Iraq* 27 (1965), 135–159.

A. K. Grayson, *Assyrian and Babylonian Chronicles,* Locust Valley, N.Y. 1975.

N. Na'aman, Chronology and History of the Late Assyrian Empire (631–619 B.C.), *ZA* 81 (1991), 243–267.

A. Millard, *The Eponyms of the Assyrian Empire 910–612 B.C. State Archives of Assyria Studies 2.* Neo-Assyrian Text Corpus Project, Helsinki 1994.

The Assyrian Administrative System

E. Forer, *Die Provinzeinteilung des assyrischen Reiches,* Leipzig 1920.

A. Alt, Das System der assyrische Provinzen auf dem Boden des Reiches Israel, *ZDPV* 52 (1929), 220–242.

M. Cogan, *Imperialism and Religion: Assyria, Judah and Israel in the Eighth and Seventh Centuries B.C.E.,* Missoula 1974.

B. Oded, Observation on Methods of Assyrian Rule in Transjordania after the Palestinian Campaign of Tiglath Pileser III, *JNES* 29 (1970), 177–186.

I. Eph'al, The Assyrian Domination of Palestine, *WHJP* (1979), 276–289.

Idem, Transjordan under Assyrian Rule, *IEJ* 4 (1984), 168–186.

J. B. Bloom, Material Remains of the Neo-Assyrian Presence in Palestine, Ph.D. diss., Bryn Mawr College, 1988.

M. Elath, International Commerce in Palestine under Assyrian Rule, in: B. Z. Kedar et al. (eds.), *Commerce in Palestine throughout the Ages,* Jerusalem 1990 (Hebrew).

N. Na'aman, Province System and Settlement Pattern in Southern Syria and Palestine in the Neo-Assyrian Period, in: M. Liverani (ed.), *Neo-Assyrian Geography,* Rome 1995, 103–115.

J. Kah-Jin-Kuan, Neo-Assyrian Historical Inscriptions and Syria-Palestine, Ph.D. diss., Hong Kong Alliance Bible Seminary, 1995.

S. Mazzoni, Settlement Pattern and New Urbanization in Syria at the Time of the Assyrian Conquest, in: M. Liverani (ed.), *Neo-Assyrian Geography,* Rome 1995, 181–191.

S. Gitin, The Neo-Assyrian Empire and Its Western Periphery: The Levant with Focus on Philistine Ekron, in: S. Parpola and R. M. Whitny (eds.), *Assyria 1995,* Helsinki 1997, 77–103.

Assyrian Campaigns to Palestine

L. L. Honor, *Senacherib Invasion of Palestine,* New York 1926.

H. Tadmor, The Campaigns of Sargon II of Assur: A Chronological-Historical Study, *JCS* 12 (1958), 22–40, 77–100.

A. Malamat, The Wars of Israel and Assyria, in: J. Liver (ed.), *The Military History of the Land of Israel in the Biblical Times,* Tel Aviv 1965, 241–260 (Hebrew).

H. Tadmor, The Conquest of Galilee by Tiglath-Pileser III, King of Assyria, in: H. J. Hirschberg (ed.), *All the Land of Naphtali,* Jerusalem 1967, 62–67 (Hebrew).

N. Na'aman, The Brook of Egypt and the Assyrian Policy on the Border of Egypt, *TA* 6 (1979), 68–90.

R. Reich, On the Identification of the "Sealed Karu of Egypt," *EI* 15 (1981), 283–287 (Hebrew).

H. Tadmor, Tiglath Pileser III in Palestine, in: M. Weinfeld (ed.), *Shnaton, an Annual for Biblical and Ancient Near-Eastern Studies* 10 (1990), 179–182 (Hebrew).

N. Franklin, The Room V Reliefs at Dur Sharukin and Sargon II's Western Campaigns, *TA* 21 (1994), 255–275.

G. Galil, A New Look at the "Azekah Inscription," *RB* 102 (1995), 321–329.

L. D. Levine, Senacherib's Southern Front, *JCS* 34 (1982), 28–58.

H. Tadmor, Senacherib's Campaign to Judah: Historical and Historiographical Considerations, *Zion* 50 (1985), 65–80 (Hebrew).

W. H. Shea, Senacherib's Second Palestinian Campaign, *JBL* 104 (1985), 401–418.

Assyrian Inscriptions

G. Beckman, Tablet Fragments from Sepphoris, *Nouvelles Assyriologiques Brèves et Utilitaires,* 1997 no. 3, 81–82.

Samaria III, 35, pl. IV:2–3.

Z. G. Kapera, The Ashdod Stele of Sargon II, *Folia Orientalia* 17 (1976), 87–99.

H. Tadmor, The History of Samaria in the Biblical Period, in: *Eretz Shomron,* Jerusalem 1973, 72, N. 16 (Hebrew).

Idem, Notes on the Stele of Sargon II from Cyprus, *EI* 25 (1996), 286–289 (Hebrew).

Y. Porath et al., *The History and Archaeology of Emek-Hefer,* Tel Aviv 1985, 58, N. 3 (Hebrew).

Hadid, Tel, 12.

N. Naʿaman, Sargon II and the Rebellion of the Cypriote Kings Against Shilta of Tyre, *Orientalia* 67 (1998), 239–247.

Gezer I, 22–29.

B. Becking, The Two Neo-Assyrian Documents from Gezer in Their Historical Context, *Jahrbericht Ex Orient Lux* 27 (1983), 76–89.

V. Donbaz, Gezer's Third Cuneiform Tablet, *State Archives of Assyria Bulletin,* no. 11/1 (1988), 6, N. 13.

M. Sigrist, Une Tablette cuneiforme de Tell Keisan, *IEJ* 32 (1982), 32–35.

Samaria HA I–II, 247, no. 1, pl. 56.

M. Cogan, A Lamashtu Plaque from the Judean Shephela, *IEJ* 45 (1995), 155–161.

The Assyrian Army

Y. Yadin, *The Art of Warfare in Biblical Lands in the Light of Archaeological Study,* New York 1963.

I. Ephʿal, On the Warfare and Military Control in the Ancient Near Eastern Empires: A Research Outline, in: H. Tadmor and M. Weinfeld (eds.), *History, Historiography and Interpretation,* Jerusalem 1983, 88–106.

S. Dalleys, Foreign Chariotry and Cavalry in the Armies of Tiglath-Pileser III and Sargon II, *Iraq* 47 (1985), 31–48.

N. Franklin, The Room V Reliefs at Dur Sharukin and Sargon II's Western Campaigns, *TA* 21 (1994), 255–275.

R. D. Barnett, The Siege of Lachish, *IEJ* 8 (1958), 161–164.

D. Ussishkin, The Camp of the Assyrians in Jerusalem, *IEJ* 29 (1979), 137–142.

Idem, The Conquest of Lachish by Senacherib, Tel Aviv 1982.

Idem, The Assyrian Attack on Lachish: The Evidence from the South-West Corner of the City, *TA* 17 (1990), 53–86.

I. Ephʿal, The Assyrian Siege Ramp at Lachish: Military and Linguistic Aspects, *TA* 11 (1984), 60–70.

B. Oded, *Mass Deportations and Deportees in the Neo-Assyrian Empire,* Wiesbaden 1979.

N. Naʾaman and R. Zadok, Sargon II's Deportations to Israel and Philistia (716–708 B.C.), *JCS* 40 (1988), 36–46.

Idem, Population Changes in Palestine Following Assyrian Deportations, *TA* 20 (1993), 104–124.

Chapter Two: The Assyrian Impact on the Material Culture of Palestine

Assyrian Documents from Palestine

Assyrian Seals

Samaria, HA I–II, 247, pl. 56:A
A. J. Sachs, Late Assyrian Royal Seal Type, *Iraq* 15 (1953), 167–170.
A. R. Milard, Royal Seal Type Again, *Iraq* 27 (1965), 12–16.
Samaria III, 87, pl. XV.
A. Spycket, La Culte du dieu-lune à Tell Keisan, *RB* 80 (1973), 384–395.
S. Geva, A Neo-Assyrian Cylinder Seal from Beth-Shan, *EI* 15 (1981), 297–300 (Hebrew).
Dor I, 139–145
Shechem I, 163, fig. 81:6.
H. Tadmor and M. Tadmor, The Seal of Bel-Ashardu—a Case of Migration, in: K. Van-Lerberyhe and A. Schoors (eds.), *Immigration and Emigration Within the Ancient Near-East—Festschrift E. Lipiński,* Leuven 1995, 345–355.
R. Reich and B. Brandl, Gezer under Assyrian Rule, *PEQ* 117 (1985), 41–54.
Beersheba I, 56–59.
W. G. Dever, Solomonic and Assyrian Period "Palaces" at Gezer, *IEJ* 35 (1985), 217–230.
M. Aharoni, An Iron Age Cylinder Seal, *IEJ* 46 (1996), 52–54.
E. Stern, Notes on the Development of Stamp-Glyptic Art in Palestine During the Assyrian and Persian Periods, *Richardson Festschrift,* 135–146.
T. Ornan, A Mesopotamian Influence on West Semitic Inscribed Seals, in: B. Saas and C. Uehlinger (eds.), *Studies in the Iconography of Northwest Semitic Inscribed Seals,* Freibourg 1993, 52–73.

Assyrian Architecture and City Planning

General

R. Amiran and I. Dunayevski, The Assyrian Open-Court Building and Its Palestinian Derivatives, *BASOR* 149 (1958), 25–32.
V. Fritz, Die Paläste während der assyrischen, babylonischen und persischen Vorherrschaft in Palästina, *MDOG* 111 (1979), 63–74.
R. Reich, Assyrian Royal Buildings in the Land of Israel, in: *Architecture,* 214–222.

Sites

R. Reich, The Persian Building at Ayyelet ha-Shahar: The Assyrian Palace at Hazor? *IEJ* 25 (1975), 233–237.
O. Lipschitz, The Date of the Assyrian Residence at Ayyelet Hashahar, *TA* 17 (1990), 96–99.
Megiddo I, 62–74, figs. 71–73, 89.
R. Reich and B. Brandl, Gezer under Assyrian Rule, *PEQ* 117 (1985), 41–54.
W. G. Dever, Solomonic and Assyrian Period "Palaces" at Gezer, *IEJ* 35 (1985), 217–230.

E. Oren, *NEAEHL,* vol. IV, 1060–1062, figs. opp. 1068.
Rishon le-Zion, 744.
Anthedon, 6–7, pls. II:7; X–XI; XXXI.
Buseirah I and *II*
C. M. Bennett, Some Reflections on Neo-Assyrian Influence in Transjordan, in: *Kenyon Festschrift,* 164–171.

Assyrian Temples and Cult

S. W. Holloway, The Case for Assyrian Religious Influence in Israel and Judah: Inference and Evidence, Ph.D. diss., University of Chicago, 1992.

Assyrian Burial Customs.

R. Amiran, A Late Assyrian Stone Bowl from Tel el-Qitaf in the Beth-Shean Valley, *'Atiqot II,* English series (1959), 129–132.
Jezreel, Tel, 33–40.
J. P. Free, The Sixth Season at Dothan, *BASOR* 156 (1959), 22–29.
Shechem II
Far'ah, Tell el-[N], 69–71, figs. 47:10–12.
J. R. Zorn, Mesopotamian Style Ceramic "Bathtub" Coffins from Tell En-Nasbeh, *TA* 20 (1993), 216–224.
Idem, More on Mesopotamian Burial Practices in Ancient Israel, *IEJ* 47 (1997), 214–219.
G. Lankester-Harding, The Tomb of Adoninur, *PEFA* 6 (1953), 48–65.
Mazar, Tell el-, 7,29; fig. 24.

Assyrian Pottery Vases

Jemmeh, Tell, 7,23; pls. XLVIII, LXV.
J. Lines (Oates), Late Assyrian Pottery from Nimrud, *Iraq* 16 (1954), 164–167.
J. Oates, Late Assyrian Pottery from Fort Shalmanesser, *Iraq* 21 (1959), 130–146.
R. Hestrin and E. Stern, Two "Assyrian" Bowls from Israel, *IEJ* 23 (1973), 152–155.
A. Gilboa, Assyrian Type Pottery at Dor and the Status of the Town During the Assyrian Occupation Period, *EI* 25 (1996), 16–121 (Hebrew).

Assyrian Metal Artifacts

J. R. Zorn, The Date of the Bronze Vase from Tell En-Nasbeh, *TA* 23 (1966), 209–211.

Chapter Three: The Assyrian Provinces of Megiddo and Samaria

The New Settlement Picture in the Megiddo Province

Dan, Tel; Hazor I-V: Kinneret; Taanach, Tel; Jezreel, Tel; Jokneam, Tel; Megiddo I
S. Geva, The Material Culture of the Region of the Kingdom of Israel During the 8th and 7th Centuries B.C.E., Ph.D. diss., Hebrew University, 1981.
E. Stern, Hazor, Dor and Megiddo in the Time of Ahab and Under Assyrian Rule, *IEJ* 40 (1990), 12–30.
Z. Gal, *Lower Galilee During the Iron Age,* Winona Lake, Ind. 1992.

W. G. Dever, Abel-Beth-Mácha: "North Gateway of Ancient Israel," in: *Horn Festschrift,* 207–222.

The Province of Samaria

General

N. Na'aman and R. Zadok, Sargon II's Deportations to Israel and Philistia (716–708 B.C.), *JCS* 40 (1988), 36–46.

N. Na'aman, The Historical Background of the Conquest of Samaria (720 B.C.), *Biblica* 71 (1990), 207–225.

J. H. Hays and J. K. Kuan, The Final Years of Samaria (730–720 B.C.), *Biblica* 72 (1991), 153–181.

I. Eph'al, The Samarian(s) in the Assyrian Sources, in: *Tadmor Festschrift,* 36–45.

B. Becking, *The Fall of Samaria: An Historical and Archaeological Study,* Leiden 1992.

G. Galil, The Last Years of the Kingdom of Israel and the Fall of Samaria, *Catholic Biblical Quarterly* 57 (1995), 52–64.

Seals

B. Brandl, An Israelite Bulla in Phoenician Style from Bethsaida (et Tell), *Bethsaida,* 141–164.

Surveys

R. Gophna and Y. Porath, Survey of the Land of Ephraim and Manasseh, in: M. Kochavi (ed.), *Judea, Samaria and the Golan, Archaeological Survey 1967–1968,* 196–243.

I. Finkelstein, Israelite and Hellenistic Farms in the Foothills and in the Yarkon Basin, *EI* 15 (1981), 331–341 (Hebrew).

A. Zertal, *The Manasseh Hill Country Survey: The Shechem Syncline,* Haifa 1992.

Sites

Dothan, Tel; Shechem I–III; Samaria HA I–II; Samaria I, III; Far'ah, Tell el- (N); Bethel; Gezer I–III; Gezer (HUCA) 1–3; Hadid, Tel

Temples and Cult Objects

A. Biran, High Places at the Gates of Dan, *EI* 25 (1996), 55–58 (Hebrew).

H. G. May, *Material Remains of the Megiddo Cult,* Chicago 1935.

N. Zori, Cult Figurines in the Eastern Plain of Esdraelon and Beth-Shan, *EI* 5 (1958), 52–54 (Hebrew).

R. Kletter, Clay Figurines and Scale Weights from Tel Jezreel, in: *Jezreel, Tel,* 110–117.

M. Popovitch, New Reading of an Egyptian Figurine from Shiloh, *JSRS* 5 (1995), 33–36 (Hebrew).

Deir 'Alla Inscription

J. Hoftijzer and G. van der Kooij, *Aramaic Texts from Deir 'Alla,* Leiden 1976.

Idem, The Balaam Text from Deir 'Alla Re-evaluated, Leiden 1991.

J. Naveh, The Date of Deir ʿAlla Inscription in Aramaic Script, *IEJ* 17 (1967), 236–238.

P. K. McCarter, The Balaam Texts from Deir ʿAlla: The First Combination, *BASOR* 239 (1980), 49–60.

J. A. Hacket, *The Balaam Text from Deir ʿAlla,* Chico, Calif. 1984.

A. Lemaire, Fragments from the Book of Balaam Found at Deir ʿAlla, *BARev* 11/5 (1985), 26–39.

B. Levine, The Balaam Inscription from Deir-ʿAlla: Historical Aspects, in: *BAT* I, 326–329.

Pottery

S. Geva, The Material Culture in the Area of the Kingdom of Israel in the 8th and 7th Centuries B.C., Ph.D. diss., Hebrew University, 1981.

D. Pakman, Late Iron Age Pottery at Tel Dan, *EI* 23 (1992), 230–240 (Hebrew).

G. Lehman, Trends in the Local Pottery Development of the Late Iron Age and Persian Period in Syria and Lebanon, ca. 700 to 300 B.C., *BASOR* 311 (1998), 7–38.

Chapter Four: The Phoenicians

The Historical Background of Phoenicia in the Assyrian Period

H. J. Kazenstein, *The History of Tyre,* Jerusalem 1973.

B. Oded, The Phoenician Cities and the Assyrian Empire in the Time of Tiglath Pilesser III, *ZDPV* 90 (1974), 38–49.

I. J. Winter, Art as Evidence for Interaction: Relations Between the Assyrian Empire and North Syria, in: H. J. Nissen and J. Renger (eds.), *Mesopotamien und seine Nachbarn,* Berlin 1982, 355–382.

G. Bunnens, Considérations géographiqes sur la place occupée par la Phénicie dans l'expansion de l'empire assyrien, in: E. Gubel and E. Lipiński (eds.), *Redt Tyrus/Sauvons Tyr, Studia Phoenicia* 1, Leuven 1983, 169–193.

J. Elayi, Les Cités phéniciennes et l'empire assyrien à l'époque d'Assurbanipal, *RA* 77 (1983), 45–58.

Idem, Les Relations entre les cités phéniciennes et l'empire assyrien sous le règne de Sennachérib, *Semitica* 35 (1985), 19–26.

A. Lemaire, Les Phéniciens et le commerce entre la Mer Rouge et la Mer Méditerranée, *Studia Phoenicia* 5, Leiden 1987, 49–60.

E. Lipiński, Le Royame de Sidon au VIIc siècle av J. C., *EI* 24 (1993), 158*–163*.

Excavations and Sites

Achzib I–II; Kabri; Acco; Keisan, Tell; Shiqmona II; Dor, I–II

E. Stern, Archaeological Background to the History of Southern Phoenicia and the Coast of the Sharon in the Assyrian Period, in: *Levine Festschrift.*

Y. Porath et al. (eds.), *The History and Archaeology of Emek-Hefer,* Tel Aviv 1985 (Hebrew).

J. F. Salles, A Propos du Niveau 4 de Tell Keisan, *Levant* 17 (1985), 203–204.

A. Gilboa, Assyrian Type Pottery at Dor and the Status of the Town During the Assyrian Occupation Period, *EI* 25 (1996), 116–121 (Hebrew).

J. Elayi and H. Sayegh, *Beirut in the Iron Age III/Persian Period: A District of the Phoenician Harbour. The Objects,* Paris, 1998.

Phoenician Architecture

E. Stern, The Excavations of Tell Mevorakh and the Phoenician Elements in the Architecture of Palestine, *BASOR* 225 (1977), 17–27.

Idem, The Phoenician Architectural Elements During the Iron Age and Persian Period, in: *Architecture,* 302–309.

Idem, The Walls of Dor, *IEJ* 38 (1988), 6–14.

Idem, New Phoenician Elements in the Architecture of Dor, in: J. Magness and S. Gitin (eds.), *Hesed Ve-Emet: Studies in Honor of E. S. Frerichs,* Atlanta 1998, 373–388.

J. Elayi, Remarques sur un type de mur phénicien, *RSF* 8 (1980), 165–180.

Idem, Nouveaux éléments sur le mur à piliers phénicien, *Trans* 11 (1996), 78–94.

G. and O. Van Beek, Canaanite-Phoenician Architecture: The Development of Two Styles, *EI* 15 (1981), 70*–77*.

I. Sharon, Phoenician and Greek Ashlar Construction Techniques at Tel Dor, Israel, *BASOR* 267 (1987), 21–42.

Idem, The Fortifications of Dor and the Transition from Israeli-Syrian Concept to the Greek Concept, *Qadmoniot* 24 (1991), 105–113 (Hebrew).

Phoenician Temples and Cult

General

R. J. Clifford, Phoenician Religion, *BASOR* 279 (1990), 55–64.

A. Lemaire, Déesses et dieux de Syrie-Palestine d'après les inscriptions (c. 1000–500 Av. N.E.), in: W. Diertrich and M. A. Klopfenstein (eds.), *Ein Gott Allein?* Freiburg 1994, 127–158.

E. Lipiński, Dieux et déesses de l'univers phénicien et punique, *Studia Phoenicia* 14, Leuven 1995.

Temples

Sarepta; Sarepta I–IV
A. Biran, High Places at the Gates of Dan, *EI* 25 (1996), 55–58 (Hebrew).

Cult Inscriptions

Acco; Dor I–II; Michal, Tel; Apollonia I–II; Jaffa I; Nebi Yunis; Jemmeh, Tell I–III
R. B. Coote, The Kition Bowl, *BASOR* 220 (1975), 47–50.

J. B. Pritchard, The Tanit Inscription from Sarepta, in: H. G. Niemeyer (ed.), *Phonizier im Westen,* Mainz am Rhein 1982, 83–94.

N. Avigad and J. C. Greenfield, A Bronze *phialē* with a Phoenician Dedicatory Inscription, *IEJ* 32 (1982), 118–128.

M. Dothan, Phoenician Inscription from 'Akko, *IEJ* 35 (1985), 81–94.

J. Naveh, Unpublished Phoenician Inscriptions from Palestine, *IEJ* 37 (1987), 25–30.

M. Delcor, Le Tarif dit de Marseille: Aspects du system sacrificiel punique, *Semitica* 38 (1990), 87–95.

J. R. Davila and B. Zuckerman, The Throne of 'Ashtart Inscription, *BASOR* 289 (1993), 67–80.

Figurines

P. J. Riis, The Syrian Astarte Plaques and Their Western Connections, *Berytus* 9 (1949), 69–90.

W. Culican, Dea Tyria Gravida, *AJBA* 1/2 (1969), 35–50.

M. Dothan, The Sign of Tanit from Tel 'Akko, *IEJ* 24 (1974), 44–49.

J. W. Betylon, The Cult of the Asherah/Elat at Sidon, *JNES* 44 (1985), 53–56.

F. O. Hvidberg-Hansen, Uni-Ashtarte and Tani-Iuno Caelestis: Two Phoenician Goddesses of Fertility Reconsidered from Recent Archaeological Discoveries, in: A. Bonano (ed.), *Archaeology and the Fertility Cult in the Ancient Mediterranean,* Amsterdam 1986, 170–195.

C. A. Meyers, Terracotta at the Harvard Semitic Museum, *IEJ* 37 (1987), 116–122.

E. Mazar, A Horsemen's Tomb at Akhziv, *Qadmoniot* 23 (1990), 104–109 (Hebrew).

N. Massika, Terracotta Figurines from Acco in the Persian and Hellenistic Periods, M.A. thesis, Hebrew University, 1996 (Hebrew).

P. R. S. Moorey and S. Flaming, Problems in the Study of the Anthropomorphic Metal Statuary from Syro-Palestine Before 330 BC, *Levant* 16 (1989), 67–90.

V. Karageorghis, *The Coroplastic Art of Ancient Cyprus, the Cypro-Archaic Period, Male Figurines,* Nicosia 1995; *Female Figurines,* Nicosia 1998.

Models of Shrines

J. H. Iliffe, A Model Shrine of Phoenician Style, *QDAP* 11 (1945), 91–92.

W. Culican, A Teracotta Shrine from Achzib, *ZDPV* 92 (1976), 47–53.

H. Seeden, A Small Clay Shrine in AUB Museum, *Berytus* 27 (1979), 7–25.

A. Mazar, Pottery Plaques Depicting Goddesses Standing in Temple Facades, *Michmanim* 2 (1985), 5–18 (Hebrew).

The Phoenician Popular Cult

E. Stern, Phoenician Masks and Pendants, *PEQ* 108 (1976), 109–118.

W. Culican, Some Phoenician Masks and Other Terracottas, *Berytus* 24 (1975–76), 47–87.

A. Ciasca, Masks and Protomes, in: S. Moscati (ed.), *The Phoenicians,* Rome 1988, 354–369.

Phoenician Burial Customs

C. N. Johns, Excavation at Pilgrims' Castle, Atlit (1933), *QDAP* 6 (1938), 121–152.

R. Saidah, Fouilles de Kaldeh, *BMB* 19 (1966), 51–90.

A. M. Bisi, *Le Stele puniche,* Rome 1967.

W. Culican, The Graves at Tell er-Ruqeish, *AJBA* 2/2 (1973), 66–105.

A. Biran, Tell er-Ruqeish, *IEJ* 24 (1974), 141–142, pl. 24:A.

M. Prausnitz, Die Nekropolen von Akhziv und die entwicklung der Keramik von 10 bis Jh. v. Chr. in Akhziv, Samaria und Ashdod, in: H. G. Niemeyer (ed.), *Phonizier im Westen,* Mainz am Rhein 1982, 45–82.

H. Sader, Phoenician Stelae from Tyre, *Berytus* 39 (1990), 105–126.

M. Gras et al., The Phoenician and Death, *Berytus* 39 (1991), 127–177.

E. Mazar, *The Achzib Burials: A Test-Case for Phoenician-Punic Burial Customs,* Ph.D. diss., Hebrew University, 1996 (Hebrew).

Phoenician Art Objects

R. A. Stucky, The Engraved Tridacna Shells, *Dedalo* 19 (1974), 1–17.

B. Brandl, The Engraved Tridacna Shell Discs, *AS* 24 (1984), 15–24.

G. Markoe, *Phoenician Bronze and Silver Bowls from Cyprus and the Mediterranean,* Berkeley 1984.

D. Barag, Phoenician Stone Vessels from the Eighth–Seventh Centuries BCE, *EI* 18 (1985), 215–232 (Hebrew).

Idem, Early Traditions in Phoenician Stone Vessels of the Eighth–Seventh Centuries BCE, *EI* 25 (1996), 82–93 (Hebrew).

Phoenician Pottery

S. V. Chapman, A Catalogue of Iron Age Pottery from the Cemeteries of Hirbet Selim, Joyah, Qraye and Qasmieh of South Lebanon, *Berytus* 21 (1972), 51–194.

W. Culican, Sidonian Bottles, *Levant* 7 (1975), 145–150.

Idem, The Repertoire of Phoenician Pottery, in: H. G. Niemeyer, *Phonizier im Westen,* Mainz am Rhein 1982, 45–82.

P. M. Bikai, *The Pottery of Tyre,* Warminster 1978.

Idem, The Late Phoenician Pottery complex and Chronology, *BASOR* 229 (1978), 47–56.

Idem, Observations on Archaeological Evidence for Trade Between Israel and Tyre, *BASOR* 258 (1985), 71–72.

Idem, The Phoenician Pottery of Cyprus, Nicosia 1987.

D. Conrad, The Akko Ware: A New Type of Phoenician Pottery with Incised Decoration, in: *Dothan Festschrift,* 127–142.

M. L. Buhl, *Sukas VII: Near Eastern Pottery and Objects from the Upper Strata,* Copenhagen 1983.

F. Braemer, La Céramique à engobe rouge de l'âge du fer à Bassit, *Syria* 63 (1986), 221–246.

Sarepta I, 139–445.

A. Gilboa, The Typology and Chronology of the Iron Age Pottery, in: *Dor II,* 1–49.

G. Lehmann, Trends in the Local Pottery Development of the Late Iron Age and Persian Period in Syria and Lebanon, ca. 700–300 B.C., *BASOR* 311 (1998), 7–37.

Chapter Five: The Philistines

The Historical Background of Philistia in the 7th Century BCE

H. Tadmor, The Campaigns of Sargon II of Assur, *JCS* 12 (1958), 22–40, 77–100.

Idem, Philistia Under Assyrian Rule, *BA* 29 (1966), 86–102.

Z. J. Kapera, Was *ya-ma-ni* a Cypriote? *Folia Orientalia* 14 (1972–1973), 207–218.

Idem, The Oldest Account of Sargon II's Campaign Against Ashdod, *Folia Orientalia* 24 (1976), 29–39.

G. Mattingly, The Role of Philistine Autonomy in Neo Assyrian Foreign Policy, *Near East Society Archaeological Bulletin* 14 (1979), 4–49, 57.

N. Na'aman and R. Zadok, Sargon II's Deportations to Israel and Philistia, *JCS* 40 (1988), 36–42.

E. D. Oren, Ethnicity and Regional Archaeology: The Western Negev Under Assyrian Rule, *BAT* II, 102–105.

S. Gitin, The Neo-Assyrian Empire and Its Western Periphery: The Levant, with Focus on Philistine Ekron, in: S. Parpola and R. M. Whitney (eds.), *Assyria 1995,* Helsinki 1997, 77–103.

Philistine Settlements and Stratigraphy

Jemmeh, Tell I–III; Ekron I–II; Anthedon
G. Van Beek, Digging Up Tel Jemmeh, *Archaeology* 36 (1983), 12–19.

R. Gophna, Some Iron Age II Sites in Southern Philistia, *'Atiqot* 6, Hebrew series (1970), 25–39.

Idem, The Boundary Between the Kingdoms of Judah, Ashkelon and Gaza in the Light of Archaeological Survey in Shiqma Valley, *Proceedings of the Seventh World Congress of Jewish Studies,* vol. I (1981), 49–52 (Hebrew).

R. Reich, On the Identification of the Sealed Karu of Egypt, *EI* 15 (1981), 283–287 (Hebrew).

L. E. Stager, The Fury of Babylon: Askelon and the Archaeology of Destruction, *BARev* 22 (1996), 56–69, 76–77.

Idem, Ashkelon and the Archaeology of Destruction: Kislev 604 BCE, *EI* 25 (1996), 61*–74*.

S. Gitin, Tel Miqne-Ekron: A Type-Site for the Inner Coastal Plain in the Iron Age II Period, in: S. Gitin and W. G. Dever (eds.), *Recent Excavations in Israel,* AASOR 49 (1989), 25–58.

Idem, Ekron of the Philistines Part II: Olive-Oil Suppliers to the World, *BARev* 16 (1990), 32–43.

Idem, The Last Days of the Philistines, *Archaeology* 45 (1992), 26–31.

Philistine Documents of the 7th Century BCE

A. Bergman (Biran), Two Hebrew Seals of "Ebed Class," *JBL* 55 (1936), 225.

J. Naveh, Writing and Scripts in the Seventh Century BCE Philistia and the New evidence from Tel Jemmeh, *IEJ* 35 (1985), 11–15.

A. Kempinski, Some Philistine Names from the Kingdom of Gaza, *IEJ* 37 (1987), 20–24.

Ekron II
A. Demski, The Name of the Goddess of Ekron—a New Reading, *JNES* 25 (1997), 1–5.

Philistine Architecture

E. D. Oren, Ashlar Masonary in the Western Negev in the Iron Age, *EI* 23 (1992), 94–105 (Hebrew).

The Philistine Cult

Ashdod I, II–III; Ekron II

I. Singer, Towards an Identity of Dagon, the God of the Philistines, *Cathedra* 54 (1989), 17–42 (Hebrew).

S. Gitin, Incense Altars from Ekron, Israel and Judah, Context, Typology and Function, *EI* 23 (1992), 43*–49*.

Idem, Tel-Miqneh-Ekron in the 7th Century BCE: The Impact of Economic Innovation and Foreign Cultural Influences on the Neo-Assyrian Vassal City-State, in: *Recent Excavations in Israel: A View to the West,* Dubuque, Iowa 1995, 57–79.

Idem, Seventh Century BCE Cultic Elements at Ekron, *BAT* II, 248–258.

A. Golani and B. Sass, Three Seventh-Century BCE Hoards of Silver Jewelry from Tel Miqne-Ekron, *BASOR* 311 (1998), 57–82.

Chapter Six: The Kingdom of Judah

Outline of History

H. Spieckermann, *Juda unter Assur in den Sargonidenzeit,* Göttingen 1982.

G. Galil, Judah and Assyria in the Sargonic Period, *Zion* 57/2 (1992), 111–133 (Hebrew).

M. Broshi, The Expansion of Jerusalem in the Reigns of Hezekiah and Manasseh, *IEJ* 24 (1974), 21–26.

M. Broshi and I. Finkelstein, The Population of Palestine in Iron Age II, *BASOR* 287 (1992), 47–60.

N. Na'aman, Sennacherib Letter to God on His Campaign to Judah, *BASOR* 214 (1974), 25–39.

Idem, Senacherib's Campaign to Judah and the Date of the *lmlk* Stamps, *VT* 29 (1979), 61–86.

Idem, Hezekiah's Fortified Cities and the *lmlk* Stamps, *BASOR* 261 (1986), 5–21.

Idem, The Negev in the Last Century of the Kingdom of Judah, *Cathedra* 42 (1987), 3–15 (Hebrew).

M. Cogan, *Imperialism and Religion, Judah and Israel in the Eighth and Seventh Centuries BCE,* Missoula, Mont. 1974.

H. Reviv, Judah from Hezekiah to Josiah, in: *WHJP,* vol. IV: *The Age of the Monarchies,* 1982, 131–139 (Hebrew).

M. Elat, The Political Status of the Kingdom of Judah Within the Assyrian Empire, in: *Lachish V,* 61–70.

S. W. Bulbach, Judah in the Reign of Manasseh, Ph.D. diss., New York University, 1981.

L. Tatum, From Text to Tell: King Manasseh in the Biblical and Archaeological Record, Ph.D. diss., Duke University, 1988.

L. Tatum, King Manasseh and the Royal Fortress at Horvat 'Usa, *BA* 54 (1991), 136–145.

A. F. Rainey, Manasseh King of Judah, in the Whirlpool of the Seventh Century B.C.E., in: R. Kutscher Memorial Book, Tel Aviv 1993, 147–164.

P. J. King, Archaeology and the Book of Jeremiah, *EI* 23 (1993), 95*–99*.

I. Finkelstein, The Archaeology of the Days of Manasseh, in: *King Festschrift,* 169–187.

S. Zmirin, *Josiah and His Period,* Jerusalem 1955 (Hebrew).

F. M. Cross and D. N. Freedman, Josiah's Revolt Against Assyria, *JNES* 12 (1953), 56–68.

A. Malamat, The Historical Background of the Assassination of Amon King of Judah, *IEJ* 3 (1953), 26–29.

Idem, The Last Kings of Judah and the Fall of Jerusalem, *IEJ* 18 (1968), 137–156.

Idem, Josiah's Bid for Armageddon, *JNES* 5 (1973), 267–278.

Idem, The Twilight of Judah in the Egyptian-Babylonian Maelstrom, *VT Supplement* 28 (1975), 123–145.

G. Galil, A New Look at the Chronology of the Last Kings of Judah, *Zion* 56/1 (1991), 1–19 (Hebrew).

Y. Yadin, The Historical Significance of Inscription 88 from Arad, *IEJ* 26 (1976), 9–14.

The Boundaries of Judah

General

Y. Yadin, The Archaeological Sources for the Period of the Monarchy, in: *WHJP,* vol. V (1979), 187–233 (Hebrew).

Y. Shiloh, *Judah and Jerusalem in the Eighth–Sixth Centuries B.C.E.,* AASOR 49 (1989), 97–105.

G. Barkai, The Redefining of Archaeological Periods: Does the Date 588/586 B.C.E. Indeed Mark the End of the Iron Age Culture? in: *BAT* II, 106–109.

R. Kletter, Observations Concerning the Material Culture of Judah at the End of the Iron Age in Connection with its Political Borders, Ph.D. diss., Tel Aviv University 1995 (Hebrew).

The Eastern Border

Vered Jericho; En-Gedi I–II; Kheleifeh, Tell el-

J. Garstang, *The Story of Jericho,* London 1940.

F. M. Cross and J. T. Milik, Explorations in the Judaean Beqe'ah, *BASOR* 142 (1956), 2–17.

L. E. Stager, Ancient Agriculture in the Judaean Desert: A Case Study, Ph.D. diss., Harvard University, 1975.

Idem, Farming in the Judaean Desert During the Iron Age, *BASOR* 221 (1976), 145–158.

K. M. Kenyon, *Excavations at Jericho,* vol. II: *The Tombs Excavated in 1955–58,* London 1965, 479–515.

T. A. Holland, *Excavations at Jericho,* vol. III: *The Architecture and Stratigraphy of the Tell,* London 1981, 11–113.

H. and M. Weippert, Jericho in der Eisenzeit, *ZDPV* 92 (1976), 105–148.

P. Bar Adon, Excavations in the Judaean Desert, *'Atiqot* 9, Hebrew series (1989).

E. Stern, The Eastern Border of the Kingdom of Judah, in: *King Festschrift,* 399–409.

The Northern Border

Sites

Shilḥah, Horvat; Michmash, Meẓad; Jib'it, Khirbet; 'Anathoth I–II; Bethel; Ful, Tell, el-I–III; Naṣbeh, Tell en-I–III; Gibeon I–IV; Gezer I–III; Gezer HUCA 1–2; Hashavyahu, Meẓad I–II; Qasile, Tell

Y. Aharoni, The Northern Boundary of Judah, *PEQ* 90 (1958), 27–31.

G. Galil, Geba'-Ephraim and the Northern Boundary of Judah in the Days of Josiah, *RB* 100 (1993), 358–367.

N. L. Lapp, Casemate Walls in Palestine and the Late Iron II Casemate at Tell el-Full (Gibeah), *BASOR* 223 (1976), 25–42.

H. Eshel, A *lmlk* Stamp from Beth-El, *IEJ* 39 (1989), 60–62.

Idem, The Late Iron Age Cemetery of Gibeon, *IEJ* 37 (1987), 1–16.

J. Seger, Tel Gezer: Phase II Excavations 1972–1994, in: *Rose Festschrift,* 113–127.

The Judaean Western Boundary

Sites

Batash, Tel; Harasim, Tel; Ṣafi, Tell eṣ-; 'Erani, Tel I; Halif, Tel; Beth-Shemesh; Bliss-Macalister [1902], Judeideh, Tell; Maresha; Lachish III, V–VII; Beit Mirsim, Tell; 'Eton, Tel I–II; Tuwein, Khirbet

A. F. Rainey, The Biblical Shephelah of Judah, *BASOR* 251 (1983), 1–22.

G. Galil, The Administrative Division of the Shefelah, *Zion* 53/1 (1988), 1–12 (Hebrew).

J. Seger, The Location of Biblical Ziklag According to the Tel Halif Excavations, in: E. Stern and D. Urman (eds.), *Man and Environment in the Southern Shephela,* Tel Aviv 1988, 139–150 (Hebrew).

Y. Dagan, The Shefelah During the Period of the Monarchy in the Light of Archaeological Excavations and Surveys, M.A. thesis, Tel Aviv University, 1992 (Hebrew).

The Southern Border

Z. Meshel, History of the Negev in the Period of the Judaean Kings, Ph.D. diss., Tel Aviv University, 1974 (Hebrew).

R. Cohen, The Iron Age Fortresses in the Central Negev, *BASOR* 236 (1979), 247–255.

Y. Yadin and S. Geva, The Cities of the Negev During Josiah's Days, in: Y. Hofman (ed.), *Encyclopedia of the Biblical World,* Jerusalem 1983, 247–255 (Hebrew).

N. Na'aman, The Negev in the Late Days of the Judaean Kingdom, *Cathedra* 42 (1987), 16–25 (Hebrew).

M. Haiman, The Iron Age II Sites of the Western Negev Highlands, *IEJ* 44 (1994), 36–61.

Sites

'Uza, Horvat; Radum, Horvat; Malḥata, Tel I–II; Qitmit; Aroer I; Arad I–III; Tov, Horvat; 'Ira, Tel; Masos, Tel; Beersheba I; Kadesh-Barnea I–II

R. Gophna and Y. Yisraeli, Soundings at Beer Sheva (Bir es Seba), in: *Beersheba I,* 115–118.

K. M. Kenyon, The Date of the Destruction of Iron Age Beer Sheba, *PEQ* 108 (1976), 63–64.

A. Mazar and E. Netzer, On the Israelite Fortress at Arad, *BASOR* 263 (1986), 88–99.

A. F. Rainey, Arad in the Later Days of the Judean Monarchy, *Cathedra* 42 (1987), 16–25 (Hebrew).

D. Ussishkin, The Date of the Judaean Shrine at Arad, *IEJ* 38 (1988), 142–157.

L. Tatum, King Manasseh and the Royal Fortress at Horvat 'Uza, *BA* (1991), 136–145.

Settlements in the Judaean Highlands

Sites

Ramat Raḥel I–II; Qom, Khirbet; Beth-Zur I–II; Hebron; Rabud, Tel
A. Ofer, The Highland of Judah During the Biblical Period, Ph.D. diss., Tel Aviv University, 1993 (Hebrew).

H. Geva, The Western Boundary of Jerusalem at the End of the Monarchy, *IEJ* 29 (1979), 84–91.

A. D. Tushingham, The Western Hill of Jerusalem Under the Monarchy, *ZDPV* 95 (1979), 39–55.

G. Barkay, Northern and Western Jerusalem in the End of the Iron Age, PD. diss., Tel Aviv University, 1985 (Hebrew).

Y. Shiloh, Judah and Jerusalem in the Eighth–Sixth Centuries B.C.E., *AASOR* 49 (1989), 97–105.

G. Edelstein and I. Milevski, The Rural Settlement of Jerusalem Reevaluated: Surveys and Excavations in the Reph'aim Valley and Mevasseret Yerushalaim, *PEQ* 126 (1994), 2–23.

S. Gibson and G. Edelstein, Investigating Jerusalem's Rural Landscape, *Levant* 17 (1985), 139–155.

I. Meitlis, The Nahal Zimri Court, *JSRS* 3 (1993), 95 (Hebrew).

J. Seligman, A Late Iron Age Farmhouse at Ras Abu Ma'aruf-Pisgat Ze'ev A, *'Atiqot* XXV, English series (1995), 63–75.

J. R. Chadwick The Archaeology of Biblical Hebron in the Bronze and Iron Ages, Ph.D. diss., University of Utah, 1992.

The Written Evidence

Ostraca and Inscriptions

R. Hestrin, *Inscriptions Reveal,* Israel Museum 1972.

A. Lemaire, Les Ostraca Hébreux de l'époque royale Israelite, PD. diss., University of Paris, 1973.

Idem, Inscriptions hébraïques, tome 1: *Les Ostraca,* Paris 1977.

J. Hoftijzer and K. Jongling, *Dictionary of the North West-Semitic Inscriptions,* vol. I, Leiden 1995.

H. Torczyner, *The Lachish Letters (Lachish I),* London 1938.

J. Naveh, The Lachish Ostraca, in: *Encyclopedia Judaica,* vol. X, 1334–1335.

Y. Yadin, The Lachish Letters—Originals or Copies and Drafts, in: H. Shanks (ed.), *Recent Archaeological Discoveries in Israel,* Jerusalem 1984, 179–186.

A. F. Rainey, Watching Out for the Signal Fires of Lachish, *PEQ* 119 (1987), 149–151.

J. Naveh, A Hebrew Letter from the Seventh Century BC, *IEJ* 10 (1960), 129–130.

Idem, More Hebrew Inscriptions from Mesad Hashavyahu, *IEJ* 12 (1962), 27–32.

F. M. Cross, Epigraphic Notes on the Hebrew Documents of the Eighth–Seventh Centuries B.C., *BASOR* 165 (1962), 36–46.

Idem, A Cave Inscription from Khirbet Beit Lei, *Glueck Festschrift,* 299–306.

W. H. Shea, The Khirbet el-Kom Inscription, *VT* 37 (1990), 50–63.

Y. Aharoni, *Arad Inscriptions,* Jerusalem 1981.

Lachish V, 19–22.

A. Demsky, The Houses of Achzib, *IEJ* 16 (1966), 211–215.

I. Beit-Arieh, The Ostracon of Ahiqam from Horvat 'Uza, *TA* 13–14 (1986–1987), 32–38.

Idem, The First Temple Period Census Document, *PEQ* 115 (1983), 105–108.

Idem, An Inscribed Jar from Horvat 'Uza, *EI* 24 (1993), 34–40 (Hebrew).

G. Barkay, The Priestly Benediction of the Ketef Hinom Plaques, *Cathedra* 52 (1989), 37–76.

H. Misgav, Two Notes on the Ostraca from Horvat 'Uza, *IEJ* 40 (1990), 216–217.

Y. Nadelman, "Chiselled" Inscriptions and Marking on Pottery Vessels from the Iron Age, *IEJ* 40 (1990), 31–41.

A. Yardeni, Remarks on Priestly Blessing of Two Ancient Amulets from Jerusalem, *VT* 41 (1991), 176–185.

P. Bordreuil et al., Deux ostraca Paleo-Hébreux de la collection Sh. Mousaieff, *Semitica* 46 (1997), 46.

Bullae and Seals

The lmlk *Seal Impressions*

Y. Yadin, The Fourfold Division of Judah, *BASOR* 163 (1961), 6–11.

D. Ussishkin, Royal Judaean Storage Jars and Private Seal Impressions, *BASOR* 223 (1976), 1–13.

Idem, The Destruction of Lachish by Sennacherib and the Date of the Royal Judean Storage Jars, *TA* 4 (1977), 28–57.

A. Lemaire, Classification des estampilles royales judéennes, *EI* 15 (1981), 54*–60*.

H. Momsen et al., The Provenience of the *"lmlk"* Jars, *IEJ* 34 (1984), 89–113.

Y. Garfinkel, A Hierarchic Pattern of the Private Seal-Impressions on the *"lmlk"* Jar Handles, *EI* 18 (1985), 108–115 (Hebrew).

Idem, 2 Chr. 11:5–10 Fortified Cities List and the *lmlk* Stamps, *BASOR* 271 (1988), 69–73.

N. Avigad, Two Hebrew "Fiscal" Bullae, *IEJ* 40 (1990), 262–266.

G. Barkai, A Group of Stamped Handles from Judah, *EI* 23 (1992), 113–128 (Hebrew).

Idem, "The Prancing Horse"—an Official Seal Impression from Judah of the 8th Century B.C.E., *TA* 19/2 (1992), 124–129.

The Rosette Impressions

J. R. Zorn, Two Rosette Impressions from Tell en Nasbeh, *BASOR* 293 (1994), 81–82.
J. M. Cahill, Rosette Stamp Impressions from Ancient Judah, *IEJ* 45 (1995), 230–252.
Idem, Rosette-Stamped Handles: Instrumental Neutron Activation Analysis, Revised Typology and Comparison with the *lmlk*-Stamped Handles, M.A. thesis, Hebrew University, 1998.

Inscribed and Ornamented Seals and Bullae

General

R. Hestrin and M. Dayagi, *Inscribed Seals: First Temple Period, from the Collection of the Israel Museum,* Jerusalem 1979.
P. Bordreuil, *Catalogue des sceaux Ouest-Sémitiques inscrits de la Bibliothèque Nationale du Musée du Louvre et du Musée Biblique de Bible et Terre Sainte,* Paris 1986.
Avigad, *Corpus,* passim.

Various Seals and Bullae

A. F. Rainey, Private Seal Impressions: A Note on Semantics, *IEJ* 16 (1966), 187–190.
F. M. Cross, Judaean Stamps, *EI* 9 (1969), 20*–27*.
Idem, The Seal of Miqneyah Servant of Yahweh, in: E. Gorelick et al., *Ancient Seals and the Bible,* Malibu 1984, 55–63.
Lachish V, 19–22; pls. 20–21.
Y. Shiloh and D. Tarler, Bullae from the City of David: A Hoard of Seal Impressions from the Israelite Period, *BA* 49 (1986), 196–209.
N. Avigad, *Hebrew Bullae from the Time of Jeremiah,* Jerusalem 1986.
Idem, New Light on the *na'ar* Seals, *Wright Festschrift,* 294–299.
J. Elayi, Name of Deuteronomy Author Found on Sealing, *BARev* 13 (1987), 54–56.
Y. Garfinkel, The Distribution of the Identical Seal Impressions and Settlement Pattern in Judah before Sennacherib's Campaign, *Cathedra* 32 (1984), 35–53 (Hebrew).
Idem, The Eliashiv Na'ar Yokin Seal Impressions, *BA* (1990), 73–79.
A. Lemaire, Royal Signature-Name of Israel's Last King Surfaces in a Private Collection, *BARev* 21/6 (1995), 30–47.
Idem, King's Command and a Widow's Plea, Two New Hebrew Ostraca of the Biblical Period, *BA* 61 (1998), 2–13.
I. Eph'al and J. Naveh, Remarks on Recently Published Moussaieff Ostraca, *IEJ* 48 (1998), 269–273.

Judaean Weights and Measures.

E. Stern, Weights and Measures, in *Encyclopedia Judaica.*
Y. Yadin, Ancient Judaean Weights and the Date of the Samaria Ostraca, *ScrHier* 8 (1960), 1–17.
Y. Aharoni, The Use of Hieratic Numerals in Hebrew Ostraca and Shekel Weights, *BASOR* 184 (1966), 13–19.

I. T. Kaufman, New Evidence of Hieratic Numerals on Hebrew Weights, *BASOR* 188 (1967), 39–41.
A. Ben-David, A Rare Inscribed *nzf* Weight, *IEJ* 23 (1973), 176–177.
G. Barkai, A Group of Iron Age Scale Weights, *IEJ* 28 (1978), 209–217.
Idem, Iron Age Gerah Weights, *EI* 15 (1981), 288–296 (Hebrew).
R. Kletter, The Inscribed Weights of the Kingdom of Judah, *TA* 18 (1991), 121–163.
J. Naveh, The Number of *bat* in the Arad Ostraca, *IEJ* 42 (1992), 52–54.

The Judaean Cult

General

J. B. Segal, Popular Religion in Ancient Israel, *JJS* 27 (1976), 1–22.
P. H. Vrijhof et al. (eds.), *Official and Popular Religion: Analysis of a Theme for Religious Studies,* The Hague 1979.
G. Ahlstrom, An Archaeological Picture of Iron Age Religions in Ancient Palestine, *Studia Orientalia* 55 (1984), 117–144.
J. S. Holladay, Religion in Israel and Judah Under the Monarchy: An Explicitly Archaeological Approach, in: *Cross Festschrift,* 249–299.
P. D. Hanson, Israelite Religion in the Early Postexilic Period, in: M. Miller et al. (eds.), *Ancient Israelite Religion,* Philadelphia 1987, 485–508.
E. M. Bloch-Smith, The Cult of the Dead in Judah: Interpreting the Material Remains, *JBL* 111 (1992), 213–224.
S. Ackerman, *Under Every Green Tree: Popular Religion in Sixth Century, Judah,* Atlanta 1992.
R. Albertz, *A History of Israelite Religion in the Old Testament Period,* Louisville, Ky. 1994.
A. Milard, The History of Israel Against the Background of Ancient Near-Eastern Religious History, in: I. Eskola et al., *From Ancient Sites of Israel: Essays in Memory of A. Saarisalo,* Helsinki 1998, 101–117.

The Sanctuaries

Y. Shiloh, Iron Age Sanctuaries and Cult Places in Palestine, in: F. M. Cross (ed.), *Symposia,* Cambridge, Mass. 1979, 147–157.

The Khirbet el Qom Inscription

W. G. Dever, Iron Age Epigraphic Material from the Area of Khirbet El-Kom, *HUCA* 40–41 (1969–1970), 139–204.
Qom, Khirbet
Z. Zevit, The Khirbet el Kom Inscription Mentioning a Goddess, *BASOR* 255 (1984), 39–48.
D. N. Freedman, Yahweh of Samaria and His Asherah, *BA* 50 (1987), 241–249.
M. O'Connor, The Poetic Inscription from Khirbet el-Kom, *VT* 37 (1987), 224–230.
J. M. Hadley, The Khirbet el-Kom Inscription, *VT* 37 (1987), 50–62.
Idem, Yahweh and "His Asherah," in: W. Dietrich et al. (eds.), *Ein Gott allein?* Freiburg 1994, 235–268.
W. H. Shea, The Khirbet el-Kom Inscription, *VT* 40 (1990), 50–63.

Cult Objects

F. M. Cross, Two Offering Bowls with Phoenician Inscriptions from the Sanctuary of Arad, *BASOR* 235 (1979), 75–78.

G. Barkai, A Bowl with the Hebrew Inscription "Qodesh," *IEJ* 40 (1990), 124–129.

Idem, "Your Poor Brother," a Note on an Inscribed Bowl from Beth-Shemesh, *IEJ* 41 (1991), 239–241.

M. Artzy, Pomegranate Scepters and Incense Stands with Pomegranates Found in Priest's Grave, *BARev* 16 (1990), 48–50.

N. Avigad, The Inscribed Pomegranate from the "House of Lord," *IMJ* 8 (1989), 7–16.

Figurines

J. B. Pritchard, *Palestinian Figurines in Relation to Certain Goddesses Known Through Literature,* New Haven 1943.

T. A. Holland, Typological and Archaeological Study of the Human and Animal Representations in Plastic Art of Palestine During the Iron Age, Ph.D. diss., Oxford University, 1975.

Idem, A Study of Palestinian Iron Age Baked Figurines with Special Reference to Jerusalem Cave I, *Levant* 9 (1977), 121–155.

J. R. Engle, *Pillar Figurines of Iron Age Israel and Asherah/Asherim,* Ph.D. diss., University of Pittsburgh, 1979.

E. Stern, What Happened to the Cult Figurines? *BARev* 15/4 (1989), 22–29, 53–54.

A. J. Amr, Ten Human Clay Figurines from Jerusalem, *Levant* 20 (1988), 185–196.

Y. Nadelman, Iron Age II Clay Fragments from the Excavations, in: B. and E. Mazar, Excavations in the South of the Temple, *Qedem* 29 (1989), 123–125.

P. Beck, A Figurine from Tel'Ira, *EI* 21 (1991), 87–93 (Hebrew).

H. J. Franken, Cave 1 at Jerusalem, in: S. Bourke et al. (eds.), *Trade Contact and the Movement of People in the Eastern Mediterranean,* Sydney 1995.

D. Gilbert-Peretz, Ceramic Figurines, in: D. J. Ariel and A. de Groot (eds.), Excavations at the City of David 1978–1985, vol. IV, *Qedem* 35 (1996), 29–34.

R. Kletter, *The Judaean Pillar Figurines and the Archaeology of the Ashera,* Oxford 1996.

The Judaean Pottery

M. and Y. Aharoni, The Stratification of Judaite Sites in the 8th and 7th Centuries BCE, *BASOR* 224 (1976), 73–87.

J. N. Tub, An Iron Age II Tomb Group from the Bethlehem Region, *B. M. Occasional Paper No. 14,* London 1980.

Gezer (HUCA) 3

O. Zimhoni, The Iron Age Pottery of Tel'Eton and Its Relation to Lachish, Tel Beit Mirsim and Arad Assemblages, *TA* 12 (1985), 63–90.

Idem, Two Ceramic Assemblages from Lachish Level III and II, *TA* 17 (1990), 3–52.

I. Eshel, *The Chronology of Selected Late Iron Age Pottery Groups from Judah,* Ph.D. diss., Tel Aviv University, 1986 (Hebrew).

Idem, The Pottery Corpus from Kenyon's Excavations on the Eastern Slope of Ancient Jerusalem, in: I. Eshel and K. Prag (eds.), *Excavations by K. M. Kenyon in Jerusalem 1961–67,* vol. IV, Oxford 1995, 1–157.

Chapter Seven: The Greek Penetration

General

Y. Garfinkel, *MLS HKRSYM* in Phoenician Inscriptions from Cyprus. The *QRSY* in Arad, *HKRSYM* in Egypt, and *BNY QYRS* in the Bible, *JNES* 47 (1988), 27–34.
P. E. Dion, Les *KTYM* de Tel Arad: Grecs ou Phéniciens? *RB* 99/1 (1992), 70–97.
J. D. Ray, Soldiers to Pharaoh: The Carians of South-West Anatolia, in: J. M. Sasson (ed.), *Civilizations of the Ancient Near East,* vol. 2, New York 1995, 1185–1194.

Sites

Al-Mina I–II; Sukas II, VI; Kabri; Keisan, Tell; Acco; Dor I–II; Meẓad Ḥashavyahu; Migdol; Qedua; Naukratis I; Defenneh; Tanis II
P. Courbin, Bassit-Posidaion in the Early Iron Age, in: J. P. Desceuders (ed.), *Greek Colonies and Native Population, A. D. Trendall Festschrift,* Oxford 1990, 503–509.
P. J. Riis, The First Greeks in Phoenicia and Their Settlement in Sukas, in: A. Parrot (ed.), *Ugaritica 6,* Paris 1969, 435–450.
E. Stern, Tel Dor—a Phoenician-Israelite Trading Post, in S. Gitin (ed.), *Recent Excavations in Israel: A View to the West,* Dubuque (1995), 81–93.

The Pottery

Sukas II; Sarepta II
S. Geva, Greek Influence on Pottery Vessels from Beer-Sheva, *EI* 18 (1985), 233–237 (Hebrew).
M. Aharoni, A Krater from Arad, *EI* 18 (1985), 200–201 (Hebrew).
J. N. Coldstream, Early Greek Pottery in Tyre and Cyprus, Some Preliminary Comparisons, *RDAC* 53 (1988), 35–48.
R. M. Cook, The Wild Goat and Fikellura Styles, Some Speculations, *Oxford Journal of Archaeology* 11/3 (1992), 255–266.
W. D. Niemeier, Greek Pottery: Evidence for Greek Mercenaries at Kabri, in: *Kabri* 7–8 (1994), 31*–38*.
J. C. Waldbaum, Early Greek Contacts with the Southern Levant 1000–600 BC: The Eastern Perspective, *BASOR* 293 (1994), 53–65.
Idem, Greeks in the East or Greeks and the East: Problems in the Definition and Recognition of Presence, *BASOR* 305 (1997), 1–17.
J. C. Waldbaum and J. Magness, The Chronology of Early Greek Pottery: New Evidence from the 7th Century BC Destruction Levels in Israel, *AJA* 101 (1997), 23–40.

Chapter Eight: Egyptians in Palestine in the 7th Century BCE

General

K. A. Kitchen, *The Third Intermediate Period in Egypt 1100–650 BC,* Warminster 1973.
Idem, Egypt and Israel during the First Millennium BC, in J. A. Emerton (ed.), *VT Supplement* 40 (1986), Leiden 107–123.

A. Sparlinger, The Year 712 BC and Its Implications for Egyptian History, *JARCE* 10 (1973), 95–101.

Idem, Esarhaddon and Egypt: An Analysis of the First Invasion of Egypt, *Orientalia* 43 (1974), 295–326.

Idem, Psametichus, King Egypt, *JARCE* 15 (1976), 133–147.

M. Elat, The Economic Relations of the Neo-Assyrian Empire with Egypt, *JAOS* 98 (1978), 20–34.

D. B. Redford, The Relations Between Egypt and Israel from El-Amarna to the Babylonian Conquest, in: *BAT* I, 192–205.

A. Maeir, Judaean Presence in Egypt, *IEJ* (forthcoming).

Inscriptions

S. Yeivin, A Hieratic Ostracon from Tel Arad, *IEJ* 16 (1966), 153–159.

Idem, An Ostracon from Tel Arad Exhibiting a Combination of Two Scripts, *JEA* 55 (1969), 98–102.

Arad I, 61–64.

O. Goldwasser, An Egyptian Scribe from Lachish and the Hieratic Tradition of the Hebrew Kingdoms, *TA* 18 (1991), 248–53.

Sites

Arad I; Kadesh-Barnea II; Ashkelon II and IV; Ekron II; Migdol

Chapter Nine: The Gilead and the Kingdom of Ammon Under Assyrian Hegemony

History

H. L. Ginsberg, Judah and the Transjordan States from 734–582 BC, *Marx Jubilee Volume,* 347–368.

H. Tadmor, The Southern Border of Aram, *IEJ* 12 (1962), 114–122.

B. Oded, Observations on Methods of Assyrian Rule in Transjordan After the Palestinian Campaign of Tiglath-Pilesser III, *JNES* 129, 177–186.

Idem, Transjordan Under Assyrian Rule, *HEI* 4 (1982), 186–188 (Hebrew).

S. Mittman, *Beitraege für Siedlung und Territorial Geschichte des mandlichen Ostjordanlandes,* Wiesbaden 1970.

M. Weipert, The Relations of the States East of the Jordan with the Mesopotamian Powers During the First Millennium B.C., in: *SHAJ* III, 97–106.

M. Ottoson, The Iron Age of Northern Jordan, in: A. Lemaire and B. Otzen (eds.), *E. Nielsen Festschrift,* Leiden 1993, 90–103.

Archaeology

N. Glueck, *Explorations in Eastern Palestine,* I–IV, AASOR 14, 15, 18–19, 25–28 (1934, 1935, 1939, 1951).

L. Harding, *The Antiquities of Jordan,* New York 1967.

N. Glueck, *The Other Side of the Jordan,* New Haven 1940.

C. M. Bennett, Some Reflections on Neo-Assyrian Influence in Transjordan, in: *Kenyon Festschrift,* 1–10.

Idem, Neo-Assyrian Influence in Transjordan, in: *SHAJ* I, 181–187.

R. H. Dornemann, *The Archaeology of Transjordan in the Bronze and Iron Ages,* Milwaukee 1983.

J. A. Sauer, Ammon, Moab and Edom, in: *BAT* I, 204–214.

Idem, Transjordan in the Bronze and Iron Ages, *BASOR* 263 (1986), 1–26.

D. Homés-Fredericq and J. B. Hennessy, *Archaeology of Jordan,* Leuven 1986.

D. Homés-Fredericq, Possible Phoenician Influences in Jordan in the Iron Age, in: *SHAJ* III, 89–96.

K. Prag, Decorative Architecture in Ammon, Moab and Judah, *Levant* 19 (1987), 121–128.

P. Bienkowski, *The Art of Jordan,* Glasgow 1991.

M. Kochavi, The Land of Geshur: History of a Region in the Biblical Period, *EI* 25 (1996), 184–201 (Hebrew).

The Kingdom of Ammon

History

W. F. Albright, The Son of Tabeel, *BASOR* 140 (1955), 34–44.

Idem, Notes on Ammonite History, in: *Horn Festschrift,* 503–509.

G. M. Lands, The Material Civilization of the Ammonites, *BA* 24 (1961), 66–86.

J. Naveh, The Scripts of Palestine and Transjordan in the Iron Age, in: *Glueck Festschrift,* 283.

F. Israel, *The Language of the Ammonites,* Leuven 1979.

D. Sivan, On the Grammar and Orthography of the Ammonite Language, *UF* 14 (1982), 219–234.

K. P. Jackson, *The Ammonite Language of the Iron Age,* Chico, Calif. 1983.

D. J. Block, Buy 'Amwn: The Sons of Ammon, *AUSS* 22 (1984), 197–213.

G. Van der kooij, The Identity of Transjordanian Alphabetic Writing in the Iron Age, in: *SHAJ* III, 107–121.

L. G. Herr, What Ever Happened to the Ammonites? *BARev* 19 (1993), 26–35, 68.

The Inscribed Ammonite Finds

S. H. Horn, Amman Citadel Inscription, *BASOR* 193 (1969), 2–13.

W. F. Albright, Some Comments on the Amman Citadel Inscription, *BASOR* 198 (1970), 38–40.

F. M. Cross, Epigraphic Notes on the Amman Citadel Inscription, *BASOR* 193 (1969), 13–19.

Idem, Notes on Ammonite Inscription from Tell Siran, *BASOR* 212 (1973), 12–15.

Idem, Ammonite Ostraca from Heshbon, *AUSS* 13 (1975), 1–20; 14 (1976), 145–148.

Idem, An Unpublished Ammonite Ostracon, in: *Horn Festschrift,* 475–490.

H. O. Thompson and F. Zayadin, The Tel Siran Inscription, *BASOR* 212 (1973), 5–11.

J. Naveh, The Ostracon from Nimrud: An Ammonite Name-List, *Maarav* 2 (1980), 163–171 (Hebrew).

W. H. Shea, The Amman Citadel Inscription Again, *PEQ* 113 (1981), 105–110.

E. Puech, L'Inscription de la statue d'Amman et la paléographie Ammonite, *RB* 92 (1985), 5–24.

K. Yassine and J. Teixidor, Ammonite and Aramaic Inscriptions from Tell el Mazar in Jordan, *BASOR* 264 (1986), 48–49.

M. O'Connor, The Ammonite Onomasticon, *AUSS* 25 (1987), 51–64.

W. E. Aufrecht, *A Corpus of Ammonite Inscriptions,* Lewiston, N.Y. 1989.

Ahituv [1992], 219–239 (Hebrew).

Ammonite Seals and Seal Impressions

N. Avigad, Seals of Exiles, *IEJ* 15 (1965), 222–232.

Idem, Two Ammonite Seals Depicting the Dea Nutrix, *BASOR* 225 (1977), 63–64.

Idem, Ammonite and Moabite Seals, in: *Glueck Festschrift,* 286–287.

K. Yassine, Ammonite Seals from Tel el Mazar, *SHAJ* I, 189–194.

P. Bordreuil, Perspectives nouvelles de l'épigraphie Sigilaire Ammonite et Moabite, *SHAJ* III, 283–286.

L. G. Herr, The Servant of Baalis, *BA* 48 (1985), 169–172.

R. Younker, Israel, Judah and Ammon and the Motifs on the Baalis Seal from Tell el-ʿUmeiri, *BA* 48 (1985), 173–183.

S. Abbadi, Ein ammonisches Siegel aus Amman, *ZDPV* 101 (1985), 30–31.

E. Porada, Two Cylinder-Seals from ʿUmeiri, Nos. 49 and 363, in: *Madaba Plains I,* 381–384.

Avigad, *Corpus* 320–371.

Excavations and Surveys in Ammon

Sites

Amman I; Saʿidiyeh, Tell es-; Mazar, Tell el- I–II; Sahab, Tel; Madaba Plains I–III

R. S. Boraas, A Preliminary Sounding at Rujm el-Malfuf, *ADAJ* 16 (1971), 31–45.

H. O. Thompson, Excavation of Khirbet al-Hajar, *ADAJ* 17 (1972), 27–72.

Idem, Rujm el-Malfuf (South), *ADAJ* 18 (1973), 47–50.

Idem, Rujm al-Malfuf Sud et Rujm al-Mekheizin, *RB* 82 (1975), 97–100.

Idem, The Ammonite Remains at Khirbet al-Hajar, *BASOR* 227 (1977), 27–34.

Idem, The Excavation of Ruzm el-Mekhezein *ADAJ* 28 (1984), 31–38.

P. E. McGovern Test Soundings at Rujm el-Henu, *ADAJ* 27 (1983), 105–41.

K. Abu Ghanimeh, Abu Nuseir Excavations, *ADAJ* 28 (1984), 305–310.

Ammonite Architecture

K. Yassine, Ammonite Fortresses Date and Function, *SHAJ* III, 11–30.

K. Prag, Decorative Architecture in Ammon, Moab and Israel, *Levant* 19 (1987), 121–127.

R. Kletter, The Rujm El Malfuf Buildings and the Assyrian Vassal State of Ammon, *BASOR* 284 (1991), 33–50.

Ammonite Cult and Cult Objects

J. H. Iliffe, A Model Shrine of Phoenician Style, *QDAP* 11 (1945), 91–92.

R. D. Barnett, Four Sculptures from Amman, *ADAJ* 1 (1951), 34–36.

R. C. O'Callaghan, A Statue Recently Found in Amman, *Orientalia* 21 (1952), 184–193.

M. M. Ibrahim, Two Ammonite Statuettes from Kh. el-Hajjar, *ADAJ* 16 (1971), 91–97.

S. Horn, The Crown of the King of the Ammonites, *AUSS* 11 (1973), 170–180.

B. S. J. Isserlin, On Some Figurines of "Lamp Goddesses" from Trans-Jordan, *Belliddo Festschrift,* 139–142.

A. J. 'Amr, A Study of the Clay Figurines and Zoomorphic Vessels of Trans-Jordan During the Iron Age with a Special Reference to Their Symbolism and Function, Ph.D. diss., University of London, 1980.

A. Abou-Assaf, Unterschungen zur ammonitischen Rundbildkunst, *UF* 12 (1980), 7–102.

R. H. Dornemann, *The Archaeology of the Transjordan in the Bronze and Iron Ages,* Milwaukee 1983, 143–162.

M. Najjar, Archaeology in Jordan, *AJA* 96 (1992), 529–531.

P. M. Daviau and P. E. Dion, El, the God of the Ammonites? The Atef-Crowned Head from Tell Jawa, Jordan, *ZDPV* 110/2 (1994), 158–167.

B. Dabrowski, Clay Figurines from Tall al-'Umayri and Vicinity (the 1987 and 1989 Seasons), in: *Madaba Plains III,* 337–349.

Ammonite Burial Customs

Mazar, Tell el- I

L. Harding, Two Iron Age Tombs at Amman, *QDAP* 11 (1945), 64–74.

Idem, Iron Age Tombs at Sahab, *QDAP* 13 (1948), 92–103.

Idem, An Iron Age Tomb at Meqabelein, *QDAP* 14 (1950), 44–48.

Idem, Two Iron Age Tombs in Amman, *ADAJ* 1 (1951), 37–40.

Idem, The Tomb of Adoninur in Amman, *APEF* 6 (1953), 48–75.

R. Dajani, An Iron Age Tomb from Amman, *ADAJ* 11 (1966), 41–47.

H. Hadad, Umm Uthaina Tomb, *ADAJ* 28 (1984), 7–16 (Arabic).

A. Hadidi, An Ammonite Tomb at Amman, *Levant* 19 (1987), 101–119.

K. Yassine, Social Religious Distinctions in Iron Age Burial Practice in Jordan, *Journal for the Study of the Old Testament Supplement Series* 24 (1983), 29–36.

The Ammonite Pottery

Amiran [1969], 294–299.

E. N. Lugenbeal and J. A. Sauer, Seventh–Sixth Century B.C. Pottery from Area B at Heshbon, *AUSS* 10 (1972), 21–69.

R. H. Dornemann, *The Archaeology of Transjordan,* 10–47.

V. A. Clark, The Iron Age IIc/Persian Pottery from Rujm al-Henu, *ADAJ* 27 (1983), 143–163.

L. G. Herr, The Late Iron Age II–Persian Ceramic Horizon at Tall al 'Umayri, *SHAJ* V, 617–619.

Chapter Ten: The Moabites

History

A. H. Van Zyl, *The Moabites,* Leiden 1960.

J. F. A. Sawyer and D. J. A. Clines (eds.), *Midian, Moab and Edom: The History and Archaeology of Late Bronze and Iron Age Jordan and North-West Arabia,* Sheffield 1983.

J. M. Miller, Moab and the Moabites, in J. A. Dearman (ed.), *Studies in the Mesha Inscription and Moab,* Atlanta 1989.

Moabite Inscriptions and Seals

R. E. Murphy, A Fragment of an Early Moabite Inscription from Dibon, *BASOR* 125 (1952), 21–24.

U. Hubner, Die ersten moabitischen Ostraca, *ZDPV* 104 (1988), 68–73.

P. Bordreuil and D. Pardee, Le Papyrus du Marzeh, *Semitica* 38 (1990), 1–10.

P. Bordreuil, Perspectives nouvelles de l'épigraphie Sigilaire Ammonite et Moabite, *SHAJ* III, 283–286.

N. Avigad, The Seal of Mefáah, *IEJ* 40 (1990), 42–43.

Idem, A New Bulla of a Moabite Scribe, *EI* 23 (1992), 92–93 (Hebrew).

Avigad, *Corpus,* 372–386.

Excavations and Surveys in Moab

J. M. Miller, Archaeological Survey of Central Moab, *BASOR* 234 (1979), 43–52.

Idem, Recent Archaeological Developments Relevant to Ancient Moab, *SHAJ* III, 169–173.

Idem (ed.), *Archaeological Survey of the Kerak Plateau,* Atlanta 1991.

F. V. Winnett and W. C. Reed, *The Excavations at Dibon in Moab,* AASOR 36–37 (1964).

A. D. Tushingham, *The Excavations at Dibon in Moab, 1952–53,* AASOR 40 (1972).

I. Negueruela, The Proto-Aeolic Capitals from Mudeibiʿa in Moab, *ADAJ* 26 (1982), 395–401.

C. Routledge, Pillared Buildings in Iron Age Moab, *BA* 58 (1995), 236.

V. Worschech, City Planning and Architecture at the Iron Age City of Al-Bluʿa in Central Jordan, *SHAJ* V, 145–149.

The Moabite Cult

S. S. Weinberg, A Moabite Shrine Group, *Muse* 12 (1978), 36–37.

G. L. Mattingly, Moabite Religion and Mesha Inscription, in: A. Dearman, (ed.), *Studies in the Mesha Inscription and Moab,* Atlanta 1989, 211–238.

Chapter Eleven: The Edomites

History

N. Glueck, The Boundaries of Edom, *HUCA* 11 (1936), 141–157.

J. Liver, The Wars of Israel and Edom, in: J. Liver (ed.), *The Military History of the Land of Israel in Biblical Times,* Jerusalem 1964, 190–205 (Hebrew).

J. R. Bartlet, The Rise and Fall of the Kingdom of Edom, *PEQ* 104 (1972), 26–37.
Idem, Edom and the Fall of Jerusalem 587 BC, *PEQ* 114 (1982), 13–24.
Idem, Edom and the Edomites, Sheffield 1989.
P. K. McCarter, Obadiah 7 and the Fall of Edom, *BASOR* 221 (1976), 87–91.
A. Millard, Assyrian Involvement in Edom, in: P. Bienkowski (ed.), *Early Edom and Moab: The Beginning of the Iron Age in Southern Jordan,* Sheffield 1992, 35–39.
I. Finkelstein, Horvat Qitmit and the Southern Trade in the Late Iron Age II, *ZDPV* 108 (1992), 156–170.
E. Stern, Edomites and Phoenicians at Tell el-Kheleifeh (Etzion Gever), in: *Eilat,* Jerusalem 1995, 141–145 (Hebrew).
Z. Meshel, Iron Age Negev Settlements as an Expression of Conflict Between Edom, Judah and Israel over Borders and Roads, in: *Eilat,* Jerusalem 1995, 169–180 (Hebrew).
I. Beit-Arieh, Edomite Advance into Judah-Israelite Defensive Fortresses Inadequate, *BARev* 22/6 (1996), 28–37.
B. Dicou, *Edom, Israel's Brother and Antagonist,* Sheffield 1994.

Edomite Inscriptions and Ostraca

D. S. Vanderhooft, The Edomite Dialect and Script: A Review of Evidence, in: D. V. Edelman (ed.), *You Shall Not Abhor an Edomite,* Atlanta 1995, 137–158.
J. Naveh, The Script of Two Ostraca from Elath, *BASOR* 183 (1966), 27–30.
N. Glueck, Tell el Kheleifeh Inscriptions, *Albright Festschrift,* 227–229.
S. Yeivin, An Ostracon from Tel Arad Exhibiting a Combination of Two Scripts, *JEA* 55 (1969), 98–102.
E. Puech, Documentes épigraphiques de Buseirah, *Levant* 7 (1977), 12–13; 9 (1979), 11–20.
I. Beit-Arieh and B. Casson, An Edomite Ostracon from Horvat 'Uza, *TA* 12 (1985), 96–101.
H. Misgav, Two Notes on the Ostraca from Horvat 'Uza, *IEJ* 40 (1990), 213–216.

Edomite Seals

Avigad, *Corpus,* 387–398.
I. Beit-Arieh, A Seal Bearing an Inscription from Edomite Shrine at Horvat Qitmit, *EI* 25 (1996), 59–64 (Hebrew).

Excavations and Surveys

Umm el-Biyara I; Buseirah I–II; Tawilan, Tell; Ghrareh.

Eastern Edom

S. Hart, The Archaeology of the Land of Edom, Ph.D. diss., Macquaire University, 1989.
Idem, The Edom Survey Project 1984–85, *SHAJ* III, 287–290.
Idem, Preliminary Thoughts on Settlement in Southern Edom, *Levant* 18 (1986), 51–58.

Idem, Five Soundings in Southern Jordan, *Levant* 19 (1987), 33–47.

M. Lindner and S. Farajat, An Edomite Mountain Stronghold North of Petra (Bája III), *ADAJ* 31 (1987), 175–185.

M. Linder et al., Es-Sadeh, an Important Edomite-Nabatean Site: A Preliminary Report, *ADAJ* 32 (1988), 75–99.

Idem, Edom Outside the Famous Excavations: Evidence from Surveys in the Greater Petra Area, in: P. Bienkowski (ed.), *Early Edom and Moab,* Sheffield 1992, 143–166.

P. Bienkowski, The Architecture of Edom, *SHAJ* V, 135–143.

Western Edom

Kheleifeh, Tell el-; Ḥazeva I–II; 'Uza, Ḥorvat; Aroer II; Qitmit; Malḥata, Tel I–II; Kadesh-Barnea II

I. Beit-Arieh, *New Data on the Relationship Between Judah and Edom Towards the End of the Iron Age,* AASOR 49 (1989), 125–131.

The Edomite Cult

Qitmit; Ḥazeva I–II

P. Beck, Transjordanian and Levantine Elements in the Iconography of Qitmit, *BAT* II, 231–236.

Idem, Horvat Qitmit Revisited via En Hazevah, *TA* 23 (1996), 102–114.

Edomite Pottery

N. Glueck, Some Edomite Pottery from Tell el-Kheleifeh, Part I, *BASOR* 188 (1967), 8–24.

Idem, Some Ezion-Geber: Elath Iron II Pottery, *EI* 9 (1969), 51–59.

M. F. Oakeshott, The Edomite Pottery, in: J. F. A. Sawyer and D. J. A. Clines (eds.), *Midian, Moab and Edom,* Sheffield 1983, 53–63.

E. Mazar, Edomite Pottery at the End of the Iron Age, *IEJ* 35 (1985), 253–269.

S. Hart and E. A. Knauf, Wadi Feinan Iron Age Pottery, *Newsletter of the Institute of Archaeology,* Yarmouk University 1986, 9–10.

J. Gunneweg and H. Mommsen, Instrumental Neutron Activation Analysis and Origin of Some Cult Objects and Edomite Vessels from Hurvat Qitmit Shrine, *Archeometry* 32 (1990), 7–18.

J. Gunneweg et al., "Edomite," "Negbite" and "Midianite" Pottery from the Negev Desert and Jordan, *Archeometry* 33 (1991), 239–253.

J. P. Zeitler, Edomite Pottery from Petra Region, in: P. Bienkowski (ed.), *Early Edom and Moab,* Sheffield 1992, 167–176.

R. H. Dornmann, Preliminary Thoughts on the Tell Nimrin Krater, *SHAJ* V, 621–628.

Edomite Art Objects

C. M. Bennett, A Cosmetic Palette from Umm el-Biyara, *Antiquity* 41 (1967), 197–201.

D. Whitcomb, *Ayla Art Industry in the Island Port of Aqaba,* Chicago 1994, 28–29.

Chapter Twelve: The Arabian Trade

I. Epha'l, *The Ancient Arabs, Nomads on the Borders of the Fertile Crescent 9th–5th Centuries B.C.,* Jerusalem 1982.

G. Ryckmans, Un Fragment de jarre avec caractères minéens à Tell el-Kheleifeh, *RB* 48 (1939), 247–249.

G. W. Van Beek and A. Jamme, An Inscribed South Arabian Clay Stamp from Bethel, *BASOR* 151 (1958), 9–16.

Y. Yadin, An Inscribed South Arabian Clay Stamp from Bethel? *BASOR* 196 (1969), 37–46.

G. W. Van Beek and A. Jamme, The Authenticity of the Bethel Stamp Seal, *BASOR* 199 (1970), 59–65.

R. L. Cleveland, More on the South Arabian Clay Stamp Found in Beitin, *BASOR* 209 (1973), 33–36.

G. W. Van Beek, Frankincense and Myrrh, *BA* 23 (1960), 70–95.

N. Groom, *Frankincense and Myrrh: A Study of the Arabian Incense Trade,* London 1981.

N. Na'aman, Pastoral Nomads in the Kingdom of Judah During the Divided Monarchy, *Zion* 52 (1987), 261–278 (Hebrew).

Y. Shiloh, South Arabian Inscriptions from the City of David, Jerusalem, *PEQ* 119 (1987), 9–18.

B. Sass, Arabs and Greeks in Late First Temple Jerusalem, *PEQ* 122 (1990), 59–61.

BIBLIOGRAPHY FOR BOOK TWO: THE BABYLONIAN PERIOD

Introduction: History of Palestine in the Babylonian Period

R. P. Dougherty, *Nabonidus and Belshazzar: A Study of the Closing Events of the Neo-Babylonian Empire,* New Haven 1929.

E. F. Weidner, Jojachin Koenig von Juda, in babylonichen Keilschrifttexten, in: *R. Dussaud Festschrift,* Paris 1939, 923–935.

W. F. Albright, King Jehoiachin in Exile, *BA* 5 (1942), 49–55.

D. J. Wiseman, *Chronicles of the Chaldean Kings (626–566 B.C.),* London 1956.

Idem, Nebuchadnezzar and Babylon, Oxford 1983.

D. N. Freedman, The Babylonian Chronicle, *BA* 19 (1956), 50–60.

C. F. Whitely, *The Exilic Age,* London and Philadelphia 1957.

J. D. Quinn, Alcaeus 48 (B16) and the Fall of Ascalon (604 B.C.), *BASOR* 164 (1961), 20–29.

P. R. Ackroyd, *Israel Under Babylon and Persia,* Oxford 1970.

A. K. Grayson, *Assyrian and Babylonian Chronicles,* New York 1975.

A. Malamat, The Twilight of Judah: In the Egyptian-Babylonian Maelstrom, *VT* 28 (1975), 123–145.

Idem, The Kingdom of Judah Between Egypt and Babylon, *Studia Theologica* 44 (1990), 65–77.

B. Oded, Judah and the Exile, in: J. H. Hays and J. M. Miller (eds.), *Israelite and Judaean History,* London 1977, 435–488.

N. Na'aman, Nebuchadnezzar's Campaign in Year 603 B.C.E., *Biblische Notizen* 62 (1992), 41–44.

Idem, Shechem and Jerusalem in the Babylonian and Persian Periods, *Zion* 58 (1993), 7–32 (Hebrew).

J. Lindsay, The Babylonian Kings and Edom 605–550 B.C., *PEQ* 108 (1976), 23–39.

I. Epha'l, The Western Minorities in Babylonia in the 6th–5th Centuries B.C.: Maintenance and Cohesion, *Orientalia* 47 (1978), 74–90.

R. Zadok, *The Jews in Babylonia During the Chaldean and Achaemenian Periods, According to the Babylonian Sources,* Haifa 1979.

B. Porten, The Identity of King Adon, *BA* 44 (1981), 36–52.

H. J. Katzenstein, Before Pharaoh Conquered Gaza, *VT* 33 (1983), 249–251.
Idem, Nebuchadnezzar's Wars with Egypt, *EI* 24 (1993), 184–186.
Idem, Gaza in the Neo-Babylonian Period (626–539) BCE, *Trans* 7 (1994), 35–49.
W. Horowitz, The Babylonian Map of the World, *Iraq* 50 (1988), 147–165.
S. Zawadzski, *The Fall of Assyria and Median-Babylonian Relations in the Light of the Nabopolassar Chronicle,* Poznan 1988.
Idem, A Contribution to the Chronology of the Last Days of the Assyrian Empire, *ZA* 85 (1995), 67–73.
P. Machinist, Palestine, Administration of, (Assyro-Babylonia), in: *The Anchor Bible Dictionary,* vol. V, New York 1992, 69–81.
A. Lemaire, Les Transformations politiques et culturelles de la Transjordanie au VIe siècle av. J.-C. *Trans* 8 (1994), 9–25.

Chapter One: Excavations and Surveys

S. S. Weinberg, Post Exilic Palestine: An Archaeological Report, *Proceedings of the Israel Academy of Sciences and Humanities,* vol. IV (1969), 78–97.
V. Fritz, Die Paläste während der assyrischen, babylonischen und persischen Vorherrschaft in Palästina, *MDOG* 111 (1979), 63–74.
G. Barkay, The Redefining of Archaeological Periods: Does the Date 588–586 B.C.E. Indeed Mark the End of the Iron Age Culture? *BAT* II, 106–109.
O. Lipschits, The "Yehud" Province Under Babylonian Rule (586–539) BCE), Historic Reality and Historiographic Conceptions, Ph.D. diss., Tel Aviv University 1997 (Hebrew).

Chapter Two: Seals and Seal Impressions

Stern [1982], 196–197.
N. Avigad, New Light on MSA Seal Impressions, *IEJ* 8 (1958), 113–119.
Idem, Seals of Exiles, *IEJ* 15 (1965), 228–230.
Idem, Two Hebrew Inscriptions on Wine Jars, *IEJ* 22 (1972), 1–9.
F. M. Cross, Epigraphical Notes on Hebrew Documents of the Eighth–Sixth Centuries B.C.: The Inscribed Jar Handles from Gibeon, *BASOR* 168 (1962), 18–23.
A. Demsky, The Genealogy of Gibeon (I Chron. 9:35–44): Biblical Epigraphic Considerations, *BASOR* 202 (1971), 16–23.
Idem, Geba Gibeah and Gibeon—an Historico-Geographic Riddle, *BASOR* 212 (1973), 26–31.
O. Goldwasser and J. Naveh, The Origin of the Tet-Symbol, *IEJ* 26 (1976), 15–19.
A. Green, A Note on the "Scorpion Man" and Pazuzu, *Iraq* 47 (1985), 75–82.
J. R. Zorn et al., The M(W)SH Stamp Impressions and the Neo-Babylonian Period, *IEJ* 44 (1994), 161–183.
Idem, Three Cross-Shaped "Tet" Stamp-Impressions from Tell En-Nasbeh, *TA* 22 (1995), 98–105.
S. Dalley and A. Goguel, The Selá Sculpture: A Neo-Babylonian Rock Relief in Southern Jordan, *ADAJ* 41 (1997), 169.

Chapter Three: Tombs and Burial Customs

Abu Ghosh; Meqabelein; Mazar, Tel el- I

R. A. S. Macalister, Some Interesting Pottery Remains, *PEFQS,* (1915), 35–37.

E. Grant and G. E. Wright, *Ain Shems Excavations,* vol. I (1931), 10, 15–16; vol. II (1933), 23–24.

A. Hadidi, An Ammonite Tomb at Amman, *Levant* 19 (1987), 101–120.

C. Dinar and G. Lipovitz, A Burial Cave from the 6th Century B.C.E. in Hurvat Almit, *Niqrot Zurim* 14 (1988), 44–51 (Hebrew).

J. R. Zorn, Mesopotamian-Style Ceramic "Bathtub" Coffins from Tell En-Nasbeh, *TA* 20 (1993), 216–224.

Chapter Four: Pottery Vessels

L. G. Herr, The Late Iron Age–Persian Ceramic Horizon at Tall al 'Umayri, *SHAJ* V, 617–619.

BIBLIOGRAPHY FOR BOOK THREE:
THE PERSIAN PERIOD

Introduction: The History of Palestine in the Persian Period

History of the Persian Empire

A. T. Olmstead, *A History of the Persian Empire,* Chicago 1948.

A. J. Toynbee, The Administrative Geography of the Achaemenian Empire, in: *A Study of History,* vol. VIIB, London 1954, 580–689.

R. Ghirshman, *Persia from the Origins to Alexander the Great,* London 1964.

W. Culican, *The Medes and the Persians,* London 1965.

R. N. Frye, *The Heritage of Persia,* New York and Toronto 1966.

A. K. Kurt, The Cyrus Cylinder and Achaemenid Imperial Politics, *Journal for the Study of the Old Testament* 25 (1983), 83–97.

J. M. Cook, *The Persian Empire,* London 1983.

D. Davies and L. Finkelstein (eds.), *The Cambridge History of Judaism,* vol. I: *The Persian Period,* London and New York 1984.

M. A. Dendamaev, *A Political History of the Achemenid Empire,* Leiden 1989.

P. Briant, *Histoire de l'Empire Perse de Cyrus à Alexandre,* Paris 1996.

History of Palestine in the Persian Period

D. Barag, The Effect of the Tennes Rebellion on Palestine, *BASOR* 183 (1966), 6–12.

A. F. Rainey, The Satrapy "Beyond the River," *AJBA* 2 (1969), 51–78.

S. S. Weinberg, Post Exilic Palestine—an Archaeological Report. *Proceedings of the Israel Academy of Sciences and Humanities,* vol. IV, no. 5 (1969).

P. R. Ackroyd, *Israel Under Babylon and Persia,* Oxford 1970.

M. Smith, *Palestinian Parties and Politics That Shaped the Old Testament,* New York 1971.

E. M. Meyers, Edom and Judah in the Sixth–Fifth Centuries B.C., in: *Albright Festschrift,* 377–392.

G. Widengren, The Persian Period, in: J. H. Hays and J. M. Miller (eds.), *Israelite and Judaean History,* Philadelphia 1977, 489–538.

H. Tadmor (ed.), *The Restoration—the Persian Period,* Jerusalem 1983 (Hebrew).

Idem, Judah, in: D. M. Lewis et al. (eds.), *Cambridge Ancient History,* 2nd ed., vol. VI: *The Fourth Century B.C.* Cambridge.

E. Stern, The Province of Yehud: The Vision and the Reality, in: L. I. Levine (ed.), *The Jerusalem Cathedra,* Jerusalem 1981, 9–21.

Idem, The Persian Empire and the Political and Social History of Palestine in the Persian Period, in: W. D. Davies and L. Finkelstein (eds.), *Cambridge History of Judaism, vol. I: Introduction; the Persian Period,* Cambridge 1984, 70–87.

S. E. McEvenue, The Political Structure in Judah from Cyrus to Nehemiah, *Catholic Biblical Quarterly* 44 (1981), 353–364.

S. Japhet, Sheshbazzar and Zerubbabel, *ZAW* 94 (1982), 66–98; 95 (1983), 218–229.

M. Kochman, Yehud Mdinta in the Light of the Yehud Stamp-Impressions, *Cathedra* 24 (1983), 3–30 (Hebrew).

J. M. Miller and J. H. Hays, *A History of Ancient Israel and Judah,* London 1986, 437–475.

I. Ephʿal, Syria-Palestina Under Achaemenid Rule, in: J. Boardman et al. (eds.), *Cambridge Ancient History,* 2nd ed., vol. IV: *Persia, Greece and the Western Mediterranean c. 525 to 479 B.C.,* Cambridge 1988, 139–164.

Idem, Changes in Palestine During the Persian Period in the Light of Epigraphic Sources, *IEJ* 48 (1998), 106–119.

H. Weippert, *Palaestina in vorhellenistischer Zeit,* Munchen 1988.

A. Lemaire, Populations et territoires de la Palestine a l'époque perse, *Trans* 3 (1990), 31–74.

J. Blenkinsopp, Temple and Society in Achemenid Judah, in: P. R. Davies (ed.), *Second Temple Studies; 1. Persian Period,* Sheffield 1991, 22–53.

J. Weinberg, *The Citizen-Temple Community,* Sheffield 1992.

K. G. Hoglund, *Achaemenid Imperial Administration in Syria-Palestine and the Missions of Ezra and Nehemiah,* Atlanta 1992.

G. W. Ahlstrom, *History of Ancient Palestine from the Paleolithic Period to Alexander's Conquest,* Sheffield 1993, 812–906.

D. F. Graf, The Persian Royal Road System in Syria-Palestine, *Trans* 6 (1993), 149–168.

A. Lemaire, Les Minéens et la Transeuphratène a l'époque perse: Une premier approche, *Trans* 13 (1997), 123–139.

The Literary and Epigraphic Evidence

Papyri

A. Cowley, *Aramaic Papyri of the Fifth Century B.C.,* Oxford 1923.

E. G. Kraeling, *The Brooklyn Museum Aramaic Papyri,* New Haven 1953.

G. R. Driver, *Aramaic Documents of the Fifth Century B.C.,* Oxford 1957.

D. M. Gropp, The Samaria Papyri from Wadi ed-Daliyeh: The Slave Sales, Ph.D. diss., Harvard University, 1986.

F. M. Cross, Samaria Papyrus 1: An Aramaic Slave Conveyance of 335 B.C.E. Found at Wadi Daliyeh, *EI* 18 (1985), 7*–17*.

F. M. Cross, A Report on the Samaria Papyri, *VT Supplement* 40 (1988), 17–26.

F. M. Cross, The Papyri and Their Historical Implications, in *Daliyeh 1,* 17–29.

B. Porten, *Archive from Elephantine,* Berkeley 1968.

B. Porten and A. Yardeni, *Textbook of Aramaic Documents from Ancient Egypt;* 1=*Letters,* Jerusalem 1986; 2=*Contracts,* Jerusalem 1989; 3=*Literature, Accounts, Lists,* Jerusalem 1993.

S. H. Eshel and H. Misgav, A Fourth Century B.C.E. Document from Ketef Yeriho, *IEJ* 38 (1988), 158–176.

J. C. Greenfield, The Aramaic Legal Texts of the Achaemenian Period, *Trans* 3 (1990), 58–59.

A. Yardeni, Maritime Trade and Royal Accountary in an Erased Customs from 475 B.C.E. on the Ahiqar Scroll from Elephantine, *BASOR* 293 (1994), 67–78.

Cuneiform Inscriptions

Mikhmoret II, 1044

S. M. Dalley, The Cuneiform Tablet from Tawilan, in: *Tawilan, Tell,* 67–68.

T. Stopler, Stele Fragments, Elamite and Akkadian, *AFO* 27 (1997), 76.

Aramaic and Phoenician Inscriptions

I. Rabinowitz, Aramaic Inscriptions of the Fifth Century B.C.E. from a North Arab Shrine in Egypt, *JNES* 15 (1956), 1–9; 18 (1959), 154–155.

F. M. Cross, A Jar Inscription from Shiqmona, *IEJ* 18 (1968), 226–233.

Idem, Two Notes on Palestinian Inscriptions of the Persian Age, *BASOR* 193 (1969), 19–24.

J. Naveh and E. Stern, A Stone Vessel with a Thamudic Inscription, *IEJ* 24 (1974), 74–83.

J. Naveh, Hebrew Texts in Aramaic Script in the Persian Period, *BASOR* 203 (1971), 27–33.

Idem, The Aramaic Ostraca, in *Beersheba I,* 79–82.

Idem, The Aramaic Ostraca from Tel Beer-Sheba (Seasons 1971–1976), *TA* 6 (1979), 182–198.

Idem, The Aramaic Ostraca from Tel Arad, in: *Arad Inscriptions,* 153–174.

Idem, Published and Unpublished Aramaic Ostraca, *'Atiqot* XVII, English series (1985), 114–121.

Idem, Aramaic Ostraca and Jar Inscriptions from Tell Jemmeh, *'Atiqot* XXI, English series (1992), 49–53.

Idem, Phoenician Ostraca from Tel Dor, in: Z. Zevit et al., *Solving Riddles and Untying Knots: Studies in Honor of J. C. Greenfield,* Winona Lake, Ind. 1995, 459–464.

N. Avigad and J. C. Greenfield, A Bronze Phiale with Phoenician Dedicatory Inscription, *IEJ* 32 (1982), 118–128.

M. Dothan, Phoenician Inscription from 'Akko, *IEJ* 35 (1985), 81–94.

M. Heltzer, The Tell el-Mazar Inscription No. 7 and Some Historical and Literary Problems of the Vth Satrapy, *Trans* 1 (1989), 111–118.

N. Dempsey, An Ostracon from Tell Nimrin, *BASOR* 289 (1993), 55–58.

R. Deutsch and M. Heltzer, New Phoenician and Aramaic Inscriptions from the Sharon Plain, in: *Forty New Ancient West Semitic Inscriptions,* Tel Aviv 1994, 69–89.

I. Eph'al and J. Naveh, *Aramaic Ostraca of the Fourth Century BC from Idumaea,* Jerusalem 1996.

J. Naveh, Gleanings of Some Pottery Inscriptions, *IEJ* 46 (1996), 44–51.

A. Lemaire, *Nouvelles inscriptions araméenne d'Idumée au Musée d'Israel,* Paris 1996.

K. Lozachmeur and A. Lemaire, Nouveaux ostraca araméens d'Idumée (Collection S. Moussaieff), *Semitica* 46 (1996), 123–142.

R. Avner and E. Eshel, A Juglet with Phoenician Inscription from a Recent Excavation in Jaffa, *Trans* 12 (1996), 59–63.

Chapter One: Excavations and Surveys

The Province of Megiddo

Hazor I, 54–63, pls. 12–19, 79–83; *Hazor III–IV,* 99–100; *Hazor V,* 156–161; *Sa'sa' Mizpe Yammim I–II; Beth-Shean I; Beth-Shean III; 'Amal, Tel; Taanek I–III; Taanach, Tel I; Kedesh, Tel; Megiddo I,* 88–91; *Jokneam, Tel; Qiri, Tel*

Phoenicia and the Coast of Galilee

Achzib I–II; Kabri; Nahariya, Tel; Philadelphia; Shavei Zion I–II; Acco; Gil'am; Keisan, Tel, 117–129; *Abu Hawam, Tell I–IV*

E. Stern, The Dating of Stratum II at Tell Abu Hawam, *IEJ* 18 (1968), 213–219.

H. J. Katzenstein, Tyre in the Early Persian Period (539–486 B.C.E.), *BA* 42 (1979), 23–34.

I. Lund, The Northern Coastline of Syria in the Persian Period: A Survey of the Archaeological Evidence, *Trans* 2 (1990), 9–12.

J. Briend, L'Occupation de la Galilée occidentale à l'époque perse, *Trans* 2 (1990), 109–123.

J. Elayi, *Economie des cités phéniciennes sous l'Empire Perse,* Napoli 1990.

Idem, Sidon, cité autonome de l'Empire Perse, Paris 1990.

J. Elayi and H. Sayegh, *Beirut in the Iron Age III/Persian Period: A District of the Phoenician Harbour. The Objects,* Paris 1998.

The Province of Dor and the Sharon Plain

Shiqmona I–II; Megadim, Tel I–II; 'Atlit; Dor I–II; Nahal Tut; 'En Hofez; Ma'agan Mikha'el-; Mikhmoret I–II; Apollonia I–II; Qasile, Tell; Kudadi, Tell; Jaffa I–II

Philistia and Northern Sinai

Ashdod I–V; Zippor, Tel; 'Erani, Tel I–II; Ashkelon I–IV; Hesi, Tell, el- I–III; Jemmeh, Tell, I–III; Far'ah, Tell el-(S); I–II; Sera', Tel; Haror, Tel; Huga, Horvat; Sinai; Ruqeish, Tel er- I–II; Anthedon

H. J. Katzenstein, Gaza in the Persian Period, *Trans* 1 (1989), 74.

The Province of Samaria

Samaria HA I–II; Samaria III; Daliyeh I–II; Qadum; Shechem I–III

E. Stern, A Phoenician Art Centre in Postexilic Samaria, *Atti Congresso Internazionale di Studi Fenici Punici,* Roma 1983, 211–212.

A. Zertal, The Pahwah of Samaria During the Persian Period, Types of Settlement, Economy, History and New Discoveries, *Trans* 3 (1990), 9–30.

The Province of Judah

The Region of Benjamin
Bethel; Naṣbeh, Tell en- I–III; Gibeon I–IV; Ful, Tell el- I–IV; Nebi Samuel

Jerusalem and the Highlands

Ramat Raḥel I–II; Beth-Zur I–III.
J. Morgenstern, Jerusalem—485 B.C., *HUCA* 27 (1956), 101–179; 28 (1957), 15–47; 31 (1960), 1–29.
A. Demsky, Pelekh in Nehemiah 2, *IEJ* 33 (1983), 242–244.
E. M. Laperrousaz, Jérusalem à époque perse, *Trans* 1 (1990), 33–66.
A. Lemaire, Zorobabel et la Judée à la lumière de l'épigraphie (fin du VIe s. av. J.C.), *RB* 103/1 (1996), 48–57.

Judah's Eastern and Western Regions

Jericho III–IV; Ketef Jericho; En-Gedi I–II; Gezer I–III; Gezer (HUCA) 1–2; Batash, Tel; Beth-Shemesh; Ḥarasim, Tel; Tuwein, Khirbet

Idumaea and the Hills

Rabud, Tel; Luzifar; Nimra, Khirbet; Lachish III, V–VII; Maresha; Ḥalif, Tel; Beersheba I; Arad I–III; Kheleifeh, Tell el-; Kadesh-Barnea I–II
Z. Meshel, The Negev in the Persian Period, *Cathedra* 4 (1977), 43–50 (Hebrew).

The Transjordanian Provinces

Sa'idiyeh, Tell es-; Mazar, Tell el- I–II; Nimrin, Tell; Heshbon; 'Umeiri, Tell el-; Umm Uthainah; Tawilan, Tell.
B. Mazar, The Tobiads, *IEJ* 7 (1957), 229–238.
P. Bienkowski, Umm El Biyara, Tawilan and Buseirah in Retrospect, *Levant* 22 (1990), 91–99.
L. G. Herr, The Late Iron Age–Persian Ceramic Horizon at Tall al 'Umayri *SAHJ* V, 617–619.

Chapter Two: Architecture

General

Stern [1982], 47–67.
P. Lampel, *Cities and Planning in the Ancient Near East,* New York 1968.
F. Castagnoli, *Orthagonal Town Planning in Antiquity,* Cambridge, Mass. 1971.
A. Segal, *The Hippodamic and Planned City,* Beersheva 1978.
E. J. Owens, *The City in the Greek and Roman World,* London and New York 1991.

Palestine

V. Fritz, Die Paläste während der assyrischen, babylonischen und persischen Vorherrschaft in Palästina, *MDOG* 111 (1979), 63–74.

G. W. and O. Van Beek, Canaanite-Phoenician Architecture: The Development and Distribution of Two Styles, *EI* 15 (1981), 70*–77*.

G. W. Van Beek, Are There Beehive Granaries at Tell Jemmeh? A Rejoinder, *BARev* 49 (1986), 245.

L. E. Stager, Climatic Condition and Grain Storage in the Persian Period, *BA* 34 (1971), 86–96.

E. Stern, The Walls of Dor, *IEJ* 38 (1988), 6–14.

Idem, The Phoenician Architectural Elements in Palestine During the Late Iron Age and the Persian Period, in: *Architecture,* 302–309.

Idem, New Phoenician Elements in the Architecture of Tel Dor, in: J. Magness and S. Gitin (eds.), *Hesed Ve-Emet: Studies in Honor of E. S. Frerichs,* Atlanta 1998, 375–388.

I. Sharon, Ashlar Construction Techniques at Tel Dor, *BASOR* 267 (1987), 21–42.

Idem, The Fortifications of Dor and the Transition from the Israeli-Syrian Concept of Defense to the Greek Concept, *Qadmoniot* 24 (1991), 105–113 (Hebrew).

J. Elayi, Remarques sur un type de mur phénicien, *RSF* 8 (1980), 165–180.

Idem, Nouveaux éléments sur le mur à piliers phéniciens, *Trans* 11 (1996), 78–94.

Tools of Siege and War

I. Shatzman, Balls from Tel Dor and the Artillery of the Hellenistic World, *Scripta Classica Israelica* 14 (1995), 52–72.

Chapter Three: Burial Customs

General

Stern [1982], 68–92.

Cist Graves

Shechem II; Mazar, Tell el- I; Ibsan, Khirbet; Gezer I, 289–299, figs. 151–157; *Jemmeh, Tell I,* 14, pls. 44–47; *Achzib I–II; 'Atlit; Bat Yam*

J. H. Iliffe, Tell Far'ah Tomb Group Reconsidered: Silver Vessels of the Persian Period *QDAP* 4 (1935), 182–186.

M. Peleg, Persian, Hellenistic and Roman Burials at Lohamei HaGetáot *'Atiqot* XX, English series (1991), 131–133.

Pit Graves

Hazor II, 45–63, pls. 80–83, 152–154; *Hazor V,* 156–161; *Michal, Tel,* 153–164; *Hesi, Tell el- III,* 325–333

E. Stern, A Burial of the Persian Period Near Hebron, *IEJ* 21 (1971), 25–30.

R. Avner and E. Eshel, A Juglet with Phoenician Inscription from Recent Excavation in Jaffa, Israel, *Trans* 12 (1996), 59–63.

A. Golani, Hajar 'Id, *ESI* 16 (1997), 122–123.

J. Elayi and M. R. Haykal, *Nouvelles decouvertes sur les usage funeraires des phéniciens d'Arwad, Supplement No. 4a Trans,* Paris 1996.

Tumuli

Y. Magen, Two Tumuli in the Jordan Valley, *EI* 18 (1985), 282–292 (Hebrew).

Chapter Four: Temples and Cult Objects

The Temples

Lachish V; Makmish; Mizpe Yammim I–II; Umm el- "Amed; Sarepta; Sukas VI
Stern [1982], 158–195.

M. Dothan, Phoenician Inscription from 'Akko, *IEJ* 35 (1985), 81–94.

Favissae

Dan, Tel, 214–216; *Shavei Zion; Stern [1982],* 159; *Bliss-Macalister [1902],* 38–41, 140, 146; *'Erani, Tel II; Zippor, Tel; Ashkelon II*

E. Stern, a Deposit of Votive Figurines from Beer-Sheba Region, *EI* 12 (1975), 91–94 (Hebrew).

Idem, A Favissa of a Phoenician Sanctuary from Tel Dor, *JJS* 33 (1982), 35–54.

Idem, Two Favissae from Tel Dor, Israel, in: C. Bonnet et al. (eds.), *Studia Phoenicia Religio Phoenicia,* Namur 1986, 277–286.

Idem, The Beginning of Greek Settlement in Palestine in the Light of the Excavations at Tell Dor, AASOR 49 (1989), 107–124.

Figurines

Stern [1982], 61–67.

W. Culican, Dea Tyria Gravida, *AJBA* 1 (1969), 35–50.

Idem, Problems in Phoenico-Punic Iconography—a Contribution, *AJBA* 1 (1970), 28–57.

M. Dothan, A Sign of Tanit from Tel 'Akko, *IEJ* 24 (1974), 43–49.

B. S. J. Isserlin, On Some Figurines of "Lamp-Goddesses" from Trans-Jordan, in: *Bel-liddo Festschrift,* 139–142.

E. Gubel, An Essay on the Axe-Bearing Astarte and Her Role in the Phoenician "Triad," *RSF* 8 (1980), 1–17.

E. Stern, What Happened to the Cult Figurines? *BARev* 15/4 (1989), 22–29, 53–54.

A. M. Bisi, Quelques remarques sur la Coroplastic à l'époque perse: Tradition locale et emprunts étrangers, *Trans* 3 (1990), 75–84.

H. Leibowitz and A. M. Dehnisch, A Mould-Made Seated Terra-Cotta Cat from Beth Gan, *IEJ* 48 (1998), 174–182.

Metal Figurines

Stern [1982] 177.

Mizpe Yammim I–II; Ashkelon I–IV; Gibeon III, 21, fig. 50:1, *Beersheba I,* 54–55; *Dan, Tel,* 214–216, fig. 175:3, pl. 39

Inscriptions and Ostraca

Sarepta, 97–110; *Mizpe Yammim II; Michal, Tel,* 381–384; *Apollonia I–II,* 259–263; *Ashkelon III, IV*

N. Avigad and J. C. Greenfield, A Bronze Phiale with a Phoenician Dedication Inscription, *IEJ* 32 (1982), 118–128.

R. B. Coote, The Kition Bowl, *BASOR* 220 (1975), 47–50.

M. Dothan, Phoenician Inscription from Akko, *IEJ* 35 (1985), 81–96.

N. Stern, A Phoenician-Cypriote Votive Scapula from Tel Dor: A Maritime Scene, *IEJ* 44 (1994), 1–12.

O. Deutch and M. Heltzer, New Phoenician and Aramaic Inscriptions from the Sharon Plain, in: *Forty New Ancient West Semitic Inscriptions,* Tel Aviv 1994, 69–88.

C. R. Conder, The Prayer of Ben Abdas on the Dedication of the Temple of Joppa, *PEFQS,* 1892, 170–174.

F. M. Cross, An Ostracon from Nebi Yunis, *IEJ* 14 (1964), 185–186.

J. Naveh and E. Stern, A Stone Vessel with Thamudic Inscription, *IEJ* 24 (1974), 79–83.

J. R. Davila and B. Zuckerman, The Throne of 'Astart Inscription, *BASOR* 289 (1993), 67–80.

Situlae

Mizpe Yammim I–II; Ashkelon IV

M. Lichtman, Situla No. 11395 and Some Remarks on Egyptian Situlae, *JNES* 6 (1947), 169–179.

P. Kyle McCarter, An Inscribed Phoenician Situla in the Art Museum of Princeton University, *BASOR* 290–291 (1993), 115–120.

The Cypriot Cult

Gjearsted, *SCE* III, 286–289.

A. Westholm, The Cypriot Temple Boys, *OP* 2 (1955), 75–77.

V. Karageorghis, Material from Sanctuary at Potamia, *RDAC,* 1979, 289–315.

Idem, The Coroplastic Art of Ancient Cyprus, vol. III: *The Cypro-Archaic Period, Large and Middle Size Sculpture,* Nicosia 1993.

Cypriot Cult in the Syro-Palestinian Coast

M. Dunnand, Les Sculptures de la favissa du Temple d'Amrit, *BMB* 7 (1944–1945), 99–108; 8 (1946–1948), 81–107.

Stern [1982], 162–165.

E. Stern, A Group of Cypriot Limestone Sculptures from Gaza Region, *Levant* 7 (1975), 104–107.

Idem, Cypriot Votive Scapula from Tel Dor, a Maritime Scene, *IEJ* 44 (1994), 1–12.

O. Masson, Pélerines Chypriotes en Phénicie (Sarepta et Sidon), *Semitica* 32 (1982), 45–49.

Ashkelon III, 109.

The Popular Apotropaic Cult

Clay Masks and Glass Pendants

P. Cintas, *Amulettes Puniques,* Publications de l'Institut des Hautes Etudes de Tunis, vol. I, 1946.

Q. Culican, Some Phoenician Masks and Terracottas, *Berytus* 24 (1975–1976), 47–87.

Idem, Phoenician Demons, *JNES* 35 (1976), 21–24.

E. Stern, Phoenician Masks and Pendants, *PEQ* 108 (1976), 109–118.

F. Spano, Pendanti Vieteri Polichromi in Sicilia, *Revista Sicilia Archeologica* 12 (1979), 25–48.

G. Simon, Phoenician Medallions from the Ha-Aretz Museum, in: R. Zeevi (ed.), *Israel. People and Land,* Museum Ha-Aretz Yearbook no. 2–3 (1985–1986), 37–46 (Hebrew).

H. Ciasca, Protomai and Masks, in: S. Moscati (ed.), *The Phoenicians,* Milano 1988, 354–369.

M. L. Ulerti, Glass, in: Moscati, ibid. 474–491.

V. Karageorghis, Notes on Some Terracotta Masks from Amathus, *RSF* 18 (1990), 3–15.

Idem, Masks, in: *The Coroplastic Art in Ancient Cyprus,* vol. III, Nicosia 1993, 105–127.

Bes Vases

E. Stern, Bes Vases from Palestine and Syria, *IEJ* 26 (1973), 183–187.

J. F. Blakely and F. L. Horton, Jr., South Palestinian Bes Vessels of the Persian Period, *Levant* 18 (1986), 111–119.

Incense Altars

Stern [1982], 183–195.

E. Stern, Note on the Decorated Limestone Altar from Lachish, *'Atiqot* XI, English series (1976), 105–109.

Idem, Limestone Incense Altars, in: *Beersheba I,* 52–53.

N. Glueck, Incense Altars, *EI* 10 (1971), 120–125 (Hebrew).

J. B. Pritchard, An Incense Burner from Tel es-Saidiyeh, Jordan Valley, in: J. W. Weavers and D. B. Redford (eds.), *Studies in Ancient Palestinian World,* Toronto 1972, 3–17.

M. O. Shea, The Small Cuboid Incense-Burner of the Ancient Near East, *Levant* 15 (1983), 76–109.

A. R. Millard, The Small Cuboid Incense-Burners: A Note to Their Age, *Levant* 16 (1984), 172–173.

Chapter Five: Pottery Vessels

The Local Pottery

Dor II, 51–92; *Michal, Tel,* 115–143; *Shechem III; Qadum; Hesi, Tell el- III,* 139–230

P. W. Lapp, The Pottery of Palestine in the Persian Period, in: *Archeologie und Altes Testament: Festschrift für Kurt Galling,* Tübingen 1970, 179–197.

Stern [1982], 93–136.

E. Stern, Achaemenid Clay Rhyta from Palestine, *IEJ* 32 (1982), 36–43.

D. Conrad, The Akko Ware: A New Type of Phoenician Pottery with Incised Decoration, in: *Dothan Festschrift*, 127*–142*.

Gezer (HUCA) 3

S. Gitin, Formulating a Ceramic Corpus: The Late Iron Age II, Persian and Hellenistic Pottery at Gezer, in: *Van Beek Festschrift*, 75–102.

L. Herr, The Late Iron Age–Persian Ceramic Horizon at Tall al-ʿUmayri, *SHAJ* V, 617–619.

G. Lehmann, Trends in the Local Pottery Development of the Late Iron Age and Persian Period in Syria and Lebanon, ca. 700–300 B.C., *BASOR* 311 (1998), 7–37.

Imported Greek Pottery

Sukas II, VI; Kabri; Dor II, 93–181; *Michal, Tel*, 145–152; *Jaffa II; Ḥashavyahu, Meẓad I–II; Ḥest, Tell el- III*, 68–137; *Ashkelon III–IV; Migdol*

C. Clairmont, Greek Pottery from the Near East, *Berytus* 11 (1954–1955), 85–139; 12 (1956–1958), 1–24.

D. Auscher, Les Relations entre la Grèce et la Palestine avant la conquête d'Alexandre, *VT* 17 (1967), 8–30.

E. Boardman, Greek Potters at Al-Mina? *AS* 9 (1959), 161–169.

Idem, The Greeks Overseas, 3rd ed., London 1980.

M. Dothan, An Attic Red-Figured Bell Krater from ʿAkko, *IEJ* 29 (1979), 148–151.

T. F. B. G. Braun, The Greeks in the Near East, in: J. Boardman and G. L. Hamond (eds.), *Cambridge Ancient History*, vol. III, Cambridge, 1982, 1–31.

A. Raban, A Group of Imported "East Greek" Pottery from Locus 46 on Tel Akko, in: *Dothan Festschrift*, 73–98.

Stern [1982], 137–142.

E. Stern, *The Beginning of the Greek Settlement in Palestine in the Light of the Excavations at Tel Dor*, AASOR 49 (1989), 107–129.

Idem, Tel Dor, a Phoenician-Israelite Trade Center, in: S. Gitin (ed.), *Recent Excavations in Israel: A View to the West*, Dubuque, Iowa 1995, 81–93.

J. Elayi, Al-Mina sur l'Oronte à l'époque perse, in: *Phoenicia and the East Mediterranean in the First Millennium, Studia Phoenicia V*, Leuven 1987, 249–266.

Idem, Pénétration grecque en Phénicie sous l'empire perse, Nancy 1988.

R. Wenning, Attische Keramik in Palestina: Ein Zwischenbericht, *Trans* 2 (1990), 157–167.

S. Yardeni, Maritime Trade and Royal Accountancy in an Erased Customs Account from 475 B.C.E. on the Ahiqar Scroll from Elephantine, *BASOR* 293 (1994), 67–78.

J. C. Waldbaum, Early Greek Contacts with the Southern Levant, ca. 1000–600 B.C.: The Eastern Perspective, *BASOR* 293 (1994), 53–66.

Idem, Greeks in the East or Greeks and the East, *BASOR* 305 (1998), 1–17.

J. C. Waldbaum and J. Magness, The Chronology of Early Greek Pottery: New Evidence from Seventh-Century B.C. Destruction Levels in Israel, *AJA* 99 (1997), 23–40.

C. M. Adelman, Greek Pottery from Ashkelon, Israel: Hints of Presence? *AJA* 99 (1995), 305.

J. Sapin, "Mortaria": Un lot inédit de Tell Keisan: Essai d'interpretation fonction-nelle, *Trans* 16 (1998), 87–120.

Chapter Six: Metal, Stone, Bone, and Glass Artifacts

Metal Vases and Furniture

Ibsan, Khirbet; Mizpe Yammim I–II; Shechem II; Ashkelon II, IV; Far'ah, Tell el- (S) I, 14, pls. 44–46

J. H. Iliffe, A Tel Far'ah Tomb Group Reconsidered: Silver Vases of the Persian Pe-riod, *QDAP* 4 (1935), 182–186.

M. Tadmor, Fragments of an Achaemenid Throne from Samaria, *IEJ* 24 (1974), 37–43.

N. Gubel, *Phoenician Furniture, Studia Phoenicia VII,* Leuven 1987.

O. Raban, A Hoard of Bronze Objects from the Sea Bottom at Athlit, *Michmanim* 6 (1992), 31–53 (Hebrew).

P. Merhav, A Bronze Leg from a Piece of Hellenistic Furniture—a Find from the Seabed Near Athlit, *EI* 25 (1996), 427–432 (Hebrew).

Chapter Seven: Seals and Seal Impressions

Babylonian Seals

P. W. Dajani, A Neo-Babylonian Seal from Amman, *ADAJ* 6–7 (1962), 124–125.

N. Avigad, Seals of Exiles, *IEJ* 15 (1965), 222–232.

Avigad, *Corpus, passim.*

Stern [1982], 196–197.

E. Stern, Assyrian and Babylonian Elements in the Material Culture of Palestine in the Persian Period, *Trans* 7 (1994), 51–62.

K. Yassin, Ammonite Seals from Tell El Mazar, *SHAJ* III, 143–153.

T. Ornan, Observations on the Glyptic Finds in Israel and Jordan: Assyrian, Baby-lonian and Achaemenian Cylinder-Seals from the First Half of the First Millenium B.C.E., M.A. thesis, Hebrew University, 1990 (Hebrew).

T. Ornan and B. Sass, A Product of Cultural Interaction: The Seal of Nergal-Selim, *IMJ* 10 (1992), 63–65.

Uninscribed Seals

Stern [1982], 199–200.

Avigad, *Corpus, Passim.*

W. Culican, The Iconography of Some Phoenician Seals and Seal Impressions, *AJBA* 1 (1968), 50–130.

Idem, A Phoenician Seal from Khaldeh, *Levant* 6 (1974), 195–198.

E. Stern, Lion Seals from the Province of Judah, *BASOR* 262 (1971), 6–16.

Idem, Notes on the Development of the Stamp Glyptic Art in Palestine During the Assyrian and Persian Periods, in: *Richardson Festschrift,* 135–146.

Dor II, 145–163.

E. Gubel, Phoenician Seals in the Allard Pierson Museum, *RSF* 16 (1988), 145–163.

B. Brandl, A Phoenician Scarab from Lohamei HaGeta'ot, *'Atiqot* XX English series (1991), 153–155.
N. Avigad, a New Seal Depicting a Lion, *Michmanim* 6 (1992), 33*-36*.

Inscribed Seals

Yehud Seals

Stern [1982], 202–213.
Ahituv [1992], *passim.*
Avigad, *Corpus, passim.*
N. Avigad, A New Class of Yehud Stamps, *IEJ* 7 (1957), 146–153.
Idem, Yehud of Háir, *BASOR* 158 (1960), 23–27.
Idem, More Evidence on the Judean Post Exilic Stamps, *IEJ* 24 (1974), 52–58.
Idem, Bullae and Seals from a Post-Exilic Judean Archive, *Qedem* 4 (1976).
F. M. Cross, Judaean Stamps, *EI* 9 (1969), 20*–27*.
E. M. Meyers, The Shlomith Seal and the Judaean Restoration: Some Additional Considerations, *EI* 18 (1985), 33*–38*.
H. G. M. Williamson, The Governors of Judah Under the Persians, *Tyndale Bulletin* 39 (1988), 59–82.
J. R. Christoph, The Yehud Stamped Jar-Handle Corpus: Implications for the History of Postexilic Palestine, Ph.D. diss., University of Michigan, 1993.
J. Naveh, Gleanings of Some Pottery Inscriptions, *IEJ* 46 (1996), 44–47.
R. Deutsch and M. Helzer, *Windows to the Past,* Tel Aviv 1997, 75–76.

Moṣah Seals

N. Avigad, New Light on the MSH Seal Impressions, *IEJ* 8 (1958), 113–119.
J. R. Zorn, The *m(w)sh* Stamp Impressions and the Neo-Babylonian Period, *IEJ* 44 (1994), 161–183.

Tet Seals

P. Colella, Les Abréviations Tet et X (XP), *RB* 80 (1973), 547–558.
O. Goldwasser and J. Naveh, The Origin of the Tet-Symbol, *IEJ* 26 (1976), 15–19.
J. R. Zorn, Cross-Shaped "Tet" Stamp Impressions, *TA* 22 (1995), 98–106.

Samaritan Seals

Daliyeh I, 28–29, 59.
Daliyeh II
E. Stern, A Hoard of Bullae of the Persian Period from the Samaria Region, *Michmanim* 6 (1992), 7–30 (Hebrew).

Phoenician Seals

F. M. Cross, Jar Inscriptions from Shiqmona, *IEJ* 18 (1968), 226–233.
N. Avigad, A Phoenician Seal with Dolphin Emblem, *Sefunim* 3 (1969–1971), 49–50.
M. Dothan, The Sign of Tanit from Tel 'Akko, *IEJ* 24 (1974), 44–49.
J. L. Greenfield, A Group of Phoenician City Seals, *IEJ* 35 (1985), 129–134.

A. Kempinski and J. Naveh, A Phoenician Seal Impression on Jar Handle from Tel Kabri, *TA* 18 (1991), 244–247.

Avigad, *Corpus passim.*

Ammonite Seals

L. G. Herr, Two Stamped Jar Impressions of the Province of Ammon from Tell El-'Umeiri, *ADAJ* 36 (1992), 163–166.

Idem, Epigraphic Finds from Tell El-'Umeiri During the 1989 Season, *AUSS* 30 (1992), 193.

D. Dempsy, Ostraca and Seal Impression from Tell Nimrin, Jordan, *BASOR* 303 (1996), 77.

Avigad, *Corpus passim.*

Egyptian Seals

R. Giveon, Seals and Seal Impressions of the XXV Egyptian Dynasty in Western Asia (751–656), in: *Belliddo Festschrift,* 133–138.

Chapter Eight: Coins

General

Stern [1982], 217–228.

M. Heltzer, The Provincial Taxation in the Achaemenian Empire and the "Forty Shekels of Silver" (Neh. 5:15), *Michmanim* 6 (1992), 15*–25*.

I. Mildenberg, On the Money Circulation in Palestine from Artaxerxes II till Ptolemy I, Preliminary Studies of the Local Coinage in the Fifth Persian Satrapy, *Trans* 7 (1994), 63–71.

J. Elayi and A. G. Elayi, *Recherches sur les Poids Phéniciens, Supplement No. 5a Trans,* Paris 1997.

Persian Coins

A. D. K. Bivar, Achaemenid Coins, Weights and Measures, *Cambridge History of Iran,* Cambridge 1985, 615–637.

A. Lemaire, Remarques à props du monnayage Cilician d'époque perse et de ses légendes araméennes, *REA* 91 (1989).

L. Mildenberg, Über das Munzwesen im Reich der Achaemeniden, *Archaeologische Mitteilungen aus Iran* 26 (1993), 55–79.

Greek Coins

Shechem I, Fig. 95.

Y. Meshorer, An Attic Archaic Coin from Jerusalem, *'Atiqot* III, English series (1961), 185.

Phoenician Coins

G. F. Hill, *A Catalogue of the Greek Coins in the British Museum, Palestine,* London 1914.

J. Baramki, A Hoard of Silver coins of Sidon and Alesander from Khirbet el Kerak, *QDAP* 2 (1943), 86–90.

A. Kindler, The Mint of Tyre—the Major Source of Silver Coins in Ancient Palestine, *EI* 8 (1967), 318–324 (Hebrew).

J. W. Betylon, *The Coinage Mints of Phoenicia, the Pre-Alexandrine Period,* Chicago 1980.

J. Elayi, Le Monnayage de Byblos avant Alexandre: Problems et perspectives, *Trans* 1 (1989), 9–20.

J. Elayi and A. G. Elayi, *Trésors de monnais phéniciennes et circulation monétaire (V–IV siècles avant J.C.),* Paris 1993.

Idem, Nouveaux trésors de monnaies phéniciennes (CH VIII), *Trans* 11 (1996), 95–114.

R. Deutsch and M. Heltzer, Numismatic Evidence from the Persian-Period from the Sharon Plain, *Trans* 13 (1997), 17–20.

Palestinian Coins

C. Lambert, Egypto-Arabian, Phoenician and Other Coins of the Fourth Century B.C. Found in Palestine, *QDAP* 1 (1932), 10–20; 2 (1933), 1–10.

A. Kindler, The Graeco-Phoenician Coins Found in Palestine in the Time of the Persian Empire, *INJ* 1 (1963), 2–6, 25–27.

Y. Meshorer, Three Gaza Coins from the Persian Period, *IMN* 12 (1977), 78–79.

Idem, The Mints of Ashdod and Ascalon During the Late Persian Period, *EI* 20 (1989), 287–291 (Hebrew).

C. M. Kraag, Some Notes on the Abu-Shusheh Hoard, *INJ* 28 (1978), 190–192.

L. Mildenberg, Baana: Preliminary Studies of the Local Coinage of the Fifth Persian Satrapy, *EI* 19 (1987), 29–35.

Idem, Gaza Mint Authorities in Persian Time: Preliminary Studies of the Local Coinage of the Fifth Persian Satrapy, *Trans* 2 (1990), 137–155.

Idem, On the Imagery of the Philisto-Arabian Coinage—a Review, *Trans* 13 (1997), 9–16.

H. Gitler, New Fourth-Century BC Coins from Ascalon, *NC* 156 (1996), 1–9.

Coins of the Province of Judah

E. L. Sukenik, Paralipomena Palaestinensia, I: The Oldest Coins of Judaea, *JPOS* 14 (1934), 178–182, pls. I–II; 15 (1935), 334–341, pl. XXIV.

L. Y. Rahmani, Silver Coins of the Fourth Century from Tel Gamma, *IEJ* 21 (1971), 148–160.

A. Kindler, Silver Coins Bearing the Name of Judah from the Early Hellenistic Period, *IEJ* 24 (1974), 73–76.

L. Mildenberg, Yehud—a Preliminary Study of the Provincial Coinage of Judaea, in: O. Morkholm and N. M. Waggoner (eds.), *Greek Numismatic and Archaeology: Essays in Honor of Margaret Thompson,* Wetteren 1979, 183–196.

Idem, Yehud-Munzen, in: *Handbuch der Archaeologie: Vorderasien,* II:1 Munich 1988, 719–728.

Y. Meshorer, *Ancient Jewish Coinage, I: Persian Period Through Hasmonaean,* New York 1982, 13–34, 98, 115–117, 160.

Idem, Ancient Jewish Coinage—Addendum I, *INJ* 11 (1990–1991), 104–106, 114–115.

Idem, A Treasury of Jewish Coins from the Persian Period to Bar-Kochba, Jerusalem 1997, 11–27 (Hebrew).

J. W. Betylon, The Provincial Government of Persian Period Judea and the Yehud Coins, *JBL* 105 (1986), 633–642.

A. Spaer, Jaddua the High Priest, *INJ* 9 (1986–1987), 1–3.

D. Barag, A Silver Coin of Yohanan the High Priest and the Coinage of Judaea in the Fourth Century B.C., *INJ* 9 (1986–1987), 4–21.

Idem, Bagoas and the Coinage of Judea, *Proceedings of the XIth International Congress,* Brussels 1991.

Chapter Nine: Weights and Measures

Stern [1982].

I. Eph'al and J. Naveh, *Aramaic Ostraca of the Fourth Century BC from Idumaea,* Jerusalem 1996.

INDEXES

Scripture Index

GENERAL INDEX

Place names with Tel or Tell are inverted. Maps, illustrations, and photographs are indicated by italic page numbers.

Apollonia, 62, 68, 76, 316, 363, 385, 386,
406, 487, 489
apotropaic cult, 17, 85, 87, 255, 479,
507–10
Apries (Hophra), Pharaoh, 305
Aqabah, Gulf of, 269
Arabia, 113, 123, 268, 289, 307, 358, 368,
369, 370, 371, 415, 421, 454
Arabians, 21, 45, 113, 114, 237, 259, 260,
267, 304, 325, 353, 369, 370, 371,
419, 420, 444, 446, 451, 460, 531,
577, 578, 581; influence of, 419; inscriptions, 297–300, *297, 298,* 366,
513; language, 446; names, 242, 298,
447; relationship with Assyria,
295–97; trade, 269, 277, 278, 293,
294, 295–300, 415, 419
Arad Ostraca, 160, 181, 191, 198–99, 203,
226, 227, 269, 270, 277, 300, 446,
452, 531, 555
Arad (Tel Arad), 10, 18, 32, 37, 41, 133,
147, 151, 152, 158–59, 161, 163,
170, 175, 178, 184, 191, 199, 200,
201, 202, 203, 204, 205, 211, 212,
215, 226, 234, 249, 269, 271, 276,
278, 279, 325, 348, 364, 372, 420,
434, 444, 446, 447, 451–52, 454,
489, 490, 531, 545, 571, 572,
579
Arad Valley, 133, 152, 161, 173,
280, 513
Arados, 386, 393
Aram, 11, 212, 269
Aram Geshur, 10
Aramaeans, xvi, 16, 116, 237
Aramaic inscriptions, 52, 91, 115, 116,
197, 238, 255, 260, 270, 335, 361,
364, *365,* 422, 446, 447, 452, 453,
456, 457, 486, 513, 545, 548, 550,
552, 564, 565, 582
Aramaic language, 14, 15, 362, 363
Aravah, 138, 154, 161, 268, 269, 273, 275,
276, 277, 278, 279, 280, 290, 293,
299, 325, 348, 446, 447, 451, 452,
458, 513
architecture: Assyrian, 23–31; Judaean,
165–68; Persian Period, 461–69;
Phoenician, 69–71
Arethusa, 565
Ariendas, 557

'Arish, el- (El-Arish), 10, 296, 366, 369,
371, 407, 415, 419, 421, 490, 491. *See
also* Ienysus
'Arish River, el-, 104, 421
Armenia, 526
Armenian Quarter (Jerusalem), 436
Arnon River, 259, 262
Aroer (Tel Aroer), 37, 40, 133, 151,
154–55, 161, 168, 191, 205, 214, 262,
263, 271, 277, 278, 290–91, 292, 293,
325
Arrian, 361, 421
arrowheads, *8,* 531–33, *532*
Arsames, 356, 357, 361
Arses (Xerxes II), li, 360
Arslan Tash, 24, 468
art objects, Phoenician, 92–100
Artabanus, 356
Artaxerxes I (Longimanus), li, 356, 357
Artaxerxes II (Memnon, Mnemon), li,
358, 359, 577
Artaxerxes III (Ochus, Okhos), li, 313,
359, 360, 376, 426, 438, 446, 561,
579
Artyphius, 356
Aruboth (Narbata), 423
Arvad, 382, 387
Arwad, 60, 61, 62, 426, 476, 556, 559, 561
Asclepius at Sarepta (Ba'al-Ashmun), 486,
489
Ashdod, 5, 9, 14, 15, 38, 76, 80, 82, 102,
105–6, 107, 109, 112, 115, 116, 117,
118, 121–22, 126, 129, 140, 144, 214,
219, 220, 229, 230, 232, 262, 268,
307, 314, 316, 317, 349, 353, 364,
366, 369, 370, 371, 407–8, 414, 417,
418, 462, 465, 486, 487, 488, 513,
529, 530, 533, 543, 556, 562, 564,
565, 570, 582
Ashdodite ware, 110, 127, 128
Ashdod-Yam, 9, 102, 105, 109, 317, 417,
418, 573, 574, 575
Asher (Tayasir), 423
Asherah, 202, 383
Asherat, 118, 119, 120, 124. *See also* 'Astarte
Ashkelon, 62, 76, 78, 83, 102, 104, 106,
109, 112, 113–14, 115, 116, 117, 118,
122, 123, 124, 126, 128, 129, 219,
221, 228, 229, 230, 232, 233, 304,